LOCAL SPIRITUAL ASSEMBLY HANDBOOK

BAHÁ'Í PUBLICATIONS
AUSTRALIA

National Spiritual Assembly of the Bahá'ís of Australia

Third Edition

BAHÁ'Í PUBLICATIONS AUSTRALIA

©National Spiritual Assembly of the Bahá'í of Australia

Published by:
Bahá'í Publications Australia
PO Box 285
Mona Vale NSW 2103
Australia
Phone: 61 2 9913 1554
Fax: 61 2 9970 6710
Email: bahaipub1@peg.apc.org

ISBN 0 909991 78 2

First Edition 1980
Second Edition 1990
Third Edition 1996

Cover Design by Wisdom Graphic Design, Wollongong
Typesetting by Wisdom Graphic Design, Wollongong

Printed and bound by CPN Publications, Canberra

TABLE OF CONTENTS

1. FORMATION OF THE LOCAL SPIRITUAL ASSEMBLY AND ITS ELECTION — 36

1.1 FORMATION - GENERAL PRINCIPLES — 36
- 1.1.1 When must a Local Spiritual Assembly be formed? — 36
- 1.1.2 Is there an obligation to form a Local Spiritual Assembly when there are nine adult believers in a civil area? — 36
- 1.1.3 What if a Local Spiritual Assembly is to be formed in a remote or unconsolidated area? — 36
- 1.1.4 Can a Local Spiritual Assembly be formed in an area where all nine believers are not actually physically resident in the area, but where believers are intending to move? — 37
- 1.1.5 Can Local Spiritual Assemblies be formed in prisons? — 37
- 1.1.6 What is the area of jurisdiction of a Local Spiritual Assembly? — 37
- 1.1.7 Where may Aboriginal Assemblies be formed? — 37

1.2 MEMBERSHIP — 37
- 1.2.1 What are the duties of a Local Spiritual Assembly member? — 37
- 1.2.2 Who can serve on the Local Spiritual Assembly? — 39
- 1.2.3 Are there any names that should not appear on the voting list? — 39
- 1.2.4 Should names of inactive believers appear on the voting list? — 39
- 1.2.5 Should names of Auxiliary Board members or their assistants appear on the voting list? — 39
- 1.2.6 Can a Hand of the Cause of God, a member of the Continental Board of Counsellors, or a member of the Auxiliary Boards, serve on an Assembly if they make up the ninth member of a community? — 40
- 1.2.7 Should the name of a believer who has asked to resign from the Faith, but whose resignation has not yet been accepted, appear on the voting list? — 40
- 1.2.8 Should the name of a believer who is mentally ill or senile be left on the voting list? — 40
- 1.2.9 Should the name of a believer who is physically incapacitated be removed from the voting list? — 40
- 1.2.10 What should a Local Spiritual Assembly do if it discovers an error in the voting list after the Assembly has been elected? — 41
- 1.2.11 Does a believer called upon to serve on a Local Spiritual Assembly, have an obligation to serve? — 41
- 1.2.12 What if a believer is unwilling to serve? — 41
- 1.2.13 What should the attitude of the community be towards a member who refuses to participate in the formation of the Assembly? — 42
- 1.2.14 May a believer resign from the Local Spiritual Assembly? — 42
- 1.2.15 Reasons that are not acceptable for proffering one's resignation include: — 42
- 1.2.16 What should believers do if pressing commitments leave them short of time to fulfil their duties on the Local Spiritual Assembly? — 43
- 1.2.17 Are there any situations that would justify a Local Spiritual Assembly removing a believer from Assembly membership? — 44

1.3 PROCEDURES FOR ELECTION — 44
- 1.3.1 How do we proceed when there are exactly nine adult believers? — 44
- 1.3.2 How do we proceed when there are more than nine adult believers? — 44
- 1.3.3 How should the Annual General Meeting be conducted? — 45

1.4 VOTING PROCEDURES — 46
- 1.4.1 How many believers must participate in the election? — 46
- 1.4.2 Does a believer eligible to vote, have an obligation to vote? — 46
- 1.4.3 .How is the Local Spiritual Assembly elected? — 46
- 1.4.4 Can a believer vote for himself? — 47
- 1.4.5 What is the procedure if a believer cannot write? — 47
- 1.4.6 What is the procedure for voting by mail? — 47

TABLE OF CONTENTS

1.4.7	How is a tie vote resolved?	47
1.4.8	Are there different procedures to follow when there is a tie vote between Bahá'ís of different races or nationalities within the community?	47
1.4.9	Is it necessary to store used ballot papers?	48
1.4.10	When must the National Spiritual Assembly be notified of the results?	48

1.5 ELECTION OF OFFICERS — **48**

1.5.1	Who convenes the first meeting of the Assembly?	48
1.5.2	When should the election of officers take place?	48
1.5.3	How are the officers elected?	48
1.5.4	What should be done if, after repeated balloting, no member receives five or more votes?	49
1.5.5	When must the National Spiritual Assembly be notified of the results?	50
1.5.6	How many officers does a Local Spiritual Assembly have?	50
1.5.7	What are the functions of the Assembly officers?	50
1.5.8	Can a believer refuse election as an office bearer?	50
1.5.9	Can an office bearer be dismissed mid-term?	50

1.6 VACANCIES — **51**

1.6.1	What is done when a vacancy occurs on a Local Spiritual Assembly?	51
1.6.2	What is the procedure for a by-election?	51
1.6.3	What is the procedure for electing a new office bearer mid-term?	51

1.7 NOTES FOR REGISTERED GROUPS — **51**

2. CONSULTATION — 52

2.1 CONSULTATION WITHIN THE LOCAL SPIRITUAL ASSEMBLY — **52**

2.1.1	What is the procedure for consultation?	52
2.1.2	Can a member abstain from voting?	53
2.1.3	In the case of a decision arrived at by majority vote, what should be the attitude of those members whose opinions were in the minority?	53
2.1.4	What if the decision of the Assembly is wrong?	54
2.1.5	Should dissenting votes be recorded in the minutes?	54
2.1.6	What is the role of the Chairman in the consultative process?	54
2.1.7	What is the function of the agenda?	54
2.1.8	Can Assembly members absent themselves from the consultation if the issue under discussion involves them personally?	55
2.1.9	Can people who are not members of the Assembly sit in on sessions?	56
2.1.10	What should the Assembly do if conflict arises between its members?	56

2.2 CONSULTATION BETWEEN THE LOCAL SPIRITUAL ASSEMBLY AND THE COMMUNITY — **57**

2.2.1	Does the Local Spiritual Assembly have an obligation to consult with the community?	57
2.2.2	What is the duty of the community with respect to decisions made by the Local Spiritual Assembly?	58

2.3 CONSULTATION BETWEEN THE LOCAL SPIRITUAL ASSEMBLY AND AN INDIVIDUAL — **59**

2.3.1	On what matters should an individual consult with the Assembly?	59
2.3.2	Can an individual bring a problem to the Local Spiritual Assembly if other parties to the problem do not wish to involve the Assembly?	59
2.3.3	Can a Local Spiritual Assembly intervene in a conflict against the will of the parties involved?	60
2.3.4	Can the Assembly delegate a committee or individual to counsel a believer?	60
2.3.5	What is the procedure for consultation between the Local Spiritual Assembly and an individual?	60

TABLE OF CONTENTS

2.4	**CONSULTATION BETWEEN THE ASSEMBLY AND ONE OF ITS COMMITTEES**	60
2.5	**THE RIGHT OF APPEAL**	60
2.5.1	What procedure must an individual follow for appealing against a decision of the Local Spiritual Assembly?	60
2.5.2	What procedure must a Local Spiritual Assembly follow for appealing against a decision of the National Spiritual Assembly?	61
2.6	**NOTES FOR REGISTERED GROUPS**	61
2.7	**SUGGESTED FURTHER READING**	62
3.	**ADMINISTRATIVE PROCEDURES**	**63**
3.1	**PRINCIPLES AND PROCEDURES**	63
3.1.1	What is the significance of the Bahá'í Administrative Order?	63
3.1.2	What is the distinction between administrative principles and procedures?	63
3.1.3	Where will it be necessary for a Local Spiritual Assembly to establish its own procedures?	64
3.1.4	What principles apply to the establishment of procedure?	64
3.2	**MEETINGS OF THE LOCAL SPIRITUAL ASSEMBLY**	64
3.2.1	How is a meeting of the Local Spiritual Assembly called?	64
3.2.2	How is a meeting of the Local Spiritual Assembly conducted?	64
3.2.3	What materials should the Secretary bring to the meetings?	65
3.2.4	How often should the Assembly meet?	65
3.2.5	What is a quorum?	65
3.2.6	What should a Local Spiritual Assembly do if it is unable to achieve a quorum?	66
3.2.7	What procedures may a Local Spiritual Assembly put in place for taking routine action between Assembly meetings?	66
3.2.8	What should a Local Spiritual Assembly do in an emergency?	66
3.2.9	What if an elected officer is absent from a meeting?	67
3.2.10	What should a Local Spiritual Assembly do if it is dissatisfied with the services of one of its officers?	67
3.2.11	What if an Assembly member is unable or unwilling to attend meetings?	67
3.2.12	Is it permissible to elect a temporary Assembly member in place of one who must be absent for a while?	70
3.3	**CONFIDENTIALITY**	70
3.3.1	Are the deliberations of a Local Spiritual Assembly confidential?	70
3.3.2	May a Local Spiritual Assembly member who receives information in confidence as an individual, share that information with the Assembly?	72
3.4	**FUNCTIONS OF THE SECRETARY**	72
3.4.1	What are the functions of the Local Spiritual Assembly Secretary?	72
3.4.2	Is it permissible for the Secretary to receive assistance from someone not on the Assembly?	73
3.5	**MINUTES**	73
3.5.1	What are the minutes?	73
3.5.2	What should be recorded in the minutes?	73
3.5.3	Must the minutes be written in English?	74
3.5.4	What principles apply to the distribution of minutes?	74
3.5.5	Should the Local Spiritual Assembly send a copy of its minutes to the National Spiritual Assembly?	75
3.5.6	Should the Local Spiritual Assembly send a copy of its minutes to the Auxiliary Board members?	75

TABLE OF CONTENTS

3.5.7	May a Local Spiritual Assembly record confidential items separately from the minutes?	75

3.6 MEMBERSHIP LIST — 75
3.6.1	How should the Local Spiritual Assembly maintain its membership list?	75
3.6.2	Should the Local Spiritual Assembly keep separate birth, death and marriage registers?	75
3.6.3	Are membership lists confidential?	76
3.6.4	Should names of believers whose address is unknown appear on the membership list?	77
3.6.5	Should the names of believers who have lost their voting rights be retained on the membership list?	77
3.6.6	How should a Local Spiritual Assembly instruct a believer who is changing his or her address?	77
3.6.7	What is the difference between the membership list and the voting list?	77

3.7 FILING — 77
3.7.1	How should a Local Spiritual Assembly organise its files?	77
3.7.2	Do all Local Spiritual Assembly members have equal access to the files?	78

3.8 ANNUAL REPORT — 78
3.8.1	When should the Local Spiritual Assembly prepare its Annual Report?	78
3.8.2	What information should the Annual Report contain?	78
3.8.3	Who prepares the Annual Report?	79
3.8.4	Do incorporated Assemblies have special requirements to meet?	79

3.9 ARCHIVES — 79
3.9.1	What is the importance of setting up local archives?	79
3.9.2	How should local archives be set up?	80
3.9.3	Who should be responsible for deciding which items to keep and which to destroy?	80
3.9.4	If a Local Spiritual Assembly lapses, what should the remaining community members do with the files?	81

3.10 COMMUNICATIONS — 81
3.10.1	Who receives and sends communications on behalf of the Local Spiritual Assembly?	81
3.10.2	What form do communications generally take?	81
3.10.3	How should communications from the Assembly be prepared?	81
3.10.4	What is the correct protocol for addressing institutions of the Faith?	82
3.10.5	How should a Local Spiritual Assembly design its letterhead?	82
3.10.6	What guidelines apply to local newsletters?	83
3.10.7	May a Local Spiritual Assembly communicate directly with the Universal House of Justice?	83
3.10.8	May an individual communicate directly with the Universal House of Justice?	83
3.10.9	May a Local Spiritual Assembly communicate directly with an overseas National Spiritual Assembly, one of its committees, or a Local Spiritual Assembly within the jurisdiction of another National Spiritual Assembly?	84
3.10.10	May Local Spiritual Assemblies communicate directly with Hands of the Cause of God, a Continental Board of Counsellors or individual Counsellors?	84
3.10.11	May individuals communicate directly with Hands of the Cause of God, a Continental Board of Counsellors or individual Counsellors?	84

3.11 INCORPORATION — 84
3.11.1	What is the value of incorporation for Local Spiritual Assemblies?	84
3.11.2	Should Local Spiritual Assemblies in Australia incorporate at the present time?	84
3.11.3	May a Local Spiritual Assembly wind up its incorporation without the permission of the National Spiritual Assembly?	84
3.11.4	What responsibilities does an incorporated Local Spiritual Assembly have?	84
3.11.5	What happens if an incorporated Assembly lapses?	85

TABLE OF CONTENTS

3.12	**NOTES FOR REGISTERED GROUPS**	**85**
	APPENDIX 1: SAMPLE FORMS	**86**
	APPENDIX 2: SAMPLE LETTERHEADS	**92**

4. BAHÁ'Í FUNDS — 95

4.1 INTRODUCTION — 95
4.1.1 Why are the Bahá'í Funds important? — 95
4.1.2 Is giving to the Bahá'í Funds an obligation? — 95
4.1.3 Are contributions voluntary? — 95
4.1.4 Who may contribute to the Bahá'í Funds? — 95
4.1.5 What if a person who is not a Bahá'í wishes to make a contribution? — 96
4.1.6 What are the spiritual principles underlying contributions to the Bahá'í Fund? — 96

4.2 THE DIFFERENT FUNDS — 97
4.2.1 How many different Funds are there? — 97
4.2.2 Should individuals and Local Spiritual Assemblies contribute to all four Funds? — 97
4.2.3 Should the believers contribute directly to the National Fund? — 98
4.2.4 Should Local Spiritual Assemblies have Area Delegates' Funds? — 99
4.2.5 What is the Bahá'í Investment Fund? — 99
4.2.6 Are donations to any of the Funds tax deductible? — 100
4.2.7 May Local Spiritual Assemblies and individuals contribute to Bahá'í projects in other countries? — 100

4.3 FORMS OF CONTRIBUTIONS — 100
4.3.1 How may contributions be made to the Funds? — 100
4.3.2 Is it permissible for Local Spiritual Assemblies and individuals to earmark donations for specific purposes? — 101
4.3.3 What principles apply to the earmarking of contributions? — 102

4.4 RESPONSIBILITIES OF THE LOCAL SPIRITUAL ASSEMBLY — 102
4.4.1 Must a Local Spiritual Assembly have a Local Bahá'í Fund? — 102
4.4.2 What is the purpose of the Local Bahá'í Fund? — 103
4.4.3 How should a Local Spiritual Assembly proceed when setting up its Fund for the first time? — 103
4.4.4 Who is responsible for managing the Fund? — 104
4.4.5 How should the Local Spiritual Assembly collect donations? — 104
4.4.6 May the National Spiritual Assembly tell a Local Spiritual Assembly how to allocate its funds? — 105
4.4.7 When should the Local Spiritual Assembly prepare its budget for the year? — 105
4.4.8 How should the Local Spiritual Assembly prepare its budget? — 105
4.4.9 When should the Local Spiritual Assembly prepare its Annual Financial Report? — 106
4.4.10 How should the Local Spiritual Assembly prepare its Annual Financial Report? — 106
4.4.11 How often should the Local Spiritual Assembly receive reports from its Treasurer? — 106
4.4.12 How often should the Local Spiritual Assembly report to its community? — 107
4.4.13 What responsibility does the Local Spiritual Assembly have for deepening the community in the importance of contributing to the Fund? — 107
4.4.14 To whom can the Local Spiritual Assembly turn for assistance? — 108

4.5 FUNCTIONS OF THE TREASURER — 108
4.5.1 What are the functions of the Treasurer? — 108

4.6 FUND-RAISING — 109
4.6.1 What is the spirit that should characterise fund-raising events? — 109
4.6.2 May fund-raising activities be held during Bahá'í feasts or on Holy Days? — 110
4.6.3 Is it permissible for Spiritual Assemblies or individual Bahá'ís to sell goods or services to the general public for the purpose of raising money for the Bahá'í Funds? — 111

TABLE OF CONTENTS

4.6.4	Is it proper for Spiritual Assemblies or individual Bahá'ís to sell goods belonging to non-Bahá'ís for the purpose of raising money for the Bahá'í Funds?	112
4.6.5	May a Local Spiritual Assembly organise a fund-raising dinner (for example) to which Bahá'ís and their non-Bahá'í friends and relatives are invited?	112
4.6.6	Are raffles, lotteries, or other games of chance appropriate methods of raising funds?	112
4.6.7	Are auctions permissible?	112
4.6.8	Is it permissible for individuals or Assemblies to establish business ventures to raise funds for the Faith?	113
4.6.9	May a Local Spiritual Assembly make appeals to its own community for funds?	114
4.6.10	May a Local Spiritual Assembly appeal to the Bahá'ís outside its area of jurisdiction for funds?	114
4.6.11	How are funds to be raised for inter-Assembly projects?	114
4.6.12	May a Local Spiritual Assembly solicit funds from Bahá'ís in other countries?	114
4.6.13	Are there any circumstances in which Bahá'ís may solicit funds from non-Bahá'ís for Bahá'í projects?	115
4.6.14	May a Local Spiritual Assembly accept funds from the Government?	115
4.6.15	May a Local Spiritual Assembly accept funds from a non-Bahá'í organisation to further the administrative work of the Faith?	116
4.6.16	May a Local Spiritual Assembly charge for services, eg. food, accommodation, to cover the costs of organising a major function such as a conference or school?	116
4.6.17	In what circumstances may a Bahá'í community raise funds on behalf of a non-Bahá'í organisation?	117
4.6.18	May an individual raise funds for non-Bahá'í institutions?	117
4.7	**ENDOWMENTS**	**117**
4.7.1	What is an endowment in the Bahá'í sense?	117
4.7.2	What form should an endowment take?	117
4.7.3	What other principles apply to the acquisition of endowments?	118
4.8	**HUQÚQU'LLÁH**	**119**
4.8.1	What is Huqúqu'lláh?	119
4.9	**NOTES FOR REGISTERED GROUPS**	**119**
5.	**TEACHING**	**120**
5.1	**INTRODUCTION**	**120**
5.1.1	What is the challenge facing the Australian Bahá'í community now?	120
5.1.2	What challenge and responsibility does the Australian Bahá'í community have to the Australasian region?	120
5.1.3	How should Local Spiritual Assemblies meet the challenge of 'entry by troops'?	121
5.1.4	What are the different aspects of teaching?	121
5.1.5	What is the administrative procedure for becoming a Bahá'í?	122
5.2	**PROCLAMATION**	**122**
5.2.1	What is the purpose of proclamation?	122
5.2.2	How does proclamation relate to expansion and consolidation?	122
5.2.3	What sort of activities does proclamation include?	123
5.2.4	What sort of information about the Faith should be made available in proclamation activities?	123
5.2.5	What standard applies to publicity campaigns?	123
5.2.6	How should Local Spiritual Assemblies organise their proclamation work?	123
5.2.7	What guidelines apply to contacting the media?	124
5.2.8	What guidelines apply to dissemination of Bahá'í literature?	124
5.2.9	Is there any particular Bahá'í literature that Bahá'ís should give to people?	125
5.2.10	What guidelines apply to holding public meetings?	125
5.2.11	What guidelines apply to making contact with local dignitaries?	126

TABLE OF CONTENTS

5.2.12	What guidelines apply to social and humanitarian activities?	126
5.2.13	What statistics should be given out in proclamation campaigns?	126

5.3 EXPANSION — 126
5.3.1	What is the purpose of expansion work?	126
5.3.2	How does expansion relate to consolidation?	127
5.3.3	What general principles apply to the teaching work?	127
5.3.4	What are the most important principles to teach a person?	128
5.3.5	What is the distinction between active teaching and proselytising?	128
5.3.6	What are some different methods of teaching?	129
5.3.7	Is door-to-door teaching acceptable?	130

5.4 CONSOLIDATION — 130
5.4.1	What is the purpose of consolidation?	130
5.4.2	What aspects of the Faith should deepening focus on?	131
5.4.3	How should the Local Spiritual Assembly nurture new believers?	131
5.4.4	How should new believers be nurtured in areas in which there have been large scale enrolments?	132
5.4.5	How do summer schools assist the teaching and consolidation work?	133
5.4.6	What is the importance of teaching institutes?	134
5.4.7	What are some other consolidation activities?	135

5.5 PIONEERING AND TRAVEL TEACHING — 135
5.5.1	What is the role of the Local Spiritual Assembly with regard to pioneering and travel teaching?	135
5.5.2	How should friends who are interested in overseas pioneering or travel teaching be advised?	135
5.5.3	What is the function of a pioneer?	135
5.5.4	What responsibility has the Local Spiritual Assembly for homefront pioneering?	136
5.5.5	What is extension teaching?	137
5.5.6	What is the function of travel teachers?	138
5.5.7	How is travel teaching organised in Australia?	138
5.5.8	How should a Local Spiritual Assembly advise a believer who wishes to undertake travel teaching within Australia?	139
5.5.9	What is the Deputisation Fund?	139

5.6 RESPONSIBILITIES OF THE LOCAL SPIRITUAL ASSEMBLY — 139
5.6.1	How should the Local Spiritual Assembly organise its teaching work?	139
5.6.2	What responsibility does the Local Spiritual Assembly have towards the local community with regard to the teaching work?	140
5.6.3	What benefit does the community receive by concentrating on the teaching work?	141
5.6.4	Should priority be given to national or locally organised teaching projects?	141
5.6.5	What is the particular role of the appointed arm in the teaching work?	142
5.6.6	What is the relationship between the Regional Teaching Committee and the Local Spiritual Assembly?	143
5.6.7	What is the relationship between individual and Local Spiritual Assembly teaching projects?	143

5.7 TEACHING MINORITIES — 143
5.7.1	Are there any minority groups in particular that the Australian Bahá'í community has been asked to teach?	143
5.7.2	What are the guidelines relating to Aboriginal teaching?	144
5.7.3	What are the guidelines relating to teaching citizens of the People's Republic of China (PRC) temporarily in Australia?	145
5.7.4	What about teaching Chinese who are residents of Australia?	147
5.7.5	What guidelines relate to teaching Muslims from the Middle-East and North Africa?	147
5.7.6	What guidelines apply to teaching Malaysians?	149
5.7.7	What guidelines apply to teaching people from Eastern Europe, Russia and the former Soviet republics?	149

TABLE OF CONTENTS

5.7.8	May sub-normal or mentally ill people be taught the Faith?	150
5.8	**NOTES FOR REGISTERED GROUPS**	**150**

6. NINETEEN DAY FEASTS AND BAHÁ'Í HOLY DAYS — 151

6.1 ORIGINS AND PURPOSE OF THE NINETEEN DAY FEAST — 151
6.1.1	What is the origin of the Nineteen Day Feast?	151
6.1.2	What is the purpose of the Nineteen Day Feast?	151

6.2 PREPARATION OF AND FOR THE FEAST — 152
6.2.1	Who hosts the Nineteen Day Feast?	152
6.2.2	What are the responsibilities of the host?	152
6.2.3	What are some other important aspects of the preparation for the Feast?	153
6.2.4	How should the believers prepare themselves for attending the Feast?	153
6.2.5	May a Local Spiritual Assembly hold a joint Feast with another community?	154
6.2.6	Who may call the Feast if the Local Spiritual Assembly is not exercising its responsibilities in this regard?	154
6.2.7	Should groups and isolated believers observe the Nineteen Day Feast?	154

6.3 PROGRAMME — 155
6.3.1	What are the three parts of the Feast programme?	155
6.3.2	What may be read during the devotional section of the Nineteen Day Feast?	155
6.3.3	What does the administrative section involve?	156
6.3.4	Who conducts the administrative section of the Feast?	157
6.3.5	How is the administrative section of the Feast organised?	157
6.3.6	What matters should the Assembly bring to the Feast for consultation?	157
6.3.7	How does the community make recommendations to the Assembly at the Feast?	158
6.3.8	Who records recommendations made at the Feast?	159
6.3.9	Does the Assembly have to read all communications received for the community, in full, at the Feast?	159
6.3.10	Should the proceedings of the Feast be translated into another language, eg. Persian, for the benefit of non-English speaking friends?	159
6.3.11	What does the social section involve?	160
6.3.12	How much flexibility is permitted in the order of the Feast and the manner of its celebration?	160
6.3.13	What kind of music may be played at the Feast?	162
6.3.14	May items be offered for sale during the Nineteen Day Feast?	162
6.3.15	Is it permissible to smoke during a Feast?	162
6.3.16	Do any of the sections of the Feast have any more importance than any other?	162

6.4 ATTENDANCE — 163
6.4.1	Who may attend the Nineteen Day Feast?	163
6.4.2	What about Bahá'ís who are citizens of the People's Republic of China (PRC)?	163
6.4.3	May Bahá'ís without voting rights attend the Feast?	163
6.4.4	Is attendance at the Feasts obligatory?	164
6.4.5	Why are non-Bahá'ís not permitted to attend the Feast?	164
6.4.6	What should be done if a non-Bahá'í comes to the Feast?	165
6.4.7	What if the Feast is held at the home of a Bahá'í with a non-Bahá'í spouse?	165
6.4.8	What should the Local Spiritual Assembly do if the administrative part of the Feast has to be postponed?	166
6.4.9	Should children of Bahá'í parents attend the Feast?	166
6.4.10	May children of non-Bahá'í parents attend Nineteen Day Feasts?	166
6.4.11	May children of Bahá'í parents who have not re-affirmed at 15, still attend the Feast?	166
6.4.12	Should children be expected to maintain good behaviour at Feasts and Holy Day celebrations?	167

TABLE OF CONTENTS

6.4.13	Who is primarily responsible for the behaviour of children at Feasts and other Bahá'í celebrations?	167
6.4.14	Does the Local Spiritual Assembly have any responsibility for the behaviour of children?	167
6.4.15	Is there specific guidance for parents as regards the discipline of children?	167
6.4.16	Should parents avoid coming to Feasts if their children misbehave?	168

6.5 TIME AND PLACE — **168**

6.5.1	When should the Nineteen Day Feast be held?	168
6.5.2	Where should the Nineteen Day Feast be held?	169
6.5.3	May Feasts be held out of doors?	169
6.5.4	Is it permissible for Local Spiritual Assemblies with very large communities to hold more than one Feast in different districts of the community?	170
6.5.5	Is it permissible to hold the Feast on the premises of another religious organisation?	171

6.6 BAHÁ'Í HOLY DAYS - GENERAL PRINCIPLES — **171**

6.6.1	What is the importance of observing the Bahá'í Holy Days?	171
6.6.2	How should the Holy Days be observed?	172
6.6.3	Should gifts be exchanged on Bahá'í Holy Days?	173
6.6.4	Is it obligatory to observe the Holy Days on the prescribed day?	173
6.6.5	Holy Day observances?	174
6.6.6	Must Holy Days be observed in each local community, or may regional functions be organised?	174
6.6.7	What responsibilities has the Local Spiritual Assembly for the Bahá'í Holy Days?	175
6.6.8	May fund-raising activities be held on Holy Days?	175
6.6.9	May marriages be celebrated on Bahá'í Holy Days?	175
6.6.10	Who may attend Holy Day observances?	175

6.7 SUSPENSION OF WORK ON BAHÁ'Í HOLY DAYS — **175**

6.7.1	On which Bahá'í Holy Days is work to be suspended?	175
6.7.2	What is meant by suspension of work?	175
6.7.3	What about Bahá'ís engaged in work that cannot be postponed?	176
6.7.4	What about work associated with the institutions of the Faith?	177
6.7.5	Should children seek to be excused from school on Holy Days on which work is suspended?	178

6.8 BAHÁ'Í ANNIVERSARIES - A BRIEF DESCRIPTION OF EACH — **178**

6.8.1	What are the Bahá'í Anniversaries?	178
6.8.2	What is the significance of the Anniversary of the Feast of Ridván?	178
6.8.3	At what time should the first, ninth and twelfth days of Ridván be celebrated?	179
6.8.4	What is the significance of the Anniversary of the Declaration of the Báb?	179
6.8.5	At what time should the Declaration of the Báb be celebrated?	179
6.8.6	What is the significance of the Anniversary of the Ascension of Bahá'u'lláh?	179
6.8.7	At what time should the Ascension of Bahá'u'lláh be commemorated?	180
6.8.8	What is the significance of the Anniversary of the Martyrdom of the Báb?	180
6.8.9	At what time should the Martyrdom of the Báb by commemorated?	180
6.8.10	What is the significance of the Anniversary of the Birth of the Báb?	180
6.8.11	At what time should the Birth of the Báb be celebrated?	181
6.8.12	What is the significance of the Anniversary of the Birth of Bahá'u'lláh?	181
6.8.13	At what time should the Birth of Bahá'u'lláh be celebrated?	181
6.8.14	What is the significance of the Anniversary of the Day of the Covenant?	181
6.8.15	Should work be suspended on the Day of the Covenant?	181
6.8.16	At what time should the Day of the Covenant be observed?	182
6.8.17	What is the significance of the Anniversary of the Ascension of 'Abdu'l-Bahá?	182
6.8.18	Should work be suspended on the Anniversary of the Ascension of 'Abdu'l-Bahá?	182
6.8.19	At what time should the Ascension of 'Abdu'l-Bahá be commemorated?	182
6.8.20	What is the significance of the Feast of Naw-Rúz?	182
6.8.21	When is Naw-Rúz celebrated in the West?	183
6.8.22	How should Naw-Rúz be celebrated?	183

TABLE OF CONTENTS

6.8.23	What is the purpose of the Fast?	183
6.8.24	What are the 'Ayyám-i-Há' - Intercalary Days?	184
6.8.25	Are there any Tablets or prayers particularly associated with the Anniversaries?	184
6.8.26	Is it necessary to stand and face the Qiblih when reciting the Tablet of Visitation?	184
6.9	**PARTICIPATION IN OTHER CULTURAL/RELIGIOUS FESTIVALS**	**185**
6.9.1	May Bahá'ís continue to participate in traditional cultural practices?	185
6.10	**NOTES FOR REGISTERED GROUPS**	**187**
7.	**RELATIONS WITH AUXILIARY BOARD MEMBERS AND ASSISTANTS**	**188**
7.1	**THE RULERS AND THE LEARNED**	**188**
7.1.1	What is the place of the Auxiliary Board within the Bahá'í Administrative Order?	188
7.1.2	How has the institution of the 'learned' evolved?	188
7.1.3	'How does the functioning of the institutions of the 'rulers' and the 'learned' differ?'	190
7.2	**FUNCTIONS OF THE AUXILIARY BOARD MEMBERS**	**191**
7.2.1	What are the distinct functions of the Propagation Board?	191
7.2.2	What are the distinct functions of the Protection Board?	192
7.2.3	What functions do the Auxiliary Boards have in common?	192
7.2.4	How do Auxiliary Board members fulfil their functions?	192
7.2.5	May an Auxiliary Board member also serve on an Assembly or committee, or be elected as a delegate to National Convention?	193
7.2.6	Are there any circumstances in which a Hand of the Cause of God, Counsellor, or Auxiliary Board member may serve in an administrative capacity?	194
7.2.7	May Hands of the Cause of God, Counsellors and Auxiliary Board members vote in elections?	194
7.2.8	How is the work of the Auxiliary Boards funded?	194
7.3	**FUNCTIONS OF THE ASSISTANTS**	**194**
7.3.1	What is the purpose of appointing assistants to the Auxiliary Boards?	194
7.3.2	What size area does an assistant function in?	195
7.3.3	What are the functions of the assistants?	195
7.3.4	Is the work of assistants confined to helping Local Spiritual Assemblies?	196
7.3.5	Are the assistants a separate institution in themselves?	196
7.3.6	How do the assistants perform their functions?	196
7.3.7	May an assistant also serve on an Assembly or committee, or be elected as a delegate to National Convention?	197
7.3.8	How does an assistant reconcile his or her roles as both an assistant to, and a member of, a Local Spiritual Assembly?	197
7.3.9	What if the assistant is serving on another elected institution?	198
7.3.10	How is the work of the assistants funded?	198
7.4	**RELATIONS BETWEEN THE LOCAL SPIRITUAL ASSEMBLY AND THE AUXILIARY BOARDS**	**199**
7.4.1	What principles govern the relationship between the Auxiliary Board members and their assistants and the Local Spiritual Assembly?	199
7.4.2	How should information be shared between the Auxiliary Board members and their assistants and the Local Spiritual Assemblies?	200
7.4.3	How should meetings be arranged between the Auxiliary Board members and their assistants and Local Spiritual Assemblies?	200
7.4.4	May a Local Spiritual Assembly refuse to meet with an Auxiliary Board member or assistant when requested to do so?	201
7.4.5	May a properly functioning Local Spiritual Assembly dispense with the services of the Auxiliary Board members and their assistants?	201

TABLE OF CONTENTS

7.4.6	When should a Local Spiritual Assembly seek collaboration with the Auxiliary Board members and their assistants?	201
7.4.7	Why is collaboration between the Auxiliary Board members and their assistants and Local Spiritual Assemblies important?	202
7.4.8	How does a Local Spiritual Assembly decide which Auxiliary Board to approach in any given instance?	203
7.4.9	May a Local Spiritual Assembly directly approach an Auxiliary Board member to carry out work that is not specifically Auxiliary Board work as such?	204
7.4.10	May a Local Spiritual Assembly directly approach an assistant to carry out work that is not Auxiliary Board work as such?	204
7.4.11	May Local Spiritual Assemblies write directly to Hands of the Cause of God, a Continental Board of Counsellors, or individual Counsellors?	204
7.5	**RELATIONS BETWEEN THE AUXILIARY BOARDS AND INDIVIDUALS**	**204**
7.5.1	What courses of action are open to an Auxiliary Board member or assistant if approached by an individual with a personal problem?	204
7.5.2	May believers report instances of misconduct by other Bahá'ís to the Auxiliary Board?	205
7.5.3	Does an assistant have a right to report information received in confidence from an individual to an Assembly or Auxiliary Board member?	205
7.6	**NOTES FOR REGISTERED GROUPS**	**205**
7.7	**SUGGESTED FURTHER READING**	**205**
8.	**MEMBERSHIP IN THE BAHÁ'Í COMMUNITY**	**207**
8.1	**DECLARATION AND ENROLMENT - GENERAL PROCEDURES**	**207**
8.1.1	What are the guidelines for determining whether an individual should be accepted into the Faith?	207
8.1.2	Does the individual have to be living a correct life, according to Bahá'í standards, before declaring?	207
8.1.3	Which laws should the individual be made aware of before enrolment in the Faith?	208
8.1.4	What steps should a Bahá'í teacher take when an individual expresses the wish to become a Bahá'í?	208
8.1.5	To whom should the completed Declaration Card be given?	208
8.1.6	What are the responsibilities of a Local Spiritual Assembly when it is given a Declaration Card?	209
8.1.7	Are there any circumstances in which a declaration should not be accepted?	209
8.1.8	What if the declarant does not live in a Local Spiritual Assembly area, or near to any members of the Regional Teaching Committee?	210
8.1.9	What if the declarant has more than one place of residence?	210
8.1.10	What should the Local Spiritual Assembly do to assist the declarant after enrolment?	210
8.1.11	What is the procedure for a person who wishes to re-enrol in the Faith?	211
8.2	**DECLARATION AND ENROLMENT - SPECIAL CASES**	**211**
8.2.1	May citizens of Israel be enrolled as Bahá'ís?	211
8.2.2	May people from Malaysia be enrolled in the Faith?	213
8.2.3	May Muslims from the Middle-East and North Africa be enrolled in the Faith?	213
8.2.4	May Chinese who are permanent residents of Australia be enrolled in the Faith?	214
8.2.5	May citizens of the People's Republic of China (PRC) be enrolled in the Faith?	214
8.2.6	May prisoners be enrolled in the Faith?	216
8.2.7	May sub-normal or mentally ill people be enrolled in the Faith?	216
8.2.8	May a person who belongs to an organisation to which Bahá'ís may not belong, be enrolled in the Faith?	217
8.2.9	May drug users or alcoholics be enrolled in the Faith?	217
8.2.10	Should a person living in an immoral relationship be accepted into the Faith?	218

TABLE OF CONTENTS

8.3	**ENROLMENT OF CHILDREN AND YOUTH**	**219**
8.3.1	Are children born of Bahá'í parents considered to be Bahá'ís?	219
8.3.2	Should the Local Spiritual Assembly register the births of children born to Bahá'í parents?	219
8.3.3	What if the child has only one Bahá'í parent?	219
8.3.4	May a Local Spiritual Assembly accept a declaration from a child, neither of whose parents are Bahá'ís?	220
8.3.5	Should the children of a couple, one or both of whom have just become Bahá'ís, be registered as Bahá'ís?	220
8.3.6	Should the children of Bahá'ís who have lost their voting rights be considered as Bahá'ís?	220
8.3.7	Can children of non-Bahá'ís attend Bahá'í functions?	220
8.3.8	What is the importance of attaining the age of 15?	221
8.3.9	What is the procedure for Bahá'í youth to re-affirm their faith when they turn 15?	221
8.3.10	What if a youth is not sure whether to re-affirm at 15 or not?	222
8.3.11	What should the attitude of the Local Spiritual Assembly be towards youth who are not sure whether to re-affirm or not?	223
8.3.12	How are youth who decide not to re-affirm to be regarded by the community?	223
8.3.13	May declarations be accepted from youth between the ages of 15 and 21 whose parents are not Bahá'ís?	223
8.3.14	Do special procedures apply to Iranian youth who wish to declare as Bahá'ís?	224
8.3.15	Does the National Spiritual Assembly require statistics of the number of youth in the community?	224
8.3.16	Can children under the age of 15 perform services for the Faith such as serving on committees?	224
8.3.17	Should children stay at home on Holy Days?	224
8.4	**INACTIVE BELIEVERS**	**224**
8.4.1	Should the names of inactive believers be removed from the register?	224
8.4.2	What is the responsibility of the Local Spiritual Assembly towards inactive believers?	225
8.4.3	What does the Local Spiritual Assembly do if it discovers that the inactive believer ceases to believe in Bahá'u'lláh?	225
8.4.4	What does the Local Spiritual Assembly do if the inactive believer is breaking Bahá'í laws and bringing the name of the Faith into disrepute?	226
8.5	**RESIGNATION OF BELIEVERS**	**226**
8.5.1	On what grounds may an individual resign from the Faith?	226
8.5.2	How should a Local Spiritual Assembly proceed if it receives a request to resign from the Faith?	226
8.5.3	Should the request to resign be put in writing?	227
8.5.4	May a person who still believes in Bahá'u'lláh resign from the Bahá'í community?	227
8.5.5	What if a person wants to resign in order to break Bahá'í law?	228
8.5.6	What is the status of a person who claims to still believe in Bahá'u'lláh, but refuses to accept some fundamental principle of the Faith, such as the authority of the administrative institutions?	229
8.5.7	What is the status of people enrolled as Bahá'ís who do not consider themselves Bahá'ís on the grounds that they did not understand the significance of what they were doing when they declared?	229
8.6	**CREDENTIALS**	**230**
8.6.1	When should credential cards be issued by the Local Spiritual Assembly?	230
8.6.2	How long are credential cards valid for?	230
8.6.3	Must credential cards be presented by believers at Bahá'í-only events?	230
8.6.4	What happens if a non-Bahá'í attends a Bahá'í-only function?	230
8.6.5	Must members of the Continental Board of Counsellors present credentials?	230
8.6.6	Must Local Spiritual Assemblies sight the credentials of visitors to their community?	231
8.6.7	How should the Local Spiritual Assembly regard visitors who cannot present current credentials?	231

TABLE OF CONTENTS

8.6.8	What should the Local Spiritual Assembly do if an overseas visitor does not have Bahá'í credentials?	231
8.6.9	What procedure does a Local Spiritual Assembly follow when believers from other communities within Australia arrive to settle in its community?	231
8.6.10	What procedure does a Local Spiritual Assembly follow when believers from overseas communities arrive to settle in its community?	231
8.6.11	Who is responsible for organising the transfer of believers into areas in which there is no Local Spiritual Assembly?	231
8.6.12	How should credentials be issued to Baha'is arriving from overseas?	232
8.6.13	Do special procedures apply when transferring in Iranian Bahá'ís?	232
8.6.14	Do special procedures apply when transferring in Southeast Asian Bahá'ís?	232
8.6.15	How does a Local Spiritual Assembly transfer Bahá'ís out of its community?	232
8.6.16	What is the procedure for a Bahá'í wishing to travel overseas?	233
8.6.17	How do Bahá'ís apply to go on pilgrimage?	233
8.6.18	How do Bahá'ís apply for a three day visit to the Holy Land?	234

8.7 NOTES FOR REGISTERED GROUPS — **234**

9. ADMINISTRATION OF BAHÁ'Í LAW — 235

9.1 GENERAL PRINCIPLES — 235

9.1.1	What is meant by the 'laws' of the Faith?	235
9.1.2	By what process are the Bahá'í laws applied to the Bahá'í community in general?	236
9.1.3	What is the primary duty of the Assembly towards its community regarding the application of Bahá'í law?	236
9.1.4	What should the Local Spiritual Assembly do when a Bahá'ís conduct is 'flagrantly contrary' to the Teachings?	237
9.1.5	How should the Local Spiritual Assembly apply Bahá'í law in specific cases?	237
9.1.6	What will the consequences be if an Assembly fails to intervene in a situation of flagrant violation of the Bahá'í laws?	238
9.1.7	What should the attitude of the Assembly be when administering justice?	238
9.1.8	How important is confidentiality?	239

9.2 LOSS OF VOTING RIGHTS — 239

9.2.1	Which institution has the right, at the present time, to remove voting rights?	239
9.2.2	What does deprivation of voting rights mean?	239
9.2.3	What is the distinction between removal of voting rights and expulsion from the Faith?	240
9.2.4	Is it possible for an individual to be barred from some activities but not others?	240
9.2.5	Can a Bahá'í who has lost his or her voting rights be subject to further sanctions for further violations of Bahá'í law?	240
9.2.6	Can a believer appeal against the loss of voting rights?	241
9.2.7	What disciplinary action can be taken against youth?	241
9.2.8	Is ignorance of the law a valid excuse?	241
9.2.9	What if a believer was given the wrong advice by a Bahá'í institution?	242
9.2.10	Can a believer avoid the application of Bahá'í law by resigning from the Faith?	242

9.3 PROCEDURES FOR ADMINISTERING A VIOLATION OF BAHÁ'Í LAW — 242

9.3.1	How should the Local Spiritual Assembly proceed when required to administer a violation of Bahá'í law?	242
9.3.2	What should a Local Spiritual Assembly do if it is not certain whether a believer has committed the misconduct brought to its attention or not?	244
9.3.3	What is the distinction between the Local Spiritual Assembly's function as a counsellor and its function as an enforcer of Bahá'í law?	244
9.3.4	What should a Local Spiritual Assembly do if a believer whose behaviour it is monitoring transfers to a new Local Spiritual Assembly area?	245
9.3.5	Which institution has jurisdiction if the situation involves believers in different Assembly areas?	245

TABLE OF CONTENTS

9.3.6	What if the believer in question is serving on a Local Spiritual Assembly?	245
9.3.7	What should an individual do if he or she becomes aware of the misconduct of another believer?	246
9.3.8	What actions is it inappropriate for a believer to take?	246

9.4 REHABILITATION AND RESTORATION OF VOTING RIGHTS — **247**

9.4.1	What responsibility has the Local Spiritual Assembly to assist believers who have lost their voting rights?	247
9.4.2	What should the attitude of the community be towards a believer without voting rights?	247
9.4.3	What steps may a community take to assist a believer without voting rights to regain them?	247
9.4.4	What must a believer do to have his or her voting rights restored?	248
9.4.5	Can the period of time for which a believer has lost his or her voting rights be extended beyond the point at which the situation is rectified?	249
9.4.6	To which institution should believers apply for restoration of their voting rights?	249
9.4.7	What if the believer has moved to a new area of jurisdiction?	249

9.5 ALCOHOL, DRUGS AND TOBACCO — **249**

9.5.1	May Bahá'ís drink alcohol?	249
9.5.2	May Bahá'ís drink 'non-alcoholic' wines?	250
9.5.3	May Bahá'í institutions serve alcohol to non-Bahá'ís?	251
9.5.4	What is the responsibility of a Bahá'í who has a non-Bahá'í spouse who wishes to serve alcohol at a function?	252
9.5.5	May Bahá'ís own businesses that sell alcohol?	252
9.5.6	May non-Bahá'ís consume alcohol on Bahá'í-owned premises?	253
9.5.7	What other guidance do the Writings provide on the use of alcohol?	253
9.5.8	May Bahá'ís take drugs?	253
9.5.9	May Bahá'ís smoke?	253
9.5.10	May a Local Spiritual Assembly ban smoking during a Bahá'í meeting?	253
9.5.11	Should new Bahá'ís be required to stop drinking alcohol or taking drugs immediately?	254
9.5.12	Should new Bahá'ís be required to stop selling alcohol immediately?	254
9.5.13	How should a Local Spiritual Assembly handle the problem of a Bahá'í who drinks alcohol or takes drugs?	254
9.5.14	What attitude should the Local Spiritual Assembly take towards a Bahá'í with a alcohol or drug problem?	255

9.6 BEHAVIOUR THAT DAMAGES THE REPUTATION OF THE FAITH OR CAUSES DISUNITY — **255**

9.6.1	What kind of behaviour does this heading include?	255
9.6.2	How should a Local Spiritual Assembly handle a flagrant violation of ethical standards?	256
9.6.3	Can a believer be deprived of voting rights for dishonest or fraudulent behaviour?	256
9.6.4	How should a Local Spiritual Assembly handle individuals whose behaviour is severely disrupting community life?	256
9.6.5	Can a believer be deprived of voting rights for failing to repay his or her debts?	258
9.6.6	Can a believer be deprived of voting rights for gambling?	258

9.7 DISOBEDIENCE TO CIVIL LAW — **259**

9.7.1	Must Bahá'ís obey the civil law?	259
9.7.2	Is a believer found guilty of a crime automatically deprived of voting rights?	259
9.7.3	How should a Local Spiritual Assembly proceed in a situation in which a Bahá'í has violated the civil law?	259
9.7.4	What guidance is there for Bahá'ís swearing an oath or affirmation in a Court of Law?	260
9.7.5	Must the oath or affirmation be sworn on a specific holy book?	260

TABLE OF CONTENTS

9.8	**DIVORCE**	**260**
9.9	**DOMESTIC VIOLENCE**	**260**
9.9.1	What is domestic violence?	260
9.9.2	Why is assault on a marriage partner wrong?	260
9.9.3	What is the law concerning domestic violence in Australia?	261
9.9.4	Should a victim or perpetrator of domestic violence take the problem to their Assembly?	261
9.9.5	How may the Local Spiritual Assembly encourage individuals to turn to the Assembly for help?	262
9.9.6	Can a Local Spiritual Assembly intervene in a domestic violence conflict against the will of the parties involved?	262
9.9.7	Should the Local Spiritual Assembly advise a couple in a domestic violence situation to separate?	262
9.9.8	What immediate action should an Assembly take to assist a victim or perpetrator of domestic violence?	263
9.9.9	What principles should a Local Spiritual Assembly bear in mind when assisting a couple in a domestic violence situation to resolve their differences?	263
9.9.10	How should the Assembly counsel the couple?	264
9.9.11	Where can the Assembly turn for further help?	264
9.9.12	Does the Local Spiritual Assembly or an individual have a responsibility to report incidences of domestic violence to the civil authorities?	265
9.9.13	If a beleiver persists in domestic violence, will that person be deprived of his or her voting rights?	265
9.9.14	What should an individual Bahá'í do if told in confidence of a domestic violence problem?	265
9.10	**MORALITY**	**265**
9.10.1	What standard of morality must Bahá'ís uphold?	265
9.10.2	How should the Local Spiritual Assembly handle problems of immorality that arise within the community?	266
9.10.3	What is meant by 'flagrant' immorality?	267
9.10.4	Is the birth of a child out of wedlock in itself sufficient reason to remove voting rights?	267
9.10.5	What is the Bahá'í stance on a man and a woman who are not married sharing the same accommodation?	268
9.10.6	What arrangements for shared accommodation are acceptable in Australia?	268
9.10.7	How should the Local Spiritual Assembly proceed in a case in which a shared accommodation arrangement is unacceptable?	269
9.10.8	How should the Local Spiritual Assembly advise believers who are living in an immoral relationship?	269
9.10.9	What is the Bahá'í stance on homosexuality?	269
9.10.10	How should a Local Spiritual Assembly handle a case of flagrant homosexuality?	270
9.11	**MARRIAGE**	**270**
9.12	**POLITICAL ACTIVITIES AND MEMBERSHIP IN UNACCEPTABLE ORGANISATIONS**	**271**
9.12.1	Are Bahá'ís permitted to become involved in political activities or the ecclesiastical activities of other groups?	271
9.12.2	How should the Local Spiritual Assembly proceed in the case of Bahá'í membership in unacceptable non-Bahá'í organisations?	271
9.13	**NOTES FOR REGISTERED GROUPS**	**272**
10.	**BAHÁ'Í TEACHINGS ON MARRIAGE**	**273**
10.1	**INTRODUCTION**	**273**

TABLE OF CONTENTS

10.1.1	What is the meaning of Bahá'í marriage?	273
10.1.2	What is the age of maturity for marriage?	273
10.1.3	What prohibitions apply to marriage between relatives?	273
10.1.4	What are the requirements for a Bahá'í marriage?	273

10.2 CONSENT OF BOTH PARTIES — **274**

10.2.1	Is the consent of both parties necessary?	274
10.2.2	Do the parties involved consent to be married to each other prior to obtaining parental consent?	274

10.3 CONSENT OF PARENTS — **274**

10.3.1	Whose consent must be obtained and why?	274
10.3.2	To what are the parents consenting?	274
10.3.3	Is there a required wording for consent?	275
10.3.4	Should the consents be given in writing?	275
10.3.5	What if the parents do not name the spouse in the letter of consent?	275
10.3.6	Must parental consents be obtained if one of the parties to the marriage is a non-Bahá'í?	276
10.3.7	Must consents be obtained if the parents are non-Bahá'ís or have been divorced for years?	276
10.3.8	Must consents be obtained in the event of a second marriage?	276
10.3.9	What is to be done if the whereabouts of the parent is unknown?	276
10.3.10	What is to be done if the identity of the father is uncertain?	277
10.3.11	What if it is dangerous to contact the parents to get their consent?	277
10.3.12	What should be done about parental consents where one of the parties to a marriage is adopted?	278
10.3.13	What should be done about parental consents where one of the parties to a marriage is fostered?	278
10.3.14	What if a Bahá'í has been born of artificial insemination?	278
10.3.15	Are there any circumstances under which parental consents are not required?	278
10.3.16	If consent of parents to a marriage is conditional on a church wedding taking place, and the couple are both Bahá'ís, can the couple proceed with the marriage?	280
10.3.17	What is the situation of Bahá'ís if they cannot obtain the consent for marriage of one or more parents?	280

10.4 BAHÁ'Í ENGAGEMENT — **281**

10.4.1	When does the Bahá'í engagement period commence?	281
10.4.2	Does the law set out in the "Kitáb-i-Aqdas" regarding the period (ie. 95 days) of engagement apply in Australia?	281
10.4.3	For those believers who are required to observe it, is it permitted to break or extend the 95 day period?	281

10.5 DOWRY — **282**

10.5.1	Is the giving of the dowry specified in the "Kitáb-i-Aqdas" binding in Australia?	282
10.5.2	When should the dowry be paid?	282
10.5.3	How much dowry should be paid?	282
10.5.4	To whom should the dowry be paid?	283

10.6 THE NATURE OF THE BAHÁ'Í MARRIAGE CEREMONY — **283**

10.6.1	What is the vow to be spoken?	283
10.6.2	What form should the ceremony take?	283
10.6.3	Is exchange of rings a necessary part of the ceremony?	283
10.6.4	Can marriages be held on Bahá'í Holy Days?	283

10.7 IMPORTANCE OF THE BAHÁ'Í MARRIAGE CEREMONY — **283**

10.7.1	Must a Bahá'í have a Bahá'í marriage ceremony?	283
10.7.2	Where one party is a non-Bahá'í, may the Bahá'í participate in the religious ceremony of the non-Bahá'í partner?	284

TABLE OF CONTENTS

10.7.3	Where there is both a Bahá'í and a non-Bahá'í ceremony, in which order should they be held?	284
10.7.4	Where two ceremonies are held, must they both be held on the same day?	285
10.7.5	Can two non-Bahá'ís be married according to the Bahá'í ceremony?	285
10.7.6	What is the relationship between Bahá'í and civil requirements for marriage?	285
10.7.7	In what order should the Bahá'í and civil requirements be completed?	285
10.7.8	What are the consequences of not obeying the Bahá'í marriage laws?	285
10.7.9	What are the necessary conditions for the restoration of voting rights, resulting from disobedience of Bahá'í marriage laws?	286
10.7.10	What are the consequences of not obeying the civil law of Australia?	286
10.7.11	What is the position when two Bahá'ís who were married before they became Bahá'ís, now wish to have a Bahá'í marriage?	286
10.7.12	What is the position when, through ignorance of Bahá'í law, two Bahá'ís fail to have a Bahá'í marriage ceremony?	287
10.7.13	Should Bahá'í believers attend weddings of Bahá'ís marrying contrary to Bahá'í Law?	287
10.7.14	What is the situation for Iranian Bahá'í couples who had only a Bahá'í marriage in Iran?	287

10.8 BAHÁ'Í MARRIAGE CELEBRANTS — **288**

10.8.1	What is a Bahá'í Marriage Celebrant?	288
10.8.2	What costs are involved in using a Bahá'í Marriage Celebrant?	288
10.8.3	What is the role of the Bahá'í Marriage Celebrant under the following conditions?	288
10.8.4	What is the responsibility of Bahá'í Marriage Celebrants towards the Bahá'í requirements of the ceremony.	289
10.8.5	Where do we obtain the names and addresses of the Bahá'í Marriage Celebrants?	289

10.9 NOTIFYING THE MARRIAGE CELEBRANT — **289**

10.9.1	How soon must the Bahá'í Marriage Celebrant be contacted?	289

10.10 RESPONSIBILITIES OF THE LOCAL SPIRITUAL ASSEMBLY FOR THE MARRIAGE — **289**

10.10.1	Which Bahá'í Institution is the responsible body?	289
10.10.2	What specific functions must the responsible Local Spiritual Assembly perform?	290
10.10.3	What responsibility does the Local Spiritual Assembly have concerning the style of the marriage ceremony?	291
10.10.4	Is there a special Bahá'í marriage form that the Assembly must fill out?	292
10.10.5	How to complete a 'notification of marriage' form.	292

10.11 DE FACTO RELATIONSHIPS — **292**

10.11.1	What constitutes a de facto relationship under Bahá'í law?	292
10.11.2	Should a couple who commenced living in a de facto relationship before becoming Bahá'ís be obliged to have a Bahá'í wedding ceremony after becoming Bahá'ís?	292

10.12 RESPONSIBILITIES OF THE LOCAL SPIRITUAL ASSEMBLY FOR MARRIAGE DEEPENING — **293**

10.12.1	What is the role of the Assembly in marriage deepening?	293
10.12.2	What is the responsibility of the Local Spiritual Assembly for marriage counselling?	294

10.13 REGISTERED GROUPS — **294**

	APPENDIX 1: CHECKLIST FOR HOLDING A BAHÁ'Í MARRIAGE IN AUSTRALIA	294
	APPENDIX 2: NOTIFICATION OF MARRIAGE FORM	301

11. RECONCILIATION AND DIVORCE — **302**

11.1 INTRODUCTION - PREVENTING DIVORCE — **302**

11.1.1	What is the Bahá'í attitude towards divorce?	302

TABLE OF CONTENTS

11.1.2	Why is divorce abhorred?	302
11.1.3	How may the Local Spiritual Assembly prevent divorce from occurring?	303
11.1.4	When should a Local Spiritual Assembly intervene in a marital conflict?	304
11.1.5	What should the attitude of the Bahá'í community be towards a couple experiencing marital difficulties?	304

11.2 RECONCILIATION — 304

11.2.1	What is the duty of the Local Spiritual Assembly if the parties to a marriage approach it asking for a divorce?	304
11.2.2	Should the Local Spiritual Assembly advise a couple in a domestic violence situation to separate?	304
11.2.3	Can one party to a marriage, acting alone, approach the Local Spiritual Assembly for a year of patience?	305
11.2.4	What procedure should the Local Spiritual Assembly follow when attempting to reconcile a couple?	305
11.2.5	Should the Assembly offer counselling to a Bahá'í without voting rights?	307

11.3 YEAR OF PATIENCE — 307

11.3.1	What is the purpose of the year of patience?	307
11.3.2	What are the primary obligations of the couple and of the Local Spiritual Assembly during the year of patience?	308
11.3.3	Who fixes the date for the beginning of the year of patience?	308
11.3.4	When does the year of patience begin?	308
11.3.5	Can the date for the beginning of the year of patience be back-dated?	309
11.3.6	Does the husband have to pay maintenance during the year of patience?	309
11.3.7	What about care of dependents during the year of patience?	309
11.3.8	Is the year of patience necessary if one party is not a Bahá'í?	309
11.3.9	What if a civil divorce is granted to the non-Bahá'í partner before the end of the year of patience?	310
11.3.10	What if the non-Bahá'í partner remarries before the end of the year of patience?	310
11.3.11	Must a believer without voting rights observe a year of patience?	310
11.3.12	Can the year of patience be extended?	310
11.3.13	Can one party, acting alone, petition for a termination of the year of patience?	310
11.3.14	What constitute acceptable social relationships during the year of patience?	311
11.3.15	Does reconciliation end the year of patience?	311

11.4 CIVIL DIVORCE LAW — 312

11.4.1	How should the information provided in this section be used by the Local Spiritual Assembly?	312
11.4.2	What is the civil law regulating divorce in Australia?	312
11.4.3	What constitute grounds for civil divorce?	312
11.4.4	When does the period of separation begin?	312
11.4.5	Does reconciliation void the period of separation?	312
11.4.6	When can application for dissolution of the marriage be made?	312
11.4.7	How is custody of the children decided?	313
11.4.8	How is division of property determined?	313
11.4.9	How are maintenance payments decided?	313

11.5 RELATIONSHIP BETWEEN BAHÁ'Í AND CIVIL DIVORCE LAWS — 313

11.5.1	What is the relationship between Bahá'í and civil divorce laws?	313
11.5.2	When is Bahá'í divorce granted?	313
11.5.3	Can civil divorce proceedings be initiated prior to the end of the year of patience?	314
11.5.4	What if civil divorce is granted before the end of the year of patience?	314
11.5.5	What if the couple become reconciled between the end of the year of patience and granting of the civil divorce?	315
11.5.6	What is the situation for a couple living in a de facto relationship, which is accepted as a marriage under Bahá'í law?	315

TABLE OF CONTENTS

11.5.7	What is the situation for Iranian couples who had only a Bahá'í marriage in Iran and wish to divorce in Australia?	315
11.5.8	What is the status of an individual who initiates civil divorce proceedings prior to becoming a Bahá'í?	315
11.5.9	What is the status of an individual who remarries without having a Bahá'í divorce due to ignorance of Bahá'í law?	315
11.5.10	Can one party interfere with the granting of the civil divorce once the year of patience has ended?	316

11.6 RESPONSIBILITIES OF THE LOCAL SPIRITUAL ASSEMBLY FOR ADMINISTERING THE YEAR OF PATIENCE — **316**

11.6.1	What procedure should the Local Spiritual Assembly follow when administering a year of patience?	316
11.6.2	What should the Local Spiritual Assembly's attitude be towards the couple whose year of patience it is administering?	317
11.6.3	Does the Local Spiritual Assembly have a counselling role or an adjudicatory role with regard to the couple?	318
11.6.4	What if the couple are unable to arrive at an amicable financial agreement during the year of patience?	318
11.6.5	Do Bahá'í sanctions apply if a party fails to abide by the agreement reached?	319
11.6.6	What if one or both parties to the year of patience are serving on the Local Spiritual Assembly?	319
11.6.7	Who administers the year of patience if one or both parties move to a new Assembly area?	319
11.6.8	Who administers the year of patience if one or both parties moves to a new country?	320

11.7 ARRANGEMENTS AFTER THE DIVORCE — **320**

11.7.1	Does Bahá'í law require the husband to pay maintenance to the wife after completion of the year of patience?	320
11.7.2	Can the husband demand refund of the dowry or marriage expenses in the event of divorce?	320
11.7.3	To what extent should the Local Spiritual Assembly involve itself in such matters as division of family assets, custody of children, etc?	321
11.7.4	What guidelines should the Local Spiritual Assembly follow when assisting a couple to make such arrangements?	321
11.7.5	What role does the Local Spiritual Assembly have in enforcing decisions of the civil court?	322
11.7.6	Do sanctions apply to Bahá'ís who do not obey decisions of the civil court?	322

11.8 ANNULMENT — **323**

11.8.1	Are there any circumstances under Bahá'í law in which a marriage can be annulled?	323

11.9 REGISTERED GROUPS — **323**

11.10 LIST OF APPROVED MARRIAGE COUNSELLING AND PRE-MARITAL EDUCATION ORGANISATIONS — **323**

11.11 FORMAT OF LETTER FOR COMMENCEMENT OF THE YEAR OF PATIENCE — **325**

11.12 FORMAT OF LETTER FOR END OF THE YEAR OF PATIENCE — **325**

11.13 FORMAT OF LETTER FOR FINALISATION OF BAHÁ'Í DIVORCE — **326**

APPENDIX 1: L.S.A. CONSULTATION ON DOMESTIC PROBLEMS — **327**

12. BAHÁ'Í WILLS AND BURIAL — 329

TABLE OF CONTENTS

12.1	**BAHÁ'Í WILLS**	**329**
12.1.1	How is the information in this Section to be used?	329
12.1.2	Does a Bahá'í have a duty to make a will?	329
12.1.3	How old should a believer be before making a will?	329
12.1.4	What is the purpose of a will?	329
12.1.5	Is a Bahá'í permitted to challenge the provisions of a will?	330
12.1.6	Should a solicitor be consulted?	330
12.1.7	Is a 'do it yourself' will a recommended alternative?	330
12.1.8	What is the executor of a will?	330
12.1.9	Who is the Public Trustee?	331
12.1.10	Should the will include reference to Bahá'í funeral requirements?	331
12.1.11	How can a Bahá'í help to ensure that he or she will receive a Bahá'í burial?	332
12.1.12	Should special provisions be made for children?	332
12.1.13	How may the Faith be made a beneficiary in a will?	332
12.1.14	How should bequests to the Faith be handled?	332
12.1.15	What should believers do with Bahá'í papers and correspondence?	333
12.1.16	Once made, should a will be periodically up-dated?	333
12.1.17	How are modifications made to a will?	333
12.1.18	Where should a will be kept?	333
12.1.19	Should pioneers make new wills when they settle overseas?	333
12.2	**BAHÁ'Í WILLS AND THE LOCAL SPIRITUAL ASSEMBLY**	**334**
12.2.1	What role has a Local Spiritual Assembly regarding the drawing up of wills?	334
12.2.2	What should a Local Spiritual Assembly do if there are provisions in a will that conflict with the laws of the Faith (eg. a provision to be cremated)?	334
12.2.3	What should a Local Spiritual Assembly do if acceptance of a bequest is dependent on fulfilling provisions in the will that are not in the best interests of the Faith?	334
12.2.4	What should a Local Spiritual Assembly do if acceptance of a bequest is dependent on fulfilling provisions in the will that conflict with Bahá'í law?	335
12.3	**BAHÁ'Í BURIAL LAWS**	**335**
12.3.1	What are the Bahá'í burial laws?	335
12.3.2	Which of the burial laws are presently binding upon believers in the West?	336
12.3.3	Which of the burial laws are presently binding on the Persian friends?	336
12.3.4	What is the meaning of 'an hour's journey'?	336
12.3.5	How should the body be prepared?	336
12.3.6	How should the shroud be wrapped?	337
12.3.7	Where may burial rings be purchased?	337
12.3.8	Why is cremation not permissible?	337
12.3.9	May a foetus be cremated?	337
12.3.10	Is there a requirement that believers be buried facing the Qiblih in 'Akká?	337
12.3.11	May the body be embalmed?	338
12.4	**BAHÁ'Í BURIAL SERVICE**	**338**
12.4.1	What is a Bahá'í burial service?	338
12.4.2	Where can the Prayer for the Dead be found?	338
12.4.3	How is the Prayer for the Dead to be read?	339
12.4.4	May non-Bahá'ís be present at a Bahá'í funeral service?	339
12.4.5	Who is responsible for organising the burial service?	339
12.4.6	Who conducts a Bahá'í burial service?	339
12.4.7	May a Bahá'í burial service be conducted for non-Bahá'í?	339
12.4.8	May Bahá'ís without voting rights have a Bahá'í burial service?	340
12.4.9	Are memorial gatherings permissible?	340
12.5	**BAHÁ'Í BURIAL LAWS AND THE LOCAL SPIRITUAL ASSEMBLY**	**340**
12.5.1	Which Bahá'í institutions should be notified when a believer passes away?	340
12.5.2	What responsibility has the Local Spiritual Assembly for the burial service?	341
12.5.3	What should a Local Spiritual Assembly or Bahá'í relatives do if they find that a believer has made plans to be cremated, or other plans that are contrary to Bahá'í law?	342

TABLE OF CONTENTS

12.5.4	How may the Local Spiritual Assembly prevent such situations from arising?	342
12.5.5	What should the Assembly and believers do if non-Bahá'í relatives organise a non-Bahá'í funeral service for a Bahá'í?	343
12.5.6	What should the Assembly and believers do if non-Bahá'í relatives have charge of the body and plan to cremate it?	343
12.5.7	How else may a Local Spiritual Assembly help to ensure that the friends receive a Bahá'í burial?	344
12.5.8	Should a Local Spiritual Assembly keep a register of deaths of community members?	344

12.6 BAHÁ'Í CEMETERIES — 344

12.6.1	Should a Local Spiritual Assembly purchase burial plots or initiate a Burial Fund?	344
12.6.2	Who is responsible for maintaining graves in which Bahá'ís are buried?	345
12.6.3	May more than one person be buried in a single grave?	345
12.6.4	How should Bahá'í graves be marked?	345
12.6.5	What other guidance is available regarding Bahá'í cemeteries?	346

12.7 OTHER MATTERS — 346

12.7.1	What happens if a Bahá'í dies at sea?	346
12.7.2	May Bahá'ís donate their bodies for medical science?	346
12.7.3	It is also possible to donate organs:-	346
12.7.4	What is the Bahá'í view on euthanasia and life-support systems?	347
12.7.5	What if a Bahá'í suicides?	347

12.8 SUMMARY OUTLINE FOR SOLICITORS — 347

12.8.1	BEQUESTS AND OTHER GIFTS TO THE FAITH	347
12.8.2	BURIAL REQUIREMENTS	348
12.8.3	LEGAL TITLE OF THE NATIONAL SPIRITUAL ASSEMBLY	348
12.8.4	INCORPORATION OF THE NATIONAL AND LOCAL SPIRITUAL ASSEMBLIES	348
12.8.5	EXECUTOR	348
12.8.6	GUARDIANSHIP	348
12.8.7	COPY	348
12.8.8	FURTHER QUESTIONS?	349

12.9 SAMPLE LETTER TO FUNERAL DIRECTORS — 349

13. INTER-COMMUNITY ACTIVITIES — 350

13.1 INTRODUCTION — 350

13.1.1	What are inter-community activities?	350
13.1.2	Does the National Spiritual Assembly encourage inter-community activities?	350
13.1.3	What is the primary purpose underlying inter-community activities?	350
13.1.4	How may inter-community activities be organised?	350
13.1.5	How should a community decide which method to use?	351
13.1.6	What factors should a community consider when deciding whether to take part in an inter-community activity?	351
13.1.7	What are some other ways in which Bahá'í communities can work together?	351
13.1.8	How should communities liaise with National Committees?	351
13.1.9	What function has the appointed arm in assisting inter-community activities?	351

13.2 ORGANISING JOINT ACTIVITIES — 352

13.2.1	What is the benefit of organising joint activities?	352
13.2.2	Who can initiate a joint activity?	352
13.2.3	How is a joint activity administered in practice?	352
13.2.4	How many projects should one committee be responsible for?	353
13.2.5	Who has financial responsibility for the joint activity?	353

13.3 NOTES FOR REGISTERED GROUPS — 353

TABLE OF CONTENTS

14.	**PROTECTION**	**354**
14.1	**THE LOCAL SPIRITUAL ASSEMBLY AS A PROTECTOR OF THE CAUSE OF GOD**	**354**
14.1.1	What responsibility has the Local Spiritual Assembly for protecting the Bahá'í community?	354
14.1.2	How can the Local Spiritual Assembly protect the Bahá'í community?	354
14.2	**ENCOURAGING UNITY**	**355**
14.2.1	What is the challenge facing the Bahá'í community at the present time?	355
14.2.2	How can the Local Spiritual Assembly encourage unity?	355
14.2.3	What are some causes of disunity?	357
14.2.4	How should the Local Spiritual Assembly handle problems of disunity?	357
14.2.5	How can the Local Spiritual Assembly determine when a problem of disunity has become so severe that it must intervene to resolve the matter?	359
14.2.6	How quickly should the Local Spiritual Assembly intervene in a situation in which the interests of the Faith are involved?	359
14.2.7	Where else may the Local Spiritual Assembly turn for assistance in overcoming problems of disunity?	360
14.2.8	What should an individual Bahá'í do if he or she has a problem with other members of the community?	360
14.3	**OPPOSITION**	**361**
14.3.1	Why does the Faith experience opposition?	361
14.3.2	What forms do attacks on the Faith take?	361
14.3.3	What attitude should the Bahá'ís take to such attacks?	362
14.3.4	What action should an individual take when he or she becomes aware of opposition to the Faith?	362
14.3.5	What action should a Local Spiritual Assembly take when it becomes aware of opposition to the Faith?	362
14.3.6	How should Bahá'ís regard books about the Faith written by well meaning but unenlightened enemies?	362
14.3.7	What about books written by enemies of the Faith placed in libraries?	363
14.4	**THE COVENANT**	**363**
14.4.1	What is the meaning of the Covenant?	363
14.4.2	What is the importance of studying the Covenant?	363
14.4.3	What is Covenant-breaking?	364
14.4.4	How should the Bahá'ís treat Covenant-breakers?	365
14.4.5	May Bahá'ís respond to claims made by Covenant-Breakers in the press?	365
14.4.6	May Bahá'ís read the writings of Covenant-breakers?	366
14.4.7	May Bahá'ís answer mail received from Covenant-breakers?	366
14.4.8	What action should an individual take if he or she becomes aware of Covenant-breaking activities?	366
14.4.9	What action should a Local Spiritual Assembly take if it becomes aware of Covenant- breaking activities?	366
14.5	**NOTES FOR REGISTERED GROUPS**	**366**
15.	**RELATIONS WITH SOCIETY**	**367**
15.1	**INTRODUCTION - GENERAL PRINCIPLES**	**367**
15.1.1	Are Bahá'ís encouraged to co-operate with non-Bahá'í movements?	367
15.1.2	What is the primary purpose of co-operation with non-Bahá'í movements?	367
15.1.3	How much time should a Bahá'í devote to non-Bahá'í movements?	368
15.1.4	What is the reason for this order of priorities?	369
15.1.5	What sort of non-Bahá'í movements should Bahá'ís co-operate with?	370

TABLE OF CONTENTS

15.1.6	May Bahá'ís be involved in political activities?	370
15.1.7	What is meant by 'political activities'?	370
15.1.8	What sanctions may be imposed on a Bahá'í who becomes involved in political activities?	372
15.1.9	Will our understanding of Bahá'í non-involvement in politics change in the future?	372
15.1.10	May Bahá'ís co-operate with movements whose methods of achieving their objectives do not accord with Bahá'í principles?	372
15.1.11	Which institution has ultimate responsibility for deciding whether Bahá'ís may be associated with a particular organisation or activity?	373
15.1.12	Are individuals bound by the same considerations as Local Spiritual Assemblies when deciding which movements to cooperate with?	373
15.1.13	Is it advisable for Bahá'ís to take steps to persuade the government to initiate plans for the world conference necessary for the establishment of the Lesser Peace?	374
15.1.14	May a Local Spiritual Assembly initiate an activity, not specifically designated as Bahá'í, in order to foster association with non-Bahá'í movements?	374
15.1.15	May association with non-Bahá'ís involve raising funds for charity?	375
15.1.16	May an individual raise funds for non-Bahá'í causes?	375
15.2	**ASSOCIATION AND AFFILIATION WITH NON-BAHÁ'Í ORGANISATIONS**	**375**
15.2.1	What is meant by 'association' with non-Bahá'í organisations?	375
15.2.2	Are Bahá'ís permitted to associate with non-Bahá'í organisations?	375
15.2.3	What is meant by 'affiliation' with non-Bahá'í organisations?	375
15.2.4	Are Bahá'ís permitted to affiliate with non-Bahá'í organisations?	375
15.2.5	May Bahá'ís affiliate with other religious organisations?	375
15.2.6	Are Bahá'ís permitted to belong to a society that practises any form of discrimination?	376
15.2.7	Are Bahá'ís permitted to belong to a secret society?	376
15.2.8	What are some issues to be considered in deciding whether to pursue association or affiliation?	376
15.2.9	Which non-Bahá'í organisations may Local Spiritual Assemblies affiliate with in Australia?	377
15.2.10	What should a Local Spiritual Assembly do if uncertain whether it is permissible to associate or affiliate with a particular organisation or not?	377
15.2.11	Are individuals bound by the same considerations as Local Spiritual Assemblies when deciding whether to associate or affiliate with a non-Bahá'í organisation?	377
15.2.12	May Bahá'ís join trade unions?	377
15.2.13	May Bahá'ís hold office in non-Bahá'í organisations such as trade unions?	377
15.2.14	What should an individual do if uncertain whether it is permissible to associate or affiliate with a particular organisation or not?	378
15.2.15	May a Local Spiritual Assembly appoint a representative to attend a non-Bahá'í consultative gathering, conference, or adhoc committee project?	379
15.2.16	What are the rules of conduct governing Bahá'í participation in consultations initiated by non-Bahá'ís?	379
15.2.17	What are the criteria for deciding whether a non-Bahá'í organisation may participate in Bahá'í activities?	380
15.3	**OTHER MATTERS - LOCAL SPIRITUAL ASSEMBLIES**	**380**
15.3.1	May Local Spiritual Assemblies publicly comment on current issues?	380
15.3.2	May Local Spiritual Assemblies make submissions to governments on any issues?	381
15.3.3	May a Local Spiritual Assembly sign an appeal or protest directed to its own and/or other governments?	382
15.3.4	May a Local Spiritual Assembly lend its support to a march or demonstration concerning a particular issue?	382
15.4	**OTHER MATTERS - INDIVIDUALS**	**383**
15.4.1	May Bahá'ís serve in government jobs?	383
15.4.2	May Bahá'ís vote in civil elections?	384
15.4.3	May Bahá'ís join the armed forces?	384
15.4.4	May Bahá'ís participate in strikes?	384
15.4.5	May Bahá'ís, as individuals, participate in coordinated campaigns such as	

TABLE OF CONTENTS

	systematic letter-writing or signing appeals?	385
15.4.6	May Bahá'ís, as individuals, participate in protests or demonstrations?	385
15.4.7	May Bahá'ís, as individuals, publicly comment on current issues?	386
15.4.8	May Bahá'ís, as individuals, write to the government to propose action on a particular issue?	386
15.4.9	How should a Bahá'í proceed to rectify an injustice?	386

15.5 NOTES FOR REGISTERED GROUPS — 387

15.6 SUGGESTED FURTHER READING — 387

15.7 UNITED NATIONS DAYS AND EVENTS — 387
15.7.1 Below is a listing of United Nations days and events that offer rich opportunities for Bahá'í-United Nations cooperation — 387

15.8 ORGANISATIONS BAHÁ'ÍS MAY BE AFFILIATE MEMBERS OF IN AUSTRALIA — 387
15.8.1 The following is a list of organisations that Bahá'ís may be affiliate members of in Australia. Both Local Spiritual Assemblies and individuals may be affiliates, except where otherwise noted. Note also the proviso that these organisations should not be acting in a political manner at the local level. — 387
15.8.2 For your further information, the National Spiritual Assembly advises that Bahá'ís are not permitted to join the following organisations: — 388

16. PLANNING — 389

16.1 INTRODUCTION — 389
16.1.1 What is the purpose of this Chapter? — 389
16.1.2 What is the importance of planning? — 389
16.1.3 What period of time does a plan cover? — 389
16.1.4 When should a Local Spiritual Assembly draw up its plan for the coming year? — 389
16.1.5 Should the Local Spiritual Assembly consult with the community when preparing its plan? — 390

16.2 THE PLANNING PROCESS — 390
16.2.1 What is the starting point for drawing up a plan? — 390
16.2.2 How should the content of the plan be determined? — 390
16.2.3 What method should the Local Spiritual Assembly use to draw up its plan? — 390
16.2.4 Should a Local Spiritual Assembly change its plan during the year? — 391

16.3 REVIEWING — 391
16.3.1 When should the plan be reviewed? — 391
16.3.2 How does a review begin? — 391
16.3.3 What method of review should be used? — 392
16.3.4 Why is reviewing essential? — 392

16.4 FEEDBACK — 393
16.4.1 What response may the Local Spiritual Assembly expect from the National Spiritual Assembly? — 393
16.4.2 What should the Local Spiritual Assembly do if it disagrees with the comments it receives from the National Spiritual Assembly? — 393
16.4.3 What about feedback from the local community? — 393

16.5 NOTES FOR REGISTERED GROUPS — 393

16.6 SAMPLE PLAN — 394
16.6.1 This sample plan assumes a community of 20 adults, 8 youth and 10 children. It also assumes a united, active and stable community. All communities are

different of course, and therefore, will have different priorities. All communities should, however, attach primary importance to developing an active teaching campaign.   394

17. LOCAL COMMITTEES   396

17.1 FUNCTIONS OF COMMITTEES   396
17.1.1 What is the purpose of setting up local committees?   396
17.1.2 Does the Local Spiritual Assembly have to implement all the procedures outlined in this Chapter?   397
17.1.3 What kinds of committees could an Assembly have?   397
17.1.4 When should local committees be appointed?   397
17.1.5 What is the difference between a committee and a working group?   398
17.1.6 What is the relationship between a local committee and other regional or national committees with similar functions? (eg. Local Teaching Committee - Regional Teaching Committee - National Bahá'í Teaching Committee)   398
17.1.7 What is the relationship between a Local Spiritual Assembly and a national committee?   398

17.2 MEMBERSHIP OF COMMITTEES   399
17.2.1 Is a believer obliged to serve on a committee if appointed?   399
17.2.2 Do committee members have to be appointed each year?   399
17.2.3 How many members should a Local Spiritual Assembly appoint to a committee?   399
17.2.4 Can Local or National Assembly members be appointed to local committees?   399
17.2.5 Can youth who have not yet reached the age of 21, serve on committees?   400
17.2.6 Can a Local Assembly appoint a person outside its area of jurisdiction to serve on a local committee or working group?   400
17.2.7 What attitude should a Local Spiritual Assembly take when disunity amongst committee members is disrupting the work?   400

17.3 DELEGATION OF AUTHORITY TO COMMITTEES   401
17.3.1 How much authority can a Local Spiritual Assembly delegate to a committee?   401
17.3.2 In what manner should authority be delegated to the committee?   402
17.3.3 How should the Local Spiritual Assembly supervise its committees?   403

17.4 THE COMMITTEE IN OPERATION   403
17.4.1 Are office bearers appointed by the Assembly or elected by the committee?   403
17.4.2 How is the first meeting of the committee convened?   403
17.4.3 How are the office bearers elected?   404
17.4.4 What are the duties of the officers?   404
17.4.5 Who is responsible for calling meetings?   404
17.4.6 How are urgent matters to be dealt with?   404
17.4.7 How should a committee organise its work?   404

17.5 NOTES FOR REGISTERED GROUPS   404

17.6 SAMPLE TERMS OF REFERENCE   404
17.6.1 Following is an example of the way in which Terms of Reference for a local committee may be set out.   404

18. INSURANCE   406

18.1 THE POLICY   406
18.1.1 What type of insurance policy does the National Spiritual Assembly have?   406
18.1.2 Who is covered by this policy?   406
18.1.3 What situations are not covered by this policy?   406
18.1.4 What should a Local Spiritual Assembly do if a claim arises?   407

TABLE OF CONTENTS

18.1.5	Where can Local Spiritual Assemblies obtain more information about the insurance policy?	407
18.2	**NOTES FOR REGISTERED GROUPS**	**408**
18.3	**APPENDIX 1 - COPY OF NATIONAL ASSEMBLY'S PUBLIC/PRODUCTS LIABILITY POLICY**	**408**
18.3.1	Attached is a copy of the National Spiritual Assembly's Public/Products Liability insurance policy. Please note that in any instance in which an Assembly is required to make copies of this policy to outside bodies, only the necessary sections of the policy should be copied. Please also check the date on the covering page to ensure that you possess the current policy, before supplying details to outside bodies.	408

19. PROPERTIES — 410

19.1 LOCAL SPIRITUAL ASSEMBLY PROPERTIES — 410

19.1.1	What forms of property may a Local Spiritual Assembly own?	410
19.1.2	What is the purpose of acquiring a local Bahá'í Centre?	410
19.1.3	What is the relationship between a local Bahá'í Centre, local Hazíratu'l-Quds and Mashriqu'l-Adhkár	410
19.1.4	Are Local Spiritual Assemblies encouraged to acquire local Bahá'í Centres?	412
19.1.5	May Local Spiritual Assemblies build Mashriqu'l-Adhkárs at the present time?	413

19.2 FACTORS TO CONSIDER BEFORE ACQUIRING A LOCAL BAHÁ'Í CENTRE — 413

19.2.1	How may a Local Spiritual Assembly acquire a Bahá'í Centre?	413
19.2.2	What general factors should a Local Spiritual Assembly take into account when deciding whether to buy, lease, or accept a donation of a Bahá'í Centre?	413
19.2.3	What financial considerations must the Local Spiritual Assembly take into account?	414
19.2.4	How can the Local Spiritual Assembly acquire, in advance, an indication of the financial support it could expect from its community for a local Centre?	416
19.2.5	Is financial assistance available from the National Spiritual Assembly?	416
19.2.6	What physical considerations need to be taken into account?	416
19.2.7	How is the Centre to be managed?	417
19.2.8	How is the Centre to be maintained?	417

19.3 OTHER MATTERS- MISCELLANEOUS — 419

19.3.1	May a Local Spiritual Assembly rent out Bahá'í property to non-Bahá'ís?	419
19.3.2	May a Local Spiritual Assembly rent its property to an organisation that may wish to bring alcohol on to the premises?	419
19.3.3	May a Local Spiritual Assembly rent its property to a political organisation?	420
19.3.4	Is dancing permitted in a local Bahá'í Centre?	420
19.3.5	Is it permissible to hold Bahá'í functions on the premises of other religious organisations?	421
19.3.6	Does the Local Spiritual Assembly have to report the acquisition of, or changes to, property holdings, to the National Spiritual Assembly?	421
19.3.7	May a Local Spiritual Assembly accept a gift of free land from a non-Bahá'í source for Bahá'í use?	421
19.3.8	How may a Local Spiritual Assembly use the proceeds from the sale of property purchased with earmarked funds?	422
19.3.9	May a Local Spiritual Assembly purchase a church for use as a Bahá'í Centre?	422
19.4	**NOTES FOR REGISTERED GROUPS**	**423**
19.5	**BIBLIOGRAPHY**	**423**

20. PUBLISHING AND DISTRIBUTION OF BAHÁ'Í LITERATURE — 424

TABLE OF CONTENTS

20.1 PUBLISHING LITERATURE — 424
20.1.1 May a Local Spiritual Assembly publish Bahá'í literature? — 424

20.2 REVIEWING LITERATURE — 425
20.2.1 Which institution is responsible for reviewing works about the Faith before publication? — 425
20.2.2 What is the purpose of review? — 425
20.2.3 What standards apply to reviewing works? — 425

20.3 COPYRIGHT — 425
20.3.1 Are Spiritual Assemblies and individuals free to quote in their publications from any of the Writings of the three Central Figures of the Faith without obtaining clearance from the copyright holder? — 425
20.3.2 What about other publications, musical and artistic works, audio-visual material (eg. video tapes), computer software programmes, and so on? — 426

20.4 DISTRIBUTING LITERATURE — 426
20.4.1 May a Local Spiritual Assembly sell works it has published outside its own area of jurisdiction? — 426
20.4.2 May a Local Spiritual Assembly set up a sales outlet? — 427

20.5 ENCOURAGING THE USE OF BAHÁ'Í LITERATURE — 427
20.5.1 How may a Local Spiritual Assembly encourage the use of Bahá'í literature within its community? — 427

20.6 NOTES FOR REGISTERED GROUPS — 427

21. BAHÁ'Í SOCIETIES AT TERTIARY INSTITUTIONS — 428

21.1 BAHÁ'Í SOCIETIES AT TERTIARY INSTITUTIONS — 428
21.1.1 What is the purpose of Bahá'í Societies at tertiary institutions? — 428
21.1.2 What is the responsibility of the Local Spiritual Assembly for Bahá'í Societies at tertiary institutions? — 428
21.1.3 What is the procedure for the formation and operation of a Bahá'í Society? — 428
21.1.4 Are there detailed terms of reference available for Bahá'í Societies at tertiary institutions? — 428
21.1.5 What is the role of the Association for Bahá'í Studies Australia Committee in relation to Bahá'í Societies at tertiary institutions? — 429

21.2 NOTES FOR REGISTERED GROUPS — 429

ADDENDUM

A STUDY GUIDE TO CHAPTER 2 OF THIS HANDBOOK — 430

INTRODUCTION — 430
What is Bahá'í consultation? — 430
Bahá'í consultation is a tool for individuals and institutions to use when making and implementing decisions on issues of concern to them. Its purpose, 'Abdu'l-Bahá has said, is "the investigation of truth." — 430
("The Promulgation of Universal Peace", p.72) — 430

CONSULTATION WITHIN THE LOCAL SPIRITUAL ASSEMBLY — 430
What are the major principles to be kept in mind during consultation? — 430

TABLE OF CONTENTS

What is the procedure for consultation?	431
Can an Assembly member absent himself from the consultation when the issue under discussion involves him personally?	433
When problems arise in consultation how can we solve them?	434

CONSULTATION BETWEEN THE LOCAL SPIRITUAL ASSEMBLY AND AN INDIVIDUAL — 438

On what matters should an individual consult with the Assembly?	438
Can an individual bring a problem to the Local Spiritual Assembly if other parties to the problem do not wish to involve the Assembly?	439
Can a Local Spiritual Assembly intervene in a conflict against the will of the parties involved?	439
Can the Assembly delegate a committee or individual to counsel a believer?	439
What is the procedure for consultation between the Local Spiritual Assembly and an individual?	439

CONSULTATION BETWEEN INDIVIDUALS — 440

How should individuals settle disputes?	440

REFERENCES — 441

WORKSHOP 1 — 442
BAHÁ'Í MARRIAGE WITHOUT CONSENT — 442

WORKSHOP 2 — 443
APPEARANCE OF DRINKING — 443

WORKSHOP 3 — 444
PREDOMINANTLY PERSIAN COMMUNITY — 444

WORKSHOP 4 — 445
DOMINANT PERSONALITIES — 445

FOREWORD

ACKNOWLEDGEMENTS

The National Spritual Assembly gratefully acknowledges the effort and work of its Members, past and present, and of those of its National Office staff and other believers, who have contributed to the writing of this Handbook.

FOREWORD

This Handbook for Local Spiritual Assemblies in Australia is designed to assist them to reach a fuller understanding of, and move closer to, their destined role in the World Order of Bahá'u'lláh. In the present programme of revision of the Handbook, the National Spiritual Assembly makes available further guidance on the day-to-day administration of the Faith. Whilst maintaining the question and answer format, it has updated the content and added new sections. The National Spiritual Assembly earlier introduced a loose-leaf page format in the hope that Local Spiritual Assemblies could update individual sections of the handbook as necessary, without disrupting its overall arrangement.

In this revision, the National Spiritual Assembly offers the complete Handbook in a printed and bound form, together with a comprehensive index. In future, it will either revise one chapter at a time, replacing the printed version chapter by chapter, or issue a completely new edition. The Handbook's pages are numbered in two ways, firstly, by page within section within chapter, and secondly, using a running page number from the start to finish. This first numbering schema is used in the Table of Contents, the second is used by the Handbook-wide Index to be found at the very end of the work. The Handbook is in no way complete or absolute in itself, but offers Spiritual Assemblies a ready reference of available guidance in an organised way, to aid their maturing role in the developing Bahá'í community. Local Assemblies should also consult the following references:-

1. By-Laws of a Local Spiritual Assembly
2. Chairman's, Secretary's and Treasurer's manuals
3. Principles of Bahá'í Administration
4. Lights of Guidance
5. Local Spiritual Assemblies (the compilation)
6. Other compilations and books mentioned in these chapters

Groups are free to follow those parts of this manual they are able to implement, within the guidance provided for them at the end of each chapter. They are not obliged to do so, but when they can they will enjoy the benefit of practising what they will have to follow when they become a Local Spiritual Assembly.

A group is considered to exist when there is more than one adult Bahá'í in good standing in a local council area. If a group wishes to be registered with the National Office it must send a request for registration to its Regional Teaching Committee. If the Regional Teaching Committee considers that the group should be registered it will send a recommendation to this effect to the National Office. The National Office will then ensure that the group receives all the materials that Spiritual Assemblies receive and it will include the group in mail-outs to Local Spiritual Assemblies.

The various principles which the National Spiritual Assembly has kept in mind throughout this review are well described in the following quotations of Shoghi Effendi and the Universal House of Justice.

> ..*They (the Spiritual Assemblies) should act like the good shepherd whom Christ mentions in His well-known parable. We also have the example of the Master*

FOREWORD

before us. The individual Bahá'ís were organic parts of His spiritual being. What befell the least one of the friends brought deep affliction and sorrow to him also. If by chance one of them erred He counselled him and increased His love and affection, if the Master saw that that friend was still stubbornly refusing to reform his ways, and that his living among the other Bahá'ís endangered the spiritual life of the rest, then He would expel him from the group. This should be the attitude of the Assemblies toward the individuals.

(From a letter written on behalf of Shoghi Effendi to a National Spiritual Assembly, dated April 11, 1933)

...National Assemblies must strongly guard against this marked tendency of laying down new rules and regulations all the time, which he considers unnecessary and injurious. In the end it will dampen the zeal and quench the spontaneity of the believers, and give the impression that the Bahá'í Faith is crystallising into set forms. Principles there must be, but they must be applied with wisdom to each case that arises, not every case covered, before it arises, by a codified set of rules. "This is the whole spirit of Bahá'u'lláh's system: rigid conformity to great essential laws, elasticity, and even a certain necessary element of diversity in secondary matters.

(From a letter written on behalf of Shoghi Effendi to a National Spiritual Assembly, dated May 18, 1948)

The divinely ordained institution of the Local Spiritual Assembly operates at the first level of human society and is the basic administrative unit of Bahá'u'lláh's World Order. It is concerned with individuals and families whom it must constantly encourage to unite in a distinctive Bahá'í Society, vitalised and guarded by the laws, ordinances and principles of Bahá'u'lláh's Revelation. It protects the Cause of God; it acts as the loving shepherd of the Bahá'í flock.

(Universal House of Justice, Message to the Bahá'ís of the World, Naw-Rúz, 1974)

National Spiritual Assembly of the Bahá'ís of Australia, April 1995

FOREWORD

INTRODUCTION

...Bahá'u'lláh ... has not only imbued mankind with a new and regenerating Spirit. He has not merely enunciated certain universal principles, or propounded a particular philosophy, however potent, sound and universal these may be. In addition to these He, as well as 'Abdu'l-Bahá after Him, has, unlike the Dispensations of the past, clearly and specifically laid down a set of Laws, established definite institutions, and provided for the essentials of a Divine Economy. These are destined to be a pattern for future society, a supreme instrument for the establishment of the Most Great Peace, and the one agency for the unification of the world, and the proclamation of the reign of righteousness and justice upon the earth.

(Shoghi Effendi, "The World Order of Bahá'u'lláh", p.19)

The role of the Local Spiritual Assembly needs to be understood within the above context. It is a divinely ordained Institution operating at the first level of human society, and is the basic administrative unit of Bahá'u'lláh's World Order. As such, it is of primary importance in the firm establishment of the Faith. As we move further into the fourth epoch of the Formative Age, the Universal House of Justice has outlined as one of the major objectives of the current Six Year Plan "further acceleration in the process of the maturation of local and national Bahá'í communities..."

(Universal House of Justice, Message to the Bahá'ís of the World, January 2, 1986).

In this process of maturation the Local Spiritual Assemblies have a crucial role to play. It is their duty to:-

1. act as a loving shepherd
2. promote unity and concord amongst the friends
3. direct the teaching work
4. protect the Cause of God
5. arrange for Feasts, Anniversaries and regular meetings of the community
6. familiarise the friends with its plans and consult with them
7. invite the community to offer its recommendations
8. promote the welfare of youth and children

Assemblies also have the duty to encourage individual believers to:-

1. study the Faith
2. teach
3. live in accordance with its laws and ordinances
4. contribute freely and regularly to the Fund
5. participate in community activities
6. seek refuge in the Assembly for advice and help when needed

The National Spiritual Assembly provides this Handbook as a contribution towards assisting the Local Spiritual Assemblies in the performance of their duties.

CHAPTER ONE

Chapter 1

1. Formation of the Local Spiritual Assembly and its Election

1.1 FORMATION - GENERAL PRINCIPLES

1.1.1 ***When must a Local Spiritual Assembly be formed?***

Local Spiritual Assemblies are formed on the first day of Ridván, which begins, according to the Bahá'í calendar, at sunset on April 20th and ends at sunset on April 21st. However, a group reaching nine or more believers, providing there has never before been a Local Spiritual Assembly in that specific area, may form their Assembly as soon as convenient, without waiting for next Ridván. It should be noted that, with the exception of Local Spiritual Assemblies in remote and unconsolidated areas [see below], a previously established Local Spiritual Assembly that has lapsed may only reform at Ridván.

1.1.2 ***Is there an obligation to form a Local Spiritual Assembly when there are nine adult believers in a civil area?***

Yes. Shoghi Effendi wrote through his Secretary:-

> *...in any locality where the number of adult believers reaches nine, a local Assembly should be established. He feels this to be an obligation rather than a purely voluntary act. Only in exceptional cases has the National Spiritual Assembly the right to postpone the formation of an Assembly...*

> ("Principles of Bahá'í Administration" p.46)

1.1.3 ***What if a Local Spiritual Assembly is to be formed in a remote or unconsolidated area?***

In a letter to all National Spiritual Assemblies, dated July 26, 1987, the Universal House of Justice said:-

> *It has been of concern to us that...there are many areas in which there are communities of nine or more believers who are left, for year after year, without the blessing of the divine institution of a Local Spiritual Assembly. This is a phenomenon of the present stage in the spread of the Faith where there has been a rapid acceptance of the Message of Bahá'u'lláh by people who, because of factors of illiteracy, unfamiliarity with the concepts of Bahá'í administration, or an attitude to the calendar and to the passage of time that is different from that of city-dwellers, fail to re-elect their Spiritual Assemblies on the First Day of Ridván...*

> *Not wishing such communities to be deprived of the bounty and experience of having Local Spiritual Assemblies, we have decided that, in such cases, when the local friends fail to elect their Spiritual Assembly on the First Day of Ridván, they should do so on any subsequent day of the Ridván Festival. This is not a general permission for all Local Spiritual Assemblies; it is intended only for those which are affected by factors such as those mentioned above, and it is for each National Assembly to decide the areas or Assemblies within its area of jurisdiction to which it will apply. The aim is still so to*

CHAPTER ONE

consolidate all communities that they will elect their Assemblies regularly on the First Day of Ridván.

1.1.4 **Can a Local Spiritual Assembly be formed in an area where all nine believers are not actually physically resident in the area, but where believers are intending to move?**

The relevant guidance is contained in a letter written on behalf of the Universal House of Justice, dated June 4, 1975, to a National Spiritual Assembly:-

The establishment of residence in a locality to the satisfaction of the National Spiritual Assembly may be accepted as a transfer of membership even though the particular individual may not physically reside at his new address immediately. Thus, the decision as to whether or not the Local Spiritual Assembly at...should be recognised is within the discretion of your Assembly.

As we can see from the above guidance, it is within the province of a National Spiritual Assembly to decide whether or not to accept such a transfer.
The National Assembly would decide if the intention to transfer physical residence was sincere and genuine, and would thus arrive at its decision concerning recognition of the Local Spiritual Assembly.

1.1.5 **Can Local Spiritual Assemblies be formed in prisons?**

The National Spiritual Assembly has adopted the policy that Local Spiritual Assemblies will not be formed in prisons.

1.1.6 **What is the area of jurisdiction of a Local Spiritual Assembly?**

The area of jurisdiction of a Local Spiritual Assembly corresponds to the recognised local government area in which it resides, whether this be a municipality, shire or city. Regional Teaching Committees maintain maps showing the boundaries of all local areas of jurisdiction in their region. Any group in doubt as to its area of jurisdiction should refer to the Regional Teaching Committee for this information.

The National Assembly, following the guidance of the House of Justice, has divided a few very large shires into two or three separate communities, each with their own Local Assembly or Group. Only the National Assembly has the power to decide to do this.

1.1.7 **Where may Aboriginal Assemblies be formed?**

In a telex to the National Spiritual Assembly of Australia, dated November 4, 1983, the Universal House of Justice said:-

As to Aboriginal Assemblies you may regard Aboriginal reserves and communities controlled by Aboriginal Councils as areas for formation Local Assemblies.

1.2 **MEMBERSHIP**

1.2.1 **What are the duties of a Local Spiritual Assembly member?**

The following quotations from 'Abdu'l-Bahá, Shoghi Effendi and the Universal House of Justice respectively, outline the duties of a Local Spiritual Assembly member:-

Obedience unto them (the Assemblies) is essential and obligatory. The members thereof must take counsel together in such wise that no

CHAPTER ONE

occasion for ill-feeling or discord may arise. This can be attained when every member expresseth with absolute freedom his own opinion and setteth forth his argument.

('Abdu'l-Bahá, quoted in "Bahá'í Administration", p.21)

The members of these Assemblies, on their part, must disregard utterly their own likes and dislikes, their personal interests and inclinations, and concentrate their minds upon those measures that will conduce to the welfare and happiness of the Bahá'í Community and promote the common weal.

(Shoghi Effendi, "Bahá'í Administration", p.41)

Their function is not to dictate, but to consult, and consult not only among themselves, but as much as possible with the Friends whom they represent...They should approach their task with extreme humility, and endeavor, by their open mindedness, their high sense of justice and duty, their candour, their modesty, their entire devotion to the welfare and interests of the Friends, the Cause, and humanity, to win, not only the confidence and the genuine support and respect of those whom they serve, but also their esteem and real affection.

(Shoghi Effendi, "Principles of Bahá'í Administration", p.44-45)

If he be a member of any Spiritual Assembly, let him encourage his Assembly to consecrate a certain part of its time, at each of its sessions, to the earnest and prayerful consideration of such ways and means as may foster the campaign of teaching, or may furnish whatever resources are available for its progress, extension, and consolidation.

(Shoghi Effendi, "The Advent of Divine Justice", p.44)

Only as individual members of Local Spiritual Assemblies deepen themselves in the fundamental verities of the Faith and in the proper application of the principles governing the operation of the Assembly will this institute grow and develop toward its full potential.

(letter from the Universal House of Justice to all National Spiritual Assemblies, dated August 11, 1970)

It is important for Assembly members to understand that their home and Assembly duties must be balanced. Development of the spiritual and family life of each believer goes hand in hand with development of the administrative institutions of the Faith and the teaching effort. Neither set of duties may be neglected:-

...Therefore it is not so much a matter of which is more important, the teaching work or family and personal responsibilities, but how we can seek a balance in our lives to accomplish both of these sacred tasks. But in addition to the progress and development of the spiritual life of each believer, individually and as a member of a family unit, the foundations of the administrative institutions of the Faith must likewise be continually strengthened...these two goals go hand in hand...

CHAPTER ONE

(letter from the Universal House of Justice to an individual, dated April 19, 1979)

1.2.2 *Who can serve on the Local Spiritual Assembly?*

With certain exceptions which are set out immediately below, any Bahá'í whose membership is in good standing, who is at least 21 years of age and is a resident of the Assembly's area of jurisdiction, is eligible to serve on the Local Spiritual Assembly. If one or more adult members of the community are such newly-declared Bahá'ís that they are not yet recorded as believers by the National Spiritual Assembly, they may take part in the formation of the Assembly, subject to later confirmation of their Bahá'í status by the National Assembly.

1.2.3 *Are there any names that should not appear on the voting list?*

The names of the following believers should not appear on the list of people eligible to be voted for:

1. Hands of the Cause of God and members of the Continental Board of Counsellors. These believers are exempt from administrative duties on elected institutions but may serve on an Assembly if they make up the ninth member of a community.
2. In the case of incorporated Assemblies, any believer who has been declared bankrupt. This is a prohibition existing under the civil laws for incorporation in Australia. It does not prevent such persons serving on committees, nor does it apply to unincorporated Assemblies. A bankrupt person may vote in elections for an incorporated Assembly.
3. Prisoners. Believers in prison may not exercise their voting rights until released.
4. Citizens of the People's Republic of China. These believers may not serve on Spiritual Assemblies, be appointed to committees, or be associated officially with Bahá'í administration. They may vote in Bahá'í elections, although they may not be voted for. They should be advised orally of the coming election, not sent a letter in the post.
5. Muslims and Israelis who have recently enrolled in the Faith who have not yet been notified of their acceptance by the National Spiritual Assembly. Such people may neither vote or be voted for, nor may they attend Bahá'í-only functions, until notified of their acceptance by the National Spiritual Assembly.
6. Believers who have transferred into the community from overseas whose transfer of membership has not yet been received at the National Office. Such people may neither vote nor be voted for, but may attend Bahá'í-only functions if they have valid international credentials. They may, however, participate in the formation of a Local Spiritual Assembly by joint declaration. The formation will be accepted by the National Spiritual Assembly, subject to this person's transfer of membership being completed at a later date.
7. Iranian Bahá'ís whose Bahá'í status has not yet been verified by the friends in Iran.
8. Believers who have previously resigned from the Faith and who have applied to re-enrol but whose re-enrolment has not yet been accepted by the National Spiritual Assembly.
9. Believers who have had their administrative right to serve on a Local Spiritual Assembly removed.

1.2.4 *Should names of inactive believers appear on the voting list?*

Yes.

1.2.5 *Should names of Auxiliary Board members or their assistants appear on the voting list?*

Yes. Auxiliary Board members, if elected, must decide whether to continue to serve on the

CHAPTER ONE

Auxiliary Board or to accept membership on an Assembly. Assistants to the Auxiliary Board, if elected to the Local Spiritual Assembly, can serve simultaneously on both institutions.

1.2.6 **Can a Hand of the Cause of God, a member of the Continental Board of Counsellors, or a member of the Auxiliary Boards, serve on an Assembly if they make up the ninth member of a community?**

Yes. In a letter to a National Spiritual Assembly, dated November 18, 1973, the Universal House of Justice said:-

> *The provisions of the Constitution of the Universal House of Justice state the principles governing the service of Counsellors and Auxiliary Board members on administrative bodies; they do not abrogate the present exception to the rule which permits a Hand of the Cause, a Counsellor or an Auxiliary Board member to serve temporarily as a member of the Local Spiritual Assembly of the locality where he or she resides, in order to help preserve its existence. If the membership of the community is exactly nine, including the Hand of the Cause, Counsellor or Auxiliary Board member, or if, subsequent to Ridván, it falls to or below nine, the above exception will come into force so long as the National Spiritual Assembly recognises the continued existence of the Spiritual Assembly. Membership of a Hand of the Cause, a Counsellor, or an Auxiliary Board member is of a temporary nature, and should cease when a replacement is available.*

1.2.7 **Should the name of a believer who has asked to resign from the Faith, but whose resignation has not yet been accepted, appear on the voting list?**

Yes. Such a person remains a Bahá'í until such time as his or her resignation is accepted.

1.2.8 **Should the name of a believer who is mentally ill or senile be left on the voting list?**

Believers' voting rights may be wholly or partially removed if they are incapable of exercising them. Shoghi Effendi advised Local Spiritual Assemblies to consult with experts before arriving at a decision:-

> *Regarding persons whose condition (ie. mental condition) has not been defined by the civil authorities after medical diagnosis, the Assembly on the spot must investigate every case that arises and, after consultation with experts, deliver its verdict. Such a verdict however, should in important cases, be preceded by consultation with the National Spiritual Assembly. No doubt, the power of prayer is very great, yet consultation with experts is enjoined by Bahá'u'lláh. Should these experts believe that an abnormal case exists, the with-holding of voting rights is justified.*

(letter from Shoghi Effendi to a National Spiritual Assembly, dated May 30, 1936)

The Local Spiritual Assembly would then have to make a recommendation to the National Spiritual Assembly for full or partial removal of voting rights. If the National Spiritual Assembly accepts that the person's right to be elected to a Bahá'í institution should be removed, the Local Spiritual Assembly should then leave that person's name off the voting list.

1.2.9 **Should the name of a believer who is physically incapacitated be removed from the voting list?**

Shoghi Effendi has said that a person may be excused from service on a Local Spiritual

Assembly on the grounds of physical incapacity:-

> *Concerning the question of refusal by certain believers to accept election to an administrative post ... Only cases of physical or mental incapacity, which, by their very nature, are extremely rare, constitute valid reasons for such an act.*
>
> ("Principles of Bahá'í Administration" p.86)

Shoghi Effendi has also said:-

> *With reference to your question whether it would be permissible for a believer to resign from the Local Assembly; under special circumstances, such as illness, one may do so, but only after, and never before he has been elected to the membership of the Assembly.*
>
> (Shoghi Effendi, "Local Spiritual Assemblies", compilation, p.13)

Based on this guidance, the names of physically incapacitated believers should not be removed from the voting list. If a believer is elected to an Assembly and is too physically incapacitated to serve, he or she should accept the election and then discuss the matter with the Assembly at the earliest opportunity. If the Assembly accepts that the believer is too physically incapacitated to serve (for a prolonged period, not just temporarily), it may, at its discretion, declare a vacancy and call a by-election.

1.2.10 What should a Local Spiritual Assembly do if it discovers an error in the voting list after the Assembly has been elected?

The voting list is determined at Ridván and all questions of eligibility are settled then by the appropriate body (the Regional Teaching Committee for a new Assembly, otherwise the Local Spiritual Assembly itself). The fact that a clerical error in the list is subsequently discovered, does not invalidate the election.

1.2.11 Does a believer called upon to serve on a Local Spiritual Assembly, have an obligation to serve?

Yes:-

> *...The Guardian wishes you to make clear to all the believers that membership in a Bahá'í Assembly or Committee is a sacred obligation which should be gladly and confidently accepted by every loyal and conscientious member of the Community, no matter how humble and inexperienced...*
>
> (letter written on behalf of Shoghi Effendi, dated July 2, 1939, quoted in "Dawn of a New Day", 1970 ed. p.79)

The only grounds on which a believer may be exempt from service on an Assembly are those of 'physical or mental incapacity' as discussed above. In a letter written on his behalf, Shoghi Effendi said:-

> *...the Guardian strongly feels that criticism, opposition, or confusion do not provide sufficient grounds for either refusal or resignation.*
>
> ("Principles of Bahá'í Administration", p.86)

1.2.12 What if a believer is unwilling to serve?

Believers cannot be excused from serving on an Assembly merely because they are unwilling to do so. Writing to a National Spiritual Assembly, the Universal House of Justice explained:-

CHAPTER ONE

The statement that it is a condition to the formation of a Local Spiritual Assembly that there be at least nine adult believers who are ready, willing and able to serve on the Local Assembly should not be taken as giving any Bahá'í the right to refuse to take part in the formation of the Assembly. It is merely a statement of a factual condition.

(letter written on behalf of the Universal House of Justice to a National Spiritual Assembly, dated June 2, 1977)

Further clarifying the matter in a letter to a National Assembly, dated June 30, 1968, the Universal House of Justice wrote:-

Within the framework of this principle it is for each National Assembly to determine in each individual case whether a Local Spiritual Assembly should be recognised. For the present, the National Spiritual Assembly has determined that the signatures of Local Assembly members on the formation form is sufficient indication of willingness to serve.

1.2.13 **What should the attitude of the community be towards a member who refuses to participate in the formation of the Assembly?**

Technically, a believer who refuses to participate in the formation of a Local Spiritual Assembly may be subject to loss of voting rights. At this stage in the development of the Faith, however, the Universal House of Justice advises that such friends should, rather, be lovingly educated as to the importance of their responsibilities:-
The following extract from a letter written on behalf of the Universal House of Justice to a National Spiritual Assembly is pertinent to the treatment of the believer, or believers, who refuse to take part in the declaration:-

It can therefore be seen that it is the duty of every Bahá'í in such a situation to take part in the joint declaration. If a Bahá'í, however, refuses to do so he should be helped to realise that he has committed a grave dereliction of his Bahá'í duty. In this stage of the development of the Cause a National Spiritual Assembly should not, generally, deprive a believer of his voting rights for such an offence, but should lovingly and patiently educate the friends in the importance of their responsibilities.

(letter written on behalf of the Universal House of Justice to a National Spiritual Assembly, dated December 2, 1980)

1.2.14 **May a believer resign from the Local Spiritual Assembly?**

A believer may resign from the Assembly if he or she has a valid reason for doing so, such as illness or travel. The believer must accept election and then discuss the matter with the Assembly at the earliest opportunity:-

With reference to your question whether it would be permissible for a believer to resign from the Local Assembly; under special circumstances, such as illness, one may do so, but only after, and never before he has been elected to the membership of the Assembly.

(Shoghi Effendi, "Local Spiritual Assemblies", compilation p.13)

1.2.15 **Reasons that are not acceptable for proffering one's resignation include:**

1. Personal differences and disagreements among Assembly members [see "Lights of Guidance" {revised edition} no.171]

CHAPTER ONE

2. A poor attendance record:-

> *Although it is highly desirable that all members of the National Assembly attend every meeting of the Assembly, the fact that a member is prevented by business or other circumstances from having a good attendance record is not a ground upon which a resignation can be accepted. It is not justified to accept a resignation or otherwise declare a vacancy on the National Assembly without a valid reason such as in the case of prolonged absence...*
>
> (letter written on behalf of the Universal House of Justice to a National Spiritual Assembly, dated November 27, 1968)

3. To give someone else the opportunity to serve:-

> *The Universal House of Justice has received your ... message .. advising that your National Assembly has accepted the resignation from the Assembly of ... for a number of reasons including the thought that his resignation was justified by "giving a chance to others to prove themselves worthy of occupying responsible posts in the administrative field". We are asked to say that ... Although the other reasons referred to in your message may have offered sufficient grounds for accepting ... resignation, the point stated above does not.*
>
> (letter written on behalf of the Universal House of Justice, to a National Spiritual Assembly, dated March 31, 1986)

A Local Spiritual Assembly may not accept a resignation from one of its members for a reason that is not valid:-

> *...the action taken by the National Spiritual Assembly in recommending to the Assembly in question the necessity of refusing to accept the resignation of any of the members, except in special circumstances such as illness, is in strict conformity with Bahá'í procedure...*
>
> (letter written on behalf of Shoghi Effendi to an individual believer, dated February 28, 1940)

1.2.16 **What should believers do if pressing commitments leave them short of time to fulfil their duties on the Local Spiritual Assembly?**

A believer in this position should strive to remain on the Assembly. He or she may ask not to be appointed as an officer or to a committee:-

> *As you know the beloved Guardian highly reprobated resignation from any office to which a believer has been elected and it is certainly best, at this present state of the Cause, for the friends to accept elective service whenever they are called upon to do so. However, there is no objection for an overburdened believer asking the Spiritual Assembly to which he may be elected not to appoint him as an officer or to a committee.*
>
> (letter from the Universal House of Justice to a National Spiritual Assembly, dated December 9, 1970)
>
> [See also "Lights of Guidance" {revised edition} no.173).]

CHAPTER ONE

1.2.17 *Are there any situations that would justify a Local Spiritual Assembly removing a believer from Assembly membership?*

A Local Spiritual Assembly may require a member to resign only on the grounds of physical incapacity or disloyalty to the Faith:-

> *...under no circumstances, has any local Assembly, or the National Spiritual Assembly the right to require a duly elected member to resign, unless he is physically incapacitated or has proved to be disloyal to the Faith.*
>
> (letter written on behalf of Shoghi Effendi to a National Spiritual Assembly, dated March 9, 1940)

Any question of the possible disloyalty of an Assembly member must be referred immediately to the National Spiritual Assembly and no action taken pending its advice. If an Assembly member's mental capacity is in doubt the Assembly would need to make a recommendation to the National Spiritual Assembly for full or partial removal of voting rights according to the procedures outlined in Chapter 9. It may be that the National Spiritual Assembly will remove the person's right to serve on an Assembly, without removing anyother rights.

1.3 PROCEDURES FOR ELECTION

1.3.1 How do we proceed when there are exactly nine adult believers?

Wherever there are nine Bahá'ís in good standing who are 21 years of age or over, resident in the same Bahá'í community on April 21st, these Bahá'ís shall form, by joint declaration, a Local Spiritual Assembly. However, a group reaching nine (provided there has never before been a Local Spiritual Assembly in that specific area), may form their Assembly at any time - not just at Ridván. Likewise, an Assembly forming in a remote and unconsolidated area, where it is affected by the factors outlined in Section 1 and has the permission of the National Assembly, may form on any subsequent day of the Ridván Festival, if it has failed to do so on the First Day of Ridván.

Whenever a group reaches nine, they, or the Regional Teaching Committee or the Local Spiritual Assembly assisting them, should write to the National Office for the necessary formation form. If all nine members are unable to come together to sign the form, an attempt must, nevertheless, be made on the day of formation, to obtain all nine signatures. Failing this, the signatures must be collected and the formation form returned to the National Office within seven days of formation. If it is not possible to collect all nine signatures within this time, the form must still be returned within seven days and there is space provided on it to explain why some signatures have not been collected. Upon receipt of the formation form, the National Spiritual Assembly will act to officially recognise the new Assembly and forward some useful materials.

1.3.2 *How do we proceed when there are more than nine adult believers?*

a) Where the Local Spiritual Assembly is being formed for the first time:-
A Local Spiritual Assembly being formed for the first time may be elected at any time during the year. When there are more than nine adult believers in a specified area, they should obtain a formation form from the National Office and follow the procedure for election by ballot as set out below.

b) Where the Local Spiritual Assembly is being re-formed:-
There is only one day of the year when a Local Spiritual Assembly can be re-formed. This is the first day of Ridván, which begins, according to the Bahá'í calendar, at sunset on April 20th and ends at sunset on April 21st. On this day the Assembly must hold its Annual General Meeting. The exception is a Local Spiritual Assembly being re-formed in a remote

and unconsolidated area, where it has the permission of the National Assembly to form on any subsequent day of Ridván.

The Annual General Meeting is the occasion for:-
1. an account of the year's activities to be presented to the community by the outgoing Assembly
2. consultation by the community on any matters pertaining to the Faith in the Assembly's area of jurisdiction
3. election of the new Assembly

As required in the Local Assembly By-Laws, all voting members of the community must receive from the Local Spiritual Assembly notice of the date, time and place of the election meeting, not less than 15 days prior to the election of the Local Spiritual Assembly. At the same time, each adult Bahá'í should be provided with a ballot which can be mailed in, should anyone be unable to attend the meeting. A current list of all believers eligible for election to the Assembly would also be useful. Following is a sample copy of an Election Call letter:-

Sample copy of an Election Call letter :-

Dear Bahá'í Friends,

The Annual General Meeting of ... Bahá'í Community will be held on (date) at (time) at the home of... We take this opportunity to call all community members to attend and participate in the election of the Spiritual Assembly which will guide and coordinate the community's activities until Ridván... The Annual General Meeting will also provide opportunity for discussion of the Assembly's summary of the Community's teaching and proclamation activities for the past year.

The Assembly urges everyone in the community to come along, to cast their vote in the election, to learn of the achievements of the community, to contribute their suggestions and discussion and to socialise with their fellow Bahá'ís in the spirit of this "Most Great Festival" during which Bahá'u'lláh announced His Mission.

Should attendance not be possible, the Assembly welcomes votes sent in by mail. Please post your ballot to the Assembly's address to be received no later than ... Please enclose your postal vote in a plain sealed envelope which is then placed in the envelope to be posted. The name of the voter MUST be indicated on or within this OUTER envelope, NOT on the envelope in which your vote is sealed. If postal votes do not have a name on or in the outer envelope they will, unfortunately, be ruled invalid.

We pray that you will be able to join us for this most joyous Holy Day.

With loving Bahá'í greetings,
In His Service

Incorporated Assemblies will be aware that their Annual General Meeting may also be the occasion for the presentation and adoption of reports required by law.

1.3.3 ***How should the Annual General Meeting be conducted?***

A suggested agenda for this annual meeting follows:-
1. Opening prayers
2. Reading of appropriate Bahá'í passages concerning elections

CHAPTER ONE

3. Appointment of tellers - there is no set limit to the number of tellers to be appointed, but there should always be at least two. It is preferable that tellers be of voting age and belong to the area of jurisdiction in which the balloting is taking place. Tellers are appointed by the retiring Chairman of the Assembly
4. Distribution of ballots
5. Prayers for the guidance of the voters
6. Election by secret ballot
7. Collection of ballots by tellers
8. Presentation of the annual reports of the Local Spiritual Assembly
9. Consultation on community affairs
10. Tellers' report of the election
11. Approval of tellers' report
12. Social activities

1.4   VOTING PROCEDURES

1.4.1   *How many believers must participate in the election?*

There is no minimum number of believers who must participate in an election:-

> *No quorum is required in the holding of an election for a Local Spiritual Assembly. This rule also applies in the case of By-elections. The mere fact that less than nine vote for the members of the Local Spiritual Assembly does not invalidate the election.*

> (letter from the Universal House of Justice to a National Spiritual Assembly, dated April 16, 1969)

1.4.2   *Does a believer eligible to vote, have an obligation to vote?*

No. Ideally, everyone eligible to vote in an election should do so, however, the right to vote is not an obligation. In a letter to a National Spiritual Assembly, dated April 28, 1935, Shoghi Effendi said:-

> *I feel I must reaffirm the vital importance and necessity of the right of voting - a sacred responsibility of which no adult recognised believer should be deprived, unless he is associated with a community that has not as yet been in a position to establish a Local Assembly. This distinguishing right which the believer possesses, however, does not carry with it nor does it imply an obligation to cast his vote, if he feels that the circumstances under which he lives do not justify or allow him to exercise that right intelligently and with understanding. This is a matter which should be left to the individual to decide himself according to his own conscience and discretion*

1.4.3   *.How is the Local Spiritual Assembly elected?*

Voting is by secret ballot. Local Spiritual Assembly members are elected on the basis of plurality, ie. the nine members receiving the highest number of votes are elected.
Each voter in an election of a Local Spiritual Assembly must vote for nine (9) different persons. A ballot is invalidated if:-
1. the same name appears more than once
2. more than nine names appear
3. less than nine names appear

If an ineligible or unidentifiable name appears in the ballot, that name is omitted and the other eight votes are counted.

CHAPTER ONE

1.4.4 *Can a believer vote for himself?*

Yes. Shoghi Effendi wrote through his Secretary ("Dawn of a New Day", pp 200-201) :-

> *A believer has the right to vote for himself during the election time, if he conscientiously feels the urge to do so. This does not necessarily imply that he is ambitious or selfish. For he might conscientiously believe that his qualifications entitle him to membership in a Bahá'í administrative body, and he might be right. The essential, however, is that he should be sincere in his belief, and should act according to the dictates of his conscience. Moreover, membership in an Assembly or committee is a form of service, and should not be looked upon as a mark of inherent superiority or a means for self-praise.*

1.4.5 *What is the procedure if a believer cannot write?*

If a believer cannot write he may privately indicate his choice to one of the tellers or to any other believer appointed to the task. That person will write out the ballot on his behalf.

1.4.6 *What is the procedure for voting by mail?*

When voting by mail the absentee ballot should be placed in two envelopes. The inner envelope should have no marking. The outer envelope should have the name and address of the sender and be marked "ballot". This enables the teller to identify the voter whilst maintaining the anonymity of the ballot. If the absentee voter mails his vote, he must mail it to the address advised on the election call and well enough in advance so that it is received before the election. Absentee ballots are opened at the election meeting, where they are counted with the votes cast at the meeting.

1.4.7 *How is a tie vote resolved?*

A tie occurs in the election of an Assembly when two or more persons receive the same number of votes for the ninth position on the Assembly. A second ballot must then be cast by those present at the election meeting unless one of the persons tied belongs to a minority (see next question). The names of those tied are announced and each voter casts a ballot for one from among those sharing the tie vote. If the tie is not resolved in this ballot then successive ballots are to be cast, all confined to the persons tied.

1.4.8 *Are there different procedures to follow when there is a tie vote between Bahá'ís of different races or nationalities within the community?*

The relevant guidance is contained in the following letter from the Universal House of Justice to a National Spiritual Assembly, dated June 30, 1966:-

> *The Guardian's instruction is clear and definite on the following point, namely that when an election results in a tied vote between persons, one of whom represents a minority, that person should unhesitatingly be accorded priority without having a re-vote to break the tie. There is no doubt on this point. What is not clearly defined, is 'majority' and 'minority'. The Guardian refers to 'various races, faiths or nationalities'. Where this is obvious, eg. in the United States a white American and a Negro, there is no problem. In all cases of doubt a re-vote should be held.*

Additional clarification was received from the International Teaching Centre (July 28, 1978 to the Australasian Counsellors):-

> *Persians, Americans and citizens of other nations living in Australia,*

CHAPTER ONE

like foreign pioneers, are not regarded as belonging to a minority in a situation involving a tie vote. As you have suggested, in all cases of doubt, further balloting should occur. The term 'minority' applies to the general community and not to the Bahá'í community. Thus, Australian Bahá'ís are not a minority, even though there may be only one or two of them within one community. Aboriginal Australian Bahá'ís, however, are a minority.

For further guidance see "Lights of Guidance" I.C:46-52, XLVII:1119-1120]

1.4.9   ***Is it necessary to store used ballot papers?***

The National Spiritual Assembly has been asked from time to time whether or not it is necessary to store used ballot papers. In December 1975, the National Spiritual Assembly put the question to the Universal House of Justice, which replied:-

> *...this is a secondary matter and left entirely to the discretion of the Spiritual Assembly.*

(letter from the Universal House of Justice to this National Spiritual Assembly, dated January 11, 1975)

1.4.10   ***When must the National Spiritual Assembly be notified of the results?***

Mail notification of the results of the election of your Local Spiritual Assembly to the National Spiritual Assembly within seven (7) days of the election. The same form is used for this as when the Assembly is formed by joint declaration. The National Assembly is responsible for confirming or determining the validity of the election of each Local Spiritual Assembly. All unusual circumstances must be reported in full to the National Spiritual Assembly.

1.5   **ELECTION OF OFFICERS**

1.5.1   ***Who convenes the first meeting of the Assembly?***

The believer receiving the highest number of votes convenes the first meeting of the Assembly and presides until the permanent Chairman is elected. When two or more people receive the same highest number of votes the convenor can be determined by the drawing of lots.

1.5.2   ***When should the election of officers take place?***

Permanent officers of the Spiritual Assembly should be elected immediately following the election or formation by joint declaration. Occasionally a meeting for the election of the officers cannot be held immediately, because of the inability on the part of one or more members to attend. The Universal House of Justice, in a letter to a National Spiritual Assembly, dated August 6, 1967, said:-

> *All members of the Assembly or committee must be given the opportunity to cast their ballots. If, therefore, all nine members of the newly elected Local Spiritual Assembly do not have the opportunity to vote for permanent officers immediately following the elections, the best procedure is to elect or appoint a temporary Chairman and Secretary immediately, who will serve until such time as all members of the Assembly can be properly notified and given the opportunity to vote*

1.5.3   ***How are the officers elected?***

The officers are elected by secret ballot. The Assembly members vote for one officer at a time. The officers are elected by the majority vote of the entire membership of the Assembly (this means at least five votes). If it is impossible for a member of the Assembly to be

CHAPTER ONE

present at the election, his vote may be received by mail or telephone:-

> *...in case of unavoidable absence, it does not contravene the spirit of the By-Laws if the member casts his ballot by mail or by telephone. All other details in the application of these principles are within the discretion of the Assembly.*
>
> (Universal House of Justice to a National Spiritual Assembly, August 6, 1967)

It should be noted, however, that receiving ballots be phone or mail will create difficulties if a second vote has to be cast because the first ballot has not produced a clear result. For this reason a member who is unable to attend the election in person should endeavour to make himself available on the phone. It is then the duty of the tellers to receive votes over the phone. In rare cases a member, having been given the opportunity to participate in the election, chooses not to do so, in person, over the phone, or by mail. In such a case the election may proceed without that member; however, the minimum number of votes required for electing an officer remains five. It follows that at least five members must be willing to vote for an election to take place. In the event of nobody receiving at least five votes, there is re-voting until this is attained. There is no such thing as a "tied vote" when voting for officers. An office of an Assembly is elected by a majority of its members and until this majority (five or more) is obtained, all members remain eligible for the position and re-voting continues. In a letter to a National Spiritual Assembly, dated January 25, 1967, the Universal House of Justice makes it clear that:-

> *The situation resulting from a tied vote occurs only in an election decided by PLURALITY vote.*

The following is a suggested procedure for conducting the election:-

1. The Convenor appoints two or more tellers
2. Tellers distribute voting slips to all members of the Assembly
3. Prayers for guidance in the election
4. The Convenor calls upon the members to vote for the one person they wish to elect to the office of Chairman
5. The tellers collect the voting slips and count the votes
6. The tellers report the results of the election to the Convenor
7. If one member of the Assembly has received a majority of five or more votes the Convenor announces that person's election as Chairman and hands over the meeting to him
8. If no member of the Assembly has received at least five votes, the Convenor reads out <u>the names</u> of all members who received votes and <u>the number</u> of votes each member received
9. All members of the Assembly remain eligible for election and a re-vote takes place, repeating the above procedure
10. Steps 2-9 are repeated until a majority of five or more votes are received for one person
11. The Chairman then follows the same voting procedure for election of Secretary, Treasurer and Vice-Chairman. This order may be varied if the Assembly so decides.

1.5.4 ***What should be done if, after repeated balloting, no member receives five or more votes?***

> *If, after repeated balloting among those present, it is found that no member receives five or more votes, the Assembly must appoint one or*

CHAPTER ONE

more temporary officers to function until the next meeting. The choice of temporary officers should be made through consultation.

(letter of the Universal House of Justice to an individual believer, June 28, 1993)

1.5.5 ***When must the National Spiritual Assembly be notified of the results?***

Ideally the National Spiritual Assembly should be notified of the results of the election for officers at the same time it is notified of the results of the election for Assembly members. Failing this, the results should be sent to the National Office as soon as possible after the election is held.

1.5.6 ***How many officers does a Local Spiritual Assembly have?***

Article VII of the By-Laws of a Local Spiritual Assembly lists four basic officers of an Assembly: Chairman, Vice-Chairman, Secretary and Treasurer. Other officers, eg. Recording-Secretary, as may be found necessary for the proper conduct of its affairs, are permitted, but these additional officers may be appointed rather than elected.

1.5.7 ***What are the functions of the Assembly officers?***

See as follows:-
- Secretary - the chapter "Administrative Procedures" and "Bahá'í Secretary's Manual"
- Treasurer - the chapter "The Bahá'í Funds" and "Bahá'í Treasurer's Manual"
- Chairman and Vice-Chairman - the chapter "Bahá'í Consultation" and "Chairman's Manual"

These manuals are readily available from the state and regional outlets of the Bahá'í Publications and Distribution Services Committee.

1.5.8 ***Can a believer refuse election as an office bearer?***

If a believer feels that there is good reason why he should not be elected to an office, he is free to put these reasons to the Assembly before the elections for office bearers take place. It is then for the Assembly to decide whether to accept his reasons or not. In a letter to an individual believer, dated February 9, 1987, the Universal House of Justice said:

...although it is the obligation of a Bahá'í to serve on an Assembly, either Local or National, when elected, on several occasions the beloved Guardian pointed out that before the election of officers, if any member had a good reason in his own opinion why he should not be elected to one of the offices of the Assembly, he was free to suggest that he should not be so elected. The House of Justice also feels that as the work of the Faith expands and the duties of officers, particularly on National Spiritual Assemblies, acquire more importance, it is permissible and at times advisable to discuss the duties incumbent upon and required of each officer before ballots are cast.

1.5.9 ***Can an office bearer be dismissed mid-term?***

An Assembly officer cannot be dismissed mid-term because of incompetence or a failure to fulfil his duties. The only circumstances in which he may be dismissed are those in which his loyalty to the Faith is in question. In such circumstances he may be dismissed following a majority vote of the members of the Assembly:-

As regards the question of what procedure the Bahá'í Assemblies should adopt when dissatisfied with the services of any of their officers. Should such dissatisfaction involve the loyalty of an Assembly officer to the Faith, he should, following a majority vote, be dismissed. But in case the dissatisfaction is due to the incompetence of a member, or simply to a neglect on his part to discharge his duties, this does not constitute sufficient justification to force his resignation or dismissal from the Assembly. He should be kept in office until new elections are held.

("Principles of Bahá'í Administration", p.50)

Prior to any such vote being taken, the matter must be referred immediately to the National Spiritual Assembly and no action taken pending its advice.

1.6 VACANCIES

1.6.1 *What is done when a vacancy occurs on a Local Spiritual Assembly?*

When a vacancy on the Local Spiritual Assembly is declared, a by-election must be held. Written notices must go to all members of the community not less than 15 days before the date of the election. In the event that the number of vacancies exceeds four, making a quorum of the Local Spiritual Assembly impossible, the election shall be under the supervision of the National Spiritual Assembly. (See "By-Laws of the Local Spiritual Assembly", Art. VIII(2)).

Where an Assembly area has fallen to below nine members, any Bahá'í in good standing who enters the community and who is aged 21 years or over, automatically becomes a member of the Assembly.

1.6.2 *What is the procedure for a by-election?*

The procedure for a by-election is the same as that for the annual election. It should be noted that the number of names to be written on the voting slip must be the same as the number of vacancies to be filled.

1.6.3 *What is the procedure for electing a new office bearer mid-term?*

If it is necessary to elect a new office bearer mid-term, the same procedure is followed as that for the initial election. It is only necessary to fill the vacancy, not to elect all new office bearers. All members of the Assembly, including existing officers, are eligible for election to the vacant office. In the event of an existing officer being elected to the vacant office, the office he previously held becomes vacant and an election must be held to fill this office also.

1.7 NOTES FOR REGISTERED GROUPS

Registered Groups, as embryonic Local Spiritual Assemblies, are encouraged to prepare themselves for the time when they become Assemblies. To this end they are encouraged to elect officers such as a Secretary, Chairman and Treasurer. It is also permissible for youth to serve as officers of Registered Groups as a group is not an official administrative institution to which the age restriction of 21 applies.

CHAPTER TWO

Chapter 2

2. Consultation

2.1 CONSULTATION WITHIN THE LOCAL SPIRITUAL ASSEMBLY

2.1.1 *What is the procedure for consultation?*

It is recommended that the following steps be used when an Assembly is consulting on a problem; however, observance of all of them is not obligatory and the Assembly should use its own discretion in deciding which steps to follow and which to leave out:-

1. **Define the matter to be decided.**
2. **Ascertain all the facts of the matter and agree on them.**

b) separate relevant from irrelevant facts and distinguish between impressions and facts
c) discover the background
d) examine different perspectives

If the Assembly finds that it does not have all the information necessary it may have to postpone discussion on the matter to another meeting.

3. **Identify the spiritual and administrative principles that relate to the issue. Available sources are:-**

c) Writings of Bahá'u'lláh, 'Abdu'l-Bahá, Shoghi Effendi and the Universal House of Justice
d) this Local Spiritual Assembly Handbook and other works mentioned in its chapters
e) Continental Counsellors, Auxiliary Board members and their Assistants
f) the National Spiritual Assembly

The first two sources listed above should be researched before consulting the remaining sources.

4. **Consult together.**
5. **Make a clear statement of the provisional conclusion.**

When it seems that the discussion has arrived at a point of conclusion the Chairman, or some other person designated by the Assembly, should summarise the discussion and make a clear statement of the tentative decision. If the Assembly feels it is necessary, the temporary decision may be expressed as a motion. This is simply a more formal way of putting the proposed decision. To put a motion before the Assembly a formal proposition must be "moved" by one member and seconded by another. The wording of the motion, if carried when voted upon, becomes the form of the decision made and recorded in the minutes. If a member wishes to alter the motion, he or she must move an amendment. This in turn must be seconded. An amendment should change the original motion by omitting or substituting words. It must not negate the original motion. If the Assembly votes against the amendment the original motion stands. There is no limit to the number of amendments that can be moved. They should be voted on in the order they are moved. A successful amendment alters the original motion and a later successful amendment alters the motion as previously amended.

6. **Make a decision by consensus or majority vote.**

If the tentative decision is read out and it is clear that everyone agrees to it, a vote will not be necessary. The Universal House of Justice has clearly stated that:-

The ideal of Bahá'í consultation is to arrive at a unanimous decision.

(letter to a National Spiritual Assembly, dated March 6, 1970)

It is clear, therefore, that unanimity is to be preferred wherever possible; however, it is not obligatory. 'Abdu'l-Bahá has said:-

CHAPTER TWO

...if, the Lord forbid, differences of opinion should arise, a majority of voices must prevail.

("Bahá'í Administration", p.64)

Therefore, if the members are not agreed the decision must be put to the vote. At this point, the Universal House of Justice states:-

When it is proposed to put a matter to the vote, a member of the Assembly may feel that there are additional facts or views which must be sought before he can make up his mind and intelligently vote on the proposition. He should express this feeling to the Assembly, and it is for the Assembly to decide whether or not further consultation is needed before voting.

(letter to a National Spiritual Assembly, dated March 6, 1970)

If the Assembly chooses not to re-open consultation, a vote must be taken and the majority opinion prevails. The instructions of Shoghi Effendi must be kept in mind at this point:-

And, when they are called upon to arrive at a certain decision, they should, after dispassionate, anxious and cordial consultation, turn to God in prayer, and with earnestness and conviction and courage record their vote and abide by the voice of the majority...

("Bahá'í Administration", p.64)

7. Record the decision in the minutes.
8. Decide how the decision will be carried out.

2.1.2 *Can a member abstain from voting?*

This issue does not arise in Bahá'í voting. Only those votes in favour of a decision are counted. A member who does not vote in favour of a decision in effect votes against it:-

Whenever it is decided to vote on a proposition all that is required is to ascertain how many of the members are in favour of it; if this is a majority of those present, the motion is carried; if it is a minority, the motion is defeated. Thus the whole question of "abstaining" does not arise in Bahá'í voting. A member who does not vote in favour of a proposition is, in effect, voting against it, even if at that moment he himself feels that he has been unable to make up his mind on the matter.

(letter from the Universal House of Justice to a National Spiritual Assembly, dated March 6, 1970)

2.1.3 *In the case of a decision arrived at by majority vote, what should be the attitude of those members whose opinions were in the minority?*

Once a vote has been taken and a decision made, that decision becomes the decision of the whole Assembly, not merely of those members who were in the majority. Those members who were in the minority must accept the decision and uphold it before the eyes of the community. They must not seek to undermine the Assembly by telling people they did not agree with the decision. In the words of 'Abdu'l-Bahá:-

'such criticism would prevent any decision from being enforced'.

("Bahá'í Administration", p.22)

CHAPTER TWO

Criticism causes disunity. Disunity prevents the decision being effectively put into practice and this in turn prevents the Assembly from receiving feedback that will assist it to do better in the future. The over-riding principle is the necessity of preserving unity.

2.1.4 *What if the decision of the Assembly is wrong?*

The decision of the Assembly must be obeyed even if it is wrong:-

> *We all have a right to our opinions, we are bound to think differently; but a Bahá'í must accept the majority decision of his Assembly, realising that acceptance and harmony - even if a mistake has been made - are the really important things, and when we serve the Cause properly, in the Bahá'í way, God will right any wrongs done in the end.*
>
> (letter written on behalf of Shoghi Effendi to an individual believer, dated October 19, 1947)

A dissenting Assembly member may ask the Assembly to reconsider its decision but, in the words of Shoghi Effendi:-

> *he has no right to force them or create inharmony because they won't change.*
>
> (letter written on behalf of Shoghi Effendi to an individual believer, dated October 19, 1947)

2.1.5 *Should dissenting votes be recorded in the minutes?*

Dissenting votes should not be recorded in the minutes:-

> *There are no dissenting votes in the Cause. When the majority of an Assembly decides a matter the minority, we are told by the Master, should accept this. To insist on having one's dissenting vote recorded is not good, and achieves no constructive end.*
>
> (letter written on behalf of Shoghi Effendi to an individual believer, dated March 19, 1950)

2.1.6 *What is the role of the Chairman in the consultative process?*

The Chairman has the following tasks:-
1. help the Secretary prepare the agenda
2. ensure meetings start and end on time
3. ensure there is agreement on the procedures to be followed
4. direct the flow of discussion
5. synthesise contributions made
6. ensure no one monopolises the discussion or intimidates others
7. confine speakers to the matter under discussion
8. ensure all members have the opportunity to contribute
9. ensure that matters are clarified for those in doubt
10. identify tentative conclusions
11. accept motions and amendments (if such a procedure is adopted)
12. determine when consensus has been reached
13. state the decision

2.1.7 *What is the function of the agenda?*

A basic function of the agenda is to bring order to consultation by listing items according to priority. The Assembly can then decide how much time should be allowed for the discussion of each issue. The Secretary should prepare the agenda in consultation with the Chairman and, ideally, send it out to the other members ahead of time. If this is not possible it should be given to each member or read aloud at the beginning of the meeting. Members should be given the opportunity to add, or make changes to, the agenda.

Following is a suggested format for the agenda:-
1. Devotional Opening
2. Approval of Minutes of previous meeting
3. Review of Agenda
4. Teaching Matters
5. Secretary's Report - letters received, etc.
6. Treasurer's Report
7. Recommendations from the last Feast
8. Committee Reports
9. Other Business
10. Devotional Close

The order of the agenda may be altered but teaching should always receive first priority.

2.1.8 ***Can Assembly members absent themselves from the consultation if the issue under discussion involves them personally?***

The relevant guidance is contained in the following statements by the Universal House of Justice:-

> *In your letter of 4 April you inquire further about the principles governing the presence of a member of the National Assembly when a matter concerning him or her personally is being discussed. The first principle to bear in mind is that every member of an Assembly has an absolute and incontrovertible right to be present at every meeting of that body and to be fully informed of every matter coming before it.*
>
> *The second principle is that of detachment in consultation. The members of an Assembly must learn to express their views frankly, calmly, without passion or rancour. They must also learn to listen to the opinions of their fellow members without taking offence or belittling the views of another. Bahá'í consultation is not an easy process. It requires love, kindliness, moral courage and humility. Thus no member should ever allow himself to be prevented from expressing frankly his view because it may offend a fellow member; and, realising this, no member should take offence at another member's statements.*
>
> *The third principle is that if a believer feels that he has been done an injustice by the Assembly, he should appeal the decision in the normal way.*
>
> (letter from the Universal House of Justice to a National Spiritual Assembly, dated August 26, 1965)
>
> *We note on page 2 that ... left the room while the National Assembly discussed ways and means of helping her. Naturally, if one wishes to absent himself while his own situation is being discussed by the*

CHAPTER TWO

National Assembly, there is no objection. The National Assembly cannot require a member to remove himself from the consultation, and he is fully entitled to remain.

(letter from the Universal House of Justice to a National Spiritual Assembly, dated February 23, 1965)

It should also be understood that a member may wish to absent himself from a meeting at which subjects in which he is personally involved are to be discussed. In such cases he may do so unless the Assembly requires him to be present.

(letter from the Universal House of Justice to the International Teaching Centre, dated January 22, 1975)

It is clear from the above statements that Assembly members have the right to remain present at all meetings of the Assembly, regardless of whether the issue under discussion involves them personally. If, however, Assembly members prefer to absent themselves they have the right to do so, unless the Assembly specifically asks them to remain. An Assembly member who feels unjustly treated by an Assembly has the right to appeal against its decision in the usual way.

2.1.9 **Can people who are not members of the Assembly sit in on sessions?**

Yes. The Assembly is free to consult with anyone it chooses when gathering information on an issue. No one not on the Assembly, however, is permitted to remain present whilst the Assembly is consulting with a view to actually making a decision:-

...it is permissible for any Spiritual Assembly to call in youth or anyone else for consultation on matters affecting the progress of the Cause. However, it is not permissible for anyone not a member of an Assembly to sit in on all sessions nor to be present at a time when the Assembly is in the actual process of consultation on a particular problem with a view to reaching a decision.

(The Universal House of Justice)

Shoghi Effendi clearly recognised the need to seek advice from non-Assembly members when, in a letter written on his behalf, he said:-

Concerning the attendance of certain individuals at the meeting of the Assemblies and at the invitation of that body. This, Shoghi Effendi considers to be as expert advice which is absolutely necessary for good administration. The members of the Assembly are not supposed to know every thing on every subject, so they can invite a person, versed in that question, to attend their meetings and explain his views. But naturally he will have no right to vote.

(letter written on behalf of Shoghi Effendi to a National Spiritual Assembly, dated October 23, 1926)

2.1.10 **What should the Assembly do if conflict arises between its members?**

If conflict arises between the members of an Assembly at a meeting, the Assembly should immediately postpone discussion of the subject until tempers have cooled and a more appropriate time is found to reopen the consultation. 'Abdu'l-Bahá makes this clear in the following statement:-

CHAPTER TWO

The honoured members of the Spiritual Assembly should exert their efforts so that no differences may occur, and if such differences do occur, they should not reach the point of causing conflict, hatred and antagonism, which lead to threats. When you notice that a stage has been reached when enmity and threats are about to occur, you should immediately postpone discussion of the subject, until wranglings, disputations, and loud talk vanish, and a propitious time is at hand.

(Universal House of Justice compilation, "Bahá'í Consultation", p.7, extract from previously untranslated Tablet)

2.2 CONSULTATION BETWEEN THE LOCAL SPIRITUAL ASSEMBLY AND THE COMMUNITY

2.2.1 *Does the Local Spiritual Assembly have an obligation to consult with the community?*

Yes. On the one hand, there is the principle that the deliberations of the Assembly are confidential and it alone has the final power of decision on any issue. On the other hand, the Assembly has a right, up until the time of actually making the decision, to consult with anyone it feels may be of assistance. In the case of the local community, this right is also a duty. The Assembly must maintain an open and honest relationship with the community, must seek its advice and have regard to its wishes. The Assembly must never act in a dictatorial manner, or create an air of secrecy around its work. Bearing the above principles in mind, it is up to the Assembly to decide just how much the local community should be told. Shoghi Effendi explains what the Assembly's attitude to the community should be in the following statement:-

The duties of those whom the friends have freely and conscientiously elected as their representatives are no less vital and binding than the obligations of those who have chosen them. Their function is not to dictate, but to consult, and consult not only among themselves, but as much as possible with the friends whom they represent. They must regard themselves in no other light but that of chosen instruments for a more efficient and dignified presentation of the Cause of God. They should never be led to suppose that they are the central ornaments of the body of the Cause, intrinsically superior to others in capacity or merit, and sole promoters of its Teachings and principles. They should approach their task with extreme humility, and endeavour, by their candour, their modesty, their entire devotion to the welfare and interests of the friends, the Cause, and humanity, to win, not only the confidence and the genuine support and respect of those whom they serve, but also their esteem and real affection. They must, at all times, avoid the spirit of exclusiveness, the atmosphere of secrecy, free themselves from a domineering attitude, and banish all forms of prejudice and passion from their deliberations. They should, within the limits of a wise discretion, take the friends into their confidence, acquaint them with their plans, share with them their problems and anxieties, and seek their advice and counsel.

("Bahá'í Administration", p.64)

The chief occasion on which consultation occurs between the Assembly and the community is the Nineteen Day Feast. Here the Assembly shares its news and receives recommendations from the community. Recommendations may be given to the Assembly after they have been passed by a majority vote of the believers present, or they may simply be noted down by the Secretary during the consultation. It is for the Assembly to decide, bearing in mind the size

CHAPTER TWO

and nature of the community, which approach would be most appropriate. The Feast is also the occasion on which the community can consult informally on matters of general interest to it.

2.2.2 **What is the duty of the community with respect to decisions made by the Local Spiritual Assembly?**

> *It is the duty of the community members to obey the decisions of the Assembly, even if they are not convinced that a decision is right. The principle of unity overrides the importance of being right:-*
>
> *The Assembly may make a mistake, but, as the Master pointed out, if the Community does not abide by its decisions, or the individual Bahá'í, the result is worse, as it undermines the very institution which must be strengthened in order to uphold the principles and laws of the Faith. He tells us God will right the wrongs done. We must have confidence in this and obey our Assemblies. He therefore strongly urges you to work directly under your Bahá'í Assembly, to accept your responsibilities as a voting member, and do your utmost to create harmony within the community.*
>
> (letter written on behalf of Shoghi Effendi to an individual believer, dated 1949)

This is not to say, however, that the believers cannot offer constructive criticism to the Assembly to improve existing conditions in the community. Indeed, they have a duty to do this. The appropriate occasion, as previously noted, is the Nineteen Day Feast. What should be avoided is negative criticism which may result in undermining the authority of the Assembly:-

> *Now with reference to your last dear letter in which you had asked whether the believers have the right to openly express their criticism of any Assembly action or policy; it is not only the right, but the vital responsibility of every loyal and intelligent member of the Community to offer fully and frankly, but with due respect and consideration to the authority of the Assembly, any suggestion, recommendation or criticism he conscientiously feels he should in order to improve and remedy certain existing conditions or trends in his local community, and it is the duty of the Assembly also to give careful consideration to any such views submitted to them by any one of the believers...*
>
> *But again it should be stressed that all criticisms and discussions of a negative character which may result in undermining the authority of the Assembly as a body should be strictly avoided. For otherwise the order of the Cause itself will be endangered, and confusion and discord will reign in the Community.*
>
> (letter written on behalf of Shoghi Effendi to an individual believer, dated 13 December, 1939)

If an individual is severely unhappy with a decision of the Assembly, he or she should take the matter up with the Assembly privately. If the matter is still not resolved an appeal against the decision can be made to the National Spiritual Assembly. The decision of the Assembly must continue to be obeyed while the appeal is in progress:-

CHAPTER TWO

> *...even if an Assembly makes an ill-advised decision it must be upheld in order to preserve the unity of the community. Appeal can be made from the Local Assembly's decision to the National Assembly ... But the principle of authority invested in our elected bodies must be upheld. This is not something which can be learned without trial and test...*
>
> (letter written on behalf of Shoghi Effendi to a National Spiritual Assembly, dated June 30, 1949)

If the community is really unhappy with the functioning of its Assembly, the appropriate response is to make changes at the next election:-

> *...The elections, specially when annual, give the community a good opportunity to remedy any defect or imperfection from which the Assembly may suffer as a result of the actions of its members. Thus a safe method has been established whereby the quality of membership in Bahá'í Assemblies can be continually raised and improved.*
>
> (letter written on behalf of Shoghi Effendi to an individual believer, dated November 15, 1935)

2.3 CONSULTATION BETWEEN THE LOCAL SPIRITUAL ASSEMBLY AND AN INDIVIDUAL

2.3.1 *On what matters should an individual consult with the Assembly?*

In any serious matter relating to the Faith, an individual should consult with the Local Assembly. An individual may also take personal matters to the Assembly if he or she so chooses; however, there is no obligation to do so:-

> *When a believer has a problem concerning which he must make a decision, he has several courses open to him. If it is a matter that affects the interests of the Faith he should consult with the appropriate Assembly or committee, but individuals have many problems which are purely personal and there is no obligation upon them to take such problems to the institutions of the Faith... A Bahá'í who has a problem may wish to make his own decision upon it after prayer and after weighing all the aspects of it in his own mind; he may prefer to seek the counsel of individual friends or of professional counsellors such as his doctor or lawyer so that he can consider such advice when making his decision; or in a case where several people are involved, such as a family situation, he may want to gather together those who are affected so that they may arrive at a collective decision. There is also no objection whatever to a Bahá'í asking a group of people to consult together on a problem facing him.*
>
> (letter to a National Spiritual Assembly, dated March 19, 1973)

2.3.2 *Can an individual bring a problem to the Local Spiritual Assembly if other parties to the problem do not wish to involve the Assembly?*

Yes. Shoghi Effendi has said:-

> *Regarding consultation: Any person can refer a matter to the Assembly for consultation whether the other person wishes to or not.*
>
> ("Principles of Bahá'í Administration", p.58)

CHAPTER TWO

2.3.3 *Can a Local Spiritual Assembly intervene in a conflict against the will of the parties involved?*

Yes. An Assembly can intervene in a matter that affects the Cause where this is necessary to protect the Faith as a whole, or individual communities or believers:-

> *In matters which affect the Cause the Assembly should, if it deems it necessary, intervene even if both sides do not want it to, because the whole purpose of the Assemblies is to protect the Faith, the Communities, and the individual Bahá'ís as well.*
>
> ("Principles of Bahá'í Administration", p.58)

2.3.4 *Can the Assembly delegate a committee or individual to counsel a believer?*

Yes. In a letter to a National Spiritual Assembly, dated March 27, 1966, the Universal House of Justice said:-

> *Although Local Spiritual Assemblies are primarily responsible for counselling believers regarding personal problems, there may be times, when in the judgement of the National or Local Assembly, it would be preferable to assign counselling or advisory duties to individuals or committees. This is within the discretion of the Assembly.*

2.3.5 *What is the procedure for consultation between the Local Spiritual Assembly and an individual?*

The following steps should be taken by the Assembly when conducting a meeting with an individual:-
1. Welcome the individual and invite him or her to say a prayer.
2. If necessary, explain the general principles of consultation to the individual.
a) Remind the individual about the importance of maintaining confidentiality
b) Mention that statements made by individual Assembly members during the consultation are not to be taken as decisions of the Assembly.
c) Conduct the interview in a courteous, orderly manner.
3. Excuse the individual from the meeting.
4. Consult on the problem, following the procedure outlined previously and arrive at and record a decision.
5. Decide how the decision of the Assembly will be communicated to the individual.
6. Have some follow up actions prepared if necessary.

The above procedure may also be followed when an Assembly itself initiates the consultation. This will occur in cases where the Assembly wishes to counsel individuals on their behaviour and assist them in obeying the laws of the Faith.

2.4 CONSULTATION BETWEEN THE ASSEMBLY AND ONE OF ITS COMMITTEES

Consultation between the Assembly and one of its committees should follow the same procedures as consultation between the Assembly and an individual. A full chapter on Local Committees may be found elsewhere in this Handbook.

2.5 THE RIGHT OF APPEAL

2.5.1 *What procedure must an individual follow for appealing against a decision of the Local Spiritual Assembly?*

An individual who is unhappy with a decision of the Local Assembly should first appeal to that Assembly for a reconsideration. If he or she is still not happy with the decision of the

CHAPTER TWO

Assembly an appeal may be made to the National Spiritual Assembly. Should the National Spiritual Assembly's decision not be satisfactory, as a final recourse, appeal can be made to the Universal House of Justice.

In all instances the appeal must be channelled through the Local Assembly and the Assembly is duty bound to pass it on. Should it not do so, appellants may take their case directly to the higher authority. On the other hand, Article X, s.4 of the By-Laws of a Local Spiritual Assembly provides that the Local Assembly has the right to complain to the National Assembly if matters falling within its jurisdiction are referred to the National Assembly before it has had an opportunity to act upon them. The procedure for making an appeal has been established in the Constitution of the Universal House of Justice:-

> (a) *Any member of a local Bahá'í community may appeal from a decision of his Local Spiritual Assembly to the National Spiritual Assembly which shall determine whether it shall take jurisdiction of the matter or refer it back to the Local Spiritual Assembly for reconsideration...*

> (b) *Any Bahá'í may appeal a decision of his National Spiritual Assembly to the Universal House of Justice which shall determine whether it shall take jurisdiction of the matter or leave it within the final jurisdiction of the National Spiritual Assembly.*

> (c) *An appellant, whether institution or individual, shall in the first instance make appeal to the Assembly whose decision is questioned, either for reconsideration of the case by that Assembly or for submission to a higher body. In the latter case the Assembly is in duty bound to submit the appeal together with full particulars of the matter. If an Assembly refuses to submit the appeal, or fails to do so within a reasonable time, the appellant may take the case directly to the higher authority.*

("The Constitution of the Universal House of Justice", pp. 14-15)

2.5.2 *What procedure must a Local Spiritual Assembly follow for appealing against a decision of the National Spiritual Assembly?*

A Local Spiritual Assembly does not have the right to publicly criticise a decision of the National Spiritual Assembly. If, however, the Assembly has reason to believe that an action of the National Spiritual Assembly is adversely affecting the welfare of its community, it may seek direct consultation with the National Assembly to resolve the difference of opinion. If the Local Assembly is not satisfied with the outcome of the consultation it may, as a final recourse, appeal to the Universal House of Justice. The appeal must be channelled through the National Spiritual Assembly. [See Article X of the By-Laws of a Local Spiritual Assembly for further information about the right of appeal within the Bahá'í community.]

2.6 NOTES FOR REGISTERED GROUPS

The consultation within a Registered Group does not cover the wide field covered by an Assembly. Its main concern is the teaching work so that the group may attain Assembly status. It does not consult on many items which may be considered by Assemblies, such as marriage, divorce, personal problems, status of believers, etc. As the same principles of consultation do apply, however, the group members should use their consultation as a means of obtaining invaluable experience.

2.7 SUGGESTED FURTHER READING

Universal House of Justice, "Bahá'í Consultation, The Lamp of Guidance" (compilation). Bahá'í Publications Australia, 1978.

J.E. Kolstoe, "Consultation, A Universal Lamp of Guidance". George Ronald, Oxford, 1985.

See also the Addendum on Consultation included at the end of this Handbook.

CHAPTER THREE

Chapter 3

3. **Administrative Procedures**

3.1 **PRINCIPLES AND PROCEDURES**

3.1.1 ***What is the significance of the Bahá'í Administrative Order?***

Shoghi Effendi explains the significance of the Administrative Order as follows:-

> *The Administrative Order, which ever since 'Abdu'l-Bahá's ascension has evolved and is taking shape under our very eyes ... will, as its component parts, its organic institutions, begin to function with efficiency and vigour, assert its claim and demonstrate its capacity to be regarded not only as the nucleus but the very pattern of the New World Order destined to embrace in the fullness of time the whole of mankind.*

("The World Order of Bahá'u'lláh", p.144)

3.1.2 ***What is the distinction between administrative principles and procedures?***

The principles and laws governing the Administrative Order are an integral part of the Teachings themselves:-

> *To dissociate the administrative principles of the Cause from the purely spiritual and humanitarian Teachings would be tantamount to a mutilation of the body of the Cause, a separation that can only result in the disintegration of its component parts, and the extinction of the Faith itself.*

(Shoghi Effendi, "The World Order of Bahá'u'lláh", p.5)

They are divine in origin, unchangeable and the same the world over, in every Bahá'í community. Procedure, on the other hand, is merely an orderly way of conducting the business affairs of the Cause, and varies from place to place. In order to enable the institutions "to function with efficiency", certain procedures are adopted from time to time. That administrative principles - the immutable laws of God - cannot be changed, and that procedures can and are changed from time to time, needs to be understood, lest disagreements and disunity come between the loved ones of God. Procedures differ from country to country and indeed from community to community. It is within the realm of each National Spiritual Assembly's authority to enact certain procedures for the efficient functioning of its national community, and it is within the realm of each Local Spiritual Assembly's authority to enact certain procedures for the efficient functioning of its local community, so long as these procedures are in no way contrary to those already established by a higher authority, and are always in conformity with the spirit of Bahá'í principles.

Examples of administrative principles include:
1. during consultation all have the right to freely express their views
2. all contributions to the Fund are voluntary
3. teaching the Cause must be given precedence in Local Spiritual Assembly meetings
4. Assembly members vote according to conscience

Examples of administrative procedures include:
1. process by which believers are enrolled

CHAPTER THREE

2. process by which believers are deepened
3. how donations to the Fund are collected and acknowledged

3.1.3 *Where will it be necessary for a Local Spiritual Assembly to establish its own procedures?*

Examples of matters on which Local Spiritual Assemblies will have to establish their own procedures include:
1. how to distribute the minutes
2. whether to appoint local committees, working groups or individuals to carry out tasks
3. how to encourage donations to the Fund

3.1.4 *What principles apply to the establishment of procedure?*

The following principles apply:
1. administrative efficiency and order should always be accompanied by an equal degree of love, of devotion and of spiritual development; both are essential to the development of the administration
2. there should be uniformity in fundamentals but diversity in the solving of local situations
3. situations should be dealt with as they arise on a case by case basis, not anticipated and procedures laid down in advance
4. over-administration can be worse for the Faith at this time than under-administration
5. the Assemblies should direct their attention to the teaching work rather than to the issuing of rules and regulations:-

> *The whole purpose of the Bahá'í administrative bodies at this time is to teach... not to create rules and regulations and impede the work through unnecessary red tape...*
>
> (letter written on behalf of Shoghi Effendi to a National Spiritual Assembly, dated July 5, 1957) [See further "Lights of Guidance" {revised edition} nos. 124, 133-36, 1344.]

3.2 MEETINGS OF THE LOCAL SPIRITUAL ASSEMBLY

3.2.1 *How is a meeting of the Local Spiritual Assembly called?*

Article VIII of the "By-Laws of a Local Spiritual Assembly" states that the first meeting of a newly-elected Assembly will be called by the member who has received the highest number of votes. All subsequent meetings:-
...shall be called by the Secretary of the Assembly at the request of the Chairman or, in his absence or incapacity, of the Vice-Chairman, or of any three members of the Assembly. ("By-Laws of a Local Spiritual Assembly", Article VIII)

A Local Spiritual Assembly should establish a regular time and place for its meetings and the Secretary is responsible for ensuring that all members are notified of the meeting in advance, preferably fourteen days in advance. In fact, some incorporated Local Spiritual Assemblies should note that the giving of fourteen days notice is a legal requirement under the Acts incorporating them.

3.2.2 *How is a meeting of the Local Spiritual Assembly conducted?*

The Secretary prepares the agenda for the meeting in consultation with the Chairman (teaching should always receive first priority). The Chairman (or Vice-Chairman) is responsible for the

CHAPTER THREE

smooth running of the meeting, which is conducted according to the principles of Bahá'í consultation. The Secretary, or a specially appointed Recording Secretary, is responsible for taking minutes.

3.2.3 **What materials should the Secretary bring to the meetings?**

The Secretary should bring the following materials to the Assembly's meetings:
1. any files and correspondence relating to the business of the meeting
2. this Handbook
3. "Lights of Guidance" {revised edition}
4. any relevant guidance received periodically from the National Spiritual Assembly
5. items in the Bahá'í Bulletin that need to be included on the agenda
6. previous Assembly minutes
7. the Local Spiritual Assembly's policy file
8. "Principles of Bahá'í Administration" (NSA of the United Kingdom)

3.2.4 **How often should the Assembly meet?**

The Spiritual Assembly should meet as often as necessary to properly carry out its functions. In practise this generally requires it to meet at least once each Bahá'í month:-

> *The Spiritual Assembly should decide how often it should meet in order to properly handle the affairs of the Cause under its jurisdiction. Twice a week or twice a month is not the point, the point is that it should be alert and carry on the work adequately.*

(letter written on behalf of Shoghi Effendi to an individual believer, dated October 23, 1949)

> *As a Local Spiritual Assembly is responsible for the organisation of Nineteen Day Feasts, and is expected to make a report of its activities to the community at the Feast, in addition to responding to suggestions submitted to it, a Local Assembly should meet at least once a Bahá'í month. However, the Universal House of Justice does not wish to draw hard and fast rules in this matter, and prefers to leave this question to the discretion of each National Assembly.*

(letter written on behalf of the Universal House of Justice to a National Spiritual Assembly, dated February 15, 1982)

The National Spiritual Assembly leaves it to the discretion of each Local Spiritual Assembly how often to meet, asking that they take note of the guidance contained in the above letter from the House of Justice. It is preferable that Local Spiritual Assemblies not meet on Bahá'í Holy Days; however, should a meeting be necessary in an emergency, it is permissible. See "Lights of Guidance" {revised edition} no.1019.

3.2.5 **What is a quorum?**

Article VIII, Section 1 of the "By-Laws of a Local Spiritual Assembly" provides that:-
Five members of the Assembly present at a meeting shall constitute a quorum, and a majority vote of those present and constituting a quorum shall be sufficient for the conduct of business, except as otherwise provided in these By-Laws, and with due regard to the principle of unity and cordial fellowship involved in the institution of a Spiritual Assembly. Ideally, all nine members of the Assembly should be present at a meeting. If only five are present a majority of three is sufficient to pass a motion; however, these three should not use the occasion to pass a motion that would violate the principle of unity and fellowship which governs the

CHAPTER THREE

operation of an Assembly:-

> *We have your letter of July 20, 1967 asking for clarification of Article VIII, Section 1 of the By-Laws of a Local Spiritual Assembly...*
>
> *A majority of the members present and constituting a quorum is sufficient to carry a motion. Thus, if only five members of the Assembly are present at a meeting, a majority vote of three is sufficient.*
>
> *However, Assemblies should take into account the last clause of the first sentence of Section 1 of Article VIII reading as follows: ...and with due regard to the principle of unity and cordial fellowship involved in the institution of a Spiritual Assembly. In other words, members of a Spiritual Assembly should not take advantage of a quorum as an expedient to pass a motion which would violate the spirit of the above quoted passage. As your National Assembly has stated, it is desirable that all nine members of a Local Spiritual Assembly be present at every meeting...*
>
> (letter from the Universal House of Justice to a National Spiritual Assembly, dated August 6, 1967)

There may be times when the Assembly prefers that all nine members be present before making a decision. ["Lights of Guidance" {revised edition} no.585].

3.2.6 **What should a Local Spiritual Assembly do if it is unable to achieve a quorum?**

If the Assembly knows in advance that there are likely to be occasions on which it is unable to achieve a quorum, thereby delaying the work of the Assembly, it may delegate authority for carrying out essential work, eg. organising Feasts. The Assembly must be very careful to ensure that individuals delegated such authority do not overstep the guidelines established by the Assembly and take on the work of the Assembly itself. The National Spiritual Assembly stresses that every effort must be made to keep the Assembly functioning.

If a Local Spiritual Assembly is having difficulty in achieving a quorum it should contact the assistants to its Auxiliary Board members for advice. If the difficulty continues over a prolonged period of time it must advise the National Spiritual Assembly. If the Assembly cannot achieve a quorum because it does not have that many adult believers left in the community it must revert to Registered Group status and cannot re-form until the following Riḍván.

3.2.7 **What procedures may a Local Spiritual Assembly put in place for taking routine action between Assembly meetings?**

The Local Spiritual Assembly may authorise an individual - for example, the Secretary - to take action on routine matters where the Assembly's policy is clearly established. The Assembly must ensure that actions on the part of individuals do not take the place of Local Spiritual Assembly meetings. All such actions taken must be brought to the Assembly for review and approval at its next meeting.

3.2.8 **What should a Local Spiritual Assembly do in an emergency?**

In emergencies the Secretary, after consultation with the Chairman or, in his absence, with the Vice-Chairman, should call a special meeting of the Assembly. In the event that it is not possible to get a quorum, the Secretary must if possible inform each member by telephone of the nature of the emergency to get a consensus upon which immediate action can be taken. An Assembly may make a provision, in advance, that in such circumstances its available

CHAPTER THREE

members may act even if a quorum cannot be obtained by telephone. Emergency actions are placed on the agenda at the next meeting for review and approval of the entire Assembly. Emergency procedures must not be allowed to take the place of Local Spiritual Assembly meetings.

3.2.9 *What if an elected officer is absent from a meeting?*

In the absence of the Chairman the Vice-Chairman chairs the meeting. If the Vice-Chairman is also absent, the Assembly may choose another member to chair the meeting (see "Lights of Guidance" {revised edition} no.103). Similarly, if the Secretary is absent, the Assembly should appoint another member to take the minutes. If an office-bearer knows that he or she will be absent from Assembly meetings for a period of time, the Assembly must make other arrangements for ensuring that the necessary work is done; for example, if the Secretary will be absent the Assembly may appoint a temporary Secretary, or may divide the Secretary's work among a number of its members. Ideally, such arrangements should be made before the officer becomes absent. If the office-bearer is going to be absent for a very long period of time, the Assembly may consider electing a new office-bearer.

3.2.10 *What should a Local Spiritual Assembly do if it is dissatisfied with the services of one of its officers?*

An Assembly officer cannot be replaced mid-term because of incompetence or because of a failure to fulfil his or her duties. Such an officer must be kept in place until new Assembly elections are held. [See further Chapter 1, Section 5, 'Can an office bearer be dismissed mid-term?']

When an Assembly officer refuses to shoulder the responsibilities of the office and is unwilling to cooperate with the Assembly for the purpose of finding a solution to the problems, it will be necessary for the Assembly to make alternate arrangements to have the duties carried out.

3.2.11 *What if an Assembly member is unable or unwilling to attend meetings?*

Although it is a condition of service on an Assembly that a member be regularly able to attend meetings, it is not a cause for concern if Assembly members are temporarily absent:-

> *It is only too obvious that unless a member can attend regularly the meetings of his local Assembly, it would be impossible for him to discharge the duties incumbent upon him, and to fulfil his responsibilities, as a representative of the community. Membership in a Local Spiritual Assembly carries with it, indeed, the obligation and capacity to remain in close touch with local Bahá'í activities, and ability to attend regularly the sessions of the Assembly.*
>
> (letter written on behalf of Shoghi Effendi to an individual believer, dated February 16, 1935)

> *Also if certain members temporarily absent themselves from meetings there is no need to dissolve the Assembly; on the contrary the reluctant ones should be educated and encouraged to reassume their spiritual obligations as believers. A spiritual Assembly is not based on nine people being available for every single meeting but on nine resident Bahá'ís doing their best to discharge their duty to the Spiritual Assembly when they are not prevented by illness or absence or some legitimate reason from doing so.*

CHAPTER THREE

(letter written on behalf of Shoghi Effendi to a National Spiritual Assembly, dated March 31, 1945)

On the other hand, if the absence is 'prolonged' or 'excessive' the Assembly will have to consider the matter. Shoghi Effendi said that no time limit should be fixed beyond which a person is automatically dropped from the Assembly; each case should be considered on its merits and, depending on the circumstances, it may be necessary to declare a vacancy and call a by-election:-

> *It is establishing a dangerous precedent to allow Assemblies to put a time limit on non-attendance of their members at meetings of the Spiritual Assembly, beyond which that person is automatically dropped from the Assembly and a vacancy declared....There should be no time limit fixed by Assemblies beyond which a person is dropped. Every case of prolonged absence from the sessions of the Assembly should be considered separately by that Assembly, and if the person is seen to not want to attend meetings, or to be held away from them indefinitely because of illness or travel, then a vacancy could legitimately be declared and a new member be elected.*

(letter written on behalf of Shoghi Effendi, in "Bahá'í News" #208, June 1948, p.7)

> *...duration of the absence of any member who has to be away. Should this period of time be excessive it is within the discretion of the Assembly to recognise a vacancy and call for a by-election. However this should not be lightly decided and the members declared elected at the Convention should remain in office unless there are insuperable difficulties which prevent it.*

(letter from the Universal House of Justice to a National Spiritual Assembly, dated December 10, 1970)

Absences generally fall into two categories: either the believers are unable or unwilling to fulfil their duties. If the Assembly ascertains that a believer is willing to serve, but, for a variety of reasons, is not able to, it may declare a vacancy. The Assembly should consult with the person concerned and make a decision based on the best interests of the Faith. A different situation arises if the Assembly feels that the believer could attend meetings but is not willing to. Absence from Assembly meetings is not, for example, justifiable, on the grounds of Assembly in harmony, eg. hurt feelings:-

> *...The Guardian strongly feels that criticism, opposition, or confusion do not provide sufficient grounds for either refusal or resignation. ...The difficulties and tests involved in the acceptance of administrative posts, far from inducing the believers to dissociate themselves from the work of the Cause, should spur them on to greater exertions and to a more active participation in the privileged task of resolving the problems that confront the Bahá'í community...The believers, for the sake of the Cause, now in the period of its infancy, should accept their duties in a spirit of self-sacrifice, and should be animated by the desire to uphold the verdict of the electorate, and to lend their share of assistance, however difficult the circumstances, to the effective administration of the affairs of the Faith.*

CHAPTER THREE

(letter written on behalf of Shoghi Effendi in "Bahá'í News" #152, April 1942, p.2)

Personal differences and disagreements among Assembly members surely afford no sufficient ground for such resignation, and certainly cannot justify absence from Assembly meetings. Through the clash of personal opinions, as 'Abdu'l-Bahá has stated, the spark of truth is often ignited, and divine guidance revealed.

(letter written on behalf of Shoghi Effendi, quoted in "Developing Distinctive Bahá'í Communities, Guidelines for Spiritual Assemblies", Chapter 3, page 10)

The remedy to Assembly in harmony cannot be in the resignation or abstinence of any of its members. It must learn, in spite of disturbing elements, to continue to function as a whole, otherwise the whole system would become discredited through the introduction of exceptions to the rule.

(letter written on behalf of Shoghi Effendi to an individual believer, dated November 20, 1941)

In any case of unwillingness of a believer to serve, the Assembly should do its utmost to discover the difficulty and lovingly assist the believer to overcome it. Steps to take could include delegating members of the Assembly to visit the believer concerned, or asking the assistant to the Auxiliary Board to act as a go-between. If all efforts fail, and the Assembly decides it is in the best interests of the Faith in its area, it may declare a vacancy and call a by-election. The decision to call a by-election rests with the Local Spiritual Assembly:-

He does not intervene in purely local administrative matters, and it is for the Assembly to decide, if the absence of a member is prolonged, when they should hold an election to replace that person. The principle is that the nine members of the Spiritual Assembly should be reasonably available for meetings. If their absence from town is prolonged, someone else must fill the vacancy.

(letter written on behalf of Shoghi Effendi to an individual believer, dated April 5, 1945)

The only circumstance in which the National Spiritual Assembly would need to be involved would be in that rare instance in which a believer, for no good reason, absolutely refused to accept his or her Bahá'í responsibilities. In such a situation the question of deprivation of voting rights could arise; however, only after the believer had been repeatedly counselled and warned. In general, the Universal House of Justice has advised that, at the present time, encouragement and education is likely to be far more beneficial than the application of sanctions:-

While it is true that refusal to serve can ultimately incur the forfeiture of administrative rights, the House of Justice feels that your Assembly should bear in mind the caution voiced on behalf of the Guardian in the letter published on pages 86 and 87 of "Principles of Bahá'í Administration": 'Only in cases where individual believers, without any valid reason, deliberately refuse the repeated exhortations, pleas, and warnings addressed to them by their Assemblies, should action be taken in removing them from the voting list.' At the present stage

CHAPTER THREE

... far more beneficial results are likely to be achieved by encouragement of the believers and by their education in the principles and significance of Bahá'í administration than by the threat or imposition of sanctions. Indeed the latter, if applied unwisely, could achieve the very opposite of what your Assembly is hoping to accomplish. Generally the membership of small local communities includes some believers who are new in the Faith and need to be lovingly nurtured in the responsibilities of being a Bahá'í, and others who are overburdened by a multitude of cares. How often one finds in small Assemblies members who, although devoted believers, have non-Bahá'í spouses and families to care for and are very limited in the time they can spend in Bahá'í administrative activities. Such believers should be encouraged, and loving appreciation should be shown for whatever services they can render, and nothing should be done, however unintentionally, to make them feel that they are living under a threat of administrative expulsion if they do not attend every Assembly meeting or decline a request to serve on a committee. There may, of course, be cases of believers who, without any good reason, refuse to shoulder the responsibilities of membership in the Bahá'í community. It is to such extreme cases that you would be justified in applying sanctions if, after 'repeated exhortations, pleas and warnings' they persist in their attitude.

(letter written on behalf of the Universal House of Justice to a National Spiritual Assembly, dated July 8, 1980)

3.2.12 **Is it permissible to elect a temporary Assembly member in place of one who must be absent for a while?**

No:-

As regards electing a temporary member to replace one who is absent the present practice of Bahá'í Administration is not in favour of this but prefers to ascertain the duration of the absence of any member who has to be away. Should this period of time be excessive it is within the discretion of the Assembly to recognise a vacancy and call for a by-election.

(letter from the Universal House of Justice to a National Spiritual Assembly, dated December 10, 1970)

3.3 **CONFIDENTIALITY**

3.3.1 **Are the deliberations of a Local Spiritual Assembly confidential?**

Yes, insofar as individual Assembly members must not share 'confidential information' acquired at an Assembly meeting with anyone else. The Assembly as a whole, for its part, must arrive at a balance between two principles in deciding whether and how much of its deliberations to share with community members.

These two principles are:
1. The Local Spiritual Assembly must avoid creating an air of secrecy around its work by never sharing anything with the community;
2. Community members must be confident that they can take sensitive matters to their Assembly and know that they will remain confidential. Bearing these two principles

in mind the Assembly must decide, in any particular instance, whether to share information or not:-

Every institution in the Faith has certain matters which it considers should be kept confidential, and any member who is privy to such confidential information is obliged to preserve the confidentiality within the institution where he learned it. Such matters, however, are but a small portion of the business of any Bahá'í institution. Most subjects dealt with are of common interest and can be discussed openly with anyone. Where no confidentiality is involved the institutions must strive to avoid the stifling atmosphere of secrecy; on the other hand, every believer must know that he can confide a personal problem to an institution of the Faith, with the assurance that knowledge of the matter will remain confidential.

(letter written on behalf of the Universal House of Justice to a National Spiritual Assembly, dated August 2, 1982)

...regarding the extent to which confidential information about believers may be shared with other believers for their protection ... we offer in reply the following considerations:

1. Any information which comes to the notice of an Assembly member, solely by reason of his membership on that Assembly may not be divulged by that member, even though the Assembly itself may later decide to share it.

2. The Assembly must itself carefully consider which information should rightly fall in the category of confidential information and which should not be shared with others, and which information may be divulged under special circumstances, and how such information may be divulged. Should confidential matters regarding personal problems be freely shared with others, upon application, the confidence of the believers in the Assembly and its members will obviously be destroyed.

3. It must be remembered that individuals can reform, and a reprehensible past does not necessarily disqualify a believer from building a better future. Within the general framework of these principles, we feel you should be able to handle each case as it may come to your attention. No hard and fast rule should be laid down in such cases, as each case requires careful handling, sound judgement and utmost discretion.

(letter written on behalf of the Universal House of Justice to a National Spiritual Assembly, dated September 18, 1968)

A Local Spiritual Assembly has a duty to 'respect requests from individuals who express the wish that certain matters be handled on a confidential basis'

(letter written on behalf of the Universal House of Justice to a Local Spiritual Assembly, dated March 2, 1987).

3.3.2 *May a Local Spiritual Assembly member who receives information in confidence as an individual, share that information with the Assembly?*

No:-

> *Members of Assemblies, whether they are assistants [to Auxiliary Board members] or not, are obviously in a position to receive confidential information as individuals from several sources. It is an important principle of the Faith that one must not promise what one is not going to fulfil. Therefore, if a Bahá'í accepts confidential information either by virtue of his profession (eg. as a doctor, a lawyer, etc.), or by permitting another person to confide in him, he is in duty bound to preserve that confidentiality.*
>
> (letter written on behalf of the Universal House of Justice to a National Spiritual Assembly, dated August 2, 1982)

If the Assembly member confided in feels that such information should come before the Assembly, he or she should encourage the believer concerned to formally take it to the Assembly. If Assembly members receive certain information, and do not undertake to keep it confidential, they may share it with the Assembly if they feel this would be in the interests of the Faith, but they are not obliged to do so. Members of the community should not assume that a matter has gone before the Assembly just because several Assembly members know about it:-

> *...It should be clear to the believers that they are not justified in assuming that because a matter is known to individual members of the Assembly it is therefore before the Assembly itself. If a believer wishes to bring a matter to the Assembly's attention he should do so explicitly and officially. If a member of the Assembly knows of a personal problem, and if he has not undertaken to keep it confidential, he may bring it to the Assembly's attention if he feels it would be in the interests of the Faith for him to do so, but he is not obliged to.*
>
> (letter written on behalf of the Universal House of Justice to a National Spiritual Assembly, dated August 2, 1982)

3.4 FUNCTIONS OF THE SECRETARY

3.4.1 *What are the functions of the Local Spiritual Assembly Secretary?*

In brief, the functions of the Local Spiritual Assembly Secretary are as follows:
1. preparation of the agenda for meetings, in conjunction with the Chairman bringing to Assembly meetings the files and letters relating to the business of the meeting
2. recording minutes of meetings
3. writing the Local Spiritual Assembly's correspondence, including the Annual Report and reports required by the National Spiritual Assembly
4. filing
5. calling community meetings, including Assembly meetings, Nineteen Day Feasts, Holy Days, the Annual General Meetings, and other community gatherings
6. distribution of newsletters to the community
7. maintaining the community membership list and notifying the National Office of any changes to the membership list
8. being aware of civil law requirements if the Assembly is incorporated
9. keeping track of items from previous minutes that require further action and other matters of an on-going nature, including responses to correspondence sent out

CHAPTER THREE

10. receiving correspondence for the Assembly
11. reporting from the Assembly to the community at the Nineteen Day Feast
12. taking notes of recommendations received at the Nineteen Day Feast
13. watching for receipt of reports and minutes from local committees, ensuring they act within their Terms of Reference and reporting to the Assembly any problems that arise
14. being aware of due dates for reports, coming Bahá'í events, and so on
15. carrying out routine work between meetings, if the Assembly delegates such authority to the Secretary

Some of the work of the Secretary may be delegated to other Assembly members if the Assembly so decides; for example, a Recording Secretary may be appointed to take the minutes.

[For further information on the work of the Secretary see the "Bahá'í Secretary's Manual"]

3.4.2 **Is it permissible for the Secretary to receive assistance from someone not on the Assembly?**

Yes:-

> *In reply to your letter of November 7th, 1973 there is no objection whatsoever to a non-member of the National Spiritual Assembly typing your Minutes or such other confidential reports. Many National Spiritual Assemblies employ typists in their national offices who are intimately connected with all the work of the National Spiritual Assembly. Of course, the person so employed should enjoy the confidence of the National Spiritual Assembly.*
>
> (letter from the Universal House of Justice to a National Spiritual Assembly, November 20, 1973)

It is preferable that the assistant be a Bahá'í and he or she must be approved by the Local Spiritual Assembly.

3.5 **MINUTES**

3.5.1 **What are the minutes?**

The minutes of the Spiritual Assembly are the permanent and official record of the community. They are the record of the on-going business of the Assembly as well as an history of the development of the community. The Local Spiritual Assembly is responsible for ensuring their accuracy.

3.5.2 **What should be recorded in the minutes?**

The following information should be recorded in the minutes:
1. name of the Assembly, venue and date of the meeting (if the Assembly is incorporated it is particularly important that the full name of the Assembly be recorded)
2. opening devotions and time meeting starts
3. names of the Assembly members present and those who were absent (with reasons); any apologies received
4. corrections to previous minutes
5. adoption of previous minutes
6. results of any by-elections or any changes in officers
7. statistical changes, eg. enrolments, transfers, resignations, deaths, divorces, marriages

approved and conducted by the Local Spiritual Assembly, including sighting of parental consents
8. any loss of voting rights of a community member
9. list of correspondence received and sent out by the Assembly since the last meeting
10. Feast recommendations
11. reports of the Secretary, Treasurer and Committees
12. all actions and decisions taken by the Assembly
13. date, time and venue of the next Assembly meeting
14. closing devotions and time meeting ended

The following points should be noted:

1. when recording the names of Assembly members and any other names in the minutes, the full name must be used, eg. Tom Brown (not just Tom)
2. the list of correspondence received and sent out should contain sufficient information to indicate the subject matter of each item
3. generally, only actions and decisions agreed upon should be recorded in the minutes, but important unresolved matters could also be included
4. background information should be brief but in sufficient detail so that anyone reading a minute will understand the decision which follows
5. incorporated Assemblies should note the importance of having a separate heading for adoption of the previous minutes, as this is a legal requirement
6. following adoption of the previous minutes they must be signed and dated by the Chairman.

[For further information on recording minutes, see pages 5-7 of the "Bahá'í Secretary's Manual" Included in that booklet is an example of minutes of a Spiritual Assembly.]

3.5.3 *Must the minutes be written in English?*

> Yes. *The Universal House of Justice advised the National Spiritual Assembly of Canada that 'Local Spiritual Assembly meetings should be conducted in English or French, as the case may be, since these are the languages of your country...'*

> (letter written on behalf of the Universal House of Justice to a National Spiritual Assembly, dated February 7, 1984).

The National Spiritual Assembly's policy with regard to minutes, therefore, is that they are to be written in English rather than, for example, Persian. If the English is not of a high standard that is not a problem. It will certainly improve with perseverance and practice.

3.5.4 *What principles apply to the distribution of minutes?*

The following guidance provided to a National Spiritual Assembly, is equally applicable to Local Spiritual Assemblies:-

Two principles apply, namely:
1. Every member of the National Spiritual Assembly is entitled to have access to the minutes of the National Assembly meetings.
2. The National Assembly must take measures to safeguard the confidential nature of many matters referred to in the minutes.

> *It is within the discretion of your National Spiritual Assembly to decide what should be done to give effect to these two principles.*

CHAPTER THREE

(letter from the Universal House of Justice to a National Spiritual Assembly, dated March 25, 1971)

Minutes of the Local Spiritual Assembly should <u>not</u> be read at the Nineteen Day Feast. However, the Assembly should decide what actions of general concern to the community should be shared with the community and how this should be accomplished.

3.5.5 ***Should the Local Spiritual Assembly send a copy of its minutes to the National Spiritual Assembly?***

Yes. A copy of the minutes should be sent to the National Office immediately after each Assembly meeting. It is not necessary that the National Spiritual Assembly have corrected minutes. Corrections to the minutes should be noted in the next set of minutes.

3.5.6 ***Should the Local Spiritual Assembly send a copy of its minutes to the Auxiliary Board members?***

The Continental Board of Counsellors for Australasia has adopted the policy that Auxiliary Board members should not ask a Local Spiritual Assembly for a copy of its minutes. The Local Spiritual Assembly is free of course, to use its own discretion in the matter and to send copies of, or extracts from, its minutes to the Auxiliary Board member if it chooses to do so.

3.5.7 ***May a Local Spiritual Assembly record confidential items separately from the minutes?***

Yes. A Local Spiritual Assembly may record confidential items separately but should note in its minutes that this has been done:-

As a general rule, all matters acted upon by an Assembly are recorded in its minutes. The Assembly may, however, record highly confidential items separately, but it should be noted in the minutes that confidential items have been separately recorded. Thus, if for any reason the Assembly is requested to supply information concerning such items and it feels that it would be preferable for the matter not to be divulged, it can express its views before acceding to the request. ...The decision about what matters should be treated confidentially is made by the Assembly, which also has the duty to respect requests from individuals who express the wish that certain matters be handled on a confidential basis.

(letter written on behalf of the Universal House of Justice to a Local Spiritual Assembly, dated March 2, 1987)

3.6 **MEMBERSHIP LIST**

3.6.1 ***How should the Local Spiritual Assembly maintain its membership list?***

The Local Spiritual Assembly should keep an up-to-date list of names, addresses and telephone numbers of all adults, youth and children in its community. The National Spiritual Assembly will periodically circulate its record of membership and the up-to-date local record should be used to correct the one circulated by the National Assembly. The Local Spiritual Assembly must advise the National Spiritual Assembly of any changes to this list on the records form provided for this purpose.

3.6.2 ***Should the Local Spiritual Assembly keep separate birth, death and marriage registers?***

The Universal House of Justice encourages Local Spiritual Assemblies to keep birth and

CHAPTER THREE

marriage registers:-

> *Local Spiritual Assemblies, which are embryonic Local Houses of Justice, should develop as rallying centres of the community. They must concern themselves not only with teaching the Faith, with the development of the Bahá'í way of life and with the proper organisation of the Bahá'í activities of their communities, but also with those crucial events which profoundly affect the life of all human beings: birth, marriage, and death. When a Bahá'í has a child it is a matter of joy to the whole local community as well as to the couple, and each Local Spiritual Assembly should be encouraged to keep a register of such births, issuing a birth certificate to the parents. Such a practice will foster the consolidation of the community and of the Assembly itself. Even if only one of the parents is a Bahá'í, the Assembly could register the birth of the child, and upon application of the Bahá'í parent issue the certificate. ... Each Assembly...must conscientiously carry out its responsibilities in connection with the...recording of Bahá'í marriages in a register kept for this purpose, and the issuing of Bahá'í marriage certificates... In some parts of the world if Local Spiritual Assemblies fail to carry out these sacred duties some believers might gradually drift away from the Faith and even pay dues to churches or other religious organisations to ensure that, when they require to register the birth of a child, to solemnise a marriage or to have a funeral service, there will be a religious institution ready to perform the necessary services. Conversely, when Local Assemblies have arisen to carry out these responsibilities, the believers have acquired a sense of security and solidarity, and have become confident that in such matters they can rely upon the agencies of the World Order of Bahá'u'lláh.*

(letter from the Universal House of Justice to all National Spiritual Assemblies, dated April 17, 1981)

Furthermore, it remains a goal of the Australian Bahá'í Community to:
Maintain registers of current members, declarations, births, transfers of members, marriages, divorces and deaths. - (Six Year Plan - goal 4.1)
It is for the Local Spiritual Assembly to decide how it will set up these registers. The register of deaths should include the date of the believer's death, the place the believer is buried and the plot number. The registers of births, marriages and deaths should be kept distinct from the membership list. Note that, although it is a function of Local Spiritual Assemblies to issue birth and marriage certificates, at present such certificates are issued under civil law only. A Bahá'í marriage or birth certificate has no legal authority. The current policy of the National Spiritual Assembly, therefore, is that no marriage or birth certificates should be issued by Local Spiritual Assemblies.

3.6.3 *Are membership lists confidential?*

Yes. A Local Spiritual Assembly may not share its membership list, or individual names from it, with any other institution or individual, Bahá'í or non-Bahá'í outside its community, without the prior consent of the believers whose names are on the list. Bahá'ís who are in business selling Bahá'í specialty items, for instance, must compile their own address lists. Lists that are no longer current should be shredded or burnt. Any Local Spiritual Assembly in doubt as to whether it should share names from its membership list in any given instance should contact the National Office for advice.

CHAPTER THREE

3.6.4 *Should names of believers whose address is unknown appear on the membership list?*

If a believer's address is unknown the Local Spiritual Assembly should make every reasonable effort to discover it, including visiting, telephoning or writing to, the person's last known address; asking neighbours; asking to see the electoral roll at the local council; and so on. If the Local Spiritual Assembly discovers the person's new address it should both place the address on its own membership list and notify the National Spiritual Assembly of it. The Assembly should take special care to maintain contact with this believer in future. If the Local Spiritual Assembly does not discover the believer's new address, it should nevertheless retain that person's name on the membership list, as he or she is still a Bahá'í. It should also advise the National Spiritual Assembly so that it will stop sending material to that believer. If the National Spiritual Assembly does not have an address for a believer, or finds that mail is being returned from the address to which it is sent, it will send mail for this believer 'care of' the Local Spiritual Assembly'. The Local Spiritual Assembly should then try to discover the person's address and notify the National Spiritual Assembly as per the above guidance.

3.6.5 *Should the names of believers who have lost their voting rights be retained on the membership list?*

Yes. A Local Spiritual Assembly must retain the names of all believers who have lost their voting rights on the membership list. It must note their status next to their names ie. whether the person has lost his or her full voting rights or only part of them and if so, which rights have been removed.

3.6.6 *How should a Local Spiritual Assembly instruct a believer who is changing his or her address?*

Local Spiritual Assemblies should advise believers who are changing their address to apply at the Post Office to have their mail re-directed. The Post Office will do this for a small fee. In this way, mail from the Bahá'í institutions will still reach them and the institutions will not lose touch with the believers.

3.6.7 *What is the difference between the membership list and the voting list?*

The membership list is a list of all adults, youth and children resident in the community, regardless of whether they are inactive, address unknown, or have lost their voting rights. Generally speaking it will also include the names of declarants who have been accepted by the Local Spiritual Assembly, but whose declarations have not yet been accepted by the National Spiritual Assembly; however, there are notable exceptions to this rule, such as declarants from Muslim or Israeli background. Other exceptions include believers who have transferred in from overseas whose transfer of membership has not yet been verified at the National Office.

The voting list, on the other hand, consists of only the adult believers eligible to serve on an Assembly. As such it does not include, for example, Hands of the Cause of God, members of the Continental Boards of Counsellors, citizens of the People's Republic of China, prisoners, or people who have lost their administrative and voting rights.

3.7 FILING

3.7.1 *How should a Local Spiritual Assembly organise its files?*

A good filing system should ensure that papers on any subject can be turned up immediately when required. The type of system used will depend on the quantity of material being handled by the Assembly. Generally speaking, Local Spiritual Assemblies will need to maintain separate files for such things as incoming or outgoing correspondence, Local Spiritual

CHAPTER THREE

Assembly policy decisions, newsletters, minutes. Other files as required may be set up for particular institutions and individuals, special projects and so on. [Further information on how to set up a filing system is available in the "Bahá'í Secretary's Manual", p.10.]

The Local Spiritual Assembly should retrieve Assembly materials such as copies of minutes, correspondence, files and so on, from anyone leaving the Assembly. If such materials are not returned voluntarily by the person, the Assembly should take action to recover them or see to it, if appropriate, that they are destroyed.

3.7.2 ***Do all Local Spiritual Assembly members have equal access to the files?***

Yes; however, the Assembly may, if it chooses, list certain items as 'confidential' and require that access to them is dependent on a specific decision of the Assembly:-

> *In reply to your letter of May 13th, 1976, the Universal House of Justice instructs us to say that all members of the Spiritual Assembly are equal and should have access to the files and minutes of the Assembly of which they are members. It is, however, within the discretion of any Spiritual Assembly to so organise its files and records that certain items could be listed as 'confidential' and access to those so classified could only be had by a specific decision of the Assembly itself.*

(letter written on behalf of the Universal House of Justice, dated June 8, 1976)

3.8 **ANNUAL REPORT**

3.8.1 ***When should the Local Spiritual Assembly prepare its Annual Report?***

The Annual Report covers the period Naw-Rúz to Naw-Rúz (March 21 - March 20) and must be prepared in time to be presented to the community at its Annual General Meeting. Note, this means the Assembly must receive its committees' reports sufficiently ahead of time to be able to incorporate them into its Annual Report [see further Chapter 17, Section 3]

3.8.2 ***What information should the Annual Report contain?***

According to Article XI, Section 4 of the "By-Laws of a Local Spiritual Assembly", the Assembly must provide its community with '...reports of the activities of the Assembly since its election, a financial statement showing all income and expenditure of its Fund, reports of its committees and presentation of any other matters pertaining to the affairs of the Bahá'í community.'

The following basic information should be included in the Assembly's Report:
1. name and location of the Assembly
2. date of report
3. period covered
4. number of adults, youth and children in community
5. results of the last annual election: Assembly membership
6. bi-elections held during the year and results
7. number of Local Spiritual Assembly meetings

Information on teaching should be included:
1. progress of the local Plan, and accomplishment of key tasks
2. the number of declarations during the year
3. a list of travel teachers and areas visited
4. a list of homefront pioneers, mentioning both the place from which they moved and the place to which they moved

CHAPTER THREE

5. major events supported or held, such as Refugee Week
6. other teaching, consolidation or proclamation activities, such as displays, deepening evenings or presentations of the Peace Message to government officials

Information on community affairs could include:
1. attendance at Feasts and Assembly meetings
2. youth and children's activities
3. women's activities
4. marriages, separations and divorces within your community during the period
5. report on what role the assistants to the Auxiliary Board members have played in relation to your Assembly during the year and what activities you have undertaken together in a collaborative fashion
6. conferences held or any other events or programmes conducted during the year for the benefit of the community

Financial information, as follows:
1. financial report, covering: total contributions received
2. expenditures
3. end of year balance sheet
4. estimate of the percentage of the community contributing to the Funds

3.8.3 *Who prepares the Annual Report?*

Preparation of the Annual Report is usually the responsibility of the Secretary; however, the Assembly as a whole has responsibility for ensuring its accuracy.

Who receives copies of the Annual Report?

The National Spiritual Assembly should be sent a copy of the Annual Report as soon as possible after April 21st, together with the Annual Financial Report, Plan and Budget. The Assembly may also send a copy to its Auxiliary Boards if it chooses.

3.8.4 *Do incorporated Assemblies have special requirements to meet?*

Incorporated Local Spiritual Assemblies will see any special requirements regarding the Annual Report which they must meet, set out in the Act that incorporated them.

3.9 **ARCHIVES**

3.9.1 *What is the importance of setting up local archives?*

Local archives provide a valuable source of information for historians of the future. The National Spiritual Assembly endorses the following statement by Hand of the Cause of God, Mr. H. Collis Featherstone:-

> *It is very evident to me that everything that gives detailed information of the development of the Faith, of special conferences, photos, reports, first meetings, etc. that indicate the building of the World Order of Bahá'u'lláh, should be preserved in a chronological order. All photographs should be set up in special albums or files identified as to persons and dates etc., the founding of local Assemblies, summer schools, acquiring of Hazíratu'l-Quds, local endowments, preservation of all legal records, all constitute archives in the sense that they are a source of information for the historians of the future in such a vast dispensation of five thousand centuries.*

CHAPTER THREE

The World Centre has said:-

> *...Bahá'ís have the opportunity - perhaps even the duty - to preserve for future generations an accurate and detailed record of how a major religion entered the world of man and became established in human society...*
>
> (extract from a letter from the Universal House of Justice Department of Library and Archival Services, dated June 11, 1986) [See also "Lights of Guidance" {revised edition} nos. 326-333.]

3.9.2 **How should local archives be set up?**

The Assembly's files should be gone through and items sorted according to the instructions given in the National Archives Committee's 'Archives Retention and Destruction Guidelines'. These are contained in Appendix 1 of this Chapter.

Once the items to be kept have been decided upon, they should be transferred to the community's archives. Items should not be transferred to the archives before they have been sorted as this will cause congestion in the collection at a later date. To set up local archives the National Archives Committee recommends that Local Spiritual Assemblies follow the guidelines in the booklet 'Guidelines for Bahá'í Archives' published by the National Spiritual Assembly of the United States. This booklet is available from the National Archives Committee for $15.00 (cost price and includes postage). The National Archives Committee may be contacted c/- the National Office.

3.9.3 **Who should be responsible for deciding which items to keep and which to destroy?**

The Universal House of Justice recommends that the Assembly appoint a committee to make recommendations to the Assembly as to which items should be kept and which destroyed, according to their historical value:-

> *It is within the discretion and jurisdiction of National or Local Assemblies to decide on which papers in their files are not of long term value and hence can be destroyed, and which papers have possible historical value. The selection of materials for archival retention or for elimination should not, however, be left to the judgement of a single person. Thus, when your Secretary or other person assigned to the task has sifted through the papers, those items marked for destruction should be passed upon by a committee appointed by your Assembly, bearing in mind the historical values of such records of national affairs. The committee's recommendations can be decided upon by your Assembly. The same principle applies to Local Assembly Archives.*
>
> (letter written on behalf of the Universal House of Justice to a National Spiritual Assembly, dated February 3, 1982)

> *...you should always bear in mind the historical value of your files. Letters which at this time seem to be of little value could prove to be of great interest to future historians of the development of the Cause of Bahá'u'lláh ...*
>
> (letter written on behalf of the Universal House of Justice to a National Spiritual Assembly, dated November 26, 1975)

Incorporated institutions are advised to make sure that all records required to be kept by the

CHAPTER THREE

Act which incorporated them are kept in an orderly and safe fashion, and are not destroyed before the statutory retention period has expired. If in doubt, seek appropriate legal advice.

3.9.4 *If a Local Spiritual Assembly lapses, what should the remaining community members do with the files?*

If a former Local Spiritual Assembly lapses back to Group status it should continue to maintain the community's archives according to the above instructions; however, should the community's numbers drop to only one or two and there seems little prospect of reforming the Assembly in the near future, the Assembly's files may be sent to the National Archives Committee (c/- National Office) for storage in the National Archives Collection. The files should be sorted first according to the instructions given in the 'Archives Retention and Destruction Guidelines' (Appendix 1). The cost of sending the files must be borne by the local community.

3.10 COMMUNICATIONS

3.10.1 *Who receives and sends communications on behalf of the Local Spiritual Assembly?*

Generally the Secretary receives and sends communications on behalf of the Local Spiritual Assembly, although the duty may be delegated to another Assembly member. All correspondence is taken to the Assembly's next meeting unless the Assembly has instructed otherwise, eg. it may instruct the Secretary that certain items can be taken directly to the Feast. The Assembly retains overall responsibility for all communications made on its behalf.

3.10.2 *What form do communications generally take?*

In-coming communications usually include:
1. written correspondence
2. spoken communications (notes should be made by the recipient and the written record kept in the Assembly's files)
3. Feast recommendations (the Secretary, or another Assembly member should take notes at the Feast and the recommendation should be treated as in-coming communications at the next Assembly meeting)

Out-going communications usually includes:
1. written correspondence (the preferred method except for minor matters)
2. spoken communications (usually followed up with a letter confirming the communication to ensure that both parties understand what has been said)
3. reports to the community at the Feast, including the Assembly's response to Feast recommendations
4. Local Spiritual Assembly newsletters

3.10.3 *How should communications from the Assembly be prepared?*

It is important that the Assembly's communications be accurate and clear; and that the tone be appropriate to the purpose of the communication, eg. if the Assembly is reprimanding a believer, the letter should be loving but also convey the authority of the Assembly. It is particularly important that the communication convey the spirit of the Faith, that is, it should be warm and loving, not cold and impersonal:-

> *We are deeply concerned that some of the letters written on behalf of your National Assembly contain brusque language, are critical in tone, lack warmth, and reflect impatience with friends whose actions have brought problems to your council chamber. We fully understand how the burdensome weight of these vexatious problems, many of which could and should have been avoided, can tax the patience of the most*

CHAPTER THREE

serene. The temptation to react sharply and defensively is very great, yet we know that, as Trustees of the Merciful, we should not do so. Not only is it contrary to the spirit of the instructions of the Master and the Guardian, with which you are thoroughly familiar, but giving vent to such reaction tends to evoke resentment rather than bringing about the desired result... ...We mention these examples only to call to your notice a reaction which may not have been apparent to those writing letters on your behalf, in the hope that ways and means can be found to insure that the manner in which you convey your views or decisions to the friends will promote the utmost unity, concord and understanding.

(letter from the Universal House of Justice to a National Spiritual Assembly, dated January 25, 1972)

Other points to note include:
1. the Assembly may require that drafts of important letters be taken to the Assembly for review and approval before being sent
2. information given to the friends at Feasts should be kept as brief as possible, eg. extracts of letters received may be read rather than the whole letter; or may be printed in the local newsletter instead
3. copies should be made of outgoing communications for the Assembly's files. [Further guidance on how to draft letters is available in the "Bahá'í Secretary's Manual", p.8-9.]

3.10.4 *What is the correct protocol for addressing institutions of the Faith?*

The full name or title of an institution should be used when that institution is being addressed:-

It has been noted that your letter of 13 June, 1972 was addressed to "The U.H.J.". It would be more fitting in addressing the institutions of the Faith that the full name or title be spelled out.

(letter written on behalf of the Universal House of Justice to a National Spiritual Assembly, dated July 6, 1972)

The International Teaching Centre has also said:-

... The House of Justice... agrees entirely ...that the friends should be advised not to allow such minor matters to become points of argument in the community, especially when the issue involved is related to the use of abbreviations or symbols in charts, maps, statistical listings, and the like.

(letter dated February 20, 1980)

3.10.5 *How should a Local Spiritual Assembly design its letterhead?*

A Local Spiritual Assembly's letterhead must read: 'The Spiritual Assembly of the Bahá'ís of ...'. If the Assembly is incorporated in New South Wales, Victoria or Tasmania, the letterhead must read: 'The Spiritual Assembly of the Bahá'ís of ... Limited', and must also include the address of the Registered Office of the Assembly. In the other states the word 'Incorporated' must replace the word 'Limited', and the Assembly may or may not have to include the address of a Registered Office depending upon the terms of the Act under which it is incorporated. The letterhead should have a simple and dignified appearance. Examples of

CHAPTER THREE

appropriate letterheads are contained in Appendix 2 of this Chapter.

3.10.6 **What guidelines apply to local newsletters?**

Local newsletters or bulletins are encouraged as a means of communication between the friends. Such newsletters should be primarily devoted to the spread of local news and activities and should always remain subordinate in importance to national newsletters or bulletins:-

> *Concerning local Bahá'í newsletters the Guardian strongly feels that they should be primarily devoted to the spread of local news and activities...They may occasionally refer to items of a national scope, but this should be done only with the view of assisting and not hindering the national body of the Cause to carry out effectively its programme and decisions. There is thus a definite line of demarcation between correspondence initiated by local and national Assemblies. Local activities should always be subordinated to those of a national character and importance. This is intended not to minimise the role of the local Assembly in the administrative order, but to establish and ensure a sane relationship between that body and the national organism of the Cause.*

> (letter written on behalf of Shoghi Effendi to an individual believer, dated May 10, 1934)

> *In certain countries, we are glad to see, there are in addition to the national newsletter, news bulletins issued on regional or district levels. The importance of these secondary organs of Bahá'í communication acquires added weight in areas where differences of language make the issue of bulletins in a local language of each area highly desirable, if not essential.*

> (letter from the Universal House of Justice to all National Spiritual Assemblies, dated May 25, 1975)

On the matter of Bahá'í newsletters being for Bahá'ís only see "Lights of Guidance" {revised edition} no.360.

3.10.7 **May a Local Spiritual Assembly communicate directly with the Universal House of Justice?**

A Local Spiritual Assembly may write directly to the Universal House of Justice and may direct invitations to attend functions to members of the Universal House of Justice. It is preferable, however, that communication be made through the National Office, as the Office has better communications facilities and may be aware of the itinerary of Universal House of Justice members. If a Local Spiritual Assembly wishes to appeal to the Universal House of Justice against a decision of the National Spiritual Assembly, the appeal must be channelled through the National Spiritual Assembly.

3.10.8 **May an individual communicate directly with the Universal House of Justice?**

Yes, with the exception of appeals:-

> *It is true, as you state in your letter of 26 May 1975, that every Bahá'í may write direct to the Universal House of Justice but this does not apply in the case of appeals which should be submitted through the National Spiritual Assembly.*

CHAPTER THREE

(letter written on behalf of the Universal House of Justice to a National Spiritual Assembly, dated June 17, 1975)

It is advisable in the first instance for individuals to communicate with the Universal House of Justice via the Australian National Office.

3.10.9 **May a Local Spiritual Assembly communicate directly with an overseas National Spiritual Assembly, one of its committees, or a Local Spiritual Assembly within the jurisdiction of another National Spiritual Assembly?**

No. In each of these instances the Local Spiritual Assembly must channel its communication through the Australian National Office. Permission can be given by the National Spiritual Assembly for regular communication between an Australian Local Spiritual Assembly and an overseas Local Spiritual Assembly.

3.10.10 **May Local Spiritual Assemblies communicate directly with Hands of the Cause of God, a Continental Board of Counsellors or individual Counsellors?**

Yes. In each of these instances it is advisable for the Assembly to communicate via the Australian National Office.

3.10.11 **May individuals communicate directly with Hands of the Cause of God, a Continental Board of Counsellors or individual Counsellors?**

Yes. Individuals may write privately to Hands of the Cause of God and to Counsellors.

3.11 **INCORPORATION**

3.11.1 *What is the value of incorporation for Local Spiritual Assemblies?*

Incorporation of Local Spiritual Assemblies constitutes legal recognition of a Bahá'í institution and affords it the legal rights and protection of an individual. Without incorporation, an Assembly is regarded under civil law as merely a group of individuals. Incorporation of the Assembly, its recognition at law as a legally constituted "Body Corporate", enables it to hold property, enter into contracts, claim certain taxation exemptions, receive bequests, etc. Incorporation is also a form of protection to the members of the Assembly, in that it limits their personal liability at law, for any acts of the Assembly.

3.11.2 *Should Local Spiritual Assemblies in Australia incorporate at the present time?*

No. The National Spiritual Assembly has been negotiating for some time now to have a Bahá'í Incorporation Act passed. These negotiations are continuing and, when successfully concluded, will enable Local Spiritual Assemblies to be incorporated more efficiently and economically than has been possible in the past. The National Spiritual Assembly will advise Local Spiritual Assemblies when the matter is finalised. Already incorporated Assemblies should, however, maintain their existing incorporations.

3.11.3 *May a Local Spiritual Assembly wind up its incorporation without the permission of the National Spiritual Assembly?*

No. If Assemblies wind up their incorporations at the present time they may jeopardise the National Spiritual Assembly's chance of having the Bahá'í Incorporation Act passed; therefore, if an Assembly, for some reason, feels a need to wind up its incorporation it must contact the National Spiritual Assembly before taking any steps.

3.11.4 *What responsibilities does an incorporated Local Spiritual Assembly have?*

Responsibilities differ from state to state according to the Act or Ordinance under which an Assembly is incorporated. For example, it is necessary in some states to have an annual audit done. In some states changes in Assembly members must be notified to the appropriate government agency within a certain specified time. Penalties for failure to comply with the law can be quite severe. Any incorporated Assembly that has not already done so, therefore, should obtain a copy of the relevant Act and familiarise itself with its contents. Any further questions regarding Assembly incorporation should be sent to the National Office.

3.11.5 *What happens if an incorporated Assembly lapses?*

If an incorporated Assembly lapses it must notify the National Spiritual Assembly <u>immediately</u>. In nearly all circumstances it is possible to continue the incorporation for a year or two even though there are less than nine adult Bahá'ís eligible to serve on the Assembly in the community.

3.12 **NOTES FOR REGISTERED GROUPS**

As Registered Groups expect to one day be Local Spiritual Assemblies, they are encouraged to practise as many of the procedures applicable to Local Spiritual Assemblies in this Chapter as are felt to be necessary. Registered Groups should, however, particularly bear in mind Shoghi Effendi's warning against over-administration and should remember to focus their energies, not on administration, but on teaching. The National Spiritual Assembly does require, however, that Registered Groups maintain their own membership lists and be responsible for transferring believers in and out of their community.

CHAPTER THREE

APPENDIX 1

Guidelines for Destruction and Preservation of Records, Files and Old Papers for Bahá'í institutions within the jurisdictions of the National Spiritual Assembly of The Bahá'ís of Australia incorporated.

1) The following is a list of those records which Local Spiritual Assemblies, Groups and Committees and Departments of the National Spiritual Assembly should keep. It has been prepared by The Australian Bahá'í National Archives Department - a Department of the National Spiritual Assembly of the Bahá'ís of Australia as a guide for all institutions within its jurisdiction

2) The list is not complete; it shows the most frequent subject classifications. However, if a particular classification is not shown, please advise the Archives Department so that it can be included in a future list, as the current list will be amended as time progresses, with new classifications.

3) Whilst a rough guideline has been given, mature judgement will be needed at all times to determine what is historical, or, what will be of future value, without causing congestion of files and space.

4) Although wise judgement is called for, it is hoped that this will not deter the culling and destruction of useless and unnecessary papers held in current and intermediate files and records.

5) Incorporated institutions are advised to make sure that all records required to be kept by the Act which Incorporated them are kept in an orderly and safe fashion, and are not destroyed before the statutory retention period has expired. If in doubt, seek appropriate legal advice.

6) Destruction, culling and cataloguing of records etc. should be completed before they are placed In your Local Archives Collection. If this is postponed to a later date, congestion in most cases invariably will occur. The records which are to be kept should be transferred to the local community's Archives.

7) Those records and files etc. belonging to Committees and Departments of the National Spiritual Assembly should be sent to The Australian Bahá'í National Archives Department, only when the following steps have been completed:

a) That the Archives Department is satisfied that the records possess temporary or permanent values warranting further preservation;

(b) That the records have been assessed according to the provision of the appropriate disposal schedule (the attached list) or other disposal agreement and that clear indication is given, at the time of transfer, of the retention period (for intermediate files and records - these are those records which are non-current and could have archival value, and are required to be kept for administrative purposes.

(c) That the records have been packed and listed for transfer in the manner prescribed by the archives Department. (Copies of the forms: AR.1. & AR.1.a. - Details of Records Packed for Filing In The National Archives Collection, is available from the Archives Department, upon request.

(d) That the rate of file return to Departments/Committees is moderate and that files returned to the Departments/committees will not, In the normal course, be retained as current records of the Department/Committee.

AR.I.

ACCESSION LIST NO: ....

Sheet:............of...............Sheets

DETAILS OF RECORDS PACKED FOR FILING IN THE NATIONAL ARCHIVES COLLECTION.

DEPARTMENT/COMMITTEE: ....

NOTE:
1. LIST ONLY THOSE RECORDS ETC. WHICH HAVE BEEN CULLED ACCORDING TO THE ARCHIVES RETENTION AND DESTRUCTION GUIDELINES.
2. LIST RECORDS IN ALPHABETICAL FILE ORDER.
3. RECORDS LISTED BELOW, IF RETURNED TO DEPARTMENT/COMMITTEE WILL NOT BE RETAINED AS CURRENT RECORDS, AND WILL BE RETURNED TO THE ARCHIVES DEPARTMENT AFTER USE.

DETAIL OF RECORD (File Title, Dates etc & File No (If Any)	BUNDLE BOX NO. (Allocated by Archives).

CHECKED BY:................................... (Lodging Dept/Com'tee)   Date: ....
CHECKED BY:................................... (Archives Dept)   Date: ....

AR.la.

ACCESSION LIST NO: ....

Sheet:............of...............Sheets

DETAILS OF RECORDS PACKED FOR FILING IN THE NATIONAL ARCHIVES COLLECTION.

DEPARTMENT/COMMITTEE: ....

DETAIL OF RECORD (File Title, Dates etc & File No (If Any)	BUNDLE BOX NO. (Allocated by Archives).

CHECKED BY:................................... (Lodging Dept/Com'tee)   Date: ....

CHECKED BY:................................... (Archives Dept)   Date: ....

ARCHIVES RETENTION AND DESTRUCTION GUIDELINES

CLASSIFICATION	ACTION TO BE TAKEN			
	KEEP	DESTROY ONE YEAR AFTER LAST DATE OF ACTION	DESTROY ONE YEAR AFTER LAST DATE OF ACTION	DESTROY AFTER STATUTORY RETENTION PERIOD HAS EXPIRED
ADMINISTRATION:				
L.S.A. Minutes	•			
Committee Reports	•			
Newsletters	•			
Minutes of Meetings	•			
Register of Believers	•			
Documents - all those documents, reports, forms, certificates required by law, as stipulated in Act of Parliament, and Regulations (for incorporated L.S.A.s)	•			
Marriage Notices/Consents	•			
Death Notices	•			
Terms of Reference	•			
Reports, including Annual General Meetings.	•			
Surveys and Statistics:-				
a) Final Report, Conclusions, Recommendations	•			
b) Old Forms and Working Papers			•	
Policy Files	•			
Correspondence to and from:-				
1) The Universal House of Justice				
2) Continental Board of Counsellors	•			
3) Hands of the Cause, Counsellors, and Auxiliary Board Members:-	•			
a) if of a routine nature			•	
b) if of a historical nature	•			
4) National Spiritual Assemblies, Local Spiritual Assemblies, Groups, Committees, Departments:-				
a) If of a routine nature		•		
b) if of a historical nature	•			
5) Individual Believers:-				
a) If of a routine nature		•		
b) if of a historical nature concerning the development of Faith	•			
c) Disputes between Believers-unless likely to have Legal implications.			•	
d) Suggestions:-				
i) if implemented			•	
ii) if rejected		•		
6) From Other Sources:-				
a) if of a routine nature		•		
b) if of a historical nature	•			

ARCHIVES RETENTION AND DESTRUCTION GUIDELINES

CLASSIFICATION	ACTION TO BE TAKEN			
	KEEP	DESTROY ONE YEAR AFTER LAST DATE OF ACTION	DESTROY ONE YEAR AFTER LAST DATE OF ACTION	DESTROY AFTER STATUTORY RETENTION PERIOD HAS EXPIRED
FINANCIAL:				
Budget Reports (Annual)	•			
Cheque Books				•
Bank Deposit Books				•
Receipt Books/Invoices				•
Book Keeping Records (Income/Expenditure/Analysis Books)	•			
Bank Statements and Reconciliations				•
Annual Financial Reports	•			
Simple Audit Reports	•			
External Audit Reports	•			
Contracts/Mortgages	•			
Insurance Papers				•
MISCELLANEOUS:				
Publicity Files - Press Releases etc				
Newspaper Clippings	•			
Scrap Books	•			
Diaries	•			
Photographs, Negatives, Movies, Videos	•			
(catalogued and indexed)	•			
Tapes, Cassettes, Records etc	•			
Artefacts and Relics	•			
Bulletins	•			
Bahá'í Magazines	•			
Maps	•			
Diagrams	•			
Construction Plans etc.	•			
Request for information on the Faith		•		

APPENDIX 2

Following are samples of recommended letterhead designs

THE SPIRITUAL ASSEMBLY OF THE BAHÁ'ÍS OF DUBBO LIMITED

Telephone: Secretary's Address:

Registered Office: First Floor, 155 Brisbane Street, Dubbo, NSW., 2830

CHAPTER THREE

The Spiritual Assembly of the Bahá'ís of Hornsby Limited

P.O. Box 406,
Pennant Hills, N.S.W. 2120
Phone: (02) 84 3827

Registered Office: 3 Pomona Street, Pennant Hills, NSW 2120

CHAPTER THREE

THE SPIRITUAL ASSEMBLY
of the
BAHÁ'ÍS of MANLY

P.O. Box 233, Manly, N.S.W. 2095. Australia

CHAPTER FOUR

Chapter 4

4. Bahá'í Funds

4.1 INTRODUCTION

4.1.1 *Why are the Bahá'í Funds important?*

The Bahá'í Funds are important because they constitute the practical means by which the work of the Cause may be advanced:-

> *...the progress and extension of spiritual activities is dependent and conditioned upon material means...*
>
> (Shoghi Effendi, "Principles of Bahá'í Administration", p. 93)

4.1.2 *Is giving to the Bahá'í Funds an obligation?*

Yes:-

> *It is the sacred obligation of every conscientious and faithful servant of Bahá'u'lláh who desires to see His Cause advance, to contribute freely and generously for the increase of that Fund.*
>
> (Shoghi Effendi, "Bahá'í Administration", p.41-2)

4.1.3 *Are contributions voluntary?*

It is important to note that contributions must be entirely voluntary. The only way in which an Assembly may seek funds is by a general appeal to its community:-

> *...I feel urged to remind you of the necessity of ever bearing in mind the cardinal principle that all contributions to the Fund are to be purely and strictly voluntary in character. It should be made clear and evident to every one that any form of compulsion, however slight and indirect, strikes at the very root of the principle underlying the formation of the Fund ever since its inception. While appeals of a general character, carefully-worded and moving and dignified in tone are welcome under all circumstances, it should be left entirely to the discretion of every conscientious believer to decide upon the nature, the amount, and purpose of his or her contribution for the propagation of the Cause.*
>
> (letter from Shoghi Effendi to a National Spiritual Assembly, dated January 10, 1926)

4.1.4 *Who may contribute to the Bahá'í Funds?*

Only Bahá'ís are permitted to contribute to the Bahá'í Funds:-

> *One of the distinguishing features of the Cause of God is its principle of non-acceptance of financial contributions for its own purposes from non-Bahá'ís: support of the Bahá'í Fund is a bounty reserved by Bahá'u'lláh to His declared followers. This bounty imposes full responsibility for financial support of the Faith on the believers alone...*
>
> (letter from the Universal House of Justice to the Bahá'ís of the World, Naw-Rúz 1974)

CHAPTER FOUR

The Writings also make the following points on this subject:-

1. Bahá'ís should not go into debt in order to contribute.
2. Children of parents, one or both of whom are not Bahá'ís, may only contribute if their parents permit them to be considered Bahá'ís.
3. Bahá'ís without voting rights may not contribute to the Funds:-

> As contributions to Bahá'í Funds are used to support the administration of the Faith, they should not be accepted from those who are deprived of their voting rights...
>
> (letter from Shoghi Effendi to a National Spiritual Assembly, dated May 8, 1947) [For further information on these points see "Lights of Guidance" {revised edition} nos. 842, 848.]

4.1.5 **What if a person who is not a Bahá'í wishes to make a contribution?**

Contributions from non-Bahá'ís may be accepted with the express provision that they will be used only for charitable and humanitarian purposes:-

> In cases...when a friend or sympathiser of the Faith eagerly insists on a monetary contribution for the promotion of the Faith, such gifts should be accepted and duly acknowledged by the elected representatives of the believers with the express understanding that they would be utilised by them only to reinforce that section of the Bahá'í Fund exclusively devoted to philanthropic or charitable purposes.
>
> (letter from Shoghi Effendi to the Bahá'ís of the United States and Canada, dated October 25, 1929) [See further "Lights of Guidance" {revised edition}, no.854]

4.1.6 **What are the spiritual principles underlying contributions to the Bahá'í Fund?**

Foremost among the spiritual principles underlying contributions to the Bahá'í Fund is that of sacrifice. By this is meant that it is the spirit of devotion in which a believer makes a contribution rather than the quantity of the contribution, that is important. The more sacrifice a person makes, the more meritorious will be the contribution in the sight of God. The following statement from Shoghi Effendi also emphasises the importance of 'universal and whole-hearted' support for the Funds:-

> As to the idea of 'giving what one can afford': this does by no means put a limit or even exclude the possibility of self-sacrifice. There can be no limit to one's contributions to the National Fund. The more one can give the better it is, especially when such offerings necessitate sacrifice of other wants and desires on the part of the donor. The harder the sacrifice the more meritorious will it be, of course, in the sight of God. For after all it is not so much the quantity of one's offerings that matters, but rather the measure of deprivation that such offerings entail. It is the spirit, not the mere fact of contributing, that we should always take into account when we stress the necessity for a universal and whole-hearted support of the various Funds of the Cause.
>
> (letter from Shoghi Effendi to an individual believer, dated December 31, 1935)

Another important principle is that of confidentiality; that is to say, the Assembly must not make contributions public.

CHAPTER FOUR

4.2 THE DIFFERENT FUNDS

4.2.1 *How many different Funds are there?*

There are four major categories of Funds established to support the work of the four major administrative institutions of the Faith.

These are:
1. Local Spiritual Assemblies - Local Funds
2. National Spiritual Assemblies - National Funds
3. Continental Board of Counsellors - Continental Funds
4. Universal House of Justice - International Funds

[Further information on the Funds can be found in the 'Deepening on the Funds' programme prepared by the National Spiritual Assembly and distributed to all Local Spiritual Assemblies in July 1985 or subsequently on formation.]

Donations to the National Funds are payable to N.S.A. Bahá'ís of Australia, and should be forwarded to:
The Treasury Department
N.S.A. Bahá'ís of Australia
PO Box 285
MONA VALE NSW 2103

All other correspondence to the National Treasurer should go to the Treasurer's Office address, should this be different from that of the National Office.

Contributions to the Continental Funds by Assemblies or individuals should be sent to the National Office for forwarding. It is most convenient if the contribution is kept quite distinct from contributions forwarded for other Funds. Cheques should be made payable to 'Continental Fund'.
Donations to the International Funds by Assemblies or individuals can be sent to the Treasury Department at the National Office, or directly, to the World Centre, payable to:

Bahá'í International Fund
PO Box 155
31 001 Haifa
ISRAEL

If the donation is for a specific Fund - for example, the Arc Fund - this should be specified. When making donations to any Bahá'í Fund, individuals and institutions must supply their name and address.

4.2.2 *Should individuals and Local Spiritual Assemblies contribute to all four Funds?*

Yes. Both Assemblies and individuals have a responsibility to contribute to all the Funds. Individuals should also be made aware that they have an obligation to contribute directly to these Funds, over and above that part of their contribution to the Local Fund which will be allocated by the Assembly to the other Funds:-

> *We therefore appeal to the friends everywhere to exercise the utmost economy in the use of the funds and to make those sacrifices in their personal lives which will enable them to contribute their share, according to their means, to the local, national, continental and international Funds of the Faith.*
>
> (letter from the Universal House of Justice to the Bahá'ís of the

CHAPTER FOUR

World, Naw-Rúz 1979)

Assemblies must likewise ensure that contributions given to them for forwarding to other Funds, are not counted in the Assembly's own budgeted allocation to that Fund:-

> *In your letter of September 28, 1953, you mentioned the sum of...as being included in the amount allocated from your Assembly's Budget to the World Centre. The principle involved is as follows: The Guardian feels that your Assembly when allocating its annual budget, and having stipulated what sum is for the purposes of the International Centre of the Faith, should immediately pigeon-hole that sum to be at the Guardian's disposal. Any monies received as contributions from the Bahá'ís for the International Centre should not be credited to this account which represents a national joint contribution, and has nothing to do with individual or local contributions forwarded to the World Centre in your care.*
>
> (letter from Shoghi Effendi to a National Spiritual Assembly, dated June 20, 1954)

The Assembly should advise the friends in its community to make the purpose of their donation quite clear; for example, that it is simply to be forwarded on their behalf to the National Fund; or that it is intended as a donation to the Local Funds. The Local Spiritual Assembly should also advise the friends in its community that contributions to special Funds established by one of the institutions of the Faith from time to time - for example, the Arc Fund - should be made in addition to contributions made to the regular Funds, and not as a substitute for them.

4.2.3 Should the believers contribute directly to the National Fund?

Yes. The progress of the Cause in Australia will come to a standstill if the friends do not contribute to the National Fund:-

> *Above all, he wishes through you to reiterate his wish, already expressed in his recent cable to the National Spiritual Assembly, that the National Fund, which undoubtedly constitutes the bedrock upon which all the activities of the Cause ultimately rest, should receive the continued and whole-hearted support of all the believers. Both the Local Assemblies and the individual believers should realise that unless they contribute regularly and generously to that Fund the progress of the Faith ... will not only be considerably retarded, but will inevitably come to a standstill. There should be a continual flow of Funds to the national treasury of the National Spiritual Assembly, if that body wishes to properly administer the manifold and ever-increasing activities of the Faith. Every Bahá'í, no matter how poor, must realise what a grave responsibility he has to shoulder in this connection, and should have confidence that his spiritual progress as a believer in the World Order of Bahá'u'lláh will largely depend upon the measure in which he proves, in deeds, his readiness to support materially the divine institutions of His Faith.*
>
> (letter written on behalf of Shoghi Effendi to a National Spiritual Assembly, dated July 17, 1937)

Individuals may send donations directly to the National Office or may give them to their local Treasurer for forwarding. In both cases the donor's name and address should be included, or a stamped self-addressed envelope enclosed, so that a receipt may be issued. The Fund the donation is for should be specified for example, the National Fund, or Yerrinbool Bahá'í School Building Fund.

4.2.4 Should Local Spiritual Assemblies have Area Delegates' Funds?

Local Spiritual Assemblies responsible for organising Unit Conventions should establish a Delegates' Fund and invite the support of the friends in their Unit Area. The relevant guidance is contained in the following statement by the Universal House of Justice:-

> ...In the matter of attendance of delegates at Conventions, the desirability of the friends themselves being self-supporting should be pointed out by the National Assembly. If a delegate cannot pay his own expenses in attending the Convention, the Local Assembly or the believers in the electoral unit from which the delegate comes should be encouraged by the National Assembly to defray such expenses, so that only when Funds are unavailable from those sources, the National Assembly is approached to consider offering financial assistance.
>
> (letter written on behalf of the Universal House of Justice to a number of National Spiritual Assemblies, dated February 9, 1967)

On the basis of this guidance the National Spiritual Assembly has formulated the following policy:

1. If the delegate cannot be self-supporting, he or she should approach the organising Local Spiritual Assembly for assistance from the Delegates' Fund.
2. All Local Spiritual Assemblies who are responsible for organising the Unit Conventions are to establish a Delegates' Fund and bring the needs of that Fund to the attention of the believers in the Unit. The believers attending the Unit Convention should discuss the Delegates' Fund and prayerfully consider their support.
3. If after 1. and 2. sufficient Funds are not available, the delegate may wish to approach the National Spiritual Assembly for financial assistance. The National Assembly will consult on the application and inform the believer of its decision.

In view of this policy it is suggested that all Local Spiritual Assemblies consider making allowance for contribution to their Delegates' Fund in their budget each year. The sum allocated must depend in part on a judgment of how likely it is that any delegate from their area will need assistance and how much his or her travel expenses will be. Travel expenses should be calculated on the basis of the cheapest, and most realistic form of transport.

4.2.5 What is the Bahá'í Investment Fund?

The Bahá'í Investment Fund is an additional Fund established by the National Spiritual Assembly to pay for and maintain capital and building items that cannot be purchased in one year from the National Fund. The Universal House of Justice advised National Spiritual Assemblies to set aside money for such purposes:-

> The Treasurer should advise the Assembly to set aside sufficient sums on a regular basis to provide for the repair and maintenance of properties owned by the Faith, so that these can be kept in good condition and so that the normal work of the Cause is not interrupted by sudden requirements of large sums for repairs. Usually the task of maintaining the properties is assigned to a special committee or committees, which should be consulted by the Assembly and can

suggest a suitable amount to be set aside annually.

(letter written on behalf of the Universal House of Justice to a
National Spiritual Assembly, dated July 13, 1981)

Individuals and Assemblies can contribute to this Fund either by making capital donations or by investing in the Fund. It should be noted, however, that contributions to this Fund are additional to donations to the National Fund and not a substitute for them. [Further information is available from the Treasury Officer at the National Office.]

4.2.6 *Are donations to any of the Funds tax deductible?*

Donations of over $2.00 to the Yerrinbool Bahá'í School Building Fund, a Fund of the National Spiritual Assembly, are income tax deductible. This is the only tax deductible Bahá'í Fund in Australia.

4.2.7 *May Local Spiritual Assemblies and individuals contribute to Bahá'í projects in other countries?*

Yes. Individuals and Assemblies are free to make donations either directly to the project concerned, or through the Bahá'í institutions:-

It is very commendable for individual believers as well as Local Spiritual Assemblies to wish to help children in developing countries by contributing towards their education costs. There are no guidelines set for this purpose. However, as we understand it, individual friends are free to make donations of this nature either directly to a school of their choice or through Local or National Spiritual Assemblies.

(letter written on behalf of the Universal House of Justice to a
National Spiritual Assembly, dated April 14, 1988)

The National Spiritual Assembly's policy is as follows:-
1. If an overseas project is an approved National Spiritual Assembly of Australia project then the monies are to be sent through the National Assembly of Australia earmarked for the project. The National Assembly will then send it in bulk to the receiving country.
2. If individuals wish to contribute to any other overseas projects they are required to organise a cheque or draft in the appropriate currency and forward this to the particular project through the regular means established by the National Assembly in that country.
3. Ear-marked contributions can also be sent to the House of Justice for certain projects and the House of Justice will forward these monies.

4.3 **FORMS OF CONTRIBUTIONS**

4.3.1 *How may contributions be made to the Funds?*

In addition to ordinary cash or cheque donations, contributions may also be made to the Funds in any of the following ways:

1. Investments - stocks, bonds, shares and so on.
Given that the Funds are under the exclusive control of the Assembly, it is for the Assembly concerned - Local or National - to determine how it will use such donations. It may sell them, or it may place them in an investment Fund. For an unincorporated Assembly, some instruments will need to be held on their behalf by the National Assembly.

2. Gifts in kind.
The Local Spiritual Assembly may sell gifts in kind and use the proceeds as it sees fit.

3. Donations 'in memory of' or 'in honour of' Bahá'í or non-Bahá'í friends.

The believers are free to make such donations. The only point to bear in mind is that donations cannot be made 'in the name of' or 'on behalf of' non-Bahá'ís.

4. Pledges

The friends may make written pledges of their hope or intention of making a contribution to the Local or National Fund. Alternatively, the Local Spiritual Assembly may call for pledges. This can be a useful means of determining in advance whether the funds will be available for the financing of a major project. Note, however, that the redemption of such pledges is entirely a matter of conscience. The Assembly may remind the donor of the pledge and ask if be possible for it to be honoured, but no pressure can be brought to bear to make the person pay:-

> *Pledges can be useful as a means of encouraging contributions attention of the friends. This method can be particularly helpful in a situation where a Spiritual Assembly has a major task to perform, such as the building of a Hazíratu'l-Quds or the establishment of a tutorial school, and needs to have some idea in advance of whether the funds for the project will be available. However, it would be entirely contrary to Bahá'í principles to bring any pressure to bear when calling for pledges or when endeavouring to collect them. Once a pledge has been given it is permissible to remind the donor, privately, of his expressed intention to contribute and to inquire courteously if it would be possible for him to honour his pledge, but Assemblies must be aware that such pledges are not an obligation in any legal sense; their redemption is entirely a matter of conscience. Lists of those making pledges must not be publicised.*

(Memorandum of Comments and Suggestions attached to a letter from the Universal House of Justice to all National Spiritual Assemblies, dated August 7, 1985)

5. Property

Local Spiritual Assemblies may accept donations of property. For an unincorporated Assembly, property will need to be held on their behalf by the National Assembly.

6. Estate Bequests

The Local Spiritual Assembly may dispose of a bequest as it considers best, within the legal terms of the will. Note that an Assembly does not have to accept a bequest if the conditions attaching to its acceptance would impose an unreasonable financial burden on the Assembly, or if fulfilment of the conditions would not be in the best interests of the Faith:-

> *In the eyes of Bahá'í Law a will is sacred and thus, when a testator makes a bequest to a Spiritual Assembly and attaches thereto certain duties and conditions, the Assembly has the responsibility to fulfil them. However, if the will imposes an unreasonable financial burden or a condition which could become an unreasonable financial burden, or if fulfilment of the conditions would be prejudicial to the best interests of the Faith, the Assembly may have no alternative to refusing the bequest, for if it accepts the bequest it is in honour bound to fulfil the conditions.*

(letter written on behalf of the Universal House of Justice to a National Spiritual Assembly, dated January 10, 1978)

4.3.2 ***Is it permissible for Local Spiritual Assemblies and individuals to earmark donations*** *for specific purposes?*

Yes:-

...any donor, Assembly or individual, has the right to specify the purpose intended for any contribution of funds or property...

(letter written on behalf of the Universal House of Justice to a National Spiritual Assembly, dated June 22, 1980)

The practise, however, is not to be encouraged, as it is better to leave the recipient free to expend the funds in the manner of most use to the Faith:-

> *Regarding your question about contributions: it is up to the individual to decide; if he wishes to devote a sum to a specific purpose, he is free to do so; but the friends should recognise the fact that too much labelling of contributions will tie the hands of the Assembly and prevent it from meeting its many obligations in various fields of Bahá'í activity.*

(letter from Shoghi Effendi to a National Spiritual Assembly, dated June 23, 1950)

4.3.3 *What principles apply to the earmarking of contributions?*

The following principles apply:-

1. A Local Spiritual Assembly does not have to accept an earmarked contribution, but is bound by the conditions of the earmarking if it does accept.
2. A Local Spiritual Assembly may not use earmarked funds for any other than their designated purpose.
3. The donor cannot change the earmarking without the agreement of the Local Spiritual Assembly, once the Assembly has accepted the donation.
4. The Local Spiritual Assembly has a duty to preserve the real value of the earmarked funds.
5. The Local Spiritual Assembly must keep earmarked funds distinct from its other funds.
6. Proceeds from the sale of earmarked property retain the earmarking of the property.
7. Should circumstances change so as to invalidate or make less relevant the original purpose of the earmarking, the Assembly should advise the donor, consult with him or her concerning the advisability of the earmarking conditions in the changed circumstances and receive the donor's advice.

[For further information on the above points, see "Lights of Guidance" {revised edition}, nos. 882-891.]

4.4 **RESPONSIBILITIES OF THE LOCAL SPIRITUAL ASSEMBLY**

4.4.1 *Must a Local Spiritual Assembly have a Local Bahá'í Fund?*

Yes:-

> *As the progress and extension of spiritual activities is dependent and conditioned upon material means, it is of absolute necessity that immediately after the establishment of local as well as National Spiritual Assemblies, a Bahá'í Fund be established, to be placed under the exclusive control of the Spiritual Assembly.*

(Shoghi Effendi, "Principles of Bahá'í Administration", p.93)

As noted in the above quotation, the Local Spiritual Assembly has 'exclusive control' over the Local Funds. The "By-Laws of a Local Spiritual Assembly" (Art. III) also state that the Assembly 'shall collect and disburse all Funds intended for the maintenance of this Corporation'.

CHAPTER FOUR

4.4.2 *What is the purpose of the Local Bahá'í Fund?*

The purpose of the Local Bahá'í Fund is to further the interests of the Cause within the Assembly's area of jurisdiction. As a general principle, Shoghi Effendi advised that it is necessary to identify that area of work which will give the greatest yield and then to appropriate the necessary funds for it:-

> *The financial questions that confront the Cause are all very pressing and important. They need a judicious administration and wise policy. We should study the needs of the Cause, find which field will give the greatest yield, and then appropriate the necessary funds. And such a task is surely most difficult and responsible.*
>
> (letter from Shoghi Effendi to an individual believer, dated December 19, 1929)

In addition he identified the following specific needs:-
1. promote the Teaching Campaign
2. help the needy
3. establish educational Bahá'í institutions
4. extend in every way possible [the Assembly's] sphere of service

(see "Bahá'í Administration", p.42)

The Local Spiritual Assembly also has an obligation to contribute to the National, International and Continental Funds. It should also set aside a portion for the Area Delegates' Fund. Regarding assistance to the needy: whilst the Assembly has a duty to care for the poor and needy - both within its own Bahá'í community and within the wider community - it must give precedence to the interests of the Cause, both because the demands of the Cause transcend those of the individual and because fostering the work of the Cause is the only sure way of alleviating the plight of the suffering in the long term.
[See "Lights of Guidance" {revised edition} nos. 411, 412]

If the Local Spiritual Assembly is responsible for the maintenance of any properties - for example, a Local Bahá'í Centre - it must ensure that a sum is regularly set aside for this.

Many Local Spiritual Assemblies find the establishment of one Fund sufficient for their needs; however, some have also established a separate Bahá'í Centre Fund and/or a Library or Bookshop Fund. At the time of formation Local Spiritual Assemblies should study their By-Laws to determine their financial obligations and how best to meet them within their community.

4.4.3 *How should a Local Spiritual Assembly proceed when setting up its Fund for the first time?*

The Local Spiritual Assembly should follow the procedure outlined below:-

1. Open a 'Society Cheque Account,' also known by Westpac as a 'Deposit Bearing Interest' Account. This type of account is interest bearing and free of bank charges.
2. If convenient, open the account with a Westpac Bank (this is the National Spiritual Assembly's bank)
3. Open the account in the name of: 'The Spiritual Assembly of the Bahá'ís of...'
4. In the event of the Assembly becoming incorporated, add the State of incorporation below the title; for example: 'Incorporated in New South Wales'
5. Signatories to the account should be the Assembly Chairman, Secretary and Treasurer

CHAPTER FOUR

6. At least two people must sign each cheque (note, however, that these two signatories may not be husband and wife)
7. Have a copy of the "Declaration of Trust and By-Laws of a National Spiritual "Assembly" and "By-Laws of a Local Spiritual Assembly" available, as the bank may need to see these when the account is being opened (copies are sent to each Assembly on formation or may be bought from Bahá'í Publications Australia)
8. Claim exemption from paying the 'Bank Accounts Debit Tax' and the 'Financial Institutions Duty' on the grounds of being a religious institution. Further information on the procedure for claiming exemption is available in the case of the Debit Tax from the bank or State Government Treasury Office, and in the case of the Financial Institutions Duty, from the local Stamp Duties Office. Should any difficulties arise in claiming exemption, the matter should be referred to the Treasury Department at the National Office for resolution.

4.4.4 **Who is responsible for managing the Fund?**

Routine management of the Fund is the delegated responsibility of the local Treasurer. The Local Spiritual Assembly, however, retains overall responsibility for authorising expenditures, ensuring that contributions are receipted and accounts properly kept:-

> *The National Spiritual Assembly has the responsibility to ensure that contributions received are properly receipted, and satisfactory accounts kept of all receipts and disbursements. While the Treasurer normally is the officer in charge of such a sacred obligation, this does not mean that other members are thereby relieved of all responsibility...*
>
> (letter written on behalf of the Universal House of Justice to a National Spiritual Assembly, dated January 11, 1977)

A corollary of this responsibility is that the Local Spiritual Assembly also retains the right of access to details relating to the Local Bahá'í Fund:-

> *...this does not mean that other members are thereby relieved of all responsibility, or are deprived of their right of access to details related to the current operation of the Assembly, in all its aspects. Such right and responsibility vested in the individual members of the Assembly do not vitiate the confidentiality of Bahá'í contributions, since the information made available to the Treasurer or other members of the Assembly is to be treated in strict confidence.*
>
> (letter written on behalf of the Universal House of Justice to a National Spiritual Assembly, dated January 11, 1977)

As a general rule the Treasurer should not provide the Assembly with the names of individual contributors. Should the Assembly need this information in any particular case, however, it can request the Treasurer for details. [For information concerning the responsibilities of the Local Spiritual Assembly for managing the Local Bahá'í Fund see "Lights of Guidance" {revised edition}, nos. 864, 867, 888. For further information see the "Bahá'í Treasurer's Manual"].

4.4.5 **How should the Local Spiritual Assembly collect donations?**

Donations are payable to the Treasurer. Alternatively, the Local Spiritual Assembly may choose to provide a receptacle:-

> *As to your question: the friends can give their contributions to the Treasurer, or, if they wish to remain anonymous and give small sums, a receptacle can be provided. The Local Assembly can decide this*

matter.

(letter written on behalf of Shoghi Effendi to an individual believer, dated September 29, 1951)

It is suggested that donations collected in a receptacle - for example, at a Feast - be counted by two (2) people: the Treasurer and one other. This provides a protection for the Treasurer against any accusations of misappropriation and relieves him of full responsibility for the contributions.

4.4.6 ***May the National Spiritual Assembly tell a Local Spiritual Assembly how to allocate its funds?***

No. The National Spiritual Assembly may make suggestions but it cannot intervene in an Assembly's plans unless a proposed action is clearly not in the best interests of the Faith:-

> *When a donation is given to a Local Assembly, the Assembly itself should decide how the funds are to be used. The National Assembly may wish to suggest to the Local Spiritual Assembly ways in which the money could be more practically spent, but the final decision regarding the use of such funds rests with the local body. National Assemblies should avoid instructing their Local Spiritual Assemblies to allocate a certain percentage or portion of their local funds towards specific purposes. They may, however, suggest that the Local Assemblies contribute funds for priority projects in the national budget and suggest that the communities try to underwrite a part of the national budget. Any National Assembly is, of course, empowered to prevent an institution under its jurisdiction from taking any action regarding the use of funds which would not be to the best interests of the Cause. Such cases, however, are rare...*

(letter written on behalf of the Universal House of Justice to an individual believer, dated October 17, 1985) [See also "Lights of Guidance" {revised edition}, no.878]

4.4.7 ***When should the Local Spiritual Assembly prepare its budget for the year?***

The budget should be prepared in February at the same time as the Assembly finalises its Plan for the coming year. The budget covers the period Naw-Rúz to Naw-Rúz; that is, March 21 to March 20. The final budget should be presented to the community at the Annual General Meeting and should serve as a recommendation from the outgoing Assembly to the newly-elected Assembly. A copy should be sent, along with the Local Spiritual Assembly's Annual Report, to the National Spiritual Assembly. A copy of the budget should also be sent, along with the Financial Report, to the National Treasurer.

4.4.8 ***How should the Local Spiritual Assembly prepare its budget?***

The Local Spiritual Assembly should prepare its budget with reference to the following factors:-
1. An estimate of the funds likely to be available for the coming year. This can be calculated by examining actual contributions over the past few years in conjunction with the relative size of the community.
2. An estimate of actual costs. This can be obtained by examining actual expenditure in previous years on items such as administration, teaching projects and so on.
3. The Assembly's proposed plans for the coming year. These, in turn, are partly dependent on the financial resources available.

CHAPTER FOUR

The task of actually drafting the budget is delegated to the Treasurer; however, the Assembly has the responsibility of reviewing and approving the budget. It is also desirable for the Local Spiritual Assembly to consult with its local community whilst formulating the budget.

4.4.9 **_When should the Local Spiritual Assembly prepare its Annual Financial Report?_**

The Annual Financial Report covers the period Naw-Rúz to Naw-Rúz (March 21 - March 20) and must be prepared in time to be presented to the community at the Annual General Meeting. Following this, a copy of the Report should be included with the Annual Report that is sent to the National Spiritual Assembly. Another copy of the Financial Report should be sent, along with the budget, to the National Treasurer.

4.4.10 **_How should the Local Spiritual Assembly prepare its Annual Financial Report?_**

The Annual Financial Report must convey the following information:-

1. total contributions received
2. total expenditures
3. an estimate of the percentage of the community contributing to the Fund

Again, although preparation of the Financial Report is delegated to the Treasurer, the Assembly as a whole has the responsibility of ensuring its accuracy.

The Local Spiritual Assembly must also arrange for an audit of all financial records:-

> *The National Spiritual Assembly should, of course, ensure that its books of account are audited annually...*
>
> (letter written on behalf of the Universal House of Justice to a National Spiritual Assembly, dated July 13, 1981)

The purpose of the audit is to relieve the Treasurer of the sole responsibility for the financial accuracy of the records, and, in the case of incorporated Local Spiritual Assemblies, to satisfy legal requirements. Unincorporated Assemblies require only a simple audit which can be carried out by members of the Assembly. Some incorporated Assemblies, however, may require external audits. [For further information see p.18 of the "Bahá'í Treasurer's Manual".]

It should be noted that the need to employ an external auditor does not violate the confidential nature of contributions to the Fund:-

> *...there is no objection to a National Spiritual Assembly's appointing auditors, whether Bahá'í or non-Bahá'í to audit its books of accounts as required by law. The function of a professional auditor is by its nature a confidential one and the fact that the auditor will have to see the records of contributions does not violate the principle of confidentiality.*
>
> (letter written on behalf of the Universal House of Justice to a National Spiritual Assembly, dated April 26, 1982)

4.4.11 **_How often should the Local Spiritual Assembly receive reports from its Treasurer?_**

The Local Spiritual Assembly should receive reports from its Treasurer at each Assembly meeting. The Assembly should record in its Minutes the current balance of the Fund, donations received, and expenditures out, since the previous meeting. It should also attach a copy of the 'Treasurer's Report Form'(see the section 'Functions of the Treasurer') to the Minutes and ensure that a copy goes with the set of Minutes sent to the National Spiritual

CHAPTER FOUR

Assembly.

4.4.12 ***How often should the Local Spiritual Assembly report to its community?***

The Universal House of Justice has encouraged Assemblies to keep in regular contact with their communities:-

> *Assemblies should take the members of their communities into their confidence, and regularly inform them of the uses to which the Fund is put and the projects for which money is needed.*
>
> (Memorandum of Comments and Suggestions attached to a letter from the Universal House of Justice to all National Spiritual Assemblies, dated August 7, 1985)

The responsibility is to advise the friends of the uses and needs not only of the Local Funds, but of all the Funds:-

> *It is...important for the Assemblies to frankly lay the financial needs of the work before the friends, to explain to them the importance of the wholehearted, universal and regular support of the Bahá'í Funds...*
>
> (letter from the Universal House of Justice, dated April 13, 1975)

The Treasurer should present a financial report to the community on behalf of the Local Spiritual Assembly at each Feast. Although the extent of the report is left to the discretion of the Assembly it should include:-
1. **A statement on the needs of the National Bahá'í Fund.**
2. **A statement of the Local Spiritual Assembly's income for the year-to-date compared with the budget for the year-to-date.**

4.4.13 ***What responsibility does the Local Spiritual Assembly have for deepening the community in the importance of contributing to the Fund?***

The Local Spiritual Assembly has the following responsibilities:-
1. **To educate the friends in the distinctive features of the Bahá'í Funds and the spiritual principles on which contributing is based:-**

> *A corollary to the sacred obligation of the friends to contribute to the Funds of the Faith, is the direct and unavoidable responsibility of each Local and National Assembly to educate them in the spiritual principles related to Bahá'í contributions. Failure to educate the friends in this aspect of the Faith is tantamount to consciously depriving them of the spiritual benefits accruing from giving in the path of God.*
>
> (letter from the Universal House of Justice to all National Spiritual Assemblies receiving assistance from the Bahá'í International Fund, dated April 13, 1975)

Deepening of new believers is particularly important:-

> *Giving to the Fund...is both a responsibility and a source of bounty. This is an aspect of the Cause which, we feel, is an essential part of the basic teaching and deepening of new believers.*
>
> (letter from the Universal House of Justice to all National Spiritual Assemblies, dated August 7, 1985)

CHAPTER FOUR

Useful deepening materials include:-
a) this Chapter
b) Universal House of Justice compilation "Lifeblood of the Cause" {revised edition} (Bahá'í Publishing Trust, UK, 1989)
c) "Lights of Guidance" {revised edition}
d) National Spiritual Assembly 'Deepening on the Funds' distributed to all Local Spiritual Assemblies in July 1985 or subsequently on formation

2. To educate those friends responsible for administering the Funds in the importance of trustworthiness:-

It is important for your Assembly...to explain to persons who are entrusted with the money of the Faith that in view of the National Assembly's obligation to protect Bahá'í Funds, the Assembly will hold them responsible for all monies they receive, and they should therefore render proper accounts to the National Spiritual Assembly, be faithful custodians of God's trust, and be assured that such honesty and faithfulness will be richly rewarded from on High.

(letter written on behalf of the Universal House of Justice to a National Spiritual Assembly, dated May 18, 1980)

3. To educate the friends in the importance of contributing to all four Funds.
On this point note "Lights of Guidance" {revised edition}, no.870 regarding the value of educating the friends in the importance of the National Funds through the example of the Local Funds.

4.4.14 *To whom can the Local Spiritual Assembly turn for assistance?*

Local Spiritual Assemblies in need of assistance in managing their Funds should not hesitate to call on the National Treasurer for advice.

4.5 **FUNCTIONS OF THE TREASURER**

4.5.1 *What are the functions of the Treasurer?*

The Treasurer is responsible to the Local Spiritual Assembly for performing the following tasks:-

1. Receiving donations and issuing receipts
A receipt must be issued for each donation received (See the "Bahá'í Treasurer's Manual", p.8-9). The Universal House of Justice has advised that this is necessary to act as a check on the possibility of defalcations or other losses:-

This relates not only to the danger of defalcations, but also to the possibility of loss either in the mails or at some other stage of the remittance. If a receipt must be issued for every contribution, and if all the friends are aware that they will always receive a receipt, this acts as a valuable check on such possibilities. As the Cause grows, it becomes increasingly necessary to follow clearly defined policies and efficient procedures in such matters.

(letter from the Universal House of Justice to a National Spiritual Assembly, dated November 10, 1981)

2. Paying bills and keeping accounts
For practical advice on how to set up a system of accounting see the "Bahá'í Treasurer's Manual".

CHAPTER FOUR

3. **Reporting regularly to the community on behalf of the Local Spiritual Assembly**
4. **Promoting unity within the community**

The following advice given to national Treasurers applies equally to local Treasurers:-

> *There is the relationship between the National Assembly and the individual believers and local communities. Through whatever correspondence he conducts with contributors to the National Fund and with committees which are drawing on the Fund for their work, the National Treasurer can be a powerful influence in establishing links of loving unity within the community.*
>
> (letter written on behalf of the Universal House of Justice to a National Spiritual Assembly, dated July 13, 1981)

5. **Providing regular, accurate financial reports to the Assembly**

These can be prepared on the 'Treasurer's Report Form' (available from Bahá'í Publications and Distribution Services). [For further information on this point see the "Bahá'í Treasurer's Manual", p.16]

6. **Preparing the Annual Financial Report and the annual budget:-**
7. **Monitoring the use of the Fund:-**

> *The Treasurer should carefully monitor the use of the Fund so that he can warn the Assembly in good time if there is danger of over-spending.*
>
> (letter written on behalf of the Universal House of Justice to a National Spiritual Assembly, dated July 13, 1981)

8. **Making sure earmarked funds are kept distinct:-**

> *In book-keeping, a system must be adopted to ensure that earmarked funds are kept absolutely distinct from those that are at the free disposition of the Assembly, and there should be safeguards to prevent the inadvertent spending of earmarked funds on matters other than those for which they are intended.*
>
> (letter written on behalf of the Universal House of Justice to a National Spiritual Assembly, dated July 13, 1981)

9. **Ensuring that any assets of the Assembly are protected:-**

In addition to keeping accurate records of income and expenditure, the Treasurer should see that the assets of the Assembly are protected and that both assets and liabilities are carefully recorded.

(letter written on behalf of the Universal House of Justice to a National Spiritual Assembly, dated July 13, 1981)

10. **Advising the Assembly to set aside sufficient sums for the repair and maintenance of any property**
11. **Educating the community in the importance of the Funds**

As the officer of the Assembly to whom responsibility for the Funds is delegated, the Treasurer assumes a major role in deepening the friends as outlined in Section 4 of this Chapter. A convenient time to do this could be during the Treasurer's report at some of the Feasts.

4.6 **FUND-RAISING**

4.6.1 *What is the spirit that should characterise fund-raising events?*

Shoghi Effendi has stated that fund-raising activities must be conducted in an appropriately dignified atmosphere in which the believers are prompted by a spirit of sacrifice to give, not by the application of psychological pressure:-

> *...gatherings for collection of funds are permissible if it is done with a true spirit of sacrifice, not when the audience is especially aroused to a frenzy and mob psychology is used to induce them to pay. Shoghi Effendi has repeatedly stated that no pressure should be used upon the friends, and psychological pressure falls under that category. But there is much difference between such gatherings, often used by religious bodies, and a true quiet, prayerful atmosphere when a person is of his own accord is aroused to make some sacrifice. The distinction is very delicate, but it is for the Chairman to use his power to see that one desirable form is not corrupted into the other. All the activities of the Cause should be carried through in a dignified manner.*
>
> (letter written on behalf of Shoghi Effendi to an individual believer, dated May 28, 1932)

The Universal House of Justice has further said that a Local Spiritual Assembly must establish a balance between maintaining the appropriate spiritual atmosphere on the one hand, and not dampening the enthusiasm of the believers, on the other:-

> *...the House of Justice feels that it is important for the friends never to lose sight of the fact that contributing to the Funds of the Faith is a spiritual responsibility and privilege of profound significance in the spiritual life of the individual believer, and care must be taken not to trivialise this aspect of Bahá'í life by applying to it too many 'gimmicks' or treating it with a lack of dignity. At the same time, the Assemblies should not dampen the enthusiasm of those friends who, having only slender financial resources, devise imaginative ways of earning money for the work of the Faith.*
>
> (letter from the Universal House of Justice to a National Spiritual Assembly, dated July 8, 1980)

It follows that there is a distinction to be drawn between those activities that individual Bahá'ís may engage in and those it would be fitting for Local Spiritual Assemblies to be involved with:-

> *Within this framework, there is clearly a difference in the range of activities open to individuals and those which it would be befitting and dignified for a Spiritual Assembly to engage in or sponsor.*
>
> (letter from the Universal House of Justice to a National Spiritual Assembly, dated July 8, 1980)

The Universal House of Justice has, for example, said that it is not permissible for the Bahá'í institutions to become involved in business ventures intended to raise funds for the Faith, although individuals may do so.

4.6.2 *May fund-raising activities be held during Bahá'í feasts or on Holy Days?*

This matter lies within the discretion of the Local Spiritual Assembly to determine; however, the guidance conveyed earlier in this Section must be particularly remembered, given the spiritual significance of such occasions. Regarding the sale of items at Bahá'í Feasts, the Universal House of Justice has expressed the preference that such sales not become habitual and that they not be conducted during the Feast itself:-

CHAPTER FOUR

As to the sale of items during the Nineteen Day Feast, we leave this to your discretion, bearing in mind that the principal purpose of holding the Feast should not be diverted and that pressure should not be placed upon the friends to participate in the purchase of articles offered for sale. Neither should it become an habitual thing. It would be better if the sale was not conducted during the Feast itself, but held at a separate time before or after the Feast proper.

(letter from the Universal House of Justice to a National Spiritual Assembly, dated April 1, 1968)

4.6.3 **Is it permissible for Spiritual Assemblies or individual Bahá'ís to sell goods or services to the general public for the purpose of raising money for the Bahá'í Funds?**

Individuals or Assemblies may sell goods or services to the general public and do with the proceeds as they please. The sale of such goods or services should not, however, be undertaken in the name of the Faith, nor be advertised as being for the benefit of the Bahá'í Fund:-

...any believer may sell personal services or property to anyone and do with the proceeds as he wishes, including giving any or all of them to Bahá'í purposes. Thus if a Bahá'í concert artist gives a concert to which admission is charged, he is free, if he so wishes, to give the money so earned to the Fund or to any charity of his choice. In giving the concert, however, he should not represent to non-Bahá'ís that the concert is for the benefit of the Bahá'í Fund or is given on behalf of Bahá'ís for a charity, which brings us to the second principle: that it is improper for Bahá'ís to solicit funds from non-Bahá'ís in the name of the Faith for any purpose.

(letter from the Universal House of Justice to a Local Spiritual Assembly, dated March 19, 1973)

It is not proper for a Bahá'í institution to sponsor a 'garage sale' of personal items contributed by believers for the benefit of a Bahá'í Fund. This is not to say that an Assembly may not sell items of property to non-Bahá'ís for fair market value, but rather that non-Bahá'ís should not be led to purchase items at a fund-raising sale on the representation that the proceeds are to be used for Bahá'í purposes.

(letter written on behalf of the Universal House of Justice to a National Spiritual Assembly, dated January 15, 1984)

Within these guidelines the manner of the sale is left to the discretion of the individual or Assembly concerned:-

As to the manner of the disposal of Bahá'í property for such purposes, and the channel through which the sale may be effected, I feel that no rigid rule should be imposed. Individual Bahá'ís are free to seek the help of private individuals or of Spiritual Assemblies to act as intermediary for such transactions. We should avoid confusion on one hand and maintain efficiency on the other, and lay no unnecessary restrictions that would fetter individual initiative and enterprise.

(letter from Shoghi Effendi to a National Spiritual Assembly, dated

CHAPTER FOUR

January 4, 1929)

4.6.4 ***Is it proper for Spiritual Assemblies or individual Bahá'ís to sell goods belonging to non-Bahá'ís for the purpose of raising money for the Bahá'í Funds?***

No. Shoghi Effendi has said:-

> *I feel that only such goods as are owned by believers, whether made by Bahá'ís or non-Bahá'ís, may be sold in the interests of the Temple or any other Bahá'í institutions, thus maintaining the general principle that non-believers are not, whether directly or indirectly, expected to contribute to the support of institutions that are of a strictly Bahá'í character.*

(letter from Shoghi Effendi to a National Spiritual Assembly, dated January 4, 1929)

4.6.5 ***May a Local Spiritual Assembly organise a fund-raising dinner (for example) to which Bahá'ís and their non-Bahá'í friends and relatives are invited?***

The National Spiritual Assembly feels that such fund-raising events are permissible provided the non-Bahá'í guests are either paid for by the Bahá'í relative or friend or permitted free entry, and provided no other fund-raising activities are conducted during the course of the event.

4.6.6 ***Are raffles, lotteries, or other games of chance appropriate methods of raising funds?***

No. The Universal House of Justice has said that these are not appropriate methods for raising funds at this time:-

> *In reviewing your Minutes...we note Item 25-B in which the Treasurer suggests a lottery as a means of disposing of a Persian carpet which has been given to you by one of the believers. We do not feel this is an appropriate way in which to raise funds...*

> *As to participation in Bingo games by a Local Spiritual Assembly with the intention of contributing to the Fund, we do not feel it is appropriate for funds for the Faith to be raised through games of chance or raffles.*

(Extracts from letters from the Universal House of Justice enclosed with a letter from the House of Justice to a National Spiritual Assembly, dated June 26, 1982)

4.6.7 ***Are auctions permissible?***

Regarding 'Dutch' or 'American' auctions, the Universal House of Justice has stated quite clearly that these are not permissible:-

> *...the House of Justice feels that the types of auctions you describe...approach too closely the nature of a raffle or a game of chance to be fitting methods of raising funds for the Faith.*

(letter from the Universal House of Justice to a National Spiritual Assembly, dated July 8, 1980)

In considering the question of 'ordinary' auctions, it is clear that both Assemblies and individuals may give goods to professional auctioneers to sell and then use the proceeds for the Fund. The manner of selling goods is left to the discretion of the Assembly or individual concerned. The Universal House of Justice has said:-

CHAPTER FOUR

There is clearly no objection to an Assembly's giving contributions in kind to a professional auctioneer to sell and then to use the proceeds for the Fund.

(letter from the Universal House of Justice to a National Spiritual Assembly, dated July 8, 1980)

The Universal House of Justice has also said that it is permissible for ordinary auctions to be held amongst Bahá'ís:-

There is no objection to the friends holding an auction among Bahá'ís for the purpose of contributing the proceeds to the Fund...

(letter written on behalf of the Universal House of Justice to a National Spiritual Assembly, dated July 8, 1984)

The holding of auctions amongst Bahá'ís is, however, dependent on the Assembly's judgement as to whether an appropriate spiritual atmosphere can be maintained. Again, although it is important that the enthusiasm of the friends not be dampened, the Universal House of Justice has said, in fact, that it prefers not to encourage such auctions:-

Whether it would be improper to hold such an "ordinary auction" among Bahá'ís would depend upon the Assembly's judgement as to whether a properly dignified atmosphere could be observed and also whether it could be construed as bringing pressure to bear upon the friends to contribute, which would, of course, be undesirable. In general the House of Justice prefers not to encourage such auctions for the Fund.

(Extracts from letters of the Universal House of Justice enclosed with a letter from the House of Justice to a National Spiritual Assembly, dated June 26, 1982)

The National Spiritual Assembly has decided that, in view of the vital importance of preserving the dignity of this part of the spiritual life of the believers, it does not wish auctions to be held at Bahá'í functions to raise funds for the Faith. The Universal House of Justice has also cautioned that auctions held without a licensed auctioneer are illegal in some countries and the National Spiritual Assembly advises that they may be illegal in New South Wales.

4.6.8 **Is it permissible for individuals or Assemblies to establish business ventures to raise funds for the Faith?**

It is permissible for individuals to establish such business ventures; however, it is not permissible for Bahá'í institutions to become involved in, or to promote, such enterprises. The Universal House of Justice advises that those friends who do participate in such a project should approach it on the basis of its viability as a business venture:-

The Universal House of Justice has received your letter of 15 February concerning the proposal by a number of Bahá'ís to establish a private company whose shares would be owned by Bahá'ís and which would be managed for the financial profit of the friends and of the Faith. We are instructed to transmit its advice. Your objective to generate funds for the Faith is, of course, praiseworthy. In the past, as you may assume, similar proposals have been made to the House of Justice, and the following guidelines may be helpful:

"Concerning the formation of a company which you and other friends

have suggested, the Universal House of Justice...has decided that the time has not yet come to have the Bahá'í institutions involved in a business transaction in the way which was suggested."

If the friends, however, are willing, spontaneously, to establish a profitable business in order to benefit themselves as well as the other friends it is meritorious and there is no objection.:

"Should such a business venture as you propose be undertaken ... and there is nothing wrong with it in principle - it would be well to advise the Bahá'ís who participate to approach it on the basis of its viability as a business project and they should not underestimate the possibilities of financial loss.

"The House of Justice feels that the institutions of the Faith should neither themselves become involved in nor promote such a private business. The use of national endowments as collateral for such a business is not permissible."

(letter written on behalf of the Universal House of Justice to a National Spiritual Assembly, dated April 5, 1982)

4.6.9 **May a Local Spiritual Assembly make appeals to its own community for funds?**

Yes. As noted in the section 'Introduction - Are contributions voluntary?', an Assembly is permitted to make general appeals to its community. If the Local Spiritual Assembly wishes to initiate a specific project for which it requires funds it may, having decided on a realistic budget for the project, draw the attention of the friends within its community to the progress they are making in meeting the budget and encourage them to achieve the agreed target.

4.6.10 **May a Local Spiritual Assembly appeal to the Bahá'ís outside its area of jurisdiction for funds?**

No. Appeals can only be made to Bahá'ís outside an Assembly's area of jurisdiction with the prior approval of the National Spiritual Assembly. In deciding whether to grant such approval the National Assembly will particularly consider the scale of the proposed activity for which the funds are required and its likely impact on behalf of the Faith beyond the local level.

4.6.11 **How are funds to be raised for inter-Assembly projects?**

Some projects go beyond the boundaries of one community. When an inter-Assembly project is agreed to by two or more communities, a budget is decided on and the method of fund-raising for the project is also agreed to by all participating communities. Thereafter, in the appropriate Bahá'í manner and within the limits of the budget and the fund-raising plan, the friends in the cooperating communities may be invited to contribute to the Fund specifically set up for the purpose. Again, if the Assemblies involved wish to appeal for funds outside the areas of their jurisdiction they must seek the approval of the National Spiritual Assembly, as explained in the previous question. [For further information on the management of inter-Assembly projects, see Chapter 13 in this Handbook on 'Inter-community Activities'.]

4.6.12 **May a Local Spiritual Assembly solicit funds from Bahá'ís in other countries?**

No:-

As regards collection of funds in other countries, the House of Justice does not wish Bahá'í institutions of any country to appeal for funds to the Bahá'ís of another country, unless the National Spiritual Assembly of that country permits it.

(letter written on behalf of the Universal House of Justice to an individual believer, dated June 6, 1985)

If individuals from other countries, of their own free will, wish to make a donation, that is another matter, and they are free to do so

4.6.13 **Are there any circumstances in which Bahá'ís may solicit funds from non-Bahá'ís for Bahá'í projects?**

The only situation in which Bahá'ís may solicit funds from non-Bahá'ís is where they are to be used for an humanitarian project which will also be of benefit to non-Bahá'ís:-

As regards the question of the Bahá'í School in India: As this institution is run by Bahá'ís but for the benefit of both Bahá'ís and any other group sending its children there, he sees no reason why a school concert should not receive money from the public attending, and use it for the school itself. It is not the same as a bazaar where the things sold are solely for the Bahá'í Fund.

(letter from Shoghi Effendi to a National Spiritual Assembly, dated June 30, 1952)

A Bahá'í school which has both Bahá'í and non-Bahá'í pupils is free to raise funds for its own development by such activities as concerts, etc., or by appeals to parents; in this instance, a humanitarian institution is clearly identified, and the funds are being collected in its name rather than in the name of the Faith.

(letter written on behalf of the Universal House of Justice to a National Spiritual Assembly, dated August 20, 1987)

4.6.14 **May a Local Spiritual Assembly accept funds from the Government?**

As a general principle, funds may be accepted from the government for the promotion of specifically humanitarian purposes. Government assistance is also acceptable in relation to institutions of community service, such as schools; however, as acceptance of government funding often necessitates also accepting a degree of governmental control, the matter must be carefully considered:-

Governments and their agencies occupy a special position because, of course, they are often very willing to assist those who are engaged in humanitarian service. Thus, where a Spiritual Assembly is undertaking a specifically humanitarian activity for which the government normally would supply financial assistance, the Assembly may accept such assistance. The activity that you instance, a meeting being held on behalf of Human Rights Day to advance one of the aims of the United Nations, is a case in point; there would be no objection to your accepting from 'INAC' its offer to pay for the invitation cards on that occasion. In relation to schools and other institutions of community service, government assistance is also acceptable, but here the Assembly needs to be aware that the acceptance of government funding often brings with it an obligation to accept a degree of governmental control, and these points must be carefully considered.

CHAPTER FOUR

(letter written on behalf of the Universal House of Justice to a
National Spiritual Assembly, dated March 6, 1983)

The National Spiritual Assembly's policy is that, if a local government body, such as a municipal or shire council, is offering funding for a project such as a peace exposition, the Local Spiritual Assembly in that civil area is permitted to directly apply to that body for funding. If the Federal or State Government, or any statutory body or department is offering such funding, the approval of the National Spiritual Assembly must be obtained before any application is made. It should also be noted that it is permissible to make application for funding from other charitable institutions, within the same guidelines applying to government funding set out above:-

> *...Bahá'í institutions are free to approach governments or institutions which hold themselves out as wishing to fund charitable activities...*

(letter written on behalf of the Universal House of Justice to a
National Spiritual Assembly, dated August 20, 1987).

The institution offering the funding would need to be investigated, however, to ensure the it was not engaging in activities of a partisan political nature, or was otherwise connected with matters with which the Faith should not be involved. Any cases in doubt should be referred to the National Spiritual Assembly.

4.6.15 **May a Local Spiritual Assembly accept funds from a non-Bahá'í organisation to further the administrative work of the Faith?**

No:-

> *...under no circumstances should the believers accept any financial help from non-Bahá'ís for use in connection with specific administrative activities of the Faith such as the Temple Construction Fund, and other local or national Bahá'í administrative Funds.*

(letter written on behalf of Shoghi Effendi to an individual believer,
dated July 12, 1938)

4.6.16 **May a Local Spiritual Assembly charge for services, eg. food, accommodation, to cover the costs of organising a major function such as a conference or school?**

The following guidance from the Universal House of Justice addressed to a National Spiritual Assembly, applies equally to Local Spiritual Assemblies:-

> *...our policy concerning registration fees for conferences, conventions and summer schools is that it is perfectly acceptable to charge reasonable fees for special services such as local transport, food, accommodation, and conference materials. It is also acceptable to charge fees for such occasions as summer schools, weekend and day schools, and even deepening and special study courses, where the friends go to receive special instruction or to undertake study. However, at conferences called by the National Spiritual Assembly where the spirit and enthusiasm of the friends themselves is the main factor in promoting the objective of the conference, no charge should be made for attendance. It would also be improper to charge a registration fee for the Convention, but general appeals may be made at the Convention for contributions to help defray Convention expenses.*

(e-mail from the Universal House of Justice to a National Spiritual

CHAPTER FOUR

Assembly, dated April 12, 1988)

A Local Spiritual Assembly may offer to perform a specific service at a major function - for example, provide meals - in order to raise funds for its own projects, only with the express approval of the organising body. For example, a Local Spiritual Assembly wishing to provide meals for sale at the National Bahá'í Conference would need the prior permission of the National Spiritual Assembly.

4.6.17 **In what circumstances may a Bahá'í community raise funds on behalf of a non-Bahá'í organisation?**

A Bahá'í community may assist in raising funds for a deserving charity providing: (a) that assisting the charity does not have partisan political implications support purposes contrary to the interests of the Faith; (b) that involvement in such activities does not divert the community's energies from the teaching work:-

> *There would be no objection to the Bahá'í community's joining with others to give a concert or undertake some similar activity to raise funds for a deserving charity. Such activities or even the making of donations to humanitarian work should be, and should be seen to be, acts of sincere assistance and cooperation. In choosing to engage in such fund-raising, a Bahá'í community would need to ensure that assisting the charity would not have partisan political implications or support purposes contrary to the interests of the Faith. It would need to watch carefully that its involvement in such activities does not divert its energies from the vital work of teaching the Faith and consolidating its institutions.*

> (letter written on behalf of the Universal House of Justice to a National Spiritual Assembly, dated August 20, 1987)

4.6.18 **May an individual raise funds for non-Bahá'í institutions?**

Individuals may be involved in fund-raising activities for deserving causes, provided they do so as individuals and not in the name of the Faith. For example, there is no objection to collecting for Red Cross or another charity so long as the collectors do not openly display their Bahá'í identity, eg. through signs or T-shirt slogans.

4.7 **ENDOWMENTS**

4.7.1 **What is an endowment in the Bahá'í sense?**

The Universal House of Justice has stated that the word 'endowment' may be used with two distinct meanings:-

> *In one sense it is taken to refer to the totality of the possessions of a National Spiritual Assembly, including its property, office furniture and fittings, vehicles, etc. In a more restrictive sense, the term is taken to refer to an item which is held as an investment for the future advantage and benefit to a National or Local Spiritual Assembly.*

> (letter written on behalf of the Universal House of Justice to a National Spiritual Assembly, dated April 12, 1988)

4.7.2 **What form should an endowment take?**

In the more restrictive sense outlined above, an endowment should take the form of real estate:-

> *An endowment should be in the form of real estate, where possible.*

CHAPTER FOUR

Thus it would not include other holdings of an Assembly, such as cash or shares.

(letter written on behalf of the Universal House of Justice to a National Spiritual Assembly, dated April 12, 1988)

In further explication of this statement the House of Justice notes that an Assembly may acquire a wide range of assets over time which it holds for the purpose of investment. Such investments would be considered endowments only in the broader sense of the term:-

However, in addition to land held as an endowment, a National or Local Spiritual Assembly may well acquire, over a period of time, a wide range of assets in the form of shares, cash, interest in businesses and the like, which are held by the Assembly for the purposes of investment. Such assets would be considered part of the Assembly's endowment, only in the broader use of the term...

(letter written on behalf of the Universal House of Justice to a National Spiritual Assembly, dated September 1, 1988)

4.7.3 **What other principles apply to the acquisition of endowments?**

The following principles apply:-
1. Endowments are usually received as gifts from believers; however, an Assembly may purchase a piece of land.
2. A contribution earmarked for investment need not be used for the purchase of real estate:-

    ...when a believer contributes funds for investment, there is no obligation for the Assembly to use these funds for the purchase of real estate, if it feels some other use would be more appropriate. The only exception would be if the contribution was specified to establish or increase the Assembly's endowment, in the sense of real estate; in such a case the Assembly would have no option but to accede to the stipulation if it accepts the contribution.

    (letter written on behalf of the Universal House of Justice to a National Spiritual Assembly, dated September 1, 1988)

3. If a Local Spiritual Assembly is not able to own property in its own name, the endowment can be held by one of the believers on behalf of the community, on condition that it be transferred legally to the Assembly when possible.
4. Endowment land cannot be used for any other specific Bahá'í purpose such as a Hazíratu'l-Quds or a Teaching Institute.
5. If a piece of land given as an endowment is large enough it may be sub-divided with one part being kept as the endowment and the other being used for some other Bahá'í purpose such as a summer school.
6. Endowment land may be farmed or otherwise developed to produce income, and the proceeds may be used for the general work of the Faith.
7. Endowment land should be purchased within the Local Spiritual Assembly's area of jurisdiction:-

    We have been asked to say that while it may be necessary in exceptional circumstances for a Local Spiritual Assembly to acquire a local endowment outside its area of jurisdiction, particularly if this is dictated by restrictive regulations, it is not generally a desirable course of action to follow.

CHAPTER FOUR

(letter written on behalf of the Universal House of Justice to a National Spiritual Assembly, dated April 3, 1975) [For further information on the above points see "Lights of Guidance" {revised edition}, nos. 722-28.]

4.8   HUQÚQU'LLÁH

4.8.1   *What is Huqúqu'lláh?*

Huqúqu'lláh (Right of God) is a spiritual obligation laid upon the believers as a privilege and bounty. As such it is a private matter and not one to be enforced by the Institutions of the Faith. The Universal House of Justice has sole discretion in determining how Huqúqu'lláh will be spent. Huqúqu'lláh is payable on a believer's assessable possessions as soon as they reach, or exceed, 19 mithqáls of gold (approximately 69.2 grammes). The amount payable is 19% of the value of the possessions after necessary expenses, such as general living expenses, have been deducted.

In Australia payments may be sent to the
Assistant to the Trustee of Huqúqu'lláh for Australasia,
Mr. Aflatoon Payman
11 Struan Street,
TOORAK VIC 3142.

Payment of Huqúqu'lláh is an obligation binding on all believers. Each Bahá'í is encouraged to study the writings on Huqúqu'lláh in order that they are fully aware of the implications and requirements of this spiritual responsibility and the appropriate method of calculating payment. Local Spiritual Assemblies, likewise, have an obligation to ensure that their communities are deepened on the subject. [Further information about Huqúqu'lláh is to be found in the Universal House of Justice compilation, "Huqúqu'lláh The Right of God {revised edition} (Bahá'í Publishing Trust, UK, 1989); and "Huqúqu'lláh A Study Guide (Bahá'í Publishing Trust, UK, 1989). Both are available from Bahá'í Publications Australia.]

4.9   **NOTES FOR REGISTERED GROUPS**

Registered Groups should establish a Bahá'í Fund. They have the same obligations as Local Spiritual Assemblies in this respect and should also manage the Fund in the same manner as outlined in this Chapter for Local Spiritual Assemblies.

CHAPTER FIVE

Chapter 5

5. Teaching

5.1 INTRODUCTION

5.1.1 *What is the challenge facing the Australian Bahá'í community now?*

Australia stands at the threshold of 'entry by troops'. In a message to the Australian Bahá'í community, dated May 24, 1988 the Universal House of Justice said:-

> *The time is now opportune for the Australian Bahá'í community to initiate a sustained teaching campaign which will bring about entry by troops in a country described by the Guardian as being "endowed with unimaginable potentialities".*

More recently, in a message dated January 16, 1990, the Universal House of Justice has called upon Australia to 'become a model' for other communities to follow by involving the rank and file of believers in the teaching work; reaching out to all strata of society; and developing specific plans to attract each ethnic and racial element of the population:-

> *The Australian Bahá'í community has the potential to become a model for others in the vitality of its teaching work, the involvement of the rank and file of the believers, the attention to reaching all strata of Australian society, and the commitment to developing and presenting teaching plans designed specifically to attract each ethnic and racial element of the population.*

5.1.2 *What challenge and responsibility does the Australian Bahá'í community have to the Australasian region?*

The Australian Bahá'í community has a responsibility to work closely with the other Bahá'í communities in the Australasian region to teach and consolidate the Faith in this part of the globe:-

> *A responsibility, at once weighty and inescapable, must rest on the communities which occupy so privileged a position in so vast and turbulent an area of the globe. However great the distance that separates them; however much they differ in race, language, custom, and religion; however active the political forces which tend to keep them apart and foster racial and political antagonisms, the close and continued association of these communities in their common, their peculiar and paramount task of raising up and of consolidating the embryonic World Order of Bahá'u'lláh in those regions of the globe, is a matter of vital and urgent importance, which should receive on the part of the elected representatives of their communities, a most earnest and prayerful consideration...*

> *...May this community [Australia] which, with its sister community in the North [North East Asia], has had the inestimable privilege of being called into being in the lifetime of, and through the operation of the dynamic forces released by the Centre of Bahá'u'lláh's Covenant, continue, with undimmed vision, with redoubled vigour, and unwavering fidelity and constancy, to discharge its manifold and ever*

increasing duties and responsibilities, and lend, as the days go by, an impetus such as it has not lent before, in the course of almost two score years of its existence, to the propagation of the Faith it has so whole-heartedly espoused and is now so valiantly serving, and play a memorable and distinctive part in hastening the establishment, and in ensuring the gradual efflorescence and ultimate fruition, of its divinely appointed embryonic World Order.

(Shoghi Effendi in 1957, in "Letters from the Guardian to Australia and New Zealand": 1923 - 1957, p.138-40)

5.1.3 How should Local Spiritual Assemblies meet the challenge of 'entry by troops'?

At Local Spiritual Assembly meetings teaching must be given first priority. It must be the first item on the agenda after approval of the previous minutes. It must also be the main topic of consultation at Feasts:-

If the meetings or Spiritual Assembly has any other occupation, the time is spent in futility. All the deliberations, all consultation, all the talks and addresses must revolve around one focal centre and that is: TEACH THE CAUSE! TEACH! TEACH! CONVEY THE MESSAGE! AWAKEN THE SOULS! NOTHING ELSE WILL BE USEFUL, TODAY...The interests of such a Glorious Cause will not advance without undivided attention. While we are carrying this load we cannot carry any other load!

('Abdu'l-Bahá, in "Bahá'í Meetings and the Nineteen Day Feast" (1976), p.9; "Lights of Guidance" {revised edition}, no.157)

Local Spiritual Assemblies must avoid becoming preoccupied with improving the administration at the expense of teaching. Rather, it must be remembered that the whole purpose of the administration is to promote the teaching work:-

As the administrative work of the Cause steadily expands, as its various branches grow in importance and number, it is absolutely necessary that we bear in mind this fundamental fact that all these administrative activities, however harmoniously and efficiently conducted, are but means to an end, and should be regarded as direct instruments for the propagation of the Bahá'í Faith. Let us take heed lest in our great concern for the perfection of the administrative machinery of the Cause, we lose sight of the Divine Purpose for which it has been created...Let this cardinal principle be ever borne in mind...

(Shoghi Effendi "Bahá'í Administration", p.103)

5.1.4 What are the different aspects of teaching?

Teaching activities fall into three categories:
1. proclamation
2. expansion
3. consolidation

Proclamation work is making the general aims of the Faith known through publicity campaigns and indirect teaching, eg. involvement in local community activities. Expansion work consists of the actual teaching programmes designed to bring people into the Faith. Consolidation is deepening the friends in the Faith to encourage them to become active in teaching and administration and to build a strong sense of Bahá'í community life. The Universal House

CHAPTER FIVE

of Justice has said:-

> ...*proclamation, expansion, and consolidation are really three different aspects of teaching which to some degree merge into one another...*
>
> (letter written on behalf of the Universal House of Justice to a National Spiritual Assembly, dated February 27, 1975)

The following sections of this Chapter explain these three aspects, in relation to teaching in Australia, in greater detail.

5.1.5 *What is the administrative procedure for becoming a Bahá'í?*

A person who wishes to become a Bahá'í normally signs a 'Declaration Card'. These are available from the National Office. If a declaration card is not available at the time, the declaration of faith may be made in some other form - for example, a letter. The person needs to make a statement to the following effect: 'I accept Bahá'u'lláh as the Manifestation of God for this Day, and wish to become a member of the Bahá'í Faith.' [For further information on enrolment procedures see Chapter 8 'Membership in the Bahá'í Community'.]

5.2 PROCLAMATION

5.2.1 *What is the purpose of proclamation?*

The Universal House of Justice has said that the purpose of proclamation *'is to make known to all mankind the fact and general aim of the new Revelation'* ("The Five Year Plan", p.5) It is essentially a publicity campaign intended to let people know of the existence and purpose of the Faith.

5.2.2 *How does proclamation relate to expansion and consolidation?*

It is essential that proclamation be coordinated with expansion and consolidation. For example, public announcements must be followed up by teaching work, otherwise people will hear about the Faith but have nowhere to turn for more information:-

> *Every effort of proclamation must be sustained by teaching, particularly locally, where public announcements should be related to such efforts. This coordination is essential, for nothing will be more disheartening than for thousands to hear of the Faith and have nowhere to turn for further information.*
>
> (Universal House of Justice, "Wellspring of Guidance", p.112-113)

Consolidation and proclamation also need to be coordinated. It needs to be considered, for example, whether it would be better to begin a teaching project in an unopened area with a publicity campaign, or whether to establish a local community first and then advertise the Faith:-

> *In all proclamation activities, follow-up is of supreme importance. ... In some places it is desirable to open a teaching campaign with publicity - in others it is wiser to establish first a solid local community before publicising the Faith or encouraging contacts with prominent people. Here, again, wisdom is needed.*
>
> (Universal House of Justice, "Wellspring of Guidance", p.118)

Each particular situation must be considered on its merits.

5.2.3 *What sort of activities does proclamation include?*

Shoghi Effendi and the Universal House of Justice have identified the following as proclamation activities:
- mass media campaigns
- public meetings
- contacts with local dignitaries
- dissemination of Bahá'í literature
- participation in social and humanitarian activities

>(See "Wellspring of Guidance", p.66-7, 117-18 and the letter of the Universal House of Justice to a National Spiritual Assembly, dated December 24, 1975.)

5.2.4 *What sort of information about the Faith should be made available in proclamation activities?*

Shoghi Effendi said the following points should be emphasised:
- the universality of the Faith
- its aims and purposes
- episodes in its dramatic history
- testimonials to its transforming power
- the character and distinguishing features of its World Order

>(Shoghi Effendi, quoted by the Universal House of Justice in "Wellspring of Guidance", p.66-7)

5.2.5 *What standard applies to publicity campaigns?*

The standard of dignity and reverence set by Shoghi Effendi must be maintained. Generally-speaking, photographs of 'Abdu'l-Bahá should not be used:-

> *Publicity itself should be well conceived, dignified, and reverent. A flamboyant approach which may succeed in drawing much initial attention to the Cause may ultimately prove to have produced a revulsion which would require great effort to overcome. The standard of dignity and reverence set by the beloved Guardian should always be upheld, particularly in musical and dramatic items; and photographs of the Master should not be used indiscriminately.*

>(Universal House of Justice, "Wellspring of Guidance", p.118)

Ways in which this standard may be maintained differ according to the conditions of each country. Any Local Spiritual Assembly in doubt as to the appropriateness of a particular activity should consult with their State Information Office before going ahead.

5.2.6 *How should Local Spiritual Assemblies organise their proclamation work?*

Local Spiritual Assemblies are encouraged to appoint local information officers. Their task is to represent the Faith to the local media and to undertake public relations work with local dignitaries. They should seize any opportunities that arise to obtain publicity for the Faith. To this end they should have on hand general information about the Faith and be prepared to make it available on request to non-Bahá'í organisations and the general public. Assistance is available from the State Information Offices and from the 'Making News' booklet distributed to all Local Spiritual Assemblies. Local information officers should also keep in touch with their Regional Teaching Committee to pass on and receive up-to-date information; and with other local information officers to coordinate publicity on a regional level where necessary.

CHAPTER FIVE

5.2.7 *What guidelines apply to contacting the media?*

The following guidelines apply:
1. Local Spiritual Assemblies, local committees and individual Bahá'ís should not contact national or state media (eg. television or radio networks, national or international wire services, newspapers or magazines, with international, national, or state-wide distribution) without first contacting their State Information Office.
2. If Bahá'ís find that programmes or articles in international, or national media contain errors about the Faith they must inform the National Spiritual Assembly. They must not contact editors or programme directors to correct the errors. Should such programmes or articles appear in local media, the friends should bring the matter to the attention of their Local Spiritual Assembly or group. Isolated believers can notify their Auxiliary Board members, their assistants, or the local Assembly whose extension teaching goals include the area where the programme or article appeared.
3. Local Spiritual Assemblies and individuals are encouraged to write letters to the editor of their local newspapers which correlate the Teachings of the Faith to the problems of the world. Such letters should be reviewed by the Local Spiritual Assembly before submission to the newspaper. Local Spiritual Assemblies and individual Bahá'ís should not write letters to state-wide or national publications before contacting their State Information Office.
4. Bahá'ís are free to write letters to the editors of publications to express their personal views if they do not identify themselves as Bahá'ís, imply that they represent the Faith or a Bahá'í community, or discuss the Bahá'í Faith. If individuals are uncertain about the relationship of their letters to the interests of the Faith, they should consult with their Local Spiritual Assembly:-

> *We feel that the crux of the problem rests on whether the expression of views on a subject affects the interests of the Cause. This applies even though believers do not identify themselves as Bahá'ís. Of course if they do so identify themselves any expression of opinion would obviously affect the interests of the Cause. Whenever the interests of the Cause may be involved, or the friends are uncertain about the matter, they should seek consultation with the administrative institution of the area in which they live and abide by its decision.*

> (letter from the Universal House of Justice to a National Spiritual Assembly, dated May 14, 1970)

It is necessary, when writing such letters, to avoid becoming involved in partisan political issues.

5.2.8 *What guidelines apply to dissemination of Bahá'í literature?*

The Universal House of Justice has provided certain guidance with regard to distributing Bahá'í literature in letter-boxes or door-to-door and has said that it is for each National Spiritual Assembly to decide what would be appropriate in its country:-

> *The principles the House of Justice wishes National Assemblies to observe in this connection are:*

> 1. *The dignity of the Faith should be carefully safeguarded in all Bahá'í activities.*
> 2. *It is important that no teaching activity should be an encroachment on people's privacy nor should it force the Teachings upon unwilling listeners.*

>> *In general the House of Justice feels that there would be no objection in principle to mailing or distributing to mail boxes such items as*

CHAPTER FIVE

invitations to meetings or introductory circular letters, or brief informative leaflets. Any leaflet used in such a way should be designed primarily to arouse the interest of the reader so that he will seek more information. It should not be intended to convince or convert the reader at that stage. A number of National Spiritual Assemblies have produced introductory circulars of this nature, which have a reply-paid card attached. It is not, of course, essential that the card be part of the leaflet provided that the leaflet itself is restrained and dignified. However, each National Spiritual Assembly must decide what is proper to be done in its own country. The quotation which you ask for is as follows: 'He feels that to distribute Bahá'í pamphlets from door-to-door...is undignified and might create a bad impression of the Faith. No doubt, it is the eagerness and devotion of the friends that led them to make this proposal, but he does not think that the best interests of the Cause are served by such a method...'

(letter written on behalf of the Universal House of Justice to a National Spiritual Assembly, dated December 6, 1981)

The National Spiritual Assembly of Australia discourages the distribution of Bahá'í materials by door knocking in all circumstances, as it would be an encroachment on people's privacy and would not be in keeping with the dignity of the Faith. As per the guidance cited above, however, invitations to Bahá'í functions may be placed in letter-boxes; also introductory circular letters or brief informative leaflets, provided they are dignified. The letter may have a reply-paid card attached. As stated above, the letter or leaflet should be designed primarily to arouse interest and should not be intended to convince or convert the reader at that stage. It is for the Local Spiritual Assembly to decide, from its knowledge of its local area, whether such a letter-boxing campaign could be conducted with dignity. The National Spiritual Assembly also discourages the indiscriminate dissemination of Bahá'í literature in public places. There is a difference between taking advantage of 'one-off' opportunities to present contacts with literature and mounting a systematic campaign to leave literature lying around. Examples of acceptable methods would be to obtain permission to place pamphlets in a public place, eg. in a library; or to offer a gift subscription, eg. "Herald of the South", to a local library.

5.2.9 **Is there any particular Bahá'í literature that Bahá'ís should give to people?**

The Universal House of Justice has strongly encouraged the dissemination of "The Promise of World Peace" as a means of introducing the Faith to people:-

..."The Promise of World Peace" is designed to open the way. Its delivery to national governmental leaders having been virtually completed, its contents must now be conveyed, by all possible means, to peoples everywhere from all walks of life. This is a necessary part of the teaching work in our time and must be pursued with unabated vigour.

(Universal House of Justice, Message to the Bahá'ís of the World, Ridván, 1988)

5.2.10 **What guidelines apply to holding public meetings?**

The following points should be noted with regard to public meetings:-
1. they should be accompanied by advance publicity and follow-up activities - for example, firesides.
2. wisdom should be exercised in the use of Iranian Bahá'í speakers, to ensure that their speaking at a public meeting will not jeopardise their interests or those of their families

CHAPTER FIVE

who may still be in Iran. Often the person invited to speak will be in the best position to judge this.

(letter written on behalf of the Universal House of Justice to selected National Spiritual Assemblies, dated November 22, 1987).

5.2.11 ***What guidelines apply to making contact with local dignitaries?***

The Local Spiritual Assembly is responsible for contacting prominent people at the local level. This is a function that could be given to the Local Information Officer. Advice on the best way to proceed may be obtained from the State Information Office. Individuals should not contact local dignitaries without consulting with the Local Spiritual Assembly.

5.2.12 ***What guidelines apply to social and humanitarian activities?***

Involvement in social and humanitarian activities constitutes a form of indirect teaching which enables our community to make contact with like-minded people, who can then gradually be introduced to the more fundamental principles of the Faith:-

> *As to your question as to what constitutes indirect teaching; it essentially consists in presenting some of the humanitarian or social Teachings of the Cause which are shared by those whom we are teaching, as a means of attracting them to those aspects of the Faith which are more challenging in character, and are specifically and solely Bahá'í. The teaching of Esperanto, for instance, has been a very useful way of presenting the Cause indirectly to many people.*

(letter written on behalf of Shoghi Effendi to an individual believer, dated May 28, 1937)

Further information about social and humanitarian activities is available in the booklet 'An Approach to Social and Economic Development', prepared by the National Bahá'í Social and Economic Development Committee of Australia and distributed to all Local Spiritual Assemblies.

5.2.13 ***What statistics should be given out in proclamation campaigns?***

In a letter written on its behalf, dated October 29, 1984, to all National Spiritual Assemblies, the Universal House of Justice said that, '*in general, it is best to provide statistics such as the number of independent countries and localities opened to the Faith, the number of national and local Spiritual Assemblies and the number of languages into which Bahá'í literature has been translated.*' If a Bahá'í is asked specifically how many Bahá'ís there are in the world, however, he or she may provide a figure. At present there are approximately six million Bahá'ís in the world. If asked specifically how many Bahá'ís there are in Australia, the figure of ten thousand may be used. This is based on a count of all adults, youth and children, including those of unknown address.

5.3 **EXPANSION**

5.3.1 ***What is the purpose of expansion work?***

The purpose of expansion work is to bring people into the Faith from every strata of society:-
The paramount goal of the teaching work at the present time is to carry the message of Bahá'u'lláh to every stratum of human society and every walk of life...

> *...No effort must be spared to ensure that the healing Word of God reaches the rich and the poor, the learned and the illiterate, the old and the young, the devout and the atheist, the dweller in the remote hills and islands, the inhabitant of the teeming cities, the suburban businessman, the labourer in the slums, the nomadic tribesman, the farmer, the university student; all must be brought consciously within*

CHAPTER FIVE

the teaching plans of the Bahá'í Community.

(letter written on behalf of the Universal House of Justice to all National Spiritual Assemblies, dated October 31, 1967)

5.3.2 **How does expansion relate to consolidation?**

Expansion and consolidation must take place at the same time. It is necessary to deepen believers to create enthusiasm for the teaching work and it is necessary to enrol new believers to provide additional manpower for the community's consolidation work:-

> *Expansion and consolidation are twin processes that must go hand in hand. The friends must not stop expansion in the name of consolidation. Deepening the newly enrolled believers generates tremendous stimulus which results in further expansion. The enrolment of new believers, on the other hand, creates a new spirit in the community and provides additional potential manpower that will reinforce the consolidation work.*

(Universal House of Justice, "Wellspring of Guidance", p.33)

Teachers involved in expansion work must ensure that it will be possible to follow up their teaching efforts with consolidation, otherwise they risk causing disillusionment amongst the newly-declared believers, thereby doing the Faith a disservice:-

> *It should be pointed out that, especially if they are assigned to expansion work, they must remember that consolidation is an essential and inseparable element of teaching, and if they go to a remote area and enrol believers whom no one is going to be able to visit again in the near future, they may well be doing a disservice to those people and to the Faith. To give people this glorious Message and then leave them in the lurch, produces disappointment and disillusionment, so that, when it does become possible to carry out properly planned teaching in that area, the teachers may well find the people resistant to the Message.*

(letter from the Universal House of Justice to all Continental Pioneer Committees, dated April 16, 1981)

5.3.3 **What general principles apply to the teaching work?**

Two principles go hand in hand and both are essential. The Local Spiritual Assembly must take a systematic, planned approach to the teaching work and it must also foster spiritual values within the community. It is the spiritual quality of the teacher which ultimately determines the success of the teaching effort:-

> *Armed with the strength of action and the cooperation of the individual believers composing it, the community as a whole should endeavour to establish greater stability in the patterns of its development, locally and nationally, through sound, systematic planning and execution of its work... May you with renewed determination and a rededication to spiritual values, seize your chance, while there is yet time, to convey the Message of Bahá'u'lláh thoughtfully, patiently and attractively to your fellow-citizens...*

(letter from the Universal House of Justice to a National Spiritual Assembly, dated Ridván 1984)

> *Whereas plans must be carefully made, and every useful means adopted in the furtherance of this work, your Assemblies must never let such plans eclipse the shining truth that it is the purity of heart, detachment, uprightness, devotion and love of the teacher that attracts the divine confirmations and enables him, however ignorant he be in this world's learning, to win the hearts of his fellowmen to the Cause of God.*
>
> (letter from the Universal House of Justice to all National Spiritual Assemblies, dated October 31, 1967)

5.3.4 *What are the most important principles to teach a person?*

The most important thing is that the person being taught should come to recognise the station of Bahá'u'lláh and catch 'the spark of faith'. In addition, he or she needs to be basically informed about the Central Figures of the Faith, and of the existence of laws to follow and of an administration that must be obeyed:-

> *The prime motive should always be the response of man to God's Message, and the recognition of His Messenger. Those who declare themselves as Bahá'ís should become enchanted with the beauty of the Teachings, and touched by the love of Bahá'u'lláh. The declarants need not know all the proofs, history, laws, and principles of the Faith, but in the process of declaring themselves they must, in addition to catching the spark of faith, become basically informed about the Central Figures of the Faith, as well as the existence of laws they must follow and an administration they must obey.*
>
> (Universal House of Justice, "Wellspring of Guidance", p.32)

Shoghi Effendi warned that obstacles should not be placed in the way of enrolments. Rather, the enrolment must be immediately followed up with deepening. Although some may then fall away, others will remain who might never have become Bahá'ís at all if the enrolment procedure had been made too strict:-

> *...As you are aware, the beloved Guardian encouraged early enrolment of new believers upon their declarations, and not the creation of obstacles to their acceptance. After declaration, follow-up with deepening is imperative, and it may be that some will fall away. However, those who remain are the true fruits of the teaching endeavour and may include persons of great merit who might have been lost to the Cause through arbitrary early judgements.*
>
> (letter written on behalf of the Universal House of Justice, to an individual believer, dated November 18, 1980)

On the other hand, Bahá'ís must not place more emphasis on getting declarations than on teaching the fundamentals of the Faith properly:-

> *Some teaching committees, in their eagerness to obtain results, place undue emphasis on obtaining a great number of declarations to the detriment of the quality of teaching.*
>
> (Universal House of Justice, "Wellspring of Guidance", p.35)

5.3.5 *What is the distinction between active teaching and proselytising?*

By proselytising is meant placing undue pressure on a person to accept the Faith. It also usually means making threats or offering material incentives to convert:-

CHAPTER FIVE

It is true that Bahá'u'lláh lays on every Bahá'í the duty to teach His Faith. At the same time, however, we are forbidden to proselytise, so it is important for all believers to understand the difference between teaching and proselytising. It is a significant difference... Proselytising implies bringing undue pressure to bear upon someone to change his Faith. It is also usually understood to imply the making of threats or the offering of material benefits as an inducement to conversion...

...They should teach with enthusiasm, conviction, wisdom and courtesy, but without pressing their hearer, bearing in mind the words of Bahá'u'lláh 'Beware lest ye contend with any one, nay, strive to make him aware of the truth with kindly manner and most convincing exhortation. If your hearer respond, he will have responded to his own behoof, and if not, turn ye away from him, and set your faces towards God's sacred Court, the seat of resplendent holiness.'

("Gleanings from the Writings of Bahá'u'lláh" CXXVIII) (extract in a letter written on behalf of the Universal House of Justice to an individual believer, dated May 5, 1982)

Shoghi Effendi explains:-

Care, however, should, at all times, be exercised, lest in their eagerness to further the international interests of the Faith they frustrate their purpose, and turn away, through any act that might be misconstrued as an attempt to proselytise and bring undue pressure upon them, those whom they wish to win over to their Cause.

("Advent of Divine Justice", p.55)

The distinction between proselytising and direct teaching is, to some extent, determined by the social environment within which it is undertaken. Street teaching, for example, is acceptable in some social environments, but not in others. Australia contains a variety of different environments and the believers must approach each particular situation with wisdom and sensitivity. A related point is that Bahá'ís must not place undue emphasis on the charitable and humanitarian aspects of the Faith to induce people to accept the Faith.

5.3.6 **What are some different methods of teaching?**

The following is a list of activities that may be undertaken by Assemblies and individuals. It is by no means exhaustive:-
1. Weave close bonds of friendship with neighbours and associates. Having won the person's trust, he or she may then gradually be taught. Ideally, every Bahá'í should choose one person each year to gradually teach in this way.
2. Hold a fireside once every nineteen days.
3. By example; that is, by living the Bahá'í life. Whilst it is important, however, for Bahá'ís to live the Bahá'í life (that is, to match their words with their deeds), nevertheless, teaching by example can never take the place of direct teaching.
4. By association with like-minded organisations to find people who appear receptive to the Faith.
5. Through the arts. Shoghi Effendi encouraged teaching through the arts to awaken the spirit:-

    That day will the Cause spread like wildfire when its spirit and Teachings are presented on the stage or in art and literature as a

CHAPTER FIVE

whole. Art can better awaken such noble sentiments than cold rationalising, especially among the mass of the people.

(letter written on behalf of Shoghi Effendi; in "Bahá'í News" #73, May 1933, p.7)

6. Through scholarship:-

...The Cause needs more Bahá'í scholars, people who not only are devoted to it and believe in it and are anxious to tell others about it, but also who have a deep grasp of the Teachings and their significance, and who can correlate its beliefs with the current thoughts and problems of the people of the world.

(letter written on behalf of Shoghi Effendi to an individual believer, dated October 21, 1943)

5.3.7 *Is door-to-door teaching acceptable?*

No. The Universal House of Justice says the following principles apply:-
1. *The dignity of the Faith. This should be carefully safe-guarded in all Bahá'í activities, and it is clear from the following quotation that the Guardian felt that door-to-door distribution of pamphlets was undignified: 'He feels that to distribute Bahá'í pamphlets from door-to-door...is undignified and might create a bad impression of the Faith. No doubt, it is the eagerness and devotion of the friends that led them to make this proposal, but he does not think that the best interests of the Cause are served by such a method...'*
2. *Bahá'u'lláh's injunction as recorded in "The Hidden Words": 'The wise are they that speak not unless they obtain a hearing...' It is important that no teaching activity should be an encroachment on people's privacy nor should it force the Teachings upon unwilling listeners.*
3. *Integrity and sincerity. If people are to be asked to answer a questionnaire it should be for the reason that it is necessary for the sponsor to know the answers. Bahá'ís should not use such a method as a subterfuge to convey the message to people.*

(letter from the Universal House of Justice to a National Spiritual Assembly, dated December 16, 1965)

The National Spiritual Assembly believes the dignity of the Faith would be compromised in Australia if the Bahá'ís mounted door-knocking teaching campaigns. The National Spiritual Assembly, strongly discourages it in all instances.

5.4 **CONSOLIDATION**

5.4.1 *What is the purpose of consolidation?*

Consolidation is concerned with deepening the knowledge of community members so that they will, of their own accord, arise to further the teaching work, make sure that the administrative institutions function, and work to develop a strong sense of community life:-

Consolidation is... that aspect of teaching which assists the believers to deepen their knowledge and understanding of the Teachings, and fans the flame of their devotion to Bahá'u'lláh and His Cause, so that they will, of their own volition, continue the process of their spiritual development, promote the teaching work, and strengthen the functioning of their administrative institutions...

...Consolidation activities promote the individual spiritual development

CHAPTER FIVE

of the friends, help to unite and strengthen Bahá'í community life, establish new social patterns for the friends, and stimulate the teaching work.

(letter written on behalf of the Universal House of Justice to all National Spiritual Assemblies, dated April 17, 1981)

It is particularly important that new believers be deepened in the Faith. The teaching of new believers should not be considered finished until those people have, of their own accord, arisen to further the teaching and administration work:-

The purpose of teaching is not complete when a person declares that he has accepted Bahá'u'lláh as the Manifestation of God for this age; the purpose of teaching is to attract human beings to the divine Message and so imbue them with its spirit that they will dedicate themselves to its service, and this world will become another world and its people another people. Viewed in this light a declaration of faith is merely a milestone along the way — albeit a very important one...

...the teaching of the believers continues until, and even after, they shoulder their responsibilities as Bahá'ís and participate in both the teaching and administrative work of the Faith.

(letter written by the Universal House of Justice to all National Spiritual Assemblies, dated May 25, 1975)

5.4.2 *What aspects of the Faith should deepening focus on?*

Deepening should focus primarily on God's purpose for man, especially His immediate purpose as revealed and directed by Bahá'u'lláh, rather than on the administration or laws of the Faith:-

A detailed and exact knowledge of the present structure of Bahá'í administration, or of the By-Laws of national and local Spiritual Assemblies, or of the many and varied applications of Bahá'í law under the diverse conditions prevailing around the world, while valuable in itself, cannot be regarded as the sort of knowledge primarily intended by deepening. Rather is suggested a clearer apprehension of the purpose of God for man, and particularly of His immediate purpose as revealed and directed by Bahá'u'lláh...

...Dearly-loved friends, this is the theme we must pursue in our efforts to deepen in the Cause. What is Bahá'u'lláh's purpose for the human race? For what ends did He submit to the appalling cruelties and indignities heaped upon Him? What does He mean by "a new race of men"? What are the profound changes which He will bring about?

(Universal House of Justice, "Wellspring of Guidance", p.113, 114)

This is not to say that the Bahá'ís should not deepen on the administration and laws - they should. It is only that such study should be placed in context and seen as secondary to the importance of studying God's purpose for man. [See further, "Lights of Guidance" {revised edition}, nos.1913-33.]

5.4.3 *How should the Local Spiritual Assembly nurture new believers?*

The Assembly should keep in touch with new believers through correspondence and visits

CHAPTER FIVE

and encouragement and assistance to attend Bahá'í conferences and other functions:-

> *After declaration, the new believers must not be left to their own devices. Through correspondence and dispatch of visitors, through conferences and training courses, these friends must be patiently strengthened and lovingly helped to develop into full Bahá'í maturity. The beloved Guardian, referring to the duties of Bahá'í assemblies in assisting the newly declared believer, has written:*
>
> *"... the members of each and every Assembly should endeavour, by their patience, their love, their tact and wisdom, to nurse, subsequent to his admission, the newcomer into Bahá'í maturity, and win him over gradually to the unreserved acceptance of whatever has been ordained in the Teachings."*
>
> (Universal House of Justice, "Wellspring of Guidance", p.32-3)

Study classes are most important; however, the new believer must also be encouraged to become fully involved in the community life, for it is not possible to catch the spirit of the Faith through reading books alone:-

> *It behoves you now to try to deepen your knowledge of the history and the Teachings of the Faith and get acquainted with the principles that stand at the basis of its present-day Administration. - The best way to attain that goal is through continued cooperation with the friends and through participation in their spiritual activities For you cannot catch the spirit of the Cause through the reading of books alone. - You should reinforce the knowledge you get through Bahá'í Writings with a whole-hearted association with the friends.*
>
> (letter written on behalf of Shoghi Effendi to an individual believer, dated August 20, 1932)

In some regions the Regional Teaching Committee may also offer courses for new believers which, of course, they should be encouraged to attend.

5.4.4 **How should new believers be nurtured in areas in which there have been large scale enrolments?**

The Universal House of Justice suggests that the new believers should be sent material immediately so that they know their declarations have been accepted and they feel that they now belong to their new Faith. Training courses of about two weeks duration, or shorter courses over a long weekend, should be held. The most capable students should be selected to attend. Transportation expenses, food, and accommodation should be paid for from the Fund if the participants can't afford the expenses. After the course the more promising students should be requested to undertake teaching projects for a limited period. These activities should be repeated as often as possible.
[See further "Wellspring of Guidance", p.31-36].

Local Spiritual Assemblies may call on travel teachers and members of the appointed arm of the Faith to assist in consolidation work by meeting with the believers and conducting deepenings.
The Universal House of Justice recommends that the following subjects be discussed at these meetings:-

1. *the extent of the spread and stature of the Faith today;*

2. *the importance of the daily obligatory prayers (at least the short prayer);*
3. *the need to educate Bahá'í children in the Teachings of the Faith and encourage them to memorise some of the prayers;*
4. *the stimulation of youth to participate in community life by giving talks, etc. and having their own activities, if possible;*
5. *the necessity to abide by the laws of marriage, namely, the need to have a Bahá'í ceremony, to obtain the consent of parents, to observe monogamy; faithfulness after marriage; likewise the importance of abstinence from all intoxicating drinks and drugs;*
6. *the local Fund and the need for the friends to understand that the voluntary act of contributing to the Fund is both a privilege and a spiritual obligation. There should also be discussion of various methods that could be followed by the friends to facilitate their contributions and the ways open to the local Assembly to utilise its local Fund to serve the interests of its community and the Cause;*
7. *the importance of the Nineteen-Day Feast and the fact that it should be a joyful occasion and rallying point of the entire community;*
8. *the manner of election with as many workshops as required, including teaching of simple methods of balloting for illiterates, such as having one central home as the place for balloting and arranging for one literate person, if only a child, to be present at that home during the whole day, if necessary;*
9. *last but not least, the all-important teaching work, both in the locality and its neighbouring centres, as well as the need to continuously deepen the friends in the essentials of the Faith. The friends should be made to realise that in teaching the Faith to others they should not only aim at assisting the seeking soul to join the Faith, but also at making him a teacher of the Faith and its active supporter. All the above points should, of course, be stressed within the framework of the importance of the Local Spiritual Assembly, which should be encouraged to vigorously direct its attention to these vital functions and become the very heart of the community life of its own locality, even if its meetings should become burdened with the problems of the community. The local friends should understand the importance of the law of consultation and realise that it is to the Local Spiritual Assembly that they should turn, abide by its decisions, support its projects, cooperate whole-heartedly with it in its task to promote the interests of the Cause, and seek its advice and guidance in the solution of personal problems and the adjudication of disputes, should any arise amongst the members of the community.*

(letter from the Universal House of Justice to all National Spiritual Assemblies Engaged in Mass Teaching Work, dated February 2, 1966)

5.4.5 *How do summer schools assist the teaching and consolidation work?*

Summer schools are essential to any teaching campaign, both because they provide the deepening in the Faith necessary for any Bahá'í to teach successfully; and because they provide an ideal forum within which people close to the Faith may learn more:-

> *The institution of the Summer School constitutes a vital and inseparable part of any teaching campaign, and as such ought to be given the full importance it deserves in the teaching plans and activities of the believers. It should be organised in such a way as to attract the attention of the non-believers to the Cause and thus become an effective medium for teaching. Also it should afford the believers themselves an opportunity to deepen their knowledge of the Teachings, through lectures and discussions and by means of close and intense community*

life.

> (letter written on behalf of Shoghi Effendi to a National Spiritual Assembly, dated October 17, 1936) [See further "Lights of Guidance" {revised edition}, nos. 1891-1907.]

The Regional Teaching Committees and the Yerrinbool School and Institutes Committee have the responsibility of organising summer and winter schools. Local Spiritual Assemblies have the responsibility of encouraging the friends in their community to make every effort to attend.

5.4.6 What is the importance of teaching institutes?

Teaching and spiritual transformation institutes are designed to prepare the friends for active participation in the expansion and consolidation work. They are centres from which large scale teaching and consolidation plans can be put into practise. Such institutes are a function rather than a building:-

> *Your Institutes should not only be seats of Bahá'í learning but also centres from which mass teaching and consolidation work over a large area must be inspired and conducted. The Institute is not merely a building, nor solely a place where Bahá'í classes can be held for a few days. It should be the centre of complex activities which systematically assist your Assembly in the achievement of its goal in teaching and consolidation.*

> (letter from the Universal House of Justice to a National Spiritual Assembly, dated June 23, 1966)

> *We have always stressed to those National Spiritual Assemblies which establish Teaching Institutes that at the present time such an Institute is a function and not necessarily a building...*

> (letter from the Universal House of Justice to an individual believer, dated April 18, 1971)

Teaching Institutes have long been in use in those parts of the world in which there has been mass teaching. They are used both to further the expansion and consolidation work after there have been mass enrolments (ie. by deepening the friends and thereby encouraging them to become active in teaching and administration); and to prepare a core group of believers to initiate a sustained teaching campaign aimed at bringing about mass enrolments:-

> *In areas where large numbers of new believers have entered the Faith, Teaching Institutes have long been used as a means of expansion and consolidation aimed at raising up workers - teachers and administrators - for the Faith. A new development has recently emerged under the guidance of the International Teaching Centre and the Continental Counsellors. In some areas individuals have initiated institutes before a large population has embraced the Faith. The purpose of these institutes is to involve a core group of believers in a systematic process that involves deepening, prayer, memorisation of the writings, and teaching. The aim is to develop the human resources necessary to initiate and sustain the process of entry by troops. The central principle of its operation is the statement from the Guardian: "Success will crown the efforts of the friends on the homefront, when they meditate on the Teachings, pray fervently for divine confirmations*

for their work, study the Teachings so they may carry their spirit to the seeker, and then act: and above all persevere in action. When these steps are followed, and the teaching work carried on sacrificially and with devoted enthusiasm, the Faith will spread rapidly."

(letter from the Universal House of Justice)

In Australia we are at the threshold of 'entry by troops' and the holding of such institutes is just beginning. Whilst Regional Teaching Committees have been given specific responsibility for organising them, this does not mean that a Local Spiritual Assembly or group of Local Spiritual Assemblies may not organise teaching institutes also. [For more information see Wellspring of Guidance", p.31-6. Further advice on how to organise such an institute is available from the National Spiritual Assembly or National Teaching Committee.]

5.4.7 **What are some other consolidation activities?**

In a letter dated December 24, 1975 to a National Spiritual Assembly, the Universal House of Justice provided the following examples of consolidation goals:
1. *improving attendance at the Nineteen Day Feast and Anniversaries*
2. *holding regular meetings for the benefit of the local friends*
3. *organising early morning prayer sessions*
4. *encouraging youth activities*
5. *establishing activities and classes for children*
6. *establishing a local Ḥaẓíratu'l-Quds*
7. *acquiring a local endowment*
8. *encouraging contributions to the local Fund*
9. *serving as a host to a district conference*
10. *issuing a regular newsletter*

5.5 **PIONEERING AND TRAVEL TEACHING**

5.5.1 **What is the role of the Local Spiritual Assembly with regard to pioneering and travel teaching?**

The Local Spiritual Assembly has a responsibility to tell its community about international and national goals and projects and to encourage the friends to help fulfil them. It also has a responsibility to assist in the fulfilment of regional and local goals in the pioneering and travel teaching fields.

5.5.2 **How should friends who are interested in overseas pioneering or travel teaching be advised?**

Friends who are interested in overseas pioneering or travel teaching should be advised to contact the Australian Overseas Pioneer Committee. Their address is available from the National Office. The Continental Pioneer Committee is also a useful source of information.

5.5.3 **What is the function of a pioneer?**

A pioneer is 'any believer who arises and leaves his home to journey to settle in another place for the purpose of teaching the Cause...'

(letter written on behalf of the Universal House of Justice to a National Spiritual Assembly, dated February 11, 1975).

The purpose in so doing is 'to establish the Faith of God securely and firmly in the hearts of people of the area and to ensure that its divinely-ordained institutions are understood, adopted and operated by them.'

CHAPTER FIVE

(letter of the Universal House of Justice to all National Spiritual Assemblies, dated June 5, 1966).

A pioneer has no special status except that in some circumstances he or she will be a channel of communication between the relevant administrative body (in Australia the Regional Teaching Committee) and the Bahá'í group as it forms. Once a Local Spiritual Assembly is formed in the area the pioneer ceases to have any special status at all:-

> *A pioneer has no special administrative status except in the case where he goes to a new area where there are no Bahá'ís. He then usually remains the channel of communication between the new Bahá'í group, as it is formed, and the National Committee in charge, until such time as a Local Spiritual Assembly is formed. At that point his special status ceases altogether. Any services he may perform in advising or teaching the new believers spring from the fact that he is an older believer, and not from his being a pioneer.*

(letter from the Universal House of Justice to a National Spiritual Assembly, dated July 2, 1965)

It is important that the pioneer work with the believers already present in the area:-

> *...all National Spiritual Assemblies receiving pioneer support should devise ways and means for the pioneers and local believers to work together in close harmony, thus taking full advantage of the help and support that pioneers are anxious to offer, often at great sacrifice, to the teaching or deepening work of the community to which they have gone, and demonstrating to a sceptical world the undivided solidarity and exemplary unity of the followers of the Most Great Name.*

(letter from the Universal House of Justice to all National Spiritual Assemblies, dated July 6, 1969)

It is also important that the pioneer teach the Faith to the local population and assist these people to arise and further the teaching work themselves, rather than allowing them to rely indefinitely on the pioneer for support:-

> *Great as are the services rendered by pioneers, and unforgettable as are the deeds they accomplish, they cannot take the places of the indigenous element which must constitute the bedrock of the Community, carry on its own affairs, build its own institutions, support its own Funds, publish its own literature, etc.*

(letter written on behalf of Shoghi Effendi to a National Spiritual Assembly, dated July 3, 1957)

5.5.4 *What responsibility has the Local Spiritual Assembly for homefront pioneering?*

If there are more than 15 adults in the community, the Local Spiritual Assembly has the duty to encourage its members to move out and help create new local Assemblies:-

> *By dispersal the Guardian means the friends should get away entirely from the large centres of population and, leaving a nucleus of about 15 Bahá'ís to maintain the Local Assembly, go settle, live and teach in new towns, cities and even villages. Naturally, it is no service to the Cause to disperse if it breaks up an existing Assembly. The purpose of dispersal is to create more Assemblies over a wider area.*

CHAPTER FIVE

(letter written on behalf of Shoghi Effendi to an individual believer, dated June 19, 1955)

In particular, the newly-arrived Iranian friends should be encouraged and assisted to move out to new territories. To have large numbers of Iranians settling in one place does little to further the teaching work and may do harm if, for example, people get the impression that the Bahá'í Faith is peculiar to Iranians:-

> *Another sacred responsibility of those dear Iranian friends now living abroad is to consult with the Assemblies and Bahá'í Institutions so that their settlement in needy areas may help the establishment and consolidation of the Faith. They must serve on the pioneer front wherever they reside. They must not allow themselves to be drawn to and congregate in areas where their relatives or friends reside, unaware of the pioneering needs of the Faith. ... Often such a congregation creates problems. For example, should the number of Iranians exceed the number of native believers in a community, they would inadvertently bring about such difficulties as might hamper the progress of the Cause of God, and the world-conquering religion of the Abhá Beauty might appear to others as a religion which is limited and peculiar to Iranians. This could but lead to a waste of time and the disenchantment of both Bahá'ís and non-Bahá'ís. Under such circumstances the dear Iranian friends would neither enjoy their stay in that place nor would they be able to serve the Faith in a befitting manner.*
>
> (translation of a letter from the Universal House of Justice addressed "to the dear Iranian believers resident in other countries throughout the world", dated February 10, 1980; quoted in letter of the Continental Board of Counsellors for Australasia to the Auxiliary Board members in Australia, dated March 29, 1987)

Where the Regional Teaching Committee has established a Pioneer and Settlement Working Group the Local Spiritual Assembly should work with this Group in assisting the Iranian friends to fulfil homefront pioneering goals. Similarly, friends wishing to homefront pioneer either within their Regional Teaching Committee area or somewhere else within Australia, should be advised to contact the Regional Teaching Committee or National Teaching Committee respectively for a list of goal areas.
Teaching

5.5.5 *What is extension teaching?*

Extension teaching is the adoption of a goal area by a Local Spiritual Assembly with the aim of raising that area to Assembly status. The Local Spiritual Assembly does not have jurisdiction over the Bahá'ís in that area; jurisdiction remains with the Regional Teaching Committee. The Local Spiritual Assembly has, however, a duty to assist them in their teaching and consolidation work:-

> *The time has come, we believe, when increasing numbers of Local Spiritual Assemblies should assume responsibility for helping the teaching work of groups, isolated believers, and other Spiritual Assemblies in their neighbourhood. Such extension teaching goals... should be carried out within the framework of the overall teaching plans of the country. It should also be made clear that by being given such goals a Spiritual Assembly is not being given any jurisdiction*

CHAPTER FIVE

over believers outside its area, still less over other Local Spiritual Assemblies, but is being called upon to collaborate with them in their work.

(letter from the Universal House of Justice to all National Spiritual Assemblies, dated Naw-Rúz 1974)

The Local Spiritual Assembly should consult with its Regional Teaching Committee as to which goal area to adopt. The Local Spiritual Assembly should also keep the Regional Teaching Committee informed of its activities in the goal area.

5.5.6 **What is the function of travel teachers?**

Travel teachers may be used in proclamation, expansion or consolidation work. Their task is not to take the place of local teaching initiatives, but to help consolidate the work that has already been done, and to encourage the believers in the locality to continue with the work:-

Visiting teachers, who are, at least in a general way, supposed to be more competent and able than the rest, are undoubtedly of great help. But these can never replace the mass of individual believers and fulfil what must be inevitably accomplished through the collective effort and wisdom of the community at large. What visiting teachers are supposed to do is to give the final touch to the work that has been done, to consolidate rather than supplement individual efforts and thereby direct them in a constructive and suitable channel. Their task is to encourage and inspire individual believers, and to broaden and deepen their vision of the task that is to be done. And this, not by virtue of any inherent spiritual right, but in the spirit of simple and whole-hearted cooperation.

(letter written on behalf of Shoghi Effendi to an individual believer, dated September 1, 1933)

Travel teachers have a highly stimulating effect on the local teaching work. The Universal House of Justice has encouraged Local Spiritual Assemblies to incorporate visits by travel teachers into their teaching plans:-

The challenge to the local and national administrative institutions of the Faith is to organise and promote the teaching work through systematic plans, involving... in addition...a constant stream of visiting teachers to every locality. The forces released by this latter process have been extolled by Bahá'u'lláh in these words: "The movement itself from place to place when undertaken for the sake of God hath always exerted, and can now exert, its influence in the world. In the Books of old the station of them that have voyaged far and near in order to guide the servants of God hath been set forth and written down."

(Universal House of Justice, "Wellspring of Guidance", p.76)

5.5.7 **How is travel teaching organised in Australia?**

The National Bahá'í Teaching Committee is responsible for organising travel teaching where the teacher is coming from overseas, or where the teacher will travel through a number of regions of Australia. The National Bahá'í Teaching Committee will normally do this by being in contact with the relevant Regional Teaching Committees and asking them to make local arrangements. The Regional Teaching Committees are responsible for organising travel teaching trips within their areas and will offer travel teachers to Local Spiritual Assemblies. The Local Spiritual Assembly is not obliged to accept a travel teacher. If it does so, however, it may be requested to provide assistance with transport, accommodation and funds, if the travel teacher is not able to organise these things. The Regional Teaching Committee will provide the Local Spiritual Assembly with background information about the travel teacher for publicity purposes and with advice as to the kind of work the teacher prefers to do, eg. interviews with the media, conducting deepenings, talks at firesides.

If the travel teacher is recommended to a Local Spiritual Assembly by the Regional Teaching Committee, it can be sure that the teacher is qualified to teach. Should it happen, however, that a Bahá'í unknown to the Local Spiritual Assembly offers, unexpectedly, to undertake teaching work in its area, the Assembly should check with the Regional Teaching Committee before accepting the offer. Local Assemblies are not obliged to assist with transport or accommodation for any travel teachers who arrive in their area without prior notification.

5.5.8 *How should a Local Spiritual Assembly advise a believer who wishes to undertake travel teaching within Australia?*

A believer who wishes to travel teach within Australia should be advised to contact either the Regional Teaching Committee of the region within which he or she intends teaching; or, if planning to teach in more than one region, the National Bahá'í Teaching Committee.

5.5.9 *What is the Deputisation Fund?*

If the friends cannot arise to pioneer or travel teach themselves, Bahá'u'lláh asks them to help others to go in their place. The Universal House of Justice and the National Spiritual Assembly of Australia have set up Deputisation Funds for this purpose, to which individuals can donate. Donations may be sent to the National Office and should be clearly marked as being for the National Spiritual Assembly or the Universal House of Justice, as the case may be. The Local Spiritual Assembly could also consider deputising friends in its community to attend summer schools, teaching institutes, and so on.

5.6 RESPONSIBILITIES OF THE LOCAL SPIRITUAL ASSEMBLY

5.6.1 *How should the Local Spiritual Assembly organise its teaching work?*

The Local Spiritual Assembly should incorporate plans for its teaching work in the coming year into the annual plan of activities it prepares The Universal House of Justice itself has provided the following outline of questions that Local Spiritual Assemblies may put to themselves in order to set their teaching goals for the coming year:-

Proclamation
1. Are mass media facilities such as radio, television, and the press available to the Local Assembly? Can a goal be adopted for such activities?
2. Can public meetings be anticipated? If so, how many?
3. What methods can be adopted for the dissemination of Bahá'í literature, such as distribution of books to local libraries?
4. Can the local community participate in the social and humanitarian activities of the society of which it forms a part? Could a modest step be taken along this line?

Expansion
1. How many new believers? The ideal is for each local community to double itself every year, since every believer should, in accordance with the wish of the Master, guide one soul to the Cause of God every year. In some areas this may be an ambitious project at the beginning, and at the outset a more modest goal could be adopted.

2. How many firesides? Shoghi Effendi urged the friends to hold one fireside every nineteen days in their homes. The friends willing to respond to this wish, could give their names to the Local Assembly.
3. Can a pledge be made to have extension teaching activities outside the local area of jurisdiction? Obviously only strong Local Assemblies can sustain such a goal.

Consolidation
1. Can the attendance of the friends at Nineteen Day Feasts be improved upon? What about the Anniversaries? Can the increase in attendance be expressed numerically, such as in terms of the percentage of those attending?
2. Can regular meetings for the benefit of the local friends be held? If so, how often and when? ... 'Abdu'l-Bahá exhorts the friends to hold such meetings as a 'constant' activity, and praises weekly meetings. He repeatedly counsels the believers to read and recite the Holy Word in such meetings and deliver speeches on the Teachings, the proofs and the history of the Faith.
3. Can daily early morning prayer sessions be held? If so, where and when? If this is not feasible every day, an effort could be made to hold such sessions less frequently.
4. Can youth activities be encouraged? If so, in what way?
5. Can activities and classes for children be established? If so, could a specific goal be adopted?
6. Can youth activities be maintained? Could this be expressed in the form of a goal?
7. How can contributions to the local and national Funds be encouraged? Can a target be adopted?
8. Can the local community serve as host to a district conference of neighbouring communities and localities?
9. Can the Local Assembly issue a regular Newsletter?
(adapted from a letter from the Universal House of Justice to a National Spiritual Assembly, dated December 24, 1975)

5.6.2 *What responsibility does the Local Spiritual Assembly have towards the local community with regard to the teaching work?*

The Local Spiritual Assembly has a duty to encourage the friends to teach. In a letter dated March 3, 1977 to all National Spiritual Assemblies , the Universal House of Justice says this may be done through sharing the following matters with the community:-
1. stories of successes achieved by some of them
2. descriptions of effective presentations found useful by them
3. examples of various ways that a Bahá'í subject could be introduced to inquirers
4. illustrations of methods which would enable the believer to relate the needs of society to our Teachings.

These ideas may be shared by any means open to the Assembly, including:-
1. at Nineteen Day Feasts
2. through a local newsletter

Another method the Assembly could use is to organise special meetings at which texts on teaching the Faith are shared. Such texts include:-
1. "Teaching the greatest gift of God" (compilation of the Universal House of Justice, 1977)
2. "A Special Measure of Love - The Importance and Nature of the Teaching Work among the Masses" (compilation of the National Spiritual Assembly of the United

States, 1974)
3. "The Individual and Teaching - Raising the Divine Call" (compilation of the Universal House of Justice, 1977)
4. "Wellspring of Guidance" Messages from the Universal House of Justice (US Bahá'í Publishing Trust, 1969)
5. "Centers of Bahá'í Learning" (compilation of the Universal House of Justice, 1980)

In addition the Local Spiritual Assembly should share news of local teaching activities in other areas and of national and international teaching activities and plans. It should encourage the friends to become involved in national and international initiatives and should know where to direct them for more information if, for example, a community member wishes to pioneer or to travel teach.

The Local Spiritual Assembly also has a duty to work to develop a spirit of real love and unity within the community. This in itself will attract people to the Faith:-

> *...the Bahá'ís... should also realise that the atmosphere of true love and unity which they manifest within the Bahá'í Community will directly affect the public, and be the greatest magnet for attracting people to the Faith and confirming them.*
>
> (letter written on behalf of Shoghi Effendi to a National Spiritual Assembly, dated April 4, 1947)

5.6.3 *What benefit does the community receive by concentrating on the teaching work?*

Teaching attracts divine assistance to the community. If a community does not teach it loses that assistance for all its activities:-

> *It is known and clear that today the unseen divine assistance encompasseth those who deliver the Message. And if the work of delivering the Message be neglected, the assistance shall be entirely cut off, for it is impossible that the friends of God could receive assistance unless they be engaged in delivering the Message.*
>
> ('Abdu'l-Bahá, "Bahá'í World Faith, p.385)

5.6.4 *Should priority be given to national or locally organised teaching projects?*

It is not a matter of priority being given to either national or local teaching projects. Rather, there should be a balance between the two and each should support the other. The appointed arm of the Faith should also be called upon to assist the teaching work of the institutions:-

> *These nationally directed projects... should be supported by locally sponsored teaching activities carried out by Local Spiritual Assemblies. By combining the two levels of Bahá'í activity, and by seeking the collaboration of the Counsellors in providing the guidance and stimulation of the Auxiliary Board members and their assistants at the local level, excellent results will be obtained and your high aspirations in the expansion and consolidation work will be fully realised.*
>
> (letter from the Universal House of Justice to a National Spiritual Assembly, dated October 7, 1975)

> *We...ask you to encourage the Counsellors to try to strike a balance between locally-sponsored teaching activities and nationally-directed*

CHAPTER FIVE

projects which should be carried out by the National Spiritual Assembly and its committees within the limits of the manpower and the financial resources at their disposal and at a speed which would enable the consolidation to be effective.

...The concentration of all teaching efforts in Local Spiritual Assemblies...is neither practical nor wise.

(letter from the Universal House of Justice to the International Teaching Centre, dated May 13, 1975)

5.6.5 **What is the particular role of the appointed arm in the teaching work?**

Whilst Local Spiritual Assemblies have the duty to organise and direct the teaching work, the role of the appointed arm - especially the Propagation Board - is to encourage and stimulate the friends in the local community to put the Assembly's teaching plans into practice:-

It is the responsibility of Spiritual Assemblies, assisted by their committees, to organise and direct the teaching work, and in doing so they must, naturally, also do all they can to stimulate and inspire the friends. It is, however, inevitable that the Assemblies and committees, being burdened with the administration of the teaching work as well as with all other aspects of Bahá'í community life, will be unable to spend as much time as they would wish on stimulating the believers. Authority and direction flow from the Assemblies, whereas the power to accomplish the tasks resides primarily in the entire body of the believers. It is the principal task of the Auxiliary Boards to assist in arousing and releasing this power...the Auxiliary Boards should work closely with the grass roots of the community: the individual believers, groups and Local Spiritual Assemblies, advising, stimulating and assisting them.

(letter from the Universal House of Justice to the Continental Boards of Counsellors and National Spiritual Assemblies, dated October 1, 1969)

To this end the Local Spiritual Assembly should ensure that its assistant for Propagation is kept well informed of its teaching plans:-

The primary tasks of the Propagation Boards...are to direct the believers' attention to the goals of whatever plans have been placed before them, to stimulate and assist them to promote the teaching work in the fields of proclamation, expansion, consolidation and pioneering, to encourage contributions to the Funds, and to act as standard-bearers of the teachers of the Faith, leading them to new achievements in the diffusion of God's Message to their fellow human beings.

(letter from the Universal House of Justice, to the International Teaching Centre, dated October 10, 1976)

The assistants to the Auxiliary Boards are also particularly useful in helping to consolidate the community, ie. by conducting deepenings, helping the friends to apply the Teachings in their daily lives, and so on:-

One of the most potent aids to the consolidation of local communities and Assemblies and the deepening of the faith of the believers, is the services of the Auxiliary Board members and their assistants. Here is

CHAPTER FIVE

an institution of the Faith, reaching into every locality, composed of firm believers who know the area they have to serve and are familiar with its problems and potentialities - an institution expressly designed to encourage and reinforce the work of the Spiritual Assemblies, to enthuse the believers, to stimulate them to study the Teachings and apply them in their lives - a body of Bahá'ís whose efforts and services will complement and support the work being done by your committees and by the Local Assemblies themselves in every sphere of Bahá'í endeavour.

(letter from the Universal House of Justice to a National Spiritual Assembly, dated December 2, 1976)

5.6.6 **What is the relationship between the Regional Teaching Committee and the Local Spiritual Assembly?**

The Regional Teaching Committee has the task of organising a regional teaching plan for the year. In doing so it should liaise closely with the Local Spiritual Assemblies in its region on such matters as extension teaching goals, homefront pioneering, visiting travel teachers, minority teaching, publicity and public relations work, the organisation of teaching institutes, and so on. The Local Spiritual Assembly has a duty, in its turn, to keep the Regional Teaching Committee informed of its teaching activities.

5.6.7 **What is the relationship between individual and Local Spiritual Assembly teaching projects?**

The Local Spiritual Assembly has a duty to organise teaching projects; however, individuals are free to pursue their own projects also. The only requirement is that they keep the Local Spiritual Assembly informed of their activities. Whilst the Local Spiritual Assembly has the right to supervise these activities it should do its utmost to encourage and assist such individual initiatives:-

Concerning individual teaching, Shoghi Effendi would urge every Bahá'í who feels the urge to exercise his right of teaching unofficially the Cause, to keep in close touch with the Local Spiritual Assembly of the locality in which he is working. The Local Spiritual Assembly, while reserving for itself the right to control such activities on the part of individual Bahá'ís should do its utmost to encourage such teachers and to put at their disposal whatever facilities they would need in such circumstances.

(Shoghi Effendi, "Principles of Bahá'í Administration", p.24)

This right of the Local Spiritual Assembly to supervise the activities of individual members must, of course, be understood within the context of the individual's right to freely express his or her views to the Assembly and the right to ask the Assembly to reconsider a decision if the individual does not agree with it.

5.7 **TEACHING MINORITIES**

5.7.1 **Are there any minority groups in particular that the Australian Bahá'í community has been asked to teach?**

As noted in the 'introduction to this chapter, Australia has been asked to develop teaching plans to attract each ethnic and racial element of the population. The Universal House of Justice has singled out the Aboriginal, Chinese, Greek and Turkish communities, for special mention:-

The achievements in the field of teaching the Aborigines and Chinese are truly noteworthy, and indicate fertile areas for sustained and diligent teaching efforts. In addition, the Outback Project stands out as an endeavour which should be given high priority to consolidate the victories already won among the Aboriginal people and establish a firm foundation for further growth in that deeply cherished community. Other groups which could be further cultivated are the Greek and Turkish communities.

(letter written on behalf of the Universal House of Justice to the National Spiritual Assembly of Australia, dated April 14, 1989)

5.7.2 *What are the guidelines relating to Aboriginal teaching?*

The National Spiritual Assembly has issued the following guidelines:-

1. Bahá'í friends planning to teach in Aboriginal areas should familiarise themselves with the guidance of the Universal House of Justice on mass teaching in "Wellspring of Guidance", p.31-and with this Chapter.
2. Travel teachers should make arrangements for their proposed teaching trip either through the National Bahá'í Teaching Committee or by contacting the Regional Teaching Committee concerned directly. Plans can then be properly coordinated and the best possible arrangements to make use of the travel teacher's abilities can be made. In some cases permission has to be obtained from the Regional Teaching Committee to travel teach in sensitive areas, and where a permit is required for entry to an Aboriginal reserve, the Regional Teaching Committee could obtain one beforehand to save the travel teacher an unnecessary delay.
3. Visiting teachers must consult with, and obey, the institutions of the Faith in whose area of jurisdiction they teach. In this way they will become aware of the teaching requirements and local conditions, and the friends of the area will be better prepared to receive and assist them, and afterwards, to follow up. The teacher should be aware that he is assisting and working with those already in the area, and that it is their joint and harmonious cooperation which will achieve results. Believers who disobey Bahá'í institutions may be debarred from subsequent teaching trips by the National Spiritual Assembly on the recommendation of the National Bahá'í Teaching Committee.
4. It is important to report back to the institutions of the area, and acquaint them with the details of the teaching trip, so that they in turn may follow on with the work.
5. From "Wellspring of Guidance", p.36:-

   The friends must teach with conviction, determination, genuine love, lack of prejudice, and a simple language addressed to the heart. Many good teachers in the field have said that particularly in teaching Aborigines a willingness to listen, and a patient and nurturing approach produce the best results. It is preferable to stay for some time in the area, to give the new Aboriginal friends a feeling of stability. Communication is not always easy; a trust needs to be built and there needs to be enough time to think as well as to speak. A letter written on behalf of Shoghi Effendi on April 9, 1955, says:-The Guardian thinks perhaps a different approach to the aborigines might attract them; one of being interested in their lives and their folklore, and of trying to become their friend, rather than trying to change them or improve them.

6. As many Aboriginal communities are still strongly based on tribal laws and customs, it would be helpful to learn about the Aboriginal protocol of an area when visiting it, and to become informed of some of the common 'dos' and 'don'ts'. If visiting teachers are aware of these matters and respectful of time honoured systems of belief and behaviour, they will be more likely to be accepted, and less in danger of causing offence.
7. In teaching the Faith no reference should be made to material benefits, such as promises of fares to conferences, etc. Only the pure Teachings should be given, and social and economic guidance provided.
8. Any promises made should be scrupulously kept.
9. Singing, music and simple audio-visual teaching aids are always a great help. However, teaching aids suited to children should not be presented to adults. The teacher's attitude should reflect equality, and should not be patronising or condescending. This is most important.
10. The process of declaration

From "Wellspring of Guidance", p.32:-

> *The declarants need not know all the proofs, history, laws, and principles of the Faith, but in the process of declaring themselves they must, in addition to catching the spark of faith, become basically informed about the Central Figures of the Faith, as well as the existence of laws they must follow and an administration they must obey.*

Before accepting a believer's declaration the Local Spiritual Assembly of the area or the Regional Teaching Committee must satisfy itself that the conditions described in the paragraph above have been fulfilled.

5.7.3 What are the guidelines relating to teaching citizens of the People's Republic of China (PRC) temporarily in Australia?

The Universal House of Justice has provided the following guidelines for teaching citizens of the People's Republic of China outside of China:-

1. Contact with Chinese Government officials:-

   > *...Bahá'ís are encouraged to foster friendships with officials of Chinese Embassies or Legations when opportunities present themselves, to acquaint these individuals with the basic tenets of the Faith and our adherence to the principle of loyalty to government. This should be carried out with discretion so that it does not appear that they are being singled out for indoctrination or conversion. If directly asked about the status of the Faith on the Chinese mainland, the friends may say that there are no Bahá'í communities or institutions established there, although there are, no doubt, individual Bahá'ís in various localities. They may also say that there are Bahá'í organisations in Hong Kong, Macau, and Taiwan.*

   (guidelines from the Universal House of Justice, dated April 19, 1989)

2. Social contacts:-

   > *Bahá'ís will undoubtedly find many occasions to meet visitors from the PRC and should certainly introduce them to the Faith and its Teachings as opportunities present themselves. However, caution and*

CHAPTER FIVE

wisdom should be exercised to avoid anything which may make these Chinese visitors uncomfortable. Attendance at Bahá'í functions should be left to their discretion, and the fact that citizens of the PRC are engaged in or participating in Bahá'í activities should not be publicised, even amongst Bahá'ís.

(guidelines from the Universal House of Justice, dated April 19, 1989)

3. Business and professional contacts:-

Individual Bahá'ís with academic, professional, or particular business credentials are urged to take advantage of natural situations in the course of their work to meet their peers from the People's Republic of China. They are also encouraged, whenever feasible, to offer their services in projects which may take them into the Chinese mainland. In this way they may be able to establish cordial contact with high officials as well as with individual Chinese citizens.

(letter written on behalf of the Universal House of Justice to a National Spiritual Assembly, dated April 19, 1989)

4. Chinese studies:-

Efforts should also be made to increase the awareness of the Bahá'í youth to the importance of meeting Chinese people at school and at work. Furthermore, they should be encouraged to take up studies in the Chinese language and culture when possible and to specialise in their respective professions on aspects related to China. Bahá'í scholars and experts on China are needed to assist in establishing the Faith in China.

(letter written on behalf of the Universal House of Justice to a National Spiritual Assembly, dated April 19, 1989)

5. Maintaining contact with Chinese Bahá'ís who have returned to the PRC:-

There is no specific way of keeping in touch with these Bahá'ís after they have returned to the PRC. It is suggested that the teacher who brings the person into the Faith assume responsibility to keep in touch with his Bahá'í friend. Prior to returning to his homeland, a Chinese Bahá'í may wish to arrange for a trusted individual overseas to forward news which he may wish to pass on to Bahá'í institutions in the future. Since mail is sometimes censored, it is advised that his Bahá'í membership or activities in the Faith not be mentioned in correspondence between the PRC and overseas. If a Bahá'í living in the PRC feels it advisable, he is free to invite Bahá'ís from overseas who travel through his country to visit him. However, overseas Bahá'ís should inform the House of Justice before making such visits. In general, Bahá'í literature should not be sent into the PRC. When Bahá'ís residing there request literature, Bahá'í publications in a language other than Chinese and which is of a general spiritual nature, such as "The Hidden Words", may be sent gradually over a period of time.

(Universal House of Justice guidelines, dated April 19, 1989)

CHAPTER FIVE

The National Chinese Teaching Committee has been appointed by the National Spiritual Assembly to take direct responsibility for teaching Chinese people. In some Regional Teaching Committee areas the National Chinese Teaching Committee has established Chinese working groups which operate in collaboration with the Regional Teaching Committee. Local Spiritual Assemblies requiring assistance in teaching Chinese people should contact the relevant working group or the National Chinese Teaching Committee.

5.7.4 **What about teaching Chinese who are residents of Australia?**

The Universal House of Justice has attached high priority to teaching Chinese residents of other countries:-

> *Increasing emphasis must also be placed on the teaching work among Chinese who have been long settled in your country as well as those who are students or long-term visitors from places with large Chinese populations such as Hong Kong, Macau, Malaysia, Singapore, or Taiwan. Historically, the Chinese overseas have been an important source of finance and expertise for their ancestral homeland. No doubt a great number of overseas Bahá'ís of Chinese background, many of whom may still have family relations in China, will be needed to take the Faith there in the future.*
>
> (letter written on behalf of the Universal House of Justice to a National Spiritual Assembly, dated April 19, 1989)

Again, assistance is available from the National Chinese Teaching Committee and its regional working groups.

5.7.5 **What guidelines relate to teaching Muslims from the Middle-East and North Africa?**

Bahá'ís are not permitted to single out Muslims from the Middle-East and North Africa, especially Iranian Muslims, to teach them the Faith. Should such a person become spontaneously attracted to the Faith he or she may, with caution, be taught. Enrolment in the Faith is, however, a different issue which must be considered on a case by case basis:-

> *The instructions of the beloved Guardian regarding teaching orientals from the Middle East are to be upheld, even more so at this time because of the present situation in Iran. Iranian Muslims in particular should not be sought out in order to teach them the Faith.*
>
> (letter written on behalf of the Universal House of Justice to a National Spiritual Assembly, dated February 6, 1986)

> *There are certain principles governing association with persons from Middle Eastern Muslim countries. Bahá'ís in the West are not to initiate any attempts to teach the Faith to Muslims from Middle Eastern countries. This includes Muslims from Iran, North Africa and Arab countries. Muslims from these countries who have become citizens of the United States or have acquired permanent resident status and who show a genuine interest in learning about the Faith may be taught the Faith but it is they who must take the initiative. If a Muslim should ask for information on the Faith, the information he seeks may be given according to the dictates of wisdom, but Bahá'ís should not exceed the request that has been made by attempting to convert the person, interest him further or invite him to Bahá'í meetings. In short, Bahá'ís are not to make a project of teaching Muslims. Although there*

CHAPTER FIVE

are certain restrictions about teaching Muslims from some countries and accepting them into the Faith, it is a different situation with Muslims from India or Pakistan as compared with those from Iran or the Near East.

(letter written on behalf of the Universal House of Justice to a National Spiritual Assembly, dated September 22, 1983)

If a person of Iranian Muslim background is spontaneously attracted to the Faith through his contact with the Bahá'ís, there would be no objection if a suitable Bahá'í friend were to assist him or her to understand the Cause. Whether or not such a person, upon claiming to accept Bahá'u'lláh and His Teachings, is enrolled in the Bahá'í community is a different issue which has to be considered separately in each case.

(guidelines issued by the Universal House of Justice, dated June 20, 1989)

This does not mean that the Bahá'ís should have no contact with Muslims, especially as some have Muslim relatives and close Muslim friends. It does mean they should not initiate attempts to teach these friends and relatives the Faith. Nor should they give information about the situation of the Bahá'ís in Iran or become embroiled in political activities:-

Furthermore, some Bahá'ís have relatives and close friends who are Iranian Muslims and who happen to reside in the West, and the Bahá'ís are not expected to relinquish these friendships nor should they cut themselves off from their Muslim relatives, as this would be contrary to the spirit of our Faith. They should, however, use wisdom and moderation in their contacts with such persons, avoid to the extent possible giving information about the activities of Bahá'ís in Iran, and take care not to become embroiled in any political activities. They should not try to teach the Faith to such people.

(guidelines from the Universal House of Justice, dated June 20, 1989)

With the above points in mind, the National Spiritual Assembly issues the following advice:
1. Individual Bahá'ís should feel free to use their own judgement in making friends with Muslims and socialising with them if they choose to do so. However, in doing so they should refrain from trying to teach them, avoid entering into arguments and disputes with them and should have the following warning from the Universal House of Justice in mind:-

   As you know, Iranians have a number of societies and organisations; some are admittedly cultural, others are politically oriented, even if seemingly cultural in purpose. These organisations are frequented by people whose standards are not compatible with those of the Faith. Obviously, association with such groups could exert a baneful influence on some of the Bahá'ís, particularly the youth.

   (letter written on behalf of the Universal House of Justice to a National Spiritual Assembly, dated February 6, 1986)

2. Invitations to Iranian Muslims to meetings set up for the specific purpose of teaching

the Faith, such as public meetings or firesides, are generally contrary to the guidance regarding teaching of Muslims. An exception to this ruling may exist, however, in the case of Muslim family members of a Bahá'í or Iranians who are permanent residents in Australia and have no apparent ulterior motives. Where such persons express a sincere interest in the Faith, Bahá'u'lláh's message may be shared with them.

3. Only close Muslim friends who know that Bahá'ís do not involve themselves in political activities and religious disputation and are willing to respect this attitude may be invited to social events such as a Naw-Rúz party and picnics organised by Bahá'í bodies.

4. Iranian Muslims living outside of Iran are becoming increasingly interested in receiving accurate information about the Faith. The best way to meet this interest is to refer such people to appropriate literature in Persian:-

> ...it has been observed that Iranian Muslims are becoming increasingly interested in receiving accurate information about the Faith which, in their homeland, has always been maligned and misrepresented by its enemies. It can only be to the advantage of the Faith if Iranian Muslims residing outside Iran are acquainted with the history and tenets of the Faith. Care must be taken, however, that in doing so, Bahá'ís do not become enmeshed in the affairs of the Iranian Muslims, nor should they spend much time participating in their social life. It is preferable that such persons be referred to appropriate literature in Persian which can be obtained from various National Spiritual Assemblies and made available to them through public libraries and universities, by mail or personal conveyance.

(guidelines from the Universal House of Justice, dated June 20, 1989)

5. As to the teaching of Muslims who come from areas other than Iran, North Africa and the Arab countries, the friends should follow the above guidance; that is, they should not go out of their way to teach them. If, through their own perseverance and effort such Muslims reach the stage of declaring, the matter must be referred to the National Spiritual Assembly.

5.7.6 *What guidelines apply to teaching Malaysians?*

Muslims from Malaysia may be informed of the Faith and given Bahá'í literature; however, they may not be enrolled as Bahá'ís if they are returning to Malaysia because it is against the law of their country. Malaysians from a non-Muslim background may be taught and may be enrolled in the Faith.

5.7.7 *What guidelines apply to teaching people from Eastern Europe, Russia and the former Soviet republics?*

Bahá'ís in Australia are encouraged to teach people from these countries who are now resident in Australia; or who are presently visiting. Bahá'í literature may be given to visitors from these countries:-

> *Another way of helping the teaching work in Eastern bloc countries is by singling out people from those countries studying, working or just visiting in your home or neighbouring communities. If they are attracted to the Teachings of the Faith they will one day take them back to their homelands.*

> *...It is certainly 'wise and legal,' in fact even desirable, to give - with wisdom - Bahá'í literature to people from the East who express interest in the Faith.*
>
> (letter written on behalf of the Universal House of Justice to an individual believer, dated February 10, 1989)

5.7.8 *May sub-normal or mentally ill people be taught the Faith?*

Bahá'ís should not make a project of teaching people who are mentally ill. Nevertheless, the Bahá'í Faith is open to all; thus sub-normal and mentally ill people are welcome and may be enrolled in the Faith except in instances of extreme illness.

5.8 NOTES FOR REGISTERED GROUPS

The main aim of Registered Groups should be to teach the Faith in their area so as to raise their status to that of a Local Spiritual Assembly as soon as possible. In so doing they should work in cooperation with their Regional Teaching Committee and, if applicable, the Local Spiritual Assembly in whose extension goal area the Group is formed.

CHAPTER SIX

Chapter 6

6. **Nineteen Day Feasts and Bahá'í Holy Days**

6.1 **ORIGINS AND PURPOSE OF THE NINETEEN DAY FEAST**

6.1.1 *What is the origin of the Nineteen Day Feast?*

> *The Nineteen-Day Feast was inaugurated by the Báb and ratified by Bahá'u'lláh, in His Holy Book, the Aqdas...*
>
> ('Abdu'l-Bahá, in "Principles of Bahá'í Administration", p.52)

The three aspects of the Feast - devotional, administrative, social - evolved in stages over time:-

> *It is notable that the concept of the Feast evolved in stages in relation to the development of the Faith. At its earliest stage in Iran, the individual friends, in response to Bahá'u'lláh's injunctions, hosted gatherings in their homes to show hospitality once every nineteen days and derived inspiration from the reading and discussion of the Teachings. As the community grew, 'Abdu'l-Bahá delineated and emphasised the devotional and social character of the event. After the establishment of Local Spiritual Assemblies, Shoghi Effendi introduced the administrative portion and acquainted the community with the idea of the Nineteen Day Feast as an institution. It was as if a symphony, in three movements, had now been completed.*
>
> (letter from the Universal House of Justice to the Followers of Bahá'u'lláh, dated August 27, 1989)

6.1.2 *What is the purpose of the Nineteen Day Feast?*

Shoghi Effendi has described the Feast as the foundation of the New World Order. It brings together at the base of society the spiritual, administrative and social processes necessary for the construction of a new civilisation. Its aim is to promote unity, ensure progress and foster joy:-

> *The World Order of Bahá'u'lláh encompasses all units of human society; integrates the spiritual, administrative and social processes of life; and canalises human expression in its varied forms towards the construction of a new civilisation. The Nineteen Day Feast embraces all these aspects at the very base of society. Functioning in the village, the town, the city, it is an institution of which all the people of Bahá are members. It is intended to promote unity, ensure progress, and foster joy...*
>
> (letter from the Universal House of Justice to the Followers of Bahá'u'lláh, dated August 27, 1989)

A properly conducted Feast should result in the spiritual restoration of the friends:-

> *As to the Nineteen Day Feast, it rejoiceth mind and heart. If this feast be held in the proper fashion, the friends will, once in nineteen days, find themselves spiritually restored, and endued with a power that is not of this world.*

CHAPTER SIX

("Selections from the Writings of 'Abdu'l-Bahá" {revised edition},
Bahá'í World Centre, 1982, sec. 51, p.91)

It also provides a forum within which the participants are educated in the essentials of responsible citizenship:-

> *...considered in its local sphere alone there is much to thrill and amaze the heart. Here [the Feast] links the individual to the collective processes by which a society is built or restored. Here, for instance, the Feast is an arena of democracy at the very root of society, where the Local Spiritual Assembly and the members of the community meet on common ground, where individuals are free to offer their gifts of thought, whether as new ideas or constructive criticism, to the building processes of an advancing civilisation. Thus it can be seen that aside from its spiritual significance, this common institution of the people combines an array of elemental social disciplines which educate its participants in the essentials of responsible citizenship.*

(letter from the Universal House of Justice to the Followers of
Bahá'u'lláh, dated August 27, 1989)

[See the above letter in "The Nineteen Day Feast", compilation of the Universal House of Justice, 1989, published by the National Spiritual Assembly of the Bahá'ís of Australia.]

6.2 PREPARATION OF AND FOR THE FEAST

6.2.1 *Who hosts the Nineteen Day Feast?*

Article XII of the "By-Laws of a Local Spiritual Assembly" places this responsibility on the Local Spiritual Assembly. The Universal House of Justice notes, however, that Local Spiritual Assemblies often call upon individuals to make the preparations:-

> *...Although the Local Spiritual Assembly is administratively responsible for the conduct of the Feast, it often calls upon an individual or a group of individuals to make preparations...Such individuals can act as hosts and are sometimes concerned with the selection of the prayers and readings for the devotional portion; they may also attend to the social portion.*

(letter from the Universal House of Justice to the Followers of
Bahá'u'lláh, dated August 27, 1989)

> *Such a practice 'is consonant with the spirit of hospitality so vital to the occasion'*

(letter from the Universal House of Justice to the Followers of
Bahá'u'lláh, cited above).

6.2.2 *What are the responsibilities of the host?*

Above all, as noted above, the host has a responsibility to provide hospitality to the friends:-

> *...the Nineteen Day Feast...is ordained in the "Kitáb-i-Aqdas" in these words: "It hath been enjoined upon you once a month to offer hospitality, even should ye serve no more than water, for God hath willed to bind your hearts together, though it be through heavenly and earthly means combined". It is clear, then, that the Feast is rooted*

CHAPTER SIX

in hospitality, with all its implications of friendliness, courtesy, service, generosity and conviviality.

(letter from the Universal House of Justice to the Followers of Bahá'u'lláh, dated August 27, 1989)

The host, with complete self-effacement, showing kindness to all, must be a comfort to each one, and serve the friends with his own hands.

('Abdu'l-Bahá, from a Tablet to an individual believer - translated from the Persian, in "The Nineteen Day Feast", compilation of the Universal House of Justice (1989), p.1)

The Universal House of Justice has also noted that:-

In small communities the aspect of personal hospitality is easy to carry out, but in large communities the Local Spiritual Assemblies, while retaining the concept of hospitality, may find it necessary to devise other measures.

(letter from the Universal House of Justice to the Followers of Bahá'u'lláh, cited above)

6.2.3 **What are some other important aspects of the preparation for the Feast?**

The Universal House of Justice has listed the following as being important aspects of the preparation for the Feast:
1. *proper selection of readings*
2. *the assignment, in advance, of good readers*
3. *a sense of decorum both in the preparation and the reception of the devotional programme*
4. *attention to the environment in which the Feast is to be held, whether indoors or outdoors*
5. *cleanliness*
6. *arrangement of the space in practical and decorative ways*
7. *punctuality*

(letter from the Universal House of Justice to the Followers of Bahá'u'lláh, dated August 27, 1989)

6.2.4 **How should the believers prepare themselves for attending the Feast?**

The believers should prepare themselves before entering the Feast by emptying their hearts of all else save God:-

But when you present yourselves in the meetings, before entering them, free yourselves from all that you have in your heart, free your thoughts and your minds from all else save God, and speak to your heart...so that you may be gathered together with the utmost love... ...Each one of you must think how to make happy and pleased the other members of your Assembly, and each one must consider all those who are present as better and greater than himself, and each one must consider himself less than the rest. Know their station as high, and think of your own station as low...

('Abdu'l-Bahá, in "Star of the West", vol. IV, no. 7 (13 July 1913), p.120)

CHAPTER SIX

6.2.5 ***May a Local Spiritual Assembly hold a joint Feast with another community?***

There is no objection to two or more communities holding joint Feasts occasionally, however, this should not be done on a regular basis, as it does not fulfil the purpose of the Nineteen Day Feast in the strict sense:-

> *With respect to your question asking whether a Local Spiritual Assembly may cancel its Nineteen Day Feast in order to attend Feast in another community the House of Justice advises that the Nineteen Day Feast should not be cancelled. However, there is no objection to two or more local communities holding a joint Nineteen Day Feast occasionally, although it is not proper to allow such joint Feasts to be held on a regular basis. If members of a community find that the plan to hold such a joint Feast would produce inconvenience to them, they should take the matter up with their Local Spiritual Assembly.*
>
> (letter written on behalf of the Universal House of Justice to an individual believer, dated April 26, 1987)

> *If a local community, under the direction of its Local Assembly, observes Nineteen Day Feasts regularly, and it occasionally has a joint Feast with one or more other communities, you may credit in your statistics each Assembly for having held its own Nineteen Day Feast. You, of course, realise that joint Feasts do not fulfil the purpose of the Nineteen Day Feast in its strict sense, and should not become a regular practice among the friends.*
>
> (letter written on behalf of the Universal House of Justice to a National Spiritual Assembly, dated February 15, 1982)

A joint Feast cannot completely fulfil the functions of a Nineteen Day Feast because the Nineteen Day Feast is intended as an opportunity for the community to discuss local affairs and make recommendations to its Assembly. Clearly this cannot be done during a combined Feast.

6.2.6 ***Who may call the Feast if the Local Spiritual Assembly is not exercising its responsibilities in this regard?***

The Universal House of Justice has said that the assistants to the Auxiliary Boards may encourage believers to come together for the Feast, as an interim measure, in communities in which the Local Spiritual Assembly is not exercising its responsibilities in this regard. A Feast can only be an official administrative occasion, however, when there is a Local Spiritual Assembly to take charge of it.

6.2.7 ***Should groups and isolated believers observe the Nineteen Day Feast?***

Yes. Groups and isolated believers are encouraged to hold their own Feasts, even though the Feast can only be an official administrative occasion when there is a Local Spiritual Assembly to take charge of it:-

> *In reply to your letter of November 8th we feel that all friends, whatever their circumstances, should be encouraged to observe the Nineteen Day Feast. Obviously it can only be an official administrative occasion where there is a Local Spiritual Assembly to take charge of it, present reports to the friends, and receive their recommendations. But groups, spontaneous gatherings of friends, and even isolated believers should*

CHAPTER SIX

certainly remember the day and say prayers together. In the case of a group it may well hold the Feast in the manner in which a Local Spiritual Assembly would do so, recognising of course that it has no official administrative standing.

(letter written by the Universal House of Justice to a National Spiritual Assembly, dated December 1, 1968)

Members of groups and isolated believers are also welcome to attend the Feast of a neighbouring community.

6.3 PROGRAMME

6.3.1 *What are the three parts of the Feast programme?*

The three parts of the Feast programme are:
1. devotional
2. administrative
3. social

What does the devotional section involve?

> *The devotional section 'entails the recitation of prayers and reading from the Holy Texts'*

(letter from the Universal House of Justice to the Followers of Bahá'u'lláh, dated August 27, 1989).

6.3.2 *What may be read during the devotional section of the Nineteen Day Feast?*

Prayers and meditations from the Writings of Bahá'u'lláh, the Báb and 'Abdu'l-Bahá may be read during the devotional section of the Feast. They may be followed by readings from other Bahá'í Sacred Writings, Holy Scriptures of previous Dispensations and the writings of Shoghi Effendi. It is clear, however, that Shoghi Effendi would not wish his writings to be interspersed with readings from Holy Scripture:-

> *...the Feast is opened with devotional readings, that is to say prayers and meditations, from the Writings of Bahá'u'lláh, the Báb and the Master. Following this passages may be read from other Tablets, from the Holy Scriptures of previous Dispensations, and from the writings of the Guardian. It is clear, however, that the beloved Guardian would not wish his own words to be read as part of an arranged devotional programme in which they would be interspersed among words of Holy Scripture. In other words, at the Nineteen Day Feast, where words of the Guardian are to be read they should follow any selections from the Scriptures and not be mixed with them. This does not mean, however, that subsequently in the Feast, any of these types of writing may not be read as suitable during the consultation.*

(letter of the Universal House of Justice to the Hands of the Cause of God, dated August 25, 1965; cited in a letter from the Universal House of Justice to an individual believer, dated October 15, 1972)

Shoghi Effendi expressed a preference that the Bahá'ís read from their own Holy Writings rather than those of other Dispensations:-

> *...he feels that although in principle there is certainly no reason why excerpts from other Sacred Scriptures should not be read in the Spiritual part of our Feasts, that as this is particularly an occasion when Bahá'ís*

CHAPTER SIX

get together to deepen their own spiritual life, it is, generally speaking, advisable for them to read from their own Holy Writings in the spiritual part of the Feast.

(letter written on behalf of Shoghi Effendi to an individual believer, dated February 18, 1954)

Note that Shoghi Effendi's Persian writings are different in character from his English writings and contain devotional passages that are suitable for reading during the devotional part of the Feast. This explains why they have been used in the devotional section of Feasts in Iran:-

Concerning the permissibility of reading selections from the writings of the beloved Guardian at Nineteen Day Feasts in Persia: it is true, as you rightly point out, that the beloved Guardian in a letter to the National Spiritual Assembly of the United States stated that only the Writings of Bahá'u'lláh and 'Abdu'l-Bahá should be read during the devotional part of the Nineteen Day Feast...

...it should be borne in mind that the Persian writings of Shoghi Effendi are unique in nature, and many of them, unlike his English letters and messages addressed to the western believers, are interspersed with supplications, prayers and homilies of a devotional character which are suitable for the spiritual part of Bahá'í Feasts.

(letter of the Universal House of Justice to an individual believer, dated October 15, 1972)

6.3.3 What does the administrative section involve?

The administrative section entails:-

...a general meeting where the Local Spiritual Assembly reports its activities, plans and problems to the community, shares news and messages from the World Centre and the National Assembly, and receives the thoughts and recommendations of the friends through a process of consultation.

(letter from the Universal House of Justice to the Followers of Bahá'u'lláh, dated August 27, 1989)

The consultative section of the Feast provides the chief opportunity the community has to discuss the affairs of the Cause and make recommendations to its Local and National Assemblies:-

The chief opportunity which the friends have for discussion on administrative questions is during the Nineteen Day Feasts, at which time the members of the Assembly can meet with the body of the believers and discuss in common the affairs of the Cause, and suggest new policies and methods...

(letter written on behalf of Shoghi Effendi to an individual believer, dated March 27, 1938)

...the Nineteen Day Feast...besides its social and spiritual aspects, fulfils various administrative needs and requirements of the Community, chief among them being the need for open and constructive criticism

CHAPTER SIX

and deliberation regarding the state of affairs within the local Bahá'í Community.

(letter written on behalf of Shoghi Effendi to an individual believer, dated December 13, 1939)

The main purpose of the Nineteen Day Feasts is to enable individual believers to offer any suggestion to the Local Assembly, which in its turn will pass it to the National Spiritual Assembly...The Convention should be regarded as a temporary gathering, having certain specific functions to perform during a limited period of time. Its status is thus limited in time to the Convention sessions, the function of consultation at all other times being vested in the entire body of the believers through the Local Spiritual Assemblies.

(letter written on behalf of Shoghi Effendi to a National Spiritual Assembly, dated November 18, 1933).

It is important to note that matters of a personal nature should not be brought up at the Feast. Also note that a Local Spiritual Assembly is not bound to pass on suggestions made by its community to the National Spiritual Assembly, but will do so at its own discretion.

6.3.4 Who conducts the administrative section of the Feast?

The Assembly Chairman, or some other appointed representative of the Assembly, conducts this section of the Feast. This person should not be a youth:-

It would not be administratively proper for a Bahá'í youth under 21 years of age to act as Chairman of the Nineteen Day Feast. However, no great issue should be made of this as it is a purely minor matter.

(letter written on behalf of the Universal House of Justice to a National Spiritual Assembly, dated February 22, 1984)

6.3.5 How is the administrative section of the Feast organised?

Typically, the Chairman of the Feast will call for reports from the Local Spiritual Assembly Secretary and Treasurer. The Chairman may then call for items to be placed on an agenda for consultation and open the meeting up for general discussion, during which time suggestions and recommendations can be made to the Assembly. The above is intended as a guide only, and is not a prescription for how this section must be organised.

6.3.6 What matters should the Assembly bring to the Feast for consultation?

A Local Spiritual Assembly will typically bring the following matters to the Feast:
1. the teaching work
2. international and national news received by the Assembly
3. correspondence from the National Spiritual Assembly or national committees
4. the Fund
5. actions of the local Assembly on community recommendations from a previous Feast
6. local committee activities
7. other items of general interest to the community
8. national communications items from the Australian Bahá'í Bulletin (which of course includes Treasurer's Report)

CHAPTER SIX

6.3.7 ***How does the community make recommendations to the Assembly at the Feast?***

Recommendations may be given to the Assembly after having been passed by a majority vote of the believers present, or they may simply be noted down during the consultation. The Assembly is bound to consider formal recommendations made by the Feast to the Assembly:-

> *If the friends at a Nineteen Day Feast agree with a recommendation, either unanimously or by a majority, it constitutes a recommendation from the Feast to the Assembly. On the other hand, if an individual believer makes a suggestion that other friends do not take up, it may still be considered by the Assembly...*
>
> (letter written on behalf of the Universal House of Justice to a National Spiritual Assembly, dated July 27, 1982)

Only adult members of the community may vote on recommendations:-

> *Bahá'í youth between the ages of 15 and 21 may certainly take part in discussions, and should be encouraged to do so, but they may not vote on recommendations to the Assembly until they are 21.*
>
> (letter written on behalf of the Universal House of Justice to a National Spiritual Assembly, dated September 16, 1979)

Visitors to the community may participate in the consultation but may not vote:-

> *As to visitors to a Nineteen Day Feast, Bahá'ís from anywhere in the world should of course be warmly welcomed, and may take part in consultation. However, only members of the local community can vote on recommendations to the Local Spiritual Assembly.*
>
> (letter from the Universal House of Justice to a National Spiritual Assembly, dated December 1, 1968)

It is for the Assembly to decide which method of accepting recommendations to adopt, based on the size and nature of its community. The important point, as laid down in the By-Laws, is that the Assembly always seeks the advice of its community and keeps it informed of all its affairs:-

> *As cited in Article IV of the By-Laws of a Local Spiritual Assembly, "While retaining the sacred right of final decision in all matters pertaining to the Bahá'í community, the Spiritual Assembly shall ever seek the advice and consultation of all members of the community, keep the community informed of all its affairs, and invite full and free discussion on the part of the community of all matters affecting the Faith."*
>
> *The actual voting on recommendations made at Nineteen Day Feasts to decide whether they should be forwarded to the Local Assembly is a secondary matter which may be left for decision by the Local Spiritual Assemblies themselves. It is not prohibited that the Local Assembly Secretary record suggestions made at Nineteen Day Feasts for consideration by the Assembly. The important point to keep in mind is the provision made in the By-Laws as mentioned above.*
>
> (memorandum written by the Universal House of Justice to the International Teaching Centre, dated January 21, 1982)

CHAPTER SIX

6.3.8 *Who records recommendations made at the Feast?*

The Secretary of the Assembly or some other appointed representative of the Assembly records the recommendations and suggestions made in order to report these to the Local Spiritual Assembly for its consideration. Whatever action is taken by the Assembly is reported to the community at a later Nineteen Day Feast.

6.3.9 *Does the Assembly have to read all communications received for the community, in full, at the Feast?*

No. Reading of long letters at a Feast can become a boring experience, especially for new believers. Other means should also be found for sharing information, eg. through a local newsletter. The number and length of local committee reports at Feasts should likewise be restricted:-

> *We note from reading your minutes that the enthusiasm of some of the new believers is being tested by the reading of long, wordy letters at Nineteen Day Feasts, and we think that something should be done about this. While it is important that the believers be informed about important messages from the Holy Land and other important items, it is true that the reading of messages at Nineteen Day Feasts can become a very boring and trying experience particularly for new believers not acquainted with many aspects of Bahá'í administration. We think you should consider other ways and means by which believers could be informed of vital and necessary information, such as through bulletins, institutes and other meetings.*
>
> (letter written by the Universal House of Justice to a National Spiritual Assembly, dated September 6, 1971)

> *...the administrative portion of the Feast should not be laborious or burdensome. It can become so because too many reports by too many local Bahá'í committees are presented at one Feast. Such reports could perhaps be conveyed in bulletins.*
>
> (letter written on behalf of the Universal House of Justice to all National Spiritual Assemblies, dated August 28, 1989)

The National Spiritual Assembly and its committees also have a responsibility not to overburden the Feast with too many items.

6.3.10 *Should the proceedings of the Feast be translated into another language, eg. Persian, for the benefit of non-English speaking friends?*

No. The Feast should be conducted in whatever is the conventional local language. There is no objection to some of the readings being in the language of the immigrants, or to the immigrants having some separate gatherings of their own, conducted in their own language; however, they should not expect official Bahá'í functions such as the Feast, to be either conducted in, or translated into, their own language. Rather, the immigrants should seek to learn the language of the country in which they are now living:-

> *The Local Spiritual Assembly of ... is correct in its decision to conduct the Nineteen Day Feasts in Spanish and to not translate the proceedings in Persian, especially in view of the fact that some of the Spanish friends are becoming alienated from the community. Although the Iranian believers should make every effort to attend the Nineteen Day Feasts, they should not expect such meetings to be conducted in Persian. They*

> *should try to learn Spanish, particularly if they are planning to make their home in Spain. There is no objection, however, to Persian friends if they so wish having special meetings for fellowship and deepening conducted in Persian.*
>
> (letter written on behalf of the Universal House of Justice to a National Spiritual Assembly, dated February 6, 1983)

> *Nineteen Day Feasts and Local Spiritual Assembly meetings should be conducted in English or French, as the case may be, since these are the languages of your country. If, however, it is possible to make arrangements for the Iranians who have not yet learned the language to benefit in some way from the topics discussed at such meetings, this factor could be taken into consideration.*
>
> (letter written on behalf of the Universal House of Justice to a National Spiritual Assembly, dated February 7, 1984)

The Universal House of Justice has also said:-

> *...it would not be appropriate for language or racial groups to hold separate Nineteen Day Feasts or to have separate Bahá'í Centres.*
>
> (letter written on behalf of the Universal House of Justice to a National Spiritual Assembly, dated August 13, 1986)

6.3.11 What does the social section involve?

The social section of the Feast:-

> *...involves the partaking of refreshments and engaging in other activities meant to foster fellowship in a culturally determined diversity of forms which do not violate principles of the Faith or the essential character of the Feast.*
>
> (letter from the Universal House of Justice to the Followers of Bahá'u'lláh, dated August 27, 1989)

For example, appropriate live entertainment might be arranged at this time; or the friends might watch videos such as the 'Bahá'í Newsreel'; or have the opportunity to socialise.

6.3.12 How much flexibility is permitted in the order of the Feast and the manner of its celebration?

It is not permissible to change the order of the Feast; however, it is permissible for the believers to gather together for a meal or social activities beforehand if they wish (eg. to welcome new believers), provided this does not take the place of the social section of the Feast itself:-

> *Regarding changing the order of the Feast, it is clear from Shoghi Effendi's instructions that the Nineteen Day Feast programme should start with the spiritual part, and not with the social part, which includes refreshments, or breaking bread together... However, if it is found that some sort of association among the friends or the serving of food and refreshments will be helpful, if this takes place at the outset, there is no objection to this practice, provided it is clear that it is not part of the Feast.*

CHAPTER SIX

(letter written on behalf of the Universal House of Justice to an individual believer, dated January 23, 1985)

We can understand the desire of some of the friends to provide a warm welcome at the Feasts to newly declared believers and particularly youth, and we see no objection to the Assembly giving a reception before the actual Feast to achieve this purpose. As the Feast is frequently held in the evening, the Assembly might consider it desirable to arrange for the believers to have a light evening meal together before the Feast is held or it could, for example, arrange for social activities of an appropriate kind while the friends are gathering prior to the actual commencement of the Nineteen Day Feast. This should not, however, take the place of the social part of the Feast itself.

(memorandum written by the Universal House of Justice to the Hands of the Cause residing in the Holy Land, dated January 21, 1973)

The Universal House of Justice has also noted that: 'Even though the observance of the Feast requires strict adherence to the threefold aspects in the sequence in which they have been defined, there is much room for variety in the total experience.'

(letter from the Universal House of Justice to the Followers of Bahá'u'lláh, dated August 27, 1989).

For instance:-

1. music may be introduced at various stages, including the devotional portion
2. 'Abdu'l-Bahá recommends that eloquent, uplifting talks be given
3. originality and variety in expressions of hospitality are possible
4. the quality and range of the consultation are critical to the spirit of the occasion

(letter from the Universal House of Justice to the Followers of Bahá'u'lláh, dated August 27, 1989)

Also:-

The effects of different cultures in all these respects are welcome factors which can lend the Feast a salutary diversity, representative of the unique characteristics of the various societies in which it is held, and therefore conducive to the upliftment and enjoyment of its participants.

(letter from the Universal House of Justice to the Followers of Bahá'u'lláh, dated August 27, 1989)

In encouraging such cultural diversity the Local Spiritual Assembly must 'be watchful that the incorporation of such elements does not lead to a degeneration of the Feast as a uniquely Bahá'í institution and, particularly, that no objectionable customs and practices begin to creep into its observance'

(letter written on behalf of the Universal House of Justice to all National Spiritual Assemblies, dated August 28, 1989).

CHAPTER SIX

6.3.13 *What kind of music may be played at the Feast?*

During the devotional portion of the Feast songs should be used whose words are from the Writings of the Báb, Bahá'u'lláh or 'Abdu'l-Bahá. Instrumental music may be used also:-

> We have noted in your Minutes of 27 December, page 1, a statement, "It was agreed to advise the friends in ... that it was not correct to sing a song composed by a Bahá'í at the devotional part of the Nineteen Day Feast." It is not clear what your framework of reference for consultation happened to be, nor if a direct question was referred to your National Assembly for decision. However, we feel that it will be helpful to you to know that songs whose words are the primary Writings of the Báb, Bahá'u'lláh or 'Abdu'l-Bahá are all quite fitting for the devotional portion of the Feast. Indeed, the Persian chants are such songs, out of a different tradition; they are a way of giving music to the holy Word, and each person who chants does it in a way which mirrors his feeling and expression of the Words he is uttering. As for songs whose words are poetic and the composition of persons other than the Figures of the Faith, these may be desirable but in their proper place, for, as you know, "music is the language of the spirit."
>
> Inasmuch as the spirit of our gathering is so much affected by the tone and quality of our worship, of our feeling and appreciation of the Word of God for this day, we would hope that you would encourage the most beautiful possible expression of the human spirits in your communities, through music among other modes of feeling.

> (letter written by the Universal House of Justice to a National Spiritual Assembly, dated February 22, 1971)

> Instrumental music may be used at the Bahá'í Feasts. There is no objection to showing appreciation by the clapping of hands.

> (letter written of behalf of Shoghi Effendi, dated August 20, 1956)

6.3.14 *May items be offered for sale during the Nineteen Day Feast?*

This matter lies within the discretion of the Local Spiritual Assembly, bearing in mind that the principal purpose of holding the Feast should not be lost sight of and that pressure should not be placed on the friends to participate in the purchase of articles offered for sale. The Universal House of Justice has expressed the preference that such sales not become habitual and that they not be conducted during the Feast itself.

6.3.15 *Is it permissible to smoke during a Feast?*

Smoking is not appropriate during the devotional part of the Feast. The Universal House of Justice has also said it is not right that believers who find smoking offensive should be made to endure it in Bahá'í meetings which they are required or expected to attend.

6.3.16 *Do any of the sections of the Feast have any more importance than any other?*

No. All are equally important and the Feast will be at its best when the three are properly combined:-

> The significance of the Nineteen Day Feast is thus threefold. It is a gathering of a devotional, social and administrative importance. When these three features are all combined, this Feast can and will surely

CHAPTER SIX

yield the best and the maximum of results.

(letter written on behalf of Shoghi Effendi to a National Spiritual Assembly, dated October 2, 1935)

6.4   **ATTENDANCE**

6.4.1   **Who may attend the Nineteen Day Feast?**

Only Bahá'ís may attend the Nineteen Day Feast:-

The Guardian wishes me to direct your attention to the fact that none of the institutions of the Faith nor its cardinal principles may be changed under any circumstances. The Nineteen Day Feast is an institution of the Cause ... These Nineteen Day Feasts are for the Bahá'ís, and the Bahá'ís exclusively, and no variation from this principle is permitted.

(letter written on behalf of Shoghi Effendi to a National Spiritual Assembly, dated May 28, 1954)

Bahá'í visitors from interstate and overseas and Bahá'ís living in isolated or group areas are welcome to attend the Feast:-

Any Bahá'í may attend a Feast — a local Bahá'í, a Bahá'í from out of town, certainly an isolated Bahá'í from the neighbourhood.

(letter written on behalf of Shoghi Effendi to a National Spiritual Assembly, dated May 27, 1957)

...Isolated believers and the members of groups may also, of course, attend the Nineteen Day Feasts of communities when they wish to.

(letter written on behalf of the Universal House of Justice to an individual believer, dated July 23, 1985)

Bahá'ís who are not members of the community may participate in the consultation but may not vote on recommendations. The Local Spiritual Assembly must, if necessary, check the credentials of visiting Bahá'ís and may not admit to the Feast visitors who are not known to the Bahá'ís and cannot show current credentials.

Shoghi Effendi also said that it 'is inconceivable and wholly inadmissible that any Bahá'í in a Community should be permitted to hold a Feast in their home and refuse admission to another believer...'

(letter written on behalf of Shoghi Effendi to a National Spiritual Assembly, dated May 27, 1957).

6.4.2   **What about Bahá'ís who are citizens of the People's Republic of China (PRC)?**

The sensitive position of Bahá'ís from the People's Republic of China must be recognised. Bahá'ís from the PRC should be introduced to each other as Bahá'ís only if they are willing for this to be done; therefore, it is recommended that it be left up to the individual to decide whether to attend functions such as the Feast, or not.

6.4.3   **May Bahá'ís without voting rights attend the Feast?**

No. Bahá'ís without voting rights may not attend Bahá'í-only functions, such as the Feast. A Bahá'í may also be barred by the National Spiritual Assembly from attending the Feast (partial loss of voting rights) if his or her behaviour is severely disrupting the Feast.

6.4.4 *Is attendance at the Feasts obligatory?*

No, but it is highly desirable:-

> *Attendance at Nineteen Day Feasts is not obligatory, but highly desirable, and effort should be made by the friends not to deprive themselves of this spiritual and communal rallying-point once in every Bahá'í month.*

(letter written on behalf of Shoghi Effendi to an individual believer, dated December 23, 1948)

The Local Spiritual Assembly has a responsibility to encourage the friends to attend the Feast; however, there are no penalties for failure to attend the Feast:-

> *In regard to the Nineteen Day Feasts, Shoghi Effendi is of the opinion that the believers should be impressed with the importance of attending these gatherings ...*
>
> *No radical action, such as the expulsion of any believer from the community, should, however, be taken in case anyone fails to attend these Feasts. It is for every individual believer to realise what the Cause requires from him in this matter.*

(letter written on behalf of Shoghi Effendi to an individual believer, dated December 22, 1934)

What if an individual has a teaching appointment at the same time as the Feast?

> *If an individual has a teaching appointment on the same evening as a Nineteen Day Feast, it is left to the individual to judge which is the most important.*

(letter written on behalf of Shoghi Effendi to an individual believer, dated August 20, 1956)

6.4.5 *Why are non-Bahá'ís not permitted to attend the Feast?*

Non-Bahá'ís are not permitted to attend because, although there is nothing secret about the Feast, it is essentially concerned with the domestic affairs of the Faith. As such, Bahá'ís should feel they have full freedom to express their views. It would also be embarrassing for any sensitive non-Bahá'í to find himself or herself in the middle of a discussion on matters of which he or she is not a part:-

> *Regarding the Nineteen Day Feast, the principle universally applicable is that non-Bahá'ís are not invited to attend, and if you are asked about this you can explain that the nature of the Feast is essentially domestic and administrative. During the period of consultation the Bahá'ís should be able to enjoy perfect freedom to express their views on the work of the Cause, unembarrassed by the feeling that all they are saying is being heard by someone who has not accepted Bahá'u'lláh and who might thereby gain a very distorted picture of the Faith. It would also be very embarrassing for any sensitive non-Bahá'í to find himself plunged into the midst of a discussion of the detailed affairs of a Bahá'í community of which he is not a part. A non-Bahá'í who asks to be invited to a Feast will usually understand if this matter is explained to him.*

CHAPTER SIX

(letter written on behalf of the Universal House of Justice to an individual believer, dated August 12, 1981)

It can be explained, in a friendly manner, that the Nineteen Day Feast is an entirely private religious and domestic occasion for the Bahá'í community when its internal affairs are discussed and its members meet for personal fellowship and worship. No great issue should be made of it for there is certainly nothing secret about the Feast but it is organised for Bahá'ís only.

(letter written on behalf of the Universal House of Justice to a National Spiritual Assembly, dated November 4, 1976)

6.4.6 **What should be done if a non-Bahá'í comes to the Feast?**

A Bahá'í should not invite a non-Bahá'í to the Feast. If, however, non-Bahá'ís come they should not be asked to leave, unless they are very close to the Faith and the request could be made without causing hurt feelings. What should be done is to omit the consultative part of the Feast:-

... when a non-Bahá'í does appear at a Feast he should not be asked to leave; rather the Assembly should omit the consultative part of the Feast, and the non-Bahá'í should be made welcome ... if the non-Bahá'í is well known to the Bahá'ís and no hurt feelings would be caused, he might be asked to retire during the consultative part. In general, however, it is much better to avoid such problems where possible...

(letter from the Universal House of Justice to an individual believer, dated March 24, 1970)

...if a non-Bahá'í does appear at a Nineteen Day Feast he should be made to feel welcome, but a Bahá'í should certainly not invite a non-Bahá'í to attend.

(letter written on behalf of the Universal House of Justice to an individual believer, dated January 23, 1985)

6.4.7 **What if the Feast is held at the home of a Bahá'í with a non-Bahá'í spouse?**

As in the case of attendance by any non-Bahá'í, the Assembly should omit the consultative part of the Feast. A non-Bahá'í spouse should, however, be permitted to attend the social and spiritual sections:-

The Universal House of Justice has noted item 13 on page 14 of your Minutes concerning a Muslim member of a family attending a Nineteen Day Feast. The following guidance on this subject was sent to a believer on 24 March 1970 by the House of Justice:

"...when a non-Bahá'í does appear at a Feast he should not be asked to leave; rather the Assembly should omit the consultative part of the Feast, and the non-Bahá'í should be made welcome."

No doubt you are familiar with this instruction. Likewise, occasionally if the Feast is held in the home of the family where the spouse is not a Bahá'í, it would be discourteous not to allow the non-Bahá'í member of the family to attend at least the social and spiritual parts of the Feast.

(letter written on behalf of the Universal House of Justice to the National Spiritual Assembly of Australia, dated January 8, 1985)

6.4.8 **What should the Local Spiritual Assembly do if the administrative part of the Feast has to be postponed?**

If the administrative part of the Feast has to be postponed, the Local Spiritual Assembly may, at its discretion, organise to hold this at another time during the Bahá'í month, or it may hold this section over until the next Feast:-

It is not quite correct to say that a Nineteen Day Feast is changed into a Unity Feast as a result of the presence of non-Bahá'í. What can happen is that the consultative portion of the Feast has to be postponed...

If it is decided to postpone part or all of the consultative portion of the Feast, the House of Justice states that it is within the discretion of the Local Spiritual Assembly to decide whether another meeting should be held during the Bahá'í month to complete it, or whether it can be postponed until the following Nineteen Day Feast.

(letter written on behalf of the Universal House of Justice to a National Spiritual Assembly, dated September 5, 1983)

6.4.9 **Should children of Bahá'í parents attend the Feast?**

Yes:-

Since children of Bahá'í parents are considered to be Bahá'ís, they are to be encouraged to attend all Feasts, there to share the reading of the Writings and prayers and be bathed in the spirit of the community. It is the hope of the House of Justice that every Feast will be a feast of love when the children will give and receive the tangible affection of the community and its individual members.

(letter written on behalf of the Universal House of Justice to the National Spiritual Assembly of Australia, dated September 20, 1982)

6.4.10 **May children of non-Bahá'í parents attend Nineteen Day Feasts?**

Yes, provided the parents agree:-

Concerning your inquiry asking if children under 15 of non-Bahá'í parents could attend Nineteen Day Feasts or other events held exclusively for Bahá'ís when the children consider themselves as Bahá'ís, such children may be permitted to attend Bahá'í functions provided their parents have given their consent. This applies only, of course, to children under the age of 15 years.

(letter written by the Universal House of Justice to a National Spiritual Assembly, dated August 4, 1970)

6.4.11 **May children of Bahá'í parents who have not re-affirmed at 15, still attend the Feast?**

Such children may continue to attend the Feast for a time. See the Chapter, "Membership in the Bahá'í community".

6.4.12 ***Should children be expected to maintain good behaviour at Feasts and Holy Day celebrations?***

Yes:-

> ...children should be trained to understand the spiritual significance of the gatherings of the followers of the Blessed Beauty, and to appreciate the honour and bounty of being able to take part in them, whatever their outward form may be.
>
> (letter written on behalf of the Universal House of Justice to a National Spiritual Assembly, dated October 14, 1982)

> While children should receive a great deal of love and understanding, they should also learn to respect those laws and ordinances governing the entire community.
>
> (letter from the International Teaching Centre to the Continental Board of Counsellors for Australasia, dated July 27, 1982)

6.4.13 ***Who is primarily responsible for the behaviour of children at Feasts and other Bahá'í celebrations?***

The parents are primarily responsible:-

> It is realised that some Bahá'í observances are lengthy and it is difficult for very small children to remain quiet for so long. In such cases one or other of the parents may have to miss part of the meeting in order to care for the child...

> In any case, the House of Justice points out that parents are responsible for their children and should make them behave when they attend Bahá'í meetings. If children persist in creating a disturbance they should be taken out of the meeting. This is not merely to ensure the properly dignified conduct of Bahá'í meetings but is an aspect of the training of children in courtesy, consideration for others, reverence, and obedience to their parents.
>
> (letter written on behalf of the Universal House of Justice to a National Spiritual Assembly, dated October 14, 1982)

6.4.14 ***Does the Local Spiritual Assembly have any responsibility for the behaviour of children?***

Yes:-

> The Spiritual Assembly can also perhaps help the parents by providing for a children's observance, suited to their capacities, in a separate room during part of the community's observance. Attendance at the whole of the adult celebration thus becomes a sign of growing maturity and a distinction to be earned by good behaviour.
>
> (letter written on behalf of the Universal House of Justice to a National Spiritual Assembly, dated October 14, 1982)

6.4.15 ***Is there specific guidance for parents as regards the discipline of children?***

The Universal House of Justice advises:-

> *In the compilation on education which was sent to your National*

CHAPTER SIX

Spiritual Assembly, there are additional extracts from letters written on behalf of Shoghi Effendi which bear upon the discipline of children. The House of Justice further notes that the Hand of the Cause of God A.A. ;Furutan's book, "Mothers, Fathers and Children" is now available from George Ronald, Publisher, and in it there is much practical advice for parents. Love, understanding, patience, along with the steady inculcation of moral principles and discipline, are keys to the nurture of the young. This character training you and your husband, as Bahá'ís, can methodically supply to your own children, even as you use prayer and consultation in resolving their problems.

(letter from the Universal House of Justice to an individual believer, dated January 7, 1981)

6.4.16 *Should parents avoid coming to Feasts if their children misbehave?*

No. As pointed out to the National Spiritual Assembly by the Continental Board of Counsellors in a letter dated September 22, 1982:-

...A danger to be avoided is where parents stop coming to Bahá'í meetings, because of their embarrassment about their children's behaviour, or where they stop bringing their children to these meetings. It is much better if the parents continue coming, with their children, and if they are helped and encouraged to supervise and train their children.

6.5 TIME AND PLACE

6.5.1 *When should the Nineteen Day Feast be held?*

Shoghi Effendi said:-

The Bahá'í day starts and ends at sunset, and consequently the date of the celebration of Bahá'í feasts should be adjusted to conform to the Bahá'í calendar time.

("Principles of Bahá'í Administration", p.56)

Furthermore:-

...the Nineteen Day Feast should be held, preferably, on the first day of the Bahá'í month, that is to say the Bahá'í day, beginning at sunset. If this is not possible for some good reason, then it may be held later, but it must fall within that same Bahá'í month and should be on the nearest possible date.

(letter written on behalf of the Universal House of Justice to a National Spiritual Assembly, dated December 4, 1985)

Also:-

As long as the meeting begins before sunset it is considered to be held on the day which comes to an end with that sunset.

(letter from the Universal House of Justice to a National Spiritual Assembly, dated June 23, 1964)

So, for example, the Feast of Jalál (Glory) that falls on April 9, is to be held between sunset on April 8 and sunset on April 9. For a list of names and dates of the Nineteen Day Feast see

CHAPTER SIX

"Principles of Bahá'í Administration", p.55. An example of a good reason for changing the date would be if it coincided with a regular public meeting evening (see "Lights of Guidance" {revised edition}, no.812.) The Universal House of Justice also recognises that the amount of time the friends can devote to the Feast is often limited and, therefore, advises that it may be permissible to hold the Feast at some other time during the Bahá'í month, if this would enable more of the friends to attend:-

> *While the House of Justice does not wish to de-emphasise the preference expressed by Shoghi Effendi that the Feast be held on the first day of the Bahá'í month, it feels that in instances of difficulty, where the friends would otherwise be unable to attend, the National Spiritual Assembly may point out to Local Assemblies that it is permissible to hold the Feast at another time within the Bahá'í month, such as on a weekend.*
>
> (letter written on behalf of the Universal House of Justice to all National Spiritual Assemblies, dated August 28, 1989)

The matter is left to the discretion of the Local Spiritual Assembly; however, the National Spiritual Assembly advises that the Feast should be held at the proper time unless insurmountable reasons prevent it. Such reasons may be of a temporary nature, eg. the illness of a community member; or of a recurrent nature, eg. the presence of elderly people in the community who cannot, for one reason or another, go out at night. Other relevant points regarding the timing of the Feast are as follows:

• it may be celebrated on one of the intercalary days or during the month of fasting provided the friends abstain from food (see "Lights of Guidance" {revised edition} no.814)
• If the Feast time has to be changed it is permissible to hold it on the preceding day (see "Lights of Guidance" {revised edition} no.813)

6.5.2 **Where should the Nineteen Day Feast be held?**

> *...[The] governing principle is that each local community should hold Nineteen Day Feasts within its own civil area.*
>
> (letter from the Universal House of Justice to a National Spiritual Assembly, dated February 10, 1986)

It is for the Local Spiritual Assembly to decide where the Nineteen Day Feast should be held. Shoghi Effendi encouraged using the Hazíratu'l-Quds where possible:-

> *The matter of where the Nineteen Day Feasts should be held is certainly one for the Spiritual Assembly to decide; but the Hazíratu'l-Quds seems the logical place on most occasions. Until the friends have a place of worship in ..., this building will also be used for devotional meetings, as well as for administrative purposes. If, under some circumstances, some special Feast is offered in the home of one of the believers, with the approval of the Spiritual Assembly, there can be no objection; but, generally speaking, he feels it is better to use the Hazíratu'l-Quds.*
>
> (letter written on behalf of Shoghi Effendi to an individual believer, dated February 18, 1954)

6.5.3 **May Feasts be held out of doors?**

Yes:-

> *There is no objection to holding meetings in the open air as long as they are conducted with dignity.*

(letter written on behalf of Shoghi Effendi to an individual believer, dated November 22, 1941)

6.5.4 ***Is it permissible for Local Spiritual Assemblies with very large communities to hold more than one Feast in different districts of the community?***

Yes. Shoghi Effendi said:-

Naturally, district Nineteen Day Feasts can be held where there are very many Bahá'ís in one city.

(letter written on behalf of Shoghi Effendi to an individual believer, dated March 31, 1949)

The Universal House of Justice has, in letters to several National Spiritual Assemblies, provided the following guidance regarding dividing up large Assembly areas for the Feast:

1. it is essential that the overall unity of the community be preserved:-

    The tendency in metropolitan areas is towards segregation, and therefore the Local Assembly should be alert to prevent a similar pattern developing in Bahá'í meetings by reason of the location of the Feast.

    (letter written by the Universal House of Justice to a National Spiritual Assembly, dated January 23, 1967)

    Given the racial and social stratification of large cities, the Spiritual Assembly would also have to exert the utmost care not to allow the Bahá'í community of ... to become, in effect, racially or socially fragmented, even though one race or stratum of society may be dominant in a sub-unit of the city. One of the questions that should remain uppermost in the minds of the Assembly, the committees and the individual friends is how to uphold at all times, through their functions and deeds, the primary principle and goal of our Faith, namely, the unity of the human race.

    (letter written on behalf of the Universal House of Justice to a National Spiritual Assembly, dated December 20, 1987)

2. *The Local Assembly should be watchful that ... control by the Local Assembly is [not] dissipated by this practice.*
    (letter written by the Universal House of Justice to a National Spiritual Assembly, dated January 23, 1967)

3. *rigid boundaries should not be established for the different areas:-*

    Difficulties of travelling to the Nineteen Day Feasts, and other occasions, which may be met in certain parishes can be overcome by your authorising the Local Assembly in such a parish to hold more than one Feast within its area. There is no need to establish rigid boundaries for such a purpose, and the friends should be allowed to attend the Feast in their parish most convenient to them...

    (letter written on behalf of the Universal House of Justice to a National Spiritual Assembly, dated January 14, 1980)

4. *it should be well understood 'that every Feast in the area is a portion of the same Feast under the jurisdiction of the Local Spiritual Assembly.'*
    (letter written on behalf of the Universal House of Justice to a

CHAPTER SIX

National Spiritual Assembly, dated January 14, 1980)

1. *Occasions should be provided for the entire Bahá'í community of the parish to meet together, and Feast days need not be excluded from such occasions.*
(letter written on behalf of the Universal House of Justice to a National Spiritual Assembly, dated January 14, 1980)

1. the number of sub-units created should be kept to a minimum:-
The sub-division of the city should be seen merely as an administrative necessity meant to serve the good of the whole community: in this sense, the Assembly should guard strenuously against creating too many sub-units, contenting itself with the minimum action in this respect.

(letter written on behalf of the Universal House of Justice to a National Spiritual Assembly, dated December 20, 1987)

Any Local Spiritual Assembly in Australia which is contemplating the sub-division of its community for the Feast should contact the National Spiritual Assembly for approval before proceeding. Alternatives to sub-division include purchasing or renting adequate facilities, rather than relying on people's homes
(guidance from letter written by the Universal House of Justice to the National Spiritual Assembly of Australia, dated August 21, 1972).

6.5.5 **Is it permissible to hold the Feast on the premises of another religious organisation?**

This is permissible provided it will not tend to identify the Faith with that religious organisation in the eyes of the public. The National Spiritual Assembly leaves the application of this principle to the discretion of the Local Spiritual Assembly.

6.6 **BAHÁ'Í HOLY DAYS - GENERAL PRINCIPLES**

6.6.1 **What is the importance of observing the Bahá'í Holy Days?**

As we are building a community life centred around the Faith the observance of the Holy Days becomes an important element in that process. These days, so intimately connected with the lives of the Central Figures of the Faith, become a part of the mortar which binds the community together and gives it strength. It is also essential that the Holy Days be properly observed by the Bahá'ís in order to enhance the influence and prestige of the Faith in the public eye. This will further assist in obtaining recognition of the Faith as an independent religion by the civil authorities:-

> *...he cannot but deplore the fact that some of the believers are reluctant to observe, as strictly as they should, the Feasts and anniversaries prescribed by the Cause. This attitude, which may be justified in certain exceptional circumstances, is fraught with incalculable dangers and harm to the community, and will, if allowed to persist, seriously endanger its influence and prestige in the public eye. Unity of action, in matters of so vital an importance as the observance of Bahá'í holidays, is essential. It is the responsibility of the National Spiritual Assembly to remind and urge the friends to faithfully carry out all such laws and precepts of the Cause, the enforcement of which does not constitute an open violation of the laws of their country.*

(Shoghi Effendi, "Dawn of a New Day", p.56)

From time to time questions have arisen about the application of the

CHAPTER SIX

law of the Kitáb-i-Aqdas on the observance of Bahá'í Holy Days. As you know, the recognition of Bahá'í Holy Days in at least ninety-five countries of the world is an important and highly significant objective of the Nine Year Plan [1964-1973], and is directly linked with the recognition of the Faith of Bahá'u'lláh by the civil authorities as an independent religion enjoying its own rights and privileges. The attainment of this objective will be facilitated and enhanced if the friends, motivated by their own realisation of the importance of the laws of Bahá'u'lláh, are obedient to them.

(Universal House of Justice, "Wellspring of Guidance", p.69)

6.6.2   ***How should the Holy Days be observed?***

Abdu'l-Bahá stated that the Holy Days should be days of enjoyment and unity:-

Briefly, every nation has a day known as a holiday which they celebrate with joy. In the sacred Laws of God, in every cycle and dispensation, there are blessed feasts, holidays and workless days. On such days all kinds of occupations, commerce, industry, agriculture etc., are not allowed. Every work is unlawful. All must enjoy a good time, gather together, hold general meetings, become as one Assembly, so that the national oneness, unity and harmony may become personified in all eyes. They should also, however, be days on which institutions should be founded of permanent benefit and value to the people:-

As it is a blessed day it should not be neglected or without results by making it a day limited to the fruits of mere pleasure. During such blessed days institutions should be founded that may be of permanent benefit and value to the people so that in current conversation and in history it may become widely known that such a good work was inaugurated on such a feast day. Therefore, the intelligent must search and investigate reality to find out what important affair, what philanthropic institutions are most needed and what foundations should be laid for the community on that particular day, so that they may be established. Such institutions should not be only for the benefit of the Bahá'ís but for all humanity:-

In all the cycles of the prophets the philanthropic affairs were confined to their respective peoples only - with the exception of small matters, such as charity, which was permissible to extend to others. But in this wonderful dispensation, philanthropic affairs are for all humanity, without any exception, because it is the manifestation of the mercifulness of God...

(above three quotations are from 'Abdu'l-Bahá, "Star of the West", vol. 9, no.1, 8-9)

The tone of these days should be festive or solemn as the occasion requires and should be conducted with a fitting sense of reverence. The believers are encouraged to be creative.

(letter written on behalf of the Universal House of Justice to the National Spiritual Assembly of Australia, dated July 10, 1988)

CHAPTER SIX

6.6.3 *Should gifts be exchanged on Bahá'í Holy Days?*

Gift giving is not an integral part of any Bahá'í Holy Day, although it is not forbidden. Bahá'u'lláh set aside the Intercalary Days as days of gift giving:-

> *The exchanging of presents among believers or the giving of gifts to children is not an integral part of any of our nine Bahá'í Holy Days. There is no prohibition against it, and it is, as you say, a custom among Persian believers such as the Bahá'í to whom you spoke, to exchange gifts at Naw-Rúz. The desire of you and your husband to associate the time of gift giving with your children's involvement in the Faith of Bahá'u'lláh is praiseworthy and it is felt that the following extract from a letter written by the Secretary of the beloved Guardian to the National Spiritual Assembly of Australia and New Zealand on December 26, 1941 will be of value to you:*
>
> *"The intercalary days are specifically set aside for hospitality, the giving of gifts, etc., Bahá'u'lláh Himself specified that they be used this way, but gave no explanation for it."*
>
> (letter written on behalf of the Universal House of Justice to an individual believer, dated January 18, 1982)

6.6.4 *Is it obligatory to observe the Holy Days on the prescribed day?*

Yes. The Holy Days must be celebrated on the prescribed day according to the Bahá'í calendar; that is to say, the Bahá'í day is between sunset and sunset, therefore, the Holy Day must be held on the prescribed day before sunset:-

> *In connection with the nine Holy Days ... the friends should consider it obligatory to celebrate them on the prescribed day before sunset.*
>
> (letter written on behalf of Shoghi Effendi to a National Spiritual Assembly, dated December 24, 1939)

> *With reference to your question in connection with the observance of Bahá'í Holy Days; the Bahá'í day begins and ends at sunset. The night preceding a Holy Day is therefore included in the day, and consequently work during that period is forbidden.*
>
> (Shoghi Effendi, in "Dawn of a New Day", p.68)

Also:

> *As long as the meeting begins before sunset it is considered to be held on the day which comes to an end with that sunset.*
>
> (letter from the Universal House of Justice to a National Spiritual Assembly, dated June 23, 1964)

If the observance must be held at a particular time on the Holy Day, this time should be fixed by counting after sunset and regardless of daylight saving time:-

> *Regarding your question of the proper time to celebrate or hold our meetings of commemoration: the time should be fixed by counting after sunset; the Master passed away one hour after midnight, which*

CHAPTER SIX

falls a certain number of hours after sunset; so His passing should be commemorated according to the sun and regardless of daylight saving time. The same applies to the Ascension of Bahá'u'lláh who passed away about eight hours after sunset.

(Shoghi Effendi, in "Principles of Bahá'í Administration", p.56-7)

Holy Days are at present celebrated at different times in the east and the west because of the different calendars in use (lunar and solar respectively). Eventually the dates of these anniversaries will be fixed according to the Bahá'í calendar; however, this is a matter for the Universal House of Justice to resolve in the future. For the present the friends must accept the calendar in use in the countries in which they live:-

The unification of eastern and western calendars in respect of the dates for observance of the Holy Days is a much more complicated matter than appears on the surface...Work is being done on this problem but the House of Justice feels that is not a matter of urgency. In the meantime, the friends must accept, for the time being, the calendar in force in the countries in which they live.

(letter written on behalf of the Universal House of Justice to an individual believer, dated April 23, 1986)

6.6.5 **Holy Day observances?**

Yes, provided they do not contravene Bahá'í principles:-

You have asked for suggestions regarding the preparation of the handbook on Bahá'í Holy Days which you are planning to publish. It is important that notwithstanding whatever details you set forth therein, it be made clear that the contents do not constitute procedures that must be rigidly adhered to. Dignity and reverence befitting the occasion should obviously characterise observances of Bahá'í Holy Days by the friends, but this does not mean that cultural traditions which do not contravene Bahá'í principles may not, and cannot, find expression in the local observances and meetings of the friends.

(letter written on behalf of the Universal House of Justice to an individual believer, dated August 1, 1983)

6.6.6 **Must Holy Days be observed in each local community, or may regional functions be organised?**

The Universal House of Justice has ruled that it may be desirable to hold regional gatherings; this is for the National Spiritual Assembly to decide:-

As to the question of holding meetings to commemorate Bahá'í Holy Days on a regional basis, the House of Justice has ruled that it may be desirable in certain areas for the believers in neighbouring localities to join together with other communities in observing Holy Days and certain events. Such matters should be referred to and determined by National Spiritual Assemblies.

(letter written on behalf of the Universal House of Justice to an individual believer, dated March 20, 1986)

The National Spiritual Assembly advises that its strong preference is for the Holy Days to be celebrated by each local community or in conjunction with a neighbouring community, as commemoration of the Holy Days is an important aspect of building a strong community life. The friends have a primary responsibility to support functions organised by the community and the Assembly should ensure that all community members are able to attend, eg. it should not charge an entry fee for a function such as Naw-Rúz celebration if that function is the only one the community is holding to observe that Holy Day. The friends may hold private gatherings and provide private hospitality but these should not interfere with the Holy Day celebration itself.

6.6.7 *What responsibilities has the Local Spiritual Assembly for the Bahá'í Holy Days?*

The Local Spiritual Assembly has the following responsibilities:
1. to deepen the believers in the meaning of the Holy Days and the importance of observing them on the designated days. Dr. B. Forghani's compilation on Holy Days, "Days to Remember" (Bahá'í Publications Australia, 1983), provides a useful starting point for understanding the meaning and significance of the Holy Days.
2. to arrange for the proper observation of the Holy Days:-

It [the Local Spiritual Assembly] shall call the meetings of the community, including the Bahá'í Anniversaries...

("By-Laws of a Local Spiritual Assembly", Article III)

6.6.8 *May fund-raising activities be held on Holy Days?*

This matter lies within the discretion of the Local Spiritual Assembly to determine, bearing in mind that both observance of the Holy Days and giving to the Fund are spiritual activities which must be carried out in an appropriately dignified atmosphere.

6.6.9 *May marriages be celebrated on Bahá'í Holy Days?*

Marriages are not prohibited on any day but the Universal House of Justice has said it would be inappropriate to hold them on sad commemorative occasions, such as the Martyrdom of the Báb or the Ascension of Bahá'u'lláh.

6.6.10 *Who may attend Holy Day observances?*

Anybody may attend Holy Day observances, including non-Bahá'ís and Bahá'ís without voting rights.

6.7 SUSPENSION OF WORK ON BAHÁ'Í HOLY DAYS

6.7.1 *On which Bahá'í Holy Days is work to be suspended?*

Work should be suspended on the following days:
1. the first day of Ridván
2. the ninth day of Ridván.
3. the twelfth day of Ridván.
4. the anniversary of the declaration of the Báb.
5. the anniversary of the birth of Bahá'u'lláh.
6. the anniversary of the birth of the Báb.
7. the anniversary of the ascension of Bahá'u'lláh.
8. the anniversary of the martyrdom of the Báb.
9. the Feast of Naw-Rúz.

(from "Principles of Bahá'í Administration", pp. 54-55)

6.7.2 *What is meant by suspension of work?*

Bahá'ís should close down their businesses or seek leave of absence from their employers on the nine Holy Days on which work is suspended:-

He wishes also to stress the fact that, according to our Bahá'í laws,

> *work is forbidden on our Nine Holy Days. Believers who have independent businesses or shops should refrain from working on these days. Those who are in government employ should, on religious grounds, make an effort to be excused from work; all believers, whoever their employers, should do likewise. If the government, or other employers, refuse to grant them these days off, they are not required to forfeit their employment, but they should make every effort to have the independent status of their Faith recognised and their right to hold their own religious Holy Days acknowledged.*
>
> (letter written on behalf of Shoghi Effendi, in "Principles of Bahá'í Administration", p.55)

This also applies to businesses owned by Bahá'ís in which non-Bahá'ís are employed:-

> *The Universal House of Justice has received your letter of 17 November 1975 and in reply to your specific question, 'May our Bahá'í-owned retail mattress store remain open in the care of our non-Bahá'í employees on the Holy Days when we refrain from working?', has instructed us to say that in shops or stores owned by Bahá'ís, the fact that they may have non-Bahá'ís in employment does not exempt the Bahá'í owners from closing their businesses on Bahá'í Holy Days.*
>
> (letter written on behalf of the Universal House of Justice to an individual believer, dated November 30, 1975)

The requirement to suspend work is binding on all believers as a matter of conscience:-

> *This distinction between institutions that are under full or partial Bahá'í control is of fundamental importance. Institutions that are entirely managed by Bahá'ís are, for reasons that are only too obvious, under the obligation of enforcing all the laws and ordinances of the Faith, especially those whose observance constitutes a matter of conscience. There is no reason, no justification whatever, that they should act otherwise... The point which should be always remembered is that the issue in question is essentially a matter of conscience, and as such is of a binding effect upon all believers.*
>
> (letter written on behalf of Shoghi Effendi dated October 2, 1935, quoted by the Universal House of Justice, in "Wellspring of Guidance", p.69-70)

Note that the period during which work is suspended is the Bahá'í day running from sunset to sunset, therefore, the night preceding the Holy Day is included in the day and consequently work during that period is forbidden.

6.7.3 What about Bahá'ís engaged in work that cannot be postponed?

In these cases the work done should be kept to the minimum necessary to provide normal essential services:-

> *The basic principle that institutions that are entirely managed by Bahá'ís are under the obligation of obeying the Bahá'í laws regarding the observance of Holy Days is clear. A problem, however, arises in relation to service institutions and work of a service nature that cannot be postponed. There are, of course, many Bahá'í activities that are carried on on the Holy Days in addition to the celebration of the Holy*

Days themselves, such as the election of Local Spiritual Assemblies on the First Day of Ridván, the holding of the National Convention, which may well coincide with one or more Holy Days, and other praiseworthy activities. It is not this kind of 'work' that is prohibited. Thus, there would be no objection to the holding of sessions of a Summer School or Weekend School on a Holy Day - although they might well be modified in form in recognition of the particular day, and would give time for the actual commemoration. In light of these considerations, and others drawn from the Sacred Texts, the House of Justice advises that, in the case of the Landegg Conference Centre, the work performed during a Bahá'í Holy Day by the household staff, whether Bahá'ís or non-Bahá'ís should be reduced to the minimum necessary to provide the normal essential services, including, of course, the work needed in connection with the celebration of the Holy Day itself. When the Manager is scheduling the booking of the premises to non-Bahá'í groups he should either try to arrange that the period of letting does not include a Bahá'í Holy Day or, if it does, he should explain to the group at the time of booking that there will be limited service rendered by the staff on the Holy Day. Of course, if no events are scheduled at the Centre on a Bahá'í Holy Day, it would be possible to close the Centre on that day.

(letter written on behalf of the Universal House of Justice to a National Spiritual Assembly, dated December 3, 1984)

He thinks it is better for Bahá'í doctors not to work on our nine Holy Days - but, of course, that does not mean they should not attend to very sick people and emergencies on these days.

(Shoghi Effendi, "Dawn of a New Day", p.116)

6.7.4 *What about work associated with the institutions of the Faith?*

Special Bahá'í functions such as the election of the Local Spiritual Assembly or the National Convention may be, and are, held on Bahá'í Holy Days. Routine work associated with the institutions of the Faith, however, should not be carried on, unless of an essential or emergency nature:-

Concerning your question about holding meetings of consultation on Bahá'í Holy Days, we have been requested to share with you an excerpt from the translation of a Persian letter from the beloved Guardian dated 3 January 1929 to an individual believer:

On the Bahá'í festivals and solemn commemorations it is preferable for Assemblies, Committees and Bahá'í Institutions to suspend their activities. However, final decision in these matters rests with the Universal House of Justice.

The Universal House of Justice feels that the above directive of the Guardian is adequate for the time being. It should be clear, however, that should emergencies occur which require the holding of meetings of Bahá'í institutions on the nine Holy Days of the Faith, this would be permissible.

(letter written on behalf of the Universal House of Justice to a

CHAPTER SIX

National Spiritual Assembly, dated July 21, 1982)

It is fully appreciated that the Bahá'í Temple must be open for worship on the Holy Days and therefore it is permitted to provide, to the minimum extent possible, essential services. Those necessary tasks, such as cleaning and other preparation of the building, which can be carried out on the previous day should be so done and only those duties which must be performed should be undertaken on the Holy Day. In the case of the Temple it is immaterial whether the workers are Bahá'í or non-Bahá'í since it is the duty of the Faith to observe, especially in respect of its own institutions, the command to cease work on the Holy Days.

(letter written on behalf of the Universal House of Justice to a National Spiritual Assembly, dated August 12, 1977)

6.7.5 **Should children seek to be excused from school on Holy Days on which work is suspended?**

Yes:-

...children under 15 should certainly observe the Bahá'í Holy Days, and not go to school, if this can be arranged on these nine days.

(letter written on behalf of Shoghi Effendi to a National Spiritual Assembly, dated October 25, 1947)

Parents should present a letter to the head of the school seeking permission for their child to be absent on those days. In Australia the right of Bahá'í children to remain at home on Holy Days has been recognised by the various State based educational authorities.

6.8 **BAHÁ'Í ANNIVERSARIES - A BRIEF DESCRIPTION OF EACH**

6.8.1 **What are the Bahá'í Anniversaries?**

The Bahá'í Anniversaries are:

1. Feast of Ridván (Declaration of Bahá'u'lláh) 21 April - 2 May 1863.
2. Declaration of the Báb, 23 May 1844.
3. Ascension of Bahá'u'lláh, 29 May 1892.
4. Martyrdom of the Báb, 9 July 1850.
5. Birth of the Báb, 20 October 1819.
6. Birth of Bahá'u'lláh, 12 November 1817.
7. Day of the Covenant, 26 November.
8. Ascension of 'Abdu'l-Bahá, 28 November 1921.
9. Period of the Fast, nineteen days beginning 2 March.
10. Feast of Naw-Rúz (Bahá'í New Year), 21 March.

(from "Principles of Bahá'í Administration", p.54)

This section also contains a description of the Intercalary Days ('Ayyám-i-Há').

[See also the "Synopsis and Codification of the Laws and Ordinances of the Kitáb-i-Aqdas" footnote 29, p.62; and any volume of "The Bahá'í World" regarding the Bahá'í Calendar and Festivals.]

6.8.2 **What is the significance of the Anniversary of the Feast of Ridván?**

The Feast of Ridván celebrates Bahá'u'lláh's declaration of His station:-

CHAPTER SIX

> *From 21 April 1863 to 2 May 1863, prior to His journey to Constantinople, Bahá'u'lláh stayed in a garden outside Baghdad, on the banks of the Tigris. Thereafter this garden was called the Garden of "Ridván" (meaning "Paradise"). It was in this Garden, that He declared Himself to be the Promised One of all ages. "As to the significance of that Declaration let Bahá'u'lláh Himself reveal to us its import. Acclaiming that historic occasion as the 'Most Great Festival', the 'King of Festivals', the 'Festival of God', He has, in His Kitáb-i-Aqdas, characterised it as the Day whereon 'all created things were immersed in the sea of purification...'*

(Shoghi Effendi, "God Passes By", pp. 153-4)

The first, ninth and twelfth days are particularly singled out as days on which work is to be suspended (see "Synopsis and Codification of the Laws and Ordinances of the Kitáb-i-Aqdas", footnote 29, p.62).

Shoghi Effendi explained the significance of these three days:-

> *As regards various matters you raised in your letters, the reason we commemorate the 1st, 9th and 12th days of Ridván as Holidays (Holy Days) is because one is the first day, one is the last day, and third one is the ninth day, which of course is associated with the number nine. All 12 days could not be holidays, therefore these three were chosen.*

(letter written on behalf of Shoghi Effendi, dated June 8, 1952 in "Lights of Guidance" 1983 edition, p.230)

6.8.3 **At what time should the first, ninth and twelfth days of Ridván be celebrated?**

Shoghi Effendi has advised that, if feasible, the first day of Ridván (April 21) should be celebrated at about 3 pm. On the ninth and twelfth days the believers are free to gather at any time during the day they find convenient ("Principles of Bahá'í Administration", p.56).

6.8.4 **What is the significance of the Anniversary of the Declaration of the Báb?**

The Declaration of the Báb ushered in the dawn of an Age that signalises the consummation of all ages:-

> *On this day, at about two hours after sunset, in an upper chamber of His house in Shiraz, the Báb revealed to Mullá Husayn that He was the promised Qa'im. "With this historic Declaration the dawn of an Age that signalises the consummation of all ages had broken. The first impulse of a momentous Revelation had been communicated to the one 'but for whom', according to the testimony of the Kitáb-i-Iqán, 'God would not have been established upon the seat of His mercy, nor ascended the throne of eternal glory'."*

(Shoghi Effendi, "God Passes By", p.7)

6.8.5 **At what time should the Declaration of the Báb be celebrated?**

Shoghi Effendi advises that, if feasible, the Declaration of the Báb should be celebrated on May 22 'at about two hours after sunset' ("Principles of Bahá'í Administration", p.56).

6.8.6 **What is the significance of the Anniversary of the Ascension of Bahá'u'lláh?**

Bahá'u'lláh passed away in the Mansion of Bahjí, at about 3 am. His Ascension marks the setting of the 'Sun of Truth' and the ending of the most momentous phase of the Heroic Age

CHAPTER SIX

of the Faith:-

> *With the Ascension of Bahá'u'lláh draws to a close a period which, in many ways, is unparalleled in the world's religious history. The first century of the Bahá'í Era had by now run half its course. An epoch, unsurpassed in its sublimity, its fecundity and duration, by any previous Dispensation, and characterised, except for a short interval of three years, by half a century of progressive Revelation, had terminated. The Message proclaimed by the Báb had yielded its golden fruit. The most momentous, though not the most spectacular phase of the Heroic Age had ended. The Sun of Truth, the world's greatest Luminary, had risen in the Síyáh-Chál of Tihrán, had broken through the clouds which enveloped it in Baghdad, had suffered a momentary eclipse whilst mounting to its zenith in Adrianople and had set finally in 'Akká, never to reappear ere the lapse of a full millennium.*

(Shoghi Effendi, "God Passes By", p.223.

6.8.7 **At what time should the Ascension of Bahá'u'lláh be commemorated?**

Shoghi Effendi advises that, if feasible, the Ascension of Bahá'u'lláh should be commemorated at 3 am on 29 May ("Principles of Bahá'í Administration", p.56).

6.8.8 **What is the significance of the Anniversary of the Martyrdom of the Báb?**

Shoghi Effendi said that the Martyrdom of the Báb was an event unparalleled in the lives of any of the Manifestations:-

> *The Báb, together with one of His disciples, Mírzá Muhammad 'Alíy-i-Zunúzí, surnamed Anís, were executed by firing squad in the barracks square in the city of Tabríz, at about midday... "It (the Martyrdom of the Báb) can ... be regarded in no other light except as the most dramatic, the most tragic event transpiring within the entire range of the first Bahá'í century. Indeed it can be rightly acclaimed as unparalleled in the annals of the lives of all the Founders of the world's existing religious systems."*

(Shoghi Effendi, "God Passes By", p.55)

6.8.9 **At what time should the Martyrdom of the Báb by commemorated?**

Shoghi Effendi advises that, if feasible, the Martyrdom of the Báb should be commemorated on July 9 'at about noon' ("Principles of Bahá'í Administration, p.56).
Work should be suspended on this day.

6.8.10 **What is the significance of the Anniversary of the Birth of the Báb?**

On this day was born the One acclaimed as:-

> *...the "Morn of Truth" and "Harbinger of the Most Great Light", Whose advent at once signalised the termination of the "Prophetic Cycle" and the inception of the "Cycle of Fulfilment", [Who] had simultaneously through His Revelation banished the shades of night that had descended upon His country, and proclaimed the impending rise of that Incomparable Orb Whose radiance was to envelop the whole of mankind.*

(Shoghi Effendi, "God Passes By", p.57).

CHAPTER SIX

6.8.11 *At what time should the Birth of the Báb be celebrated?*

The believers are free to observe this Holy Day at any time during the day they find convenient ("Principles of Bahá'í Administration", p.56).

6.8.12 *What is the significance of the Anniversary of the Birth of Bahá'u'lláh?*

The Birth of Bahá'u'lláh marked the arrival of One described by Shoghi Effendi as:-

> ...the Judge, the Lawgiver and Redeemer of all mankind, as the Organizer of the entire planet, as the Unifier of the children of men, as the Inaugurator of the long-awaited millennium, as the Originator of a new "Universal Cycle," as the Establisher of the Most Great Peace, as the Fountain of the Most Great Justice, as the Proclaimer of the coming of age of the entire human race, as the Creator of a new World Order, and as the Inspirer and Founder of a world civilisation.

("God Passes By", p.93-4)

6.8.13 *At what time should the Birth of Bahá'u'lláh be celebrated?*

The believers are free to observe this occasion by gathering at any time during the day they find convenient ("Principles of Bahá'í Administration", p.56).

6.8.14 *What is the significance of the Anniversary of the Day of the Covenant?*

This Day was given to the friends by 'Abdu'l-Bahá. November 26 is observed as the day of the appointment of the Centre of the Covenant.

The explanation of how November 26th came to be substituted in relation to the Birthday of 'Abdu'l-Bahá, for May 23rd, is related by the late Hand of the Cause H.M. Balyuzi in his book, "Abdu'l-Bahá" (p.523):

Abdu'l-Bahá told the Bahá'ís that this day was not, under any circumstances, to be celebrated as His day of birth. It was the day of the Declaration of the Báb, exclusively associated with Him. But as the Bahá'ís begged for a day to be celebrated as His, he gave them November 26th, to be observed as the day of the appointment of the Centre of the Covenant. It was known as Jashn-i-A'zam - (The Greatest Festival), because He was Ghusn-i-A'zam - (The Greatest Branch). In the West it is known as the 'Day of the Covenant.

> He ('Abdu'l-Bahá) is and should for all time be regarded, first and foremost, as the Centre and Pivot of Bahá'u'lláh's peerless and all-enfolding Covenant...

(Shoghi Effendi, "Dispensation of Bahá'u'lláh", p.44.)

6.8.15 *Should work be suspended on the Day of the Covenant?*

No. Observance of this day is obligatory but suspension of work is not:-

> *The Day of the Covenant Nov. 26th, and the Day of the Ascension, Nov. 28th, anniversaries of the birth and the Ascension of 'Abdu'l-Bahá must be observed by the friends coming together, but work is not prohibited. In other words the friends must regard observance of these two anniversaries as obligatory - but suspension of work is not to be regarded as obligatory.*
>
> *(letter written on behalf of Shoghi Effendi to the National Spiritual Assembly of Australia and New Zealand, dated January 21, 1951)*

> ...*the anniversaries of the birth and the ascension of 'Abdu'l-Bahá are not to be regarded as days on which work is prohibited. The celebration of these two days is however obligatory."* - These are the words of the Guardian. We really have eleven Holy Days but as stated, work is only prohibited on the first nine mentioned in the Tablet.
>
> (Written on behalf of Shoghi Effendi, in "Letters from the Guardian to Australia and New Zealand", p.94)

6.8.16 **At what time should the Day of the Covenant be observed?**

The believers are free to observe the occasion by gathering at any time during the day they find convenient ("Principles of Bahá'í Administration", p.56).

6.8.17 **What is the significance of the Anniversary of the Ascension of 'Abdu'l-Bahá?**

'Abdu'l-Bahá's passing marked the close of the Heroic Age of the Faith:-

> 'Abdu'l-Bahá passed away at 1 am in Haifa.. *"Thus was brought to a close the ministry of One Who was the incarnation, by virtue of the rank bestowed upon Him by His Father, of an institution that has no parallel in the entire field of religious history, a ministry that marks the final stage in the Apostolic, the Heroic and most glorious Age of the Dispensation of Bahá'u'lláh."*
>
> (Shoghi Effendi, "God Passes By", p.314)

6.8.18 **Should work be suspended on the Anniversary of the Ascension of 'Abdu'l-Bahá?**

Observance of this Holy Day is obligatory but work is not to be suspended.

6.8.19 **At what time should the Ascension of 'Abdu'l-Bahá be commemorated?**

Shoghi Effendi advises that, if feasible, the Ascension of 'Abdu'l-Bahá should be commemorated at 1 am on November 28 ("Principles of Bahá'í Administration", p.56)

6.8.20 **What is the significance of the Feast of Naw-Rúz?**

Naw-Rúz' means 'New Day' and is the Bahá'í New Year. 'Abdu'l-Bahá explains its significance as follows:-

> *At this moment the sun appears at the meridian and the day and night are equal. Until today the North Pole has been in darkness. Today the sun appears on the horizon of the North Pole. Today the sun rises and sets at the equator and the two hemispheres are equally illumined. This sacred day, when the sun illumines equally the whole earth, is called the equinox, and the equinox is the symbol of the Manifestation of God. The Sun of Truth rises on the horizon of Divine Mercy and sends forth its rays. This day is consecrated to commemorate it. It is the beginning of spring. When the sun appears at the equinox, it causes a movement in all living things. The mineral world is set in motion, plants begin to shoot, the desert is changed into a prairie, trees bud and every living thing responds, including the bodies of animals and men.*
>
> ('Abdu'i-Bahá, quoted in "Star of the West", vol. 5, no.1, p.4, in "Days to Remember", compiled by Dr. B. Forghani, p.21-2)

CHAPTER SIX

6.8.21 *When is Naw-Rúz celebrated in the West?*

Bahá'ís in the West celebrate Naw-Rúz according to the Gregorian calendar on March 21st each year, until such time as the Universal House of Justice fixes the meridian:-

> *It has been decided that until the Universal House of Justice fixes the meridian, the friends in the West should observe Naw-Rúz on the 21st day of March each year according to the Gregorian calendar ... regardless of the date and the hour of the vernal equinox.*

> (letter from the Universal House of Justice to a National Spiritual Assembly, dated October 28, 1971)

6.8.22 *How should Naw-Rúz be celebrated?*

The National Spiritual Assembly urges the friends to celebrate Naw-Rúz at the community level by appropriate gatherings of a dignified and festive nature. Private gatherings and hospitality should not be permitted to interfere with the holding of the Feast of Naw-Rúz.

With regard to giving cards at Naw-Rúz Shoghi Effendi has said:-

> *There is no objection to individual Bahá'ís sending Naw-Rúz cards if they want to; also the National Spiritual Assembly can send them out occasionally, but it should not become a fixed custom.*

> ("Letters of the Guardian to Australia and New Zealand", p.65)

The Persian friends have a custom of giving gifts on Naw-Rúz and there is nothing wrong with this; however, it is not an integral part of the Holy Day

It should also be noted that Naw-Rúz and the Nineteen Day Feast that fall on the same date are separate functions:-

> *...The Naw-Rúz Feast should be held on March 21 before sunset and has nothing to do with the Nineteen Day Feast. The Nineteen Day Feast is administrative in function whereas the Naw-Rúz is our New Year, a Feast of hospitality and rejoicing.*

> (letter written on behalf of the Shoghi Effendi to a National Spiritual Assembly, dated June 30, 1949)

6.8.23 *What is the purpose of the Fast?*

The Fast is obligatory for all believers (with certain exceptions) between the ages of 15 and 70. The Fast period is nineteen days. It begins on March 2, (after the Intercalary Days) and ends on March 20 (followed by the Feast of Naw-Rúz). During this time no food or drink may be taken from sunrise to sunset. The Fast is essentially a period of spiritual recuperation and serves as a symbolic reminder of abstinence from selfish and carnal desires (see "Principles of Bahá'í Administration", p.9). 'Abdu'l-Bahá has also explained that during the time a Manifestation is receiving the Divine Revelation He abstains from food and drink, therefore, the friends also fast in commemoration of this time (see "Lights of Guidance" {revised edition}, no.779).

For a summary of the laws relating to the Fast, see the "Synopsis and Codification of the Laws and Ordinances of the Kitáb-i-Aqdas", p.38-39. Note, however, that the following are not yet binding on believers in the West:
- to abstain from smoking at the same time one abstains from food and drink
(see "Lights of Guidance" {revised edition} no.782)
- the definition of travellers for the purpose of exemption from fasting.

Instead, the friends should follow the guidance given by Shoghi Effendi in "Principles of Bahá'í Administration", p.9-10.
* the law regarding exemption from fasting granted to women in their courses
(from letter written on behalf of the Universal House of Justice to a National Spiritual Assembly, dated June 9, 1974)
* The law regarding fasting, whilst obligatory, is the responsibility of the individual. A Local Spiritual Assembly cannot enforce it on the friends:-

> *But while a universal obligation, the observance of the nineteen day fast has been made by Bahá'u'lláh the sole responsibility of the individual believer. No Assembly has the right to enforce it on the friends, or to hold anybody responsible for not observing it. The believer is free, however, to ask the advice of his Assembly as to the circumstances that would justify him to conscientiously break such a fast. But he is by no means required to do so.*

(letter written on behalf of Shoghi Effendi to an individual believer, dated March 9, 1937)

[For further information about the Fast see: - "Lights of Guidance" {revised edition} nos. 775-784 - "Principles of Bahá'í Administration", pp. 8-10]

6.8.24 What are the 'Ayyám-i-Há' - Intercalary Days?

The Intercalary Days are from February 26 to March 1 inclusive (four in ordinary and five in leap years). They immediately precede the Fast and are to be devoted to feasting, rejoicing and charity:-

> *Bahá'u'lláh designated those days as the 'Ayyám-i-Há' and ordained that they should immediately precede the month of 'Alá', which is the month of fasting. He enjoined upon his followers to devote these days to feasting, rejoicing and charity. Immediately upon the termination of these intercalary days, Bahá'u'lláh ordained the month of fasting to begin.*

(in 'Additional Material Gleaned from Nabíls Narrative (Vol. II), Regarding the Bahá'í Calendar', "The Bahá'í World", Vol. XV, p.691)

The Intercalary Days are also designated as a time of gift-giving and hospitality.

6.8.25 Are there any Tablets or prayers particularly associated with the Anniversaries?

The 'Tablet of Visitation of Bahá'u'lláh' is frequently used to commemorate the Anniversaries of the Báb and Bahá'u'lláh. The 'Prayer of Visitation of 'Abdu'l-Bahá' may be used to commemorate the Anniversaries of 'Abdu'l-Bahá. There are also Tablets and prayers revealed specifically for such occasions as Naw-Rúz, Ridván, the Fast and the Intercalary Days. These can be found in most available prayer books. A useful starting point for locating readings appropriate to the Holy Days is "Days to Remember", a compilation on Bahá'í Holy Days by Dr. B. Forghani (Bahá'í Publications Australia, 1983)

6.8.26 Is it necessary to stand and face the Qiblih when reciting the Tablet of Visitation?

No:-

> *In letters to several enquirers the House of Justice has stated that nothing has been found in the Writings requiring the friends to stand and face the Qiblih every time the Tablet of Visitation is recited. It*

CHAPTER SIX

adds that it is very important that no issue be made about such minor details. When, however, one is actually in, or within the precincts of, one of the Holy Shrines, it is an act of simple reverence to stand and face the Shrine when the Tablet of Visitation is recited.

(letter written on behalf of the Universal House of Justice to the National Spiritual Assembly of Australia, dated January 11, 1990)

6.9 PARTICIPATION IN OTHER CULTURAL/RELIGIOUS FESTIVALS

6.9.1 *May Bahá'ís continue to participate in traditional cultural practices?*

Yes, provided the practice has cultural, rather than religious connotations, and does not contravene the principles of the Faith:-

Bahá'ís should obviously be encouraged to preserve their inherited cultural identities, as long as the activities involved do not contravene the principles of the Faith. The perpetuation of such cultural characteristics is an expression of unity in diversity. Although most of these festive celebrations have no doubt stemmed from religious rituals in bygone ages, the believers should not be deterred from participating in those in which, over the course of time, the religious meaning has given way to purely culturally oriented practices. For example, Naw-Rúz itself was originally a Zoroastrian religious festival, but gradually its Zoroastrian connotation has almost been forgotten. Iranians, even after their conversion to Islam, have been observing it as a national festival. Now Naw-Rúz has become a Bahá'í Holy Day and is being observed throughout the world, but, in addition to the Bahá'í observance, many Iranian Bahá'ís continue to carry out their past cultural traditions in connection with this Feast. Similarly, there are a number of national customs in every part of the world which have cultural rather than religious connotations. Bahá'ís must guard against the extremes of, on the one hand, dissociating themselves needlessly from harmless cultural practices and risking alienation from family and friends; and, on the other hand, undermining the independence of the Faith by participating in observances belonging to abrogated dispensations:-

In deciding whether or not to participate in such traditional activities, the Bahá'ís must guard against two extremes. The one is to disassociate themselves needlessly from harmless cultural observances and thus alienate themselves from their non-Bahá'í families and friends; the other is to continue the practice of abrogated observances of previous dispensations and thus undermine the independence of the Bahá'í Faith and create undesirable distinctions between themselves and their fellow-Bahá'ís. In this respect a distinction is to be drawn between what the Bahá'ís do in relation to one another and what they do in relation to their non-Bahá'í relatives and friends:

For example, in a letter written on behalf of the Guardian there appears the following guidance:

As regards the celebration of the Christian Holidays by the believers, it is surely preferable and even highly advisable that the Friends should

CHAPTER SIX

in their relation to each other discontinue observing such holidays as Christmas and New Year, and to have their festival gatherings of this nature instead during the intercalary days and Naw-Rúz. There is no objection to Bahá'ís attending other religious marriage ceremonies, provided that in doing so they do not contravene Bahá'í law, eg. by drinking alcohol.

Further, there is no objection for Bahá'ís to attend religious marriage ceremonies of their friends and relatives or take part in festivities usually connected with these events, provided that in doing so they do not contravene Bahá'í Law. For example, if consuming alcoholic beverages is part of such activities, the Bahá'ís, of course, would be obliged to refrain from partaking of such drinks. There are some exclusive religious ceremonies in which Bahá'ís should not be involved in order to preserve the independence of the Faith. In this respect the Bahá'ís must maintain a balance between their adherence to the Cause and their role in society:-

There are some exclusive religious ceremonies in which Bahá'ís should not participate, in order to safeguard the independence of the Faith. In this regard, the beloved Guardian has given the following advice to an individual believer: 'In these days the friends should, as much as possible, demonstrate through their deeds the independence of the Holy Faith of God, and its freedom from the customs, rituals and practices of a discredited and abrogated past.' In observing this principle, the House of Justice advises the Bahá'ís to maintain a balance between their adherence to the Cause and obedience to its laws on the one hand, and their role in society on the other. Bahá'ís must continue to show respect for their former religion but must guard against anything that could imply their membership in another religion or which would be contrary to Bahá'í principles:-

When an individual becomes a Bahá'í he acquires, as you are aware, wider loyalty to the Manifestations of God. Having found this new way of life, he should be careful not to isolate himself from his family and his people, and he should show respect for his former religion. The Bahá'ís should, of course, avoid performing any acts which could be considered as implying their membership in another religion or which are contrary to Bahá'í Principles. There is a clear distinction between participating in festive and cultural events, as opposed to performing religious ceremonies and rituals. The institutions of the Faith must strike a balance between not allowing the Faith to be compromised, on the one hand; and not insisting too rigidly, on the other, on Bahá'ís immediately abandoning customs that have been established in their communities over centuries:-

It should also be remembered that the weaning away of the Bahá'ís from customs and traditions, which have been established among communities for centuries, takes time and is a gradual process. Therefore, while the National Assembly should avoid rigidity in these matters, it should also not compromise when the interests of the Faith

CHAPTER SIX

and its integrity and independence are at stake.

(the above quotations are taken from a letter written on behalf of the Universal House of Justice to a National Spiritual Assembly, dated May 26, 1982)

[See also Chapter 14, Section 2 'Encouraging Unity' and "Lights of Guidance" {revised edition} nos. 460-66.]

6.10 **NOTES FOR REGISTERED GROUPS**

Groups are encouraged to hold their own Feasts even though they cannot be official administrative occasions in the absence of an Assembly to conduct the Feast. The Universal House of Justice has also noted:-

Any Bahá'í, whether an isolated believer or a member of a local community or group, may convey his suggestions and recommendations to the National Spiritual Assembly at any time and thus take part in the consultative aspect of Bahá'í community life.

(letter written on behalf of the Universal House of Justice to an individual believer, dated July 23, 1985)

Bahá'ís in Group areas are also welcome to attend the Feasts of neighbouring communities. Groups are, in addition, encouraged to observe the Holy Days in their own community, according to the principles set out in this Chapter, or to attend the observances arranged by neighbouring communities.

CHAPTER SEVEN

Chapter 7

7. Relations with Auxiliary Board Members and Assistants

7.1 THE RULERS AND THE LEARNED

7.1.1 *What is the place of the Auxiliary Board within the Bahá'í Administrative Order?*

The Bahá'í Administrative Order is described by the Universal House of Justice in these terms:-

> *This Administrative Order consists, on the one hand, of a series of elected councils, universal, secondary and local, in which are vested legislative, executive and judicial powers over the Bahá'í community and, on the other, of eminent and devoted believers appointed for the specific purposes of protecting and propagating the Faith of Bahá'u'lláh under the guidance of the Head of that Faith.*

("The Constitution of the Universal House of Justice, p.8")

The Auxiliary Boards are numbered among the 'eminent and devoted believers' charged with 'protecting and propagating the Faith'. The Hands of the Cause of God and the Continental Boards of Counsellors also belong to this branch of the Administrative Order. They may be considered as separate institutions in themselves or as parts of one institution designated by Bahá'u'lláh as the 'learned'. The elected councils belong to the institution of the 'rulers':-
In the Kitáb-i-'Ahd (the Book of His Covenant) Bahá'u'lláh wrote "*Blessed are the rulers and the learned among the people of Bahá*", and referring to this very passage the beloved Guardian wrote on 4 November 1931:

> *In this holy cycle the 'learned' are, on the one hand, the Hands of the Cause of God, and, on the other, the teachers and diffusers of His Teachings who do not rank as Hands, but who have attained an eminent position in the teaching work. As to the 'rulers' they refer to the members of the Local, National and International Houses of Justice. The duties of each of these souls will be determined in the future.*

(Translated from the Persian).

> *The Hands of the Cause of God, the Counsellors and the members of the Auxiliary Boards fall within the definition of the "learned" given by the beloved Guardian. Thus they are all intimately interrelated and it is not incorrect to refer to the three ranks collectively as one institution. However, each is also a separate institution in itself...*

(letter from the Universal House of Justice to the Continental Boards of Counsellors and National Spiritual Assemblies, dated April 24, 1972)

7.1.2 *How has the institution of the 'learned' evolved?*

The institution of the Hands of the Cause of God was first brought into existence by Bahá'u'lláh. When 'Abdu'l-Bahá proclaimed and established the Bahá'í Administrative Order in His 'Will and Testament' the institution of the Hands of the Cause was given the functions of protecting and propagating the Faith and made an auxiliary institution of the Guardianship. Shoghi Effendi appointed the first living Hands of the Cause in 1951 and gave them responsibilities on a continental level. When he launched the Ten Year World Crusade in 1953 Shoghi

CHAPTER SEVEN

Effendi gave the Hands of the Cause the duty *'to assist National Spiritual Assemblies of the Bahá'í world in the specific purpose of effectively prosecuting the World Spiritual Crusade'* (cablegram, June 4, 1957)

> *In 1957 he added to this 'the primary obligation to watch over and insure protection to the Bahá'í world community, in close collaboration with these same National Assemblies...'*

(cablegram, June 4, 1957)

To assist with this work Shoghi Effendi authorised the appointment of two Auxiliary Boards on each continent to serve as *'deputies, assistants and advisers' to the Hands in that continent.* (cablegram to the Hands of the Cause and all National Spiritual Assemblies, dated April 6, 1954)

The first Auxiliary Board was given responsibility for propagation of the Faith; the second for protection of the Faith. The Auxiliary Boards were not given administrative functions but had the tasks of stimulating, counselling and assisting the local assemblies, groups and individuals within their assigned areas through visits and correspondence. They were to report on the progress of the Faith in their areas to their respective Hands. The Hands and National Spiritual Assemblies, in turn were urged

> *'to establish ... direct contact and deliberate, whenever feasible, as frequently as possible, to exchange reports to be submitted by their respective Auxiliary Boards and national committees, to exercise unrelaxing vigilance and carry out unflinchingly their sacred, inescapable duties'*

(cablegram, June 4, 1957)

Following the passing of Shoghi Effendi the Universal House of Justice determined from the Writings that it was not possible for it to make further appointments of Hands of the Cause; however, there was a need to extend their functions into the future, within the structure of the administrative order. In 1968, therefore, the Universal House of Justice appointed Continental Boards of Counsellors to operate in specified zones throughout the world. These Boards were to

> *'operate in a manner similar to that set forth by the beloved Guardian for the Hands of the Cause...'*

(letter from the Universal House of Justice to Continental Boards of Counsellors, dated June 24, 1968)

Their responsibilities included:

> *'directing the Auxiliary Boards in their respective areas, consulting and collaborating with National Spiritual Assemblies, and keeping the Hands of the Cause and the Universal House of Justice informed concerning the conditions of the Cause in their areas.'*

The Auxiliary Boards from now on reported to their respective Continental Board of Counsellors and were appointed by that Board. The Hands, released from administration of the Boards, now operated increasingly on an intercontinental level. From the time of his first appointment of Hands of the Cause, Shoghi Effendi had maintained a small nucleus of Hands in the Holy Land. Their tasks included assisting Shoghi Effendi with the work of the Faith in the Holy Land and serving as liaison between himself and the Hands in each continent.

In 1973, the extension into the future of the functions of the Hands in the Holy Land was ensured by the establishment of the International Teaching Centre. Its members were all the Hands of the Cause of God, whether resident in the Holy Land or not, and Counsellors appointed by the Universal House of Justice for five year terms of office. Its functions include: directing the work of the Continental Boards of Counsellors; serving as liaison between these Boards and the Universal House of Justice; watching over the teaching work in all parts of the world; and watching over the security of the Faith in all parts of the world.

In 1973 also, the Universal House of Justice took a further step in the development of the institution of the 'learned' by giving the Boards of Counsellors the right to authorise individual Auxiliary Board members to appoint assistants. This step was made necessary by the growth of the Bahá'í community. The assistants are appointed for terms of a year or two, function in a localised area only and report to the Auxiliary Board member for whom they work. The appointment of assistants enables the institution of the Counsellors to reach to the grassroots of the community and to further the work of protection and propagation on a practical, day-to-day basis.

7.1.3 **'How does the functioning of the institutions of the 'rulers' and the 'learned' differ?'**

The functioning of the institutions of the 'rulers' and the 'learned' differ in the following ways:-

1. The 'rulers'

> *'function as corporate bodies'; that is, their actions are governed by the decision of the entire Assembly through majority vote. The 'learned', on the other hand, 'operate primarily as individuals.'*

> (letter from the Universal House of Justice to the Continental Boards of Counsellors and National Spiritual Assemblies, dated April 24, 1972).

2. The role of the 'learned' is to stimulate, counsel and assist Local Spiritual Assemblies, groups and individual believers. They '*have no legislative, administrative or judicial authority...*'(letter from the Universal House of Justice to the Continental Boards of Counsellors and National Spiritual Assemblies, dated April 24, 1972). These are functions of the Spiritual Assemblies.

a) the 'learned' do not participate in the decision-making process. Their role is confined to consultation and giving advice on matters relating to legislation; but they cannot be present in an Assembly meeting when the Assembly is consulting with a view to making a decision:-

> *A non-member of an Assembly should not be present while the Assembly is in the process of arriving at a decision...Normally, an Auxiliary Board member would be present only during the period necessary for his consultation with the Assembly and then he would absent himself during the time when the Assembly is in process of discussing the matter with the view to arriving at a decision.*

> (letter from the Universal House of Justice to the Hands of the Cause of God in the Holy Land, dated May 10, 1970)

An exception to this role exists when an assistant to an Auxiliary Board member consulted is also a member of the Assembly.

b) the 'learned' do not carry out any administrative functions. Their role is confined to stimulating the friends to take part in projects organised by the Assemblies and to advise the Assemblies on administrative principles. The Universal House of Justice provides the following examples:-

> ...when Auxiliary Board members arouse believers to pioneer, any believer who expresses his desire to do so should be referred to the appropriate committee which will then organise the project. Counsellors and Auxiliary Board members should not, themselves, organise pioneering or travel teaching projects.
>
> ...if an Auxiliary Board member finds a Local Spiritual Assembly functioning incorrectly he should call its attention to the appropriate Texts...
>
> (letter from the Universal House of Justice to Continental Boards of Counsellors and National Spiritual Assemblies, dated October 1, 1969)

c) the 'learned' do not have the function of issuing warnings, applying sanctions, or investigating alleged violations of Bahá'í law. Their role is confined to advising, counselling and educating Assemblies and individuals regarding the principles of the Faith:-

> We feel that instead of having Board members investigate the private lives of believers, the Board members should be called upon to educate the believers regarding the principles of the Faith and that problems involving alleged immorality or irregularities in marital status should be dealt with only when they arise. These problems should not be sought out.
>
> (letter from the Universal House of Justice to the Hands of the Cause in the Holy Land, dated August 14, 1967)

> The Protection Board does have a role to 'keep constantly a watchful eye on those who are known to be enemies or to have been put out of the Faith [and to] discreetly investigate their activities...'
>
> (Universal House of Justice, quoted in a letter from the International Teaching Centre to the Continental Boards of Counsellors, dated October 14, 1976).

> This is a function that will become more prominent in the future when opposition to the Faith increases. It is a specialised role that does not extend to the investigation of believers who appear to be violating Bahá'í laws or endangering the interests of the Faith by their behaviour. This, as well as the application of sanctions, is a function of the Assemblies. It should also be noted that the 'learned' 'are entirely devoid of priestly functions or the right to make authoritative interpretations.'
>
> (letter from the Universal House of Justice to the Continental Boards of Counsellors and National Spiritual Assemblies, dated April 24, 1972).

7.2 FUNCTIONS OF THE AUXILIARY BOARD MEMBERS

7.2.1 *What are the distinct functions of the Propagation Board?*

The Universal House of Justice has set out four primary tasks for the Propagation Board:-
1. to direct the believers' attention to the goals of whatever plans have been placed

before them,
2. *to stimulate and assist them to promote the teaching work in the fields of proclamation, expansion, consolidation and pioneering,*
3. to encourage contributions to the Funds,
4. *to act as standard bearers of the teachers of the Faith, leading them to new achievements in the diffusion of God's Message to their fellow human beings.*
(quoted in letter of the International Teaching Centre to all Boards of Counsellors, dated October 14, 1976)

7.2.2 **What are the distinct functions of the Protection Board?**

The Universal House of Justice has enumerated the functions of the Protection Board as follows:-
1. *Above all ... concentrate on deepening the friends' knowledge of the Covenant and increasing their love and loyalty to it,*
2. *clearly and frankly answering, in conformity with the Teachings, whatever questions may trouble any of the believers,*
3. *fostering the spiritual profundity and strength of their Faith and certitude,*
4. *promoting whatever will increase the spirit of loving unity in Bahá'í communities,*
5. *warn intelligently the friends of the opposition inevitably to come,*
6. *explain how each crisis in God's Faith has always proved to be a blessing in disguise,*
7. *prepare them for the 'dire contests' which are 'destined to range the Army of Light against the forces of darkness'*
(quoted in letter of the International Teaching Centre to all Boards of Counsellors, dated October 14, 1976)

There are other functions which will be applicable in the future, when enemies of the Faith are more active. At the present time, the actions of enemies are sporadic and are handled by specific actions of the Protection Board, determined in consultation with the Counsellors.

7.2.3 **What functions do the Auxiliary Boards have in common?**

The Auxiliary Boards have functions in common in the areas of consolidation and deepening:-

> *In implementing their functions the members of the two Auxiliary Boards will often be promoting the same thing; moreover, many of their functions are held in common especially in the areas of consolidation and deepening, and it is left to each Board of Counsellors to determine the range of responsibility assigned to each Auxiliary Board member so that in the circumstances of each area maximum collaboration is achieved.*

(letter of the Universal House of Justice to the International Teaching Centre, dated October 10, 1976) [See also Section 3, 'What are the functions of the assistants?']

7.2.4 **How do Auxiliary Board members fulfil their functions?**

Auxiliary Board members fulfil their functions by:-

> *...[building] up a warm and loving relationship between themselves and the believers in their area so that the Local Spiritual Assemblies will spontaneously turn to them for advice and assistance.*

(letter from the Universal House of Justice to the Continental Boards of Counsellors and National Spiritual Assemblies, dated October 1, 1969)

It is their responsibility to be well informed of the relative strengths and weaknesses of each locality and to send reports and recommendations to the Continental Board of Counsellors on a regular basis:-

> *Each Auxiliary Board member who is allotted a specific area in which to serve, should establish contact with the Local Spiritual Assemblies and other localities of his area, encourage and guide all such centres in the implementation of the goals of the Plan, become informed of the relative strength and weakness of each locality, and feel responsible before God in the discharge of his responsibilities. Should he lose contact with a particular Local Spiritual Assembly or locality, he should use his initiative in finding a satisfactory solution to the problem. He should also send his reports and recommendations to the Counsellors on a regular basis.*
>
> (from a summary of points prepared by the Universal House of Justice, based on a letter to a National Spiritual Assembly, dated May 20, 1970)

Auxiliary Board members do not need the permission of the Counsellors to establish contact with a Local Spiritual Assembly:-

> *...as a general principle Auxiliary Board members are not only free, but are urged, in accordance with the writings of the beloved Guardian, to have direct contact with the individual friends, as well as the Local Spiritual Assemblies.*
>
> (letter from the Universal House of Justice to a National Spiritual Assembly, dated December 15, 1965)

Nor do they need the permission of the National Spiritual Assembly. In addition, much of the contact between the Auxiliary Boards and the Local Spiritual Assemblies is now through the assistants to the Auxiliary Board members, who have a duty to become well acquainted with the progress of the Faith in their assigned areas and to send regular reports to the Auxiliary Boards.

7.2.5 May an Auxiliary Board member also serve on an Assembly or committee, or be elected as a delegate to National Convention?

An Auxiliary Board member, if elected to an administrative post, must decide whether or not to accept the election. If the Board member chooses to accept the election, he or she must resign from the Auxiliary Board:-

> *...concerning the eligibility of Auxiliary Board members for election to local Spiritual Assemblies, as delegates to the national Convention, and to the National Spiritual Assembly. In all three areas of election, Auxiliary Board members are eligible to be elected. Therefore, a ballot should not be invalidated because it contains the name of a member of an Auxiliary Board. The basic principle involved is that the Board member himself must decide whether or not to accept his election.*
>
> *...a Board Member should be allowed a reasonable time to make his choice and should feel no compulsion to resign immediately after the results of the election are announced.*
>
> (letter from the Universal House of Justice to a National Spiritual Assembly, dated March 25, 1966)

CHAPTER SEVEN

An Auxiliary Board member is eligible for any elective office but if elected to an administrative post on a national or local level must decide whether to retain membership on the Board or accept the administrative post, since he may not serve in both capacities at the same time.

(The Constitution of the Universal House of Justice, p.16)

Members of Auxiliary Boards should be freed from administrative responsibilities including serving on Committees...

(letter from the Universal House of Justice to all National Spiritual Assemblies, dated November 1964)

7.2.6 **Are there any circumstances in which a Hand of the Cause of God, Counsellor, or Auxiliary Board member may serve in an administrative capacity?**

If the membership of a local community, including the Hand of the Cause, Counsellor or Auxiliary Board member is exactly nine, or if, subsequent to Riḍván it falls to, or below, nine, the member of the learned arm may serve temporarily on the Local Spiritual Assembly to preserve its existence until a replacement can be found. See "Lights of Guidance" {revised edition}, no.571.]

7.2.7 **May Hands of the Cause of God, Counsellors and Auxiliary Board members vote in elections?**

Yes:-

All adult Bahá'ís, including members of the Auxiliary Board, are eligible to vote in elections for delegates or in elections for members of the Local Spiritual Assembly.

(letter from the Universal House of Justice to a National Spiritual Assembly, dated April 10, 1966)

7.2.8 **How is the work of the Auxiliary Boards funded?**

The work of the Auxiliary Boards is funded by the Continental Funds. All Assemblies and individuals have a responsibility to contribute directly to these Funds.

7.3 **FUNCTIONS OF THE ASSISTANTS**

7.3.1 **What is the purpose of appointing assistants to the Auxiliary Boards?**

The purpose of appointing assistants is to enable the Auxiliary Boards to remain in close touch with the communities and individual believers in their areas. Assistants aid the consolidation of local communities:-

The House of Justice has repeatedly linked the appointment of assistants in various localities with Assembly consolidation. As the use of assistants is broadened 'it should prove to be the most potent force in consolidating Local Spiritual Assemblies and in aiding them to function properly - a process that will, in turn, foster and channel the devotion and activities of the individual believers.'

(communication of the Universal House of Justice to a National Spiritual Assembly, dated November 5, 1974)

CHAPTER SEVEN

7.3.2 ***What size area does an assistant function in?***

The International Teaching Centre has noted that the assistants function in a '*localised area' only* (statement attached to a letter to Continental Boards of Counsellors, dated August 28, 1984).

> *An assistant is appointed by an Auxiliary Board member for a term of a year or two, 'to help in a specified area of the territory and he functions as an assistant only in relation to that area.'*
>
> (letter written on behalf of the Universal House of Justice to a National Spiritual Assembly, dated August 2, 1982)

7.3.3 ***What are the functions of the assistants?***

The Auxiliary Board members must decide whether to assign their assistants the general responsibility of helping them with their work or whether to give an assistant a specific task - for example, increasing the participation of women in community life:-

> *There is scope for considerable diversity and creativity in the use of the assistants... He can be given a general responsibility to assist the Auxiliary Board member in the performance of his functions or he can also be assigned to concentrate on a specific task, such as stimulating greater attention to the teaching of children, development of youth activities, increasing the participation of women in community life, attainment of property goals, social and economic development, and so on.*
>
> (statement from the International Teaching Centre, 'Role of Auxiliary Board members in Working with Assistants', November 1986)

The following have been designated as specific functions of the assistants:
1. *to activate and encourage Local Spiritual Assemblies*
2. *to call the attention of Local Spiritual Assembly members to the importance of holding regular meetings*
3. *to encourage local communities to meet for the Nineteen Day Feasts and Holy Days*
4. 4. *to help deepen their fellow-believers' understanding of the Teachings*
5. *generally to assist the Auxiliary Board members in the discharge of their duties*

(letter from the Universal House of Justice to the Bahá'ís of the World, dated October 7, 1973)

The Universal House of Justice has said that the assistants may encourage believers to come together for the Feast in communities in which the Local Spiritual Assembly is not exercising its responsibilities in this regard:-

> *As you rightly point out, in many such communities the fostering of the Feast is an effective aid to community development. Feasts may, in turn, lead to other activities such as children's classes, and gradually help in the activation of the Local Assembly. Assistants may therefore assume the important role of encouraging the believers to gather for the Feast as an interim measure when the Local Spiritual Assembly is not functioning, although the Nineteen Day Feast can be an official administrative occasion only when there is a Local Spiritual Assembly to take charge of it...*
>
> *It should nevertheless be borne in mind that the goal is for the Local Assembly to be strengthened in order that it may itself assume*

responsibility to conduct the Feast.

(quoted in a letter written on behalf of the Universal House of Justice to all National Spiritual Assemblies, dated September 26, 1989)

7.3.4 Is the work of assistants confined to helping Local Spiritual Assemblies?

No. Assistants may also work in goal areas and with groups and isolated believers:- The work of the assistants is not only confined to helping Local Spiritual Assemblies, or believers in areas where a Local Spiritual Assembly exists. The Universal House of Justice, on one occasion, offered:-

...the suggestion that perhaps the Counsellors could consider asking their Auxiliary Board members to assign an assistant to work in each goal area where a new Assembly is to be formed.

(communication from the Universal House of Justice to the International Teaching Centre, dated February 8, 1977 - included in a statement from the International Teaching Centre, 'Role of Auxiliary Board members in Working with Assistants', November 1986)

The Supreme Body also wrote:

...As to the function of encouraging groups and isolated believers, as well as Local Spiritual Assemblies, not only do national committees normally attend to such duties, but more recently Auxiliary Board members and their assistants have been assuming, in most parts of the world, a far greater measure of responsibility for providing personal support and stimulation to the efforts of the friends residing in these localities.

(letter written on behalf of the Universal House of Justice to an individual believer, dated November 28, 1977)

7.3.5 Are the assistants a separate institution in themselves?

No. The assistants are part of the institution of the Auxiliary Board:-

The assistants to the Auxiliary Board members are part of that institution...An assistant should obey the instructions of the Auxiliary Board member in carrying out assignments for him.

(letter from the International Teaching Centre to all Counsellors, dated April 14, 1974)

An assistant works for a particular Auxiliary Board member, not for the Auxiliary Board generally.

7.3.6 How do the assistants perform their functions?

The assistants function in the same way as the Auxiliary Boards; that is, an assistant has a duty 'to foster loving relationships and an atmosphere of trust and mutual respect with the Local Spiritual Assemblies in his area.'

(letter from the International Teaching Centre to all Counsellors, dated April 14, 1974)

CHAPTER SEVEN

They should maintain direct contact with the local communities and individuals in their area of responsibility and report regularly to their Auxiliary Board member. They do not need to be specifically deputised by their Auxiliary Board member to meet with a Local Spiritual Assembly. They may also carry out specific assignments on behalf of their Auxiliary Board member:-

> *There seems to be no particular need for an Auxiliary Board member to specifically deputise an assistant to meet with a Spiritual Assembly on his behalf because such meetings are part of the normal work of an assistant. The assistant should be meeting with Local Spiritual Assemblies in the normal course of his duties without having to have special instructions from the Auxiliary Board member on each occasion, but, of course, if the Auxiliary Board member asks him to meet with a particular Assembly about some matter, he will do so.*
>
> (letter from the International Teaching Centre to all Counsellors, dated April 14, 1974)

7.3.7 *May an assistant also serve on an Assembly or committee, or be elected as a delegate to National Convention?*

Yes:-

> *Believers can serve at the same time both as assistants to Auxiliary Board members and on administrative institutions.*
>
> (letter from the Universal House of Justice to the Counsellors, dated June 8, 1973)

> *...Appointment of a believer as a Board member's assistant does not require the resignation of the appointee from a Spiritual Assembly or a committee. The House of Justice leans towards 'assistants' not retiring from administrative work, although in consultation with their Spiritual Assembly it may be quite in order; it would be preferable, however, for the suggestion to come from the appointee and not from the Spiritual Assembly.*
>
> (letter written on behalf of the Universal House of Justice to a National Spiritual Assembly, dated November 10, 1975)

7.3.8 *How does an assistant reconcile his or her roles as both an assistant to, and a member of, a Local Spiritual Assembly?*

A Bahá'í who is both an elected member of a Local Spiritual Assembly and who has been appointed to serve as an assistant to that Local Spiritual Assembly, has a primary duty to help that Spiritual Assembly to function harmoniously and efficiently. It is not the assistant's function to report all the proceedings of the Assembly's meetings to his or her Auxiliary Board member:-

> *An assistant can, of course, be a member of a Local Spiritual Assembly, but his task here as an assistant is to help the Spiritual Assembly to function harmoniously and efficiently in the discharge of its duties and this will hardly succeed if he gives the Assembly the feeling that he is reporting privately everything it does to the Auxiliary Board member. He should, on the contrary, do all he can to foster an atmosphere of warm and loving collaboration between the Local Assembly and the Board member.*

(letter written on behalf of the Universal House of Justice to a National Spiritual Assembly, dated August 2, 1982)

7.3.9 *What if the assistant is serving on another elected institution?*

As an assistant does not function as such outside his or her assigned area, an assistant serving on another institution of the Faith has the same duty to preserve the confidentiality of its consultations as any other believer:-

> *An assistant serves in this capacity only within the area assigned to him. Hence it would be improper for a believer who is an assistant to regard himself as having the responsibility to report his activities to the Auxiliary Board member, irrespective of where he is carrying out these activities. If serving on an Assembly or committee, his responsibility at that time is to the body on which he is serving.*

(International Teaching Centre statement 'Work of Members of the Auxiliary Boards', p.5, attached to a letter of 28 August 1984)

> *In the relationship between assistants and the National Spiritual Assembly no problems should arise, because the functions are entirely separate. An assistant is appointed by an Auxiliary Board member to help him in a specified area of the territory and he functions as an assistant only in relation to that area. Assistants, like Auxiliary Board members, function individually, not as a consultative body. Assistants who are members of a National Assembly or a national committee do not function as assistants in relation to that body, and they have the same duty to observe the confidentiality of its consultations, and of matters considered by the Assembly to be confidential, as does any other member.*

(letter written on behalf of the Universal House of Justice to a National Spiritual Assembly, dated August 2, 1982)

7.3.10 *How is the work of the assistants funded?*

The localised nature of the work of the assistants means that they should not normally require funding; however, if funds are required they should be supplied by the Local Spiritual Assembly or the Continental Board of Counsellors, depending upon on whose behalf the assistant is working:-

> *Normally the localised nature of the work of the assistants should enable them to carry it out without assistance from the Fund.*

(letter from the Universal House of Justice to the Counsellors, dated June 8, 1973)

> *...it is the hope of the Supreme Body that the work of the assistants will, for the most part, require no financial assistance. But if it does become necessary, it would seem obvious that when executing a task for the Local Spiritual Assembly he would be reimbursed out of the local Fund, and when engaged on a project for the Auxiliary Board member he would be reimbursed by the Continental Fund.*

(letter from the International Teaching Centre to all Counsellors, dated April 14, 1974)

CHAPTER SEVEN

7.4 RELATIONS BETWEEN THE LOCAL SPIRITUAL ASSEMBLY AND THE AUXILIARY BOARDS

7.4.1 *What principles govern the relationship between the Auxiliary Board members and their assistants and the Local Spiritual Assembly?*

The relationship between the Auxiliary Boards and the Local Spiritual Assembly is the same as that between the Continental Boards of Counsellors and the National Spiritual Assemblies in their zones of operation; that is, the Auxiliary Board members and their assistants have the necessary rank to ensure that they are kept informed of the Assemblies' activities and that the Assemblies will give due consideration to their advice and recommendations; however, they cannot tell Spiritual Assemblies what to do, or direct their work. The essence of the relationship between the Auxiliary Boards and Local Spiritual Assemblies should be one of loving cooperation:-

> *The statement that the Boards of Counsellors outrank the National Institutions of the Faith has a number of implications. A Board of Counsellors has the particular responsibility of caring for the protection and propagation of the Faith throughout a continental zone which contains a number of national Bahá'í communities. In performing these tasks it neither directs nor instructs the Spiritual Assemblies or individual believers, but it has the necessary rank to enable it to ensure that it is kept properly informed and that the Spiritual Assemblies give due consideration to its advice and recommendations. However, the essence of the relationships between Bahá'í institutions is loving consultation and a common desire to serve the Cause of God rather than a matter of rank or station.*
>
> (letter written on behalf of the Universal House of Justice to all National Spiritual Assemblies, dated March 27, 1978) [See also Lights of Guidance {revised edition}, nos. 1091-98.]

Another important principle is that the relationship between the Auxiliary Board members and their assistants and Local Spiritual Assemblies should not be hampered by rules and regulations:-

> *...we feel it important to stress that the relationship between Auxiliary Board members and Local Spiritual Assemblies should not be hampered by regulations; the methods of submitting information - either by minutes or otherwise - are optional...The relationship between Auxiliary Board members and Local Spiritual Assemblies should not be a matter of rights and prerogatives; it should be one of loving and wholehearted collaboration, in the spirit of the beloved Guardian's statement that 'the keynote of the Cause of God is not dictatorial authority but humble fellowship, not arbitrary power, but the spirit of frank and loving consultation'.*
>
> (memorandum from the Universal House of Justice to the Hands of the Cause of God in the Holy Land, dated October 7, 1970)

The Universal House of Justice has stressed that hard and fast lines of distinction should not be drawn between the functions of the assistants and other institutions:-

> *...the House of Justice has stressed that the work of the assistants should be kept on as informal a basis as possible, and that to draw hard and fast lines of jurisdiction and authority, or to overstress distinctions between this institution and that institution, are not only unnecessary*

CHAPTER SEVEN

but would be detrimental to the spirit of loving collaboration and encouragement which is essential to the progress of the work.

(letter from the International Teaching Centre to all Counsellors, dated April 14, 1974)

7.4.2 How should information be shared between the Auxiliary Board members and their assistants and the Local Spiritual Assemblies?

It is left to the Auxiliary Board members and their assistants and Assemblies to decide between themselves how best to share information. One option is for the Assembly to share its minutes with the Auxiliary Boards, however, it is not under any obligation to do so:-

It should be left to the discretion of the Local Spiritual Assemblies whether they send a complete copy of their minutes or report extracts from the minutes to the Auxiliary Board member in their zone.

(letter from the Universal House of Justice to a National Spiritual Assembly, dated December 21, 1969)

Other items that may be shared with the Auxiliary Board members and their assistants include local community newsletters, copies of the Assembly's Annual Report, Plan and Budget, programmes of local deepening and spiritualisation institutes, and so on. Another option is for the assistants (or Auxiliary Board members) to attend occasional meetings of the Local Spiritual Assembly or gatherings of the community.

7.4.3 How should meetings be arranged between the Auxiliary Board members and their assistants and Local Spiritual Assemblies?

Both the Auxiliary Boards and the Local Spiritual Assemblies have the right to request a meeting, which should then be arranged in a manner mutually convenient to both parties. It is not necessary to obtain the consent of the National Spiritual Assembly for such meetings:-

The National Spiritual Assembly should by all means encourage close cooperation and collaboration between the Auxiliary Board members and the Local Spiritual Assemblies, but it is not required that an Auxiliary Board member be present at all Local Assembly meetings. At occasional meetings, when the Local Spiritual Assembly wishes to discuss matters regarding the progress of the Cause in certain areas, for instance, attendance by a member of the Auxiliary Board would be of assistance, but such matters should be left to the discretion of the Local Spiritual Assemblies concerned. Of course whenever an Auxiliary Board member feels it necessary to consult with the Local Spiritual Assembly, he or she may request the Assembly to hold a meeting in his presence for the particular subject.

(letter written on behalf of the Universal House of Justice to a National Spiritual Assembly, dated July 13, 1986)

...it is not necessary that a member of the Continental Board of Counsellors or an Auxiliary Board member obtain the consent of the National Spiritual Assembly before contacting a Local Spiritual Assembly. However, an attitude of courtesy, respect and understanding on the part of both the administrative institutions and the Counsellors and their Auxiliary Board members should characterise their relationships to each other. Thus when a member of the Auxiliary Board wishes to meet with a Local Spiritual Assembly, both the Board

member and the Local Spiritual Assembly should try to arrange a mutually satisfactory time as far in advance as possible.

(from a communication of the Universal House of Justice to the Hands of the Cause in the Holy Land, dated May 10, 1970)

The above principles apply equally to meetings between assistants to Auxiliary Board members and Local Spiritual Assemblies.

7.4.4 **_May a Local Spiritual Assembly refuse to meet with an Auxiliary Board member or assistant when requested to do so?_**

No. As noted above in 'What principles govern the relationship between the Auxiliary Boards and their assistants and the Local Spiritual Assembly?' the Auxiliary Boards outrank the Local Spiritual Assemblies, therefore, the Assemblies cannot refuse to meet with an Auxiliary Board member or his or her assistant. Emphasis must be placed, however, on the attitude of loving cooperation that should exist between the institutions of the Faith, rather than on issues of rank.

7.4.5 **_May a properly functioning Local Spiritual Assembly dispense with the services of the Auxiliary Board members and their assistants?_**

No:-

When a Local Spiritual Assembly begins to function properly, it does not mean it can dispense with the service and work of Auxiliary Board members and their assistants, who can and should continue to provide stimulation and inspiration not only generally to the Assembly and local Bahá'í activities, but to individual believers as well.

(letter written on behalf of the Universal House of Justice to an individual believer, dated June 9, 1980)

7.4.6 **_When should a Local Spiritual Assembly seek collaboration with the Auxiliary Board members and their assistants?_**

A Local Spiritual Assembly should seek collaboration with the Auxiliary Board or with their assistant in the following matters:

1. When developing the local plan and budget for the coming year. The Spiritual Assemblies have the responsibility to formulate and execute plans of action; the Auxiliary Boards must be informed of these so that they can encourage the friends to support them:-

   It is the Spiritual Assemblies who plan and direct the work, but these plans should be well known to the Counsellors and Auxiliary Board members, because one of the ways in which they can assist the Assemblies is by urging the believers continually to support the plans of the Assemblies. If a National Spiritual Assembly has adopted one goal as pre-eminent in a year, the Auxiliary Board members should bear this in mind in all their contacts with the believers and should direct their attention to the plans of the National Assembly, and stimulate them to enthusiastically support them.

   (letter from the Universal House of Justice to the Continental Boards of Counsellors and National Spiritual Assemblies, dated October 1, 1969

2. When organising teaching and consolidation activities. The Spiritual Assemblies have the responsibility to organise and direct the teaching work; the Auxiliary Boards have the responsibility to stimulate the believers to carry out the work:-

> *It is the responsibility of Spiritual Assemblies, assisted by their committees, to organise and direct the teaching work, and in doing so they must, naturally, also do all they can to stimulate and inspire the friends. It is, however, inevitable that the Assemblies and committees, being burdened with the administration of the teaching work as well as with all other aspects of Bahá'í community life, will be unable to spend as much time as they would wish on stimulating the believers.*
>
> *Authority and direction flow from the Assemblies, whereas the power to accomplish the tasks resides primarily in the entire body of the believers. It is the principal task of the Auxiliary Boards to assist in arousing and releasing this power. This is a vital activity...*
>
> (letter from the Universal House of Justice to the Continental Boards of Counsellors and National Spiritual Assemblies, dated October 1, 1969)

There should be regular consultation on effective teaching methods between the Assembly and their Auxiliary Board members and assistants.

3. When the Assembly is handling any matter related to the protection of the Faith. The Spiritual Assemblies and the Auxiliary Boards should both be promptly informed of serious matters involving the protection of the Faith and should work together to resolve them:-

> *...both the administrative institutions on the one hand, and the Hands of the Cause and the institution of the Counsellors on the other, should be informed promptly of serious matters involving the protection of the Faith, particularly Covenant-breaking, and these institutions should cooperate in discharging the needed functions of protection. The point which should be emphasised is that the institutions of the Faith should keep each other informed on problems relating to the protection of the Cause, including in particular those involving Covenant-breaking.*
>
> (letter from the Hands of the Cause in the Holy Land to all Continental Boards of Counsellors, dated December 5, 1971)

4. When the Assembly is having difficulty in carrying out its routine responsibilities, eg. organising the Nineteen Day Feast or Holy Day celebrations, carrying out routine administrative work, and so on.
5. When the Assembly needs advice on the applicable spiritual and administrative principles relevant to a particular matter it is handling.
6. When the Assembly is handling a problem of disunity or any other matter that may adversely affect the interests of the Faith within the Bahá'í community; for example, flagrant violations of Bahá'í law.

7.4.7 Why is collaboration between the Auxiliary Board members and their assistants and Local Spiritual Assemblies important?

The Auxiliary Board members and their assistants and the Local Spiritual Assemblies are

CHAPTER SEVEN

both responsible for the protection and propagation of the Faith. This is why it is essential that they consult with one another:-

> *Since the functions of the propagation and the protection of the Faith are among the duties of Spiritual Assemblies, wholehearted collaboration and regular, continuous and full consultation between these Assemblies and the institution of the Counsellors are necessary. It should not be assumed that these two arms act independently of each other and are not in need of the essential support which each must give to the other. The functions are indeed complementary.*
>
> (from summary of points prepared by the Universal House of Justice, based on a letter to a National Spiritual Assembly, dated May 20, 1970)

The Universal House of Justice has noted that the existence of the 'learned' arm of the Faith is a feature not found in any of the religions of the past and it will take time for the Bahá'í community to fully recognise the value of the vital interdependence between the 'rulers' and the 'learned':-

> *The existence of institutions of such exalted rank [the 'learned']... is a feature of Bahá'í administration unparalleled in the religions of the past. The newness and uniqueness of this concept make it difficult to grasp; only as the Bahá'í Community grows and the believers are increasingly able to contemplate its administrative structure uninfluenced by concepts from past ages, will the vital interdependence of the 'rulers' and 'learned' in the Faith be properly understood, and the inestimable value of their interaction be fully recognised.*
>
> (letter from the Universal House of Justice to the Continental Boards of Counsellors and National Spiritual Assemblies, dated April 24, 1972)

The believers must understand that both the Local Spiritual Assemblies and the Auxiliary Boards are at a very early stage in their evolution; that both will develop and the relations between them change, as the Faith itself grows and changes. The Local Spiritual Assemblies, in particular, must understand the importance of persevering in cultivating relations with the Auxiliary Boards, according to the principles outlined in this Chapter.

7.4.8 ***How does a Local Spiritual Assembly decide which Auxiliary Board to approach in any given instance?***

Assemblies and individuals should feel free to refer a matter to either Board and the Board member or assistant concerned will decide whether it should be handled by his or her Board, or whether it would be better referred to another institution:-

> *The question has been raised as to how Local Spiritual Assemblies and individual believers are to know which matters they should refer to which Auxiliary Board member. We feel that this will be worked out at the local level in the light of experience, and that meanwhile the Assemblies and believers should not concern themselves unduly about it. They should feel free to refer to either Board, and if the Auxiliary Board member feels that the matter would better have been referred to his colleague, he can either himself pass the question on, or suggest the different approach to the Assembly or believer. This is similar to the situation, already familiar to Board members, when*

CHAPTER SEVEN

they have referred to them a matter which should properly be dealt with by a National Spiritual Assembly or one of its committees.

(letter from the Universal House of Justice to the International Teaching Centre, dated October 10, 1976)

7.4.9 **May a Local Spiritual Assembly directly approach an Auxiliary Board member to carry out work that is not specifically Auxiliary Board work as such?**

Yes:-

A National Spiritual Assembly, National Committee or Local Spiritual Assembly may directly request an Auxiliary Board member to perform such tasks as speaking at Summer Schools, appearing on television, etc. It should, of course, be left to the discretion of the Auxiliary Board member to determine whether such a request would clash with his other commitments.

(letter written on behalf of the Universal House of Justice to a National Spiritual Assembly, dated October 10, 1981)

7.4.10 **May a Local Spiritual Assembly directly approach an assistant to carry out work that is not Auxiliary Board work as such?**

Yes. A Local Spiritual Assembly can ask assistants to carry out specific tasks as individuals, without requiring the prior approval of the Auxiliary Board or a counsellor:-
A Spiritual Assembly is free to approach a believer who is an assistant without prior approval from the Auxiliary Board member or from a Counsellor. The guidance of the Universal House of Justice is:

Assistants can function simultaneously in both arms of the administration; therefore, if the National Assembly or a Local Spiritual Assembly requests a believer who happens to be an assistant to undertake a specific task, it is asking him in his capacity as an individual believer, not as an assistant.

(letter written on behalf of the Universal House of Justice to a National Spiritual Assembly, dated October 10, 1983)

7.4.11 **May Local Spiritual Assemblies write directly to Hands of the Cause of God, a Continental Board of Counsellors, or individual Counsellors?**

Local Spiritual Assemblies may write directly to Hands of the Cause of God, to a Continental Board of Counsellors or to any Counsellor. They may direct invitations to attend functions to these institutions. It will, however, be more effective if they communicate through the National Office. Better facilities of communication are available through the National Office, and it may be aware of the itinerary of members of these institutions. The National Assembly strongly encourages local communities, therefore, to communicate via the National Office with these institutions, although they are not forbidden to do otherwise. As to the International Teaching Centre, however, neither Local Spiritual Assemblies nor the National Spiritual Assembly have any direct communications with it. In the case of the International Teaching Centre, all communications must be directed through the Universal House of Justice. Individual believers may write privately to Hands of the Cause of God and to Counsellors.

7.5 **RELATIONS BETWEEN THE AUXILIARY BOARDS AND INDIVIDUALS**

7.5.1 **What courses of action are open to an Auxiliary Board member or assistant if approached by an individual with a personal problem?**

An assistant or Auxiliary Board member who is asked for advice by an individual on a personal matter may advise the believer to turn to his or her Assembly; give advice to the believer personally; or he or she may personally report the matter to the Counsellor or the Local Spiritual Assembly:-

> *If a believer turns to an assistant or Auxiliary Board member for advice on a personal matter it is for the assistant or Auxiliary Board member to decide whether he should advise the believer to turn to his Spiritual Assembly, whether he should himself give advice and, in either case, whether he should report the matter to the Counsellors, or to the Local Assembly, which, of course, would depend upon the degree of confidentiality he had undertaken to observe. Likewise, it is for the Counsellor to decide whether it is a matter of which the National Assembly should be informed. All this is, of course, within the general context that, apart from matters which ought to remain confidential, the more freely information is shared between the institutions of the Faith the better.*
>
> (letter written on behalf of the Universal House of Justice to a National Spiritual Assembly, dated August 2, 1982)

Within the terms of the above guidance it is clear that a Local Spiritual Assembly member may, as an individual, discuss any matter he or she chooses with the Auxiliary Board. For example, an Assembly member who is experiencing some difficulty related to his or her Assembly work, is free to discuss this with an Auxiliary Board member or assistant.

7.5.2 *May believers report instances of misconduct by other Bahá'ís to the Auxiliary Board?*

Individuals may consult their Auxiliary Board member or assistant regarding instances of misconduct on the part of other Bahá'ís (The Auxiliary Board member or assistant must then decide how to handle the situation within the terms of the Board's designated functions. For example, options may include reporting the matter to the Local Spiritual Assembly, or tactfully drawing the believer concerned into Bahá'í activities with the hope that this will lead to an improvement in conduct; however, members of the Auxiliary Board may not issue warnings, apply sanctions, or investigate alleged violations of Bahá'í law, as these are functions of the administrative institutions.

7.5.3 *Does an assistant have a right to report information received in confidence from an individual to an Assembly or Auxiliary Board member?*

No. A Bahá'í who promises to keep a matter confidential, regardless of the capacity in which he or she serves, must preserve that confidentiality. [See further Chapter 3, Section 3 'May a Local Spiritual Assembly member who receives information in confidence as an individual, share that information with the Assembly?']

7.6 **NOTES FOR REGISTERED GROUPS**

As noted in this Chapter, the Auxiliary Boards have the function of assisting groups and individuals as well as Local Spiritual Assemblies. Registered Groups should, therefore, consult with their Auxiliary Boards on matters relating to the propagation and protection of the Faith in their area.

7.7 **SUGGESTED FURTHER READING**

For further information on the evolution and functioning of the institution of the 'learned', Local Spiritual Assemblies are referred to the following works:

CHAPTER SEVEN

1. "The Continental Board of Counsellors", compilation of the National Spiritual Assembly of the United States (Bahá'í Publishing Trust, Wilmette, 1981)
2. Eunice Braun, "The March of the Institutions", A Commentary on the Interdependence of Rulers and Learned (George Ronald, Oxford, 1984)

CHAPTER EIGHT

Chapter 8

8. Membership in the Bahá'í Community

8.1 DECLARATION AND ENROLMENT - GENERAL PROCEDURES

8.1.1 *What are the guidelines for determining whether an individual should be accepted into the Faith?*

As stated on the 'Enrolment Card' they must:

1. have a sincere belief in Bahá'u'lláh
2. recognise the station of the Báb and 'Abdu'l-Bahá
3. be informed of the existence of laws that would affect their personal conduct
4. be informed of the existence of an administration they must follow

It is important to note that, whilst individuals must have a full understanding of the fundamentals, as outlined above, they do not need to know all the proofs, history, laws and principles of the Faith:-

> *The prime motive should always be the response of man to God's Message, and the recognition of His Messenger. Those who declare themselves as Bahá'ís should become enchanted with the beauty of the Teachings, and touched by the love of Bahá'u'lláh. The declarants need not know all the proofs, history, laws, and principles of the Faith, but in the process of declaring themselves they must, in addition to catching the spark of faith, become basically informed about the Central Figures of the Faith, as well as the existence of laws they must follow and an administration they must obey.*
>
> (Universal House of Justice, "Wellspring of Guidance", p.32)

Shoghi Effendi has warned of the need to avoid the extremes of, on the one hand, allowing people to come into the Faith before they have understood its meaning; and, on the other, making the conditions of entry too difficult:-

> *The believers must discriminate between the two extremes of bringing people into the Cause before they have fully grasped its fundamentals and making it too hard for them, expecting too much of them, before they accept them. This requires truly keen judgement, as it is unfair to people to allow them to embrace a movement the true meaning of which they have not fully grasped. It is equally unfair to expect them to be perfect Bahá'ís before they can enter the Faith.*
>
> (letter written on behalf of Shoghi Effendi to an individual believer, dated November 22, 1941) [See further "Lights of Guidance" {revised edition} nos. 232-66.]

8.1.2 *Does the individual have to be living a correct life, according to Bahá'í standards, before declaring?*

No. It is not necessary that individuals be living according to Bahá'í standards at the time of their declaration, provided they are told of the laws that would affect their personal conduct and it is understood that they must take steps to conform to those laws after declaring:-

> *The acceptance of a person into the Bahá'í community should be based not on whether he is leading an exemplary life, but on whether the*

> *Assembly is reasonably certain that he is sincere in his declaration of faith in Bahá'u'lláh and that he knows of the laws which would affect his personal conduct, so that he does not enter the community under a misapprehension.*
>
> (letter written on behalf of the Universal House of Justice to a National Spiritual Assembly, dated April 19, 1981)

8.1.3 *Which laws should the individual be made aware of before enrolment in the Faith?*

The individual should be made aware of those laws relating to:
- Marriage and Divorce
- Avoidance of Drinking Alcohol
- Avoidance of Use of Drugs (including marijuana)
- Obedience to the Law of the Land
- Non-Involvement in Politics
- Chastity
- Daily Prayers
- Fasting

It is particularly important that the individual is made aware of these laws, otherwise problems are likely to arise after enrolment:-

> *A person wishing to join the Faith should be told of the laws which affect his personal conduct, in the process of his acceptance into the Faith. Sometimes a Bahá'í teacher is afraid to do this, for fear of scaring the person away; under these circumstances, the person is being admitted under a misapprehension, and future problems often result.*
>
> (International Teaching Centre, letter dated December 11, 1978)

8.1.4 *What steps should a Bahá'í teacher take when an individual expresses the wish to become a Bahá'í?*

The Bahá'í teacher should use the following procedure:-

1. the teacher should be satisfied in his or her own mind that the individual has a proper understanding of the Faith, as outlined above.
2. the teacher should ask the individual to sign a 'Declaration Card'.

Declaration Cards are available from Local Assemblies, Regional Teaching Committees, or the National Office, on request. If a Declaration Card is not available at the time, the declaration of faith may be made in some other form - for example, a letter. The person needs to make a statement to the following effect: 'I accept Bahá'u'lláh as the Manifestation of God for this Day, and wish to become a member of the Bahá'í Faith.' Completion of the Declaration Card should be treated as an important and significant event and not one to be handled in a light or hasty manner. Note also that the signing of the Declaration Card is an administrative matter enabling the declarant to become a member of the Bahá'í community. The spiritual implications of a declaration of faith are between the individual and God.

8.1.5 *To whom should the completed Declaration Card be given?*

If the declarant lives in a Local Spiritual Assembly area the Declaration Card or letter should be given to the Local Spiritual Assembly. If the declarant does not live in a Local Spiritual Assembly area the Card or letter should be given to the Regional Teaching Committee for that area.

CHAPTER EIGHT

8.1.6 ***What are the responsibilities of a Local Spiritual Assembly when it is given a Declaration Card?***

The Local Spiritual Assembly has the following duties:-

1. It is responsible for checking that individuals are sincere in their declaration of faith and have a proper grasp of the fundamentals of the Faith, as outlined above. Arrangements should therefore be made for declarants to meet either with the full institution, or with representatives of it. The meetings also serve the following purposes:-
    a) they provide declarants with an opportunity to ask questions
    b) they introduces declarants, to the administrative body with which they w i l l have dealings
2. If it is satisfied that a declaration should be accepted, the Assembly must complete the confirmation of enrolment section on the reverse side of the Declaration Card and forward to the National Office. Completion of this section of the card certifies that representatives of the Local Spiritual Assembly have met with the individual concerned and have satisfied themselves that the person is sincere and has a knowledge of the fundamentals of the Faith. It also provides useful information for the National Spiritual Assembly's records. The purpose of this card is entirely administrative. It should be sent with any comments the Assembly wishes to add in a letter, to the National Spiritual Assembly. The final decision concerning acceptance of a declaration lies with the National Spiritual Assembly.
3. Whilst waiting for the decision of the National Spiritual Assembly, declarants should be regarded as Bahá'ís. This means, if of age, they may be elected to an Assembly, become a delegate, or be appointed to a committee, and may exercise the right to vote; in short, all the rights and responsibilities of Bahá'ís in good standing. They may be appointed to a committees. If attending a Bahá'í-only function at which credentials must be shown they may be vouched for by other believers.
4. When the National Spiritual Assembly has approved a declaration it will send a letter of welcome to the individual along with a card on Requisites for Spiritual Growth.
5. A copy of the letter will be sent to the Assembly which will authorise the issuing of Bahá'í credentials to the declarant.
6. The Feast may be a fitting time to present the letter of welcome to the new declarant. The Assembly may also like to give a gift. One suggestion is a free subscription to "Herald of the South".
7. The new declarant should be entered on the Assembly's membership list.
8. In rare instances the National Spiritual Assembly will not accept a declaration. Should this occur, the Assembly will be advised and will be given guidance on the steps to take.
9. Exceptions to the above procedures exist in the case of individuals of certain backgrounds. These exceptions are outlined in later in this Chapter.

8.1.7 ***Are there any circumstances in which a declaration should not be accepted?***

An Assembly may refuse to accept a declaration if it feels that the person does not meet the guidelines set out above. For instance, the International Teaching Centre has advised that:-

> *An Assembly can refuse to enrol a person if they feel he does not really believe in Bahá'u'lláh as a Manifestation (rather than as a wise man, or an inspired man). In other words, it (the Assembly) does not have to accept someone, just because he wishes to enter.*
>
> (letter dated December 11, 1978)

CHAPTER EIGHT

The Universal House of Justice has also noted that:-

> *...an individual may be encouraged to become better acquainted with the spirit, laws, and principles of the Faith before submitting his application...*
>
> (letter written on behalf of the Universal House of Justice to a Local Spiritual Assembly, dated April 4, 1977)

As Shoghi Effendi has advised against being too rigid in our requirements, it should not often happen that a declaration is refused. Nevertheless, should the Assembly feel it has good reason not to accept a declaration, it has the right to do so. If the declarant still wishes to become a Bahá'í and believes the Assembly has made a wrong decision, the Bahá'í teacher involved may refer the matter to the National Spiritual Assembly. The Local Assembly is not required to advise the National Spiritual Assembly that it has refused a declaration. There are some exceptional situations in which it may be advisable to postpone enrolment, even though the Assembly is satisfied as to the sincerity of the declarant's belief. These situations are covered later in this Chapter.

8.1.8 **What if the declarant does not live in a Local Spiritual Assembly area, or near to any members of the Regional Teaching Committee?**

If the new declarant is not in an Assembly area and lives far away from the members of the Regional Teaching Committee, the Regional Teaching Committee may request a nearby Local Spiritual Assembly or someone responsible who lives near the new declarant, to conduct the interview.

8.1.9 **What if the declarant has more than one place of residence?**

If the declarant has more than one place of residence he or she should make a choice as to which address should be recorded on the membership roll. The declarant will then be considered a member of that community and will be enrolled by the Bahá'í institution having responsibility for that area.

8.1.10 **What should the Local Spiritual Assembly do to assist the declarant after enrolment?**

After enrolment it is essential that new believers are deepened in the Faith; encouraged to bring their lives into conformity with Bahá'í law; and moved to become active participants in the administrative and teaching work. The teaching and deepening work must go hand in hand:-

> *Above all, the utmost endeavour should be exerted by your Assembly to familiarise the newly enrolled believers with the fundamental and spiritual verities of the Faith, and with the origins, the aims and purposes, as well as the processes of a divinely appointed Administrative Order, to acquaint them more fully with the history of the Faith, to instil in them a deeper understanding of the Covenants of both Bahá'u'lláh and of 'Abdu'l-Bahá, to enrich their spiritual life, to rouse them to a greater effort and a closer participation in both the teaching of the Faith and the administration of its activities, and to inspire them to make the necessary sacrifices for the furtherance of its vital interests. For as the body of the avowed supporters of the Faith is enlarged, and the basis of the structure of its Administrative Order is broadened, and the fame of the rising community spreads far and wide, a parallel progress must be achieved, if the fruits already garnered are to endure, in the spiritual quickening of its members and the deepening of their inner life.*

CHAPTER EIGHT

> (letter written on behalf of Shoghi Effendi to a National Spiritual Assembly, dated June 26, 1956)

> *When enrolling new believers, we must be wise and gentle, and not place so many obstacles in their way that they feel it impossible to accept the Faith. On the other hand, once accorded membership in the Community of the followers of Bahá'u'lláh, it must be brought home to them that they are expected to live up to His Teachings, and to show forth the signs of a noble character in conformity with His Laws. This can often be done gradually, after the new believer is enrolled.*

> (letter written on behalf of Shoghi Effendi to a National Spiritual Assembly, dated June 25, 1953) [For further information and suggestions on how to deepen new believers see "Wellspring of Guidance", p.31-36}

8.1.11 **What is the procedure for a person who wishes to re-enrol in the Faith?**

If a person has resigned from the Faith and then wishes to rejoin, the Local Spiritual Assembly should follow the normal declaration procedure, except that the person is not be considered as a Bahá'í and may not attend Bahá'í-only functions until the National Spiritual Assembly notifies the Local Spiritual Assembly that it has accepted the re-declaration. The Local Spiritual Assembly must, when recommending the person's acceptance to the National Spiritual Assembly, note that he or she is seeking to 're-enrol'. An explanation of how the person has overcome the problems that led to his or her resignation in the first place would also be useful. It must be made clear to the applicant that the decision to enrol in the Faith is a serious one and not to be taken lightly. The Local Spiritual Assembly must be quite sure of the person's sincerity before recommending his or her re-enrolment.

8.2 **DECLARATION AND ENROLMENT - SPECIAL CASES**

8.2.1 **May citizens of Israel be enrolled as Bahá'ís?**

The Bahá'í Faith is not taught in Israel and there is no Bahá'í community in Israel apart from those serving at the World Centre. Israelis who learn about the Faith outside of Israel and wish to become Bahá'ís may be enrolled only if they intend living permanently outside of Israel. They must, however, be advised that it is not possible for them to return to Israel, even for a brief visit, without the prior permission of the Universal House of Justice. They would also have to be willing to accept the restriction placed on teaching the Faith in Israel. The Local Spiritual Assembly should satisfy itself that the declarants' depth of understanding is sufficient to enable them to appreciate their situation and to remain firm in the Faith under these circumstances. If they intend to return to Israel formal enrolment is not possible. This, of course, does not affect the status of their personal belief in Bahá'u'lláh:-

> *As you know, it has been a policy of long standing that we do not enrol believers in the Holy Land. The Writings and Teachings of Bahá'u'lláh are available for everyone, including those who live here. However, when it comes to enrolment, those deeply interested in the Faith must be lovingly informed that aside from the World Centre, there is no Bahá'í community in the Holy Land and that for many reasons it is not propitious to establish local Bahá'í communities here. Furthermore, Bahá'ís are only permitted to come to the Holy Land for pilgrimage or for brief visits. Only those associated with the work at the World Centre are permitted to reside here. Therefore, if they ...*

CHAPTER EIGHT

expect to return to the Holy Land for purposes of residence, they should be counselled that they cannot be formally enrolled. What they do about Bahá'u'lláh and His Teachings as a matter of personal belief, is another matter.

(letter from the Universal House of Justice to a National Spiritual Assembly, dated August 11, 1972)

In the case of an Israeli, of whatever background, you should explain that the Faith is not taught in Israel; that if he is planning to return to Israel to reside, he cannot be accepted into the Bahá'í community; and that if he is planning to continue to reside outside Israel he may be accepted but that he will be subject to the same restrictions as other Bahá'ís with respect to visiting Israel, namely he could do so only with the express permission of the Universal House of Justice. In any event, the Universal House of Justice should be informed of such declaration.

(letter from the Universal House of Justice to a National Spiritual Assembly, dated March 8, 1974)

For your further information, when Israeli citizens who are permanently resident elsewhere learn of the Faith, study it and wish to become Bahá'ís, they may be welcomed and accepted fully into the Bahá'í community. Before such a declaration is accepted, however, certain steps must be taken. The respective Spiritual Assembly should satisfy itself that the declarants' depth of understanding is sufficient to enable them to appreciate the particular problems that will face them as Israeli Bahá'ís, and is satisfied they will remain firm under these circumstances. As in the case of all Bahá'ís, they would not be permitted to reside permanently in Israel, although they would normally be given permission to come and visit any family members they may have here, whenever they wish to do so. They would also have to understand that Bahá'ís do not teach the Faith in Israel, and be willing to abide by this restriction. The reasons for this should be explained in a loving way by the Spiritual Assembly concerned.

(letter written on behalf of the Universal House of Justice to a National Spiritual Assembly, dated September 5, 1990)

Israelis who are permanently resident outside of Israel, who wish to become Bahá'ís, should complete a Declaration Card in the usual way. The Local Spiritual Assembly should meet with them to assess their knowledge and sincerity; to advise them of the particular situation facing Israeli Bahá'ís, as outlined above; and to assess whether the declarants' would remain firm under these circumstances. If the Assembly believes they fulfil all these conditions, it should send the completed Declaration and Enrolment Cards to the National Spiritual Assembly, together with full background information about the declarants' situation and a written recommendation that they believe the declarant to be sincere, and willing and able to abide by the above guidelines. The National Spiritual Assembly must refer the declarations to the Universal House of Justice and obtain its consent to the declarants' enrolment; therefore, until a reply has been received from the National Spiritual Assembly, the Local Assembly should treat the declarants with kindness and friendship, but they must not be considered as Bahá'ís. That is to say, they may not attend Bahá'í-only functions or exercise any of the rights and duties of a Bahá'í in good standing.

CHAPTER EIGHT

8.2.2 *May people from Malaysia be enrolled in the Faith?*

Muslims from Malaysia may not be enrolled in the Faith if they are planning to return to Malaysia. They may, however, be given Bahá'í literature. Malaysians who are not Muslims may be enrolled:-

> *In reply to your letter of 2 January 1985, the Universal House of Justice has requested us to advise you that the Muslim Malaysian students at the University of Tasmania may be informed of the Faith and be given Bahá'í literature. If they are returning to Malaysia, they may not be registered as Bahá'ís, because it is against the law of their country. However, Malaysians from non-Muslim background can be registered if they accept the Cause, since the law in Malaysia prohibits teaching other religions to Muslims only.*

(letter from the Universal House of Justice to a National Spiritual Assembly, dated January 21, 1985)

8.2.3 *May Muslims from the Middle-East and North Africa be enrolled in the Faith?*

As a general principle Bahá'ís should not seek out Muslims from the Middle-East and North Africa, especially Iranian Muslims, to teach them the Faith [see further Chapter 5 on 'Teaching' in this Handbook]. Should people from this background wish to become Bahá'ís, however, they should fill out a Declaration Card in the usual way and the Local Spiritual Assembly should meet with them to assess their knowledge and sincerity. Iranians should be made aware of the problems they may face if returning to Iran as Bahá'ís; for example, they may then find themselves unable to leave Iran. The Assembly should send the completed Declaration and Enrolment Cards to the National Spiritual Assembly, together with a written recommendation that they believe the declarant to be sincere.

This letter should also include the following information about the declarant:
- country of origin
- ethnic background
- date of leaving the country
- previous address in the country
- names and addresses of one or two people they knew in the country

Depending on the circumstances it is likely that the National Spiritual Assembly will have to refer the application to the Universal House of Justice. Exceptions to this rule exist in the following cases:-

1. *Applications from Iranian Muslim spouses and close relatives of Bahá'ís who have shown sincere interest in the Faith and have never engaged in any kind of opposition or animosity toward it.*
2. *Applications from Iranian Muslims who have been permanent residents in a country outside Iran before the Iranian Revolution (ie. before 1 January 1979), provided they are sincere in their wish to become Bahá'ís and have no ulterior motive such as obtaining refugee status and the like.*

(guidelines from the Universal House of Justice, dated June 20, 1989)

In these two instances the National Spiritual Assembly may make a decision without reference to the Universal House of Justice. Until a reply has been received from the National Spiritual Assembly the person concerned should be treated with kindness and friendship, but must not be considered as a Bahá'í; that is to say, he or she may not attend Bahá'í-only functions or exercise any of the rights and duties of a Bahá'í in good standing.

Given the various factors that must be taken into consideration - for example, the reactions of Muslim relatives - it may be that the enrolment will have to be postponed. Should this happen the person concerned should continue to be treated with friendship and helped to deepen in the Faith. The Universal House of Justice has said:-

> *In such instances it could be explained to them that although they have accepted the Faith in their hearts and are regarded as Bahá'ís in belief, their enrolment must be postponed because of the situation in Iran. Meanwhile, the Bahá'ís should maintain friendly contacts with them and deepen them in their knowledge of the Faith.*
>
> (letter written on behalf of the Universal House of Justice to a National Spiritual Assembly, dated February 6, 1986)

The above policy also applies to Muslims from the Middle-East and North Africa who are only visiting Australia; that is, they may be enrolled according to the above procedure. When the time comes for them to return to their home country, their membership must be transferred through the Universal House of Justice, see later in this Chapter. This policy does not apply to people from the Middle-East and North Africa who are not Muslims. They may be enrolled according to the ordinary procedure already set out. Again, if they are returning to their home country, the transfer of their membership must be affected through the Universal House of Justice. As to the enrolment of Muslims who come from any part of the world other than the Middle-East and North Africa, the friends should follow the above guidance; that is, they should be interviewed and the above-listed information sent to the National Spiritual Assembly. They should not be regarded as Bahá'ís until notification of their acceptance is received from the National Spiritual Assembly.

8.2.4 *May Chinese who are permanent residents of Australia be enrolled in the Faith?*

Yes. Chinese who are permanent residents of Australia may be enrolled according to the ordinary enrolment procedure already outlined. The Local Spiritual Assembly should work closely with the National Chinese Teaching Committee and its working groups when teaching and enrolling Chinese residents; for example, it may be helpful to have someone from this Committee, who understands the Chinese culture, present, when the Local Spiritual Assembly is interviewing the person.

8.2.5 *May citizens of the People's Republic of China (PRC) be enrolled in the Faith?*

Yes. Citizens of the PRC may be enrolled in the Faith. They may participate in the social life of the community, in Feasts and deepenings, and should be shown the usual Bahá'í hospitality and friendship. Citizens of the PRC are, however, in a sensitive position as the Faith is not formally established on the Chinese mainland. For their own protection, and for the sake of the future of the Faith in the PRC, the Universal House of Justice has established the following policies with regard to their participation in Bahá'í community life:

1. Chinese believers who are citizens of the PRC should be introduced to each other as Bahá'ís only if they are willing for this to be done. Given the possibility of meeting other Chinese citizens at Bahá'í functions, it is recommended that it be left up to the individual believer to decide which functions to attend.
2. Whilst citizens of the PRC may participate in the social life of the Bahá'í community in a normal manner they should not be singled out for undue attention or be subjected to public gaze.
3. Citizens of the PRC may not serve on Spiritual Assemblies, be appointed to committees, or be associated officially with Bahá'í administration. Note, however, that they may vote in Bahá'í elections (although they may not be voted for). They may also be included in the meetings and activities of local committees as long as their names are not published or recorded in the minutes and they are not considered members of a committee.

CHAPTER EIGHT

4. Literature published in Taiwan may be given to citizens of the PRC. Bahá'ís from Taiwan are free to meet with citizens of the PRC in natural situations. Likewise, Bahá'ís who are citizens of the PRC when overseas, may, at their own discretion, share the Teachings of Bahá'u'lláh with the Chinese from Taiwan. (from guidelines from the Universal House of Justice, dated April 19, 1989 and a letter written on behalf of the Universal House of Justice to a National Spiritual Assembly, dated October 2, 1989)

When enrolling citizens of the PRC in the Faith the following procedure (based on the guidelines of the Universal House of Justice, dated April 19, 1989) must be observed:

1. The Bahá'í teacher should not ask the person wishing to declare to sign a Declaration Card but should pass on his or her expressed wish to declare orally to the Local Spiritual Assembly. Note, however, that the person may make a written declaration of Faith if he or she so wishes.
2. The Local Spiritual Assembly should appoint one or two of its members who have, if possible, some experience with Chinese people, to meet with the new declarant and the teacher and (if necessary) a member of the National Chinese Teaching Committee or working group. This meeting should be conducted in a very informal manner, bearing in mind that citizens of the PRC, because of their background, are often suspicious and afraid of being interviewed by officials. This is the reason the full Assembly should not meet with the individual.

At this meeting the Assembly representatives must make an assessment of the person's knowledge and sincerity and collect the following information:
- the person's full name in Chinese script
- full name in Roman alphabet
- current address
- home address in China
- date of declaration
- occupation

The Assembly representatives should fill out and sign the Enrolment Card on behalf of the Local Spiritual Assembly. The Enrolment Card and above particulars must be sent to the National Spiritual Assembly. The National Spiritual Assembly, in turn, will forward this information to the Universal House of Justice for the membership records at the World Centre.

3. While waiting for the decision of the National Spiritual Assembly the person should be regarded as a Bahá'í and encouraged to participate in Bahá'í activities to the extent possible within the terms of the above guidance of the Universal House of Justice.
4. It should be made clear to citizens of the PRC that there is no Bahá'í administration in China and, therefore, at this time Bahá'í laws of personal status are not binding nor are they required to withdraw from membership in other associations. Laws of personal status have been defined to mean such things as change in marital status in a letter written on behalf of the Universal House of Justice to a National Spiritual Assembly, dated February 21, 1988. 'Other associations' have been defined as 'religious or political' in a letter written on behalf of the Universal House of Justice to a National Spiritual Assembly, dated September 17, 1987. Citizens of the PRC should, however, endeavour to learn about Bahá'í laws and principles and should, as a matter of conscience, endeavour to practice these to the best of their ability. They should also be advised of the caution needed regarding teaching the Faith on the Chinese mainland and be asked to observe it for their own protection as well as the future of the Faith there.

5. The National Spiritual Assembly will advise the Local Spiritual Assembly by letter when the declaration is accepted. No letter of welcome will be sent to the declarant.
6. The Local Spiritual Assembly should advise the person of their acceptance orally. No credential card may be issued.
7. The person's name and address should be entered on the community's membership list but it must be kept separate from the voting list and must not be publicised.

The Local Spiritual Assembly must also note the following points:
1. All communications with Bahá'ís from the PRC must be oral. It could be dangerous for them to have any form of written identification of their membership in the Faith upon them. This means they must not be sent official correspondence - for example, election calls or community newsletters - through the post. The National Spiritual Assembly does not send the Bahá'í Bulletin or any other mailouts to these believers. The best way of keeping in touch with the Chinese friends is through an informal social network.
2. The Local Spiritual Assembly should work closely with the National Chinese Teaching Committee (NCTC) or its working groups. If the Assembly knows it will have to handle continuing enrolments of citizens of the PRC it may consider appointing permanent liaison officers on the Assembly whose tasks would include liaising with the NCTC or one of its working groups, meeting with new declarants, and keeping in touch with Bahá'ís from the PRC in the local community.

8.2.6 *May prisoners be enrolled in the Faith?*

Yes. Prisoners may be enrolled in the Faith in the same manner as anyone else; however, they cannot exercise their voting rights until released from prison:-

> *You are free to accept declarations of faith from inmates of a prison, but their participation as voting believers can take place only after they have been discharged from prison. The fact of having been in prison does not deprive a Bahá'í from exercising his voting rights when he is released and there is no need for a probationary period. However, if there is some other factor which would indicate to the National Assembly that in a particular case the voting rights should be suspended, the National Assembly may then exercise its discretion.*

(letter from the Universal House of Justice to a National Spiritual Assembly, dated December 8, 1969)

Should the Local Spiritual Assembly concerned feel that there are particular circumstances which could necessitate the withholding of voting rights once the prisoner has been released, it should send a full report to the National Spiritual Assembly.

8.2.7 *May sub-normal or mentally ill people be enrolled in the Faith?*

Yes. Only in cases of extreme illness should membership be denied such a person:-

> *The question of mental instability has no bearing upon the acceptance of an enrolment unless it is of such a nature that it affects the ability of the declarant to judge whether or not he believes in Bahá'u'lláh.*

(letter written on behalf of the Universal House of Justice to a National Spiritual Assembly, dated April 19, 1981)

In a letter written on his behalf to a National Spiritual Assembly, dated May 15, 1940, Shoghi Effendi said that by mental unfitness was meant a condition much more serious than any temperamental deficiency or disinclination to conform to the principle of majority rule. He said:

> 'Only in rare cases when a person is actually unbalanced, and is admittedly proved to be so, should the right of membership be denied him. The greatest care and restraint should be exercised in this matter.'

8.2.8 *May a person who belongs to an organisation to which Bahá'ís may not belong, be enrolled in the Faith?*

In considering the enrolment of a person who belongs to an organisation to which Bahá'ís may not belong, the Assembly has two choices. It may enrol the person in the usual way, making sure that he or she is aware that continued membership in the organisation is not permissible under Bahá'í law. The person should then be given a reasonable time to withdraw from the organisation. Should the person not do so, nor pay attention to the Local Spiritual Assembly's warnings on the matter, the question of deprivation of voting rights may arise. This is the normal procedure. The alternative is to advise the person of the Bahá'í law on the matter and suggest that enrolment be postponed until he or she has had the opportunity to withdraw from the organisation. This option may be preferable for a person holding a political post, for example:-

> *In the case of people who accept the Faith while living in a situation which is not morally acceptable, or while being a member of an organisation to which it is not permissible for a Baha'i to belong, the normal procedure is for the Assembly to accept the declaration of faith so that the new believer may become a member of the Bahá'í community and his newly-born belief in Bahá'u'lláh can be nurtured, and at the same time for the Assembly to explain that his situation is one that must change within a reasonable time. If the believer does not rectify his situation as a result of the Assembly's exhortations and assistance, and following due warnings when the time limit expires, the Assembly would have to consider depriving him of his administrative rights. It may well be, however, that in a particular case, it is preferable to explain the matter to the individual concerned and advise the postponement of the registration of his acceptance of the Faith until such time as he has been able to rectify his situation. This has happened, for example, in some countries where a person who holds a prominent political post has accepted the Faith and needs to complete his term of office before being able to withdraw honourably from politics.*

(letter written on behalf of the Universal House of Justice to an individual believer, dated June 18, 1985)

However the Assembly chooses to handle the matter, it should be wary of placing too many obstacles in the way of a person's enrolment. It is generally expected that individuals will gradually adjust their lives to conform to the Bahá'í standards after they enrol.

8.2.9 *May drug users or alcoholics be enrolled in the Faith?*

Yes. The same guidelines as above should be applied; that is, the individual should be made aware of the relevant Bahá'í principles at the time of enrolment; he or she should be given sufficient time to rectify the situation after becoming a Bahá'í; should the person not rectify the situation within a reasonable time, the question of deprivation of voting rights may arise. The Local Spiritual Assembly should provide the person with every assistance and should also encourage him or her to seek professional help:-

CHAPTER EIGHT

Concerning the acceptance into the Faith of individuals who have mental problems or are drug addicts, etc., the House of Justice instructs us to say that if the Assembly is satisfied that the person is sufficiently in command of his faculties to understand what his declaration of faith implies, he may be accepted as a believer. In other words you should apply the normal guidelines of acceptance of new believers. In such cases, however, you may have to ensure that special steps are taken to deepen the understanding of the new Bahá'í. A drug addict or alcoholic should, of course, be told that the taking of drugs and alcohol is strictly forbidden in Bahá'í law, and he will have to do whatever is necessary to break himself of the addiction. You may find it necessary and helpful to put him in touch with organisations which specialise in helping such cases. If a case is severe you may have to warn the person that if he does not overcome this problem within a reasonable time you may have to consider depriving him of his voting rights.

(letter written on behalf of the Universal House of Justice to a National Spiritual Assembly, dated May 12, 1982)

The Local Spiritual Assembly may also consider the possibility of postponing enrolment until the problem is overcome, if it is severe.

8.2.10 Should a person living in an immoral relationship be accepted into the Faith?

Yes. Again, the conditions outlined above apply:-

The young lady in question should be advised by you or the believer with whom she has been studying that the decision as to whether or not she wishes to enrol in the Faith rests with her and her alone. Your Assembly should not prevent her from enrolling should she so decide, but if she does apply for membership in the community, she obviously should understand that she will be expected to conduct herself as a Bahá'í by adjusting her relationship to the man with whom she is presently living. This means that either they must become legally married or she should sever the existing relationship between them. Your Local Spiritual Assembly is responsible to guide and assist this young lady...

(letter written on behalf of the Universal House of Justice to a Local Spiritual Assembly, dated April 4, 1977)

If the other party to the relationship does not wish to become a Bahá'í it may nevertheless be desirable to consult with that person at the same time so that any doubtful points can be cleared up. Note also that if the couple plan to adjust their relationship by getting married, it is not necessary for them to separate in the meantime:-

As the friends are very new in the Faith and are willing to abide by the Bahá'í laws regarding marriage, it would be better not to be rigid in this case by insisting that the couple separate until legally married.

(letter from the Universal House of Justice to a National Spiritual Assembly, dated December 8, 1974)

CHAPTER EIGHT

8.3 ENROLMENT OF CHILDREN AND YOUTH

8.3.1 *Are children born of Bahá'í parents considered to be Bahá'ís?*

Yes. Although at the age of 15 children of Bahá'ís are asked to make their own declaration of faith, and do not automatically inherit the Faith of their parents, they are nevertheless regarded as Bahá'ís from the time of their birth unless there is some reason to suppose otherwise:-

> *Unlike the children of some other religions, Bahá'í children do not automatically inherit the Faith of their parents. However, the parents are responsible for the upbringing and spiritual welfare of their children, and Spiritual Assemblies have the duty to assist parents, if necessary, in fulfilling these obligations, so that the children will be reared in the light of the Revelation of Bahá'u'lláh, and from their earliest years will learn to love God and His Manifestations and to walk in the way of God's Law. It is natural, therefore, to regard the children of Bahá'ís as Bahá'ís unless there is a reason to conclude the contrary. It is quite wrong to think of Bahá'í children as existing in some sort of spiritual limbo until the age of 15 at which time they can 'become' Bahá'ís.*
>
> (letter written on behalf of the Universal House of Justice to a National Spiritual Assembly, dated July 19, 1982)

8.3.2 *Should the Local Spiritual Assembly register the births of children born to Bahá'í parents?*

Yes:-

> *Children born to a Bahá'í couple are regarded as Bahá'ís from the beginning of their lives, and their births should be registered by the Spiritual Assembly.*
>
> (letter written on behalf of the Universal House of Justice to a National Spiritual Assembly, dated July 19, 1982)

The National Spiritual Assembly needs to be informed of all children who are registered as Bahá'ís in order to keep the national membership list up to date. It also needs to pass these statistics on to the Universal House of Justice. Should there be a reason for the parents not to want their children to be registered as Bahá'ís, the Local Spiritual Assembly may, at its own discretion, decide not to register them:-

> *...although children of Bahá'í parents, under age 15, are generally considered Bahá'ís, there may be circumstances in which they should not be registered as such, and this is also left to your discretion. Local Spiritual Assemblies should help by advising the parents to consider it one of their primary obligations to raise their children in a spirit of love and dedication towards the Faith.*
>
> (letter written on behalf of the Universal House of Justice to a National Spiritual Assembly, dated October 3, 1976)

8.3.3 *What if the child has only one Bahá'í parent?*

The child should be registered as a Bahá'í unless the non-Bahá'í parent objects:-

> *The birth of a child to a couple, one of whom is a Bahá'í, should also be registered unless the non-Bahá'í parent objects.*

CHAPTER EIGHT

(letter written on behalf of the Universal House of Justice to a
National Spiritual Assembly, dated July 19, 1982)

8.3.4 **May a Local Spiritual Assembly accept a declaration from a child, neither of whose parents are Bahá'ís?**

Yes. The Local Spiritual Assembly may register such a child as a Bahá'í, provided the parents agree:-

> *A Spiritual Assembly may accept the declaration of faith of a child of non-Bahá'í parents, and register him as a Bahá'í child, provided the parents give their consent.*

(letter written on behalf of the Universal House of Justice to a
National Spiritual Assembly, dated July 19, 1982)

8.3.5 **Should the children of a couple, one or both of whom have just become Bahá'ís, be registered as Bahá'ís?**

The situation of children whose parents have just declared must be determined by the reactions of the children in each case. The Local Spiritual Assembly should, on the one hand, ensure that family unity is maintained; and, on the other, ensure that such children are made welcome at Bahá'í gatherings:-

> *In the cases of children whose parents become Bahá'ís, much depends upon the ages and reactions of the children concerned. They will require great love and understanding, and each case must be judged on its own merits. This applies to an added degree, of course, if only one of the parents has accepted the Faith, in which case the attitude of the other parent is an important factor; the aim of the Bahá'ís should be to foster family unity. The important thing is that the children, whether registered as Bahá'ís or not, should be made to feel welcome at Bahá'í children's classes and other community gatherings.*

(letter written on behalf of the Universal House of Justice to a
National Spiritual Assembly, dated July 19, 1982)

8.3.6 **Should the children of Bahá'ís who have lost their voting rights be considered as Bahá'ís?**

Yes. Such children should be made welcome by the Bahá'í community and permitted to attend Bahá'í children's classes:-

> *Mr....whose administrative rights were withdrawn...has written to the Universal House of Justice to say that his child wished to go to the Bahá'í children's class, but had been denied admission because of the father's status. We are asked to inform you that the House of Justice recommends that children of such Bahá'ís, whose parents wish to educate them as Bahá'ís, may be welcomed by the Bahá'í community in the Bahá'í children's classes.*

(letter written on behalf of the Universal House of Justice to a
National Spiritual Assembly, dated October 28, 1985)

8.3.7 **Can children of non-Bahá'ís attend Bahá'í functions?**

Yes, if the parents give permission:-

> *If non-Bahá'í parents permit a child of less than 15 to attend Bahá'í meetings, and in fact, be a Bahá'í, this is likewise permissible.*

CHAPTER EIGHT

(letter from Shoghi Effendi to a National Spiritual Assembly)

8.3.8 **What is the importance of attaining the age of 15?**

Children born to a Bahá'í couple are regarded as Bahá'ís from the beginning of their lives...

(letter written on behalf of the Universal House of Justice to a National Spiritual Assembly, dated July 19, 1982)

At the age of 15 a Bahá'í reaches spiritual maturity. Although Bahá'ís do not acquire voting rights until they turn 21, they are, from the age of 15 obliged to uphold the laws of the Aqdas in their personal lives. At 15, therefore, Bahá'í youth become responsible for declaring their Faith on their own behalf. If they choose not to do so, they can no longer be considered members of the Bahá'í community:-

Regarding the age of 15 fixed by Bahá'u'lláh; this relates only to purely spiritual functions and obligations and is not related to the degree of administrative capacity which is a totally different thing, and is, for the present, fixed at 21.

(letter written on behalf of Shoghi Effendi to a National Spiritual Assembly, dated May 15, 1940)

Regarding children at 15 a Bahá'í is of age as far as keeping the laws of the Aqdas is concerned - prayer, fasting, etc.

(letter written on behalf of Shoghi Effendi to a National Spiritual Assembly, dated October 25, 1947)

...upon attaining the age of 15 a child becomes spiritually mature and is responsible for stating on his own behalf whether or not he wishes to remain a member of the Bahá'í community. If he does not then reaffirm his faith, he must be treated, administratively, as a non-Bahá'í.

(letter written on behalf of the Universal House of Justice to a National Spiritual Assembly, dated December 12, 1975)

8.3.9 **What is the procedure for Bahá'í youth to re-affirm their faith when they turn 15?**

The Universal House of Justice has stated that the procedure to be followed is for the National Spiritual Assembly of each country to decide. It has, however, provided the following guidelines:-

1. A Bahá'í child is not becoming a Bahá'í at that age, but is simply affirming his faith on his own behalf'

(letter written on behalf of the Universal House of Justice to a National Spiritual Assembly, dated July 19, 1982)

2. In whatever procedure it adopts a National Spiritual Assembly must wisely steer a course between seeming to doubt the faith of a child who has been brought up as a devout Bahá'í on the one hand, and seeming to compel a child to be a member of the Bahá'í community against his will, on the other.

(letter written on behalf of the Universal House of Justice to a

CHAPTER EIGHT

National Spiritual Assembly, dated July 19, 1982)

Bearing this guidance in mind, the National Spiritual Assembly has decided that youth may re-affirm their belief in Bahá'u'lláh in one of three ways:-
1. sign a Re-affirmation or Declaration Card and give the Card to the Local Spiritual Assembly (Re-affirmation Cards are available from the National Office on request)
2. write a letter affirming their belief to their Local Spiritual Assembly or write similarly to the National Spiritual Assembly
3. orally indicate to their Local Spiritual Assembly that they re-affirm their Faith

The Local Spiritual Assembly should adopt the following procedure:-
1. Communicate with youth in their community well before they turn 15, either orally or in writing, to prepare them for the Bahá'í responsibilities and privileges which come with reaching the age of spiritual maturity. As noted above, they should be advised that they have all the rights and responsibilities of Bahá'í adults, except the right to vote or to be elected to an administrative position (they may serve on committees). Youth who re-affirm in group areas may serve as office holders. Youth should also be advised at this time of the above choices open to them for re-affirming their Faith.
2. If the youth decides to re-affirm in any of the above ways the Assembly should fill out an Enrolment Card and send it to the National Office in the usual way. It is not necessary to interview the youth as one would a new declarant. Alternatively the National Assembly should be written to informing it that the youth has re-affirmed.
3. When the National Spiritual Assembly has accepted the youth re-affirmation it will send a letter of welcome to the Assembly to be presented to the youth.
4. In the intervening period between the time the youth re-affirms his or her faith and notification of acceptance is received from the National Spiritual Assembly, the youth should be regarded as a full member of the community. Those Bahá'í youth who do not wish to re-affirm at 15 have the opportunity to make their position clear at any point after the Assembly communicates with them.

8.3.10 *What if a youth is not sure whether to re-affirm at 15 or not?*

Youth who are not sure whether to re-affirm at 15 but wish, for the time being, to still be regarded as Bahá'ís, may attend Feasts and other functions. Their parents and the Assembly have a duty to deepen them in the Faith; however, they must also advise such youth that they must soon make their position clear:-

> *It may happen that a Bahá'í child, on reaching the age of 15 is not entirely sure in his own mind. This can well happen if one of the parents is not a Bahá'í or if the parents have accepted the Faith not long before. In such a case the Assembly should not assume automatically that he is not a Bahá'í. If the youth wishes to attend Feasts and is content to continue to be regarded as a Bahá'í as he was when a child, this should be permitted, but in the process of deepening his understanding of the Faith his parents and the Assembly should explain to him that it is his responsibility to soon make his position clear.*

(letter written on behalf of the Universal House of Justice to a National Spiritual Assembly, dated July 19, 1982)

The Local Spiritual Assembly must decide how much time youth should be given to make up their minds, given the individual circumstances in each case. Without in any way being rigid about it, the National Spiritual Assembly suggests that twelve months should be sufficient time. Beyond that time each case should be treated carefully and on its merits.

8.3.11 ***What should the attitude of the Local Spiritual Assembly be towards youth who are not sure whether to re-affirm or not?***

The Local Spiritual Assembly should maintain a loving and nurturing attitude towards such youth. It has a responsibility, with their parents, to deepen them and assist them to arrive at a decision.

8.3.12 ***How are youth who decide not to re-affirm to be regarded by the community?***

Youth who decide not to re-affirm should not be regarded as members of the Bahá'í community. They should, however, be treated with the same warmth and friendship as any other non-Bahá'í who is close to the community:-

> *If the Assembly ascertains from a youth that he does not, in fact, accept the Faith, even if he has been brought up in a Bahá'í family, it should not register him as a Bahá'í youth, and such a youth, since he is now mature and responsible for his own actions, would be in the same situation as any other non-Bahá'í youth who is in close contact with the Bahá'í community. He should be treated with warmth and friendship.*
>
> (letter written on behalf of the Universal House of Justice to a National Spiritual Assembly, dated July 19, 1982)

8.3.13 ***May declarations be accepted from youth between the ages of 15 and 21 whose parents are not Bahá'ís?***

Yes. From the age of 15 youth may declare their Faith without requiring their parents' consent. They must, however, consider their parents' wishes in deciding how much involvement they will have in Bahá'í activities:-

> *Declarations of faith from non-Bahá'í youth between the ages of 15 and 21, whose parents are not Bahá'ís, may be accepted without the consent of their parents unless this is contrary to the civil law. However, the importance of respect for one's parents must not be forgotten, and such youth may need to be counselled to give heed to their parents' wishes as far as the degree of their activity on behalf of the Faith is concerned, and even, if the parents are very antagonistic, to be completely inactive for a time.*
>
> (letter written on behalf of the Universal House of Justice to a National Spiritual Assembly, dated July 19, 1982)

If the youth was a member of a church and the parents object to their child's withdrawal from the church then, for the sake of family unity, membership may be retained in the church until the age of 21:-

> *Your letter of 25th October has been received and we fully appreciate the problem, posed in the case of youth who accept Bahá'u'lláh but whose parents strongly oppose their withdrawal from the Church. In such cases where the parents oppose their withdrawal and insistence upon it by the youth would undermine the unity of the family it is permissible for the withdrawal to be postponed until the youth attain the age of 21. This would not, of course, in any way affect his acceptance into the Bahá'í community. As you mention, this is the*

very time at which such a newly-declared believer needs all the deepening and confirmation he can receive.

(letter from the Universal House of Justice to a National Spiritual Assembly, dated November 6, 1972)

8.3.14 **Do special procedures apply to Iranian youth who wish to declare as Bahá'ís?**

Yes. Iranian youth who have arrived in Australia after they turn 15 and who wish to declare are to be handled under the special procedures outlined in the section named - 'May Muslims from the Middle-East and North Africa be enrolled in the Faith?'
May children of Iranian Bahá'í families whose members are not yet recognised as Bahá'ís in good standing be enrolled in the Faith?
Yes. Such children should be enrolled in the usual manner.

8.3.15 **Does the National Spiritual Assembly require statistics of the number of youth in the community?**

Yes. The Universal House of Justice also requires these statistics, therefore, Local Spiritual Assemblies must be sure to keep their register of youth in their community up to date, and to regularly keep the National Office informed of changes in their community membership.

8.3.16 **Can children under the age of 15 perform services for the Faith such as serving on committees?**

Yes:-

Both children of Bahá'í parents, and children who, with their non-Bahá'í parents' consent, declare their faith in Bahá'u'lláh before they are 15 years old, are regarded as Bahá'ís and it is within a Spiritual Assembly's discretion to request such children to undertake work of which they are capable in the service of the Faith, such as service on suitable committees.

(letter written on behalf of the Universal House of Justice to a National Spiritual Assembly, dated December 12, 1975)

8.3.17 **Should children stay at home on Holy Days?**

Yes:-

...children under 15 should certainly observe the Bahá'í Holy Days and not go to school, if this can be arranged on these nine days.

(letter written on behalf of Shoghi Effendi to a National Spiritual Assembly, dated October 25, 1947)

8.4 **INACTIVE BELIEVERS**

8.4.1 **Should the names of inactive believers be removed from the register?**

No:-

Your Assembly should not remove the names of Bahá'ís from the voting list just because they do not attend meetings or just because their addresses are unknown. It is hard to make Bahá'ís; and you must try and help them and reactivate them, and find those whose addresses are unknown if you can.

(letter written on behalf of Shoghi Effendi to a National Spiritual Assembly, dated September 26, 1957)

CHAPTER EIGHT

8.4.2 *What is the responsibility of the Local Spiritual Assembly towards inactive believers?*

The Local Spiritual Assembly has a responsibility to maintain contact with inactive Bahá'ís and find out the reasons why they are inactive. Each individual case should be considered on its own merits:-

> ...people who are inactive should not automatically be removed from that list. Each case should be considered on its own merits. In some cases a spark of faith may be found which with care may be fanned into flame. Patience and good judgement are called for.
>
> (letter written on behalf of the Universal House of Justice to an individual believer, dated July 10, 1975)

> It may be that the person still believes in Bahá'u'lláh but cannot be active for personal reasons. For example, the Universal House of Justice notes that 'a Bahá'í who is married to a non-Bahá'í may well have to limit his activities to some degree in order to maintain the unity of his family.'
>
> (letter written on behalf of the Universal House of Justice to a National Spiritual Assembly, dated May 7, 1975)

Alternatively, a person may have a very firm belief in Bahá'u'lláh, but be too immature to take an active role in the Faith. Such people should be shown love and encouragement:-

> It is very discouraging to find inactive and unresponsive believers; on the other hand we must always realise that some souls are weak and immature and not capable of carrying on an active administrative burden. They need encouragement, the love of their fellow Bahá'ís and assistance. To blame them for not doing more for the Cause is useless, and they may actually have a very firm belief in Bahá'u'lláh which with care could be fanned into flame. If some of these isolated and inactive people gradually turn to other work than the Cause we should not always blame them - they probably needed more help, more stimulating, more teaching and Bahá'í comradeship than they received.
>
> (letter written on behalf of Shoghi Effendi to an individual believer, dated April 25, 1947)

8.4.3 *What does the Local Spiritual Assembly do if it discovers that the inactive believer ceases to believe in Bahá'u'lláh?*

If the Local Spiritual Assembly finds that the inactive believer has ceased to believe in Bahá'u'lláh and wishes not to be a member of the Bahá'í community, this fact should be communicated to the National Spiritual Assembly. If at all possible, the inactive believer should make his or her resignation in writing:-

> If during this process of encouragement it becomes apparent that the Bahá'í in question has in fact ceased to believe in Bahá'u'lláh and wishes not to be a member of the Bahá'í community, the Assembly would be fully justified in accepting his withdrawal.
>
> (letter written on behalf of the Universal House of Justice to a National Spiritual Assembly, dated May 7, 1975)

> A distinction is to be made between those who are interested in the

CHAPTER EIGHT

Faith but remain inactive and those whose inactivity indicates complete lack of interest in the Faith to the extent that they have in fact ceased to be Bahá'ís In this latter instance removal from the list is simply recognition of this fact.

(letter written on behalf of the Universal House of Justice to a National Spiritual Assembly, dated December 18, 1974)

8.4.4 **What does the Local Spiritual Assembly do if the inactive believer is breaking Bahá'í laws and bringing the name of the Faith into disrepute?**

If the Local Spiritual Assembly finds that the inactive believer is breaking Bahá'í laws and bringing the name of the Faith into disrepute, the Local Spiritual Assembly should help the believer to mend his or her ways. Should these efforts fail, the Local Spiritual Assembly should report the matter to the National Spiritual Assembly. If the believer is not in an Assembly area, the Regional Teaching Committee is responsible for counselling the person and, if these efforts fail, reporting the matter to the National Spiritual Assembly:-

As to certain of your voting members who have long been inactive, and whose conduct you disapprove of, he suggests you make an effort to find out if they still believe in the Faith, and if they do, and wish to be members of it, then they should be helped to mend their ways. If this patient and loving method does not prove successful and they refuse to identify themselves with the Faith, they should be removed from the voting list.

(letter written on behalf of Shoghi Effendi to a National Spiritual Assembly, dated May 8, 1947)

8.5 **RESIGNATION OF BELIEVERS**

8.5.1 *On what grounds may an individual resign from the Faith?*

Resignations are only accepted from people who have ceased to satisfy the requirements set out for membership in the Bahá'í community. In essence such a person no longer accepts the authority and sovereignty of Bahá'u'lláh. This should be clearly indicated by the person at the time of resignation.

8.5.2 *How should a Local Spiritual Assembly proceed if it receives a request to resign from the Faith?*

A Local Spiritual Assembly should consider each request to resign on its merits. The Universal House of Justice has specifically advised that 'the expressed wish to withdraw from the Faith should not be acted upon in a routine or bureaucratic manner.'

(letter written on behalf of the Universal House of Justice to a National Spiritual Assembly, dated September 2, 1987)

On the one hand, the Assembly should not pry unduly into a believer's personal affairs in order to find out the reason why he or she wishes to resign. In a letter written on his behalf, Shoghi Effendi said:-

...if a person makes it quite clear that he does not wish to be a Bahá'í, his name should be removed from the membership list. Normally, therefore, tenders of resignation, however they are expressed, may be accepted.

CHAPTER EIGHT

(cited in a letter from the Universal House of Justice to a National Spiritual Assembly, dated November 10, 1971)

On the other hand, the Assembly may feel that consultation with the believer could resolve his or her difficulties with the Faith, in which case it should make the attempt:-

If, for example, it is felt that loving consultation will clear up misunderstandings and possibly lead to reaffirmation of faith, the Spiritual Assembly should be free, within the limits of discretion, to make an attempt.

(letter from the Universal House of Justice to a National Spiritual Assembly, dated November 10, 1971)

If it seems advisable, the Universal House of Justice has said that the Assembly may give a believer: 'An opportunity to remain on the rolls, becoming inactive if he wishes, for as long as may be necessary under the circumstances.' (letter to a National Spiritual Assembly, dated January 16, 1971)

If the Assembly does not resolve the believer's difficulties and he or she still wishes to resign, the resignation should be forwarded to the National Spiritual Assembly with a report on the person concerned and a recommendation as to whether it should be accepted. If the National Spiritual Assembly accepts the resignation it will advise the Local Spiritual Assembly that it has removed the person's name from the national membership list and ask that this information be passed on to the person concerned. In some instances it may also send the person's Declaration Card to be returned to them as a reminder of the promise made at the time of declaration. If an individual writes directly to the National Spiritual Assembly asking to resign and the National Spiritual Assembly accepts that resignation it will advise the person directly and also notify the relevant Assembly.

8.5.3 **Should the request to resign be put in writing?**

The request to resign should be put in writing if possible. If the person does not comply with this request, however, the Local Spiritual Assembly must consult on the verbal resignation and decide whether to recommend to the National Spiritual Assembly that it be accepted.

8.5.4 **May a person who still believes in Bahá'u'lláh resign from the Bahá'í community?**

No. A resignation may only be accepted if the person genuinely no longer believes in Bahá'u'lláh:-

Any member of the Bahá'í Community who finds that he does not believe in Bahá'u'lláh and His Revelation is free to withdraw from the Faith and such a withdrawal should be accepted. But a Bahá'í who continues to believe in Bahá'u'lláh cannot withdraw from the Bahá'í Community. While he believes in this Revelation he is subject to its laws. Therefore your National Spiritual Assembly was not correct in accepting Mr....'s withdrawal from the Faith. In his very letter of withdrawal Mr.... reaffirmed his belief in the Faith. You should, therefore, immediately reinstate him and so inform him. Of course, he may well wish to remain inactive, and if so his wish should be respected, but he should know that he is a member of the Bahá'í community.

(letter from the Universal House of Justice to a National Spiritual Assembly, dated July 8, 1970)

CHAPTER EIGHT

It has happened, for instance, that people have been upset by incidents that have occurred within the Bahá'í community and, therefore, have decided to resign. In this instance, consultation with the person concerned may remove the difficulty:-

> *When a person wishes to withdraw, he may state that he no longer accepts the claim of Bahá'u'lláh. The Assembly must then determine, to the extent possible, whether this really is the case, or whether in fact he is making this statement for other reasons; for example, he may be a believer who is reacting to the distress he is experiencing from an unfortunate occurrence in his Bahá'í community life...*
>
> (letter written on behalf of the Universal House of Justice to a National Spiritual Assembly, dated September 2, 1987)

When consulting with people in this position the Local Spiritual Assembly should point out the grave spiritual implications of resigning from the Faith:-

> *...believers need to be educated to realise that resignation from the Faith is a serious step which has a profound effect on their spiritual development, since it involves a repudiation of the claim of Bahá'u'lláh. Believers who express their disagreement with a decision of an Assembly, local or national, by resigning from the Faith, should be urged to consider carefully the implications of their actions in light of the Covenant of Bahá'u'lláh.*
>
> (letter written on behalf of the Universal House of Justice to a National Spiritual Assembly, dated October 14, 1988)

If, after consultation, the person still wishes to resign, the matter must be referred to the National Spiritual Assembly. If the Local Spiritual Assembly is not convinced that the person really lacks belief in Bahá'u'lláh, it must note this in its report to the National Spiritual Assembly. The Universal House of Justice has also noted that resignations may not be accepted from people on the grounds that they have caused disunity within the community:-

> *...resignations from the Faith should be accepted only if the Assembly feels that the person does not believe in the Manifestation of God; that an individual has been a trouble-maker, or has seriously disturbed the unity of the community, is not sufficient reason to accept his resignation from the Faith, unless the Assembly feels that his actions provide sufficient evidence of a lack of belief in the claim of Bahá'u'lláh.*
>
> (letter written on behalf of the Universal House of Justice to a National Spiritual Assembly, dated October 14, 1988)

8.5.5 *What if a person wants to resign in order to break Bahá'í law?*

It is not permissible to accept resignations from people who still believe in Bahá'u'lláh but who want to resign in order to avoid the consequences of breaking Bahá'í law. If a person breaks Bahá'í law in such a way that the loss of voting rights is justified, he or she will continue to be regarded as a Bahá'í, but not one who is, administratively, in good standing:-

> *To deny that one is a Bahá'í while one still believes in Bahá'u'lláh is not withdrawal, it is dissimulation of one's faith, and Bahá'í law does not countenance the dissimulation of a believer's faith for the purpose of breaking the law. If a believer who did not like a particular law were to be permitted to leave the community to break the law, and then rejoin with impunity, this would make a mockery of the Law of*

CHAPTER EIGHT

God...It is abundantly clear from his letters that he has continually believed in Bahá'u'lláh, that he knew the law that marriage is conditioned on the consent of parents, that he dissimulated his faith in order to be able to break this law with impunity. He must, therefore, be regarded as a Bahá'í without administrative rights...

(letter written by the Universal House of Justice to a National Spiritual Assembly, dated May 15, 1967)

If a Local Spiritual Assembly has reason to believe that a Bahá'í is attempting to dissimulate his or her faith, it should advise the National Spiritual Assembly of this when forwarding the resignation. Care should be taken in all such instances, however, to make a distinction between people who are deliberately attempting to evade Bahá'í law and those who are breaking the law because they no longer believe in Bahá'u'lláh:-

As you know, a believer cannot escape administrative expulsion by the ruse of resigning from the Faith in order to break its law with impunity. However, the Assembly should be satisfied that there was indeed such an ulterior motive behind the withdrawal. A believer's record of inactivity and his general attitude to the Faith may well lead the Assembly to conclude that his withdrawal was bonafide, even though immediately succeeded by marriage, and in such a case withdrawal may be accepted.

(letter written by the Universal House of Justice to a National Spiritual Assembly, dated May 20, 1971)

8.5.6 What is the status of a person who claims to still believe in Bahá'u'lláh, but refuses to accept some fundamental principle of the Faith, such as the authority of the administrative institutions?

The Universal House of Justice has pointed out that denial of a basic principle of the Faith is, in fact, denial of the authority of Bahá'u'lláh. This is so, even if the person still claims to believe in Bahá'u'lláh; for example, a person cannot claim to believe in Bahá'u'lláh but not accept the authority of the Administrative Institutions:-

...To accept the Cause without the administration is like to accept the Teachings without acknowledging the divine station of Bahá'u'lláh. To be a Bahá'í is to accept the Cause in its entirety. To take exception to one basic principle is to deny the authority and sovereignty of Bahá'u'lláh, and therefore is to deny the Cause...

(letter written on behalf of Shoghi Effendi to a National Spiritual Assembly, dated May 30, 1930)

Any Assembly confronted with this sort of problem should refer the matter to the National Spiritual Assembly.

8.5.7 What is the status of people enrolled as Bahá'ís who do not consider themselves Bahá'ís on the grounds that they did not understand the significance of what they were doing when they declared?

The Local Spiritual Assembly should try to deepen these people; however, if they still feel, after receiving more information, that they wish to resign, their names should be removed from the membership list:-

With regard to those who do not consider themselves Bahá'ís on the basis of the argument that they signed the Declaration Card without

CHAPTER EIGHT

actually knowing the significance of what they were doing, you should determine who these people are. You should then deepen their knowledge of the Faith. If they feel, after receiving sufficient information, that they do not wish to be Bahá'ís, then their names should be removed from the Bahá'í membership list.

(letter written on behalf of the Universal House of Justice to a National Spiritual Assembly, dated June 23, 1985)

8.6 CREDENTIALS

8.6.1 *When should credential cards be issued by the Local Spiritual Assembly?*

New credential cards should be issued at the beginning of the Bahá'í year (March 21) to all adults and youth (that is, 15 years and over) in the Bahá'í community, in good standing. The Regional Teaching Committee is responsible for issuing credentials within its area of jurisdiction, to people who are not in Local Spiritual Assembly areas.

8.6.2 *How long are credential cards valid for?*

Credential cards are valid for one Bahá'í year.

8.6.3 *Must credential cards be presented by believers at Bahá'í-only events?*

Yes. Any Bahá'í institution organising a function for Bahá'ís only must establish a registration procedure in which those attending are required to show valid Bahá'í credentials, or have a Bahá'í with credentials vouch for them.

8.6.4 *What happens if a non-Bahá'í attends a Bahá'í-only function?*

Should it happen that a non-Bahá'í attends a Bahá'í-only function, the organising institution should use its discretion in deciding how to act. In general, the same principle applies here as applies to non-Bahá'í attending the Feast; that is:-

> *...if a non-Bahá'í does appear at a Nineteen Day Feast he should be made to feel welcome, but a Bahá'í should certainly not invite a non-Bahá'í to attend.*

(letter written on behalf of the Universal House of Justice to an individual believer, dated January 23, 1985)

A non-Bahá'í who can be vouched for by a believer should, therefore, be permitted to remain. Any person whom the organisers have reason to suspect may have an ulterior motive for attending, however, should be quietly asked to leave, on the grounds that this is a function for Bahá'ís only. A Bahá'í without voting rights should also be asked to leave.

8.6.5 **Must members of the Continental Board of Counsellors present credentials?**

Counsellors travelling within their own zone need not present credentials. Counsellors travelling outside their own zone, however, should have credentials issued to them by the National Spiritual Assembly of their country of residence:-

> *When Counsellors travel within their zone, they do not normally need credentials nor identification cards. When they travel outside their zones, they should carry with them credentials issued by the National Spiritual Assembly of the country of their residence.*

(letter from the Universal House of Justice to the International Teaching Centre, dated May 13, 1974)

CHAPTER EIGHT

8.6.6 Must Local Spiritual Assemblies sight the credentials of visitors to their community?

Yes. The Local Spiritual Assembly must sight the current credential card of the visitor before that person may be admitted to the Feast or any other function restricted to Bahá'ís only. This applies both if the person is visiting from another community within Australia and if he or she is visiting from overseas. In the case of an overseas visitor current credentials may be in the form of a card or a letter of introduction signed by their National Secretary and stating that this person is a Bahá'í in good standing.

8.6.7 How should the Local Spiritual Assembly regard visitors who cannot present current credentials?

Visitors who cannot present current credentials should be regarded as non-Bahá'ís and may not attend Bahá'í-only functions.

8.6.8 What should the Local Spiritual Assembly do if an overseas visitor does not have Bahá'í credentials?

Overseas visitors who do not have credentials must be advised that it is their responsibility to obtain international credentials from their former National Spiritual Assembly. In the meantime, the Local Spiritual Assembly must advise the Australian National Spiritual Assembly that the particular individual is in the country, and is endeavouring to obtain his or her credentials. If the person is not in a Local Spiritual Assembly area, it is for the Regional Teaching Committee to advise the individual and the Australian National Spiritual Assembly accordingly.

8.6.9 What procedure does a Local Spiritual Assembly follow when believers from other communities within Australia arrive to settle in its community?

Believers arriving to settle from other communities from within Australia must present their current credentials to the Local Spiritual Assembly Secretary, who will issue them with new credentials. The Local Spiritual Assembly is also advised to notify its Regional Teaching Committee that this person has moved into its community.

8.6.10 What procedure does a Local Spiritual Assembly follow when believers from overseas communities arrive to settle in its community?

Believers transferring in from overseas should have asked their former National Spiritual Assembly to transfer their membership to Australia before leaving. Such believers should also have some form of Bahá'í identification on them, eg. international credentials, when they arrive in Australia. The Secretary of the Local Spiritual Assembly in the area to which the believers move should sight these before allowing them to attend Bahá'í-only functions. To transfer such believers in, the Secretary should fill out the appropriate section of the membership form and send this, together with the believers' credentials, or copies of them, to the National Office. A copy of the form is also to go to the Regional Teaching Committee. If believers arrive from overseas without credentials, the Secretary should contact the National Office. If a transfer form has arrived at the National Office from the believers' previous National Spiritual Assembly, they may be enrolled and the Local Spiritual Assembly should notify the Regional Teaching Committee accordingly. If a transfer form has not been received the believers will be advised to write to their former National Spiritual Assembly and ask it to send the form. Until the transfer is completed the believers cannot attend Bahá'í-only functions.

8.6.11 Who is responsible for organising the transfer of believers into areas in which there is no Local Spiritual Assembly?

Registered Groups have this responsibility in their areas. The Regional Teaching Committee has this responsibility in group and isolated areas.

CHAPTER EIGHT

8.6.12 ***How should credentials be issued to Baha'is arriving from overseas?***

If a person arrives from overseas, please notify the National Office of their name, previous country of residence, country of birth, ethnic origin, date of birth and current address and phone number in Australia. If the person has an introductory or credential letter in their possession please send a copy to the National Office. We will then arrange for a transfer. When the transfer form has arrived and the status of the person has been verified, the Records Department will inform the person's community that he or she is a Bahá'í in good standing and may be issued local credentials..

If an Iranian arrives from Pakistan and has a credential card issued in Pakistan, please send the original card, current address and phone number in Australia and date of birth, ethnic origin and country of birth to the Records Department. If you want, the original card to be returned after verification please let the Records Department know.

If an Iranian arrives from Pakistan or Iran with no credentials, it is necessary for them to complete a questionnaire, and return the completed form as soon as possible to the National Office for processing. It may take several weeks to several months to complete the verifying of credentials of friends from Iran. When the status has been verified the Local Spiritual Assembly or Bahá'í Regional Teaching Committee concerned will be advised to issue credentials.

8.6.13 ***Do special procedures apply when transferring in Iranian Bahá'ís?***

Special procedures may apply in some cases. Iranian Bahá'ís who have come to Australia via Pakistan and have been issued with blue credential cards may be admitted to the community immediately as Bahá'ís in good standing. The transfer should be completed in the normal fashion outlined above. In other instances, Iranian Bahá'ís may not have been issued with credentials; however, a transfer form may have been sent to the National Spiritual Assembly of Australia. The Secretary of the Local Spiritual Assembly should, therefore, contact the National Office in the first instance. If a transfer form has been received at the National Office the Local Spiritual Assembly may register the Bahá'í concerned immediately and complete the transfer procedure in the ordinary way. If an Iranian Bahá'í arrives in a community without credentials and no transfer form has been sent to the National Spiritual Assembly, the Assembly Secretary must advise the National Office so that a questionnaire may be sent to the person concerned. This questionnaire will be used by the National Spiritual Assembly to determine from the friends in Iran whether the person concerned should be registered as a Bahá'í in good standing. While waiting for the reply, such people are not permitted to attend Bahá'í-only functions. The friends should also be advised that it may take some time for a reply to be received. Once a reply is received, the person may be registered, or not, according to the usual procedure. Local Spiritual Assemblies should also note that Iranian friends who come to Australia via Pakistan may have been issued with white pass cards. These are not credentials and such people should not be admitted into the Bahá'í community until their status has been checked according to the above procedure.

8.6.14 ***Do special procedures apply when transferring in Southeast Asian Bahá'ís?***

Bahá'ís from countries in Southeast Asia such as Vietnam, Laos or Kampuchea who do not have current credentials may have had their Bahá'í status verified in a letter sent to the National Spiritual Assembly. Local Spiritual Assembly Secretaries should, therefore, check with the National Office in the first instance. If it is not possible to verify a person's credentials and that person wishes to belong to the Bahá'í community, he or she should be asked to declare in the usual manner.

8.6.15 ***How does a Local Spiritual Assembly transfer Bahá'ís out of its community?***

The procedure for transferring a Bahá'í out of the community is to complete the relevant

CHAPTER EIGHT

section of the 'Bahá'í Records and Membership Form' and send it to the National Office. If the person is transferring to a new community within Australia, a copy of this form should be sent to the new community (or Regional Teaching Committee if there is no Assembly). A Local Spiritual Assembly should also send a copy of the form to its own Regional Teaching Committee. If the person is transferring to a new community overseas the National Office will advise the relevant National Spiritual Assembly, or the Universal House of Justice if the country is 'sensitive' for Bahá'ís. Again, the Local Spiritual Assembly should send a copy of the form to its own Regional Teaching Committee.

8.6.16 *What is the procedure for a Bahá'í wishing to travel overseas?*

Bahá'ís travelling overseas must obtain international credentials before leaving. International credentials are available from the National Office. Applicants must send a passport size photograph, $5.00 and their signature on a separate piece of paper. The credentials will be valid for the rest of the current Bahá'í year and the next Bahá'í year. Applicants are advised to give the National Office as much notice as possible to issue the card. Should a Bahá'í be overseas without current credentials he or she should contact the Australian National Office for advice. It is not possible to attend Bahá'í-only functions overseas without international credentials. Local credentials are not sufficient. It should be noted that if a Bahá'í intends to be overseas for six months or more, he or she should arrange for a transferral of Bahá'í membership to the new country, rather than applying for international credentials. It is also important to note that some countries are 'sensitive' in relation to the Faith. Bahá'ís should first check with the National Office if planning to travel in the Middle East, North Africa, Russia and the former Soviet republics, Eastern Europe, China, Indo-China, or any other part of the world in which, for some reason, it has not been possible to establish a Bahá'í community.

8.6.17 *How do Bahá'ís apply to go on pilgrimage?*

Applications for pilgrimage should be sent to:
    The Office of Pilgrimage
    Bahá'í World Centre
    P.O. Box 155
    31001 Haifa
    Israel

Applications must be in writing. They may be sent by fax (972-4-358-507) or electronic mail (internet address: - pilsched@bwc.org)

The letter should state:
- the complete mailing address
- the full name of each family member
- date of birth of all those applying
- Bahá'í identification number for each individual (if applicable)
- the date of any previous application for pilgrimage (if applicable)

There is to be a lapse of at least five years from the date of completion of a believer's pilgrimage before a subsequent request for pilgrimage is submitted. Believers may not exchange their places in the pilgrimage queue, give up their places for friends or relatives, or transfer their pilgrimage invitation to another person.

Requests to be invited for specific pilgrimage dates cannot be accommodated..
Parents are discouraged from bringing children under ten years of age. Parents should also consider the fact that if they take young children with them they may have to spend time minding them, as there are no child-minding facilities at the World Centre. They may, therefore, miss part of the pilgrimage.
[Further information can be found in a letter from the Universal House of Justice to all

CHAPTER EIGHT

Bahá'ís contemplating pilgrimage to the Holy Land, dated March 1, 1994 - a copy of this letter has been sent to all Local Spiritual Assemblies and Registered Groups]

8.6.18 *How do Bahá'ís apply for a three day visit to the Holy Land?*

Request for three day visits may be submitted either through the National Assembly or directly to the Bahá'í World Centre.

8.7 **NOTES FOR REGISTERED GROUPS**

As Registered Groups are not administrative institutions the duties outlined in this Chapter are the responsibility either of the Regional Teaching Committee or the National Spiritual Assembly. In areas where there is no Local Spiritual Assembly the Regional Teaching Committee has the responsibility of admitting new believers, handling resignations and problems with inactive believers and youth re-affirmations. Registered Groups should note, however, that they should maintain their own membership lists and they do have responsibility for transferring believers in and out of their area according to the procedures set out in this Chapter.

CHAPTER NINE

Chapter 9

9. Administration of Bahá'í Law

9.1 GENERAL PRINCIPLES

9.1.1 *What is meant by the 'laws' of the Faith?*

The general term 'laws' can be used to refer to a variety of laws, ordinances, exhortations and principles, covering the spiritual, ethical, moral and administrative aspects of the Faith. All are important to the life of the community and the individual, but they are applied differently. Broadly speaking, there are three categories:

1. Those which:-

   ...affect society and social relationships and the Spiritual Assemblies are responsible for their enforcement. If a believer breaks such a law, he is subject to the imposition of sanctions.

2. Those which:-

   ...although of very great importance, are not sanctionable, because their observance is a matter of conscience between the individual and God; among these fall the laws of prayer and fasting and the law of Huqúqu'lláh.

3. Those:-

   ... high ethical standards to which Bahá'u'lláh calls His followers, such as trustworthiness, abstention from backbiting, and so on; generally speaking obedience to these is a matter for individual conscience, and the Assemblies should not pry into people's lives to see whether or not they are following them; nevertheless, if a believer's conduct falls so far below the standard set by Bahá'u'lláh that it becomes a flagrant disgrace and brings the name of the Faith into disrepute, the Assembly would have to intervene, to encourage the believer to correct his ways, to warn him of the consequences of continued misconduct, and possibly, if he does not respond, to deprive him of his administrative rights.

   (the above three quotations are extracts from a letter from the Universal House of Justice, quoted in a letter from the National Spiritual Assembly of the Hawaiian Islands to its Local Spiritual Assemblies, dated February 1, 1988)

Although these laws are equally binding on the believers it is important that the Local Spiritual Assembly be able to distinguish between those laws it has a duty to enforce and those it does not:-

...the friends should realise the importance of following all the Teachings, and not assume that merely because an offence is not punishable it is therefore less grave. Assemblies, on the other hand, should distinguish clearly between those laws which it is their duty to enforce, those which should be left strictly to the conscience of the individual, and those in which it may have to intervene if the

CHAPTER NINE

misbehaviour is blatant and injurious to the good name of the Faith.

(extract from a letter from the Universal House of Justice, contained in a letter from the National Spiritual Assembly of the Hawaiian Islands to its Local Spiritual Assemblies, dated February 1, 1988)

This Chapter deals with those laws the Local Spiritual Assembly has a duty to enforce and with those situations in which it may have to intervene if an individual's behaviour is injurious to the Faith.

9.1.2 **By what process are the Bahá'í laws applied to the Bahá'í community in general?**

The application of Bahá'í law is an evolutionary process, dependent upon various factors, such as the prevailing conditions of society and the present capacity of the Bahá'ís in different parts of the world to uphold particular laws. This means, for example:
1. some laws are binding on Bahá'ís in some parts of the world at the present time, but not binding on Bahá'ís in other parts of the world.
2. some laws, such as the punishments for arson, adultery, murder, and theft, set out in the "Kitáb-i-Aqdas" are designed for a future state of society. At present such matters are usually covered by the civil laws of each country.
3. there are some matters which the Universal House of Justice has yet to legislate on. In this case, the final decision is left to the individual to make in accordance with certain fundamental principles. Examples include the Bahá'í laws on abortion and birth control. [for further information on these subjects see "Lights of Guidance" {revised edition}, nos.1154-55, 1160-70]

9.1.3 **What is the primary duty of the Assembly towards its community regarding the application of Bahá'í law?**

The Assembly has a primary duty to counsel and educate the believers. Imposition of sanctions should be a last resort:-

> *Generally, administrative rights should not be suspended because of the birth of a child out of wedlock. The questions to be considered are whether the party is guilty of blatant and flagrant immorality, whether such conduct is harming the Faith, and whether the believer has refused or neglected to improve her conduct despite repeated warnings. As you no doubt know, deprivation of administrative rights is a very serious sanction, and the beloved Guardian repeatedly cautioned that it should be exercised only in extreme situations. In a letter written on behalf of the Universal House of Justice to another National Spiritual Assembly which asked similar questions, it was pointed out that it was the task of the institutions to provide both counsel and education for the believers, and thereafter it is for the individual Bahá'í to determine his course of conduct in relation to the situations of his daily life.*

(letter written on behalf of the Universal House of Justice, dated March 23, 1983)

See also "Lights of Guidance" {revised edition}, no.213]

Assistance in educating the believers about the Bahá'í laws is available from the Auxiliary Board.

CHAPTER NINE

9.1.4 *What should the Local Spiritual Assembly do when a Bahá'í's conduct is 'flagrantly contrary' to the Teachings?*

Although the Local Spiritual Assembly's primary duty is to counsel and educate the believers, it cannot tolerate conduct 'flagrantly contrary' to the Teachings. When it becomes aware of such conduct the Assembly must intervene, to warn the friends concerned and, if necessary, recommend deprivation of their voting rights to the National Spiritual Assembly:-

> *He feels that your Assembly must keep before its eyes the balance specified by Bahá'u'lláh, Himself, in other words, justice, reward and retribution. Although the Cause is still young and tender, and many of the believers inexperienced, and therefore loving forbearance is often called for in the place of harsh measures, this does not mean that a National Spiritual Assembly can under any circumstances tolerate disgraceful conduct, flagrantly contrary to our Teachings, on the part of any of its members, whoever they may be and from wherever they come. You should vigilantly watch over and protect the interests of the Bahá'í Community, and the moment you see that any Bahá'ís ... are acting in a way to bring disgrace upon the name of the Faith, warn them, and if necessary, deprive them immediately of their voting rights if they refuse to change their ways. Only in this way can the purity of the Faith be preserved.*

(letter written on behalf of Shoghi Effendi to a National Spiritual Assembly, dated August 14, 1957)

9.1.5 *How should the Local Spiritual Assembly apply Bahá'í law in specific cases?*

Each case of a violation of Bahá'í law must be considered on its own merits. The Universal House of Justice has provided the following examples of factors to be taken into account:
- the circumstances of the individual
- the degree to which the good name of the Faith is involved
- whether the offence is blatant and flagrant:-

> *There are certain Teachings and exhortations the observance of which is solely between the individual and God; the non-observance of other laws and ordinances incurs some form of sanction. Some of these violations incur punishment for a single offence, while others are punished only after repeated warnings have failed to remedy the violation. It is not possible to establish a single rule applicable automatically and invariably. Every case is different, and there is more than one variable consideration to take into account, for example, the circumstances of the individual, the degree to which the good name of the Faith is involved, whether the offence is blatant and flagrant. Over and over again the Guardian urged Assemblies to be extremely patient and forbearing in dealing with the friends. He pointed out on many occasions that removal of administrative rights is the heaviest sanction which the Assemblies may impose at the present time... it is for the Assembly to determine at what point the conduct is blatant and flagrant or is harmful to the name of the Faith. They must determine whether the believer has been given sufficient warning before the imposition of sanctions.*

(letter written on behalf of the Universal House of Justice to an individual believer, dated February 20, 1977)

A consequence of applying the above principles is that a similar violation of Bahá'í law by two individuals would result in different treatment by the Assembly, because of differences in the circumstances of the two individuals. Reference to the way in which the laws and principles were applied in previous cases may be of general assistance to the Assembly but cannot provide a fixed precedent for making a decision in the case presently before it. Further guidance on how to apply Bahá'í law is available from the Auxiliary Board.

9.1.6 **What will the consequences be if an Assembly fails to intervene in a situation of flagrant violation of the Bahá'í laws?**

If the Assembly does not intervene promptly it risks the following:

a) backbiting amongst the friends
b) loss of prestige for the Faith in the eyes of Bahá'ís and non-Bahá'ís
c) loss of morale by the friends
d) believers developing an attitude of disregard for the laws:-

> *Whenever it becomes known that one of the believers is flagrantly disobeying the Teachings of the Faith, whether spiritual, ethical, moral or administrative, the Assemblies should not allow such a situation to become a source of backbiting among the friends or deteriorate into either the loss of dignity of the Teachings in the eyes of the Bahá'ís and non-Bahá'ís, or the eventual inactivity of the believer.*
>
> (letter from the Universal House of Justice, dated November 12, 1965)

> *It is obvious that a continuous condoning of acts of disobedience of the Laws of God on the part of the Administration will result in an attitude of increasing disregard of these laws on the part of the believers.*
>
> (letter from the Universal House of Justice, dated November 12, 1965)

9.1.7 **What should the attitude of the Assembly be when administering justice?**

Assembly members have a responsibility to place the interests of the Faith above their own interests and to combine an attitude of love towards their fellow-believers with a determination to act with justice at all times:-

> *The members of these Assemblies, on their part, must disregard utterly their own likes and dislikes, their personal interests and inclinations, and concentrate their minds upon those measures that will conduce to the welfare and happiness of the Bahá'í Community and promote the common weal.*
>
> (Shoghi Effendi, "Bahá'í Administration", p.41)

> *The administrators of the Faith ... [should be] ... motivated by a true sense of love for their fellow-brethren coupled with a firm determination to act with justice in all the cases which are submitted to them for their consideration.*
>
> (letter written on behalf of Shoghi Effendi to an individual believer, dated March 9, 1934)

9.1.8 *How important is confidentiality?*

The importance of ensuring that the consultation of the Assembly remains confidential cannot be over-emphasised. Failure to maintain confidentiality will make the friends unwilling to entrust sensitive personal issues to their Assembly's care. [See further Chapter 3, Section 3.]

It is suggested that any letters written concerning allegations or warnings about breaking Bahá'í law be marked 'PRIVATE AND CONFIDENTIAL' and the envelope also. This will lessen the likelihood of such letters being read by unauthorised persons.

9.2 LOSS OF VOTING RIGHTS

9.2.1 *Which institution has the right, at the present time, to remove voting rights?*

At the present time only the National Spiritual Assembly has the right to remove voting rights:-

> *It will be noted that the model By-Laws for Local Spiritual Assemblies sent to you...provide for Local Assemblies to exercise [the] function of withdrawing or restoring voting rights of individual believers under their jurisdiction. This provision was made in the By-Laws because this is inherently a Local Assembly function. However, for the present, National Assemblies should continue to exercise this function, and should so inform Local Assemblies under their jurisdiction, if they have not already done so.*
>
> (letter from the Universal House of Justice to all National Spiritual Assemblies, dated January 5, 1965)

The Local Spiritual Assembly has a responsibility to recommend to the National Spiritual Assembly when it feels removal of voting rights (or the application of partial sanctions) is necessary, but may not make the decision itself.

9.2.2 *What does deprivation of voting rights mean?*

1. The Universal House of Justice has explained deprivation of voting rights as follows:-*One who has lost his voting rights is considered to be a Bahá'í but not one in good standing. The following restrictions and limitations apply to such a believer:*
    - *a) He cannot attend Nineteen Day Feasts or other meetings for Bahá'ís only, including International Conferences, and therefore cannot take part in consultation on the affairs of the community.*
    - *b) He cannot contribute to the Bahá'í Fund.*
    - *c) He cannot receive newsletters and other bulletins whose circulation is restricted to Bahá'ís.*
    - *d) He cannot have a Bahá'í marriage ceremony and therefore is not able to marry a Bahá'í.*
    - *e) He may not have a Bahá'í pilgrimage.*
    - *f) Although he is free to teach the Faith on his own behalf, he should not be used as a teacher or speaker in programmes sponsored by Bahá'ís.*
    - *g) He is debarred from participating in administrative matters, including the right to vote in Bahá'í elections.*
    - *h) He cannot hold office or be appointed to a committee.*
    - *i) He should not be given credentials.*
2. *Although generally speaking a believer deprived of his voting rights is not restricted except as stated above, the following privileges have been expressly stipulated as not denied:*

CHAPTER NINE

a) He may attend the observances of the nine Holy Days.
b) He may attend any Bahá'í function open to non-Bahá'ís.
c) He may receive any publication available to non-Bahá'ís.
d) He is free to teach the Faith as every individual believer has been enjoined by Bahá'u'lláh to teach.
e) Association with other believers is not forbidden.
f) He may have the Bahá'í burial service if he or his family requests it, and he may be buried in a Bahá'í cemetery.
g) Bahá'í charity should not be denied him on the ground that he has lost his voting rights.
h) Bahá'í institutions may employ him, but should use discretion as to the type of work he is to perform.
i) He should have access to the Spiritual Assembly.

(from an attachment to a letter written on behalf of the Universal House of Justice to a National Spiritual Assembly, dated December 9, 1985)

9.2.3 What is the distinction between removal of voting rights and expulsion from the Faith?

Expulsion from the Faith has grave spiritual implications and the person concerned cannot be considered even nominally as a Bahá'í. Loss of voting rights, on the other hand, is merely an administrative sanction and a believer without voting rights is, nevertheless, still a Bahá'í. [See further "Lights of Guidance {revised edition}, no. 198.]

Only the Universal House of Justice can, on the recommendation of the Hands of the Cause of God resident in the Holy Land, spiritually expel a person from the community.

9.2.4 Is it possible for an individual to be barred from some activities but not others?

Yes:-

It is also quite permissible for a National Spiritual Assembly to debar an individual believer from serving on a Local Spiritual Assembly without removing his or her voting rights and they may also debar a believer from attending the consultative part of a Nineteen Day Feast. You may also debar a believer from voting in elections without imposing all the other administrative sanctions involved in administrative expulsion.

(letter from the Universal House of Justice to a National Spiritual Assembly, dated January 31, 1972)

Limited sanctions are most commonly applied in cases where the individual disrupts the unity of the community, or is mentally unfit however, their application is not limited to these situations. In any instance the sanction applied must be relevant to the misconduct that has occurred. Note that only the National Spiritual Assembly may apply limited sanctions.

9.2.5 Can a Bahá'í who has lost his or her voting rights be subject to further sanctions for further violations of Bahá'í law?

No:-

A Bahá'í who has lost his administrative rights is administratively expelled from the community and therefore is not subject to the jurisdiction of the Spiritual Assembly in the matter of laws of personal status, such as divorce... His observance of such laws is a matter of conscience and he would not be subject to further sanctions for non-observance of Bahá'í laws during the period he is without voting rights.

(letter written on behalf of the Universal House of Justice, dated April 6, 1982)

In the case of partial sanctions, however, it is possible for further sanctions to be applied, where some additional infraction occurs.

In rare cases, where the National Spiritual Assembly determines that such a measure is necessary, a believer without voting rights may be debarred from attending functions which they would normally be permitted to attend. This would only occur in cases affecting the protection of the community, eg. protecting the children of a community.

9.2.6 *Can a believer appeal against the loss of voting rights?*

Yes. A believer may make an appeal to the National Spiritual Assembly for the restoration of their voting rights.

9.2.7 *What disciplinary action can be taken against youth?*

The Universal House of Justice has provided the following guidance on this matter:-

With reference to the question in your second letter as to what disciplinary action can be taken against youth who are not of voting age, it must be remembered that the removal of his voting rights is administrative expulsion. In addition to being deprived of his right to vote, the believer cannot attend Feasts or other meetings for Bahá'ís only; cannot contribute to the Fund; or, cannot have a Bahá'í marriage ceremony. The restrictions against voting would become operative when the young offender reaches voting age.

(letter from the Universal House of Justice to a National Spiritual Assembly, dated April 14, 1965)

It is clear from this reference that if a youth disobeys sanctionable law, such as the law requiring the consent of parents to a marriage, or if a youth acts in a flagrantly disobedient manner, bringing disrepute upon the Faith, the National Assembly may remove that youth's voting rights. This removal of rights will not differ in any respect from the removal of voting rights imposed upon an adult.

9.2.8 *Is ignorance of the law a valid excuse?*

Yes:-

In all matters concerning the deprivation of voting rights your Assembly should bear in mind that at the present time, when Bahá'í laws are being progressively applied and when a large proportion of the community consists of newly declared believers, you may accept ignorance of the Bahá'í Law as a valid excuse if your Assembly is fully convinced that such ignorance existed.

(letter from the Universal House of Justice to a National Spiritual Assembly, dated October 11, 1965)

9.2.9 *What if a believer was given the wrong advice by a Bahá'í institution?*

The same principles as above apply:-

> *...you should take into account a believer's good intention if he acted in accordance with incorrect advice or instructions given to him by his Local Spiritual Assembly or another Bahá'í institution.*
>
> (letter from the Universal House of Justice to a National Spiritual Assembly, dated October 11, 1965)

9.2.10 *Can a believer avoid the application of Bahá'í law by resigning from the Faith?*

No. It is not permissible for a Bahá'í who still believes in Bahá'u'lláh to resign in order to break Bahá'í law. Such an act amounts to dissimulation of one's faith, which is forbidden. If a person breaks Bahá'í law in such a way that the loss of voting rights is justified, he or she will continue to be regarded as a Bahá'í but not one who is, administratively, in good standing. It is important, however, that the Assembly distinguish between situations in which a person wishes to resign in order to break Bahá'í law and situations in which a person breaks Bahá'í law because he or she has ceased to believe in Bahá'u'lláh. In the former case the person should be counselled by the Assembly to correct or prevent a violation of Bahá'í law. In the latter case the issue of resignation would arise.

9.3 PROCEDURES FOR ADMINISTERING A VIOLATION OF BAHÁ'Í LAW

9.3.1 *How should the Local Spiritual Assembly proceed when required to administer a violation of Bahá'í law?*

The Local Spiritual Assembly should follow the general guidance on consultation set out elsewhere in this Handbook. Shoghi Effendi also provided the following particular guidance on handling violations of Bahá'í law:-

> *He has informed, some years ago, the American National Spiritual Assembly that, before anyone is deprived of their voting rights, they should be consulted with and lovingly admonished at first, given repeated warnings if they do not mend their immoral ways, or whatever other extremely serious misdemeanour they are committing, and finally, after these repeated warnings, be deprived of their voting rights.*
>
> (letter written on behalf of Shoghi Effendi to a National Spiritual Assembly, dated March 3, 1955)

Following is a suggested procedure a Local Spiritual Assembly may follow based on the above guidance. The Local Spiritual Assembly may use this general procedure in conjunction with the guidance on specific matters contained in following sections of this Chapter.

These sections cover the following topics:
- Alcohol, Drugs and Tobacco
- Behaviour that Damages the Reputation of the Faith or Causes Disunity
- Disobedience to Civil Law
- Divorce
- Domestic Violence
- Immorality
- Marriage
- Political Activities and Membership in Unacceptable Organisations

Note that the above is not an exhaustive list of situations. Also note that some violations of Bahá'í law (eg. participation in politics) may call for immediate and decisive action, rather than the extended process of counselling and warning outlined here.

CHAPTER NINE

1. Consult with the person or persons concerned to determine whether there has been a violation of Bahá'í law with which the Assembly should concern itself. The Assembly should:
   a) ensure that the person has a clear understanding of the law has violated and what steps to take in order to remedy the violation. The Assembly should share relevant passages from the Writings with the individual in a loving manner;
   b) if applicable, provide practical assistance to the person; for example, if the person has an alcohol problem the Assembly may be able to put the believer in touch with a counselling service;
   c) meet with the believer periodically to monitor his or her progress in complying with the law. The Assembly may offer the person the option of meeting with individual members of the Assembly, rather than with the Assembly as a whole, or the Assembly may decide to appoint an adhoc committee for this purpose;
   d) the Assembly's attitude at this stage should be that of a loving parent. It should give the believer time to respond.
2. If counselling fails the Assembly may gently reprove the believer for his or her failure to rectify the situation, pointing out the harm such behaviour causes to the Faith and urging compliance with the law.
3. If gentle reproofs fail the Assembly may issue one or more warnings that continued failure to comply with Bahá'í law will result in the Local Spiritual Assembly recommending to the National Spiritual Assembly the imposition of partial or full sanctions (ie. loss of voting rights). The Assembly should ensure that the believer fully understands what this means and that the warning is not being issued lightly. It may be helpful to produce a prepared statement that could be read to the individual or individuals concerned. This statement could review the problem and the steps taken so far to resolve it. It could also review the relevant Bahá'í principles relating to the law in question, the responsibilities of individual Bahá'ís to uphold the law, and the responsibility of the Assembly to enforce it. It should culminate in a clear warning to the believer. The Assembly could also write to the National Spiritual Assembly at this point to advise of the situation and request support from the National Spiritual Assembly. If the National Spiritual Assembly feels it is warranted, it may also issue a warning to the person or persons concerned.
4. If warnings do not succeed in making the person comply, the Local Spiritual Assembly should pass the matter over to the National Spiritual Assembly. The Local Spiritual Assembly's report must contain the following:
   a) a comprehensive explanation of the situation and the steps the Local Spiritual Assembly has taken to try and remedy it;
   b) a recommendation to the National Spiritual Assembly as to how the matter should be dealt with. Note that the penalty should fit the transgression and it is possible in some cases to impose partial sanctions.
5. The National Spiritual Assembly will advise the Local Spiritual Assembly in writing of its decision and request the Local Spiritual Assembly to advise the believer concerned; or the National Spiritual Assembly may contact the believer directly.
   The names of people who lose their voting and administrative rights will be published in the first Bahá'í Bulletin after the National Spiritual Assembly's decision. This will be done for the protection of the Bahá'í community.
   When advising believers of their loss of voting rights, an Assembly must also indicate to them, in writing, the need to repent of their action before voting rights can be restored.
6. The Assembly should remain in touch with the believer to offer spiritual and practical support to remedy the situation and to monitor the person's progress in doing so. It is often advisable to appoint one or two people from the Assembly, who can develop a rapport with the believer concerned, to carry out this task. New credential cards must not be issued to a Bahá'í without voting rights. Credential cards may be provided to believers who have had part of their voting rights removed.

CHAPTER NINE

7. The Assembly must ensure that members of the community maintain a loving attitude towards the individual concerned and do not gossip or backbite about his or her situation.
8. If the believer applies to the Local Spiritual Assembly to have his or her voting rights restored the Assembly, or its representatives, must meet with the person concerned to determine:
   a) whether he or she has rectified the situation that led to loss of voting rights;
   b) whether the believer is sincerely repentant of his or her conduct.
   c) In its report to the National Spiritual Assembly the Assembly must outline:
   d) the steps the believer has taken to rectify the situation;
   e) the assistance the Assembly has provided to the believer;
   f) its recommendation as to whether voting rights should be restored.

Any applications made by believers for restoration of their voting rights must be forwarded to the National Assembly regardless of whether the Local Assembly believes the application is justified. It must provide its own assessment of the situation in an accompanying letter.

9.3.2 *What should a Local Spiritual Assembly do if it is not certain whether a believer has committed the misconduct brought to its attention or not?*

A Local Spiritual Assembly is not required to decide whether a person is 'guilty' or 'not guilty' in any given case. The responsibility of the Assembly is to take whatever action it feels is justified based on the evidence before it:-

> *...the House of Justice asks us to point out that a Spiritual Assembly, unlike a civil court of law, is not required to return a verdict of "guilty" or "not guilty" in such cases. It would be perfectly in order for you to say to such a person that, in view of the evidence before you, you feel that there is a strong probability that he acted as described, which justifies your issuing a warning to him. If, as he maintains, he is innocent, all the better, but you are responsible to take the action that you deem to be justified in the circumstances.*
>
> (letter written on behalf of the Universal House of Justice to the National Spiritual Assembly of Australia, dated November 7, 1989)

The Universal House of Justice advises Spiritual Assemblies to follow the advice of Shoghi Effendi:-

> *...when they are called upon to arrive at a certain decision, they should, after dispassionate, anxious, and cordial consultation, turn to God in prayer, and with earnestness and conviction and courage record their vote...*
>
> (quoted in letter written on behalf of the Universal House of Justice to the National Spiritual Assembly of Australia, dated November 7, 1989)

9.3.3 *What is the distinction between the Local Spiritual Assembly's function as a counsellor and its function as an enforcer of Bahá'í law?*

In its role as a counsellor a Spiritual Assembly may give an individual some advice; however, it is up to the individual whether or not to accept it. The Assembly cannot recommend the imposition of sanctions for a failure to obey such advice:-

> *The National Spiritual Assembly should distinguish between its functions as an adviser and counsellor of the friends and its role as the enforcer of Bahá'í Law. For example, it is quite in order for the Assembly to advise a believer to consult a psychiatrist or any other*

CHAPTER NINE

doctor, if it feels this is necessary, but such advice should not be linked with any deprivation of voting rights which may have to be imposed for flagrant immorality. You may feel it advisable to give such advice to a person who is being deprived of his voting rights, but the two actions should be clearly separate - one is administrative, the other is advice given for the person's own good which he may or may not accept as he wishes.

(letter from the Universal House of Justice, dated September 21, 1965)

For example, a Bahá'í living in an immoral relationship with another person may be advised that this is contrary to Bahá'í law and asked to find another place to live and to cease the relationship. Failure to do this could result in loss of voting rights. At the same time, the Local Spiritual Assembly may advise the believer to seek counselling because it feels that a psychological reason underlies the immoral behaviour. It is up to the believer to decide whether to follow this advice or not and sanctions could not be imposed for a failure to do so.

9.3.4 **What should a Local Spiritual Assembly do if a believer whose behaviour it is monitoring transfers to a new Local Spiritual Assembly area?**

The Local Spiritual Assembly should either advise the National Office so that the Office can inform the new Assembly of the situation, or it should advise the new Assembly directly in writing and copy its letter to the National Spiritual Assembly. The National Spiritual Assembly may decide that the original Local Spiritual Assembly should retain responsibility over the matter in some circumstances. If the believer moves to an area without an Assembly the National Office must be advised as the matter will then fall under the jurisdiction of the National Spiritual Assembly itself.

9.3.5 **Which institution has jurisdiction if the situation involves believers in different Assembly areas?**

If the situation involves believers in different Assembly areas the Assemblies concerned should consult together to determine the best method of handling the situation. If they cannot decide the matter between themselves, the National Spiritual Assembly should be consulted. If one of the parties is not in an Assembly area, the National Spiritual Assembly must be informed as that person comes under the National Assembly's jurisdiction.

9.3.6 **What if the believer in question is serving on a Local Spiritual Assembly?**

If the believer is serving on the Assembly he or she may not feel comfortable discussing the matter before fellow Assembly members. In this case, the Assembly may consider delegating investigation to an individual or sub-committee of the Assembly. The Assembly should also bear in mind the guidance concerning the presence of an Assembly member at a consultation in which that member's personal affairs are being discussed. In certain circumstances the National Spiritual Assembly may appoint an ad hoc committee to handle the matter, which could be made up of members of the community concerned and other nearby communities:-

In reply to your letter of February 4th asking whether you may assign personal problems which a Local Spiritual Assembly is unable to deal with to a nearby Local Spiritual Assembly, we feel that in such cases it would be better for your National Spiritual Assembly to appoint an ad hoc committee for each case, the membership of which could be drawn from one or two nearby communities as well as the community where the particular problem exists.

(letter from the Universal House of Justice to a National Spiritual Assembly, dated October 22, 1984)

Such a committee would report directly to the National Spiritual Assembly.

9.3.7 *What should an individual do if he or she becomes aware of the misconduct of another believer?*

The way in which an individual should behave in any given situation is dependent upon the circumstances of that situation:-

> *While it can be a severe test to a Bahá'í to see fellow believers violating Bahá'í laws or engaging in conduct inimical to the welfare and best interests of the Faith, there is no fixed rule that a believer must follow when such conduct comes to his notice. A great deal depends upon the seriousness of the offence and upon the relationship which exists between him and the offender.*

(letter written on behalf of the Universal House of Justice to an individual believer, dated February 20, 1977)

The following are some options the individual may pursue, as described in the above letter:
1. *If the misconduct is blatant and flagrant or threatens the interests of the Faith the believer to whose attention it comes should immediately report it to the Local Spiritual Assembly. Once it is in the hands of the Assembly the believer's obligation is discharged and he should do no more than pray for the offender and continue to show him friendship and encouragement - unless, of course, the Spiritual Assembly asks him to take specific action.*
2. *Sometimes...the matter does not seem grave enough to warrant reporting to the Spiritual Assembly, in which case it may be best to ignore it altogether.*
3. *....he could foster friendly relations with the individual concerned, tactfully drawing him into Bahá'í activities in the hope that, as his knowledge of the Teachings and awareness of the Faith deepens, he will spontaneously improve his patterns of conduct.*
4. *...perhaps the relationship is such that he can tactfully draw the offender's attention to the Teachings on the subject - but here he must be very careful not to give the impression of prying into a fellow-believer's private affairs or of telling him what he must do, which would not only be wrong in itself but might well produce the reverse of the desired reaction.*
5. *If a believer faced with knowledge of another Bahá'í's misconduct is unsure what course to take, he can, of course, always consult his Local Spiritual Assembly for advice. If, for some reason, he is reluctant at that stage to inform his Spiritual Assembly, he can consult an Auxiliary Board member or assistant.*

(a letter written on behalf of the Universal House of Justice to an individual believer, dated February 20, 1977)

9.3.8 *What actions is it inappropriate for a believer to take?*

Bahá'ís must not spread gossip about a situation or discuss it with others behind the person's back:-

> *Whatever steps are taken, it is vital that the believers refrain from gossip and backbiting, for this can only harm the Faith, causing perhaps more damage than would have been caused by the original offence.*

CHAPTER NINE

(letter written on behalf of the Universal House of Justice to an individual believer, dated February 20, 1977)

9.4 **REHABILITATION AND RESTORATION OF VOTING RIGHTS**

9.4.1 *What responsibility has the Local Spiritual Assembly to assist believers who have lost their voting rights?*

Bahá'ís without voting rights have the right of access to their local Assembly. The Assembly, for its part, has a duty to assist these believers to rectify their mistakes:-

> *The deprivation of a person's voting rights should only be [resorted to] when absolutely necessary...sometimes, to protect the Cause, it must be done, but he feels that if the believer so deprived makes an effort to mend his ways, rectifies his mistakes, or sincerely seeks forgiveness, every effort should be made to help him and enable him to re-establish himself in the Community as a member in good standing.*

(letter written on behalf of Shoghi Effendi to a National Spiritual Assembly, dated May 18, 1948)

9.4.2 *What should the attitude of the community be towards a believer without voting rights?*

Community members must at all times remember that relations between individuals in the Bahá'í community are governed by love and forbearance. The believers have no right to pass judgement on one another. Reaching a judgement and applying it is a function restricted to the Bahá'í institutions in their capacity as the administrators of Bahá'í law:-

> *...there is a distinction drawn in the Faith between the attitudes which should characterise individuals in their relationship to other people, namely, loving forgiveness, forbearance, and concern with one's own sins, not the sins of others, and those attitudes which should be shown by the Spiritual Assemblies, whose duty is to administer the law of God with justice.*

(letter from the Universal House of Justice to all National Spiritual Assemblies, dated February 6, 1973)

Bahá'ís are also forbidden to gossip and backbite. This means the friends should not busy themselves discussing the circumstances of a Bahá'í who has lost his or her voting rights. The Local Spiritual Assembly has a duty to educate the friends about their responsibilities in such matters. [Further information is available in Chapter 14 on 'Protection' in this Handbook.]

9.4.3 *What steps may a community take to assist a believer without voting rights to regain them?*

As to the steps a community should take to assist a member without voting rights to regain them, this must depend upon the circumstances of each individual case:-

> *The degree to which a community should be active or passive towards a believer who is deprived of his voting rights depends upon the circumstances in each individual case. Obviously, it is desirable that such a person should come to see the error of his ways and rectify his condition. In some cases friendly approaches by the Bahá'ís may help to attain this; in other cases the individual may react more favourably if left to his own devices for a time.*

CHAPTER NINE

(letter from the Universal House of Justice to a National Spiritual Assembly, dated November 1, 1973)

9.4.4 **What must a believer do to have his or her voting rights restored?**

Bahá'ís who have lost their voting rights must understand that this is a severe sanction and not one that can be lightly removed. Restoration is dependent on believers showing real repentance for their act of disobedience:-

> *The Assembly must exercise great care to ensure that Bahá'ís do not come to regard Bahá'í Laws as mere technicalities which they can break and later easily have the sanctions removed.*

(letter from the Universal House of Justice to a National Spiritual Assembly, dated October 11, 1965)

> *In all cases of application for restoration of voting rights the Assembly should satisfy itself that the believer is sincerely repentant of his act of disobedience - not merely that he regrets the unhappy condition he is in and wishes to re-enter the Bahá'í Community.*

(letter from the Universal House of Justice to a National Spiritual Assembly, dated October 11, 1965)

Each application must be considered on its merits; the repentance required differs from case to case. Often it is sufficient for the person to simply rectify the error and to then apply for re-instatement. On the other hand, there are circumstances in which an open expression of regret and repentance is important. Consider the following cases:

> *Each case must be considered on its own merits and no hard and fast rules can be laid down. It is for your Assembly to determine, in each case, whether the facts justify restoration of voting rights. Restoration of voting rights often requires repentance by the offender...the repentance required to be shown differs in degree and form from case to case. At one extreme is the case of a believer who is no longer able to rectify the wrong he has committed - for example when he has lost his voting rights for marrying without parental consent and the parents have since died - in such a case the factor of repentance is particularly important. At the other extreme is the case of a believer who has been deprived of his voting rights because the Assembly is convinced by the evidence that he was guilty of the offence, but who maintains that, in spite of all appearances to the contrary, he is innocent. There is no requirement that such a believer admit guilt before the voting rights can be restored. The believer must, however, comply with the Assembly's instructions as to his behaviour. In between these extremes are many cases where the very rectifying of the error can be held to constitute repentance.*

(letter from the Universal House of Justice to a National Spiritual Assembly, dated July 12, 1979)

> *It can happen, for example, that voting rights are removed mistakenly and the incorrect action of the Assembly is the basis for the believer's application for their restoration. If the voting rights have been removed justifiably it is generally sufficient for the believer to take the necessary actions to have them restored; his application for restoration and*

CHAPTER NINE

compliance with the requirements of Bahá'í law are sufficient evidence of repentance.

(letter from the Universal House of Justice to a National Spiritual Assembly, dated September 21, 1976)

9.4.5 **Can the period of time for which a believer has lost his or her voting rights be extended beyond the point at which the situation is rectified?**

Yes, but only in such rare instances as when the believer shows an attitude of contempt for the Bahá'í laws and the violation has been serious:-

If the voting rights have been removed justifiably it is generally sufficient for the believer to take the necessary actions to have them restored; his application for restoration and compliance with the requirements of Bahá'í law are sufficient evidence of repentance. However, if the Assembly sees that the believer does not understand the reason for the deprivation and has a rebellious attitude it should endeavour to make the matter clear to him. If his attitude is one of contempt for the Bahá'í law and his actions have been in serious violation of its requirements, the Assembly may even be justified in extending the period of deprivation beyond the time of the rectification of the situation - but such cases, by their nature, are very rare.

(letter from the Universal House of Justice to a National Spiritual Assembly, dated September 21, 1976)

9.4.6 **To which institution should believers apply for restoration of their voting rights?**

Applications for restoration of voting rights must be made through the Local Spiritual Assembly to the National Assembly, as the Local Spiritual Assembly has responsibility for monitoring the behaviour of the person If the believer does not live in a Local Spiritual Assembly area the application may be made directly to the National Spiritual Assembly.

9.4.7 **What if the believer has moved to a new area of jurisdiction?**

If the believer has moved to a new area of jurisdiction the application for restoration of voting rights must be made through the new Local Spiritual Assembly. If the believer not moved to an area without an Assembly, the application should be made directly to the National Spiritual Assembly. If the believer moves to the area of jurisdiction of a different National Spiritual Assembly he or she must make application for restoration of voting rights to that National Assembly, which will then contact the believer's old National Assembly for details of the case [see "Lights of Guidance" {revised edition}, no. 209].

9.5 **ALCOHOL, DRUGS AND TOBACCO**

9.5.1 **May Bahá'ís drink alcohol?**

No. Bahá'ís are prohibited from drinking alcohol. This prohibition also extends to the consumption of foods which contain alcohol:-

Under no circumstances should Bahá'ís drink. It is so unambiguously forbidden in the Tablets of Bahá'u'lláh that there is no excuse for them even touching it in the form of a toast, or in a burning plum pudding; in fact, in any way.

(letter written on behalf of Shoghi Effendi to an individual believer, dated March 3, 1957)

> *With reference to your question whether those foods which have been flavoured with alcoholic liquors such as brandy, rum, etc. should be classified under the same category as the intoxicating drinks, and consequently be avoided by believers, the Guardian wishes all the friends to know that such foods, or beverages, are strictly prohibited.*

(letter written on behalf of Shoghi Effendi to an individual believer, dated January 9, 1939)

> *The reason for the prohibition is that alcohol 'leadeth the mind astray and causeth the weakening of the body.'*

('Abdu'l-Bahá, Tablet to an individual believer - translated from the Persian)

> *Intellect and the faculty of comprehension are God's gifts whereby man is distinguished from other animals. Will a wise man want to lose this Light in the darkness of intoxication? No, by God! This will not satisfy him! He will, rather, do that which will develop his powers of intelligence and understanding, and not increase his negligence, heedlessness and decline. This is an explicit text in the Perspicuous Book, wherein God hath set forth every goodly virtue, and exposed every reprehensible act.*

('Abdu'l-Bahá, Tablet to an individual believer - translated from the Persian)

The only exception to this rule is taking alcohol on medical advice:-

> *Concerning your question with regard to the use of alcohol for rubbing; the believers can make any use of alcohol for any such treatments, provided they do not drink it, unless, of course, they are compelled to do so, under the advice of a competent and conscientious physician, who may have to prescribe it for the cure of some special ailment.*

(letter written on behalf of Shoghi Effendi to an individual believer, dated July 25, 1938)

> *Concerning your inquiry about a Bahá'í keeping brandy in his home for emergency use on the advice of a doctor, the House of Justice feels there is no objection to this.*

(letter written on behalf of the Universal House of Justice to a National Spiritual Assembly, dated March 2, 1978)

9.5.2 *May Bahá'ís drink 'non-alcoholic' wines?*

The friends must use their own judgement in deciding whether to drink 'alcohol-free' wines:-

> *In the matter of abstaining from intoxicating beverages, as in many other laws, there is a border area between that which is permissible and that which is prohibited where exact definition would lead to hair-splitting and infinite complications. As you point out in your letter, some of the beverages which are now being sold as "alcohol-free" may not be entirely so, but a greater percentage may well be present naturally in fruit juices which no one would think to query.*

The friends should be familiar with the principle given in the Bahá'í law and should, at this time, be left free to make their own determination of borderline cases. No issue should be made of the matter in such cases.

(letter from the Universal House of Justice to a National Spiritual Assembly, dated October 8, 1987)

9.5.3 **May Bahá'í institutions serve alcohol to non-Bahá'ís?**

No:-

No Bahá'í institution should serve alcohol to non-Bahá'ís under any circumstances.

(statement issued by the Universal House of Justice, dated January 31, 1982)

May Bahá'ís, as individuals, serve alcohol to non-Bahá'ís?
The Universal House of Justice has provided the following guidelines:-

1. *If an individual Bahá'í is entertaining an individual guest or a small group of guests as an official representative of the Bahá'í community, he should not serve alcohol in his own home, but must use his discretion whether or not to do so if the entertaining is taking place in a restaurant.*

2. *No Bahá'í should serve alcohol at any function or reception given by him, such as a wedding reception or a party to which a number of people are invited.*

3. *When a Bahá'í is privately entertaining an individual non-Bahá'í or a small group of guests in his own home, he must himself judge whether or not to serve alcohol. This will depend to a great degree on the customs of the country in which he is living, the individuals concerned, and the host's relationship to his guests. Obviously it is better for the Bahá'ís not to serve alcohol if possible, but against this he must weigh the probable reaction of the guest in the circumstances which prevail and in the particular situation. In some countries there would be no problem in failing to provide alcohol to a guest; in others it would be regarded as extremely peculiar and anti-social and would immediately raise a barrier to further contact. It is not desirable to make a major issue of the matter.*

4. *When such private entertaining of an individual or small group of non-Bahá'ís is taking place in a restaurant the same general principles as in point [3] above apply, except that in such a public place a failure to provide alcoholic drinks would be less easily understood than in a private home, and the Bahá'í must use his discretion accordingly.*

(statement issued by the Universal House of Justice, dated January 31, 1982)

CHAPTER NINE

9.5.4 ***What is the responsibility of a Bahá'í who has a non-Bahá'í spouse who wishes to serve alcohol at a function?***

This is a matter for the couple to decide between them. In principle, the rights of the non-Bahá'í must be preserved and the Bahá'í partner must guard against imposing his or her standards of conduct on the non-Bahá'í spouse. The Universal House of Justice offered the following guidance with regard to a christening:-

> *The future christening of the child should present no problem, for the Bahá'í parent should have no objection to the baptism of his child if the Catholic mother wishes it. Similarly, the use of champagne upon that occasion is a matter which she is free to undertake, but of course the Bahá'ís would not partake of alcoholic beverages.*
>
> (letter written on behalf of the Universal House of Justice to a National Spiritual Assembly, dated December 7, 1977)

9.5.5 ***May Bahá'ís own businesses that sell alcohol?***

No:-

> *Alcohol must not be served in a restaurant or other business which is wholly owned by Bahá'ís.*
>
> (statement issued by the Universal House of Justice, dated January 31, 1982)

In the case of a business involving the sale of alcoholic beverages in which a Bahá'í is a partner with non-Bahá'ís, it is up to the conscience of the individual to decide how to act, taking into account the spirit of the Teachings and the circumstances of the case. A Bahá'í who is not already involved in such a partnership, should not enter into one:-

> *We have found no explicit text or instruction of the beloved Guardian on such a situation (the sale of alcoholic beverages by a business in which a Bahá'í is a partner with non-Bahá'ís) and feel that it is one in which no hard and fast rules should be drawn at the present time...We feel that this is a matter which needs to be decided in each case in the light of the spirit of the Teachings and the circumstances of the case, and unless the situation is one which is endangering the good name of the Faith or is obviously a ruse on the part of a believer to evade the Bahá'í law, it should be left to the conscience of the believer concerned who should, of course, be informed of the Bahá'í Teachings concerning alcohol and should make every effort to dissociate himself from such an activity. The above concerns Bahá'ís who are already in partnership dealing in such matters. It is, however, obvious that a Bahá'í who is not in such a situation should not enter into it.*
>
> (memorandum from the Universal House of Justice to the International Teaching Centre, dated January 15, 1976)

The House further clarified the above guidance in the following statement, written on its behalf to a National Spiritual Assembly, dated February 8, 1982:-

> *You will note in the enclosed quotations a reference to a Bahá'í being in partnership with non-Bahá'ís, and the instruction that each such case should be judged on its own merits. The House of Justice instructs us to state here that in the partnership of Mr..., Mrs..., Mr..., and Mr..., the fact that Mrs... is not a Bahá'í is no justification for the majority*

of the partners, who are Bahá'ís, permitting the service of alcohol in their restaurant.

9.5.6 **May non-Bahá'ís consume alcohol on Bahá'í-owned premises?**

The Universal House of Justice has said:-

> ...there is no objection if patrons bring their own alcoholic beverages and consume them on the premises, as long as there has been no advertising, signs posted or invitations extended, suggesting that they may do so.

(letter written on behalf of the Universal House of Justice to the National Spiritual Assembly of Australia, dated March 16, 1987)

9.5.7 **What other guidance do the Writings provide on the use of alcohol?**

The following matters have been left to individual believers to decide:
1. whether to use cake flavourings such as rum extracts in cooking or whether to work in factories that manufacture such extracts [see "Lights of Guidance" {revised edition} no.1174].
2. whether a Bahá'í may prepare advertisements for alcohol. {see "Lights of Guidance" {revised edition} no. 1181].
3. whether to remain in employment involving the sale of alcohol. [see "Lights of Guidance" {revised edition} no.1177, pt.7]

9.5.8 **May Bahá'ís take drugs?**

No. In a letter written on his behalf to an individual believer, dated November 4, 1926, Shoghi Effendi said:-

> ...in the Book of Aqdas we are definitely forbidden to take not only wine, but every thing that deranges the mind. Bahá'ís may not use marijuana, LSD, peyote or any other hallucinogenic agent. [See further "Lights of Guidance" nos. 1183-88.]

9.5.9 **May Bahá'ís smoke?**

'Abdu'l-Bahá strongly discouraged smoking but it is not forbidden and the Bahá'ís have no right to prevent anyone from smoking. An issue should not be made of the matter. [See further, "Lights of Guidance" {revised edition} nos. 1189-93.]

9.5.10 **May a Local Spiritual Assembly ban smoking during a Bahá'í meeting?**

A Local Spiritual Assembly may ban smoking at a meeting held under its auspices. The Universal House of Justice offers the following guidelines:-

> Believers have also raised the question about smoking during Bahá'í meetings. It is entirely within the authority of Local and National Spiritual Assemblies to prohibit smoking in meetings held under their auspices. An Assembly may well feel that it does not wish to raise an additional barrier to seekers by prohibiting smoking at public meetings in a society where it is the accepted practice to smoke. On the other hand, it might be wise for the Assembly to caution the Bahá'ís to restrain their smoking at teaching meetings and firesides in case it is offensive to some seekers. In the case of Nineteen Day Feasts or meetings of Assemblies or committees, it is not right that friends who find smoking offensive should be made to endure it in Bahá'í meetings which they are required or expected to attend. If certain individuals

CHAPTER NINE

feel that they must smoke, then arrangements, such as a break in the meeting, could be made for their convenience. It would, of course, be entirely inappropriate to smoke during the devotional part of a Feast, or at any other devotional gathering

(letter from the Universal House of Justice to a National Spiritual Assembly, dated March 4, 1974)

9.5.11 **Should new Bahá'ís be required to stop drinking alcohol or taking drugs immediately?**

No. New Bahá'ís should be made aware of the relevant Bahá'í principles and should be given sufficient time to bring their lives into conformity with the Teachings. Should a person not do so within a reasonable time and the problem is severe, deprivation of voting rights may have to be considered. The Local Spiritual Assembly should provide loving support to the person, and if necessary, encourage him or her to seek professional assistance.

9.5.12 **Should new Bahá'ís be required to stop selling alcohol immediately?**

No. The new believer should be given a reasonable time to dispose of the business and only if such time has lapsed and the new believer has made no effort to comply with Bahá'í law, should deprivation of voting rights be considered:-

...as he is a new believer and was engaged in this business before becoming a Bahá'í, he should be given a reasonable opportunity to find another means whereby he can earn a living and should be given every assistance by the National Spiritual Assembly to do so. He should be treated with patience and understanding, especially if he is making efforts to dispose of this business and to seek other employment. However, if after a reasonable time has elapsed and no effort has been made to comply with the Bahá'í law, then, as a last resort, the Assembly would have no alternative but to suspend his administrative rights.

(letter from the Universal House of Justice to a National Spiritual Assembly, dated March 13, 1974)

9.5.13 **How should a Local Spiritual Assembly handle the problem of a Bahá'í who drinks alcohol or takes drugs?**

If a Local Spiritual Assembly has a problem with a Bahá'í who drinks or takes drugs it must first decide whether the offence is flagrant. If it decides that the offence is flagrant, the believer must be lovingly exhorted, warned and eventually, if necessary, a recommendation may be made to the National Spiritual Assembly for deprivation of voting rights. If the offence is not flagrant the Assembly need take no action at all:-

As to those believers who continue to drink, they should be lovingly exhorted, then firmly warned and eventually deprived of their voting rights. The number of times a person is exhorted and warned is a matter left to the discretion of each Local Spiritual Assembly, in consultation with the National Spiritual Assembly. The policy you adopt should not be one of removing the administrative rights of the believers in a bureaucratic and automatic way, as this would be unwise and unjust. Your Assembly as well as all Local Spiritual Assemblies should courageously and continuously remind the friends of their obligation in this respect, handle firmly all flagrant cases, and use such cases, in a way that by force of example, they exert their influence upon the other believers.

(letter from the Universal House of Justice to a National Spiritual Assembly, dated November 12, 1965)

In the case of a believer who continues to take alcoholic drinks the Assembly should decide whether the offence is flagrant, and, if it is, should try to help him to understand the importance of obeying the Bahá'í law. If he does not respond he must be repeatedly warned and, if this is unsuccessful, he is subject to loss of his voting rights. In the case of an alcoholic who is trying to overcome his weakness the Assembly must show especial patience, and may have to suggest professional counselling and assistance. If the offence is not flagrant, the Assembly need take no action at all.

(letter written on behalf of the Universal House of Justice to a National Spiritual Assembly, dated September 26, 1978)

As noted above, the Assembly should, if necessary, help the believer to obtain professional counselling. The Local Spiritual Assembly may also place the believer in touch with the 'Bahá'ís in Recovery Fellowship' which provides support for Bahá'ís overcoming dependency problems. It is run along similar lines to the Twelve Step Programmes of Alcoholics Anonymous, Al Anon, Co-Da, and so on; and has the endorsement of the Universal House of Justice and the National Spiritual Assembly of Australia.

The responsibility of the believer in this situation is to get expert advice, to follow that advice, and to pray. [See "Lights of Guidance" {revised edition} no. 1180.]

9.5.14 ***What attitude should the Local Spiritual Assembly take towards a Bahá'í with a alcohol or drug problem?***

The Assembly must draw a distinction between, on the one hand, being gentle and patient with a believer who is trying to overcome an alcohol or drug habit; and, on the other hand, not tolerating a prolonged and flagrant disregard of the Bahá'í Teachings:-

The Assemblies must be wise and gentle in dealing with such cases (ie. Bahá'ís using alcoholic beverages), but at the same time must not tolerate a prolonged and flagrant disregard of the Bahá'í Teachings as regards alcohol.

(letter written on behalf of Shoghi Effendi to a National Spiritual Assembly, in "Bahá'í News", June 1958)

It must be made clear to the Local Assemblies that they should be willing to cooperate with the believers affected by such drinking habits, when any such believer promises gradually and systematically to reduce his drinking with the objective in mind of entirely abandoning this habit.

(letter from the Universal House of Justice to a National Spiritual Assembly, dated November 12, 1965)

9.6 **BEHAVIOUR THAT DAMAGES THE REPUTATION OF THE FAITH OR CAUSES DISUNITY**

9.6.1 ***What kind of behaviour does this heading include?***

This heading includes behaviour such as flagrant violations of Bahá'í ethical standards; or severe disruptions to community life caused by people with negative behavioural traits (eg.

CHAPTER NINE

strongly critical or contentious personalities); or difficulties caused by people suffering from emotional or psychological problems. Essentially these are matters that only become the concern of the Local Spiritual Assembly if the behaviour is so flagrant as to damage the reputation of the Faith or to cause disunity within the community.

9.6.2 **How should a Local Spiritual Assembly handle a flagrant violation of ethical standards?**

The Universal House of Justice provides the following guidance:-

> *Then there are those high ethical standards to which Bahá'u'lláh calls His followers, such as trustworthiness, abstention from backbiting, and so on; generally speaking obedience to these is a matter for individual conscience, and the Assemblies should not pry into people's lives to see whether or not they are following them; nevertheless, if a believer's conduct falls so far below the standard set by Bahá'u'lláh that it becomes a flagrant disgrace and brings the name of the Faith into disrepute, the Assembly would have to intervene, to encourage the believer to correct his ways, to warn him of the consequences of continued misconduct, and possibly, if he does not respond, to deprive him of his administrative rights.*

> (extract from a letter from the Universal House of Justice, contained in a letter from the National Spiritual Assembly of the Hawaiian Islands to its Local Spiritual Assemblies, dated February 1, 1988)

9.6.3 **Can a believer be deprived of voting rights for dishonest or fraudulent behaviour?**

Yes, if the interests of the Faith require it. Shoghi Effendi once ordered the removal of voting rights of a believer who was actively teaching the Faith, and in the public eye, and who was also displaying gravely dishonest characteristics:-

> *Regarding Mr....: it was with the approval of the Guardian that his name was removed from the voting list. It is very bad for the Cause to have a member of the Community, actively in the public eye, teaching the Faith, and at the same time showing dishonest characteristics. We cannot possibly say that because a person also has many virtues, faults as grave as lying and dishonourable conduct regarding money can be overlooked! This means that we tolerate as representatives of our Faith people who flagrantly disobey its laws and fundamental Teachings. This does not mean there is no hope for Mr....; let him change his conduct, if he really loves the Cause, and then a way will be opened for him to again be active. But the change must be real and obvious; mere protestations will serve no purpose.*

> (letter written on behalf of Shoghi Effendi, in "Arohanui: Letters from Shoghi Effendi to New Zealand", p.52)

9.6.4 **How should a Local Spiritual Assembly handle individuals whose behaviour is severely disrupting community life?**

If counselling, admonitions and warnings have not remedied, or cannot remedy, the behaviour, the Local Spiritual Assembly may recommend partial sanctions to the National Spiritual Assembly. For example, if the person is continually disrupting the Feast, he or she may be forbidden to attend the Feast:-

CHAPTER NINE

> *Limited sanctions (ie. restrictions on one's eligibility to serve on institutions or participate in community events) are usually imposed in cases where the individual disrupts the unity of the community, or is mentally unfit and unable to exercise judgment or behave responsibly. The Universal House of Justice has clearly indicated that a National Spiritual Assembly may debar an individual from serving on a Local Spiritual Assembly without removing his administrative rights.*
>
> (letter written on behalf of the Universal House of Justice, dated January 31, 1972)

If the person has psychological or emotional problems the Local Spiritual Assembly should assist the believer to find a professional counselling service and should provide loving support to the believer whilst he or she is undergoing counselling. If the person's mental illness is so severe as to make the responsible exercising of his or her administrative rights impossible, these may be removed, not as a punishment, but as a recognition of the person's incapacity to properly use them. Again, depending upon the nature of the illness, the withdrawal of rights may be partial rather than total. Professional advice should be sought and each case must be decided on its own merits. If the person's mental health is restored, voting rights would then be reinstated:-

> *We are asked to say that a National Spiritual Assembly has a wide range of options available to it in handling the difficulties created by a believer who is suffering from a mental disability. The restrictions imposed by the National Assembly are determined by recognition of the believer's inability to exercise the normal range of administrative rights or by the need to avoid disruption of community activities. In the most extreme case, the voting rights of the believers would be suspended due to mental illness. However, this is a very serious measure, and its application would be governed by the guidance provided in letters written on behalf of the Guardian, to the effect that:*
>
> *'Only people who are very seriously deranged mentally and confined to institutions or under constant supervision should be deprived of their voting rights.'*
>
> *'Only in rare cases when a person is actually unbalanced, and is admittedly proved to be so, should the right of membership be denied him.'*
>
> *If the situation is not so serious as to warrant such a step, but the participation of a believer is causing grave problems for the community, it is permissible for a National Spiritual Assembly to debar him from those activities which are giving rise to the distress of the community: such restrictions could include interdicting his attendance at the Nineteen Day Feast, service on the Local Spiritual Assembly or committees or representing the Faith in public.*
>
> (letter written on behalf of the Universal House of Justice to a National Spiritual Assembly, dated June 1, 1987)

The National Spiritual Assembly has the authority to suspend the voting rights of a believer if it is satisfied that he is not mentally capable of exercising the right to vote in Bahá'í elections or of serving as a member of a Bahá'í Institution. Such an action should be taken only in serious cases where it is clearly evident that such a mental incapacity exists. The withdrawal of voting rights in a case of this nature is not a sanction, but merely a recognition that the believer's condition renders him incapable of exercising these rights. Depending on the particular circumstances, the Assembly may permit him to continue to receive Bahá'í news journals, or even to attend the Nineteen Day Feasts and contribute to the Fund. Each case should be decided on its own merits. If the believer's mental health is restored, voting rights would then be reinstated, unless there were some other reason for withholding them.

(letter written on behalf of the Universal House of Justice to the National Spiritual Assembly of Australia, dated October 14, 1988)

Regarding persons whose condition (ie. mental condition) has not been defined by the civil authorities after medical diagnosis, the Assembly on the spot must investigate every case that arises and, after consultation with experts, deliver its verdict. Such a verdict however, should in important cases, be preceded by consultation with the National Spiritual Assembly. No doubt, the power of prayer is very great, yet consultation with experts in enjoined is Bahá'u'lláh. Should these experts believe that an abnormal case exists, the with-holding of voting rights is justified.

(letter from Shoghi Effendi to a National Spiritual Assembly, dated May 30, 1936)

[See also Chapter 14 on 'Protection', Section 2.]

9.6.5 **Can a believer be deprived of voting rights for failing to repay his or her debts?**

No. Believers have a moral obligation before God to repay their debts, but this obligation is not enforceable by the Bahá'í institutions:-

As regards ...., the Guardian never gave him any 'mission'. He feels, however, that your Assembly should not deprive him of his voting rights on this pretext, or because he cannot, or will not, liquidate his debts. If once the precedent is established that a Bahá'í can be deprived of his voting rights on such grounds as these, you can see for yourself where it would lead.

(letter written on behalf of Shoghi Effendi to a National Spiritual Assembly, dated June 20, 1954)

9.6.6 **Can a believer be deprived of voting rights for gambling?**

Generally speaking the prohibition on gambling in the Writings is, at present, a matter left to the individual conscience of the believer. It may become a matter of concern to the Assembly if a believer's behaviour is so flagrant as to bring the name of the Faith into disrepute. [See further "Lights of Guidance" {revised edition} nos. 1201-04.]

CHAPTER NINE

9.7 DISOBEDIENCE TO CIVIL LAW

9.7.1 *Must Bahá'ís obey the civil law?*

Yes:-

> ...Bahá'ís obey the law, Federal or state, unless submission to these laws amounts to a denial of their Faith.
>
> (letter from the Universal House of Justice to a National Spiritual Assembly, dated March 30, 1965)

The National Spiritual Assembly particularly draws to the attention of the friends the need to obey the following laws:
- laws relating to taxation
- laws relating to social security benefits and payments
- laws relating to sales tax and customs duties
- copyright laws
- laws relating to immigration and visas

9.7.2 *Is a believer found guilty of a crime automatically deprived of voting rights?*

No. Violations of civil law are handled by the civil courts. Generally speaking the Bahá'í institutions do not have a role in enforcing decisions of the civil courts. The question of deprivation of voting rights only arises if the person's actions conspicuously disgrace the Faith and seriously injure its reputation. Every case must be considered on its merits:-

> *We have carefully reviewed your letter of April 18, 1967 inquiring about the attitude to be adopted by your National Assembly regarding believers who have been charged with criminal offences, suspected to have committed such offences, or convicted by the court. The principle to bear in mind is that each case falling in any of the aforementioned categories should be considered separately and on its own merits. No hard and fast rule should be applied. If the believer's actions conspicuously disgrace the Faith and such actions seriously injure its reputation, the National Assembly may in its discretion apply the sanction of deprivation of voting rights. ... it should be realised that the application of Bahá'í sanctions is not an automatic action in response to a verdict of the court.*
>
> (letter from the Universal House of Justice to a National Spiritual Assembly, dated May 3, 1967)

> *...you cite violations of the criminal laws of the state. These cases are handled in the civil courts, and may or may not be subject to Bahá'í administrative action depending upon the nature of the offence and its effect on the Faith. Generally speaking the development of the Administrative Order has not progressed to the point where Bahá'í institutions enforce criminal laws.*
>
> (letter of the Universal House of Justice to a National Spiritual Assembly, dated May 7, 1974)

9.7.3 *How should a Local Spiritual Assembly proceed in a situation in which a Bahá'í has violated the civil law?*

A Local Spiritual Assembly must advise the National Spiritual Assembly promptly if a believer is charged with a serious offence. The Local Spiritual Assembly should act immediately to ascertain the facts of the case and send in a full report to the National Spiritual Assembly, together with any supporting documentation, eg. press clippings. The Local Spiritual Assembly should continue to monitor the case and keep the National Spiritual Assembly informed. It must also recommend to the National Spiritual Assembly whether full or partial sanctions should be applied to the Bahá'í concerned or not. As noted above, the Local Spiritual Assembly does not have the role of enforcing civil law and it must not take any steps that would interfere with the established civil law procedures.

9.7.4 *What guidance is there for Bahá'ís swearing an oath or affirmation in a Court of Law?*

As there is nothing specific in the Bahá'í writings on this subject the National Spiritual Assembly advises that there is no objection to Bahá'ís swearing an oath or affirmation such as:

- "I (name), do solemnly, sincerely and truly declare and affirm that the evidence I shall give to the court shall be the truth, the whole truth and nothing but the truth."

Indeed Bahá'ís should not find such an oath or affirmation difficult since they are required to be truthful at all times, regardless of the formality of the law. There cannot be, therefore, any objection to Bahá'ís conforming to the requirements of the law courts.

9.7.5 *Must the oath or affirmation be sworn on a specific holy book?*

The Universal House of Justice advises that Bahá'ís may take an oath, if required, on any sacred book, although it may be preferable for them to do so on a Bahá'í book, if possible.

9.8 DIVORCE

For information on the laws relating to divorce see Chapter 11 of this Handbook and "Lights of Guidance" {revised edition}, nos. 182, 1302-38.

9.9 DOMESTIC VIOLENCE

9.9.1 *What is domestic violence?*

Domestic violence generally takes place behind the closed doors of family homes and is often the result of family tension erupting into physical violence whether it be in the form of bullying, bashings, beatings or sexual abuse. In some instances, the abuse may be verbal or psychological. This violence against another human being may also be the result of the aggressor thinking they have superior rights over another human being. Domestic violence is the most common form of assault in Australia. Women are usually the victims of such violence; however, in some cases men are the victims. Domestic violence occurs across all age groups, income levels, nationalities, religions and races. Usually it gets worse if no action is taken. This form of violence, as with all forms of violence, affects people physically, emotionally, spiritually and psychologically. It leads to the destruction of the family unit.

9.9.2 *Why is assault on a marriage partner wrong?*

Assault on a marriage partner is wrong because it is contrary to the Bahá'í principles of mutual respect and equality that should govern relations between husband and wife. Often the perpetrator of domestic violence views himself (or herself) as a person who has a problem which he or she has tried to solve in other ways which have failed, therefore, violence is now being used as a last resort; however, this is contrary to the fundamental Bahá'í principle that conflicts should be resolved through consultation, not violence:-

> *...the stress laid in the statements of Bahá'u'lláh and 'Abdu'l-Bahá*

on love and harmony as the hallmark of marriage, and in view of 'Abdu'l-Bahá's exhortation that each member of the family must uphold the rights of the others, makes it clear that violence in the family is contrary to the spirit of the Faith and a practice to be condemned. It is clear that no husband should subject his wife to abuse of any kind, whether emotional, mental or physical. Such a reprehensible action would be the very antithesis of the relationship of mutual respect and equality enjoined by the Bahá'í writings — a relationship governed by the principles of consultation and devoid of the use of any form of abuse, including force, to compel obedience to one's will.

(letter written on behalf of the Universal House of Justice to the National Spiritual Assembly of Australia, dated April 12, 1990)

...there are times when the husband and the wife should defer to the wishes of the other. Exactly under what circumstances such deference should take place, is a matter for each couple to determine.

(letter written on behalf of the Universal House of Justice to an individual believer, dated May 16, 1982)

The National Spiritual Assembly will not tolerate acts of domestic violence within the Bahá'í community in Australia.

9.9.3 **What is the law concerning domestic violence in Australia?**

In all the States of Australia, any form of assault which is committed in the home is considered a crime. Various State Governments have passed specific legislation concerning domestic violence which gives added protection and rights to the victim. Local Spiritual Assemblies will need to contact various State Government Offices for particular details of legislation. New legislation is being enacted all the time, and amendments are being made to previous legislation. For example, in New South Wales the Crimes (Domestic Violence) Amendment Act came into force on April 18, 1983 and amendments to the law were made in December 1983. The law was changed to give added protection to victims of domestic violence, eg. police can now obtain warrants quickly to enter a home where there has been domestic violence. There are court orders which can be given if a person is afraid they will be assaulted; police now lay charges; the victim's role is now one of a witness to an assault case. Men or women can be charged with assault and either can be a victim (from 'Domestic Violence' - NSW Government Publication).

9.9.4 **Should a victim or perpetrator of domestic violence take the problem to their Assembly?**

Yes. Bahá'ís are encouraged to turn to their Local Spiritual Assembly for solutions to their problems and, individuals may take a problem to their local Assembly even if other parties to the problem do not wish to involve the Assembly:-

When a Bahá'í wife finds herself in such a situation [of domestic violence] and feels it cannot be resolved through consultation with her husband, she could well turn to the Local Spiritual Assembly for advice and guidance...

(letter written on behalf of the Universal House of Justice to the National Spiritual Assembly of Australia, dated April 12, 1990)

> *Often with cases of domestic violence, individuals do not take their problems to the Assembly for a number of reasons. They may be embarrassed to do so as it will indicate that they have been violated as a human being; they feel it might bring shame to their families; they are frightened if they do, domestic violence will be even more severe; or they may feel that the Assembly is not competent in dealing with this problem of theirs. There may be other reasons. If individuals feel that they cannot tell their Local Assembly, they should go to the National Spiritual Assembly. Such a situation may arise if, for example, one of the parties to the conflict is serving on the Local Spiritual Assembly. The Universal House of Justice also notes that a person in this situation 'might ... find it highly advantageous to seek the assistance of competent professional counsellors.'*

(letter written on behalf of the Universal House of Justice to the National Spiritual Assembly of Australia, dated April 12, 1990)

9.9.5 How may the Local Spiritual Assembly encourage individuals to turn to the Assembly for help?

The Local Spiritual Assembly should educate the believers in the value of turning to the Assembly for assistance with their serious problems. At the same time, Assembly members must be made aware of the importance of maintaining complete confidentiality at all times:-

> *Regarding the question of confidentiality, the believers should be educated to a deeper understanding of the value of their turning to their institutions for assistance with such problems, confident that by this means justice will prevail. Together with that, it is essential that the members of the Assemblies be fully aware of the obligation imposed upon them to avoid any leakage of information from the Assembly meeting to other believers who have no legitimate reason to be so informed.*

(letter written on behalf of the Universal House of Justice to the National Spiritual Assembly of Australia, dated April 12, 1990)

9.9.6 Can a Local Spiritual Assembly intervene in a domestic violence conflict against the will of the parties involved?

Yes. An Assembly can intervene in a matter that affects the protection of individual Bahá'ís:-

> *In matters which affect the Cause the Assembly should, if it deems it necessary, intervene even if both sides do not want it to, because the whole purpose of the Assemblies is to protect the Faith, the Communities, and the individual Bahá'ís as well.*

(Shoghi Effendi, "Principles of Bahá'í Administration", p.58)

9.9.7 Should the Local Spiritual Assembly advise a couple in a domestic violence situation to separate?

At present the prevailing method in Australia of treating domestic violence is to advise the couple to separate and to seek treatment from professional counselling services. It is suggested that Assemblies follow this method of treating domestic violence also. The Universal House of Justice has said:-

> *There is no obligation on a wife, who is being subjected to beating by her husband, to continue living with him; she has the freedom to leave*

CHAPTER NINE

him and to live in a separate domicile if she feels it necessary to do so.

(letter written on behalf of the Universal House of Justice to the National Spiritual Assembly of Australia, dated April 12, 1990)

If, alternatively, the couple is counselled to remain together to try and reconcile their differences, there can be no guarantee that the violence will not recur, in which case the Assembly could appear, inadvertently, to be condoning it. If the couple separate, however, the role of the Assembly can then become that of providing an independent forum within which the couple can come together and try to resolve their differences. It is imperative that action be taken and the couple undergoes counselling. If no intervention takes place the 'cycle of violence' may very well repeat itself. This may be obscured by remorse and guilt; or a feeling of helplessness and self-blame on the victim's part, followed by apparent good relations between the couple which they confirm. However, left untreated, violence has the possibility of surfacing again.

9.9.8 **What immediate action should an Assembly take to assist a victim or perpetrator of domestic violence?**

It is recommended that Local Spiritual Assemblies take the following actions immediately in domestic violence cases:

1. If help is sought from a victim -
   a) Believe them.
   b) Telephone the police if necessary. Advise the victim of his or her rights.
   c) Arrange for medical, welfare and refuge services.
   d) Provide an immediate Local Spiritual Assembly contact person.
   e) Establish a support network which will offer information, protection and safety.
2. If help is sought from a perpetrator -
   a) Advise the perpetrator that his or her act is an offence under Bahá'í and Australian law. The consequences, if the behaviour continues, should be explained.
   b) Provide an immediate Local Spiritual Assembly contact person.
   c) Arrange for counselling and a support network.

9.9.9 **What principles should a Local Spiritual Assembly bear in mind when assisting a couple in a domestic violence situation to resolve their differences?**

The Local Spiritual Assembly should be aware of the procedure for consultation set out elsewhere in this Handbook and the general procedure for administering a violation of Bahá'í law set out earlier in this Chapter. In addition it should bear the following principles in mind: eg.-
a) individual pressures: low self-esteem, inability to control anger, inability to express one's feelings
b) relationship pressures: sexist attitudes, jealousy, unrealistic marital expectations
c) economic pressures: unemployment and financial stress
d) cultural pressures: the view of one sex by the other within the context of specific cultures

It is vital that the Assembly not be influenced by the personalities or the public perception of the individuals and their standing in the community and that they be objective in their assessment of the problem.

The Local Spiritual Assembly needs to be optimistic about the resolution of the problem due to the all-encompassing Bahá'í belief in the potential within each individual for the transformation of human character. Many of the issues raised can be traced back to lack of spirituality in the lives of believers and recognition of this enables the Assembly to be enthusiastic about positive strategies for change.

Trust by the couple in the Assembly. This results in effective change. To achieve this state the Assembly needs to ensure absolute confidentiality and to be impartial in its dealings with both parties. While it is a function of the Assembly to administer justice it is also a function to be a loving shepherd to all parties and not to rush to judgement without full knowledge of the facts.

9.9.10 *How should the Assembly counsel the couple?*

A programme of treatment or counselling on the Assembly's part may include:
- education in the non-violent resolution of conflict (consultation);
- spiritualisation of the individual and couple.

a) Couples should attempt to solve domestic conflicts through practising Bahá'í consultation:-

> *Bahá'u'lláh also stressed the importance of consultation. We should not think this worthwhile method of seeking solutions is confined to the administrative institutions of the Cause. Family consultation employing full and frank discussion, and animated by awareness of the need for moderation and balance, can be the panacea for domestic conflict. Wives should not attempt to dominate their husbands, nor husbands their wives.*

(letter written on behalf of the Universal House of Justice to an individual believer, dated August 1, 1978)

b) The Bahá'í Writings repeatedly emphasise the development of a spiritual relationship:-

> *O ye two believers in God! The Lord, peerless is He, hath made woman and man to abide with each other in the closest companionship, and to be even as a single soul. They are two helpmates, two intimate friends, who should be concerned about the welfare of each other. If they live thus, they will pass through this world with perfect contentment, bliss, and peace of heart, and become the object of divine grace and favour in the Kingdom of heaven. But if they do other than this, they will live out their lives in great bitterness, longing at every moment for death, and will be shamefaced in the heavenly realm. Strive then, to abide, heart and soul, with each other as two doves in the nest, for this is to be blessed in both worlds.*

("Selections from the Writings of 'Abdu'l-Bahá", p.122)

9.9.11 *Where can the Assembly turn for further help?*

There are a number of government and private services available in Australia which can assist Assemblies. The following organisations or places can be contacted:
- Local Courts and Chamber Magistrates
- Legal Aid Centres
- Community Legal Centres
- Women's Refuges
- Women's Health Centres
- Housing Department
- Community Health Centres
- Department of Social Security
- Police Departments
- Independent Medical Practitioners

CHAPTER NINE

- Marriage and Family Counselling Services

9.9.12 ***Does the Local Spiritual Assembly or an individual have a responsibility to report incidences of domestic violence to the civil authorities?***

According to legal advice received by the National Spiritual Assembly a person is not in general required to act to prevent the occurrence of a criminal harm; the law does not impose any such general duty. This, however, is only a general rule and it is subject to some specific exceptions which include:
1. A parent's responsibility to safeguard the health and life of his or her young dependent child.
2. A police officer's responsibility to protect a citizen from serious assault.
3. An employee's responsibility to intervene to prevent a fellow employee from stealing their employer's property.

Clearly, none of these exceptions are applicable to the situation faced by Bahá'í institutions in relation to domestic violence. A further exception to the general rule may be found in the old common law offence of misprision of felony, which still exists in New South Wales and South Australia, where the distinction between felonies and misdemeanours has been retained. This offence is committed by any person who fails to report to the police or anyone else in lawful authority an unreported felony known to him or her. Most serious assaults are classified as felonies.

9.9.13 ***If a beleiver persists in domestic violence, will that person be deprived of his or her voting rights?***

The Universal House of Justice has said:-

> *If the husband is also a Bahá'í, the Local Spiritual Assembly can bring to his attention the need to avoid abusive behaviour and can, if necessary, take firmer measures to compel him to conform to the admonitions of the Teachings.*
>
> (letter written on behalf of the Universal House of Justice to a National Spiritual Assembly, dated April 12, 1990)

The National Spiritual Assembly regards domestic violence as a serious matter which may result in the immediate removal of voting rights.

9.9.14 ***What should an individual Bahá'í do if told in confidence of a domestic violence problem?***

As a general principle, if an individual has been given information after promising to keep it confidential, it is not permissible to break that promise. What the individual should do is encourage the person to take the problem to their Local Spiritual Assembly.

There may, however, be circumstances, as noted previously, in which the individual is obliged to report the matter to the civil authorities.

9.10 **MORALITY**

9.10.1 ***What standard of morality must Bahá'ís uphold?***

The Bahá'í standard is one of strict chastity before marriage and complete faithfulness to one's spouse after marriage:-

> *The question you raise as to the place in one's life that a deep bond of love with someone we meet other than our husband or wife can have*

is easily defined in view of the Teachings. Chastity implies both before and after marriage an unsullied, chaste sex life. Before marriage absolutely chaste, after marriage absolutely faithful to one's chosen companion. Faithful in all sexual acts, faithful in word and in deed.

(letter written on behalf of Shoghi Effendi to an individual believer, dated September 28, 1941)

[See further "Lights of Guidance" {revised edition} nos.1205 - 1220.]

9.10.2 *How should the Local Spiritual Assembly handle problems of immorality that arise within the community?*

The Local Spiritual Assembly should be loving rather than sternly judgemental when faced with problems of immorality. It has a duty to deepen the friends in the moral Teachings of the Faith and to exhort them to follow those Teachings. Only if a believer's conduct is blatantly and flagrantly immoral, and therefore harmful to the good name of the Faith - and all attempts at counselling and warning have failed - should the Assembly recommend the application of sanctions to the National Spiritual Assembly:-

In sexual morality, as in other realms of behaviour, people often stumble and fall short of the ideal. It is the task of Spiritual Assemblies to ensure that the friends are deepened in their understanding of the Teachings, and are exhorted to apply them in their lives. In caring for its community, a Spiritual Assembly should act as a loving father rather than as a stern judge in such matters. Nevertheless, if a believer's behaviour is blatantly and flagrantly immoral and, therefore, is harmful to the good name of the Faith, the Assembly must counsel him (or her), urge him to reform his conduct, warn him of the consequences if he does not mend his ways and, ultimately, if the believer persists in misbehaviour, the Assembly must deprive him of his administrative rights. This deprivation remains in force until such time as the believer repents of his actions and is able to satisfy the Spiritual Assembly that he has rectified his behaviour.

(letter written on behalf of the Universal House of Justice to a National Spiritual Assembly, dated June 5, 1986)

Any blatant acts of immorality on the part of the Bahá'ís should be strongly censured; the friends should be urged to abandon such relationships immediately, straighten out their affairs, and conduct themselves as Bahá'ís; if they refuse to do this, in spite of the warnings of the Assembly, they should be punished through being deprived of their voting rights.

(letter written on behalf of Shoghi Effendi to a National Spiritual Assembly, dated July 20, 1946)

We wish to emphasise ... that although all immorality is condemned in the Teachings, it is only flagrant immorality that is sanctionable. You should not pry into people's affairs, and only in cases of flagrant immorality should you consider imposing sanctions, and then only after you have patiently explained to the believers concerned the Bahá'í Laws involved and given them ample time to comply. Particularly in the application of these laws to indigenous people should you be patient and forbearing. The emphasis should be on education rather than on rigid enforcement of the law immediately.

(letter from the Universal House of Justice to a National Spiritual Assembly, dated June 23, 1969)

The sanctions imposed may be partial rather than full, depending on the circumstances of the case:-

Regarding those whose conduct is immoral... If the conduct of the believer does not improve and continues to be a disgrace to the Faith, the National Spiritual Assembly may decide merely to remove him from the membership of the Local Assembly, if he is a member of it, or to apply the full sanction of depriving him of his voting rights, depending upon the circumstances in each case. It is impossible and unwise to lay down a general ruling to cover all circumstances.

(letter written on behalf of the Universal House of Justice to a National Spiritual Assembly, dated January 14, 1966)

9.10.3 **What is meant by 'flagrant' immorality?**

By 'flagrant' is meant an act that occurs more than once, is generally known and reflects badly on the name of the Faith:-

As to deprivation of voting rights for immorality, while we may not have written to you on the subject it should be clear that sanctions should not be imposed for isolated acts of immorality. Only extreme cases involving acts of blatant and flagrant immorality reflecting on the name of the Faith and repeated time after time in spite of warnings should be taken as a basis for suspension of voting rights.

(letter from the Universal House of Justice to a National Spiritual Assembly, dated June 14, 1967)

If the acts of immorality are not generally known and are discoverable only on investigation, a serious question is raised as to whether this immorality is 'flagrant'.

(letter from the Universal House of Justice to a National Spiritual Assembly, dated August 20, 1969)

9.10.4 **Is the birth of a child out of wedlock in itself sufficient reason to remove voting rights?**

No:-

...in reply to your letter of 8 April 1981 requesting guidance on how to deal with problems involving Bahá'í women who have had children out of wedlock. Normally administrative rights should not be suspended because of the birth of a child out of wedlock. The questions to be considered are whether the party is guilty of blatant and flagrant immorality, whether such conduct is harming the Faith, and whether the believer has refused or neglected to improve her conduct despite repeated warnings. If you find that the girls in question are responding to the exhortations of the Assembly and have corrected their behaviour, you should consider the matter closed and restore their administrative rights. Your Assembly should, of course, provide for the proper

CHAPTER NINE

deepening of the friends, and in a loving and patient manner attempt to instil in them a respect for Bahá'í Laws.

(letter written on behalf of the Universal House of Justice to a National Spiritual Assembly, dated May 6, 1981)

9.10.5 **What is the Bahá'í stance on a man and a woman who are not married sharing the same accommodation?**

The situation of a man and a woman who are not married to each other occupying the same household raises a number of issues of which individual Bahá'ís and Local Spiritual Assemblies should be aware.

The following Bahá'í principles are involved:-
1. The high station of marriage in the Bahá'í Teachings must be preserved:-

    The institution of marriage is upheld and strengthened in the Bahá'í Teachings, being described by Bahá'u'lláh as a 'fortress for well-being and salvation.' It is contrary to Bahá'í law for a couple to commence to live together in an unmarried state when either one or both are Bahá'ís.

    (letter from the Universal House of Justice to a National Spiritual Assembly, dated May 3, 1987)

2. Chastity must be observed in all our relationships:-

    A chaste and holy life must be made the controlling principle in the behaviour and conduct of all Bahá'ís, both in their social relations with members of their own community, and in their contact with the world at large.

    (Shoghi Effendi, "Advent of Divine Justice", p.25)

3. The good name of the Faith must be upheld, taking account of the way our actions are likely to be perceived in the general community:-

    The Cause in...is growing very rapidly, and the more it spreads the more the attention of the public will be fixed upon it. This imposes a heavy responsibility on the believers...

    (letter written on behalf of Shoghi Effendi, in "Living the Life", p.26)

The Local Spiritual Assembly should share these three principles with Bahá'ís who intend sharing accommodation and are uncertain about the appropriateness of their plans.

9.10.6 **What arrangements for shared accommodation are acceptable in Australia?**

The National Spiritual Assembly feels that the following arrangements for shared accommodation would be acceptable in many parts of Australia:
- where one of the parties is a bona fide housekeeper
- where the believer lives in a boarding house, residential college, hostel, nurses' quarters, etc.
- where the believer lives in rented accommodation that is shared by at least two other tenants
- where a believer lives with a family.

In doubtful cases it is the responsibility of the Local Spiritual Assembly

CHAPTER NINE

to determine the acceptability of living arrangements within its area of jurisdiction in the light of the three principles given above. It should be noted that the Universal House of Justice has said 'the age of the parties or their capacity to father or conceive children' are not relevant criteria.

(letter from the Universal House of Justice to a National Spiritual Assembly, dated September 3, 1974).

9.10.7 **How should the Local Spiritual Assembly proceed in a case in which a shared accommodation arrangement is unacceptable?**

If the Local Spiritual Assembly decides, upon investigation, that the believer's living arrangements are not commonly accepted in the community, or are likely to be perceived as suggesting an illegitimate sexual relationship, it must tactfully counsel the believers on the need to change their living arrangements. Patience is particularly called for when dealing with a new believer or one who is not deepened. It is clear that the customs of the society in which we live are still to varying degrees influencing the behaviour of Bahá'ís. Because of this the Local Spiritual Assembly must be actively involved in educating and promoting the deepening of the friends in their respective areas and not merely imposing the laws of the Faith in an abrupt manner. On the other hand, in cases of flagrant disregard for laws that are well understood by the believers involved, the Local Spiritual Assembly's stand should be much firmer. It may call for clear warnings that if the matter is not rectified within a reasonable time it will be referred to the National Spiritual Assembly.

9.10.8 **How should the Local Spiritual Assembly advise believers who are living in an immoral relationship?**

If believers are living in an immoral relationship, they must be advised either to separate or to have a Bahá'í marriage ceremony to legitimise the relationship. Failure to do so, after repeated warnings, must result in loss of voting rights:-

...it is not permissible for Bahá'ís to enter into such an immoral relationship and ... any believers who do so must be counselled by the Assembly and warned to correct their conduct, either by separating or by having a Bahá'í marriage ceremony in accordance with the provision of Bahá'í Law. If, after repeated warnings, the believers concerned do not conform to Bahá'í Law, the Assembly has no choice but to deprive them of their voting rights.

(letter written on behalf of the Universal House of Justice to a National Spiritual Assembly, dated September 7, 1981)

9.10.9 **What is the Bahá'í stance on homosexuality?**

The Bahá'í Teachings centre on marriage and the family as the bedrock of society, therefore, homosexuality is not a permissible way of life:-

Amongst the many other evils afflicting society in this spiritual low water mark in history is the question of immorality, and over-emphasis of sex. Homosexuality, according to the Writings of Bahá'u'lláh, is spiritually condemned. This does not mean that people so afflicted must not be helped and advised and sympathised with. It does mean that we do not believe that it is a permissible way of life; which, alas, is all too often the accepted attitude nowadays.

(letter written on behalf of Shoghi Effendi to an individual believer, dated May 21, 1954)

CHAPTER NINE

> *Bahá'í Teachings on sexual morality centre on marriage and the family as the bedrock of the whole structure of human society and are designed to protect and strengthen that divine institution. Thus Bahá'í Law restricts permissible sexual intercourse to that between a man and the woman to whom he is married. Thus, it should not be so much a matter of whether a practicing homosexual can be a Bahá'í as whether, having become a Bahá'í, the homosexual can overcome his problem through knowledge of the Teachings and reliance on Bahá'u'lláh.*
>
> (letter from the Universal House of Justice to an individual believer, dated March 14, 1973)

9.10.10 ***How should a Local Spiritual Assembly handle a case of flagrant homosexuality?***

The Local Spiritual Assembly should primarily seek to assist the person through loving advice and repeated warnings. Only if the behaviour does not improve and becomes a matter of public knowledge may the Assembly take the step of recommending removal of voting rights. The principle to be followed is that the practice of homosexuality is immoral and should be dealt with no more and no less harshly than other kinds of immorality:-

> *The question of how to deal with homosexuals is a very difficult one. Homosexuality is forbidden in the Bahá'í Faith by Bahá'u'lláh; so, for that matter, are immorality and adultery. If one is going to start imposing heavy sanctions on people who are the victims of this abnormality, however repulsive it may be to others, then it is only fair to impose equally heavy sanctions on any Bahá'ís who step beyond the moral limits defined by Bahá'u'lláh. Obviously at the present time this would create an impossible and ridiculous situation. He feels, therefore, that, through loving advice, through repeated warnings, any friends who are flagrantly immoral should be assisted, and, if possible, restrained. If their activities overstep all bounds and become a matter of public scandal, then the Assembly can consider depriving them of their voting rights. However, he does not advise this course of action and feels it should only be resorted to in very flagrant cases.*
>
> (letter written on behalf of Shoghi Effendi to a National Spiritual Assembly, dated August 20, 1955) [Further information to assist in counselling a believer who is homosexual is available in "Lights of Guidance" {revised edition} nos. 185, 1221-30.]

9.11 **MARRIAGE**

For information on the laws relating to marriage see the chapter on Marriage in this handbook and "Lights of Guidance" {revised edition} nos. 1231-1301, 180, 190, 191, 199, 208. Note that there is a difference between violation of Bahá'í marriage laws and violation of many other laws of the Faith in that a knowing violation of the marriage laws must result in immediate loss of voting rights. Nevertheless, removal of voting rights is not an automatic procedure and the Assembly must first make sure that the person concerned knew all the requirements for Bahá'í marriage and his or her responsibilities in connection with them, before recommending the application of sanctions to the National Spiritual Assembly:-

> *...For the present, your Assembly should follow the guidance already given by the beloved Guardian, keeping in mind that suspension of voting rights is not an automatic procedure. In all marriage cases,*

including those you list, your Assembly must first ascertain if the Bahá'í in question was informed of the requirements for Bahá'í marriage, and of his own responsibilities in connection therewith. In cases involving disregard of Bahá'í Laws other than that of marriage, you should be slow to impose this severe sanction.

(letter from the Universal House of Justice to a National Spiritual Assembly, dated April 14, 1965)

9.12 POLITICAL ACTIVITIES AND MEMBERSHIP IN UNACCEPTABLE ORGANISATIONS

9.12.1 *Are Bahá'ís permitted to become involved in political activities or the ecclesiastical activities of other groups?*

For information on the laws relating to Bahá'í involvement in political and ecclesiastical activities, see the chapter in this handbook, 'Relations with Society'. Bahá'ís who refuse to dissociate themselves from unacceptable political and ecclesiastical activities are subject to loss of voting rights. According to the gravity of the situation they must be immediately warned and, if they do not desist, the matter must be reported to the National Spiritual Assembly without delay:-

The same sanction (ie. removal of voting rights) should apply to those who persistently refuse to dissociate themselves from political and ecclesiastical activities.

(letter written on behalf of Shoghi Effendi, in "Principles of Bahá'í Administration", p.87)

Your understanding and attitude regarding participation in politics is correct, namely, you immediately warn and quickly remove the voting rights, as such prompt action is necessary to protect the interests of the Faith.

(letter from the Universal House of Justice to a National Spiritual Assembly, dated November 12, 1965)

9.12.2 *How should the Local Spiritual Assembly proceed in the case of Bahá'í membership in unacceptable non-Bahá'í organisations?*

The Universal House of Justice has advised that the believers be first properly deepened in the relevant principles and then given a reasonable time to withdraw from these organisations. Each case must be considered on its own merits. Should a believer refuse to withdraw within a reasonable time, deprivation of voting rights will have to be considered. New believers must be advised of the need to withdraw from such organisations either before they become Bahá'ís or within a reasonable time after declaring:-

Your Assembly is advised to carefully inform the friends of these principles and to deepen them in their understanding and appreciation of them. Having made certain that all friends, especially those directly concerned, have been so deepened, your Assembly should then set a time limit by which the friends must obey your directive to withdraw their membership in the organisation. Each case will have to be considered on its own merits. Some of the friends may have to fulfil certain commitments as officers before they can withdraw with honour. The time limit should make allowance in such cases. Whereas persistence in membership in these and in similar organisations is

CHAPTER NINE

ample ground for deprivation of voting rights, your Assembly is advised to give sufficient time for each of the friends to be thoroughly deepened, and to comply with the principles before any disciplinary action is taken.

(letter from the Universal House of Justice to a National Spiritual Assembly, dated December 26, 1963)

In the case of new believers, it should be made clear to them in the course of teaching them the Faith that one cannot be a Bahá'í and also a member of another religious organisation. This is simply a matter of straight-forwardness and honesty...

You should not formalise the method by which the withdrawal from the church is to be made, and certainly nothing should be added to a declaration form if you use one. It should be left to the Local Spiritual Assembly which is accepting the declaration to satisfy itself, as it deems best in each case, that the new believer has already resigned from the church, or does so within a reasonable time of his declaration. In regard to the old believers, your Assembly should tactfully, and in a kindly way, make the Bahá'í position clear to them and gently persuade them to resign from their former churches. This is a matter for great tact and discretion. If such a believer remains adamant you will have to consider depriving him of his voting rights.

(letter from the Universal House of Justice to a National Spiritual Assembly, dated November 21, 1968)

9.13 NOTES FOR REGISTERED GROUPS

Any serious problems of violation of Bahá'í laws that arise within Groups should be referred to the National Spiritual Assembly. The National Spiritual Assembly will normally refer the matter to a neighbouring Assembly to handle.

CHAPTER TEN

Chapter 10

10. Bahá'í Teachings on Marriage

10.1 INTRODUCTION

10.1.1 *What is the meaning of Bahá'í marriage?*

> *The true marriage of Bahá'ís is this, that husband and wife should be united both physically and spiritually, that they may ever improve the spiritual life of each other, and may enjoy everlasting unity throughout all the worlds of God. This is Bahá'í marriage.*
>
> ('Abdu'l-Bahá, "Selections from the Writings of 'Abdu'l-Bahá", p.118)

In the "Kitáb-i-Aqdas", Bahá'u'lláh states that the purpose of marriage is to establish a family:-

> *Enter into wedlock, O people, that ye may bring forth one who will make mention of Me...*
>
> ("Synopsis and Codification of the Laws and Ordinances of the Kitáb-i-Aqdas", p.17)

10.1.2 *What is the age of maturity for marriage?*

In the "Synopsis and Codification of the Laws and Ordinances of the Kitáb-i-Aqdas" (p.39) it is stated that the age of maturity for marriage is 15. It is unlawful for a couple to become engaged if either party has not reached the age of maturity. Australian civil law, which has an over-riding effect at this time, states that for both males and females the marriageable age is 18, with approval needed from a Judge or Magistrate if one is under 18 but over 16.

10.1.3 *What prohibitions apply to marriage between relatives?*

Australian civil law previously forbade marriage between first cousins, but has now lifted this restriction. Where the ties are closer than that of first cousin, marriage is forbidden. Australian civil law permits marriage between a son and his stepmother and between a daughter and her stepfather. These marriages are, however, forbidden in Bahá'í law:-

> *It is apparent from the Guardian's writings that where Bahá'u'lláh has expressed a law as between a man and a woman it applies, mutatis mutandis, between a woman and a man unless the context should make this impossible. For example the text of the Kitáb-i-Aqdas forbids a man to marry his father's wife (ie. his step-mother), and the Guardian has indicated that likewise a woman is forbidden to marry her stepfather*
>
> .(letter from the Universal House of Justice to an individual believer, dated April 28, 1974)

10.1.4 *What are the requirements for a Bahá'í marriage?*

There are three major requirements:-
Bahá'u'lláh has made marriage conditional on
1. the consent of both parties
2. the consent of all living parents, and
3. the holding of a Bahá'í marriage ceremony.

CHAPTER TEN

10.2 CONSENT OF BOTH PARTIES

10.2.1 *Is the consent of both parties necessary?*

Yes. Bahá'u'lláh has commanded this in the "Kitáb-i-Aqdas".

> *"Verily in the Book of Bayan (the Báb's Revelation) the matter is restricted to the consent of both (bride and bridegroom). As We desired to bring about love and friendship and the unity of the people, therefore We made it conditional upon the consent of the parents also, that enmity and ill-feeling might be avoided."*
>
> (quoted in "Bahá'u'lláh and the New Era", p.176-77)

10.2.2 *Do the parties involved consent to be married to each other prior to obtaining parental consent?*

Yes. On this point 'Abdu'l-Bahá wrote to an enquirer:-

> *As for the question regarding marriage under the Law of God: first thou must choose one who is pleasing to thee, and then the matter is subject to the consent of father and mother. Before thou makest thy choice, they have no right to interfere.*
>
> ("Selections from the Writings of 'Abdu'l-Bahá", p.118)

10.3 CONSENT OF PARENTS

10.3.1 *Whose consent must be obtained and why?*

The consent of all living parents must be obtained, no matter what the age of the couple intending to marry. The purpose is to strengthen the ties of unity in both family and society generally; and to create a sense of gratitude in the hearts of the children towards their parents:-

> *Bahá'u'lláh has clearly stated the consent of all living parents is required for a Bahá'í marriage. This applies whether the parents are Bahá'ís or non-Bahá'ís, divorced for years, or not. This great law He has laid down to strengthen the social fabric, to knit closer the ties of the home, to place a certain gratitude and respect in the hearts of children for those who have given them life and sent their souls out on the eternal journey towards their Creator.*
>
> (letter written on behalf of Shoghi Effendi, published in "U.S. Bahá'í News", No.202, Dec. 1947, p.2)

10.3.2 *To what are the parents consenting?*

The parents consent only to the marriage. They do not have to give their consent for the Bahá'í ceremony; however, if they refuse to allow the marriage because there must be a Bahá'í ceremony, the marriage cannot take place. The decision of the parents is binding and they are responsible to God alone:-

> *Although a Bahá'í ceremony is required, it is not necessary that the parents consent to the ceremony; the only requirement is that they consent to the marriage. However, if consent be withheld because a Bahá'í ceremony is to be conducted, this must be accepted. The freedom of the parents in giving or refusing consent is unrestricted and unconditioned. They may refuse consent on any ground and they are responsible to God alone.*

CHAPTER TEN

(letter from the Universal House of Justice to an individual believer, dated January 18, 1972)

[See also "Lights of Guidance", Nos. 742, 746, 751]

10.3.3 *Is there a required wording for consent?*

No. There are a number of ways in which consent can be expressed. Because the consent is to the marriage itself, it is not necessary that it be sought in a way which suggests that a non-Bahá'í parent is being asked to approve a Bahá'í marriage ceremony or to observe Bahá'í laws:-

> *If it had been understood that Bahá'í law requires parental consent to marriage and not to the Bahá'í ceremony, Mrs. — consent might have been asked for in such a way as not to have incurred her displeasure. The request could have been quite casual without her son's even mentioning that he had to have it to fulfil a requirement of Bahá'í law...*

(letter written on behalf of the Universal House of Justice to an individual believer, dated September 16, 1981)

If parents give their blessing to a marriage, or express approval of or happiness with the marriage plans of their son or daughter, this may be accepted as consent:-

> *...Perhaps a different climate can be created so that, without violating any of her religious convictions, a happy family relationship can be established by Mrs. — simply saying that she approves of — being married to —*

(letter written on behalf of the Universal House of Justice to an individual believer, dated September 16, 1981)

10.3.4 *Should the consents be given in writing?*

It is preferable that consent of parents be given in writing; however, if this is not possible, verbal consent may be given in the presence of two persons acceptable to the Spiritual Assembly. Written statements of these witnesses should be filed by the Spiritual Assembly in place of the written consent. The witnesses do not need to be Bahá'ís:-

> *It is not necessary for the consent to be in writing if you are satisfied with verbal consent given in the presence of witnesses acceptable to your National Assembly.*

(letter from the Universal House of Justice to a National Spiritual Assembly, dated December 12, 1965)

10.3.5 *What if the parents do not name the spouse in the letter of consent?*

Such a letter may be accepted by the Spiritual Assembly:-

> *...the responsibility of the parents in giving their consent is unrestricted and unconditioned, but in discharging this duty they are responsible for their decision to God. Should the parents in their letter of consent...not name a specific future spouse, the House of Justice states that it could be accepted and it would be permissible to perform a Bahá'í marriage ceremony on the basis of such a letter.*

(letter written on behalf of the Universal House of Justice to an individual believer, dated October 9, 1975)

10.3.6 ***Must parental consents be obtained if one of the parties to the marriage is a non-Bahá'í?***

Yes. The consent of all parents is required:-

> *Regarding the question whether it is necessary to obtain the consent of the parents of a non-Bahá'í participant in a marriage with a Bahá'í; as Bahá'u'lláh has stated that the consent of the parents of both parties is required in order to promote unity and avoid friction, and as the Aqdas does not specify any exceptions to this rule, the Guardian feels that under all circumstances the consent of the parents of both parties is required...*

(letter written on behalf of Shoghi Effendi, quoted in "Principles of Bahá'í Administration", p.13)

10.3.7 ***Must consents be obtained if the parents are non-Bahá'ís or have been divorced for years?***

Yes. Shoghi Effendi states:-

> *This applies whether the parents are Bahá'ís or non-Bahá'ís, divorced for years, or not.*

(letter written on behalf of Shoghi Effendi, published in "U.S. Bahá'í News", No. 202, December 1947, p.2)

10.3.8 ***Must consents be obtained in the event of a second marriage?***

Yes:-

> *About the consent of parents for marriage...It is also required in the event of a second marriage, after the dissolution of the first whether through death or through divorce.*

(letter from Shoghi Effendi to an individual believer, dated October 10, 1936)

10.3.9 ***What is to be done if the whereabouts of the parent is unknown?***

Consent must be obtained unless the parent is dead. This law is not conditional on the relationship the parent has with the child:-

> *...As long as the parents are alive, the consent must be obtained; it is not conditioned on their relationship to their children. If the whereabouts of the parents is not known legally, in other words, if they are legally dead, then it is not necessary for the children to obtain their consent, obviously. It is not a question of the child not knowing the present whereabouts of its parents, it is a question of a legal thing - if the parents are alive, they must be asked.*

(letter written on behalf of Shoghi Effendi, in "Messages to Canada" p.59-60)

The child has an obligation to exhaust every possible way of finding his or her parent, before the requirement to gain that parent's consent can be waived:-

> *Since there is evidence to presume that his father is alive, there is no alternative but for Mr.— to continue efforts to locate the father through all avenues of investigation which may be open to him, including advertising. The investigation should continue until the only*

CHAPTER TEN

conclusion which can be reached is that the father is dead.

(letter from the Universal House of Justice to a National Spiritual Assembly, dated March 18, 1965)

In the case of a parent who abandons his family and disappears without trace or support, this does not constitute disowning a child. Every effort should be made to trace the parent and secure consent for marriage. If, however, the Assembly is satisfied that every avenue of search has been exhausted and the missing parent has not been found, the marriage can take place.

(letter written on behalf of the Universal House of Justice to a National Spiritual Assembly, dated March 23, 1987)

If need be, advice from the National Spiritual Assembly should be sought in particular cases.

10.3.10 What is to be done if the identity of the father is uncertain?

If the law of the country presumes that the name on the birth certificate is that of the father, then the person so named must give consent to the marriage. If the law of the country does not presume conclusively that the name on the birth certificate is that of the father the child does not need to seek the consent of that man. The only exception is if he has been legally certified as the parent of the child by some other means:-

Furthermore, if the assumed natural father denies that he is the father of the child the following principles apply: if his name appears on the birth certificate of the child and if the law of the country presumes that the name on the birth certificate is that of the father, then he should be considered as the father for the purpose of obtaining consent. If the name of the father given on the birth certificate is not a conclusive presumption of parenthood and if the man in question has always denied that he is the father of the child, the child is not required to seek the consent of this man unless it has been legally established that he is the father notwithstanding the denial.

(letter from the Universal House of Justice to a National Spiritual Assembly, dated October 24, 1965)

Australian law does not conclusively presume that the name on the birth certificate is that of the father, therefore, if that man has always denied that he is the father, it is not necessary to obtain his consent for the marriage. Nor is there any obligation to search for the true father. If doubts arise as to the correct course of action in any particular situation, the advice of the National Spiritual Assembly should be sought.

10.3.11 What if it is dangerous to contact the parents to get their consent?

Even so, a Bahá'í must get the consent of his or her parents. If necessary, arrangements should be made to get in contact with the parents through other people:-

Please inform Mr. — that it is necessary that he have the consent of his parents as long as they are alive. We agree that it is dangerous for him to attempt to contact them himself, but we suggest the possibility of securing their consent through others. There are Bahá'ís who make trips to —, and these are known to the National Assembly of —. Please assist Mr. — in contacting that National Assembly and in making arrangements for someone who is going to — to see his parents on his behalf and secure their consent.

(letter from the Universal House of Justice to a National Spiritual Assembly, dated August 3, 1965)

10.3.12 What should be done about parental consents where one of the parties to a marriage is adopted?

Under Australian Adoption Laws, adoption involves an explicit legal severance of all parental rights and obligations in regard to the child, voluntarily enacted by one or both parents. This being so, there is no need to obtain consents from the natural parents of the adopted child:-

We are asked to say that if the adoption law cuts all ties between the child and its parents, as it seems to do in Australia, there is no need to obtain parental consent.

(letter written on behalf of the Universal House of Justice, to the National Spiritual Assembly of the Bahá'ís of Australia, dated March 23, 1987)

Recent changes to adoption laws in Australia which allow adopted children access to the names of their natural parents, do not affect the matter. It is the nature of the original adoption, which cuts all ties, that makes it unnecessary for the adopted person to obtain the consent of his or her parents. The fact that the names of these parents may now be discovered is irrelevant. It is not necessary to obtain the consent of the adopting parents, although the child may do so if he or she wishes. The right to grant consent to a marriage can never be transferred to anyone else by the natural parents. If only one of the parties to a proposed marriage is adopted, then the consents of the parents of the other party are still required.

10.3.13 What should be done about parental consents where one of the parties to a marriage is fostered?

Parental consents are still required in the case of one party to the marriage having been fostered:-

...[concerning] the situation where parents have had their children fostered by another family by an agreement under which they do not give up their rights and obligations as natural parents. Under such a situation the consents of the natural parents would be required. In no circumstances can the responsibility for giving or withholding consent for marriage be transferred to the foster parents.

(letter from the Universal House of Justice, to a National Spiritual Assembly, dated November 18, 1986.)

10.3.14 What if a Bahá'í has been born of artificial insemination?

A Bahá'í parent is permitted to use artificial insemination only if the husband of the mother is the donor. In these circumstances there is no doubt as to the identity of the natural parents and their consent is required. In other circumstances, where a non-Bahá'í mother has used artificial insemination, doubt may arise as to the identity of the father. If need be, advice from the National Spiritual Assembly should be sought in particular cases.

10.3.15 Are there any circumstances under which parental consents are not required?

The Universal House of Justice has said that parental consents are not required in the following circumstances:-

1. *If the parent is dead.*

CHAPTER TEN

2. If the parent has absented himself to the degree that he can be adjudged legally dead.
3. If the parent is certified insane and therefore legally incompetent to give consent.
4. If the parent is a Covenant-breaker.
5. It is possible under Bahá'í Law, in certain very rare cases, to recognise that a state of disownment exists...

(letter from the Universal House of Justice to a National Spiritual Assembly, dated May 30, 1971)

Under Bahá'í law, adoption in Australia is an act of disownment, as in clause 5 above. This is the reason why an adopted child does not need to obtain the consent of his or her natural parents. It should also be noted that the right to give or withhold consent cannot be transferred. That is, the persons adopting a child never acquire this right from the natural parents. Any other application of the principle of disownment other than that of adoption can only occur with the prior approval of the National Spiritual Assembly.

6. If incest or other forms of sexual abuse have been committed by one of the parents against one of the parties to be married.

(letter from the Universal House of Justice to the National Spiritual Assembly of Australia, March 4, 1985)

1. When a parent adopts the point of view that the child is an adult, free to marry whomsoever she or he wishes, and the parent sees no reason for being asked for consent.
2. When the parents state that they have such confidence in their children that they have given them general consent to marry whomsoever they wish.

> *However, a quite different situation exists when a parent adopts the point of view that the child is an adult, free to marry whomsoever he or she wishes, and the parent sees no reason for being asked for consent. Such an attitude, if clearly established, is tantamount to the parent's renunciation of the right to give or withhold consent and can be accepted by the Assembly as freeing the child from the requirement to obtain consent from that parent. Another possibility is that parents state that they have such confidence in their children that they have given them general consent to marry whomsoever they wish; in this instance, such general consent would suffice to satisfy the requirements for Bahá'í marriage. In neither circumstances is there disownment, but the statement of the parent opens the way for the requirement of Bahá'í law to be satisfied.*

(letter from the Universal House of Justice to the National Spiritual Assembly of Australia, dated September 5, 1993)

In each of these cases, consent is not required from the parents concerned, but is still required from all other living parents.

Regarding points 5, 6, 7 and 8, all such cases must be referred to the National Spiritual Assembly with all the relevant information. Local Spiritual Assemblies at this time are not permitted to make rulings in these cases.

In the case of point 6, it will be referred on to the Universal House of Justice as it handles each of these cases individually.

CHAPTER TEN

10.3.16 ***If consent of parents to a marriage is conditional on a church wedding taking place, and the couple are both Bahá'ís, can the couple proceed with the marriage?***

No. If the couple are both Bahá'ís and consent is withheld because there is not going to be a church wedding, the marriage cannot take place:-

> *We have considered your letter of 13 August 1971 asking about the consent of parents to a marriage which is given on the condition that a church wedding take place. The instruction of the beloved Guardian in the letter to your Assembly as quoted in your letter is controlling. The Guardian stated over and over again that there must be no commingling of the old forms with the new, and that where two Bahá'ís are to be married there can be no religious ceremony except the Bahá'í ceremony. Likewise, the freedom of parents in giving or refusing consent is unrestricted and unconditioned. They may refuse consent on any ground, and they are responsible to God alone. While the parties are free to appeal to the parents to give consent without the condition, if consent is withheld because no church ceremony is to take place, this must be respected by the parties.*
>
> (letter from the Universal House of Justice to a National Spiritual Assembly, dated August 29, 1971)

It is permissible to attend a church in order to pray for the success of the marriage, provided the couple do not go through a form of marriage ceremony:-

> *If the parents of a Bahá'í couple are, for example, Christians, there is no objection to their attending church with their parents and their parents' friends and relations, if their parents so wish, in order to pray for the future of the marriage, but such attendance should not involve any form of marriage ceremony or simulated marriage ceremony.*
>
> (letter from the Universal House of Justice to a National Spiritual Assembly, dated January 19, 1975)

10.3.17 ***What is the situation of Bahá'ís if they cannot obtain the consent for marriage of one or more parents?***

Bahá'ís who cannot obtain the consent for marriage of one or more parents may consult with their Local Spiritual Assembly to see if they have any suggestions for changing the attitudes of the parents involved. If no way can be found to change the parents' attitudes, however, the believers have no alternative but to submit to the will of God:-

> *Bahá'ís who cannot marry because of lack of consent of one or more parents could consult with their Local Spiritual Assembly, to see whether it may suggest a way to change the attitude of any of the parents involved. The believers, when faced with such problems, should put their trust in Bahá'u'lláh, devote more time to the service, the teaching and the promotion of His Faith, be absolutely faithful to His injunctions on the observance of an unsullied, chaste life, and rely upon Him to open the way and remove the obstacle, or make known His will.*
>
> (letter from the Universal House of Justice to an individual believer, dated September 9, 1969)

> *While we have the greatest sympathy for the individuals involved in*

CHAPTER TEN

these unfortunate circumstances, we can reach no other conclusion but that consent of parents must be obtained in all cases before marriage can take place. Obedience to the laws of Bahá'u'lláh will necessarily impose hardships in individual cases. No one should expect, upon becoming a Bahá'í, that his faith will not be tested, and to our finite understanding of such matters these tests may occasionally seem unbearable. But we are aware of the assurance which Bahá'u'lláh Himself has given the believers that they will never be called upon to meet a test greater than their capacity to endure.

(letter from the Universal House of Justice to a National Spiritual Assembly, dated January 29, 1970)

10.4 BAHÁ'Í ENGAGEMENT

10.4.1 *When does the Bahá'í engagement period commence?*

The Bahá'í engagement period commences when the couple and their parents have signified their consent.

10.4.2 *Does the law set out in the "Kitáb-i-Aqdas" regarding the period (ie. 95 days) of engagement apply in Australia?*

The law regarding the ninety-five day engagement period applies to Persian Bahá'ís in Australia, but not to Australian Bahá'ís generally. It also applies to the children of Persian believers in Australia where they have been brought up in the Persian tradition. Where the engagement is between a Persian and an Australian believer, it does not apply. Regarding the Persian believers, the Universal House of Justice has said:-

> *...the law of the Kitáb-i-Aqdas that the lapse of time between engagement and marriage should not exceed ninety-five days is binding on Persian believers wherever they reside, if both parties are Persian. This law is not applicable, however, if one of the parties is a western believer.*

> *Concerning the question as to how the term "Persian believer" should be defined in applying this law, you should be guided as follows. The law applies to Persian believers wherever they have established residence after leaving Iran...in cases where children born to such parents are brought up in the Persian tradition, speak Persian, and are thoroughly conversant with the laws of the Kitáb-i-Aqdas, they will obviously feel an obligation, and should be assisted, to observe this and other laws of the Kitáb-i-Aqdas as circumstances permit.*

(e-mail to a National Spiritual Assembly, dated October 23, 1987)

[See also "Lights of Guidance", no.736]

10.4.3 *For those believers who are required to observe it, is it permitted to break or extend the 95 day period?*

Yes:-

> *...the breaking of an engagement, though not always desirable, does not violate Bahá'í Marriage Law.*

(from the Universal House of Justice, to a National Spiritual Assembly, dated November 11, 1969)

CHAPTER TEN

If the reason for breaking or extending the engagement period is judged valid by the Local Spiritual Assembly, it should extend every assistance to the couple to resolve the problem so that the marriage can proceed according to Bahá'í Law. If, however, the decision to break or extend the engagement does not seem valid to the Assembly, the matter should be referred to the National Spiritual Assembly, which in turn must consult on the validity of the reasons offered and decide whether an extension of time should be permitted. All cases of doubt should be referred to the National Spiritual Assembly:-

> *In principle, according to the decisive text of 'Abdu'l-Bahá, the period of ninety-five days should commence only when the two parties have been betrothed, and the marriage is agreed. Therefore, the breaking of an engagement, although possible, should rarely occur. The Assemblies should, when the reason for breaking, or extending, the fixed period of engagement is valid, render every assistance to the parties involved to remove their difficulties and facilitate their observance of the ordinance of the Book. However, if the revoking, extending, or renewing of engagement, in the judgement of the Assembly, is an intentional disregard of the law of the Book, then the National Spiritual Assembly should, in each case, carefully consult and carry out whatever action they may decide...*
>
> (letter from the Universal House of Justice to a National Spiritual Assembly, dated June 29, 1971)

10.5   DOWRY

10.5.1   *Is the giving of the dowry specified in the "Kitáb-i-Aqdas" binding in Australia?*

> *If both parties are Persians giving of dowry is binding, but at this time Bahá'í institutions should not involve themselves in such matters.*
>
> (e-mail from the Universal House of Justice to a National Spiritual Assembly, dated July 15, 1986)

10.5.2   *When should the dowry be paid?*

The dowry should be paid during the 95 day engagement period:-

> *Following the agreement for marriage and its official public announcement, that is, the statement to the effect that the two parties have been betrothed, the period of engagement must not exceed ninety-five days during which marriage should take place, and the verse be recited, and the dowry paid.*
>
> (extract from untranslated tablet of 'Abdu'l-Bahá, in Universal House of Justice unpublished compilation, "Requirements for Bahá'í Marriage")

10.5.3   *How much dowry should be paid?*

According to the "Synopsis and Codification of the Laws and Ordinances of the Kitáb-i-Aqdas"(p.40), the dowry is fixed at 19 mithqáls of pure gold for city-dwellers and 19 mithqáls of silver for village-dwellers. The place of residence for the purpose of calculating the dowry is that of the husband. It is forbidden to pay more that 95 mithqáls. It is preferable that a man content himself with 19 mithqáls of silver. If full payment of the dowry is not possible it is permissible to issue a promissory note. One mithqál is equivalent to a little over three and a half grammes. Calculation of the appropriate amount of dowry can be made on this basis. At current gold prices (August, 1995), 19 mithqáls is worth approximately

CHAPTER TEN

A$1200.00.(Check the current value of Gold when calculating the exact amount of the dowry).

10.5.4 *To whom should the dowry be paid?*

...*the dowry is to be paid by the bridegroom to the bride.* [handwritten: P 33 Study guide Kitab-i-Aqdas]

(e-mail from the Universal House of Justice to a National Spiritual Assembly, dated November 15, 1988)

10.6 THE NATURE OF THE BAHÁ'Í MARRIAGE CEREMONY

10.6.1 *What is the vow to be spoken?*

...the bride and groom, before two witnesses, must state 'We will all, verily, abide by the Will of God.'

(letter from the Universal House of Justice to a National Spiritual Assembly, dated August 8, 1969)

10.6.2 *What form should the ceremony take?*

The ceremony should remain as simple as possible and there should be no mixing of old marriage ceremony forms with the new one of Bahá'u'lláh:-

As you know there is no ritual, according to the Aqdas, and the Guardian is very anxious that none should be introduced at present and no general form accepted. He believes this ceremony should be as simple as possible, the parties using the words ordained by Bahá'u'lláh [quoted above], and excerpts from the writings and prayers being read if desired. There should be no commingling of the old forms with the new and simple one of Bahá'u'lláh, and Bahá'ís should not be married in the Church or any other acknowledged place of worship of the followers of other Faiths.

(letter written on behalf of Shoghi Effendi to an individual believer, dated March 13, 1944)

(Also see "Lights of Guidance", no.774, regarding use of the 'Marriage Tablet'.)

10.6.3 *Is exchange of rings a necessary part of the ceremony?*

No. The exchange of rings is not required by Bahá'í or civil law but may be included in the program.

10.6.4 *Can marriages be held on Bahá'í Holy Days?*

There is nothing in the Writings prohibiting the celebration of a Bahá'í marriage on any day, but the Universal House of Justice, in a letter written on its behalf to a National Spiritual Assembly, dated November 28, 1983, states that:-

...it would be inappropriate for Bahá'í celebrants to schedule a marriage on such sad occasions as the day for the observance of the Martyrdom of the Báb or of the Ascension of Bahá'u'lláh.

10.7 IMPORTANCE OF THE BAHÁ'Í MARRIAGE CEREMONY

10.7.1 *Must a Bahá'í have a Bahá'í marriage ceremony?*

Yes:-

CHAPTER TEN

> *When a Bahá'í marries, he must have a Bahá'í marriage ceremony.*
>
> (letter from the Universal House of Justice to a National Spiritual Assembly, dated March 23, 1966)

Further:-

> *The instructions of the beloved Guardian are clear on this point. When two Bahá'ís are married they may not be married by the religious ceremony of another Faith.*
>
> (from the Universal House of Justice to a National Spiritual Assembly, dated May 20, 1968)

10.7.2 **Where one party is a non-Bahá'í, may the Bahá'í participate in the religious ceremony of the non-Bahá'í partner?**

Yes, provided the Bahá'í does not make a vow contrary to Bahá'í law; nor can the right to bring up the children as Bahá'í be forfeited. There must be a Bahá'í ceremony; however, Bahá'í law does not specify that it must be the public ceremony:-

> *There is no objection to a Bahá'í participating in a religious ceremony of the non-Bahá'í partner provided that the Bahá'í does not undertake a vow contrary to Bahá'í law as, for example, a vow to raise the children of the marriage in the Catholic Faith. Furthermore, there must be a Bahá'í ceremony... There is no requirement that the Bahá'í ceremony... be the public ceremony...*
>
> (letter from the Universal House of Justice to a National Spiritual Assembly, dated September 4, 1972)

Note also the letter of the the Universal House of Justice dated 30 May 1988.

It must be made perfectly clear that the Bahá'í partner is not taking on the religion of the non-Bahá'í partner; nor can the Bahá'í make a declaration of faith in any other religion other than the Bahá'í faith:-

> *If a Bahá'í marries a non-Bahá'í who wishes to have the religious ceremony of his own sect carried out, it must be quite clear that, first, the Bahá'í partner is understood to be a Bahá'í by religion, and not to accept the religion of the other party to the marriage through having his or her religious ceremony; and second, the ceremony must be of a nature which does not commit the Bahá'í to any declaration of faith in a religion other than his own.*
>
> (letter written on behalf of Shoghi Effendi to a National Spiritual Assembly, dated June 20, 1954)

[See also "Lights of Guidance", nos. 762, 767, 768]

10.7.3 **Where there is both a Bahá'í and a non-Bahá'í ceremony, in which order should they be held?**

In order to meet the requirements of Australian civil law, the ceremony which fulfils the requirements of Australian civil law should be held last. This generally means the Bahá'í ceremony should be held before, for example, a church ceremony in which the priest will complete the civil requirements. [See further below, the question, 'In what order should the Bahá'í and civil requirements be completed?']

CHAPTER TEN

10.7.4 ***Where two ceremonies are held, must they both be held on the same day?***

Yes:-

> *As to the holding of the Bahá'í and civil marriage ceremonies on the same day, as consummation of the marriage should not take place until both ceremonies have been held, a night should not intervene between the two ceremonies.*

>> (letter from the Universal House of Justice to an individual believer, dated April 23, 1971)

10.7.5 ***Can two non-Bahá'ís be married according to the Bahá'í ceremony?***

Yes:-

> *There is no objection to performing a Bahá'í marriage for two non-Bahá'ís, if they desire to have our simple ceremony. This, on the contrary, is yet another way of demonstrating our liberality.*

>> (letter written on behalf of Shoghi Effendi to a National Spiritual Assembly, dated October 25, 1947)

If a non-Bahá'í couple choose to have a Bahá'í ceremony they must also comply with the Bahá'í law of obtaining parental consents.

10.7.6 ***What is the relationship between Bahá'í and civil requirements for marriage?***

All marriages in Australia must be celebrated according to civil law. The operative Act is the Marriage Act, 1961-73. This is a Commonwealth Act, which, in 1963, superseded the old State Acts, and applies to the whole of Australia. Bahá'ís in Australia therefore have two sets of requirements to comply with:-

a) Those given to us by Bahá'u'lláh, as amplified by 'Abdu'l-Bahá, Shoghi Effendi and the Universal House of Justice.
b) The civil law of Australia, as required by the Marriage Act, 1961-73.

10.7.7 ***In what order should the Bahá'í and civil requirements be completed?***

Bahá'í law does not specify which should come first. Australian civil law, however, requires that the Bahá'í vows be be held first, otherwise the civil law forbidding a couple to be married when already legally married may be breached. If a Bahá'í ceremony is held after civil requirements have been fulfilled, the form 'STATEMENT pursuant to Section 113(5) of THE MARRIAGE ACT, 1961', must be filled out and sent to the National Assembly . This is a Bahá'í form, not a civil form and is necessary in order to protect the reputation of the Faith from the accusation of having breached civil law. A copy of the form is kept in the individual's file in the National Office. The Bahá'í Marriage Celebrant will be able to supply this form to the couple. Such a situation has been known to occur when a couple who have married in a civil ceremony without fulfilling Bahá'í law and who have, therefore, lost their voting rights, subsequently apply to have their voting rights restored. In this case they are required by Bahá'í law to have a Bahá'í ceremony immediately after their voting rights are restored. In order to do this they must fill out the above form. Likewise it is not a requirement of Bahá'í law that the Bahá'í ceremony must be held before the ceremony of another faith. In practice, however, in Australia, the religious ceremony of another faith usually incorporates the civil requirements. For this reason the Bahá'í ceremony is to be held first.

10.7.8 ***What are the consequences of not obeying the Bahá'í marriage laws?***

It should be realised that non-compliance with a marriage law of Bahá'u'lláh can lead to loss

CHAPTER TEN

of Bahá'í status - a most serious deprivation. Voting rights may be lost in the following circumstances, where:-
rights
[For further information on sanctions see "Lights of Guidance", nos. 130-33, 142, 149-53, 750-52, 758, 775-6, 784-5]

Only the National Spiritual Assembly can actually remove the voting rights of a believer. Where a believer is found to have been in real ignorance of a particular law, the National Assembly may excuse the transgression.

10.7.9 **What are the necessary conditions for the restoration of voting rights, resulting from disobedience of Bahá'í marriage laws?**

> *"We have your letter of October 9, 1971 informing us of your action to deprive..... of his voting rights for violation of Bahá'í marriage law ion that he married without having consent of all living parents. It is noted that he had a civil ceremony and a Catholic ceremony. The question you have asked deals with possible restoration of his voting rights.*
>
> *In cases involving only a civil ceremony, voting rights may be restored if the Assembly feels that the believer is truly repentant and wishes to comply with the Bahá'í law previously broken. The civil marriage ceremony itself is not contrary to Bahá'í law, and therefore the dissolution of the civil marriage is not a prerequisite to restoration of full voting rights. In such cases the Bahá'í marriage ceremony may take place if the parents now give their consent to the marriage and the Assembly is satisfied that the consent has been genuinely and freely given and is not conditioned by the fact that the parties have already had a civil ceremony. In such cases the Assembly would restore the voting rights immediately before the Bahá'í ceremony on the condition that it be performed should..... apply for restoration of his voting rights, and should your Assembly feel that he is truly repentant, you should offer assistance in arranging the other details including helping him in obtaining the consents of parents.*
>
> (From a letter of the Universal House of Justice to the National Spiritual Assembly of Ecuador, November 18, 1971)

10.7.10 **What are the consequences of not obeying the civil law of Australia?**

Bahá'ís are also required to obey the civil law of Australia concerning marriage. Failure to obey the Marriage Act, 1961-73, can lead to fines of $1,000 and/or 6 months imprisonment. The Bahá'í Marriage Celebrants are familiar with all civil law requirements and their advice should be sought by anyone in doubt as to their duty under the civil law.

10.7.11 **What is the position when two Bahá'ís who were married before they became Bahá'ís, now wish to have a Bahá'í marriage?**

Marriages entered into under civil, religious or tribal law are generally recognised as valid under Bahá'í law, therefore, there is no need to hold a Bahá'í ceremony after a couple become Bahá'ís. In fact, it is forbidden under Bahá'í law:-

> *...there is no question of a couple's having a Bahá'í wedding ceremony subsequently because, as the Guardian says, 'Bahá'í marriage is*

> *something you perform when you are going to be united for the first time, not long after the union takes place.' If, however, such a couple would like to have a meeting of their friends at which Bahá'í prayers and readings are said on behalf of their marriage now that they are Bahá'ís, there is no objection to their doing so, although it must be understood that this does not constitute a Bahá'í marriage ceremony.*

(letter from the Universal House of Justice to a National Spiritual Assembly, dated June 23, 1969)

> *In general marriages entered into by parties prior to their enrolment in the Faith are recognised as valid under Bahá'í law, and in such cases an additional Bahá'í marriage ceremony is not permitted. This applies whether the marriage was established under civil or religious law or under tribal custom.*

(letter from the Universal House of Justice to a National Spiritual Assembly, dated March 5, 1978)

10.7.12 What is the position when, through ignorance of Bahá'í law, two Bahá'ís fail to have a Bahá'í marriage ceremony?

Bahá'ís who, through ignorance of the law, marry without having a Bahá'í marriage ceremony should be considered married and are not required to rectify the omission by having a Bahá'í ceremony at a later date:-

> *At the present state in the development of the Bahá'í Community, Bahá'ís who failed to have a Bahá'í marriage through ignorance of the law are in a different category altogether from those who wittingly broke the law. The latter must have a Bahá'í ceremony in order to regain their voting rights; but the former should be treated in the same manner as those Bahá'ís who married before they entered the Faith and those Bahá'ís who married without a Bahá'í ceremony before the law was applied; they should be considered married and not be required to have a Bahá'í ceremony.*

(letter from the Universal House of Justice to a National Spiritual Assembly, dated January 20, 1966)

10.7.13 Should Bahá'í believers attend weddings of Bahá'ís marrying contrary to Bahá'í Law?

Bahá'ís are not encouraged to attend a wedding of Bahá'ís marrying contrary to Bahá'í Law.

> *If it is known beforehand that a believer is violating such laws, it would be inappropriate for the friends to attend the ceremony. This is out of respect for Bahá'í Law. However, if without realising the situation believers find themselves in attendance at a ceremony in the course of which it is apparent that such a violation is occurring, they should not make an issue of it.*

(letter from the Universal House of Justice to a National Spiritual Assembly, dated November 11, 1974)

10.7.14 What is the situation for Iranian Bahá'í couples who had only a Bahá'í marriage in Iran?

The present situation for such Iranian Bahá'í couples is as follows:-

1. They receive de facto recognition of their marital status in Australia.
2. They do not presumably face any inconvenience in their situation.
3. They are not legally disadvantaged in matters such as inheritance.

The National Spiritual Assembly, however, strongly advises the friends to obey the law of the Faith and have a will prepared. If this is done then inheritance is protected. Any individuals uncertain as to the application of this advice in their particular circumstances should contact the National Office. In particular, anyone who was both married and divorced in Iran and now intends re-marrying in Australia, should contact the National Office before they re-marry.

10.8 BAHÁ'Í MARRIAGE CELEBRANTS

10.8.1 *What is a Bahá'í Marriage Celebrant?*

A Bahá'í Marriage Celebrant is a person nominated by the National Spiritual Assembly and licensed under the Australian Marriage Act 1974 to solemnize marriages according to Bahá'í Law in Australia. This allows the Bahá'í and civil marriage requirements to be completed at the same time, in the same place. It is, therefore, desirable, although not obligatory, for the civil requirements of the marriage ceremony to be conducted by a Bahá'í Celebrant. One common exception is that of a marriage being held at a location remote from any of the appointed Celebrants.

10.8.2 *What costs are involved in using a Bahá'í Marriage Celebrant?*

Non-Bahá'í civil celebrants and registrars charge a fee for their services, as required under the Marriage Act, 1961-73. Bahá'í Marriage Celebrants, by direction of the National Spiritual Assembly, and with the consent of the Attorney-General, do not receive these fees however the Bahá'í Marriage Celebrant may need to recover the purchase cost of the Marriage Certificate and other legal forms. Check with the Baha'i Marriage Celebrant to obtain the most recent costs.. If the Bahá'í Marriage Celebrant has to travel, however, he or she should be reimbursed for the cost in advance. Expenses are kept to a minimum and do not include costs for members of the Celebrant's family who may travel with the Celebrant. Where a Celebrant must stay overnight, accommodation must be provided, but the Celebrant will accept Bahá'í hospitality if offered. Should a Celebrant choose to select alternative accommodation, he or she will be responsible for the cost.

10.8.3 *What is the role of the Bahá'í Marriage Celebrant under the following conditions?*

1. Where the civil requirements are conducted by a Bahá'í Marriage Celebrant: - the Bahá'í requirements and civil requirements may be fulfilled in the one ceremony, or as arranged with the Celebrant. The Bahá'í marriage Celebrant is required by civil law to be present for the entire ceremony including Bahá'í requirements and civil requirements.
2. Where the marriage is held in a registry office or conducted by a civil celebrant:- a Bahá'í Marriage Celebrant is not essential in such circumstances as responsibility for the ceremony is in the hands of the Local Spiritual Assembly.
3. Where there is another religious ceremony as well as the Bahá'í ceremony: - it will be necessary to clarify whether the member of the clergy (who will be a marriage celebrant) or the Bahá'í Celebrant carries out the civil requirements. Usually the member of the clergy insists on doing this. In this case a Bahá'í Celebrant is not necessary.

CHAPTER TEN

10.8.4 *What is the responsibility of Bahá'í Marriage Celebrants towards the Bahá'í requirements of the ceremony.*

The Bahá'í Marriage Celebrant has responsibility for civil requirements of the marriage ceremony, and is not required by civil law, to be present for the entire ceremony. The Local Spiritual Assembly has responsibility for the overall ceremony and the Bahá'í requirements in particular. Since it is desirable that they do not appear to be like a "clergy", the Bahá'í Marriage celebrant should not be asked to act as the Master of Ceremonies or Chairperson, should one be required. They should not be asked to give any short introductory talk that may be part of the program. They do not usually read in the program. They would usually stand to one side, possibly with the readers, and should only come forward when necessary for the civil requirements. These measures should be carefully followed, particularly when non-Bahá'ís are in attendance at the ceremony.

10.8.5 *Where do we obtain the names and addresses of the Bahá'í Marriage Celebrants?*

The names and addresses of all Bahá'í Marriage Celebrants should be issued regularly in a directory of all committees circulated to Local Spiritual Assemblies. Alternatively, the names and addresses are available from the National Office.

10.9 NOTIFYING THE MARRIAGE CELEBRANT

10.9.1 *How soon must the Bahá'í Marriage Celebrant be contacted?*

It is essential to contact the Bahá'í Marriage Celebrant early, before other arrangements are made, to ensure that the Celebrant will be available. Under the provisions of the Marriage Act, the Notice of Intended Marriage form must be in the hands of the Celebrant at least one calendar month and one day before the marriage can take place. The Celebrant is bound by Australian law and cannot shorten this time. The following timetable is suggested to ensure compliance with Bahá'í and civil law:-

1. The engagement commences when the couple agree to marry and obtain their parental consents.
2. Contact the Bahá'í Marriage Celebrant as soon as possible to:-
   a) ascertain when the Bahá'í Marriage Celebrant will be available.
   b) complete necessary forms and ensure that all personal documents are in order. This is particularly important for Iranians and others born outside Australia to give time to clarify any matter in doubt. Such documents include -
      i) Notice of Intended Marriage form
      ii) Declaration of Conjugal Status
      iii) Birth Certificates, copies or extracts; or passport if not Australian-born
      iv) Death Certificate of spouse or Decree Absolute (not Nisi) of divorce if either party has been previously married
      v) any other documents required
   c) the Celebrant can supply and witness all necessary forms, or advise where they can be obtained, and by whom they can be witnessed
   d) fix date and venue for marriage
3. At the same time, consult with the Local Spiritual Assembly responsible for the marriage and also with any other Spiritual Assembly involved.

10.10 RESPONSIBILITIES OF THE LOCAL SPIRITUAL ASSEMBLY FOR THE MARRIAGE

10.10.1 *Which Bahá'í Institution is the responsible body?*

The Local Spiritual Assembly within whose area of jurisdiction the marriage is to take place is the Institution responsible for arranging the marriage. Therefore, if the couple live within the jurisdiction of one Local Spiritual Assembly, but get married within the jurisdiction of another Local Spiritual Assembly, the responsible Institution is the one in which the marriage takes place. As marriage affects the status of the parties, however, the Assembly or Assemblies in whose area(s) the couple reside, will vouch to the responsible Assembly for the status of the couple. After the marriage, the responsible Assembly will notify the Local Spiritual Assembly where the couple are to reside that the Bahá'í requirements have been complied with. If the marriage is to take place in an area where there is no Local Spiritual Assembly, the National Spiritual Assembly must assume responsibility for the marriage and fulfil the obligations, listed below, that devolve upon the Local Spiritual Assembly. The National Spiritual Assembly may choose to do this by appointing a nearby Local Spiritual Assembly to be responsible. If a couple intend marrying in an area outside their own area of residence, they should be encouraged by their Local Spiritual Assembly/ies to contact, as soon as possible, the Assembly within whose area of jurisdiction they intend marrying.

10.10.2 ***What specific functions must the responsible Local Spiritual Assembly perform?***

The Local Spiritual Assembly has exclusive authority to conduct Bahá'í marriage ceremonies within its area of jurisdiction. This authority does not include the responsibility of determining whether the marriage should take place or not, as this is a matter left entirely to the discretion of the couple concerned and their parents, to determine. The Assembly's responsibility is to ensure that the civil and Bahá'í requirements for the marriage are met:-

> *The obligation of the Spiritual Assembly is to ascertain that all requirements of civil and Bahá'í law have been complied with, and having done so, the Assembly may neither refuse to perform the marriage ceremony nor delay it.*

(letter from the Universal House of Justice to a National Spiritual Assembly, dated March 30, 1967)

In Australia the Bahá'í Marriage Celebrant has the task of ensuring that the civil law requirements are met; however, ultimate responsibility remains vested in the Local Spiritual Assembly. The specific functions of the Assembly are as follows:-

1. Ensure that the couple understand the spiritual and administrative principles applying to marriage and are aware of the sanctions that they may incur if they do not obey the administrative requirements. [
2. Ascertain consent of parents. The Assembly must ensure that the parents have given their consent freely, before the marriage can take place:-

> *With reference to the matter of the consent of the parents to a Bahá'í marriage: as this is a vital binding obligation, it is the duty of the Assemblies to ascertain, before giving their sanction, that the consent obtained has been given freely by the parents themselves.*

(Shoghi Effendi, in "Principles of Bahá'í Administration", p.59)

If the marriage is taking place within an Assembly area different from that in which the couple reside, all Assemblies concerned should satisfy themselves that consent has been given.

3. The Local Spiritual Assembly should advise and encourage believers to contact the Bahá'í Marriage Celebrant early, certainly prior to fixing a date for the marriage.
4. Appoint two witnesses to the marriage. The parties may consult with the responsible Spiritual Assembly regarding the appointment of two witnesses, but the Assembly has the final responsibility. The witnesses may be any two people acceptable to the Spiritual Assembly, Bahá'ís or non-Bahá'ís. Parents of the parties may act as witnesses and may be encouraged to do so. Civil law requires that two witnesses, over the age of 18 observe the civil requirements and sign documentation. The National Spiritual Assembly requests that the witnesses appointed by the Assembly also be the civil

witnesses. Concerning the witnesses, the Universal House of Justice has said:-

> *...you state that the two witnesses at the marriage must be Bahá'ís. Although this is the usual practice, it is not essential. The witnesses can be any two trustworthy people whose testimony is acceptable to the Spiritual Assembly under whose jurisdiction the marriage is performed. This fact makes it possible for a lone pioneer in a remote post to have a Bahá'í marriage.*

(letter from the Universal House of Justice to a National Spiritual Assembly, dated August 8, 1969)

5. If either party has been divorced, the Local Spiritual Assembly must ensure that all Bahá'í and civil divorce requirements have been fulfilled. In particular, if one of the parties to the marriage is an Iranian Bahá'í who has previously been both married and divorced in Iran, he or she should be advised to contact the National Office before proceeding with the marriage.
6. Ascertain that Bahá'ís wishing to be married are in good standing.
7. Inform the Bahá'í Marriage Celebrant when the above steps have been taken.
8. Record the full details relating to the above steps in the Assembly's minutes. Also record the marriage in the Assembly's marriage register.
9. Issuing of a Bahá'í marriage certificate - at present, in Australia, marriage certificates may only be issued under civil law. A Bahá'í marriage certificate has no legal authority. The current policy of the National Spiritual Assembly, therefore, is that no Bahá'í marriage certificate should be issued by Local Spiritual Assemblies.
10. The Bahá'í Marriage Celebrants keep copies of a document called 'Bahá'í Marriage in Australia' to give to couples intending to marry. The document is available in both English and Iranian. It provides a basic outline of the Bahá'í and civil requirements for Bahá'í marriage in Australia. Local Spiritual Assemblies may also find it useful to keep copies of this document on hand. If your Assembly would like some copies, please contact the National Office.

10.10.3 **What responsibility does the Local Spiritual Assembly have concerning the style of the marriage ceremony?**

Regarding arrangements for the wedding itself, the Universal House of Justice has said that these should be left to the bride and groom without interference from the Assembly, unless the Assembly is quite certain that the Cause will really be harmed if it does not intervene:-

> *An Assembly has the overriding duty to protect the good name of the Faith in relation to any activity of the friends, but it should always exercise great care not to restrict the individual's freedom of action unnecessarily. Normally the size of the wedding celebration, the place in which it is to be held and who is to be invited are all left entirely to the discretion of the bride and groom and an Assembly should interpose an objection only if it is quite certain that the Cause will really be injured if it does not do so.*

(letter from the Universal House of Justice to a National Spiritual Assembly, dated January 20, 1966)

The Assembly should ensure that details of the ceremony do not cause any participating Bahá'í Marriage Celebrant to appear to be like "clergy" in the Faith. {See also Section 8}

CHAPTER TEN

10.10.4 *Is there a special Bahá'í marriage form that the Assembly must fill out?*

Yes. Following the ceremony, the 'Notification of Marriage' form is to be filled out and signed by the Secretary of the Local Spiritual Assembly and the witnesses to the marriage. The original copy is to be retained by the Local Spiritual Assembly and the duplicate sent to the National Spiritual Assembly. You may request copies of this Bahá'í form from the National Office. Following the civil ceremony, the Register and Marriage Certificates must also be signed by the witnesses, as arranged by the Bahá'í Marriage Celebrant.

10.10.5 *How to complete a 'notification of marriage' form.*

When completing a 'Notification of Marriage' form for Bahá'ís use the legal name as used on the birth certificate or passport. Please advise the records department of any differences in the spelling of the name if it is not the same as on the membership list. If you are unsure of the spelling please, contact the individuals concerned or the secretary of their local community.

When members of your community are getting married please send any change of name and/or address to the National Office.

10.11 DE FACTO RELATIONSHIPS

10.11.1 *What constitutes a de facto relationship under Bahá'í law?*

The Universal House of Justice recognises that a de facto relationship exists under the following circumstances:-

> *Because of unusual conditions in certain countries and certain cases, it sometimes happens that a person will become a Bahá'í when he or she is living in a situation... for example, where a couple have established firm ties of union and are living together in such a way that they appear to be married and are accepted as such by those around them; the union has stood the test of time and there may even be children, and yet, in fact, the couple are not actually married in any of the ways defined above.*
>
> (letter from the Universal House of Justice to a National Spiritual Assembly, dated March 5, 1978)

> *...people who are living in an immoral relationship at the time when they accept the Faith. It may be that such a relationship, although immoral, is of long standing. Because of the current attitudes in society a couple may have settled down as man and wife without getting married, but with the intention of making a home together, and may even have had children.*
>
> (letter from the Universal House of Justice to a National Spiritual Assembly, dated March 5, 1978)

> *Such a situation must be distinguished from a relationship that is not only immoral in the above sense, but quite unacceptable such as a temporary liaison or recently established companionate marriage.*
>
> (letter from the Universal House of Justice to a National Spiritual Assembly, dated March 5, 1978).

10.11.2 *Should a couple who commenced living in a de facto relationship before becoming Bahá'ís be obliged to have a Bahá'í wedding ceremony after becoming Bahá'ís?*

No. The Universal House of Justice says that in this case, the couple should be accepted as married under Bahá'í law. They should, however, be encouraged to have a civil ceremony:-

> *In such cases where the situation, although immoral, is settled and accepted, the Assembly should not attempt to go back into the past and undo a union that was cemented before the couple became Bahá'ís, but should accept their condition as being a marriage in the eyes of Bahá'í law. To compel them to separate, or to celebrate a Bahá'í ceremony at such a late date, could cause serious injustice; it might well be impossible for the couple, for example, to obtain parental consent and a united, happy family could thus be disrupted, the very opposite of the intention of the law. When a situation is thus recognised as a marriage in the eyes of Bahá'í law, the question of having a Bahá'í ceremony does not arise. If, however, the couple are able to regularise their situation in the eyes of the civil law by having a civil ceremony, they should be encouraged to do so for the sake of the good name of the Faith.*
>
> (letter from the Universal House of Justice to National Spiritual Assembly, dated March 5, 1978)

These latter situations must be dealt with in the same way as any other case of immoral behaviour:-

> *A couple living together merely as man and mistress when either or both become Bahá'ís are not married in the eyes of Bahá'í law, and must either have a Bahá'í marriage in accordance with the provisions of Bahá'í law, or cease living together. In other words, the Assembly must deal with the situation as it would any other case of immoral behaviour, explaining the requirements of the law, giving repeated warnings, and ultimately, if the offender does not comply, he must forfeit his voting rights.*
>
> (letter from the Universal House of Justice to a National Spiritual Assembly, dated March 5, 1978)

Local Assemblies should bear in mind that this is a particularly sensitive issue. It must ensure, on the one hand, that it does not countenance thoroughly immoral behaviour, thus making a mockery of Bahá'í law and principles. On the other hand, it must not apply Bahá'í standards so strictly that it causes the break-up of what is in fact, if not in law, a well established family. All cases of doubt should be referred to the National Assembly.

For further information about procedures for dealing with immoral relationships see the Chapter, 'The Local Spiritual Assembly as a Loving Shepherd'.

10.12 RESPONSIBILITIES OF THE LOCAL SPIRITUAL ASSEMBLY FOR MARRIAGE DEEPENING

10.12.1 *What is the role of the Assembly in marriage deepening?*

The Local Spiritual Assembly has an on-going responsibility to deepen its community in the marriage laws:-

> *Local Assemblies are responsible for making certain that the members of their community understand both the requirements of Bahá'í marriage law and the nature of the sanctions which can be imposed when the laws are violated - (It should be noted that this is not a matter of information to be checked at the time of enrolment, but rather represents a continuing L.S.A. responsibility for deepening the Bahá'í community.)*

CHAPTER TEN

(letter from the Universal House of Justice to a National Spiritual Assembly, dated April 14, 1965)

The Assembly should refer to the following works for deepening materials on marriage:-

- this Handbook
- <u>Family Life</u> (compilation by Universal House of Justice)
- <u>Divorce</u> (compilation by Universal House of Justice)
- <u>Marriage: A Fortress for Well-Being</u>
- <u>Prescription for Living</u>
- <u>Preserving Bahá'í Marriages</u> (compilation by Universal House of Justice)
- <u>Lights of Guidance</u>
- <u>WOMEN Equality and Development</u> (compilation by Universal House of Justice)

By law the Bahá'í Marriage Celebrants are required to give couples preparing to marry, two pamphlets (a) 'Marriage Counselling and Pre-Marital Education - Approved Organizations'; (b) 'Marriage and You'. The Assembly should make sure it knows the contents of these pamphlets.
The Local Spiritual Assembly should also consult the Bahá'í Marriage Celebrants.

10.12.2 **What is the responsibility of the Local Spiritual Assembly for marriage counselling?**

In addition to its on-going responsibility to deepen the believers in the Marriage laws, the Assembly also has a particular responsibility to counsel believers who are experiencing marital problems. Further information about appropriate procedures for marriage counselling can be found in this handbook in the chapter, "Bahá'í Teachings on Divorce". This chapter also contains a list of non-Bahá'í marriage guidance services approved under the provisions of the Family Law Act and the Marriage Act.

10.13 **REGISTERED GROUPS**

Registered groups do not have the authority to perform marriages. They do, however, have the responsibility of ensuring that their members are deepened in the Bahá'í marriage laws. Bahá'ís wishing to marry in an area under the jurisdiction of a Registered Group, should contact the National Spiritual Assembly, which is the responsible body in this situation. The National Assembly will normally appoint a nearby Local Spiritual Assembly to take responsibility for the marriage.

CHAPTER TEN

APPENDIX 1

CHECKLIST FOR HOLDING A BAHÁ'Í MARRIAGE IN AUSTRALIA

Australia is a country in which there is freedom of religion. Church and State are separated. All marriages In Australia MUST be celebrated in accordance with Australian civil law (Marriage Act 1961-73). All Bahá'í' marriages MUST be celebrated in accordance with Bahá'í' law. Most churches in Australia have a marriage ceremony which combines the religious and civil requirements into one. The clergy are registered Marriage Celebrants. So too, the Bahá'í Marriage Celebrants are registered under the Marriage Act to carry out civil ceremonies. The Spiritual Assembly remains the responsible authority for the Bahá'í marriage; however, having a Bahá'í Marriage Celebrant enables the two ceremonies to be combined and held at the one place at the one time.

The following Bahá'í and civil requirements must be complied with:

BAHÁ'Í REQUIREMENTS	CIVIL REQUIREMENTS
BEFORE THE MARRIAGE:	
(1) Contact your Spiritual Assembly.	(1) Contact the Bahá'í Celebrant early.
(2) Set the date you want.	(2) Check to see if the Celebrant is available on the date you choose. Have alternative dates in mind.
(3) If two Persians are marrying, the 95 days engagement period applies. Remember this in relation to par. 3 Civil Requirements.	(3) Notice of Intended Marriage. This form MUST be in the hands of the Celebrant at least one calendar month and one day before marriage can take place. The Celebrant cannot shorten this time.
(4) Parental consents of all living natural parents. The Assembly must approve these and notify the Bahá'í Celebrant.	
(5) The Spiritual Assembly where the marriage takes place is the responsible Assembly. Each party's own Assembly has the duty of viewing parental consents.	(4) If the girl is under 18 the consent of parents or legal guardian is required. Legal age for marriage is 18 years for boys, 16 years for girls.
If outside a Local Spiritual Assembly area, the National Spiritual Assembly is responsible.	(5) Parties must produce their birth certificates or copies or extracts to the Celebrant. If not Australian-born, a passport is acceptable. Check with the Celebrant.
(6) The Assembly conducting the marriage has the duty of notifying the Marriage Celebrant that all the Bahá'í requirements for the marriage are in order. The Assembly must appoint two witnesses. In practice the witnesses are usually Bahá'í, but they do not have to be. The National Spiritual Assembly recommends that these also be the civil witnesses.	(6) If either party has been previously married the Death Certificate of the spouse or Decree Absolute (not Nisi) of divorce must be produced for the Celebrant.
	(7) Declaration of Marital Status must be completed on the official Marriage Certificate.
	(8) Two witnesses over the age of 18 years must be appointed (see para.6 Bahá'í Requirements).

CHAPTER TEN

DURING THE CEREMONY

(1) The Bahá'í vows are: "We will all, verily, abide by the Will of God."

2) The Bahá'í Notification of Marriage form is to be filled out and signed by the Secretary of the Local Spiritual Assembly and the witnesses. The Assembly keeps the original and forwards a copy to the National Office.

(1) Bahá'í vows should generally come before civil vows. In special cases the order may be reversed. The Local Spiritual Assembly Handbook explains these cases.

(2) The civil vows are: "I call upon the persons here present to witness that I ... take thee ... to be my lawful wedded wife/husband."

(3) Register and Marriage Certificates must be signed.

It should be noted that the exchange of rings is not required by Bahá'í or civil law. If required these can be exchanged after either set of vows. It is not desirable to interrupt the ceremony with photographs. The Celebrant will co-operate with a re-run to allow photos to be taken, and these can be posed.

EXPLANATORY NOTES

Your own Spiritual Assembly/ies need to view and approve your parental consents. The Spiritual Assembly of the areas in which the marriage takes place is also responsible to approve your consent. In addition it is responsible for the marriage - to ensure that the service is dignified, and to appoint witnesses. The Assembly should advise the Celebrant that these are in order before the marriage. The marriage cannot take place unless you have complied with these Bahá'í requirements.

As an alternative to a Bahá'í Marriage Celebrant, the civil marriage ceremony may be carried out in a Registry Office or by a civil Marriage Celebrant. However all the Bahá'í requirements have to be observed. The Universal House of Justice advises that a night must not intervene between separate ceremonies. If you have separate ceremonies, the Bahá'í ceremony should come first, and then the civil ceremony, held on the same calendar day. If you use a civil Celebrant, be careful that he does not use a pseudo religious ceremony which may not accord with the Faith.

Civil Celebrants and Registrars make a charge for their services. Bahá'í Celebrants do not, but you are responsible for the Bahá'í Celebrants travelling expenses and reasonable accommodation if he/she has to stay overnight.

Failure to comply with civil law or making a false declaration or statement can bring heavy penalties of fines and/or jail. Failure to comply with Bahá'í law can lead to loss of administrative status and voting rights.

If you are marrying a non-Bahá'í it is in order for you to take part in the ceremony of his/her Faith, providing the Bahá'í does not undertake a vow contrary to Bahá'í law. However you must also have a Bahá'í marriage. It will be necessary to clarify whether the clergyman (who will be a Marriage Celebrant), or the Bahá'í Celebrant, carries out the civil requirements. Usually the clergyman insists he should do this. In this case a Bahá'í Celebrant is not necessary and the Bahá'í ceremony, which is under the authority of the Spiritual Assembly, should be held first.

The Celebrant can supply and witness all necessary forms, or advise where they can be obtained, and by whom they can be witnessed.

These brief notes do not cover all contingencies. Further information can be obtained

CHAPTER TEN

from the Celebrants, and your Spiritual Assembly. It is particularly important to contact the Celebrant early, where there are unusual circumstances and problems, to give time to clarify the position.

16 October 1989

CHAPTER TEN

شرایط لازم برای برگزاری مراسم ازدواج بهائی در استرالیا

CHECKLIST FOR HOLDING A BAHÁ'Í MARRIAGE IN AUSTARLIA

در کشور استرالیا دیانت آزاد است و قوانین مذهبی از قوانین ایالتی جدا میباشد. تمام ازدواجها در استرالیا باید مطابق قانون مدنی این کشور انجام شود. اغلب کلیساها مراسم ازدواجشان طوری است که مقررات دینی و قوانین کشوری هر دو را در بر میگیرد و بصورت مراسم واحدی انجام میشود. روسای ادیان در عین حال عاقدین شناخته شده از طرف دولت نیز هستند. عاقدین بهائی نیز از جانب حکومت برای اجرای مراسم ازدواج کشوری برسمیت شناخته شده اند. محفل روحانی مسئول اجرای مراسم ازدواج بهائی است و وجود عاقد بهائی سبب میشود که هر دو مراسم در یک محل و همزمان انجام گیرد.

موارد ذیل که شامل مقررات بهائی و کشوری است باید کاملا رعایت شود:

مقررات کشوری	مقررات بهائی

قبل از ازدواج

۱ـ هر چه زودتر با عاقد بهائی تماس بگیرید	۱ـ با محفل محلی خود تماس بگیرید
۲ـ اطمینان حاصل نمائید که عاقد میتواند در روز تعیین شده در مراسم شرکت کند. در صورت احتیاج روز دیگری را پیش بینی نمائید.	۲ـ روز ازدواج را تعیین نمائید
۳ـ تکمیل فرم Notice of Intended Marriage برای اینکه مراسم ازدواج در روز تعیین شده انجام گیرد این فرم باید حداقل یکماه و یک روز قبل از روز تعیین شده برای ازدواج بدست عاقد برسد. باید توجه داشته باشید که عاقد نمیتواند این مدت را کوتاهتر کند.	۳ـ اگر دو نفری که با هم ازدواج میکنند هر دو بهائی ایرانی هستند باید مهلت ۹۵ روز بین نامزدی و عقد را مراعات نمایند. در این مورد ماده ۳ از مقررات کشوری را در نظر داشته باشید.
۴ـ اگر سن دختر کمتر از ۱۸ سال باشد اجازه پدر و مادر یا قیم قانونی وی لازم خواهد بود. سن قانونی ازدواج برای پسران ۱۸ و برای دختران ۱۶ سال است.	۴ـ تهیه رضایت نامه های والدین حقیقی طرفین ازدواج که در حیات دارند. محفل محلی باید این رضایت نامه ها را تصویب نموده و عاقد بهائی را مطلع سازد.
۵ـ طرفین ازدواج باید ورقه گواهی تولد (شناسنامه یا خلاصه آنرا در اختیار ما قرار دهند. اگر طرفین ازدواج در خارج از استرالیا متولد شده با شندبجای شناسنامه میتوانند گذرنامه های خود را ارائه دهند. در این مورد بهتر است که این موضوع را با عاقد در میان بگذارند.	۵ـ محفل روحانی محلی که ازدواج در آنجا انجام میگیرد مسئول اجرای مراسم است. محافل روحانی که طرفین ازدواج در آنجا ساکن هستند وظیفه دارند که رضایت نامه های والدین را رویت نمایند. اگر ازدواج در محلی خارج از حوزه حاکمیت محفل روحانی انجام میگیرد محفل روحانی ملی مسئول اجرای مراسم ازدواج است.

CHAPTER TEN

و ـ محفلی که مسئول اجرای مراسم ازدواج است موظف میباشد که ماقد را مطلع سازد که تمام مقررات بهائی برای انجام مراسم رعایت شده است. محفل روحانی محلی باید دو نفر شاهد تعیین نماید. شاهدین غالبا بهائی هستند اما این شرط ضروری نیست. محفل روحانی ملی توصیه میکند که این دو نفر، شاهدین مراسم ازدواج کشوری نیز باشند.

و ـ در مورتیکه یکی از طرفین قبلا ازدواج کرده باشد ورقه گواهی فوت همسر قبلی یا گواهی طلاق Decree Absolute را باید در اختیار ماقد بگذارد. (توجه داشته باشد که منظور حکم طلاق موقت نیست).

7ـ اطلاعات مربوط بوضع ازدواج باید در ورقه قانونی ازدواج ثبت شود.

8ـ تعیین دو نفر شاهد که از 18 سال بیشتر داشته باشند (به ماده 6 از مقررات بهائی مراجعه نمائید).

در حین اجرای مراسم

1ـ قرائت آئین:

"We will all, verily, abide by the Will of God"

2ـ فرم

"Notification of Bahá'í Marriage"

باید بوسیله منشی محفل روحانی محلی و شاهدین پر شده و امضاء شود. محفل محلی فرم اصلی را نگاه داشته و رونوشت آن را به دفتر محفل ملی ارسال میدارد.

1ـ قرائت آئین معمولا قبل از اظهار عبارتی که لازمه مقد کشوری است انجام میگیرد. در شرایط خاصی ممکن است که آئین بعدا خوانده شود. برای آگاهی به این شرایط به Local Spiritual Assembly Handbook مراجعه نمائید.

2ـ عبارتی که اظهار آن لازمه مقد کشوری است بشرح زیر میباشد.

"I call upon the persons here present to witness that I.............. take thee............... to be my lawful wedded wife/husband."

3ـ دفتر و ورقه گواهی ازدواج باید امضاء شود

باید توجه داشت که مبادله انگشتر از شرایط مراسم ازدواج بهائی و یا کشوری نیست. اگر مبادله انگشتر لازم باشد این کار ممکن است پس از تلاوت آئین و یا بعد از مراسم مقد کشوری انجام گیرد. شایسته نیست که مراسم ازدواج را با عکس برداری مختل کرد. ماقدین معمولا موافقت میکنند که بعدا مراسم را برای عکس برداری تکرار نمایند.

CHAPTER TEN

توضیحــات

محفل روحانی محلی که شما در حوزه حاکمیت آن ساکن هستید باید رضایت نامه های والدین را روایت و تائید نماید. محفل روحانی محلی که مراسم ازدواج در آن انجام میگیرد نیز مسئول تصویب رضایت نامه هاست علاوه، این محفل مسئول اجرای مراسم ازدواج و تصویب برنامه و تعیین شاهدین بهائی نیز میباشد. همچنین این محفل باید ما قدرا مطلع سازد که ترتیب امور قبل از روز ازدواج داده شده است. اگر مقررات بهائــــی مراعات نشده باشد برگزاری مراسم ازدواج امکان پذیر نخواهد بود.

در صورت عدم استفاده از عاقد بهائی مراسم ازدواج کشوری ممکن است در دفتر رسمی ازدواج Registry Office وسیله عاقد کشوری انجام گیرد. در هر حال باید کلیه مقررات بهائی و کشوری رعایت شده باشد. مطابق امریه بیت العدل اعظم الهی نباید بین اجرای مراسم بهائی و کشوری یک شب فاصله باشد. اگر مراسم بهائــــی و کشوری بطور جداگانه برگزار میشوند اول باید مراسم بهائی و بعد در همان روز مراسم کشوری انجام گیـــرد. اگر مراسم بعقد و سیله عاقد کشوری انجام میشود باید مواظب باشید که عاقد مراسمی اجرا ننماید که با اصــول دیانت بهائی مغایرت داشته باشد.

عاقدین ازدواج کشوری و مسئولین دفتر ازدواج Registrars برای خدمتی که انجام میدهند حق الزحمه دریافت میدارند. عاقدین بهائی این حق الزحمه را نمیگیرند ولی طرفین ازدواج باید متوجه باشند کـــه مسئول خرج مسافرت آنان بوده و اگر لازم باشد که عاقد بهائی شب در محل بماند محل مناسبی برای اقامت ایشان تهیه نمایند.

تخلف از اجرای مقررات کشوری و یا تسلیم اظهار نامه مخالف حقیقت و یا بیان مطالب نادرست جریمه هـای سنگین و یا زندان بدنبال خواهد داشت. عدم مراعات مقررات بهائی نیز منجر به طرداداری و از دست دادن حق رای در جامعه بهائی خواهد شد.

اگر شما با فرد غیر بهائی ازدواج میکنید ما نعی ندارد که در مراسم ازدواج دینی طرف غیر بهائی خود شرکت کنیـد. بشرط اینکه اظهاری و یا تعهدی که مباین با مقررات بهائی باشد ننمائید. در هر صورت شما باید مراسم ازدواج بهائی را هم انجام دهید. این مطلب باید قبلا روشن شود که پیشوای مذهبی طرف غیر بهائی (که در عیـــن حال عاقد دولتی هم خواهد بود) یا عاقد بهائی کدام یک مراسم عقد دولتی را انجام خواهند داد. معمـولا نماینده مذهبی طرف غیر بهائی امر را ردک اینکار را انجام دهد در این صورت نیازی به عاقد بهائی نخواهد بود و مراسم ازدواج بهائی که تحت نظر محفل روحانی است باید اول انجام شود.

عاقد میتواند تمام اوراق لازم را در اختیار طرفین ازدواج قرارداده و آنها را گواهی کند و یا راهنمائی های لازم را در مورد اینکه از کجا آنها را تهیه کرده و یا چه کسی میتواند آنها را گواهی کند در اختیارشان بگذارد.

این نکات که به اختصار ذکر شد جوابگوی تمام موارد و احتمالات نمیباشد. اطلاعات بیشتر را میتوانید از عاقدین و محفل روحانی محل خویش بدست بیاورید. این نکته مهم را باید مخصوصا بخاطر داشت که لازم است با عاقد بهائی زودتر تماس گرفت تا اگر موارد غیر عادی و مسائل پیچیده ای پیش بیاید وقت کافی برای روشن شـــدن آنها موجود باشد.

STATEMENT pursuant to Section 113 (5) of
THE MARRIAGE ACT, 1961

We, the undersigned, having been duly married in a civil ceremony In accordance with the marriage Act, I961, now wish to participate in a Bahá'í ceremony of marriage.
We state that:

(I)   This day we went through a ceremony of Marriage under the Marriage Act 1961 with each other

at..

....(Town)..(State).........................

(2)   We are the parties mentioned in the Certificate of Marriage produced with this statement to........
(Full name of Chairman of Spiritual Assembly or other officer
who is conducting the Bahá'í proceedings)

(3)   We have no reason to believe that we are not legally married to each other.

....
(Full name of Husband)   (Signature)

....
(Full name of Wife)   (Signature)

....
(Address)

....

....

....(Signature of Witness)

....(Office Held)

....(Name of Spiritual Assembly)

....(Address of Witness)

(FORM to be used when a Bahá'í ceremony follows a civil marriage, i.e. a marriage celebrated by a Civil Celebrant or in a church ceremony which includes civil marriage under the Marriage Act 1961. TO BE FILLED IN DUPLICATE - 1 copy for the Spiritual Assembly conducting the Bahá'í proceedings and one for that Assembly to forward to the National Spiritual Assembly).

CHAPTER ELEVEN

Chapter 11

11. Reconciliation and Divorce

11.1 INTRODUCTION - PREVENTING DIVORCE

11.1.1 *What is the Bahá'í attitude towards divorce?*

Divorce is legally permitted within the Bahá'í community but only as a last resort. Bahá'u'lláh has said:-

> *God doth verily love union and concord, and abhorreth separation and divorce.*
>
> (extract from previously unpublished Tablet, in "Divorce" compilation by Universal House of Justice, published by National Spiritual Assembly of the Bahá'ís of Australia, 1980, p.3)

To 'abhor' something is to shrink from it or to strongly dislike it. This is essentially the Bahá'í attitude towards divorce. A couple should seek a divorce only if every possible means to reconciliation has been attempted and has failed:-

> *For while, according to the Bahá'í law, divorce is permissible, yet it is highly discouraged, and should be resorted to only when every effort to prevent it has proved to be vain and ineffective.*
>
> (letter written on behalf of Shoghi Effendi to an individual believer, dated September 11, 1938)

11.1.2 *Why is divorce abhorred?*

Divorce is abhorred for two major, interrelated reasons:
1. (1) it has a negative effect on the children of the marriage because it causes them to suffer from conflicting loyalties and influences their own attitudes to marriage in the future:-

> *He feels that you should by all means make every effort to hold your marriage together, especially for the sake of your children, who, like all children of divorced parents cannot but suffer from conflicting loyalties, for they are deprived of the blessings of a father and mother in one home, to look after their interests and love them jointly.*
>
> (letter written on behalf of Shoghi Effendi to an individual believer, dated March 6, 1953)

> *The presence of children, as a factor in divorce, cannot be ignored, for surely it places an even greater weight of moral responsibility on the man and wife in considering such a step. Divorce under such circumstances no longer just concerns them and their desires and feelings but also concerns the children's entire future and their own attitude towards marriage.*
>
> (letter written on behalf of Shoghi Effendi to an individual believer, dated December 19, 1947)

2. *Bahá'u'lláh came to bring unity to the world and a fundamental unity is that of the family. Divorce disrupts the family and leads to the disintegration of society:-*

> *Regarding the Bahá'í Teachings on divorce. While the latter has been made permissible by Bahá'u'lláh yet He has strongly discouraged its practice, for if not checked and seriously controlled it leads gradually to the disruption of family life and to the disintegration of society.*
>
> (letter written on behalf of Shoghi Effendi to an individual believer, dated November 16, 1936)

> *...the foundation of the Kingdom of God is based upon harmony and love, oneness, relationship and union, not upon differences, especially between husband and wife.*
>
> ('Abdu'l-Bahá, previously unpublished Tablet, in "Divorce" compilation, p.5)

It should also be noted that 'Abdu'l-Bahá has predicted 'great difficulties' for anyone responsible for causing divorce:-

> *If one of these two [husband or wife] becomes the cause of divorce, that one will unquestionably fall into great difficulties, will become the victim of formidable calamities and experience deep remorse.*
>
> ('Abdu'l-Bahá, previously unpublished Tablet, in "Divorce" compilation, p.5)

11.1.3 *How may the Local Spiritual Assembly prevent divorce from occurring?*

The Local Spiritual Assembly is responsible for deepening the community in the importance of the marriage laws:-

> *The Spiritual Assembly should always be concerned that the believers in its community are being deepened in their understanding of the Bahá'í concept of marriage, especially the young people, so that the very thought of divorce will be abhorrent to them.*
>
> (letter written on behalf of the Universal House of Justice to an individual believer, dated November 3, 1982)

The Local Spiritual Assembly also has the responsibility of offering counselling to believers on personal problems, including marital ones, if approached by the individuals concerned for advice:-

> *He feels, in regard to your family problems, that you should take these matters up with your Assembly, if you desire advice; one of the duties of these assemblies is to advise and aid the friends, and it is your privilege to turn to your Assembly.*
>
> (letter written on behalf of Shoghi Effendi to an individual believer, dated April 10, 1947)

If problems are resolved as they arise, matters should not reach a point where the couple concerned feel it is necessary to apply for a divorce.

11.1.4 *When should a Local Spiritual Assembly intervene in a marital conflict?*

The Local Spiritual Assembly can only intervene if requested to do so by the parties involved:-

> *There should be no intervention into the marital affairs of individuals in a Bahá'í community unless and until the parties themselves bring a problem to the Assembly. Prior to that it is not the business of the Assembly to counsel the parties.*
>
> (letter written by the Universal House of Justice to a National Spiritual Assembly, dated March 22, 1968)

As with any dispute between believers, it is permissible for one party to bring the matter to the Assembly, regardless of whether the other party wishes it or not.
In counselling the couple concerned, the Assembly should encourage them to consult a professional marriage counselling service if necessary.

11.1.5 *What should the attitude of the Bahá'í community be towards a couple experiencing marital difficulties?*

The Local Spiritual Assembly must ensure that the community maintains an impartial attitude towards the couple experiencing such difficulties. In the words of Shoghi Effendi:-

> *The Bahá'ís must learn to forget personalities and to overcome the desire - so natural in people - to take sides and fight about it.*
>
> (letter written on behalf of Shoghi Effendi to a National Spiritual Assembly, dated June 30, 1949)

11.2 RECONCILIATION

11.2.1 *What is the duty of the Local Spiritual Assembly if the parties to a marriage approach it asking for a divorce?*

An Assembly that is approached by a party or parties to a marriage requesting a divorce, has the duty of impartially investigating the matter with a view to bringing about a reconciliation:-

> *When a Spiritual Assembly receives an application for Bahá'í divorce, the Assembly has the duty of trying to reconcile the parties before setting the date for the beginning of the year of patience.*
>
> (letter from the Universal House of Justice to a National Spiritual Assembly, dated March 29, 1966)

> *When an application for divorce is made to a Spiritual Assembly, its first thought and action should be to reconcile the couple and to ensure that they know the Bahá'í Teachings on the matter. God willing, the Assembly will be successful and no year of waiting need be started.*
>
> (letter written on behalf of the Universal House of Justice to an individual believer, dated November 3, 1982)

11.2.2 *Should the Local Spiritual Assembly advise a couple in a domestic violence situation to separate?*

At present the prevailing method in Australia of treating domestic violence is to advise the couple to separate and to seek treatment from professional counselling services. It is suggested that Assemblies follow this method of treating domestic violence also. The Universal House of Justice has said:-

CHAPTER ELEVEN

> *There is no obligation on a wife, who is being subjected to beating by her husband, to continue living with him; she has the freedom to leave him and to live in a separate domicile if she feels it necessary to do so.*
>
> (letter written on behalf of the Universal House of Justice to the National Spiritual Assembly of Australia, dated April 12, 1990)

If, alternatively, the couple is counselled to remain together to try and reconcile their differences, there can be no guarantee that the violence will not recur, in which case the Assembly could appear, inadvertently, to be condoning it. If the couple separate, however, the role of the Assembly can then become that of providing an independent forum within which the couple can come together and try to resolve their differences. It is imperative that action be taken and the couple undergoes counselling. If no intervention takes place the 'cycle of violence' may very well repeat itself. This may be obscured by remorse and guilt; or a feeling of helplessness and self-blame on the victim's part, followed by apparent good relations between the couple which they confirm. However, left untreated, violence has the possibility of surfacing again.

11.2.3 *Can one party to a marriage, acting alone, approach the Local Spiritual Assembly for a year of patience?*

Yes:-

> *Either party may apply for the year of waiting without the consent of the other.*
>
> (letter from the Universal House of Justice to a National Spiritual Assembly, dated November 23, 1970)

11.2.4 *What procedure should the Local Spiritual Assembly follow when attempting to reconcile a couple?*

It is recommended that the following steps be followed, as far as is practicable, when the Assembly is attempting to reconcile a couple.

1. advise the couple that the Assembly has the duty to try and bring about a reconciliation:-

   > *...Bahá'ís who apply for divorce should be so counselled and left in no doubt that it is the duty of the Spiritual Assembly concerned, according to the emphatic command of our Scripture, to do everything possible to bring about a reconciliation.*
   >
   > (letter from the Universal House of Justice to a National Spiritual Assembly, dated August 3, 1981)

2. remember that the Local Assembly must maintain an impartial attitude at all times:-

   > *Its members [of an Assembly] must at ALL TIMES put the interests of the Faith above personality and impartially go into any matter brought to its attention.*
   >
   > (letter written on behalf of Shoghi Effendi to a National Spiritual Assembly, dated June 30, 1949)

   The Assembly should also reassure the couple as to the confidential nature of the consultation. As noted in the 'Introduction - Preventing Divorce', the Assembly must further ensure that the community does not become involved, and take sides, in the conflict.

CHAPTER ELEVEN

3. review the Bahá'í Teachings on divorce with the couple. In particular, point out that divorce is abhorred in the Writings and that it can only be granted if the condition of 'irreconcilable antipathy' is found to exist:-

> *In the strict legal sense there are no 'grounds' for a Bahá'í divorce. No question of misbehaviour of either party is involved and the only condition under which a Bahá'í divorce may be considered is the irreconcilable antipathy of the parties.*
>
> (letter from the Universal House of Justice to a National Spiritual Assembly, dated May 24, 1972)

The couple should be made aware that the following <u>do not</u> constitute valid grounds for a Bahá'í divorce:
physical incompatibility:-

> *For the Bahá'í Teachings do not only preclude the possibility of bigamy, but also, while permitting divorce, consider it a reprehensible act, which should be resorted to only in exceptional circumstances, and when grave issues are involved...transcending such...considerations as physical attraction or sexual compatibility and harmony. The Institution of marriage, as established by Bahá'u'lláh, while giving due importance to the physical aspect of marital union considers it as subordinate to the moral and spiritual purposes and functions with which it has been invested by an all-wise and loving Providence.*
>
> (letter written on behalf of Shoghi Effendi to an individual believer, dated May 8, 1939)

lack of love for one's spouse:-

> *Irreconcilable antipathy arising between the parties to a marriage is not merely a lack of love for one's spouse but an antipathy which cannot be resolved.*
>
> (letter from the Universal House of Justice to a National Spiritual Assembly, dated September 3, 1969)

service to the Cause:-

> *...he does not feel that any believer, under any circumstances whatsoever, can ever use the Cause or service to it as a reason for abandoning their marriage; divorce, as we know, is very strongly condemned by Bahá'u'lláh, and only grounds of extreme gravity justify it.*
>
> (letter written by Shoghi Effendi to an individual believer, dated April 7, 1947)

4. whilst interviewing the parties, make an effort to ascertain the reason for their differences and encourage a reconciliation. Note, however, that it is not necessary for the Local Assembly to know the reasons behind the marriage breakdown if the couple really do not wish to discuss the matter:-

> *Assemblies are, or course, discouraged from probing unnecessarily into details of personal lives and the examination of a divorce problem should not go beyond what is necessary to ascertain whether or not such*

antipathy does, indeed, exist.

(letter written on behalf of the Universal House of Justice to a National Spiritual Assembly, dated May 30, 1983)

Depending on the circumstances, the couple may be advised to:-
i) reflect further on the advice of the Local Spiritual Assembly
ii) seek counselling from professional Bahá'í or non-Bahá'í counsellors
iii) consider a period of separation rather than initiating a year of patience

5. note that if only one party wishes to initiate a year of patience, the Assembly should attempt to meet with the other party before setting a date for its beginning; also that the Universal House of Justice has said:

'The Assembly may meet with the couple together or separately in its attempts to reconcile them.'

(letter written on behalf of the Universal House of Justice to a National Spiritual Assembly, dated June 20, 1977)

6. if one party to the marriage is a non-Bahá'í the Assembly needs to consider whether it is practicable to attempt to meet with that person.
7. if the Assembly is not able to reconcile the couple, it must conclude that a condition of 'irreconcilable antipathy' exists, in which case it has no choice but to set the date for the beginning of the year of patience:-

...if the Assembly finds that it is unable to persuade the party concerned to withdraw the application for divorce, it must conclude that, from its point of view, there appears to be an irreconcilable antipathy, and it has no alternative to setting the date for the beginning of the year of waiting.

(letter written on behalf of the Universal House of Justice to an individual believer, dated November 3, 1982)

It is important to note from the above guidance of the Universal House of Justice, that the Assembly only needs to be satisfied that the party or parties concerned will not withdraw their application for divorce, in order to conclude that a condition of 'irreconcilable antipathy' exists.

11.2.5 *Should the Assembly offer counselling to a Bahá'í without voting rights?*

Yes. The Universal House of Justice has said:-

...a Bahá'í who has lost his administrative rights is not required to observe the year of waiting before divorce, but he may do so if he wishes. The Assembly should offer counselling on the divorce in any case.

(letter written to a National Spiritual Assembly, dated March 18, 1975)

11.3 YEAR OF PATIENCE

11.3.1 *What is the purpose of the year of patience?*

The year of patience is a period of separation during which time the couple contemplating divorce have the opportunity to reflect upon their situation and consider means of reconciliation:-

CHAPTER ELEVEN

It is understood that two Bahá'ís who reach the point of strain where they feel a divorce is necessary need time to cool down and reflect, which is, of course, the purpose of the year of waiting.

(letter written on behalf of the Universal House of Justice to a National Spiritual Assembly, dated August 3, 1981)

11.3.2 ***What are the primary obligations of the couple and of the Local Spiritual Assembly during the year of patience?***

During the year the couple have the responsibility of attempting to reconcile their differences, and the Assembly has the duty to help them.

(letter written on behalf of the Universal House of Justice to an individual believer, dated November 3, 1982)

11.3.3 ***Who fixes the date for the beginning of the year of patience?***

According to the Universal House of Justice:-

It is for the Local Spiritual Assembly, or the National Assembly, as the case may be, to fix the date for the beginning of the year of patience...

(letter to a National Spiritual Assembly, dated August 26, 1965)

While a Local or National Assembly may request the advice of the Continental Board of Counsellors and their Board members, and should be grateful for their assistance, it is the Assembly's responsibility to conduct its own investigation and come to a decision.

(letter written on behalf of the Universal House of Justice to a National

If a couple do not live in a Local Spiritual Assembly area, the National Spiritual Assembly becomes the responsible body. The National Assembly may choose to appoint a nearby Local Assembly to assume responsibility.

11.3.4 ***When does the year of patience begin?***

Normally the date for the beginning of the year of patience is that on which the party or parties have separated and applied to the Assembly for divorce. By separation is meant no longer sharing the same home. It is for the couple between them to decide who will leave the family home:-

The Bahá'í Law requires that the parties separate for one full year before the divorce may be realised. This contemplates complete physical separation in the sense that they should not reside in the same dwelling.

(letter from the Universal House of Justice to a National Spiritual Assembly, dated April 23, 1964)

The couple must realise that the year of patience cannot begin to run unless and until they are living apart, and it is for them to decide between them which will leave the home.

(letter from the Universal House of Justice to a National Spiritual Assembly, dated December 2, 1965)

11.3.5 *Can the date for the beginning of the year of patience be back-dated?*

If the Assembly believes there is sufficient reason it may set the date for the year of patience earlier than that on which the party or parties apply to the Assembly for the divorce, but it can never be set earlier than the last date on which the couple actually separated with the intention to divorce:-

> *The Spiritual Assembly may, if it is satisfied that there is sufficient reason for doing so, establish the date for the beginning of the year of waiting retroactively. Whether established retroactively or not, the date set for the beginning of the year of waiting cannot be prior to the last date when the couple actually separated for the purpose of obtaining a divorce.*
>
> (letter from the Universal House of Justice to a National Spiritual Assembly, dated September 26, 1972)

11.3.6 *Does the husband have to pay maintenance during the year of patience?*

Generally, yes:-

> *The husband is obligated to support the wife and children until the granting of the Bahá'í divorce.*
>
> (letter from the Universal House of Justice to a National Spiritual Assembly, dated January 13, 1983)

There may be situations in which both husband and wife were contributing financially towards the marriage, or the wife was the bread-winner. The procedure then is that the financial arrangements that stood during the marriage should form the basis for an amicable agreement between the couple during the year of patience:-

> *The House of Justice views it as a basic principle of Bahá'í law that the husband is responsible for the support of his wife and children as long as they are married, ie. until the granting of a divorce. There may be particular circumstances in which the wife is the bread-winner of the family, or both husband and wife are earning income; such situations should not be ignored, or changed merely because the couple is in a year of waiting.*
>
> (letter from the Universal House of Justice to a National Spiritual Assembly, dated May 19, 1989)

11.3.7 *What about care of dependents during the year of patience?*

> *The Assembly...has the duty to see that just arrangements are made for the support of dependents during the year of patience.*
>
> (letter from the Universal House of Justice to a National Spiritual Assembly, dated March 29, 1966)

11.3.8 *Is the year of patience necessary if one party is not a Bahá'í?*

Yes:-

> *With regard to the question of Bahá'í divorce, the year of separation is necessary even though the non-Bahá'í partner to the marriage is the one instituting the divorce proceedings...*
>
> (letter from the Universal House of Justice to a National Spiritual Assembly, dated January 28, 1966)

11.3.9 *What if a civil divorce is granted to the non-Bahá'í partner before the end of the year of patience?*

Even if a civil divorce is granted to the non-Bahá'í partner before the end of the year of patience, the Bahá'í partner must wait until the end of that year before Bahá'í divorce can be granted:-

> *If, as in the case cited, a civil divorce is granted to a non-Bahá'í partner before the end of the year of patience, Bahá'í divorce cannot be granted until the end of that year.*
>
> (letter from the Universal House of Justice to a National Spiritual Assembly, dated January 23, 1966)

11.3.10 *What if the non-Bahá'í partner remarries before the end of the year of patience?*

If the non-Bahá'í partner remarries the Bahá'í divorce should be granted immediately:-

> *Should the non-Bahá'í partner remarry before the year of separation is over, the Bahá'í partner is released from further waiting and a Bahá'í divorce may be granted.*
>
> (letter from the Universal House of Justice to a National Spiritual Assembly, dated January 28, 1966)

11.3.11 *Must a believer without voting rights observe a year of patience?*

No:-

> *...a Bahá'í who has lost his administrative rights is not required to observe the year of waiting before divorce, but he may do so if he wishes.*
>
> (letter from the Universal House of Justice to a National Spiritual Assembly, dated March 18, 1975)

11.3.12 *Can the year of patience be extended?*

No. The waiting period only extends beyond one year if the civil divorce has not yet been finalised:-

> *...if, at the end of the year, harmony is not established, the Bahá'í divorce becomes effective, unless further waiting is necessary before the civil divorce is granted since the Bahá'í divorce cannot be granted before the civil divorce is finalised. Other than this, there is no possibility for extending the period of waiting. Moreover, Bahá'ís should not prolong the process longer than is necessary.*
>
> (letter from the Universal House of Justice to an individual believer, dated July 12, 1979)

11.3.13 *Can one party, acting alone, petition for a termination of the year of patience?*

No:-

> *One party to a divorce, acting alone, cannot petition for a termination of the year of waiting.*
>
> (letter from the Universal House of Justice to a National Spiritual Assembly, dated May 1, 1967)

That is to say, there can be no reconciliation except by the agreement of both parties.

CHAPTER ELEVEN

11.3.14 *What constitute acceptable social relationships during the year of patience?*

Normal friendships with members of the opposite sex are permissible during the year of patience, but these should not progress to dating in the spirit of courtship. To do so is to contravene the purpose of the year of patience which is to bring about a reconciliation between the couple concerned:-

> *It is always the hope that, during the year of patience, affection between the couple will recur and that divorce will not be necessary. Therefore, although normal social relationships between each of the partners and members of both sexes are permissible, it is quite contrary to the spirit of the Teachings for either party to be courting a new partner during the year of waiting.*
>
> (letter from the Universal House of Justice to an individual believer, dated March 6, 1974)

If one party to a year of patience is known to be dating another person, he or she should be counselled by the Assembly that such behaviour is inappropriate. Sanctions, however, should not be applied, unless the person's behaviour is flagrantly immoral.

> *...this is not an area in which the Assembly should resort to sanctions if either or both of the pair disregard this principle. Naturally, if one of the parties conducts himself or herself in a way that is blatantly or flagrantly immoral the matter should be handled as any other similar case would be.*
>
> (letter from the Universal House of Justice to an individual believer, dated March 6, 1974)

Any case in doubt should be referred to the National Spiritual Assembly.

11.3.15 *Does reconciliation end the year of patience?*

Yes. If a couple are reconciled, the process of divorce is considered to be abandoned. If the couple again wish to apply for divorce, the year of patience must begin anew:-

> *If at any time during the waiting period affection should recur, the marriage tie is valid. If this reconciliation is followed by estrangement and divorce is again desired, a new year of waiting will have to be commenced.*
>
> (Bahá'u'lláh, "Synopsis and Codification of the Laws and Ordinances of the Kitáb-i-Aqdas", p.42)

Whether sharing a common residence temporarily could void the year of patience must be determined by the Assembly, according to whether it judges that the purpose of the year of patience has been preserved or not:-

> *Regarding the question of voiding the year of waiting, should a couple share a common residence for one or two nights when the residence belongs to a third party, the House of Justice does not wish to make a ruling on such a general basis. In the case you mention involving temporary residence in the home of the parents of one of the parties who are in a year of waiting, the House of Justice suggests you try to verify whether or not the purpose of the year of waiting has been preserved and if satisfied this is so, make your decision accordingly.*
>
> (letter from the Universal House of Justice to a National Spiritual

CHAPTER ELEVEN

Assembly, dated August 2, 1981)

11.4 CIVIL DIVORCE LAW

11.4.1 *How should the information provided in this section be used by the Local Spiritual Assembly?*

The information contained in this section is taken from "The Law Handbook" (3rd edition) published by Redfern Legal Centre. It should be used by Local Spiritual Assemblies as a guide to basic civil law in the area of divorce. In any particular instance in which an Assembly needs to utilise such knowledge, it should contact the Attorney-General's Department, or other legal referral agencies in its respective State. This is necessary to ensure that the Assembly has the most recent and accurate information concerning divorce when handling any particular case.

11.4.2 *What is the civil law regulating divorce in Australia?*

The law relating to divorce is laid out in the Family Law Act 1975 (Commonwealth). Divorce cases come before the Family Court.

11.4.3 *What constitute grounds for civil divorce?*

The only civil ground for divorce is: IRRETRIEVABLE BREAKDOWN OF MARRIAGE [s. 48(1) of the Family Law Act]. This is shown when the parties have lived separately and apart for twelve months and there is no reasonable likelihood of their getting back together [ss. 48(2),(3)]. The granting of a divorce dissolves the legal bonds of marriage between the parties. It does not deal with matters such as custody of, or access to, children; maintenance; or division of property. If a couple wish the Family Court to make rulings on these matters they must make separate application to the Court. This is explained in further detail below.

11.4.4 *When does the period of separation begin?*

The twelve month period of separation begins the day both or one party leaves the marriage and must be complete at the time of filing for dissolution of the marriage. One party does not usually have to inform the other that the period of separation has begun. Under certain conditions it may be considered in civil law that the couple have been living separately and apart although still under the same roof.

11.4.5 *Does reconciliation void the period of separation?*

The parties concerned can resume the marital relationship after separation has commenced and continue to live as husband and wife for one period of up to three months, without having to re-start the separation period. [Family Law Act, s.50(1) and (2)]. The separation period stands still during this time and recommences if and when the parties separate again before three months is completed. Note that this provision is at variance with Bahá'í Law (see previous section).

11.4.6 *When can application for dissolution of the marriage be made?*

An application for dissolution of the marriage cannot be filed until the twelve month separation period is over. Either party may apply, regardless of whether the other wants a divorce, or they can apply together. When the Court finds that the separation requirements have been satisfactorily met, it grants a "decree nisi". This becomes a "decree absolute" one month later. If the parties become reconciled during the intervening period they must apply to the Court to have the "decree nisi" set aside. "Decree absolute" dissolves the marriage.

CHAPTER ELEVEN

11.4.7 *How is custody of the children decided?*

During the twelve month separation period, the couple remain equally responsible for care of the children. If they cannot decide with whom the children should live, either parent can apply for custody to the Court. The parent without custody can apply to see the children. The Court will not usually grant a divorce unless the parties have made suitable arrangements for any children under 18 years of age who were living as part of the family when the parties separated. The judge has to approve these arrangements but they do not become orders of the Court enforceable by the Court. It is preferable that the couple make their own arrangements about custody of, and access to, the children. They may, if the agreement is in writing, submit it to the Court to be registered. Once registered the agreement has effect as if it was an order of the Court but the Court may still vary, set aside or refuse to enforce the agreement if it thinks it is not in the best interests of the child. If the couple cannot agree between themselves on custody of the children, they must make an application to the Court, which is separate to that made for dissolution of the marriage.

11.4.8 *How is division of property determined?*

It is preferable that the couple make their own arrangements regarding division of property. This can be done during the separation period and then submitted to the Court according to provisions outlined in the Family Law Act. If the couple are unable to agree, they can make separate application to the Court for a decision. Such actions can be started before the divorce or separation period commences. After the divorce is finalised proceedings should be begun within 12 months of granting the "decree absolute".

11.4.9 *How are maintenance payments decided?*

A couple may make their own agreement concerning maintenance of the spouse and any children and submit it to the Court according to provisions outlined in the Family Law Act. Alternatively, either spouse may apply to the Family Court or Local Court for a maintenance order against the other spouse at any time during the marriage or separation period leading up to divorce; or during the twelve month period following granting of the "decree absolute". Application for maintenance for the children can be made at any time. The parents of a child have a primary duty to support the child. To be granted maintenance applicants will have to show that they are not able to support themselves properly because they are caring for children or unable to work because of old age, sickness, or some other reason. They will also have to show that their spouse is reasonably able to pay maintenance. Maintenance is not an automatic right. A separated woman (or man) not caring for children and able to work will probably not be granted maintenance.

11.5 RELATIONSHIP BETWEEN BAHÁ'Í AND CIVIL DIVORCE LAWS

11.5.1 *What is the relationship between Bahá'í and civil divorce laws?*

As Bahá'í divorce is not legally recognised in Australia, a Bahá'í couple must obtain a civil divorce as well as a Bahá'í divorce.

11.5.2 *When is Bahá'í divorce granted?*

According to Bahá'í law, divorce is granted automatically at the end of the year of patience if there has been no reconciliation. As Bahá'ís must also obey civil law, however, the Bahá'í divorce cannot be granted until civil divorce is granted:-

> *If the Assembly ascertains that the couple have not been able to become reconciled and that the year of patience has truly been completed, then it is possible for a Bahá'í divorce to be granted. However, as Bahá'í law in these matters is subordinated to civil law, the Bahá'í*

CHAPTER ELEVEN

divorce does not become effective until the civil divorce is granted.

(letter from the Universal House of Justice to a National Spiritual Assembly, dated December 2, 1965)

The civil divorce decree granted must be "decree absolute", not "nisi":-

You should make it clear that a Bahá'í divorce cannot be granted prior to the granting of a final divorce decree in the civil action nor before the expiration of the year of patience.

(letter from the Universal House of Justice to a National Spiritual Assembly, dated June 5, 1966)

11.5.3 *Can civil divorce proceedings be initiated prior to the end of the year of patience?*

Civil divorce proceedings should not be initiated prior to the end of the year of patience unless special circumstances make this necessary. It is not, however, a sanctionable offence if it occurs:-

...it is more within the spirit of Bahá'í Law for Bahá'ís to postpone the initiation of civil proceedings, (if the law of the country requires a civil divorce) until the end of the year of waiting. However, if such postponement gives rise to inequity or to a legal prejudice against the possibility of a civil divorce, it is, of course, permissible for the civil proceedings to be initiated during the year of waiting.

(letter written on behalf of the Universal House of Justice to a National Spiritual Assembly, dated June 20, 1977)

There is no Bahá'í law requiring the removal of voting rights for obtaining a civil divorce before the end of the year of waiting. It is, of course, preferred that civil divorce action not be instituted or completed before the end of the year unless there are special circumstances justifying such action.

(letter from the Universal House of Justice to a National Spiritual Assembly, dated August 20, 1974)

11.5.4 *What if civil divorce is granted before the end of the year of patience?*

Although the civil divorce is granted, Bahá'í divorce cannot be granted before the end of the year of patience. This means that it is not yet possible to re-marry. Should a Bahá'í do so he or she will be subject to sanctions:-

... the believer will be subject to sanctions if he should marry a third party within the year of patience, not only because it is a violation of the year of patience itself, but also because even though a civil divorce has been granted, the Bahá'í divorce cannot be granted until the end of the year of patience. For this reason no marriage is possible during the running of the year of patience unless the parties to the divorce re-marry each other in a civil ceremony.

(letter written on behalf of the Universal House of Justice to a National Spiritual Assembly, dated July 18, 1973)

CHAPTER ELEVEN

11.5.5 ***What if the couple become reconciled between the end of the year of patience and granting of the civil divorce?***

In this instance, according to Bahá'í law, there is no need for the couple to re-marry:-

> *...should the couple be reconciled during the period between the end of the year of waiting and the time when the civil divorce would become effective, there would be no need for the parties to remarry according to Bahá'í law.*

(letter from the Universal House of Justice to a National Spiritual Assembly, dated May 1, 1967)

11.5.6 ***What is the situation for a couple living in a de facto relationship, which is accepted as a marriage under Bahá'í law?***

People who are living in a de facto relationship which has been recognised as a valid marriage under Bahá'í law should have a Bahá'í divorce if they separate; that is, they are bound by the requirement to go through the year of patience but, obviously, do not need a civil divorce.

11.5.7 ***What is the situation for Iranian couples who had only a Bahá'í marriage in Iran and wish to divorce in Australia?***

Application of Australian civil divorce law is uncertain in such cases, therefore, the Local Spiritual Assembly should advise the party or parties concerned to contact the National Office.

11.5.8 ***What is the status of an individual who initiates civil divorce proceedings prior to becoming a Bahá'í?***

When an individual has initiated civil divorce proceedings prior to becoming a Bahá'í, he or she does not have to observe Bahá'í divorce law:-

> *You ask about the contact who wishes to declare her faith, having already initiated legal steps to divorce her husband. As this case is already in process before her declaration she does not have to observe Bahá'í divorce law.*

(letter from the Universal House of Justice to a National Spiritual Assembly, dated May 21, 1968)

11.5.9 ***What is the status of an individual who remarries without having a Bahá'í divorce due to ignorance of Bahá'í law?***

If the Local Spiritual Assembly is satisfied that the individual was genuinely ignorant of Bahá'í law, no sanctions should be applied and their situation should be considered the same as that of a Bahá'í who was divorced before becoming a Bahá'í:-

> *In cases in which your Assembly has decided that the believer was ignorant of the law requiring him to have a Bahá'í divorce before marrying another, and a civil divorce has already been obtained, your Assembly may in its discretion excuse him and he would be regarded as in the same status as one who obtained a divorce before becoming a Bahá'í.*

(letter from the Universal House of Justice to a National Spiritual Assembly, dated March 14, 1976)

CHAPTER ELEVEN

11.5.10 *Can one party interfere with the granting of the civil divorce once the year of patience has ended?*

No:-

> *When a year of waiting ends without re-establishment of the marriage relationship, it is not in the spirit of the Faith for one party to delay or interfere with the civil divorce which thereafter must occur in order to legalise the Bahá'í divorce.*
>
> (letter from the Universal House of Justice to a National Spiritual Assembly, dated August 1, 1978)

11.6 RESPONSIBILITIES OF THE LOCAL SPIRITUAL ASSEMBLY FOR ADMINISTERING THE YEAR OF PATIENCE

11.6.1 *What procedure should the Local Spiritual Assembly follow when administering a year of patience?*

A suggested procedure is outlined below:-
1. attempt a reconciliation between the parties.
2. set the date for the beginning of the year of patience, notify both parties in writing, and record the date in the minutes (see 11.11 at the end of this Chapter for a suggested format for the letter).
3. ascertain that the extent of the husband's obligation to support his wife and any children of the marriage during the year of patience has been clarified.
4. ensure that suitable arrangements have been made for taking care of the children and any other dependents.
5. ensure that the couple are aware of the rules of conduct during the year of patience.
6. determine a suitable method of consultation with the couple to attempt reconciliation during the year.

The Universal House of Justice has said:-

> *Attempts at reconciliation should continue during the year of waiting.*
>
> (letter written on behalf of the Universal House of Justice to a National Spiritual Assembly, dated June 20, 1977)

This implies that the Local Spiritual Assembly should arrange such consultations more than once during the year. Further points to consider are as follows:-
   a) whether the couple will be counselled together or separately
   b) whether the Assembly will offer counselling as an Assembly or whether it will delegate the responsibility either to an individual or sub-committee of the Assembly, or to someone not on the Assembly, eg. a mature, deepened Bahá'í couple. If the Assembly does decide to delegate the responsibility for counselling, it nevertheless retains overall responsibility for ensuring that the matter is handled appropriately
   c) in determining the best procedure to follow the Local Spiritual Assembly should seek the advice and assistance of professional counsellors in the same way it would seek the advice of experts in other fields
7. if one party to the year of patience is a non-Bahá'í, the Assembly needs to consider its relationship to that person. Obviously, consultation with the non-Bahá'í spouse is desirable if possible.
8. advise the couple of marriage counselling services available and encourage them to use such a service. Ideally, Bahá'ís should be referred to Bahá'í marriage counsellors. Where none are available, however, it is recommended that the Local Spiritual

Assembly seek first to ascertain whether a particular counselling service holds views that are compatible with the Faith. Essentially this means that the counselling service should be focussing on trying to reconcile the couple. It would also be most helpful for the counsellor concerned to be made aware of the Bahá'í principles and teachings on divorce. Again, the Local Spiritual Assembly retains overall responsibility for any counselling process that is implemented. The National Spiritual Assembly is in the process of establishing a register of Bahá'í and non-Bahá'í agencies with expertise in counselling. A list of non-Bahá'í agencies is contained in 11.10.

9. send a copy of the letter granting the year of patience to the National Spiritual Assembly.
10. note the date on which the year of patience ends and record this date in the minutes.
11. notify the couple accordingly and remind them that the Local Spiritual Assembly must be given a copy of the civil "decree absolute" (not "nisi") before a Bahá'í divorce can be approved (see 11.12 at the end of this Chapter for a suggested format for such a letter).
12. file a copy of the "decree absolute", note the date on which it was granted in the minutes, and advise the couple concerned that their Bahá'í divorce is now finalised (see 11.13 at the end of this Chapter for a suggested format for such a letter).
13. send a copy of the letter granting the Bahá'í divorce to the National Spiritual Assembly.
14. the Local Spiritual Assembly should also advise the National Assembly in writing if the year of patience ends because the couple have been reconciled.

11.6.2 What should the Local Spiritual Assembly's attitude be towards the couple whose year of patience it is administering?

> *The administrators of the Faith of God must be like unto shepherds. Their aim should be to dispel all the doubts, misunderstandings and harmful differences which may arise in the community of the believers. And this they can adequately achieve provided they are motivated by a true sense of love for their fellow-brethren coupled with a firm determination to act with justice in all the cases which are submitted to them for their consideration.*
>
> (letter written on behalf of Shoghi Effendi to an individual believer, dated March 9, 1934)

The Local Spiritual Assembly needs to be aware of the following points when counselling a couple:-

1. Objectivity - it is important that the Local Spiritual Assembly remain completely objective in its assessment of the problem and not allow itself to be influenced by the personalities or views of those whom it is counselling.
2. Confidence - the Local Spiritual Assembly needs to show the couple that it is confident of its ability to provide effective counselling. This will be greatly facilitated if the Local Spiritual Assembly deepens on the relevant principles before the consultation.
3. Confidentiality - it is imperative that neither the local Assembly members, nor the parties being counselled, discuss the consultation outside the Assembly meeting. If the Local Spiritual Assembly appoints other believers in the community to counsel the couple it must ensure that they also are aware of the above principles and will abide by them. The Assembly must also ensure that the community as a whole observes these principles and does not take sides in the conflict.

CHAPTER ELEVEN

11.6.3 *Does the Local Spiritual Assembly have a counselling role or an adjudicatory role with regard to the couple?*

The Local Spiritual Assembly's role is advisory only. Its function is to assist the couple to work out their differences. Its function is not to lay down the law and tell the couple what they must do:-

> *In the opening paragraphs of your letter you speak of your Committee adjudicating upon divorce settlements, and the House of Justice feels that the use of the word 'adjudicate' may lie at the root of some of the problems that the committee is facing. In a country like the United Kingdom, where divorce is subject to the civil law, the function of the Assembly (or its committee) in dealing with a divorce case is not primarily a matter of adjudication. Its first duty is to try to reconcile the couple. If it finds that it is unable to do this, it then sets the beginning of the year of waiting and continues, as circumstances permit and wisdom dictates, throughout the running of the year, its attempts at reconciliation.*
>
> (letter written on behalf of the Universal House of Justice to a National Spiritual Assembly, dated February 24, 1983)

It is important to note that this applies to all aspects of the year of waiting and any subsequent divorce settlement: that is to say, the Local Spiritual Assembly has a counselling role in assisting the couple to reconcile; in assisting them to arrive at an amicable financial agreement during the year of patience; and to assist them in arriving at a just settlement relating to division of assets, custody of children, and so forth after the year of patience.

11.6.4 *What if the couple are unable to arrive at an amicable financial agreement during the year of patience?*

If the couple are unable to arrive at an amicable financial agreement, and the Local Spiritual Assembly is unable to assist them to arrive at such an agreement, the matter must be referred to the civil court for decision:-

> *One of the duties of the committee is to see that the requirements of Bahá'í Law governing the year of waiting are not violated - that is to say, that the two parties live apart and that proper provisions are made for the financial support of the wife and children. As you will see from the enclosures, this is a matter that needs to be considered for [each] case on its own merits. If the matter can be amicably arranged between the parties, well and good. If not, the basic principle of Bahá'í Law is that the husband is responsible for the support of his wife and children so long as they are married; that is until the granting of the divorce. In a particular case, however, it may have been the wife who was the bread-winner of the family or both the husband and wife may have been earning income. The Assembly should not ignore such specific situations and change them merely because a year of waiting is running. The application of these principles should not be in the form of an adjudication which the Assembly will require the couple to accept, but as a basis for an arrangement which the couple will amicably agree to and present to the Court for endorsement. If the Assembly is unable to get the couple to agree, it should leave the matter to the civil court.*
>
> (letter written on behalf of the Universal House of Justice to a

National Spiritual Assembly, dated February 24, 1983)

It follows from the above that the Local Spiritual Assembly should not insist upon seeking an amicable agreement over an extended period of time. If the Assembly has tried to achieve such an agreement and failed, it should, without further delay, advise the parties concerned to turn to the civil courts for a remedy.

11.6.5 *Do Bahá'í sanctions apply if a party fails to abide by the agreement reached?*

No. In the event of one or other party failing to abide by the financial agreement reached, Bahá'í sanctions do not apply, although civil sanctions do:-

> *While it is obvious that the Assembly should encourage the husband to honour his Bahá'í responsibilities in paying the required support money, matters of support may be covered by the civil courts when a civil divorce is applied for, and, in such a case, the wife would, of course, be able to invoke whatever civil remedy is available. In any case, at the present time National Spiritual Assemblies should not normally apply sanctions in cases of failure to comply with support requirements.*
>
> (letter written on behalf of the Universal House of Justice to a National Spiritual Assembly, dated February 6, 1978)

11.6.6 *What if one or both parties to the year of patience are serving on the Local Spiritual Assembly?*

Where one or both parties to the year of patience are serving on the Assembly, they may not feel comfortable discussing personal problems before their fellow Assembly members. In this case, the Assembly may consider the options outlined above, of delegating counselling either to an individual or sub-Committee of the Assembly, or to a mature, married couple not on the Assembly. The Assembly should also bear in mind the guidance contained in Chapter 2 on 'Consultation' concerning the presence of an Assembly member at a consultation in which that member's personal affairs are being discussed. In certain circumstances the National Spiritual Assembly may appoint an ad hoc committee to handle the matter, which could be made up of members of the community concerned and other nearby communities:-

> *In reply to your letter of February 4th asking whether you may assign personal problems which a Local Spiritual Assembly is unable to deal with to a nearby Local Spiritual Assembly, we feel that in such cases it would be better for your National Spiritual Assembly to appoint an ad hoc committee for each case, the membership of which could be drawn from one or two nearby communities as well as the community where the particular problem exists.*
>
> (letter from the Universal House of Justice quoted in a letter written on behalf of the Universal House of Justice to a National Spiritual Assembly, dated October 22, 1984)

Such a committee would report directly to the National Spiritual Assembly.

11.6.7 *Who administers the year of patience if one or both parties move to a new Assembly area?*

If one or both parties move to a new Assembly area the Local Spiritual Assemblies concerned should consult together on the best means by which to attempt a reconciliation. If the reconciliation fails they should decide between themselves which Assembly will be responsible

CHAPTER ELEVEN

for administering the year of patience. If they cannot decide this matter between themselves the National Spiritual Assembly must decide:-

> *When Bahá'í couples wish to establish year of waiting and they reside in different communities, it is incumbent on both local Assemblies to consult with each other and make an effort to effect a reconciliation with parties. If unsuccessful and they cannot agree on which Assembly should assume jurisdiction, it is within jurisdiction of National Assembly to decide.*
>
> (message from the Universal House of Justice, to a National Spiritual Assembly, dated May 14, 1987)

If one or both parties move to an area without a Local Assembly, the details must be sent to the National Spiritual Assembly and the parties informed accordingly.

11.6.8 **Who administers the year of patience if one or both parties moves to a new country?**

As a general principle it is not in the spirit of the Faith for a party to move so far away that attempts at reconciliation are not possible. The Local Spiritual Assembly should inform the party or parties concerned accordingly. If one or both parties insist upon moving, however, the Local Spiritual Assembly cannot prevent them from doing so. In the event of this occurring the Local Spiritual Assembly should contact the National Office for advice.

11.7 **ARRANGEMENTS AFTER THE DIVORCE**

11.7.1 **Does Bahá'í law require the husband to pay maintenance to the wife after completion of the year of patience?**

No. Bahá'í law only requires maintenance to be paid during the year of patience. On completion of that year, the Local Assembly has the duty to assist the couple to arrive at a just financial settlement:-

> *The only provision in Bahá'í Law regarding the support of the wife is that which makes the husband responsible for her support during the year of waiting. This does not mean, however, that further support is prohibited; all such matters will require legislation in the future. At the present time, it is the responsibility of the Assembly to arrange an amicable and just financial settlement between the couple, and any such arrangement must, obviously, take into consideration the financial situation of both parties and their relative responsibilities.*
>
> (letter from the Universal House of Justice to a National Spiritual Assembly, dated April 5, 1970)

11.7.2 **Can the husband demand refund of the dowry or marriage expenses in the event of divorce?**

No. Shoghi Effendi has said:-

> *Concerning...divorce: He has no right to demand from his wife a refund of the marriage expenses he incurred. In the Aqdas it is quite clear that the husband must not only give the dowry but must support his wife until the time when the divorce is completed. In view of this she is not required to repay expenses of the marriage, etc.*
>
> ("Dawn of a New Day", p.118)

11.7.3 **To what extent should the Local Spiritual Assembly involve itself in such matters as division of family assets, custody of children, etc?**

The Assembly should assist the couple concerned to reach agreement on these matters. This agreement then need only be submitted to the civil courts for ratification. If it is not possible to reach an agreement the parties concerned must take the matter to the civil court:-

> *...it is preferable for the Spiritual Assembly to try to arrange some amicable agreement between the parties concerning such matters as division of family assets, the custody of children and their support and education, rather than to let these things become the subject of dispute between the Bahá'ís in the law courts. Should a settlement be agreed, provision should be made for this to be submitted to the civil court for its endorsement and ratification, both to ensure that it complies with civil law and to avoid problems in case of a dispute in the future. If however, it proves impossible to reach an amicable agreement, the only recourse the couple will have will be to submit the matter to the decision of the civil courts.*
>
> (letter written on behalf of the Universal House of Justice to a National Spiritual Assembly, dated March 14, 1980)

Again, the Assembly must not unduly delay the parties from seeking a civil remedy if it is unable to bring about an agreement between them.

11.7.4 **What guidelines should the Local Spiritual Assembly follow when assisting a couple to make such arrangements?**

The Universal House of Justice has provided the following guidelines:-

> 1. *The decisions in each case must be made in light of the particular conditions of that case. The guidelines given below are general in nature and should be applied as far as possible unless there are compelling reasons to the contrary.*
>
> 2. *"Custody of Children"*
>
> a) *It is preferable that the couple should amicably agree on the custody of the children and submit their agreement to the Assembly for endorsement. Normally in the case of very young children custody is given to the mother unless there are compelling reasons which make this inadvisable.*
>
> b) *Regardless of which parent is given custody, the children should be so educated that they may develop a proper Bahá'í attitude towards, and due regard for, both parents. Fair and practical arrangements should be made to protect the rights of the parent not having custody to associate with the children and spend time with them.*
>
> c) *Usually custody arrangements continue until the child comes of age unless, of course, new circumstances transpire during this period which call for a review of the arrangements.*

CHAPTER ELEVEN

> 3. *"Financial Support"*
>
> *a) The husband is obligated to support the wife and children until the granting of the Bahá'í divorce. This normally takes place at the end of the year of waiting unless it has to be postponed pending the granting of a civil divorce.*
>
> *b) Following the granting of the divorce the father continues to be under the obligation of providing the necessary funds for the support of the children, but he has no continuing obligation to support his former wife.*
>
> (letter from the Universal House of Justice to a National Spiritual Assembly, dated January 13, 1983)

11.7.5 What role does the Local Spiritual Assembly have in enforcing decisions of the civil court?

Once the civil court has made its decision regarding financial settlement, etc., the couple, as Bahá'ís, have the obligation to obey it. Should they not do so, the Assembly should counsel them to obey:-

> *Once the divorce decree with its related provisions has been handed down by the court, it is the obligation of both parties, as good Bahá'ís, to obey it and, if either is lax in so doing, the Assembly should advise him or her about his or her duties and press for their fulfilment.*
>
> (letter written on behalf of the Universal House of Justice to a National Spiritual Assembly, dated January 13, 1983)

This does not negate the right of the wronged party to also appeal to the civil court for enforcement of its decision:-

> *The wronged party, however, should at the same time be left free to apply to the civil authorities for the enforcement of the decision. Unfortunately, such enforcement is notoriously difficult, especially when the parties subsequently reside in different countries. It is here that the action of the Spiritual Assembly, reinforcing the decision of the civil courts, can be of help.*
>
> (letter written on behalf of the Universal House of Justice to a National Spiritual Assembly, dated January 13, 1983)

11.7.6 Do sanctions apply to Bahá'ís who do not obey decisions of the civil court?

Sanctions only apply if the disobedience is particularly severe or if it involves failure to provide support for the children. Otherwise, enforcement should be left to the civil court:-

> *Except in circumstances of unusual gravity or cases where the responsible party fails to obey a court decision to provide support for the children, an Assembly should not contemplate imposing sanctions for lack of compliance in these matters. Actual enforcement should normally be left to the action of the civil courts.*
>
> (letter written on behalf of the Universal House of Justice to a National Spiritual Assembly, dated January 13, 1983)

All such cases must be referred to the National Spiritual Assembly for a decision.

CHAPTER ELEVEN

11.8 **ANNULMENT**

11.8.1 *Are there any circumstances under Bahá'í law in which a marriage can be annulled?*

A marriage may be annulled if an irreconcilable antipathy develops between the couple after the marriage ceremony and before the marriage is consummated:-

> *Should either party, following the recital of the specifically revealed verse and the payment of the dowry, take a dislike to the other, before the marriage is consummated, the period of waiting is not necessary prior to a divorce. The taking back of the dowry, however, is not permitted.*

(Bahá'u'lláh, "Synopsis and Codification of the Laws and Ordinances of the Kitáb-i-Aqdas", p.41)

Should any such case arise it must be referred to the National Spiritual Assembly.

11.9 **REGISTERED GROUPS**

Registered Groups do not have the authority to administer Bahá'í divorces. They do, however, have the responsibility of ensuring that their members are deepened in Bahá'í law. Bahá'ís wishing to apply for a year of patience in an area under the jurisdiction of a Registered Group, should contact the National Spiritual Assembly, which is the responsible body in such a situation.

11.10 **LIST OF APPROVED MARRIAGE COUNSELLING AND PRE-MARITAL EDUCATION ORGANISATIONS**

Following is a list of approved marriage counselling and pre-marital education organisations:-

NEW SOUTH WALES

Catholic Family Welfare Bureau 2 Hornsey Road HOMEBUSH WEST 2140 Ph: 764 4666

Church of England Marriage Guidance Centre 7th Floor, Fletcher Building 491 Kent Street SYDNEY 2000 Ph: 61 3946, 61 3214 (also regional office at Wollongong)

Family Life Movement of Australia 41 The Boulevarde LEWISHAM 2049 Ph: 560 3377 (also regional offices at Coffs Harbour, Dubbo, Gosford and Tamworth)

Marriage Guidance Council of New South Wales 36 Alfred Street, South, MILSONS POINT 2061 Ph: 929 7122 (also regional offices at Newcastle, Taree and Wollongong)

Methodist Marriage Guidance Council Pilgrim House 264 Pitt Street SYDNEY 2000 Ph: 26 3826

VICTORIA

Cairnmillar Institute Department of Marriage and the Family 100 Collins Street MELBOURNE 3000 Ph: 63 9876, 63 5853, 63 6269

Citizens Welfare Service of Victoria 197 Drummond Street CARLTON 3053 Ph: 3478933

Marriage Guidance Council of Victoria 46 Princess Street KEW 3101 Ph: 86 8512, 86 5354 (also regional offices at Albury, Ballarat, Bendigo, Echuca, Geelong, Horsham, Morewell, Sale, Shepparton, and Warragul)

Catholic Family Welfare Bureau 491 Nicholson Street NORTH CARLTON 3054 Ph: 347 6066 (also regional office at Geelong Church of England)

Marriage Guidance and Education Council 3rd Floor, Nicholas Building 37 Swanston Street MELBOURNE 3000 Ph: 63 7360, 63 7091

TASMANIA
Catholic Family Welfare Bureau 11 Harrington Street HOBART 7000 Ph: 23 2428, 23 2429

Tasmanian Marriage Guidance Council 24 Antill Street HOBART 7000 Ph: 23 6041 (also regional offices at Launceston and Penguin)

SOUTH AUSTRALIA
Adelaide Central Mission Marriage Counselling and Education Service 43 Franklin Street ADELAIDE 5000 Ph; 51 5355 (also regional offices at Mildura, Murray Bridge and Christies Beach)

Catholic Family Welfare Bureau 33 Wakefield Street ADELAIDE 5000 Ph: 223 6313

Marriage Guidance Council of South Australia 55 Hutt Street ADELAIDE 5000 Ph: 223 4566 (also regional centre at Elizabeth)

WESTERN AUSTRALIA
Catholic Marriage Guidance Council 27 Victoria Square PERTH 6000 Ph: 25 4232

Marriage Guidance Council of Western Australia 32 Richardson Street WEST PERTH 6005 Ph: 21 8904, 21 5058 (also regional offices at Bunbury and Fremantle)

QUEENSLAND
Catholic Family Welfare Bureau Morgan Street FORTITUDE VALLEY 4006 Ph: 52 4371/2 (also regional office at Burleigh Heads)

Queensland Marriage Guidance Council 159 St. Paul's Terrace BRISBANE 4000 Ph: 221 2005 (also regional offices at Cairns, Mackay, Gladstone, Rockhampton, Toowoomba and Townsville)

AUSTRALIAN CAPITAL TERRITORY
Canberra Marriage Guidance Council 115 London Ci rcuit CANBERRA CITY 2601 Ph: 48 0530, 47 0603

Catholic Welfare Organisation Strangways Street CURTIN 2605 Ph: 81 3999

NORTHERN TERRITORY
Darwin Marriage Guidance Council City Mutual Building Cavenagh Street DARWIN 5794 Ph: 81 8924

11.11 FORMAT OF LETTER FOR COMMENCEMENT OF THE YEAR OF PATIENCE

Below is a suggested format for a letter advising a couple of the date of the commencement of their year of patience:-

Dear Bahá'í Friend,

This is to advise you that the Assembly has accepted ... as the date for the commencement of your year of patience. In order to arrange appropriate counselling procedures for you during the year of patience, the Local Spiritual Assembly would like to meet with you both on .... The meeting will be at ...'s home, at ....pm. At this meeting the Local Spiritual Assembly also wishes to ensure that you have arrived at an amicable financial agreement and that arrangements are in place for taking care of the children. Should you have any queries please do not hesitate to contact the undersigned on ....

With loving Bahá'í greetings,

(Secretary)

cc National Spiritual Assembly

11.12 FORMAT OF LETTER FOR END OF THE YEAR OF PATIENCE

Following is a suggested format for a letter notifying a couple that their year of patience has ended:-

Dear Bahá'í Friend,

The Local Spiritual Assembly would like to advise you that your year of patience has expired as at ... There only remains for the Assembly to be given a copy of your decree absolute so that we may notify the National Spiritual Assembly and finalise your Bahá'í divorce. The Local Spiritual Assembly is responsible for the spiritual well being of the community, therefore, if there is anything that we can do for you, please feel free to contact us, with the assurance that any such consultation will remain completely confidential.

With loving Bahá'í greetings,

(Secretary)

cc National Spiritual Assembly

11.13 FORMAT OF LETTER FOR FINALISATION OF BAHÁ'Í DIVORCE

Following is a suggested format for a letter advising a couple that their Bahá'í divorce is now finalised:-

Dear Bahá'í Friend,

At the Assembly's meeting held on ... the Assembly noted the copy of the decree absolute certificate forwarded by ... as confirmation of civil divorce having been finalised. As this requirement has now been fulfilled, we wish to notify you that according to Bahá'í law, the Bahá'í divorce is now effective. With our loving prayers and best wishes for your future

With loving Bahá'í greetings,

(Secretary)

cc National Spiritual Assembly

CHAPTER ELEVEN

APPENDIX 1

L.S.A. CONSULTATION ON DOMESTIC PROBLEMS

(A Keynote address to national convention, BE146, by Auxiliary Board Member, Saffoura Chittleborough.)

Recently I attended a workshop on Marital Counselling conducted by Professor Neil Jacobson a renowned marital therapist from the United States, who has been working with couples for the last 15 years.

A number of points emerged in his Modes Approach that I feel are equally pertinent when we look at L.S.A.'s handling of domestic problems; be it, marital conflict, or interpersonal problems between Bahá'ís in the Community or the L.S.A.

The first point he emphasized which he saw crucial in effective counselling is:

1) Definition of the Problem

He stressed that therapists need to be extremely wary that they do not accept the couples definition of the problem, in that each partner views the other as the problem and the only way the marriage can be salvaged is for the therapist to become the arbitrator and prove them right and rebuke the other partner and demand them to change.

He emphasized that it is important to get the couple to view the problem in the relationship as Mutually Caused. Thus each partner needed to make changes to improve their marital satisfaction.

This point is most pertinent when the L.S.A. deals with marital and interpersonal conflicts. Invariably one party sees the other at fault and thus their agenda is for the L.S.A. to support them and mete out justice to the perceived transgressor.

In this process, often the friends attempt to direct and prescribe what course of action the L.S.A. needs to take.

It is vital that the L.S.A. is not influenced by personalities and is objective in its assessment of the problem and acts in accordance with the principles and teachings of the Faith.

The second point raised by him related to what he deemed.

2. Characteristics of good therapist
a) enthusiasm; b) optimism

To be effective the therapist needs to communicate enthusiasm and optimism about what he/she is doing. He pointed out effectiveness in therapy is not so much what technique you use but confidence in the technique. Thus if one is confident in one's approach and believes in it and communicates this with enthusiasm and optimism, this has a far greater impact.

This point is equally important in the L.S.A.'s approach in dealing with domestic problems. The L.S.A. needs to be confident about its ability to assist with the resolution of personal problems. One way it can achieve this is to ensure that :-

a) L.S.A. members are well informed about, principles teachings and policies. Preparation by members in reading the relevant text before meetings can certainly facilitate effective communication.

The sense of confidence is also engendered when:-

b) The L.S.A. members are cognizant of the following quote of 'Abdu'l-Bahá:

"These Spiritual Assemblies are aided by the Spirit of God. Their defender is Abdu'l-Bahá. Over them he spreadth His wings. What bounty is there greater than this?... They indeed, are the potent sources of the progress of man, at all times and under all conditions." (L.S.A. Compilation, p.3)

Thus confidence is engendered knowing there is divine assistance to draw on.

The third point raised by him was, one of the key factors for helping individuals to solve their personal problems is having:

3. Faith in the therapist
Unless the individual has confidence in the therapist, effective change will not occur.
Again relating this point to the L.S.A.'s effective intervention in personal problems, it is vital that the L.S.A. wins the confidence of the friends. Two factors are crucial.
a) Impartiality
If the friends are to develop confidence in their L.S.A.'s, then it is imperative that L.S.A. Members do not take sides. As this further fuels the existing conflict when <u>factions</u> are built and the community becomes polarized.
b) Confidentiality;
This is breached in two ways. i) When L.S.A. members talk about L.S.A. matters. ii) When members meeting with the L.S.A. talk outside the deliberation of the L.S.A.
On the issue of confidentiality, it cannot be overemphasised, as often breaches of this principle has caused havoc in the community and undermined the implementation of L.S.A. decisions.
The beloved Guardian warned:
"What makes the Bahá'ís think that when they sacrifice the spiritual laws the administrative laws are going to work? (Living the Life, p.31)

Thus recapitulating the 3 points mentioned
1. The L.S.A. defining the problem and not the individuals.
2. The L.S.A. being a) confident, b) enthusiastic and c) optimistic in discharging its responsibilities in accordance with the Divine Text.
3. The L.S.A. winning the confidence of the friends by being impartial and observing confidentiality.
I would like to end with the following quote of the Guardian in reference to Spiritual Assemblies.
"The administrators of the Faith of God must be like unto Shepherds. Their aim should be to dispel all the doubts, misunderstandings and harmful differences which may arise in the community of the believers. And this they can adequately achieve provided they are motivated by a true sense of love for their fellow brethren coupled with a firm determination to act with justice in all cases which are submitted to them for their consideration."

Saffoura Chittleborough
Auxiliary Board Member
for Protection for S.A. and N.T.

CHAPTER TWELVE

Chapter 12

12. Bahá'í Wills and Burial

12.1 BAHÁ'Í WILLS

12.1.1 *How is the information in this Section to be used?*

The information in this section is provided for the general guidance of the friends. It does not constitute legal advice; or advice on how to draw up a Bahá'í will. The Universal House of Justice has not issued specific instructions on how Bahá'ís should draw up their wills and has advised Assemblies against giving out legal advice. As noted below, believers should be advised to consult a solicitor for specific information about their particular situation.

12.1.2 *Does a Bahá'í have a duty to make a will?*

Yes:-
In the "Kitáb-i-Aqdas" Bahá'u'lláh has stated:

> *It is incumbent upon everyone to write his testament...*
>
> (quoted in a letter written on behalf of the Universal House of Justice to a National Spiritual Assembly, dated September 4, 1982)

12.1.3 *How old should a believer be before making a will?*

It is important for a person of legal age (at present, in Australia, 18 years), single or married, to make a will. It is a wise precaution and not a death warrant, and the best time to act is obviously when one is healthy, relaxed and not under pressure of any kind. Avoid rushing it.

12.1.4 *What is the purpose of a will?*

The purpose of a will is to enable individuals to:
- decide to whom their assets should go
- decide in what manner their assets should be distributed
- appoint an executor and trustee to carry out their wishes, eg. by investing wisely on behalf of an infant beneficiary.

The Universal House of Justice has said:-

> *According to the Teachings of Bahá'u'lláh, the making of a will is essentially an obligation of the individual Bahá'í. Each believer is free to dispose of his estate in whatever manner he chooses, within the limits imposed by civil law and after payment of burial expenses and other debts and obligations.*
>
> (letter written on behalf of the Universal House of Justice to a National Spiritual Assembly, dated October 1, 1980)

The friends should note that they are bound by the laws of the "Kitáb-i-Aqdas", which require that provision be made for payment of Huqúqu'lláh also:-

> *Any person is at liberty to will his possessions as he sees fit provided he makes provisions for the payment of Huqúqu'lláh and the discharge of his debts.*
>
> ("Synopsis and Codification of the Laws and Ordinances of the Kitáb-i-Aqdas", page 46)

CHAPTER TWELVE

In the "Kitáb-i-Aqdas" Bahá'u'lláh provided for the division of an estate if a believer did not leave a will. This is outlined in pages 43-6 in the section on 'Inheritance' in the "Synopsis and Codification of the Laws and Ordinances of the Kitáb-i-Aqdas". It should be noted that these provisions are not intended as advice for Bahá'ís to follow in creating a will. The inheritance laws revealed by Bahá'u'lláh cannot have any effect in Australia where, if an individual dies without leaving a will, statutes (ie. legislation passed by Parliament), govern the distribution of an estate.

12.1.5 *Is a Bahá'í permitted to challenge the provisions of a will?*

No:-

> *A person's will is sacred and therefore a Bahá'í is not permitted to challenge the provisions of another's will.*
>
> (letter written on behalf of the Universal House of Justice to a National Spiritual Assembly, dated September 4, 1986)

12.1.6 *Should a solicitor be consulted?*

Yes. The Universal House of Justice encourages this:-

> *The civil law in relation to the making of wills is sometimes quite complex. It is, therefore, highly advisable for an individual to consult a lawyer when he makes his will to ensure that his intention is not nullified by some possible breach of the requirements of the law in the drawing up or execution of the will.*
>
> (letter written on behalf of the Universal House of Justice to a National Spiritual Assembly, dated September 4, 1986)

Solicitors are trained to handle the intricacies of will-making and it is not an expensive service. A solicitor's expert advice can make substantial savings for the estate. A solicitor will also ensure that a document is signed and witnessed properly (very important for wills), that it will 'hold up' legally and that it expresses the person's intentions. Before consulting a solicitor, believers should think over what they want in their wills. The solicitor can then advise how this would best be done, or how to vary it if legally advisable. 12.8 contains material relating to Bahá'í matters that may be applicable in drawing up a will - for example, a legally valid clause for leaving a bequest to the National Spiritual Assembly. Local Spiritual Assemblies should make this statement known to Bahá'ís in their community and be prepared to make copies for any Bahá'í in the process of drawing up a will. Any queries should be directed to the National Office.

12.1.7 *Is a 'do it yourself' will a recommended alternative?*

Believers are advised not to use 'do it yourself' or 'home-made' will forms because of problems of interpretation or validity that may arise. So far as New South Wales law is concerned, for example, the Redfern Legal Centre advises that:
If a person draws up her or his own will, great care must be taken. If the formal requirements are not met, the will is not valid and when the will-maker dies, it is as if no will has been made.
("The Law Handbook", 3rd edition, p.671)

12.1.8 **What is the executor of a will?**

> *The executor of a will is the person named in the will to be responsible for carrying out its requirements after death. The will is primarily an instrument dealing with the transfer of assets to beneficiaries. The*

CHAPTER TWELVE

executor is bound to distribute assets as he or she is directed by the will, although State legislation allows the executor some flexibility in the manner in which this is to be done. Burial or funeral requirements, on the other hand, are not binding on the executor, although a sympathetic executor would endeavour to abide by the will-maker's wishes. It is, therefore, wise to appoint one or more Bahá'ís as executors, in order to ensure that the Bahá'í burial requirements are followed. It is important to provide copies of the will to the executors, as often the will is not located and read until after the funeral. It is important to note that, in the words of the Universal House of Justice, "neither the National or Local Spiritual Assemblies should be named as executor of a will."

(letter to a National Spiritual Assembly, dated January 4, 1971)

This prohibition also applies to the officers of an Assembly in their official capacity. Individuals should be appointed to fulfil this function..

12.1.9 **Who is the Public Trustee?**

In most states there are officials such as a Public Trustee and his local representatives who will draw up a will without charge, but this is on condition that the Public Trustee is made the sole executor. The Public Trustee will make a charge for acting in this capacity when the estate is probated and the conditions of the will carried out.

12.1.10 **Should the will include reference to Bahá'í funeral requirements?**

Yes, and the inclusion of this requirement in the will should be made known to the believer's Local Spiritual Assembly and relatives:-

The friends should be strongly advised to make Wills specifying that they want their funerals to be conducted under the auspices of the Bahá'í Faith or at least in conformity with its requirements and they should make this known both to the Local Spiritual Assembly and to their own relatives, while they are still alive. In this way it is quite possible that agreements may be reached with non-Bahá'í relatives before death takes place.

(letter from the Universal House of Justice, dated August 18, 1972)

As noted in the above statement, believers should seek the agreement of non-Bahá'í relatives to the Bahá'í funeral requirements, before death. Following is an example of how this part of a will may be worded:-
It is my desire that upon my death my body shall be buried in accordance with the ordinances of the Bahá'í Faith, that is to say that my body shall not be cremated nor should any embalming process be used, but that my body shall be buried at a place within one hour's journey from the place of my death and after a Bahá'í burial service arranged under the auspices of the Bahá'í Faith, or at least in conformity with its requirements.
If a Bahá'í wishes to leave his or her body to medical science, Shoghi Effendi suggested that the following provision be made in the will (drafted in appropriate terms by a solicitor):-

...that you wish your body to be of service to mankind in death, and that, being a Bahá'í, you request that your remains not be cremated and not be taken more than an hour's journey from the place you die.

(letter written on behalf of Shoghi Effendi to an individual believer,
dated March 22, 1957)

CHAPTER TWELVE

12.1.11 *How can a Bahá'í help to ensure that he or she will receive a Bahá'í burial?*

As wills are usually not read until after the funeral, each Bahá'í, especially where there are non-Bahá'í relatives, should give letters of instruction requesting a Bahá'í burial and the carrying out of Bahá'í law concerning the dead, to the following people and institutions:
- family members
- executor
- Local Spiritual Assembly

The letter should also include reference to leaving the body to medical science, or donating organs, if applicable. Bahá'ís should note, however, that letters of instruction are not legally binding. It is advisable, therefore, to seek the agreement of non-Bahá'í relatives to Bahá'í burial requirements before death.

12.1.12 *Should special provisions be made for children?*

If parents wish to make provision for the possibility of both pre-deceasing their children, they may state in their wills whom they wish to be guardians. Bahá'ís may wish their executors to also act as guardians of their children; or sometimes two Bahá'í couples may make a mutual arrangement to act as guardians for each others' children. Any such provision made in a will provides a strong indication of the wishes of the will-makers as to whom they wish to be guardians of their children. The National Spiritual Assembly requests the Bahá'ís not to appoint the Bahá'í institutions or their officers as guardians of infant children, and advises that if possible, they select individual Bahá'ís for this purpose, periodically up-dating the will if necessary. If they so choose, they might include a charge upon the guardians that the children have full access during their infant years to the Bahá'í community and Teachings. This would not be legally binding on the guardians, however; therefore, any Bahá'í wishing to include this charge should ensure that the appointed guardians are sympathetic.

12.1.13 *How may the Faith be made a beneficiary in a will?*

The Faith may be made a beneficiary in various ways, including the following:
1. a bequest
2. a percentage of a believer's gross estate designated to be made payable to the Faith
3. a residuary gift in which believers make specific bequests to provide for their families with the residue or remainder of the estate being given to the Faith
4. a remainder interest in a testamentary trust, wherein a believer gives a person the right to reside in a house until that person remarries, wishes to move elsewhere or dies; or the believer leaves a 'life estate' in the property to a person, eg. spouse, unmarried child, disabled person. On the beneficiary dying, etc., the 'remainder interest' may pass elsewhere, eg. to the Faith.

12.1.14 *How should bequests to the Faith be handled?*

Bequests to the Faith may be made to recognised Bahá'í Funds - local, national, continental or international. Believers wishing to bequeath funds to the Universal House of Justice should specify the National Spiritual Assembly as the beneficiary with the clear understanding that the National Spiritual Assembly is to receive the funds on behalf of the Universal House of Justice. Similar provision should be made for bequeathing property of a personal nature, or in the form of real estate, etc. Believers wishing to bequeath contributions in kind are asked by the Universal House of Justice to first make provision for their sale and then bequeath the proceeds (note this does not apply to items of historical and/or sentimental value to the Cause or to articles for the use of the World Centre, not intended to be sold). Bequests to the Continental Board of Counsellors for Australasia should be made to the 'Continental Bahá'í Fund for Australasia'. Bequests to the National Fund should be made through insertion into the will of the following clause:-

CHAPTER TWELVE

I give, devise and bequeath (insert details of bequest here) to the "National Spiritual Assembly of the Bahá'ís of Australia Incorporated", for the purpose of the promotion, protection and propagation of the Bahá'í Faith.

This clause covers bequests of funds, property, stocks, securities, and so on. Bequests to a local Fund should be made through insertion of a similar clause using the full legal name of the Local Spiritual Assembly. Bequests of property, money, stocks, securities, and so on, to unincorporated Local Spiritual Assemblies should be made to the National Spiritual Assembly 'on behalf of The Spiritual Assembly of the Bahá'ís of ...' (full title), as it is necessary that the National Spiritual Assembly hold the property on behalf of the Local Spiritual Assembly. Incorporated Local Spiritual Assemblies may receive bequests of property and cash directly. It is permissible, but not encouraged, to ear-mark bequests, eg. for a particular teaching programme, a special building project, and so on. A bequest may also include articles of interest to the Bahá'í archives, as well as books, documents and other papers of general Bahá'í interest.

12.1.15 *What should believers do with Bahá'í papers and correspondence?*

Believers are asked to make careful provision for Bahá'í documents in their wills, especially if they have non-Bahá'í relatives, by either bequeathing them to a Bahá'í institution or a trusted individual or authorising such an institution or individual to destroy or otherwise dispose of the papers in a fit manner.

12.1.16 *Once made, should a will be periodically up-dated?*

Yes. A will should be reviewed periodically and, if necessary, altered to cover changed circumstances. Note, for instance, that marriage automatically invalidates a will made prior to the marriage. Divorce or separation of the parties does not have the same effect. A will may be made prior to a marriage and expressed to be made in anticipation of the marriage between the will-maker and the intended spouse. A will made in this way will not be invalidated by that marriage.

12.1.17 *How are modifications made to a will?*

Modifications are usually made by drawing up a new will. Believers should consult their solicitors before making any changes.

12.1.18 *Where should a will be kept?*

It is necessary that people know where to find a will. Photocopies of the original executed will should be provided to the executors and a notation made on the copy as to the whereabouts of the original. Believers may want to give a copy to their Local Spiritual Assembly and to their relatives. The important point is that someone - either family, Local Spiritual Assembly, or executor - should know where to find it quickly. Copies should only be given to the National Spiritual Assembly, the Continental Board of Counsellors for Australasia or the Universal House of Justice if one of these institutions is to be the recipient of a bequest.

12.1.19 *Should pioneers make new wills when they settle overseas?*

Believers pioneering overseas are advised to inquire about the requirements regarding wills in their new country, as it may be necessary to make a new will.

CHAPTER TWELVE

12.2 BAHÁ'Í WILLS AND THE LOCAL SPIRITUAL ASSEMBLY

12.2.1 *What role has a Local Spiritual Assembly regarding the drawing up of wills?*

The Local Spiritual Assemblies do not have a role in:
- prescribing provisions for wills
- giving legal advice about the making of wills

They do have a role in:
- drawing to the believers' attention the obligation to make a will
- advising individuals to consult a solicitor in order to draw up a will
- supporting and enforcing the provisions of a will unless they are in conflict with the principles of the Faith
- informing individuals of the advisability of depositing copies of their wills with the Assembly:-

> *Shoghi Effendi urged Local Spiritual Assemblies to admonish the friends not to overlook the importance of wills. In letters written on his behalf we find the following important points.*
>
> 1. *The friends are free to formulate the provisions of their wills as they please, and the Spiritual Assembly has the obligation to support and enforce these provisions unless, of course, they are in conflict with the principles of the Faith.*
> 2. *While it is appropriate and advisable for the friends to deposit a copy of their wills with the Spiritual Assembly, they should not be required to do so, but should be left free in this matter.*
> 3. *It is not necessary for the Spiritual Assembly to publish the text of a 'model' will. Each believer should compose his will according to his own wish.*
>
> (letter written on behalf of the Universal House of Justice to a National Spiritual Assembly, dated September 4, 1986)

> *The Universal House of Justice has not issued specific instructions on the form and content of Wills of Bahá'ís. National and Local Spiritual Assemblies should likewise refrain, at this time, from issuing specific instructions on Wills. They may draw the attention of the believers, in a general way, to the obligation to make a Will, but should not prescribe provisions. Assemblies should not become involved in giving legal advice about the making of Wills, but may suggest that a qualified attorney be consulted.*
>
> (letter written on behalf of the Universal House of Justice to a National Spiritual Assembly, dated October 1, 1980)

12.2.2 *What should a Local Spiritual Assembly do if there are provisions in a will that conflict with the laws of the Faith (eg. a provision to be cremated)?*

Where a provision in a will conflicts with the laws of the Faith neither the Local Spiritual Assembly nor the Bahá'í relatives are permitted to fulfil it.

12.2.3 *What should a Local Spiritual Assembly do if acceptance of a bequest is dependent on fulfilling provisions in the will that are not in the best interests of the Faith?*

A Local Spiritual Assembly is honour bound to fulfil the provisions of a will if it accepts a bequest, therefore, if a provision would impose an unreasonable financial burden on an Assembly, or not be in the best interests of the Faith, the Assembly will have to refuse to accept the bequest:-

> *In the eyes of Bahá'í Law a will is sacred and thus, when a testator*

CHAPTER TWELVE

makes a bequest to a Spiritual Assembly and attaches thereto certain duties and conditions, the Assembly has the responsibility to fulfil them. However, if the will imposes an unreasonable financial burden or a condition which could become an unreasonable financial burden, or if fulfilment of the conditions would be prejudicial to the best interests of the Faith, the Assembly may have no alternative to refusing the bequest, for if it accepts the bequest it is in honour bound to fulfil the conditions.

(letter written on behalf of the Universal House of Justice to a National Spiritual Assembly, dated January 10, 1978)

12.2.4 *What should a Local Spiritual Assembly do if acceptance of a bequest is dependent on fulfilling provisions in the will that conflict with Bahá'í law?*

If a provision is contrary to Bahá'í law a Local Spiritual Assembly may not fulfil it, even if this means it cannot receive the bequest. If it is possible for the Assembly to refuse to fulfil a provision contrary to Bahá'í law and still receive the bequest, then it may do so:-

On the other hand, if the testator, being a Bahá'í, makes a provision in his will that is contrary to Bahá'í Law (eg. to bury his remains in a place more than one hour's journey from the place of death), that provision is null and void in Bahá'í Law and the Assembly must not fulfil it even if failure to do so would cause the bequest to be revoked in civil law. If failure to fulfil such a condition does not cancel the bequest in civil law, the Assembly is not required to refuse the bequest as it would have to do in the case of failure to fulfil a valid condition.

(letter written on behalf of the Universal House of Justice to a National Spiritual Assembly, dated January 10, 1978)

12.3 BAHÁ'Í BURIAL LAWS

12.3.1 What are the Bahá'í burial laws?

The Bahá'í burial laws are as follows:-

1. *...it is forbidden to carry the body for more than one hour's journey from the place of death...*

2. *...the body should be wrapped in a shroud of white silk or cotton...*

3. *...on [the body's] finger should be placed a ring bearing the inscription "I came forth from God, and return unto Him, detached from all save Him, holding fast to His Name, the Merciful, the Compassionate"...*

4. *...the coffin should be of crystal, stone or hard fine wood...*

5. *A specific Prayer for the Dead is ordained, to be said before interment.*

6. *..this law prohibits cremation of the dead...*

7. *The formal prayer and the ring are meant to be used for those who have attained the age of maturity.*

CHAPTER TWELVE

("Synopsis and Codification of the Laws and Ordinances of the Kitáb-i-Aqdas" note 30, pages 62-3)

12.3.2 *Which of the burial laws are presently binding upon believers in the West?*

The Universal House of Justice has said that the following laws are presently binding upon believers in the West:-

1. *to bury the body (not to cremate it)...*

2. *not to carry it more than a distance of one hour's journey from the place of death...*

3. *to say the Prayer for the Dead if the deceased is a believer over the age of 15...*

(letter from the Universal House of Justice to a National Spiritual Assembly, dated June 9, 1974)

12.3.3 *Which of the burial laws are presently binding on the Persian friends?*

All the burial laws are binding on the Persian friends. This Section, therefore, contains information regarding all the burial laws, not just those presently binding on the friends in the West. For a definition of a Persian believer see Chapter 10, Section 4, 'Does the law of the "Kitáb-i-Aqdas" regarding the period (ie. 95 days) of engagement apply in Australia?'

12.3.4 *What is the meaning of 'an hour's journey'?*

The Universal House of Justice has said that the distance of one hour may be calculated from the city limits of the city or town in which the believer passes away; and the journey may be undertaken by any method ie. land, sea or air. It is most important, however, to bear in mind the spirit of the law, which is that the body should be buried soon and in a nearby place:-

In the "Kitáb-i-Aqdas" Bahá'u'lláh states:

> *"It is forbidden you to carry the body more than an hour's distance from the town; bury it with tranquillity and cheer in a nearby place."*

The law applies to transportation by land as well as by sea, whether it be an hour's distance by boat or train. The purpose is the time-limit of one hour, no matter what means of conveyance is employed. However, the sooner the burial takes place, the more fitting and preferable. The Universal House of Justice advises that the place of death may be taken to be the city or town in which the believer passes away, and therefore the hour's journey may be calculated from the city limits to the place of burial. However, it should be borne in mind that the spirit of Bahá'u'lláh's law is to be buried near where one dies.

> *In light of the above, while transportation of the body by air is permissible, due consideration should always be given to the preference expressed by Bahá'u'lláh for the body to be buried soon and in a nearby place.*

(letter written on behalf of the Universal House of Justice to an individual believer, dated July 6, 1988)

12.3.5 *How should the body be prepared?*

> *The preparation for the body for burial is a careful washing, and placing in a shroud of white cloth, silk preferably.*

(letter written on behalf of Shoghi Effendi to an individual believer,

dated April 2, 1955)

Arrangements can be made with the Funeral Director for the members of a deceased person's family to wash and enshroud the body at the mortuary section of the funeral parlour. If someone passes away in hospital, the body is subsequently removed to a mortuary. In the case of someone passing away at home, the preparations may be carried out at home by members of the family. This would, however, only be done after a doctor has issued a certificate stating the cause of death, or an interim certificate.

12.3.6 *How should the shroud be wrapped?*

The Universal House of Justice has said:-

> *Although the Kitáb-i-Aqdas ordains that the body be wrapped in a shroud, there is nothing in the Writings to define how the wrapping is to be done. As to the wrapping of the body in the five pieces of the shroud, the friends are free to use their judgment in the matter until such time as the House of Justice may choose to legislate on it. In a letter dated 1 July 1943 to an individual believer, the beloved Guardian stated that if it is not possible to have five pieces, it is permissible to use one piece, either in silk or in cotton. No text has been seen permitting the dead to be dressed, instead of being wrapped in a shroud.*

(letter written on behalf of the Universal House of Justice to an individual believer, dated April 10, 1989)

12.3.7 *Where may burial rings be purchased?*

Burial rings may be purchased from Bahá'í Distribution Services Australia. Western friends are free to use burial rings if they wish. [On the purpose of the ring see "Lights of Guidance" {revised edition} no. 649.]

12.3.8 *Why is cremation not permissible?*

'Abdu'l-Bahá has explained that, according to the natural order and Divine Law, as the body has been formed gradually, so too it should be decomposed gradually. [See further "Lights of Guidance" {revised edition}, nos. 666, 668, 669.]

12.3.9 *May a foetus be cremated?*

It is preferable that a foetus not be cremated if this can be prevented:-

> *The letter from the Spiritual Assembly of ... indicates that the miscarriage took place when the mother was approximately four months into her pregnancy, therefore, they could have been assured that they did the right thing in having the foetus buried. Also, it would have been helpful for the Assembly to know that the hospital policy of incinerating a naturally aborted foetus is not in keeping with Bahá'í law which prohibits cremation.*

(letter written on behalf of the Universal House of Justice to a National Spiritual Assembly, dated December 3, 1973)

[See also "Lights of Guidance" {revised edition} no.641.]

12.3.10 *Is there a requirement that believers be buried facing the Qiblih in 'Akká'?*

The Universal House of Justice has said:-

CHAPTER TWELVE

The position of the body in the grave should be with the feet pointing toward the Qiblih, which is Bahjí in 'Akká'.

(letter from the Universal House of Justice to a National Spiritual Assembly, dated May 4, 1972)

The National Spiritual Assembly advises, however, that the position of the body in the grave is not an issue in Australia. The Universal House of Justice expects us to follow the customs of burial in Australia so that it should not be thought that strange rituals or customs are followed by Bahá'ís. Within the general guidance we have been given, it is up to the individual or the Assembly to decide what is most appropriate in the circumstances. There is no requirement for the coffin to face 'Akká', nor is this forbidden.

12.3.11 *May the body be embalmed?*

The body should not be embalmed unless it is a requirement of civil law, or circumstances do not permit the interment of the body to occur very soon after passing, in which case some form of temporary embalming may be used:-

Under the Bahá'í Teachings it seems clear that the body is not to be embalmed...The practice in the Orient is to bury the person within 24 hours of the time of death; sometimes even sooner; although there is no provision in the Teachings as to the time limit.

(letter written on behalf of Shoghi Effendi to an individual believer, dated April 2, 1955)

Embalming is not a requirement in Australian civil law.

12.4 BAHÁ'Í BURIAL SERVICE

12.4.1 *What is a Bahá'í burial service?*

The only obligatory part of the Bahá'í burial service is to read the Prayer for the Dead prescribed in the "Kitáb-i-Aqdas", before burial if the believer is 15 years of age or more. Further selections from the Writings may also be read. The Guardian strongly warned the believers against developing a definite system of rituals or practices. Rather, the service must be kept extremely simple:-

Regarding the Bahá'í funeral service: it is extremely simple, as it consists only of a congregational prayer to be read before burial!... your National Spiritual Assembly should take great care lest any uniform procedure or ritual in this matter be adopted or imposed upon the friends. The danger in this, as in some other cases regarding Bahá'í worship, is that a definite system of rigid rituals and practices be developed among the believers. The utmost simplicity and flexibility should be observed, and a selection from the Bahá'í Sacred Writings would serve the purpose at the present time, provided this selection is not rigidly and uniformly adopted on all such occasions.

(letter written on behalf of Shoghi Effendi, in "Principles of Bahá'í Administration" , p.14)

12.4.2 *Where can the Prayer for the Dead be found?*

The Prayer for the Dead can be found in "Prayers and Meditations" by Bahá'u'lláh, no.CLXVII, or in most available prayer books.

CHAPTER TWELVE

12.4.3 *How is the Prayer for the Dead to be read?*

The following guidance applies:-

> *The Prayer for the Dead is ... the only Bahá'í obligatory prayer which is to be recited in congregation; it is to be recited by one believer while all present stand. There is no requirement to face the Qiblih when reciting this prayer.*
>
> ("Synopsis and Codification of the Laws and Ordinances of the Kitáb-i-Aqdas", note 11, page 58)

> *The Prayer for the Dead should be read in its entirety by one person, while all others stand in silence. It is not the practice for those present to repeat any part of the prayer in unison.*
>
> (letter written on behalf of the Universal House of Justice to a National Spiritual Assembly, dated May 22, 1987)

[See also "Lights of Guidance" {revised edition} no.1503.]

Note that it is permissible to change the gender of the pronoun when reading the Prayer for the Dead (see "Lights of Guidance" {revised edition} no.660).

12.4.4 *May non-Bahá'ís be present at a Bahá'í funeral service?*

Yes:-

> *There is no objection whatsoever to non-Bahá'ís being present when the long prayer for the dead is read, as long as they respect our manner of reading it by rising and standing as the Bahá'ís do on this occasion. Nor, indeed, is there any objection to non-Bahá'ís being present during the reading of any Bahá'í prayer for the departed.*
>
> (letter written on behalf of Shoghi Effendi to a National Spiritual Assembly, dated July 20, 1946)

12.4.5 *Who is responsible for organising the burial service?*

The relatives of the deceased and/or the executor of the will are responsible for organising the burial service. The Local Spiritual Assembly is responsible for ensuring that this is done according to Bahá'í law. It is desirable, therefore, that there be cooperation between the family and the relevant Local Spiritual Assembly. [See further Section 5 of this Chapter.]

12.4.6 *Who conducts a Bahá'í burial service?*

It is for the relatives and/or the executor to decide who will conduct the service:-

> *As a funeral is not a legal ceremony...the family of the deceased may want some particular Bahá'í friend to officiate.*
>
> (letter written on behalf of Shoghi Effendi to a National Spiritual Assembly, dated July 20, 1946)

12.4.7 *May a Bahá'í burial service be conducted for non-Bahá'í?*

There is no objection to Bahá'ís organising a funeral service for a non-Bahá'í, consisting of readings from the Bahá'í Writings, if requested to do so; however, the Prayer for the Dead may only be said for Bahá'ís over the age of 15:-

> *An official Bahá'í funeral service should only be given for a believer,*

but there is no objection to the reading of Bahá'í prayers, or indeed to a Bahá'í conducting the funeral service of a non-Bahá'í, if this has been requested.

(letter written on behalf of Shoghi Effendi to a National Spiritual Assembly, dated July 20, 1946)

Concerning your question whether a Bahá'í burial service can be conducted for non-Bahá'ís if requested by them; if non-Bahá'ís desire that the believers should conduct such a service, there is no objection at all.

(letter written on behalf of Shoghi Effendi to a National Spiritual Assembly, dated April 19, 1941)

12.4.8 *May Bahá'ís without voting rights have a Bahá'í burial service?*

Yes:-

He [a believer deprived of his voting rights] may have the Bahá'í burial service if he or his family requests it ...

(from an attachment to a letter written on behalf of the Universal House of Justice to a National Spiritual Assembly, dated December 9, 1985)

12.4.9 *Are memorial gatherings permissible?*

The Universal House of Justice advises:-

As you know, the offering of prayers on behalf of the departed, whether Bahá'ís or non-Bahá'ís, is encouraged in our Teachings, as such prayers are conducive to the progress of their souls in the world beyond. As to the holding of memorial gatherings at regular intervals, there is nothing in the Teachings specifically prohibiting such gatherings, but we find general guidelines in the letters of the beloved Guardian, in which he warns the believers against adhering to the rites and customs of past systems and of former religions, and instead urges them to show forth the Bahá'í way of life and demonstrate the independent character of the Teachings of the Faith. Advertising memorial gatherings by the family is entirely a personal matter for the family to decide. It is left to the discretion of your National Spiritual Assembly whether Local Spiritual Assemblies may permit the use of their Bahá'í Centres for such gatherings.

(letter written on behalf of the Universal House of Justice to a National Spiritual Assembly, dated May 24, 1974)

12.5 BAHÁ'Í BURIAL LAWS AND THE LOCAL SPIRITUAL ASSEMBLY

12.5.1 *Which Bahá'í institutions should be notified when a believer passes away?*

The Local Spiritual Assembly of the area in which the believer lives should be immediately notified. The Local Spiritual Assembly of the area in which the believer passed away should also be notified (if this is different from the area of residence). The wishes of the relatives and the practicalities of the situation will determine which Assembly should be contacted regarding burial arrangements. It would also be courteous to contact the Local Spiritual Assembly of the area in which the believer is to be buried, if this is different again. If the believer does not live in a Local Spiritual Assembly area, or passes away in an area in which there is no Assembly, the National Spiritual Assembly should be notified.

12.5.2 *What responsibility has the Local Spiritual Assembly for the burial service?*

The relatives of the deceased and/or the executor of the will are responsible for organising the burial service. The Local Spiritual Assembly is responsible for ensuring that this is done according to Bahá'í law:-

> *Local Spiritual Assemblies, which are embryonic Local Houses of Justice, should develop as rallying centres of the community. They must concern themselves not only with teaching the Faith, with the development of the Bahá'í way of life and with the proper organisation of the Bahá'í activities of their communities, but also with those crucial events which profoundly affect the life of all human beings: birth, marriage, and death...*
>
> *The burial of the dead is an occasion of great solemnity and importance, and while the conduct of the funeral service and the arrangements for the interment may be left to the relatives of the deceased, the Local Spiritual Assembly has the responsibility for educating the believers in the essential requirements of the Bahá'í law of burial as at present applied, and in courteously and tactfully drawing these requirements to the attention of the relatives if there is any indication that they may fail to observe them...In some parts of the world, if Local Spiritual Assemblies fail to carry out these sacred duties, some believers might gradually drift away from the Faith and even pay dues to churches or other religious organisations to ensure that, when they require to register the birth of a child, to solemnise a marriage or to have a funeral service, there will be a religious institution ready to perform the necessary services. Conversely, when Local Assemblies have arisen to carry out these responsibilities, the believers have acquired a sense of security and solidarity, and have become confident that in such matters they can rely upon the agencies of the World Order of Bahá'u'lláh.*
>
> (letter from the Universal House of Justice to all National Spiritual Assemblies, dated April 17, 1981)

It is desirable, therefore, that there be cooperation between the family and the relevant Local Spiritual Assembly. Assemblies should particularly note their responsibility to keep in touch with elderly believers who are no longer able to be active in the community. Where this has not been done it has been known for such believers to pass away without the Local Spiritual Assembly becoming aware of it until months afterwards. In such instances, non-Bahá'í families have sometimes made funeral arrangements either disregarding or in ignorance of the Bahá'í laws regarding burial. Also note that if the family is not able to provide for a proper burial, the Local Spiritual Assembly has a responsibility to do so:-

> *When a Bahá'í in a community has passed away, for whatever cause, the Local Spiritual Assembly, or the National Spiritual Assembly, as the case may be, does have a responsibility to provide for a proper burial which cannot be provided for either by the family or by insurance.*

CHAPTER TWELVE

(letter from the Universal House of Justice to a National Spiritual Assembly, dated August 17, 1969)

12.5.3 **What should a Local Spiritual Assembly or Bahá'í relatives do if they find that a believer has made plans to be cremated, or other plans that are contrary to Bahá'í law?**

Neither a Local Spiritual Assembly, nor Bahá'í relatives, may be involved in burial arrangements that contravene Bahá'í law. Rather, the Bahá'í law must be followed, unless there is some reason in civil law that prevents this from being done. The Assembly may not be involved in arrangements that contravene Bahá'í law even if they are required by the civil law:-

> *As was explained to your Assembly in a letter written on behalf of the Universal House of Justice on 10 January 1978, if a Bahá'í makes a provision in his will that is contrary to Bahá'í Law, that provision is null and void in Bahá'í Law, and neither the Bahá'í relatives nor the Spiritual Assembly are permitted to fulfil it. Thus, if a Bahá'í states in his will that his remains are to be cremated he should, nevertheless, be buried in accordance with Bahá'í Law unless there is some element of the civil law [that] would prevent such an occurrence - in which case the civil law would have to be followed, but the Assembly, as indicated above, could take no part in it...*

(letter written on behalf of the Universal House of Justice to a National Spiritual Assembly, dated December 9, 1984)

> *Obviously a Spiritual Assembly cannot itself arrange for the cremation of the remains of a Bahá'í even if it was that person's wish that his body be disposed of in this way. Bahá'í relatives, likewise, are under the obligation of obeying the Bahá'í law and must not agree to the cremation of a Bahá'í.*

(letter written on behalf of the Universal House of Justice to a National Spiritual Assembly, dated December 9, 1984)

> *On the other hand, if the testator, being a Bahá'í, makes a provision in his will that is contrary to Bahá'í law (eg. to bury his remains in a place more than one hour's journey from the place of death), that provision is null and void in Bahá'í law and the Assembly must not fulfil it...*

(letter written on behalf of the Universal House of Justice to a National Spiritual Assembly, dated January 10, 1978)

12.5.4 **How may the Local Spiritual Assembly prevent such situations from arising?**

The Local Spiritual Assembly has a responsibility to educate believers in the burial requirements so that such situations do not arise:-

> *...the Local Spiritual Assembly has the responsibility for educating the believers in the essential requirements of the Bahá'í law of burial as at present applied...*

(letter from the Universal House of Justice to all National Spiritual Assemblies, dated April 17, 1981)

> *Whereas believers should be informed of the Bahá'í law of burial and*

CHAPTER TWELVE

urged to ensure that their remains are not cremated this is a matter of education and not one involving the imposition of sanctions.

(letter from the Universal House of Justice)

12.5.5 **What should the Assembly and believers do if non-Bahá'í relatives organise a non-Bahá'í funeral service for a Bahá'í?**

The Assembly should attempt to persuade the non-Bahá'í relatives to permit a Bahá'í funeral service to take place. Should it not succeed, however, the Bahá'ís may still attend the service and should attempt to offer Bahá'í prayers for the progress of the believer's soul, either at the service or at another time:-

Concerning the burial of a Bahá'í youth, if the burial has not taken place and there is time to do so, the non-Bahá'í family should be advised that the deceased is a Bahá'í (assuming they do not already know it), and every effort should be made to induce the family to allow the body of their deceased Bahá'í relative to be buried according to the requirements of his Faith. However, if they remain adamant, or if the burial has already taken place, there is nothing which can be done except, perhaps, to say prayers for the deceased.

(letter from the Universal House of Justice to a National Spiritual Assembly, dated December 20, 1976)

There is no objection to Bahá'ís attending the non-Bahá'í funeral service of a Bahá'í whose non-Bahá'í relatives have prevented the Bahá'í funeral from taking place. The Bahá'ís should, however, endeavour to offer Bahá'í prayers for the progress of the soul of their departed friend, if circumstances permit. If they cannot be offered on the occasion of the funeral they should be offered at another time.

(letter from the Universal House of Justice to a National Spiritual Assembly, dated May 4, 1966)

12.5.6 **What should the Assembly and believers do if non-Bahá'í relatives have charge of the body and plan to cremate it?**

As above. If the Assembly discovers that the non-Bahá'í relatives intend to cremate the body, the Local Spiritual Assembly should do all it can to explain the Bahá'í attitude to the relatives and prevent the cremation. If the Assembly is not successful, the friends may, nevertheless, attend the service and cremation, and may offer prayers for the progress of the departed soul. The Assembly may not be officially involved in the cremation, but may arrange a meeting at a different time to say the Prayer for the Dead:-

Where non-Bahá'í relatives of the deceased Bahá'í have charge of the body and are proposing to cremate the remains, the responsible Spiritual Assembly should do all it can to explain the Bahá'í attitude to the relatives in an effort to prevent the cremation. If these efforts fail, the Assembly can have nothing officially to do with the cremation of the body; the believers, however, are free to do as they wish about attending the funeral and the cremation and they may certainly offer a prayer for the progress of the soul of the deceased. The Assembly could, if it seemed appropriate, arrange a meeting at a time other than the funeral, at which the Prayer for the Dead could be said on behalf of the deceased.

CHAPTER TWELVE

(letter written on behalf of the Universal House of Justice to a National Spiritual Assembly, dated December 9, 1984)

12.5.7 ***How else may a Local Spiritual Assembly help to ensure that the friends receive a Bahá'í burial?***

Local Spiritual Assemblies may like to provide local funeral directors in their area with information about the Faith and Bahá'í burial laws. 12.9 contains a sample letter that may be sent to funeral directors.

12.5.8 ***Should a Local Spiritual Assembly keep a register of deaths of community members?***

Yes. The Local Spiritual Assembly should maintain a register in which should be entered the date of the believer's death, the place the believer is buried and the plot number. The Local Spiritual Assembly must also notify the National Spiritual Assembly of the death on the records form provided for this purpose.

12.6 BAHÁ'Í CEMETERIES

12.6.1 ***Should a Local Spiritual Assembly purchase burial plots or initiate a Burial Fund?***

In making such a decision the following points need to be considered:-
1. In a letter written on his behalf Shoghi Effendi said:-

> *The Guardian thinks the ideal thing would be for the believers to have a cemetery.*

(letter to an individual believer, dated September 5, 1950)

2. Funds should not be diverted from the goals of the current Plan to acquire cemeteries or burial plots:-

> *While it is desirable that the Bahá'ís have their own cemeteries or burial plots, funds needed to attain the objectives of the Nine Year Plan should not be diverted to this purpose.*

(letter from the Universal House of Justice to the National Spiritual Assembly of Australia, dated August 28, 1967)

3. There is no requirement that Bahá'ís be buried in plots specifically allocated or purchased for Bahá'ís:-

> *Mr. and Mrs. ... are naturally quite free to be buried in their own plot in the Cemetery, if that is what they desire.*

(letter written on behalf of Shoghi Effendi to a National Spiritual Assembly, dated July 20, 1946)

> *There is no objection to Bahá'ís being buried in the general section of a cemetery.*

(letter from the Universal House of Justice to a National Spiritual Assembly, dated August 28, 1967)

4. At present, in Australia, individuals usually purchase their own burial plots.
   It is permissible to accept free plots of land from government authorities for use as Bahá'í cemeteries.

In Australia, it is often possible to arrange to have sections of a cemetery allocated to particular religious groups, free of charge, and some Bahá'í communities have done this.

CHAPTER TWELVE

5. Only incorporated Local Spiritual Assemblies may own property - including burial plots or cemeteries - in Australia.
6. Bahá'í cemeteries or burial plots, once acquired, must be properly maintained which will require expenditures of time, money, and human resources. Local Spiritual Assemblies should consider carefully the above factors before making a decision to acquire a cemetery or burial plots. One option an Assembly may consider is to start up a local Fund to acquire a cemetery or plots in the future.

12.6.2 *Who is responsible for maintaining graves in which Bahá'ís are buried?*

Local Spiritual Assemblies should ensure that Bahá'í graves in cemeteries within their area of jurisdiction are being properly maintained. Where they are not owned by the Assembly and are the responsibility of the civic authorities, the Assembly should check that the civic authorities are taking proper care of them.

12.6.3 *May more than one person be buried in a single grave?*

Shoghi Effendi expressed a preference for individuals to have their own graves; however, this is not a binding ruling and the friends may decide for themselves:-

Regarding burying more than one person in a single grave, the Guardian's statement that 'It is better and more appropriate to assign a grave for every dead person' expresses a preference, but is not given as a binding ruling. Moreover, the House of Justice has not legislated upon the question of what exactly constitutes a 'grave', nor does it wish to legislate on such details of the burial laws at the present time. Individual friends, therefore, are free to use their own discretion.

(letter written on behalf of the Universal House of Justice to an individual believer, dated April 10, 1989)

12.6.4 *How should Bahá'í graves be marked?*

There is no requirement in the Bahá'í Writings that Bahá'í graves be marked. Normally the family of the deceased is responsible for any marker erected. Shoghi Effendi has indicated that excerpts from the Sacred Writings may be used on tombstones, as may the nine pointed star; however, it would be inappropriate to use any form of the Most Great Name or the ringstone symbol:-

The Universal House of Justice has received your letter of 22 August 1975, about the marking of Bahá'í graves. We have been asked to tell you that nothing has been found in the Writings making this a requirement. However, in Bahá'í cemeteries in 'Akká' and Haifa, the graves are marked and some of the words on the headstones are those of Bahá'u'lláh, 'Abdu'l-Bahá and Shoghi Effendi. As you know, Shoghi Effendi indicated that the Most Great Name would not be appropriate for gravestones and has suggested that such inscriptions as a nine pointed star and extracts from the Writings would be suitable.

(letter written on behalf of the Universal House of Justice to a National Spiritual Assembly, dated November 13, 1975)

There is no reason why the word Bahá'í should not appear in the centre of a nine-pointed star on the tombstone of dear ... but the ringstone emblem should not be used, nor the Greatest Name. Shoghi Effendi feels it is better not to put the Greatest Name on Bahá'í graves.

CHAPTER TWELVE

It is not forbidden to do so, but inappropriate.

(letter written on behalf of Shoghi Effendi to an individual believer, dated September 30, 1955)

Normally the building of structures or headstones on graves should be left to the family of the deceased, and all expenses should be covered by them.

(letter from the Universal House of Justice to a National Spiritual Assembly, dated May 4, 1972)

[See also "Lights of Guidance" {revised edition} nos. 656, 672.]

12.6.5 *What other guidance is available regarding Bahá'í cemeteries?*

The following guidance is available in "Lights of Guidance" {revised edition}:
1. the appearance of the cemetery - see no. 654
2. Bahá'ís without voting rights may be buried in Bahá'í cemeteries - see - no.655
3. non-Baha'is may be buried in Bahá'í cemeteries - see no.655

12.7 OTHER MATTERS

12.7.1 *What happens if a Bahá'í dies at sea?*

At present, death at sea is covered by the relevant civil or maritime laws; however, the burial should take place on land whenever possible.
[See further "Lights of Guidance" {revised edition}, no. 643.]

12.7.2 *May Bahá'ís donate their bodies for medical science?*

Yes, provided that the remains are buried according to Bahá'í law. Bahá'ís who wish to do this should make appropriate provision in their wills:-

There is nothing in the Teachings against leaving our bodies to medical science. The only thing we should stipulate is that we do not wish to be cremated, as it is against our Bahá'í laws. As many people make arrangements to leave their bodies to medical science for investigation, he suggests that you inquire, either through some lawyer friend or through some hospital, how you could do this, and then make the necessary provision in your will, stipulating that you wish your body to be of service to mankind in death, and that, being a Bahá'í, you request that your remains not be cremated and not be taken more than an hour's journey from the place you die. The spirit has no more connection with the body after it departs, but as the body was once the temple of the spirit, we Bahá'ís are taught that it must be treated with respect.

(letter written on behalf of Shoghi Effendi to an individual believer, dated March 22, 1957)

12.7.3 *It is also possible to donate organs:-*

Concerning your question about the Teachings of the Faith in connection with donating or receiving human organs, in a letter dated 6 September 1946 written on behalf of the beloved Guardian, it was stated that there was nothing in the Teachings which would forbid a Bahá'í to bequeath his eyes to another person for a hospital, adding

CHAPTER TWELVE

that it seemed a noble thing to do.

(letter written on behalf of the Universal House of Justice to a
National Spiritual Assembly, dated October 1, 1984)

12.7.4 **What is the Bahá'í view on euthanasia and life-support systems?**

Generally, the Writings indicate that God, the giver of life, may alone dispose of it. Until such time as the Universal House of Justice legislates on these matters, however, it is left to the consciences of those responsible:- As to whether a Bahá'í may stipulate in his will, that the life-supporting medical equipment by turned off, in the event of a very serious accident that would deprive him of his mental faculties and where there is no chance of recovery, the following excerpt from a letter written on behalf of the Universal House of Justice to a Local Spiritual Assembly, bears on this subject:

> *...we are asked to say that, in general, our Teachings indicate that God, the Giver of life, can alone dispose of it as He deems best. The Universal House of Justice has found nothing in the Sacred Text about the matter of withholding or removing life support in disabling or terminal illnesses where intervention prolongs life. Therefore, until such time as the House of Justice considers legislation on these matters, it is left to the conscience of the individual concerned whether or not to subscribe to a 'living will'.*

(from the Research Department to the Universal House of Justice,
dated October 22, 1985)

[See also "Lights of Guidance" {revised edition} no.985.]

12.7.5 **What if a Bahá'í suicides?**

Although suicide is condemned, a person does not cease to be a Bahá'í because he or she has committed suicide. This means that such a person should still be buried according to Bahá'í law. [See also "Lights of Guidance" {revised edition} nos. 674-78.]

12.8 **SUMMARY OUTLINE FOR SOLICITORS**

The Bahá'í Faith is a world religion, founded in 1844 in Iran, whose central principles are a belief in one God, oneness of religion, and the unification of mankind. Its main tenets include independent search for truth, eradication of all prejudices, the equality of men and women, universal education, and establishment of a universal auxiliary language. Bahá'u'lláh, the Prophet-Founder of the Bahá'í Faith made it incumbent upon every Bahá'í to have a Will.

12.8.1 **BEQUESTS AND OTHER GIFTS TO THE FAITH**

Bequests to the Faith may be made to recognised Bahá'í Funds - local, national, continental or international. When bequeathing funds to the Universal House of Justice (the international head of the Faith) the National Spiritual Assembly should be specified as the beneficiary with a clear direction that the National Spiritual Assembly is to receive the funds on behalf of the Universal House of Justice. Similar provision should be made for bequeathing property of a personal nature, or in the form of real estate, etc. If the bequest is to be a contribution in kind, provision should first be made for the sale of the item, then the proceeds from the sale may be bequeathed (note this does not apply to items of historical and/or sentimental value to the Faith or to articles for the use of the Bahá'í World Centre, not intended to be sold). Bequests to the Continental Board of Counsellors for Australasia should be made to the 'Continental Bahá'í Fund for Australasia'. Bequests to the National Spiritual Assembly Fund should be made through insertion into the will of the following clause:-

CHAPTER TWELVE

I give, devise and bequeath (insert details of bequest) to the "National Spiritual Assembly of the Bahá'ís of Australia Incorporated", for the purpose of the promotion, protection and propagation of the Bahá'í Faith.

This clause covers bequests of funds, property, stocks, securities, and so on. Bequests to a local Fund should be made through insertion of a similar clause using the full legal name of the Local Spiritual Assembly. Bequests of property to unincorporated Local Spiritual Assemblies should be made to the National Spiritual Assembly 'on behalf of The Spiritual Assembly of the Bahá'ís of ...' (full title), as it is necessary that the National Spiritual Assembly hold the property on behalf of the Local Spiritual Assembly. Incorporated Local Spiritual Assemblies may receive bequests of property directly.

12.8.2 BURIAL REQUIREMENTS

Bahá'ís are recommended to make provision in their wills to be buried according to the Bahá'í burial laws. The necessary information is contained in the following statement, which is also an example of how a reference in the will may be worded:-
It is my desire that upon my death my body shall be buried in accordance with the ordinances of the Bahá'í Faith, that is to say that my body shall not be cremated nor should any embalming process be used, but that my body shall be buried at a place within one hour's journey from the place of my death and after a Bahá'í burial service conducted under the auspices of the Bahá'í Faith, or at least in conformity with its requirements.

12.8.3 LEGAL TITLE OF THE NATIONAL SPIRITUAL ASSEMBLY

The full title of the National Spiritual Assembly is 'National Spiritual Assembly of the Bahá'ís of Australia Incorporated'. This is also the title of the body corporate. The registered office of the National Spiritual Assembly is:
Bahá'í Temple Gardens
Mona Vale Road
INGLESIDE NSW 2101

12.8.4 INCORPORATION OF THE NATIONAL AND LOCAL SPIRITUAL ASSEMBLIES

The National Spiritual Assembly is incorporated under the laws of the Australian Capital Territory. However, Local Spiritual Assemblies are incorporated within their respective States; for example, the Spiritual Assembly of the Bahá'ís of Brisbane Incorporated is incorporated under Queensland law.

12.8.5 EXECUTOR

Neither the National Spiritual Assembly or any Local Spiritual Assemblies, or their officers, should be made executors of a will.

12.8.6 GUARDIANSHIP

Neither the National Spiritual Assembly or any Local Spiritual Assemblies, or their officers, should be made guardians of infant children.

12.8.7 COPY

If the National Spiritual Assembly has been made a beneficiary of the will please send a copy to:
National Spiritual Assembly of the Bahá'ís of Australia
PO Box 285
MONA VALE NSW 2103

If the Continental Board of Counsellors for Australasia, or the Universal House of Justice have been made beneficiaries of the will, copies may be sent to the above address for forwarding to the appropriate institution if the believer so chooses.

12.8.8   **FURTHER QUESTIONS?**

If you have any questions please contact:
Bahá'í National Office
PO Box 285
MONA VALE NSW 2103
Ph: (02) 913 2771/2
Fax: (02) 913 2169

12.9   **SAMPLE LETTER TO FUNERAL DIRECTORS**

Dear

The Local Spiritual Assembly of the Bahá'ís of ..... is the local governing body of the Bahá'í community of ..... We are writing to provide you with some information for your files regarding Bahá'í funeral requirements as we anticipate you may need this information some time in the future. The Bahá'í Faith is a world religion, founded in 1844 in Persia, whose central principles are a belief in one God, oneness of religion, and the unification of mankind. Its main tenets include independent search for truth, eradication of all prejudices, the equality of men and women, universal education, and establishment of a universal auxiliary language. Bahá'u'lláh, the Prophet-Founder of the Bahá'í Faith, laid down the following laws regarding burial:

a) it is a law of the Bahá'í Faith that a Bahá'í is to be buried within one hour's journey from the place of death;
b) it is a law of the Bahá'í Faith that a Bahá'í is not to be cremated;
c) Bahá'ís are not to be embalmed;

The Spiritual Assembly named on this letterhead should be contacted immediately in order that a Bahá'í funeral may be arranged in association with the deceased's family; further laws that may be applicable in certain situations may be advised by the above Bahá'í institution.

We trust that this information will be of assistance to you. Should you require any further details, please do not hesitate to contact the undersigned. We enclose, for your information, a pamphlet on the Bahá'í Faith.

Yours sincerely,

Spiritual Assembly of the Bahá'ís of .....
Secretary

CHAPTER THIRTEEN

Chapter 13

13. Inter-Community Activities

13.1 INTRODUCTION

13.1.1 *What are inter-community activities?*

Inter-community activities are projects involving collaboration between Local Spiritual Assemblies, groups and isolated believers. They include such things as:
- advertising campaigns in major newspapers, radio and television
- the opening and maintaining of an information centre
- entering a float in a parade
- mounting an exhibition at a show
- organising a peace exposition
- organising a major teaching campaign into unopened areas

13.1.2 *Does the National Spiritual Assembly encourage inter-community activities?*

Yes. The National Spiritual Assembly recommends inter-community cooperation whenever this will serve the best interests of the Faith.

13.1.3 *What is the primary purpose underlying inter-community activities?*

The primary purpose underlying these activities, as with all activities, is teaching the Faith:-

> *The all-important thing of course is that every activity ... is for the purpose of teaching the Faith and confirming people.*
>
> (letter written on behalf of Shoghi Effendi to an individual believer, dated June 1, 1951)

13.1.4 *How may inter-community activities be organised?*

There are basically two methods of organising an inter-community activity:
1. An Assembly or group may initiate a project and retain complete authority for its planning and responsibility, merely inviting other communities to support and cooperate in the project. There are many examples of successful inter-community activities that are centred on one Spiritual Assembly; for example, a children's class organised and run by one Assembly but attended by children from neighbouring areas. Funding for such a project may be sought from all participating communities according to the guidelines set out in the chapter, on 'The Bahá'í Funds' in this Handbook.

A Local Spiritual Assembly or group considering such a project is advised to find out the degree of support other communities are willing to provide, and to seek their suggestions for its operation, before proceeding. An Assembly or group that does not do this must be willing to assume full responsibility for the ultimate cost, rather than expect to recover it later by appeals to other communities.

2. A number of communities may agree to collaborate to carry out a specific project. In this case each community will generally nominate one or two representatives as members of the project committee. The communities should agree on one Local Spiritual Assembly to assume primary responsibility for the supervision of the project committee (that is, to have the power of final decision in all matters related to the project), including management of Funds. Detailed information on how to organise such an activity is contained later in this Chapter.

CHAPTER THIRTEEN

13.1.5 *How should a community decide which method to use?*

Communities should consider the scale of the project and their own resources in deciding which method to use. Activities organised according to method (2) above are generally on a scale beyond the resources of one community. Activities that can realistically be handled by one community should be run by one community and not split between multiple communities just for the sake of having a joint project.

13.1.6 *What factors should a community consider when deciding whether to take part in an inter-community activity?*

There are three factors to consider:
1. whether the activity is in the best interests of the Faith;
2. whether the essential independence of the community will be strengthened, not weakened, by its involvement;
3. whether it will cause the individual goals of the community to be set aside in favour of the inter-community activity. Inter-community activities should be 'additional to' not 'in place of' the community's own activities.

13.1.7 *What are some other ways in which Bahá'í communities can work together?*

In addition to organising specific activities, communities may set up 'sister-community' relationships with other Bahá'í communities either within Australia or overseas. Some of the more affluent communities, for example, have formed relationships with poorer communities to provide them with material assistance and to exchange news and ideas. After the cyclone in the Solomon Islands in 1986, a number of communities within Australia 'adopted' Bahá'í communities in the Solomons, again to provide them with material assistance and to exchange news and ideas. Communities within Australia are free to form such relationships with one another without reference to the National Spiritual Assembly. Communities wishing to form relationships with Bahá'í communities outside Australia should make their request, in the first instance, through the National Spiritual Assembly which, in turn, will correspond with the National Spiritual Assembly of the country concerned.

13.1.8 *How should communities liaise with National Committees?*

> *Shoghi Effendi said that National Committees are intended to serve the needs of Local Spiritual Assemblies and 'not to dictate arbitrarily to them'. Furthermore, Local Spiritual Assemblies 'should certainly cooperate with National Committees and not refuse their assistance'*
>
> (letter written on behalf of Shoghi Effendi to a National Spiritual Assembly, dated November 5, 1948)

National Committees can make themselves useful to local communities in many ways - for example, through publication of newsletters, deepening materials, and handbooks on particular subjects organising seminars and conferences; appointing state or regional resource people to whom communities can turn for information and assistance. National Committees and Local Spiritual Assemblies are also strongly encouraged to work together on joint projects, for example, teaching projects.

13.1.9 *What function has the appointed arm in assisting inter-community activities?*

Communities organising joint activities should not overlook the role of the appointed arm in educating and encouraging the believers to fulfil the goals of the administrative institutions. To this end, they should keep their assistants fully informed of their inter-community activities.

CHAPTER THIRTEEN

13.2 ORGANISING JOINT ACTIVITIES

13.2.1 *What is the benefit of organising joint activities?*

The benefit of organising joint activities is that projects of much larger scope than could be arranged by one community, may be embarked upon. This means that more challenging goals can be attempted and a wider variety of projects undertaken; for example, specific projects for children and youth and for other sets of believers with special needs or interests can be arranged. All this will assist in the teaching work as it gains momentum.

13.2.2 *Who can initiate a joint activity?*

Any community - Assembly, group or isolated believer - may initiate an joint activity. The decision as to which communities will participate rests with the communities themselves, and will be influenced primarily by practical considerations, such as transportation and access, as well as the factors outlined above.' The community initiating the project should take responsibility for organising a meeting between the different communities or their representatives and take care of the administrative requirements ie. issuing an agenda, supplying the Chairman, ensuring that minutes, or a report, are circulated to the participating communities afterwards.

13.2.3 *How is a joint activity administered in practice?*

A joint activity is administered according to the following procedure:

1. Ideally there should be an Assembly willing to become the sponsoring body; that is, to administer the funds and assume final responsibility for the project (ie. have the final say in all decisions made). If a number of Bahá'í communities wish to come together to organise a project, however, and there is no Local Spiritual Assembly able to participate, a group - preferably Registered - may take on the role of sponsorship.
2. A committee must be established made up of members of each of the participating communities.
3. The participating communities must give the committee terms of reference on the following matters:
- the limits of its authority and responsibilities
- approved/disapproved lines of communication
- who is the sponsoring body; that is, the Assembly or group to which the committee should report
- the term of appointment
- administrative requirements; for example, how the committee is to keep the sponsoring body informed of its work
- the budget for the project.
4. The committee should elect officers according to need; for example, if a large amount of money is involved the committee will need a Treasurer to work in close liaison with the sponsoring body's Treasurer.
5. The sponsoring body has a duty to see that the committee complies with its terms of reference. This Assembly or group must find a moderate path between the extremes of overly interfering in the committee's work, on the one hand, and ignoring it, on the other.
6. Any proposed revision to the committee's terms of reference must be referred to the sponsoring body, which in turn, must refer it to the cooperating communities for their agreement.
7. The sponsoring body is responsible for dissolving the committee once the project is complete.

13.2.4 *How many projects should one committee be responsible for?*

Any committee set up should be given a specific project; for example, organising youth activities, or a regional advertising campaign, or managing the regional Bahá'í centre. One committee should not be given more than one of these projects, otherwise there is a risk of it becoming a form of regional Assembly, which would not be appropriate.

13.2.5 *Who has financial responsibility for the joint activity?*

As already noted, the sponsoring body is responsible for the funds. At the time of setting up the project the participating communities must work out how much money is needed and how it will be raised. The communities involved may, for example, allocate a sum from their budgets, or they may appeal to the believers in their areas for donations. If the communities involved wish to appeal for funds outside their areas of jurisdiction, they must seek approval from the National Spiritual Assembly. In deciding whether to grant approval the National Assembly will particularly consider the scale of the proposed activity for which the funds are required and its likely impact on behalf of the Faith beyond the local level. When the budget and method of fund raising are decided upon, the sponsoring body should then set up a separate Fund for the project and disburse money to the committee in the same way that it would to any other local committee. Proper accounting records showing all sources of income and all types of expenditure must be kept for the project. Progress reports on the financial position of the project should be made to the sponsoring body with a final financial report being submitted at the conclusion of the project to the sponsoring body.

13.3 NOTES FOR REGISTERED GROUPS

As explained in this Chapter, any Bahá'í community may initiate or participate in an inter-community activity. In the absence of a Local Spiritual Assembly, a Registered Group may sponsor a joint activity.

CHAPTER FOURTEEN

Chapter 14

14. Protection

14.1 THE LOCAL SPIRITUAL ASSEMBLY AS A PROTECTOR OF THE CAUSE OF GOD

14.1.1 *What responsibility has the Local Spiritual Assembly for protecting the Bahá'í community?*

The Local Spiritual Assembly has a duty to maintain the prestige of the Faith in the eyes of the public:-

> ...the Assemblies...should act with more vigilance and a greater sense of community responsibility towards every situation that may damage the prestige of the Faith in the eyes of the public.
>
> (letter written on behalf of Shoghi Effendi to an individual believer, dated March 13, 1944)

The duty to be vigilant, however, must be balanced against the need to refrain from prying into the private affairs of individual believers:-

> The Local Assemblies should neither be like private agents prying into the lives of the believers and seeking out their personal problems, nor should they condone glaring disregard of the Holy Laws.
>
> (letter from the Universal House of Justice to a National Spiritual Assembly, dated November 12, 1965)

14.1.2 *How can the Local Spiritual Assembly protect the Bahá'í community?*

The Local Spiritual Assembly can protect the community in the following ways:
1. Encourage deepening
2. The Assembly can do this by:
   a) establishing formal deepening classes
   b) encouraging informal deepenings by the friends
   c) encouraging private study
   d) reminding the friends of their obligation to read the Writings every night and morning
3. Apply Bahá'í laws and administer justice
4. This involves a twofold responsibility of education and the wise administration of justice:-

> It is a vital and urgent duty of the Assemblies, both national and local, not only to apply the Laws of Bahá'u'lláh with justice and firmness, but to increase the believers' understanding of and devotion to these Laws. In this way they will obey them not through fear of punishment but out of love for Bahá'u'lláh and because their whole lives have been transformed and re-oriented in the Way of God.
>
> (letter from the Universal House of Justice to a National Spiritual Assembly, dated October 11, 1965)

5. The Assembly must also:
   a) encourage unity between community members.
   b) review Bahá'í literature. This is necessary in order to protect the Faith from misrepresentation at this early stage of its existence when comparatively few people have any knowledge of it.

c) encourage non-involvement by Bahá'ís in politics. If Bahá'ís become involved in politics they risk associating the Faith in the public mind with warring sects and factions, thereby obscuring its essential message of unity.
d) guard against opposition to the Faith.
e) increase the friends understanding of, and commitment to, the Covenant.

14.2 ENCOURAGING UNITY

14.2.1 *What is the challenge facing the Bahá'í community at the present time?*

The challenge facing the Bahá'í community at the present time is to maintain a high degree of unity without suppressing cultural diversity:-

> *The Bahá'í Faith seeks to maintain cultural diversity while promoting the unity of all peoples. Indeed, such diversity will enrich the tapestry of human life in a peaceful world society. The House of Justice supports the view that in every country it is quite appropriate for the cultural traditions of the people to be observed within the Bahá'í community as long as they are not contrary to the Teachings... At the present time, the challenge to every Bahá'í community is to avoid suppression of those culturally-diverse elements which are not contrary to the Teachings, while establishing and maintaining such a high degree of unity that others are attracted to the Cause of God.*

(letter written on behalf of the Universal House of Justice to an individual believer, dated July 25, 1988)

14.2.2 *How can the Local Spiritual Assembly encourage unity?*

The Local Spiritual Assembly can encourage unity in the following ways:
1. Encouraging informal social interaction between the friends:-

> *In their relations amongst themselves as fellow-believers, let them not be content with the mere exchange of cold and empty formalities often connected with the organising of banquets, receptions, consultative assemblies, and lecture-halls. Let them rather, as equal co-sharers in the spiritual benefits conferred upon them by Bahá'u'lláh, arise and, with the aid and counsel of their local and national representatives, supplement these official functions with those opportunities which only a close and intimate social intercourse can adequately provide. In their homes, in their hours of relaxation and leisure, in the daily contact of business transactions, in the association of their children, whether in their study-classes, their playgrounds, and clubrooms, in short, under all possible circumstances, however insignificant they appear, the community of the followers of Bahá'u'lláh should satisfy themselves that in the eyes of the world at large and in the sight of their vigilant Master they are the living witnesses of those truths which He fondly cherished and tirelessly championed to the very end of His days.*

(Shoghi Effendi, "Principles of Bahá'í Administration", p.15)

2. Assisting new believers to integrate into the community.
3. Assisting Bahá'í immigrants to integrate into the community This involves encouraging them to learn English, where necessary, as the Universal House of Justice has said that official Bahá'í functions must be conducted in the native language of the country. At the same time, however, it is permissible to hold some conferences and social

CHAPTER FOURTEEN

gatherings in the language of the immigrants, provided this does not hinder their integration into the community or create problems of disunity or estrangement between community members:-

The International Teaching Centre has sent us a copy of your letter of 10 October 1982 asking about language problems brought about by the influx of Iranians who do not understand English. It is important that the Iranian friends be encouraged to make the effort to learn the language used in the country and become integrated into the life and activities of the community. The Nineteen Day Feasts and other official gatherings of the friends should be conducted in whatever is the conventional local language. This does not mean, of course, that at such gatherings some of the readings could not be in the language of the immigrants, or that, if these friends so wish, some classes and conferences may not be held and conducted in their own language for their benefit. The essential thing is, as stated above, to promote the integration of the immigrants into the community and avoid feelings of estrangement or disunity on account of language.

(letter written by the Universal House of Justice to an individual believer, dated November 10, 1982)

...it would not be appropriate for language or racial groups to hold separate Nineteen Day Feasts or to have separate Bahá'í Centres. This, however, does not preclude providing a meeting room or building where particular language or racial groups would feel comfortable, as long as it does not discourage their integration into the community. Such a meeting place could serve as a means of attracting them to the Faith or to provide much-needed social activities for those already enrolled. This is particularly true of the dear friends who have declared their Faith while in refugee camps. The refugees should be dealt with very wisely and patiently, and should be carefully nurtured until they feel at one with their Bahá'í brothers and sisters, and can freely participate in Bahá'í community life.

(letter written on behalf of the Universal House of Justice to a National Spiritual Assembly, dated August 13, 1986)

The National Spiritual Assembly particularly requests that Local Spiritual Assemblies arrange deepenings in Persian for the newly-arrived Persian friends.

4. Being sensitive to possible conflicts between tribal practices and Bahá'í law. The Universal House of Justice has said that a Local Spiritual Assembly should distinguish between aspects of tribal life which are related to fundamental laws of the Faith and those which are of lesser importance and from which the friends can be weaned away gradually:-

The House of Justice has given the advice to Spiritual Assemblies faced with questions of possible conflict between tribal practices and Bahá'í law, that such Assemblies should distinguish between aspects of tribal community life which are related to fundamental laws (such as monogamy) and matters of lesser importance, from which the friends can and should extricate themselves gradually. Furthermore, the House of Justice has offered the advice that: The institutions of the Faith should

CHAPTER FOURTEEN

be careful not to press the friends to arbitrarily discard those local traditions which are harmless and often colourful characteristics of particular peoples and tribes. Were a new Bahá'í suddenly to cease following the customs of his people, it is possible that they might misunderstand the true nature of the Bahá'í Faith, and the Bahá'í could be regarded as having turned against the traditions of the land...

(letter written on behalf of the Universal House of Justice to two believers, dated October 25, 1987)

14.2.3 ***What are some causes of disunity?***

The following problems have the ability to cause disunity within a community:
1. criticism of individuals and institutions
2. disputes between individuals
3. backbiting and gossip
4. disruptive behaviour at community functions
5. disobeying Assembly decisions

14.2.4 ***How should the Local Spiritual Assembly handle problems of disunity?***

Depending upon the nature and severity of the problem the Local Spiritual Assembly may resolve the situation in any one of the following ways, or a combination of them:
1. Deepening the friends in the standard of conduct expected of Bahá'ís and in the Covenant. Deepening in the Covenant is particularly important because it is, above all, obedience to the Covenant that protects the Faith from schism. See "Lights of Guidance" {revised edition}, nos. 304-325, 1339-50 for general guidance on the standard of conduct expected of Bahá'ís and advice on how they can overcome problems such as backbiting, gossip, and damaging criticism.]
2. Encouraging the friends to take their problems to the Assembly:-

   Over and over, in going through the correspondence he received from your Assembly he was struck by the fact that the friends acted so unadministratively. Instead of taking up their accusations and problems and unhappy feelings with their local Assembly, or the National Assembly, they referred to individuals or individual members of the Assembly, or they refused to meet with the Assembly. The first thing a believer should do is turn to an Assembly — That is why we have assemblies! He feels this trouble would never have arisen if the Bahá'ís utilised their assemblies as they should.

   (letter written on behalf of Shoghi Effendi to a National Spiritual Assembly, dated June 30, 1949)

Shoghi Effendi said it was preferable that disputes between believers, even over non-Bahá'í matters, be taken to the Local Spiritual Assembly rather than the civil courts. If the Local Spiritual Assembly cannot resolve the dispute, however, there is no objection to the matter being taken to the civil court; nor can the Assembly prevent believers from taking a matter to the civil court if they choose to do so:-

The Guardian wishes to emphasise the importance of avoiding (reference to civil courts) of cases of dispute between believers, even in non-Bahá'í issues. It is the Assembly's function to endeavour to settle amicably such disputes, both in order to safeguard the fair name and prestige of the Cause, and to acquire the necessary experience for the extension of its functions in the future.

CHAPTER FOURTEEN

(letter written on behalf of Shoghi Effendi to a National Spiritual Assembly, dated May 30, 1936)

...The House of Justice ... states that believers should take their differences to the Spiritual Assembly and abide by the decision of the Assembly. However, if Bahá'ís cannot negotiate a settlement of a dispute between them, and if the Spiritual Assembly cannot succeed in arbitrating a solution to the dispute, then there is no objection to the Bahá'ís having recourse to the civil courts...However, the Assembly does not have the authority to prohibit a believer from having recourse to the civil courts if he decides to do so.

(cited in a letter written on behalf of the Universal House of Justice to a National Spiritual Assembly, dated February 9, 1983)

The Assembly must also distinguish between matters which it is authorised to handle and matters which fall within the scope of the civil authorities and must be dealt with by the civil courts. The Assembly may not interfere in matters in which the State claims a prior interest and has already laid down the procedures to be followed:-

Your Assembly should make a distinction between those actions which can be dealt with at present by the Bahá'í administrative institutions and those which are criminal in character and fall within the purview of the civil authorities. In general, misconduct on the part of individual Bahá'ís and differences between the friends should be adjudicated by Spiritual Assemblies, and the friends should obey the Assemblies' decisions. However, in criminal matters in which the State claims a prior interest and has clearly laid down the procedures to be followed, and the action of Assemblies would amount to interference with these procedures, such matters must be referred to the civil authorities.

(letter written on behalf of the Universal House of Justice to a National Spiritual Assembly, dated June 5, 1985)

Shoghi Effendi also noted that the Bahá'ís should not take up too much of an Assembly's time with their disputes. Rather, they should put the past behind them, unite, and concentrate on serving the Faith:-

He does not want the friends to form the habit of taking up a kind of Bahá'í litigation against each other. Their duties to humanity are too sacred and urgent in these days, when the Cause is struggling to spread and assert its independence, for them to spend their precious time, and his precious time, in this way. Ask them, therefore, to unite, forget the past, and serve as never before.

(letter written on behalf of Shoghi Effendi to a National Spiritual Assembly, dated July 22, 1947)

3. Intervening directly to counsel and warn believers. In extreme cases the Local Spiritual Assembly may even need to recommend to the National Spiritual Assembly partial or total removal of voting rights of the believers concerned. As a general principle, however, it is better for the Local Spiritual Assembly to resolve problems of disunity by educating the friends, rather than by adjudication. With regard to gossip, for example, the Universal House of Justice has said:-

We realise that a great problem is presented by gossip when it occurs in Bahá'í communities, and the poison it can instil into the relationship between the friends. However, deprivation of voting rights is usually of little help in such circumstances and should be resorted to only after other remedies have been tried and failed. We think it would be much better for the National Assembly to provide for the proper deepening of the friends and in a loving and patient manner attempt to instil in them a respect for Bahá'í laws. Rash action can dampen the zeal of the community, and this must be avoided at all costs.

(letter from the Universal House of Justice to a National Spiritual Assembly, dated August 20, 1969)

14.2.5 *How can the Local Spiritual Assembly determine when a problem of disunity has become so severe that it must intervene to resolve the matter?*

The Local Spiritual Assembly must intervene in any matter that affects the interests of the Faith, regardless of whether those involved wish it to or not. The decision to intervene must be made on a case by case basis. As a general guide, however, a problem of disunity between believers may be said to be harming the interests of the Faith when it begins to visibly disrupt community life. Warning signs to look for include:
- repeated absence of community members from functions
- absence of Assembly members from Assembly meetings (if a person misses a number of meetings with no explanation, the Assembly should find out why)
- withdrawal of children from Bahá'í childrens' classes
- visible distress shown by community members

Such a situation is to be distinguished from a situation in which, for example, two believers do not get along well together, but do not allow their personal differences to disturb the community. If the Assembly was to intervene in that instance it could justly be accused of prying into the private affairs of individuals. When the above signs are present the Assembly should seriously consider what steps it can take to overcome the problem. If it feels that direct intervention is necessary, it should make arrangements to meet with the believers concerned to ascertain the facts of the situation; counsel them; and, if the situation is not remedied within a reasonable time, issue warnings about possible loss of voting rights. Often it is better for the Local Spiritual Assembly to delegate one or two of its members to have a private talk with the believers concerned. This sometimes makes it easier to get to the bottom of a matter. If the situation is particularly grave and the Assembly has tried every means possible to remedy it without success, it will have to report the matter to the National Spiritual Assembly and recommend the application of sanctions. Information on how to administer such a situation is available in the Chapter, 'Administration of Bahá'í Law'. The Assembly must also be alert to prevent gossip about the situation spreading throughout the community, for this may cause more damage than the original problem:-

Whatever steps are taken (to handle misconduct) it is vital that the believers refrain from gossip and backbiting, for this can only harm the Faith, causing perhaps more damage than would have been caused by the original offence.

(letter from the Universal House of Justice, dated February 20, 1977)

14.2.6 *How quickly should the Local Spiritual Assembly intervene in a situation in which the interests of the Faith are involved?*

It is important that the Local Spiritual Assembly intervene promptly in such a situation. Failure to do so may lead to backbiting amongst the friends; a loss of dignity for the Faith in the eyes of Bahá'ís and non-Bahá'ís; and/or the eventual inactivity of the believers. Any one

CHAPTER FOURTEEN

of these consequences will prevent the Faith from progressing.

14.2.7 **_Where else may the Local Spiritual Assembly turn for assistance in overcoming problems of disunity?_**

The Local Spiritual Assembly may call upon the advice and assistance of the Protection Board:-

> *It is the duty of Local and National Spiritual Assemblies to refer to the Auxiliary Board members for protection matters which may involve ...... problems of disunity within the community, the removal of voting rights or any other matters in which you feel the guidance and advice of the Protection Boards may be helpful to the institutions of the Faith... You are free at any time to refer to the Continental Board of Counsellors and the Auxiliary Board members for protection any matters about which you are not clear involving the security of the Faith in your area and you will always find them willing to assist you in dealing with such problems.*
>
> (letter written on behalf of the Universal House of Justice to a National Spiritual Assembly, dated October 1, 1979)

Note that the Protection Board cannot take over handling of a matter, nor can it tell the Assembly what its decision should be. It can, however, advise the Assembly on procedures for dealing with it and draw the Assembly's attention to the relevant texts in the Writings.

14.2.8 **_What should an individual Bahá'í do if he or she has a problem with other members of the community?_**

It is not permissible for Bahá'ís to express critical opinions of other people to one another. If a Bahá'í has a problem with an individual in the community and wishes to consult on the matter with a friend, he or she should strive to do so without mentioning names. If the problem is so severe as to endanger the interests of the Faith, the individual should take it to the Local Spiritual Assembly or a member of the appointed arm of the Faith:-

> *You ask in your letter for guidance on the implications of the prohibition on backbiting and more specifically whether, in moments of anger or depression, the believer is permitted to turn to his friends to unburden his soul and discuss his problem in human relations. Normally, it is possible to describe the situation surrounding a problem and seek help and advice in resolving it, without necessarily mentioning names. The individual believer should seek to do this, whether he is consulting a friend, Bahá'í or non-Bahá'í, or whether the friend is consulting him. 'Abdu'l-Bahá does not permit adverse criticism of individuals by name in discussion among the friends, even if the one criticising believes that he is doing so to protect the interests of the Cause. If the situation is of such gravity as to endanger the interests of the Faith, the complaint, as your National Spiritual Assembly has indicated, should be submitted to the Local Spiritual Assembly, or as you state to a representative of the institution of the Counsellors, for consideration and action. In such cases, of course, the name of the person or persons involved will have to be mentioned.*
>
> (letter written on behalf of the Universal House of Justice to an individual believer, dated September 23, 1975)

[See also "Lights of Guidance" {revised edition}, no.308.]

14.3 OPPOSITION

14.3.1 *Why does the Faith experience opposition?*

The Faith experiences opposition because its growing influence challenges the position of powerful social institutions such as the Church. As the Faith grows in strength, so too will the opposition of these institutions:-

> *For let every earnest upholder of the Cause of Bahá'u'lláh realise that the storms which this struggling Faith of God must needs encounter, as the process of the disintegration of society advances, shall be fiercer than any which it has already experienced. Let him be aware that so soon as the full measure of the stupendous claim of the Faith of Bahá'u'lláh comes to be recognised by those time-honoured and powerful strongholds of orthodoxy, whose deliberate aim is to maintain their strangle-hold over the thoughts and consciences of men, this infant Faith will have to contend with enemies more powerful and more insidious than the cruellest torture-mongers and the most fanatical clerics who have afflicted it in the past. What foes may not in the course of the convulsions that shall seize a dying civilisation be brought into existence, who will reinforce the indignities which have already been heaped upon it!*
>
> (Shoghi Effendi, "The World Order of Bahá'u'lláh", p.17)

The Faith also suffers from what Shoghi Effendi describes as the

> *storm of mischief with which they who apostasize their faith or claim to be its faithful exponents assail it from to time.'*
>
> ("The World Order of Bahá'u'lláh", p.15)

Such attacks are necessary because they enable the Faith to grow:-

> *Instead of undermining the Faith, such assaults, both from within and from without, reinforce its foundations, and excite the intensity of its flame. Designed to becloud its radiance, they proclaim to all the world the exalted character of its precepts, the completeness of its unity, the uniqueness of its position, and the pervasiveness of its influence.*
>
> (Shoghi Effendi, "The World Order of Bahá'u'lláh", p.15-16)

[See further "Crisis and Victory" (compilation of the Universal House of Justice), - Bahá'í Publications Australia, 1988.]

14.3.2 *What forms do attacks on the Faith take?*

Opposition to the Faith is expressed in many forms. In the West it is generally expressed through the publication of books which attack or deliberately misrepresent the Faith, through the publication of articles in the press, or through correspondence which the believers sometimes receive from Covenant-breakers or enemies of the Faith. The Bahá'ís of the West have been warned to expect 'severe mental tests' in the future:-

> *...How often we seem to forget the clear and repeated warnings of our beloved Master, who, in particular during the concluding years of His mission on earth, laid stress on the 'severe mental tests' that would inevitably sweep over His loved ones of the West - tests that would*

CHAPTER FOURTEEN

purge, purify and prepare them for their noble mission in life.

(Shoghi Effendi, "Bahá'í Administration", p.50)

14.3.3 ***What attitude should the Bahá'ís take to such attacks?***

As the Bahá'ís know that the Faith will ultimately triumph over its enemies they should be calm in the face of such attacks and use them both for their own spiritual upliftment and for the promotion of the Cause. They should be confident, wise and moderate in their actions and, above all, should not do anything provocative:-

> *The friends should, therefore, not assume an attitude of mere resignation in the face of persecutions, they should rather welcome them, and utilise them as means for their own spiritual uplift and also for the promotion of the Cause. As the Faith grows stronger and attracts the serious attention and consideration of the world outside, the friends must expect a similar, if not a greater, increase in the forces of opposition which from every direction, both secular and religious, will be massed to undermine the very basis of its existence. The final outcome of such a struggle, which will be surely gigantic, is clear to us believers. A Faith born of God and guided by His Divine and all-pervasive spirit cannot but finally triumph and firmly establish itself, no matter how persistent and insidious the forces with which it has to contend. The friends should be confident, and act with the utmost wisdom and moderation, and should particularly abstain from any provocative act. The future is surely theirs.*

(letter written on behalf of Shoghi Effendi to an individual believer, dated June 24, 1936)

When dealing with enemies of the Faith the Bahá'ís must be impartial and fair:-

> *Such a rectitude of conduct must...be demonstrated in the impartiality of every defender of the Faith against its enemies, in his fair-mindedness in recognising any obligations he may have towards him.*

(Shoghi Effendi, "The Advent of Divine Justice", p.22)

14.3.4 ***What action should an individual take when he or she becomes aware of opposition to the Faith?***

The individual Bahá'ís should report the matter immediately to the Local Spiritual Assembly or Auxiliary Board member (or assistant) for Protection. If the Bahá'í lives outside a Local Spiritual Assembly area the matter should be reported immediately to the National Assembly.

14.3.5 ***What action should a Local Spiritual Assembly take when it becomes aware of opposition to the Faith?***

Whenever an Assembly becomes aware of any form of opposition to the Faith it should contact the National Spiritual Assembly for advice. The Auxiliary Board member for Protection should also be contacted. The Assembly must guide the believers in the community to react wisely and calmly according to the principles set out in this section.

14.3.6 ***How should Bahá'ís regard books about the Faith written by well meaning but unenlightened enemies?***

> *Books written by such people are to be distinguished from those written by Covenant-breakers. They may be read 'so as to refute [the] charges'*

made in them

(letter written on behalf of Shoghi Effendi to an individual believer, dated March 19, 1945)

14.3.7 *What about books written by enemies of the Faith placed in libraries?*

Books written be enemies of the Faith found in libraries should not be destroyed or removed. Rather, they should be ignored:-

In reply to your letter of September 20, 1975 the Universal House of Justice instructs us to say that the friends should be advised to ignore these books and any similar ones which might be written by enemies of the Faith. There should certainly be no attempt made to destroy or remove such books from libraries. On the other hand there is no need at all for the friends to acquire them and, indeed, the best plan is to ignore them entirely.

(referring to books written by Hermann Zimmer and William Miller. Letter written on behalf of the Universal House of Justice to a National Spiritual Assembly, dated October 2, 1975)

14.4 THE COVENANT

14.4.1 *What is the meaning of the Covenant?*

The Universal House of Justice explains the meaning of the Covenant as follows:-

There is, for example, the Greater Covenant which every Manifestation of God makes with His followers, promising that in the fullness of time a new Manifestation will be sent, and taking from them the undertaking to accept Him when this occurs. There is also the Lesser Covenant that a Manifestation of God makes with His followers that they will accept His appointed successor after Him. If they do so, the Faith can remain united and pure. If not, the Faith becomes divided and its force spent...It is a Covenant of this kind that Bahá'u'lláh made with His followers regarding 'Abdu'l-Bahá, and that 'Abdu'l-Bahá perpetuated through the Administrative Order that Bahá'u'lláh had already created.

(letter from the Universal House of Justice to an individual believer, dated March 3, 1975)

The authority of the Covenant was perpetuated after the passing of 'Abdu'l-Bahá through the institutions of the Guardianship and the Universal House of Justice. Today, the Universal House of Justice is 'the head of the Faith and the supreme institution to which all must turn'

("Constitution of the Universal House of Justice", p.4)

14.4.2 *What is the importance of studying the Covenant?*

If the believers are deepened in the Covenant they will be better able to withstand the attacks of the enemies of the Faith, both from within and without:-

...the believers need to be deepened in their knowledge and appreciation of the Covenants of both Bahá'u'lláh and 'Abdu'l-Bahá.

CHAPTER FOURTEEN

> *This is the stronghold of the faith of every Bahá'í, and that which enables him to withstand every test and the attacks of the enemies outside the Faith, and the far more dangerous, insidious, lukewarm people inside the Faith who have no real attachment to the Covenant, and consequently uphold the intellectual aspect of the Teachings while at the same time undermining the spiritual foundation upon which the whole Cause of God rests.*
>
> (letter written on behalf of Shoghi Effendi to an individual believer, dated April 15, 1949)

A firm grounding in the Covenant also prevents conflicts arising over personalities and matters of secondary importance, and therefore assists the smooth functioning of the Administration:-

> *Some of the younger believers, from letters and reports received here, seem to lack a firm grounding on such matters as the Will and Testament and the deeper spiritual Teachings of the Faith. Whenever the grasp of these fundamentals is weak, the friends are almost sure to pay undue attention to secondary procedures, to quibble over details, to lose themselves in personalities, and to founder in a sea of unnecessary inharmony. This has nothing to do with their devotion, their loyalty, their zeal, their eagerness to serve. It is merely a question of not having received, perhaps through lack of sufficient teachers to carry on the all-important work of deepening the friends in their own faith, a strong enough education in the Covenant before the duties and responsibilities of the Administrative Order were thrust upon them.*
>
> (letter written on behalf of Shoghi Effendi to a National Spiritual Assembly, dated June 26, 1956)

For these reasons it is essential that Local Spiritual Assemblies deepen their communities in the Covenant. The following texts are useful:-
- "Will and Testament of 'Abdu'l-Bahá"
- "The Covenant" (compilation of the Universal House of Justice, 1989)
- "The Power of the Covenant", vols. 1,2 and 3 (National Spiritual Assembly of the Bahá'ís of Canada)
- "The Covenant: Its Origins and our Attitudes Towards It" (a study guide)

The assistance of the Auxiliary Board for Protection should be sought for such deepening as this Institution has the specific responsibility of deepening the friends in the Covenant and preparing them for the opposition that must inevitably come.

14.4.3 *What is Covenant-breaking?*

A Covenant-breaker is someone who, having declared his or her belief in Bahá'u'lláh, then turns around in a contradictory fashion and attacks Bahá'u'lláh or the Central Institution of the Faith ordained by Bahá'u'lláh in His Covenant (ie. 'Abdu'l-Bahá, the Centre of the Covenant; Shoghi Effendi, the Guardian of the Faith; or the Universal House of Justice, the Head of the Faith):-

> *When a person declares his acceptance of Bahá'u'lláh as a Manifestation of God he becomes a party to the Covenant and accepts the totality of His Revelation. If he then turns round and attacks Bahá'u'lláh or the Central Institution of the Faith he violates the Covenant. If this happens every effort is made to help that person to*

see the illogicality and error of his actions, but if he persists he must, in accordance with the instructions of Bahá'u'lláh Himself, be shunned as a Covenant-breaker.

(letter from the Universal House of Justice to an individual believer, dated March 23, 1975)

It is important to understand that the following people are NOT Covenant-Breakers:
- those who break a Bahá'í law and lose their voting rights.
- those who withdraw from the Faith
- those who reject Bahá'u'lláh's claim to be a Manifestation of God

The decision to expel or reinstate a Covenant-breaker is made by the Hands of the Cause of God subject to the approval of the Universal House of Justice:-

Authority for the expulsion and reinstatement of Covenant-breakers remains with the Hands of the Cause of God. All such matters will be investigated locally by the relative Continental Board of Counsellors in consultation with any Hand or Hands who may be in the area. The Continental Board of Counsellors and the Hands concerned will then make their reports to the International Teaching Centre where they will be considered. The decision whether or not to expel or reinstate will be made by the Hands of the Cause residing in the Holy Land who will, as at present, submit their decision to the Universal House of Justice for approval.

(letter of the Universal House of Justice to the Bahá'ís of the World, dated June 8, 1973)

14.4.4 *How should the Bahá'ís treat Covenant-breakers?*

Bahá'ís must shun Covenant-breakers entirely in order to preserve the unity of the Faith. Covenant-breakers are like people with a serious disease. Their association with healthy people cannot make them well but they may infect the healthy people. The only thing to be done for Covenant-breakers is to pray for them:-

...One of the greatest and most fundamental principles of the Cause of God is to shun and avoid entirely the Covenant-breakers, for they will utterly destroy the Cause of God, exterminate His Law and render of no account all efforts exerted in the past.

('Abdu'l-Bahá, "Will and Testament", p.3)

Bahá'u'lláh and the Master in many places and very emphatically have told us to shun entirely all Covenant-breakers...they have also told us, however, to pray for them. These souls are not lost forever. In the Aqdas, Bahá'u'lláh says that God will forgive Mirzá Yahyá if he repents. It follows, therefore, that God will forgive any soul if he repents. Most of them don't want to repent, unfortunately...

(written on behalf of Shoghi Effendi, in "Principles of Bahá'í Administration", p.22) [See further "Lights of Guidance", no.621-29.]

14.4.5 *May Bahá'ís respond to claims made by Covenant-Breakers in the press?*

No:-

In areas where Covenant-breakers are active...the friends should avoid confrontation with them before the public, especially in news columns such as 'Letters to the Editor'.

(letter from the Universal House of Justice to a National Spiritual Assembly, dated February 21, 1973)

14.4.6 *May Bahá'ís read the writings of Covenant-breakers?*

Reading the writings of Covenant-breakers is not forbidden, but it is strongly discouraged:-

To read the writings of Covenant-breakers is not forbidden to the believers and does not constitute in itself an act of Covenant-breaking...However, the friends are warned in the strongest terms against reading such literature because Covenant-breaking is a spiritual poison and the calumnies and distortions of the truth which the Covenant-breakers give out are such that they can undermine the faith of the believer and plant the seeds of doubt unless he is fore-armed with an unshakeable belief in Bahá'u'lláh and His Covenant and a knowledge of the true facts.

(letter from the Universal House of Justice to a National Spiritual Assembly, dated October 29, 1974)

14.4.7 *May Bahá'ís answer mail received from Covenant-breakers?*

No. Such mail should be passed on to the Local Spiritual Assembly, preferably unopened. Alternatively, if recognised for what it is before being opened, it should be marked 'return to sender' and returned.

14.4.8 *What action should an individual take if he or she becomes aware of Covenant-breaking activities?*

As with other instances of opposition, the individual Bahá'ís should report the matter immediately to the Local Spiritual Assembly or Auxiliary Board member (or assistant) for Protection. If the Bahá'í lives outside a Local Spiritual Assembly area the matter should be reported immediately to the National Assembly.

14.4.9 *What action should a Local Spiritual Assembly take if it becomes aware of Covenant-breaking activities?*

As with other instances of opposition, the Assembly should contact the National Spiritual Assembly for advice. The Auxiliary Board member for Protection should also be contacted. Again, the Assembly must guide the believers in the community to react wisely and calmly according to the principles set out in this section.

14.5 NOTES FOR REGISTERED GROUPS

If problems of disunity arise within a Registered Group the matter should be reported directly to the National Spiritual Assembly or the Auxiliary Board member or assistant. Problems of opposition or Covenant-breaking should be reported immediately to the National Spiritual Assembly and Auxiliary Board member.

CHAPTER FIFTEEN

Chapter 15

15. Relations with Society

15.1 INTRODUCTION - GENERAL PRINCIPLES

15.1.1 *Are Bahá'ís encouraged to co-operate with non-Bahá'í movements?*

Yes. Bahá'u'lláh said:-

> *Consort with all men, O people of Bahá, in a spirit of friendliness and fellowship.*
>
> ("Gleanings from the Writings of Bahá'u'lláh", UK Revised Edition, 1978, p.287-88)

- The Universal House of Justice has said:-

> *...the believers should, at all times, be alert to opportunities to do whatever is within their power to make the conditions of human life better; by this means they will manifest that commitment to action exemplified by the Master, will demonstrate the relevance of Bahá'í principles to the issues of contemporary society, and will attract the receptive and discerning to the Bahá'í Teachings.*
>
> (letter written on behalf of the Universal House of Justice to the National Spiritual Assembly of Australia, dated October 24, 1990)

With the emergence of the Faith from obscurity the Universal House of Justice has said that the time has come for the Bahá'í community to become more involved in the world around it by:-

> *1. exerting its influence towards unity*
>
> *2. demonstrating its ability to settle differences by consultation rather than by confrontation, violence or schism*
>
> *3. declaring its faith in the divine purpose of human existence*
>
> (letter from the Universal House of Justice to the Bahá'ís of the World, dated Riḍván 1985)

Examples of successful co-operation between Bahá'ís and non-Bahá'í organisations include participation in Interfaith Services, Peace and Environment Expositions; giving addresses about the Faith at meetings of non-Bahá'í organisations; participating in committees and conferences designed to promote activities in accord with the principles of the Faith, section 7 contains a list of United Nations days and events which offer rich opportunities for Bahá'í-United Nations collaboration. The field of social and economic development also offers opportunities for constructive association with non-Bahá'í movements.

15.1.2 *What is the primary purpose of co-operation with non-Bahá'í movements?*

The primary purpose of co-operation with non-Bahá'í movements is to teach the Faith, in the broadest sense of the word 'teach':-

> *They should always bear in mind, however, the dominating purpose of such a collaboration which is to secure in time the recognition by*

CHAPTER FIFTEEN

those with whom they are associated of the paramount necessity and the true significance of the Bahá'í Revelation in this day.

(Shoghi Effendi, "Bahá'í Administration", p.126)

We go forward confident that the wholehearted involvement of the friends in these [social and economic development] activities will ensure a deeper consolidation of the community at all levels. Our engagement in the technical aspects of development should however, not be allowed to supplant the essentials of teaching, which remains the primary duty of every follower of Bahá'u'lláh. Rather should our increased activities in the development field be viewed as a reinforcement of the teaching work, as a greater manifestation of faith in action. For, if expansion of the teaching work does not continue, there can be no hope of success for this enlarged dimension of the consolidation process.

(letter from the Universal House of Justice to the Bahá'ís of the World, dated October 20, 1983)

15.1.3 *How much time should a Bahá'í devote to non-Bahá'í movements?*

Shoghi Effendi said that the major task of the Bahá'í institutions is the formation and consolidation of the Bahá'í administrative order. Association with non-Bahá'í movements should be regarded as a minor task, but one that is, nevertheless, equally necessary. The two tasks should be seen as complementary and as each, in their own way, fulfilling a vital function:-

Whilst chiefly engaged in the pursuit of their major task, consisting chiefly in the formation and the consolidation of Bahá'í administrative institutions, they should endeavour to participate, within recognised limits, in the work of institutions which though unaware of the claim of the Bahá'í Cause are prompted by a sincere desire to promote the spirit that animates the Faith. In the pursuit of their major task their function is to preserve the identity of the Cause and the purity of the mission of Bahá'u'lláh. In their minor undertaking their purpose should be to imbue with the spirit of power and strength such movements as in their restricted scope are endeavouring to achieve what is near and dear to the heart of every true Bahá'í...These twofold obligations devolving upon organised Bahá'í communities, far from neutralising the effects of one another or of appearing antagonistic in their aims, should be regarded as complementary and fulfilling, each in its way, a vital and necessary function.

(Shoghi Effendi, "Bahá'í Administration", p.126)

Individuals must, likewise, give first priority to supporting the Bahá'í institutions and, only when they have fulfilled this duty, devote time to non-Bahá'í activities:-

In their collaboration with such associations they would extend any moral and material assistance they can afford, after having fulfilled their share of support to those institutions that affect directly the interests of the Cause.

(Shoghi Effendi, "Bahá'í Administration", p.125-6)

CHAPTER FIFTEEN

15.1.4 *What is the reason for this order of priorities?*

The reason for this order of priorities is that the World Order of Bahá'u'lláh provides the only sure means of alleviating the problems of the world today and only the Bahá'ís can build it:-

> *The Faith of God is the sole source of salvation for mankind today. The true cause of the ills of humanity is its disunity. No matter how perfect may be the machinery devised by the leaders of men for the political unity of the world, it will still not provide the antidote to the poison sapping the vigour of present-day society. These ills can be cured only through the instrumentality of God's Faith. There are many well-wishers of mankind who devote their efforts to relief-work and charity and to the material well-being of man, but only Bahá'ís can do the work which God most wants done. When we devote ourselves to the work of the Faith we are doing a work which is the greatest aid and only refuge for a needy and divided world.*
>
> (letter from the Universal House of Justice to National Spiritual Assemblies in Africa, dated February 8, 1970)

> *The well-being of humanity is a reflection of its spiritual state, and any enduring change for the better in its material affairs requires a change in its spiritual condition. For this reason the principal concern and contribution of the followers of Bahá'u'lláh is the spiritual transformation of human society, with full confidence that by this means they are making a most valuable and most fundamental contribution to the betterment of the world and the rectification of its many problems.*
>
> (letter written on behalf of the Universal House of Justice to the National Spiritual Assembly of Australia, dated October 24, 1990)

> *We Bahá'ís should, in other words, arm our minds with knowledge in order to better demonstrate to, especially, the educated classes, the truths enshrined in our Faith. What the Guardian, however, does not advise the friends to do is to dissipate their time and energies in serving movements that are akin to our principles but not, we believe, capable of solving the present spiritual crises the world finds itself in. We can co-operate with such movements and their promoters to good effect, while at the same time openly standing forth as Bahá'ís with a specific programme to offer society.*
>
> (letter written on behalf of Shoghi Effendi to an individual believer, dated July 5, 1949)

The Local Spiritual Assembly has a responsibility to assist the believers to understand this connection between promoting the Faith and improving human society:-

> *It is the responsibility of the institutions of the Faith to assist the believers in their endeavours to acquire an accurate and profound understanding of the indissoluble connection between their efforts to propagate the Faith and consolidate its institutions and their commendable desire to contribute to improvement in the quality of human life. They should realise also that their approach to the solution*

of the world's problems will not be understood, and may even be disparaged by the idealistic materialists whose labours are directed so assiduously to improvement in the material welfare of humanity, and to whom material good is the only standard by which the condition of society is assessed.

(letter written on behalf of the Universal House of Justice to the National Spiritual Assembly of Australia, dated October 24, 1990)

15.1.5 *What sort of non-Bahá'í movements should Bahá'ís co-operate with?*

Bahá'ís should associate with those movements that are seeking to promote the same principles as the Faith:-

> *...they should endeavour to participate, within recognised limits, in the work of institutions which though unaware of the claim of the Bahá'í Cause are prompted by a sincere desire to promote the spirit that animates the Faith...such movements as in their restricted scope are endeavouring to achieve what is near and dear to the heart of every true Bahá'í.*

(Shoghi Effendi, "Bahá'í Administration", p.126)

They must guard against becoming associated with any matter that would involve the slightest departure from the fundamental principles of the Faith:-

> *...the broad principle that the followers of Bahá'u'lláh will, under no circumstances, suffer themselves to be involved, whether as individuals or in their collective capacities, in matters that would entail the slightest departure from the fundamental verities and ideals of their Faith.*

(Shoghi Effendi, "The World Order of Bahá'u'lláh", p.66)

15.1.6 *May Bahá'ís be involved in political activities?*

No. Bahá'ís, both individuals and Assemblies, have been commanded to 'shun politics like the plague':-

> *I feel it, therefore, incumbent upon me to stress, now that the time is ripe, the importance of an instruction which, at the present stage of the evolution of our Faith, should be increasingly emphasised, irrespective of its application to the East or to the West. And this principle is no other than that which involves the non-participation by the adherents of the Faith of Bahá'u'lláh, whether in their individual capacities or collectively as local or national Assemblies, in any form of activity that might be interpreted, either directly or indirectly, as an interference in the political affairs of any particular government...*

(Shoghi Effendi, "The World Order of Bahá'u'lláh", p.63-4)

[See also "Lights of Guidance {revised edition} no.1449]

15.1.7 *What is meant by 'political activities'?*

Each of the following may be considered a political activity. Bahá'ís must not:
a) seek *'to impose Bahá'í Teachings upon others by persuading the powers that be to enact laws enforcing Bahá'í principles'*

(letter from the Universal House of Justice to a National Spiritual Assembly, dated July 21, 1968)

CHAPTER FIFTEEN

It follows that it is not permissible for the Faith to be associated with political lobby groups.
b) associate the Faith with a discussion of political affairs:-

> *He hath even prohibited the believers from discussing political affairs.*
>
> ('Abdu'l-Bahá, quoted in a letter from the Universal House of Justice, dated July 7, 1976)

This ban extends to even mentioning the names of political figures in public talks:-

> *The Guardian wishes me to draw the attention of the Friends through you that they should be very careful in their public addresses not to mention any political figures - either side with them or denounce them. This is the first thing to bear in mind. Otherwise they will involve the friends in political matters, which is infinitely dangerous to the Cause.*
>
> (Shoghi Effendi, "Principles of Bahá'í Administration", p.32)

c) associate the Faith with protests against the policies of any government. Apartheid provides an example. Whilst the Bahá'ís must uphold the fundamental principle of racial equality, we must not engage in protests against the specific policies of any government:-

> *In reply to your letter of 15 July seeking further clarification on the issue of apartheid, the Universal House of Justice has instructed us to point out that as the policy of apartheid derives from racial discrimination, it cannot be accepted by Bahá'ís wherever, and in whatever form, it may be practised. While the friends should, of course, support the principles of the Faith, including those advocating the oneness of mankind, and may associate with groups and engage in activities which promote these principles, they must scrupulously take care not to become involved in political issues. As stated in the letter to you dated 16 April 1985, participation in anti apartheid demonstrations and protest activities could be construed as involvement in politics, and therefore should be avoided. ...The world around us is seething with unrest caused by the conflicting interests of Governments, peoples, races and individuals. Each of these contending parties has some good and some evil on its side, and, whereas we will unhesitatingly uphold Bahá'í principles, we will never become embroiled in these internecine conflicts by identifying ourselves with one or other of the parties, however much in our hearts we may sympathise with its aims.*
>
> (letter written on behalf of the Universal House of Justice to a National Spiritual Assembly, dated August 18, 1985)

d) associate the Faith with breaking the law:-

> *...Bahá'ís obey the law, Federal or State, unless submission to these laws amounts to a denial of their Faith.*
>
> (letter from the Universal House of Justice to a National Spiritual Assembly, dated March 30, 1965) [For further information see "Lights of Guidance {revised edition} nos. 1454, 1455, 1456]

e) associate the Faith with movements

CHAPTER FIFTEEN

'identified in the public mind with partisan political stances'.

(letter from Bahá'í International Community Office of Public Information, Haifa, to an individual believer, dated July 26, 1989).

15.1.8 **What sanctions may be imposed on a Bahá'í who becomes involved in political activities?**

A Bahá'í who refuses to disengage from political activities may lose his or her voting rights:-

> *Your understanding and attitude regarding participation in politics is correct, namely, you immediately warn and quickly remove the voting rights, as such prompt action is necessary to protect the interests of the Faith.*
>
> (letter from the Universal House of Justice to a National Spiritual Assembly, dated November 12, 1965)

Any situation in which voting rights are at risk should be referred promptly to the National Spiritual Assembly for decision [See "Lights of Guidance" {revised edition} , nos. 183, 1443, 1448)

15.1.9 **Will our understanding of Bahá'í non-involvement in politics change in the future?**

Yes. The Universal House of Justice has noted that, as the Faith emerges from obscurity and as political systems undergo change, the meaning of Bahá'í non-involvement in politics will also change. For the time being, however, it reiterates the advice of Shoghi Effendi cited in "The World Order of Bahá'u'lláh"

> *The general policy already enunciated by Shoghi Effendi in "The World Order of Bahá'u'lláh", pages 63-67, should be scrupulously upheld by the friends. However, as the Faith emerges from obscurity, the application of certain aspects of this policy will require the clarification of the House of Justice. With the passage of time, practices in the political realm will definitely undergo the profound changes anticipated in the Bahá'í writings. As a consequence, what we understand now of the policy of non-involvement in politics will also undergo a change; but as Shoghi Effendi has written, this instruction, 'at the present stage of the evolution of our Faith, should be increasingly emphasised, irrespective of its application to the East or to the West.'*
>
> (letter written on behalf of the Universal House of Justice to an individual believer, dated June 23, 1987)

15.1.10 **May Bahá'ís co-operate with movements whose methods of achieving their objectives do not accord with Bahá'í principles?**

No. Bahá'ís must not become involved in the 'adversarial approach' commonly used by people today to achieve their objectives:-

> *Not only is the Bahá'í perspective unique, so too are the methods used by the believers to achieve their objectives. Unity and co-operation are important values which should be the watchwords for activities in which the believers engage. As a consequence, Bahá'ís eschew the adversarial approach of dispute and confrontation, and seek rather the methods of consultation, with its commitment to informed discussion and mutual respect, and with its goal the achievement of consensus in the pursuit of truth. Bahá'ís aim to persuade others of*

CHAPTER FIFTEEN

the correctness of their views through their example and the use of reason, and shun the techniques of pressure, condemnation and abuse which are a deplorable feature of much of the present-day quest for social justice.

(letter written on behalf of the Universal House of Justice to the National Spiritual Assembly of Australia, dated October 24, 1990)

This means that even if the aims of the movement are compatible with those of the Faith. Bahá'ís may not associate with them if their methids are confrontational

15.1.11 *Which institution has ultimate responsibility for deciding whether Bahá'ís may be associated with a particular organisation or activity?*

The National Spiritual Assembly has this responsibility:-

It is for the National Spiritual Assembly in each country, in the light of local conditions, to decide whether a particular issue is one Bahá'ís can associate themselves with, or whether it is a political one in which they should take no sides.

(letter from the Universal House of Justice to a National Spiritual Assembly, dated December 22, 1981)

15.1.12 *Are individuals bound by the same considerations as Local Spiritual Assemblies when deciding which movements to cooperate with?*

As a general principle the same considerations apply to individuals as apply to Local Spiritual Assemblies. That is:-

The injunction to avoid participation in political controversies, identification with political pursuits, or involvement in partisan political affairs is binding on all believers, whether they act as individuals or as representatives of the Bahá'í community.

(letter written on behalf of the Universal House of Justice to the National Spiritual Assembly of Australia, dated October 24, 1990)

However:-

Within those bounds, there is a wide range of possible activities open to them in participating with other groups which aim to promote measures entirely in accord with the Bahá'í principles, such as improvement in race relations, the emancipation of women, conservation of the earth's resources, the promotion of world peace, and so on. The institutions of the Faith are generally subject to a greater restriction in the issues with which they would choose to identify themselves, since their involvement will necessarily have a direct implication for the reputation of the Faith and for its possible misrepresentation by its adversaries.

(letter written on behalf of the Universal House of Justice to the National Spiritual Assembly of Australia, dated October 24, 1990)

It should also be noted that Shoghi Effendi has specifically warned individuals against committing the Faith as a whole to projects that they have taken an interest in as individuals:-

It is very good that the individual friends should support the different societies that are furthering the cause of peace and good will, but they should be on their guard not to commit the Cause as a whole. The Cause is, as we believe, of far greater importance than any such society. It has, therefore, to preserve its dignity and never assent to any compromise with the views of others.

(letter written on behalf of Shoghi Effendi to an individual believer, dated September 7, 1926)

15.1.13 Is it advisable for Bahá'ís to take steps to persuade the government to initiate plans for the world conference necessary for the establishment of the Lesser Peace?

No. If the Bahá'ís were to become involved in attempting to have the calling of this conference implemented they would embroil themselves in partisan politics; also the Bahá'í Writings clearly state that the Lesser Peace will be brought about without the direct involvement of the Bahá'ís:-

It is not advisable for Bahá'í institutions or individuals to initiate actions designed to prod government leaders to urge their governments or the leaders of other governments to convene the world conference called for by Bahá'u'lláh and echoed in "The Promise of World Peace". Two points should be borne in mind in this regard:

1. *Because of the political gravity of the decisions implied by this call and the differing political attitudes which it evokes, such actions on the part of the Bahá'í community would embroil the friends in partisan politics. There is quite a difference between identifying, as does the Peace Statement, the need for a convocation of world leaders and initiating the political processes towards its realisation.*

2. *In the writings of the Faith (eg., the closing passages of "The Promised Day is Come"), it is clear that the establishment of the Lesser Peace, of which the conference leaders will be a related event, will come about independently of any direct Bahá'í plan or action.*

(letter from the Universal House of Justice, dated August 13, 1987)

What the Bahá'ís can and should be doing, in order to promote world peace, is to disseminate the Peace Message and the more recently published "The Prosperity of Humankind as far and wide as possible.

15.1.14 May a Local Spiritual Assembly initiate an activity, not specifically designated as Bahá'í, in order to foster association with non-Bahá'í movements?

A Local Spiritual Assembly may initiate its own non-Bahá'í activities if, after careful consideration, it determines that such an approach is the best means of furthering the interests of the Faith:-

It would even appear at times to be advisable and helpful as a supplement to their work for the Bahá'ís to initiate any undertaking, not specifically designated as Bahá'í, provided they have ascertained that such an undertaking would constitute the best way of approach to those whose minds and hearts are as yet unprepared for a full acceptance of the claim of Bahá'u'lláh.

(Shoghi Effendi, "Bahá'í Administration", p.126)

CHAPTER FIFTEEN

The Assembly may, for example, initiate an Interfaith Service as a means of proclamation to people of other Faiths; or it may organise a series of public meetings with non-Bahá'í speakers on topics of general interest to the community.

15.1.15 *May association with non-Bahá'ís involve raising funds for charity?*

The Universal House of Justice has said that a Bahá'í community may assist in raising funds for a deserving charity provided that such assistance would not have political overtones or be in any way detrimental to the Faith; and provided involvement in such an activity does not divert the community's energies from the teaching work.

15.1.16 *May an individual raise funds for non-Bahá'í causes?*

Individuals may raise funds for deserving causes provided they do so as individuals and do not identify the Faith with their activities.

15.2 **ASSOCIATION AND AFFILIATION WITH NON-BAHÁ'Í ORGANISATIONS**

15.2.1 *What is meant by 'association' with non-Bahá'í organisations?*

To associate with an organisation is to work with it towards some common goal or purpose. The association may be long term or only temporary, and does not necessarily imply support for all the organisation's principles or practices.

15.2.2 *Are Bahá'ís permitted to associate with non-Bahá'í organisations?*

Yes. Bahá'ís may associate with non-Bahá'í organisations according to the general principles outlined in the first section of this Chapter.

15.2.3 *What is meant by 'affiliation' with non-Bahá'í organisations?*

By 'affiliation' is meant becoming a paying member of an organisation and, therefore, a supporter of 'all its principles and activities'.

15.2.4 *Are Bahá'ís permitted to affiliate with non-Bahá'í organisations?*

Bahá'ís may only affiliate with organisations whose aims and methods are wholly reconcilable with the Faith. Shoghi Effendi said:-

> *Formal affiliation with and acceptance of membership in organisations whose programs or policies are not wholly reconcilable with the Teachings is of course out of the question...*

(Shoghi Effendi, "Bahá'í Procedure", p.14)

15.2.5 *May Bahá'ís affiliate with other religious organisations?*

Generally, no. It is not possible for the Teachings of another religion to be fully compatible with the Teachings of the Faith. Affiliation with another religious organisation therefore implies only partial acceptance of the Faith:-

> *Concerning membership in non-Bahá'í religious associations. The Guardian wishes to re-emphasise the general principle...that no Bahá'í who wishes to be a wholehearted and sincere upholder of the distinguishing principles of the Cause can accept full membership in any non-Bahá'í ecclesiastical organisation. For such an act would necessarily imply only a partial acceptance of the Teachings and laws of the Faith, and an incomplete recognition of its independent status, and would thus be tantamount to an act of disloyalty to the verities it enshrines. For it is only too obvious that in most of its fundamental*

assumptions the Cause of Bahá'u'lláh is completely at variance with outworn creeds, ceremonies and institutions. To be a Bahá'í and at the same time accept membership in another religious body is simply an act of contradiction that no sincere and logically-minded person can possibly accept...

(letter written on behalf of Shoghi Effendi to a National Spiritual Assembly, dated June 15, 1935)

It is, of course, permissible to associate with other religious organisations, eg. in Interfaith Services, Peace Expos, and so on, provided the independent character of the Bahá'í Faith is maintained. It is also permissible for Bahá'ís to join certain religious organisations in which the independent character of the Bahá'í Faith is recognised, eg. the World Conference on Religion and Peace with which the Bahá'í International Community is affiliated.

15.2.6 **Are Bahá'ís permitted to belong to a society that practises any form of discrimination?**

No. Shoghi Effendi said:-

Bahá'ís should certainly not belong to clubs or societies that practice any form of discrimination.

("Lights of Guidance" {revised edition}, no.1393)

15.2.7 **Are Bahá'ís permitted to belong to a secret society?**

No:-

...Generally speaking the friends should not enter secret societies. It is certainly much better for the believers to dissociate themselves from such organisations...

(letter written on behalf of Shoghi Effendi to a National Spiritual Assembly, dated March 2, 1951)

15.2.8 **What are some issues to be considered in deciding whether to pursue association or affiliation?**

The following issues should be considered:-

1. The need to preserve the independent status of the Faith in the eyes of the world:-

    ...the Bahá'ís should be absolutely independent, and stand identified only with their own Teachings. That is why they are requested to withdraw from membership in the church, the synagogue, or whatever other previous religious organisation they may have been affiliated with, to have nothing whatsoever to do with secret societies, or with political movements etc. It protects the Cause; it reinforces the Cause, and it asserts before all the world its independent character.

    (letter written on behalf of Shoghi Effendi to an individual believer, dated February 12, 1956)

2. The need for the Bahá'ís to be able to disassociate themselves if an apparently innocent movement drifts into politics:-

    ...because present world conditions are so unstable, many seemingly innocent movements can drift away from their course, and the issues they propound become political platforms or take on political overtones.

CHAPTER FIFTEEN

(letter written on behalf of the Universal House of Justice to a National Spiritual Assembly, dated December 22, 1981)

15.2.9 **Which non-Bahá'í organisations may Local Spiritual Assemblies affiliate with in Australia?**

The National Spiritual Assembly's policy is that, should the Bahá'í International Community be affiliated with an international organisation then, provided the local or regional branches of the association are not acting in a partisan political manner, Local Spiritual Assemblies may obtain formal representation in such branches by joining them as a body and nominating a representative to attend meetings. Other proposals of affiliation with non-Bahá'í organisations should be referred to the National Spiritual Assembly on a case by case basis. The National Spiritual Assembly should be sent a copy of the organisation's Constitution and stated aims and objectives, together with any other relevant background material; for example, a description of its recent activities, copies of recent policy statements. A list of organisations with which Local Spiritual Assemblies may presently affiliate is contained in section 8 of this Chapter.

15.2.10 **What should a Local Spiritual Assembly do if uncertain whether it is permissible to associate or affiliate with a particular organisation or not?**

Any Local Spiritual Assembly in doubt as to whether it should associate with a particular organisation should consult the National Spiritual Assembly. The National Spiritual Assembly should be sent a copy of the organisation's Constitution and stated aims and objectives, together with any other relevant background material; for example, a description of its recent activities, copies of recent policy statements, and so on.

15.2.11 **Are individuals bound by the same considerations as Local Spiritual Assemblies when deciding whether to associate or affiliate with a non-Bahá'í organisation?**

As a general principle, the same considerations apply to individuals as apply to Local Spiritual Assemblies . [See further Section 1 of this Chapter.] Clearly, however, there is a wide range of organisations - from professional, to community service, to leisure - that individuals are free, not only to associate with, but to become affiliate members of. Such organisations are, generally-speaking, not the concern of the Bahá'í institutions.

15.2.12 **May Bahá'ís join trade unions?**

Bahá'ís as individuals may belong to trade unions, provided the trade union is not affiliated with any particular political party:-

> *As long as the trade unions are not members of any particular political party, there does not seem to be any objection to the Bahá'ís belonging to them.*

(letter written on behalf of Shoghi Effendi to an individual believer, dated February 2, 1951)

15.2.13 **May Bahá'ís hold office in non-Bahá'í organisations such as trade unions?**

If a Bahá'í is able to belong to such an organisation, then he or she may also hold office and may participate in its election procedures, even though these may differ from Bahá'í election procedures:-

> *As long as this and other associations, such as the special interest groups you mention, are not affiliated with any political party and are not involved in political activities there is no objection to Bahá'ís belonging to them nor to their holding office in them. As for participation in elections of non-Bahá'í organisations which are open*

to Bahá'ís but which employ election methods different from Bahá'í practices, believers need not avoid the election procedures carried out in such organisations.

(letter written on behalf of the Universal House of Justice to a National Spiritual Assembly, dated January 4, 1979)

The specific principles to be borne in mind are contained in the following guidance from the Universal House of Justice to a National Spiritual Assembly, concerning the question of whether Bahá'ís may be elected Barrio Captains or may serve on a Barrio local Council:-

> 1. *He is not required to become a member of a political party.*
>
> 2. *Service as a Barrio Captain or as a member of the Barrio Council does not involve him in partisan politics.*
>
> 3. *That he does not campaign for election to office. There is no objection to allowing one's name to be placed in nomination if required by law. If nominations are not obligatory and the voter is allowed to write on the ballot paper and vote for the names of those he wishes to be elected, this procedure should be followed by the Bahá'ís.*

(letter of the Universal House of Justice dated April 24, 1972)

15.2.14 What should an individual do if uncertain whether it is permissible to associate or affiliate with a particular organisation or not?

Individuals who are uncertain whether or not it is permissible to associate with a particular organisation should consult their Local Spiritual Assemblies. If the Local Spiritual Assembly is uncertain it must consult the National Spiritual Assembly. In the matter of association with governments in particular, the Universal House of Justice has noted the growing necessity for Bahá'í communities to establish some form of relationship. In view of the complex situations that are bound to arise, it is most important that the authorised institutions of the Faith, rather than individuals, determine what form those relationships will take:-

> *In view of the necessity of the Bahá'í community to relate to governments, whether for reasons of defending its persecuted members, or of responding to opportunities to be of service, a correct understanding of what is legitimate Bahá'í action in the face of the policy of non-interference with government affairs is bound to be difficult to achieve on the part of individual friends. The force of circumstances, operating internally and externally, is pressing the Bahá'í community into certain relationships with governments. Hence, it is important that decisions as to the conduct of such relationships be made by authorised institutions of the Faith and not by individuals. In matters of this kind, given the utter complexity of human affairs with which the Bahá'í community must increasingly cope with spiritually and practically, individual judgment is not sufficient.*

(letter written on behalf of the Universal House of Justice to an individual believer, dated June 23, 1987)

A list of organisations with which individuals may affiliate is contained in section 8 of this Chapter.

CHAPTER FIFTEEN

15.2.15 *May a Local Spiritual Assembly appoint a representative to attend a non-Bahá'í consultative gathering, conference, or adhoc committee project?*

Yes. If the Local Spiritual Assembly has determined that association is desirable according to the principles outlined above, it may appoint a representative to such a gathering, where that gathering is local in nature and taking place within the Assembly's area of jurisdiction. If the function is regional in nature, the prerogative of appointing a representative lies with the Regional Teaching Committee. At the national level the National Spiritual Assembly has the responsibility. It should be noted that the State Information Offices also have the responsibility of fostering cordial relations with State Government Departments and non-governmental organisations at the State and regional level. Local Spiritual Assemblies may, therefore, like to consult with their State Information Office to share ideas and plans.

15.2.16 *What are the rules of conduct governing Bahá'í participation in consultations initiated by non-Bahá'ís?*

The following guidance, provided by the Universal House of Justice to the Bahá'í International Community, is useful here:-

> 1. *Bahá'ís should not hesitate to present the positive Bahá'í Teachings on a subject but should refrain from taking sides in a debate. When partisan political stances are presented in the form of resolutions, Bahá'ís must refrain from voting:-*
>
> *Bahá'ís should not become involved in controversial political issues affecting any nation. When such issues are presented in the form of resolutions, Bahá'í representatives have no choice but to abstain from voting. During the consultation however, they may, indeed they should, present the positive Bahá'í teaching on the subject and refrain from siding with those who openly criticise and seek to oppose the specific policy of any nation.*
>
> (letter from the Universal House of Justice to Bahá'í International Community, dated February 2, 1970)

> 2. Bahá'ís may make motions in such consultations *'provided everything said and done is fully compatible with the Teachings.'* (quoted from Shoghi Effendi in letter from Bahá'í International Community to National Spiritual Assembly of Australia, dated January 4, 1983).
> 3. Bahá'ís should not use the identifying names of policies that will be connected with particular governments [apartheid is an example]. They may, however, support positive activities aimed at counteracting such policies, provided this will not appear to align them for or against any particular government:-

> *...while all activities to do with human welfare can be manoeuvred by political interests, there are certain issues which, in the world today, are identified with the policies of particular governments ...The identifying names of such policies should obviously not be used, although United Nations activities aimed at dissolving the particular problem of prejudice involved can be supported wholeheartedly by the Bahá'í community. We must not appear to become aligned with or against the policies of any particular government, but should always support activities to promote the oneness of mankind.*
>
> (letter written on behalf of the Universal House of Justice to Bahá'í

CHAPTER FIFTEEN

International Community, dated May 8, 1975)

15.2.17 **What are the criteria for deciding whether a non-Bahá'í organisation may participate in Bahá'í activities?**

The over-riding criteria is that the non-Bahá'í organisation not be involved in political activities:-

> In order to decide whether it would be appropriate for a Bahá'í community to invite the participation of another organisation in a Bahá'í sponsored event, one would have to determine whether the organisation in question was in fact non-political, that is to say, not identified in the public mind with partisan political stances.

> (letter from the Bahá'í International Community to an individual believer, dated July 26, 1989)

15.3 **OTHER MATTERS - LOCAL SPIRITUAL ASSEMBLIES**

15.3.1 *May Local Spiritual Assemblies publicly comment on current issues?*

Local Spiritual Assemblies are encouraged to find ways of correlating the Teachings of the Faith to the problems of the world, as a means of furthering the teaching work:-

> *The Cause needs more Bahá'í scholars, people who not only are devoted to it and believe in it and are anxious to tell others about it, but also who have a deep grasp of the Teachings and their significance, and who can correlate its beliefs with the current thoughts and problems of the people of the world.*

> (letter written on behalf of Shoghi Effendi to an individual believer, dated October 21, 1943)

> *With the approach of the Year of Peace and the rapidly growing awareness among thinking people of the need for world-wide solutions to the problems threatening humankind, the House of Justice feels that there is a need for research and the writing of books and papers on subjects which are of immediate interest to the leaders of thought and the generality of mankind.*

> (letter written on behalf of the Universal House of Justice to the Association for Bahá'í Studies, Canada, dated March 13, 1985)

So, for example, they may write letters to the editor of their local newspaper along these lines. What they may not do is issue public statements touching on the controversial and political issues of the day. To do so is to risk involving the Faith in complex issues that are no concern of ours, and which may not only divert our energies from the teaching work, but also run the risk of identifying the Faith, in the public mind, with particular sects or factions, thus obscuring its essential message of unity:-

> *Touching the publication of articles and pamphlets bearing on the controversial and political issues of the day, I desire to remind my dearly-beloved fellow-workers that at the present stage when the Cause is still in its infancy, any minute and detailed analysis by the Friends of subjects that are in the forefront of general discussion would often be misconstrued in certain quarters and give rise to suspicions and misunderstandings that would react unfavourably on the Cause. They would tend to create a misconception of the real object, the true*

CHAPTER FIFTEEN

mission, and the fundamental character of the Bahá'í Faith. We should, while endeavouring to uphold loyally and expound conscientiously our social and moral principles in all their essence and purity, in all their bearings upon the divers phases of human society, insure that no direct reference or particular criticism in our exposition of the fundamentals of the Faith would tend to antagonise any existing institution, or help to identify a purely spiritual movement with the base clamourings and contentions of warring sects, factions and nations.

(Shoghi Effendi, "Principles of Bahá'í Administration", p.32)

Whereas a general statement on the Bahá'í principle of equal rights for men and women of every race, nation, class and creed is perfectly in order, it is dangerous to start making comments on specific items of legislation because so many complex questions arise. For example, it is Bahá'í law that an individual has an indefeasible right to will his property in any way he wishes, and that a valid will may not be challenged; would we therefore be justified in publicly opposing legislation which makes for compulsory bequests to widows and children of a deceased?...It should be the aim of the Bahá'ís to avoid becoming involved in such matters so that their primary purpose of leading men to Bahá'u'lláh is not obscured.

(letter from the Universal House of Justice to a National Spiritual Assembly, dated July 21, 1968)

A method of commenting on current issues that might appropriately be used is that employed by Shoghi Effendi in his "Goal of a New World Order". In this work he analyses political theory rather than political practice, thereby avoiding condemnation of existing institutional organisations. As a clear cut line cannot always be drawn between theory and practice, however, it is advisable to use this method, and any others that may be conceived, with care. [see further "Lights of Guidance" {revised edition} nos. 1468, 1469].

15.3.2 ***May Local Spiritual Assemblies make submissions to governments on any issues?***

The National Spiritual Assembly's policy is that Local Spiritual Assemblies may respond to an inquiry from a governmental body requesting the Bahá'í viewpoint on a particular subject, if the subject is local, or if local opinion is being deliberately sought. If a Local Spiritual Assembly is approached for an opinion on a matter that is not purely local, it must refer the inquiry to the National Spiritual Assembly. The National Spiritual Assembly may then guide the Assembly as to how to respond or ask the Assembly to refer the inquirer to the National Spiritual Assembly. If making a submission the following criteria must be adhered to:
1. It must be a matter of vital interest to the Faith:-

It is perfectly in order for Bahá'í institutions to present the Bahá'í view or recommendations on any subject of vital interest to the Faith which is under the consideration of a government...

(letter from the Universal House of Justice to Bahá'í International Community, dated November 21, 1971)

2. The government must either invite or be open to receive recommendations:-

...on any subject of vital interest to the Faith which is under the consideration of a government, if the governmental authority itself

CHAPTER FIFTEEN

invites such a submission, or if it is open to receive recommendations.

(Letter as above.)

3. The Bahá'í institution can only submit its views; it cannot press their acceptance on the government:-

   The Bahá'í Assemblies should, however, refrain from bringing pressure to bear on the authorities in such matters, either separately or in concert with others. The Bahá'ís will submit their views, if permissible, expressing them as cogently and forcefully as the occasion warrants, but will not go beyond this to the stage of pressing the authorities to adopt these views...

   (letter from the Universal House of Justice to Bahá'í International Community, dated November 21, 1971)

4. The submission must not be critical of any particular party or faction or in any other way divisive:-

   ...the Assembly must ensure that it does not, by any minute or detailed analysis of a situation 'needlessly alienate or estrange any individual, government or people,' or involve the Faith in 'the base clamourings and contentions of warring sects, factions, and nations.'

   (letter from the Universal House of Justice to Bahá'í International Community, dated November 21, 1971)

15.3.3 May a Local Spiritual Assembly sign an appeal or protest directed to its own and/or other governments?

It is permissible for Bahá'í institutions to make appeals on behalf of the Bahá'ís themselves:-

   When the protest or appeal is being made on behalf of the Bahá'í themselves there is no problem. This is the sort of activity in which Assemblies have been engaged all over the world on behalf of their persecuted fellow brethren in Iran. The guiding consideration here is wisdom, and this is why believers in certain countries have not been asked by the Universal House of Justice to make any appeals; for them to do so would have been disadvantageous to the Cause in their own countries, or would have had a negative effect in Iran.

   (letter written on behalf of the Universal House of Justice to a National Spiritual Assembly, dated December 22, 1981)

Should a Local Spiritual Assembly have occasion to make such an appeal, it should first obtain the approval of the National Spiritual Assembly. If the appeal is being made on behalf of a non-Bahá'í organisation, a Local Spiritual Assembly may only associate itself with the appeal if it is satisfied it will meet all the criteria outlined in Section 1 of this chapter.

15.3.4 May a Local Spiritual Assembly lend its support to a march or demonstration concerning a particular issue?

As previously noted in Section 1, the Faith cannot be associated with protests aimed against specific government policies. On the other hand, Shoghi Effendi has said that the Bahá'ís may take part in demonstrations intended to promote a fundamental principle of the Faith, such as equal race relations:-

   ...a number of Bahá'í students at the University of Chicago joined a

CHAPTER FIFTEEN

protest against racial prejudice and carried a placard with the word 'Bahá'í' on it. Mr. Ellsworth Blackwell asked the Guardian: 'Is there anything wrong in the protesting of Bahá'í student groups against racial prejudice along with other student organisations?' The beloved Guardian replied through his Secretary (January 1948):

'He does not see any objection to Bahá'í students taking part as Bahá'ís in protests such as that mentioned in the (newspaper) clipping. On the contrary, he does not see how they could remain indifferent when fellow students were voicing our own Bahá'í attitude on such a vital issue and one we feel so strongly about.'

("Bahá'í News", Insert, June 1964) ("The American Bahá'í," May 1983, p.28)

[See also "Lights of Guidance" {revised edition}, no. 1804]

In deciding whether or not to lend its support to a march or demonstration concerning a particular issue, the "vital distinction the Assembly must make is between a protest against attitudes and practices prevalent in some quarters of society, on the one hand, and protests antagonistic to the government, on the • other. The former may be acceptable (if all other criteria for involvement are satisfied - see Section 1). The latter is not:-

As your letter points out, there are instances where the Guardian endorsed Bahá'ís identifying themselves with protest activities on vital issues which the Bahá'í Teachings illuminate. It must be remembered that there is an important distinction between protest against attitudes and practices prevalent in some quarters of society and protest antagonistic to the government. The Bahá'í Faith directs its attention principally to the promotion of attitudinal change consequent to acceptance of the claim of Bahá'u'lláh, confident that the transformation of attitudes and values will, in due course, yield its fruit in measures which will resolve the problems with which humanity is now burdened.

(letter written on behalf of the Universal House of Justice to the National Spiritual Assembly of Australia, dated October 24, 1990)

15.4 OTHER MATTERS - INDIVIDUALS

15.4.1 *May Bahá'ís serve in government jobs?*

Yes. It is necessary to distinguish between posts that are purely administrative in character and posts that are diplomatic or political. Service in purely administrative posts is one way in which Bahá'ís can demonstrate their love for their country:-

This love for their country the Bahá'ís show by serving its well-being in their daily activity, or by working in the administrative channels of the government instead of through party politics or in diplomatic or political posts.

(letter from the Universal House of Justice to National Spiritual Assemblies in Africa, dated February 8, 1970)

Purely administrative posts are those that are 'under no circumstances...affected by the changes and chances that political activities and party government in every land, must necessarily involve'

(Shoghi Effendi, "The World Order of Bahá'u'lláh", p.65).

15.4.2 *May Bahá'ís vote in civil elections?*

Bahá'ís may vote in civil elections provided they can do so without identifying themselves with one party or another. They must make their choice according to the merits of the individual and not according to the party he or she belongs to:-

> *It remains for the individuals to so use their right to vote as to keep aloof from party politics, and always bear in mind that they are voting on the merits of the individual, rather than because he belongs to one party or another. The matter must be made perfectly clear to the individuals, who will be left free to exercise their discretion and judgment.*

(Shoghi Effendi, "Principles of Bahá'í Administration", p.29-30)

Voting in State and Federal elections in Australia is compulsory for Australian citizens. In some parts of Australia voting in local elections is also compulsory. Bahá'ís are therefore obliged to vote and should bear the above guidance in mind when doing so.

15.4.3 *May Bahá'ís join the armed forces?*

Bahá'ís may only join the armed forces if it is quite certain they can do so in a non-combatant capacity. This principle is not altered by the fact that joining the armed forces is a useful means of acquiring a trade or skill:-

> *The Universal House of Justice has received your recent letter requesting advice about Bahá'ís who wish to volunteer for military service for the sake of the trade or skill they can learn. It instructs us to say that the principle has been clearly established. A Bahá'í may not volunteer to serve in the army or other armed service if, by so doing, he makes himself liable to undertake combatant service. Your Assembly should therefore, in the light of the regulations governing military service in Australia, give permission for Bahá'ís to enlist only if you are sure that they will thereby in no way jeopardise their non-combatant status.*

(letter written on behalf of the Universal House of Justice to National Spiritual Assembly of Australia, dated October 31, 1978)

The National Spiritual Assembly has contacted the Department of Defence and been advised that the Australian Defence Force does not enlist professed non-combatants. All elements of the Defence Force can be committed, at relatively short notice, to active duty. Bahá'í youth should therefore be discouraged from enlisting or registering for apprenticeships within any of the Services.

15.4.4 *May Bahá'ís participate in strikes?*

Bahá'ís may participate in strikes called by recognised authorities, such as trade unions. The decision is left to the individual and the Universal House of Justice has advised National Spiritual Assemblies not to lay down any more rules on the subject:-

> *Regarding the participation of Bahá'ís in strikes, the beloved Guardian, in his letter to your National Spiritual Assembly dated 11th July 1956, expressed approval of your understanding of this matter. As you know, 'Abdu'l-Bahá in general disapproved of strikes. Briefly stated, the Bahá'í attitude is that when the law recognises strikes as legal, as*

CHAPTER FIFTEEN

> *when called by a properly constituted authority such as a trade union, the Bahá'í teaching neither requires nor forbids an individual to participate in the strike but leaves him free to decide for himself what is the proper course of action in the particular circumstance.*
>
> *This ruling, we feel, applies by its nature only to so-called official strikes and when Bahá'ís are members of a trade union. However, as essentially this question is a matter of conscience your Assembly should be very careful, in the words written on behalf of the Guardian in the above-mentioned letter to your Assembly, to "avoid becoming rigid and laying down any more rules and regulations of conduct".*

(letter from the Universal House of Justice to a National Spiritual Assembly, dated August 9, 1969)

15.4.5 **May Bahá'ís, as individuals, participate in coordinated campaigns such as systematic letter-writing or signing appeals?**

The Universal House of Justice has said:-

> *In considering whether they should participate in coordinated campaigns such as letter writing, or signing petitions, Bahá'ís should be guided by their Spiritual Assemblies, and are encouraged to accept this guidance in a spirit of radiant acquiescence. The Assemblies should give careful consideration to the motives of the originators of the activity and the methods which are being used. Bahá'ís should avoid contention and strife, and are to be distinguished by their honesty and fair-mindedness, and their respect for the rule of law. They should carefully avoid being involved in partisan activities which are sponsored by a political organisation, and are warned to "beware lest they allow themselves to become the tools of unscrupulous politicians, or to be entrapped by the treacherous devices of the plotters and the perfidious among their countrymen."*

(letter written on behalf of the Universal House of Justice to the National Spiritual Assembly of Australia, dated October 24, 1990)

15.4.6 **May Bahá'ís, as individuals, participate in protests or demonstrations?**

The following matter, on which a Local Spiritual Assembly in Australia sought guidance, was referred to the Universal House of Justice. Our National Spiritual Assembly wrote:-

> *Members of the Assembly have noted that individual Bahá'ís have participated in or attended recent rallies in ... relating to environmental issues, which clearly have confrontationist aims and are currently dividing the general community. ...Often these activities are not 'political' in the pure sense of party divisions and because of this the friends feel they are free to join in, according to their own private views on the question. But these issues are usually confrontationist and often involve a certain degree of opposition to government policy. In referring the matter to the Universal House of Justice the National Spiritual Assembly particularly asked whether it would be possible for Bahá'ís to participate in such activities as individuals ie. provided they did not formally associate the Faith with the activity.*

CHAPTER FIFTEEN

The Universal House of Justice replied:-

...Bahá'ís eschew the adversarial approach of dispute and confrontation, and seek rather the methods of consultation, with its commitment to informed discussion and mutual respect, and with its goal the achievement of consensus in the pursuit of truth... ...in light of the Bahá'í approach to the search for truth, it would not be proper for a Bahá'í to become involved in environmental activities which are confrontationist. The concern of the ... Bahá'ís for conservation is highly commendable, but they should be aided to find other, more productive, means to express this concern; a study of the recently prepared compilation on conservation of the earth's resources may well be of benefit to them in this regard.

(letter written on behalf of the Universal House of Justice to the National Spiritual Assembly of Australia, dated October 24, 1990)

15.4.7 **May Bahá'ís, as individuals, publicly comment on current issues?**

As noted in Section 3, 'May Local Spiritual Assemblies publicly comment on current issues?', Bahá'ís are encouraged to find ways of correlating the Teachings of the Faith to the problems of the world, as a means of furthering the teaching work. So, for example, Bahá'ís may write letters to the editor of their local newspapers along these lines. Bahá'ís may also write letters to the editors of publications to express their personal views on issues if they do not identify themselves as Bahá'ís, imply that they represent the Faith or a Bahá'í community, or discuss the Bahá'í Faith. Bahá'ís, as individuals, are under the same constraints as Local Spiritual Assemblies regarding controversial and political issues of the day; that is, generally speaking, they may not discuss them, regardless of whether they are acting as representatives of the Bahá'í community or purely as individuals.

15.4.8 **May Bahá'ís, as individuals, write to the government to propose action on a particular issue?**

Yes:-

Like other citizens, Bahá'ís are free to write to their governments in order to propose action on environmental or other problems. Such approaches are considered non-partisan in nature, because they are normally addressed to the appropriate government department or to a Member of Parliament. It would not be appropriate for a Bahá'í to attempt to enlist the support of one party for initiatives that are known to be opposed by others.

(letter from the Bahá'í International Community to an individual believer, dated July 26, 1989)

15.4.9 **How should a Bahá'í proceed to rectify an injustice?**

The Bahá'ís should work within the existing legal system. They must not resort to political action:-

It is contrary to Bahá'í principles for a believer to resort to partisan political action in asserting his rights or in seeking to obtain justice... Bahá'ís are free to work within the existing political and legal system. There is no objection to any Bahá'í making a legal claim to property or rights through the courts or administrative agencies to which he has access.

CHAPTER FIFTEEN

(letter from the Universal House of Justice to a National Spiritual Assembly, dated November 19, 1974)

15.5 NOTES FOR REGISTERED GROUPS

As Registered Groups do not have any administrative status they should follow the guidelines set out in this Chapter for Bahá'ís as individuals.

15.6 SUGGESTED FURTHER READING

It is suggested that Local Spiritual Assemblies also consult:-
"Lights of Guidance" {revised edition}, esp. the sections on 'Churches', 'Organisations, Non-Bahá'í', and 'Politics and Government'. P.J. Khan, 'Political Non-Involvement and Obedience to Government', A compilation of messages from the Universal House of Justice (Bahá'í Publications Australia, 1979)

15.7 UNITED NATIONS DAYS AND EVENTS

15.7.1 *Below is a listing of United Nations days and events that offer rich opportunities for Bahá'í-United Nations cooperation*

International Women's Day	March 8
World Health Day	April 7
World Environment Day	June 5
International Literacy Day	September 8
International Day of Peace	September 19
Universal Children's Day	First Monday in October
World Food Day	October 16
United Nations Day	October 24
World Disarmament Week	October 24-30
International Week of Science and Peace	November
International Volunteer Day for Economic and Social Development	December 5
Human Rights Day	December 10

Note that additional 'Days' and 'Weeks' are announced from time to time and that, therefore the above list will not be complete.

15.8 ORGANISATIONS BAHÁ'ÍS MAY BE AFFILIATE MEMBERS OF IN AUSTRALIA

15.8.1 *The following is a list of organisations that Bahá'ís may be affiliate members of in Australia. Both Local Spiritual Assemblies and individuals may be affiliates, except where otherwise noted. Note also the proviso that these organisations should not be acting in a political manner at the local level.*

1. United Nations Association of Australia
2. UNICEF
3. Men of the Trees
4. World Wide Fund for Nature
5. National Council of Women (National Bahá'í Women's Committee is a member of the Council)
6. Women's International League for Peace and Freedom - individuals only

7. Australian Conservation Foundation - individuals only and they are to be advised against it, although not forbidden
8. One World Campaign - individuals only
9. World Conference on Religion and Peace

15.8.2 ***For your further information, the National Spiritual Assembly advises that Bahá'ís are <u>not permitted</u> to join the following organisations:***

1. Amnesty International
2. Women's Electoral Lobby
3. People for Nuclear Disarmament
4. Brahma Kumaris
5. Results

This list is obviously not complete. If in doubt, contact the National Office.

Proposals by Local Spiritual Assemblies for affiliation with non Bahá'í organisations not already approved by the National Spiritual Assembly should be referred to the National Spiritual Assembly on a case by case basis. The National Spiritual Assembly should be sent a copy of the organisation's Constitution and stated aims and objectives, together with any other relevant back ground material; for example, a description of its recent activities, copies of recent policy statements, and so on.

Detailed guidance on the relevant criteria for determining whether Bahá'ís may associate with an organisation in a particular activity is contained in Chapter 15 of the Handbook. In matters of association, therefore, Local Spiritual Assemblies should first consult this Chapter and then, if it has any doubts, seek guidance from the National Assembly, providing the same information as listed above for affiliation.

CHAPTER SIXTEEN

Chapter 16

16. Planning

16.1 INTRODUCTION

16.1.1 *What is the purpose of this Chapter?*

The purpose of this Chapter is to suggest how adoption, by Local Spiritual Assemblies, of a method of planning similar to that implemented by the National Spiritual Assembly and its national committees, may assist the work of the Local Assemblies. To this end, the method of planning used at the national level has been adapted for the use of Local Assemblies in the sections that follow. Briefly, it is a method by which a Local Spiritual Assembly can work out a set of goals for the coming year; formulate them into an annual plan; implement them; and review the plan's progress in achieving the goals set, with the assistance of considered comments from its local community and the National Spiritual Assembly. Assemblies are encouraged to follow the method outlined in this Chapter as closely as possible. Full observance is not, however, obligatory, and it is ultimately for the Local Spiritual Assembly to decide how much of this method it will put into practise. Local Spiritual Assemblies may also like to consider implementing aspects of this method of planning with their local committees.

16.1.2 *What is the importance of planning?*

The importance of planning is that it enables the Local Spiritual Assembly to '*see the end in the beginning*' (Bahá'u'lláh, "The Seven Valleys and the Four Valleys", US paperback edition, p.15); that is, it enables the Local Spiritual Assembly to have a vision of what it wants to achieve and to steadily work towards that vision. The Universal House of Justice has noted that:-

> *The adoption of a local plan by the Local Assembly can exert a far-reaching influence on its work and on the life of the community.*

> (letter to a National Spiritual Assembly, dated December 24, 1975)

By developing a plan and a budget for the year ahead, a Local Spiritual Assembly can bring order into its efforts and have a measure of its progress. Without a set of clear goals to aim at, efforts are spread here and there, with little effect. 'Abdu'l-Bahá expresses this principle in the following passage:-

> *So long as the thoughts of an individual are scattered he will achieve no results, but if his thinking be concentrated on a single point wonderful will be the fruits thereof.*

> ("Selected Writings of 'Abdu'l-Bahá", p.110-11)

Just so, if a Local Spiritual Assembly draws up an annual plan, each agreed element of the plan becomes a 'single point' on which the Assembly's attention can be concentrated.

16.1.3 *What period of time does a plan cover?*

The method of planning outlined below operates over twelve months. It is prepared in advance and put into practice following Ridvan.

16.1.4 *When should a Local Spiritual Assembly draw up its plan for the coming year?*

Local Spiritual Assemblies should draw up their annual plan for the following year in February,

CHAPTER SIXTEEN

at the same time they draw up their budget for that year. Developing the two together has obvious advantages, as the Assembly must take its financial resources into account in deciding on its activities. The final plan should be presented to the community at the Annual General Meeting and should serve as a recommendation from the outgoing Assembly to the newly-elected Assembly. A copy should also be sent, along with the Local Spiritual Assembly's Annual Report, to the National Spiritual Assembly.

16.1.5 ***Should the Local Spiritual Assembly consult with the community when preparing its plan?***

Yes. It is essential for the Local Spiritual Assembly to consult with its community at an early stage in the development of the plan. Article XI, s.4 of the "By-Laws of a Local Spiritual Assembly" provides that:-

> *The Assembly, both preceding and following the annual election, shall invite discussion and welcome suggestions from the community, in order that its plans may reflect the community mind and heart.*

16.2 **THE PLANNING PROCESS**

16.2.1 ***What is the starting point for drawing up a plan?***

The starting point for all Assemblies' plans is to refer to and study the current Plan of the National Spiritual Assembly. That document will highlight those issues which are of primary importance and will suggest approaches which may be followed.
Other tasks for Local Spiritual Assemblies are to be found in the "By-Laws of a Local Spiritual Assembly" and in letters from the National Spiritual Assembly specifically addressed to them from time to time. As well, the thoughts of the Regional Teaching Committee and its wishes in relation to teaching goals should be taken into account.

16.2.2 ***How should the content of the plan be determined?***

The plan should be kept "simple and should be set out as an action list; that is, it should be a list of specific things to do, rather than general ideas. In this way, an Assembly's annual plan will be quite different from the wording of the current National Plan itself. As an example, one of the goals may be to:-

- ***Encourage Local Spiritual Assemblies and believers to consider ways in which they can advance the social and economic development of their communities.***

If an Assembly wanted to work towards such a goal, it might decide on the following:-

- ***Foster closer association with a local environmental group by assisting in their activities, eg. tree planting projects; appoint an Assembly member to liaise with the group.***

By listing things to do rather than writing down vague and general ideas, each Assembly will have to come to terms with what it feels it can actually achieve in one year. The list then becomes something against which real progress can be measured. It will also aid the Assembly to allocate its funds.

16.2.3 ***What method should the Local Spiritual Assembly use to draw up its plan?***

There are different methods that may be used for drawing up a plan. One possible method - but by no means the only one - is outlined below:-

1. Ensure that each member of the community has a copy of the current National Plan and has read it. Be aware, also, of your "By-Laws" and of the wishes of your

CHAPTER SIXTEEN

Regional Teaching Committee.

2. Organise a community meeting. Local Spiritual Assemblies are strongly encouraged to invite the assistants to their Auxiliary Board member to be present.
3. At this meeting write up the major headings of the goals Local Spiritual Assemblies have been asked to work towards on large sheets of paper.
4. Have an open consultation at which all members of the community are encouraged to come up with ideas for activities. Focus on teaching, the primary task of all Assemblies. Write down all ideas under their appropriate headings, regardless of how unrealistic some may seem.
5. At the next Local Spiritual Assembly meeting review the ideas that have come up by considering how, when, by whom, each idea could be implemented. Check the estimated cost against the community's estimated budget for the year. Examining each idea from these different perspectives will help to determine how realistic the proposal is and what value would be derived from implementing it. Again, Local Spiritual Assemblies are strongly encouraged to invite the assistants to their Auxiliary Board member to be present. The Assembly should also refer to any guidance received from the National Spiritual Assembly and to its "By-Laws".
6. Gradually eliminate those ideas that don't seem feasible until the Assembly is left with a number of specific items that it is satisfied are constructive and able to be achieved by the community.
7. Write the plan down and submit it to the community for comments. Once these have been received and considered by the Local Spiritual Assembly, the plan can be finalised and submitted to the community at the Annual General Meeting. An example of how a final plan may look is contained in section 6. Further information on how to draw up a plan can be found in the booklet 'An Approach to Social and Economic Development' prepared by the National Bahá'í Social and Economic Development Committee and previously sent to all Local Spiritual Assemblies.

16.2.4 *Should a Local Spiritual Assembly change its plan during the year?*

It may be that, as a result of a mid-year review of the plan, or as a result of recommendations received from the community during the year, the Local Spiritual Assembly may decide to modify its plan. Circumstances change and Assemblies should remain flexible enough to respond to new opportunities as they arise. As a general principle, however, a Local Spiritual Assembly should not make major changes to its plan once it is finalised. It is far preferable to persevere with the major tasks of a plan. Most goals need some persistent work before any result is seen. Chopping and changing can result in a waste of effort.

16.3 REVIEWING

16.3.1 *When should the plan be reviewed?*

As the Local Spiritual Assembly is required to submit its Annual Report to its community at the Annual General Meeting it should review progress with its plan prior to this date, as an aid to preparing the Report. It is also necessary to make an assessment of last year's plan in order to have a measure of the community's achievements to date before preparing the following year's plan. The review should, therefore, take place some time early in, or prior to, February. The Assembly may also like to consider conducting a review part way through the year, in order to assess its progress.

16.3.2 *How does a review begin?*

The method of review outlined below is based on the reporting format the Universal House of Justice requests National Spiritual Assemblies to use when submitting their reports to the Universal House of Justice. A serious review has as its starting point the list of things to do

CHAPTER SIXTEEN

set out in the Local Spiritual Assembly's annual plan. It is a mistake to simply list what the Assembly has done without reference to what was planned to be done. The plan should therefore be gone through, item by item. If it is discovered that the Assembly has achieved other things that were not in the plan, these should be added to the end of the review and a note made to include them for consideration when the Assembly draws up its next plan.

16.3.3 *What method of review should be used?*

The Local Spiritual Assembly should first decide what progress has been made with each item. This requires simply an evaluation of whether it has been achieved, partially achieved, or not even started. The Assembly should then list briefly the steps that have been taken in relation to each item. For example, if a goal of the plan is:-

- ***Foster closer association with a local environmental group by assisting their activities, eg. tree planting projects; appoint an Assembly member to liaise with the group. the Assembly might begin by noting:-***
Achieved.
- ***John Brown has met with the group and made arrangements for the community to participate in two tree planting projects. The first of these projects took place on a weekend in June. The second project is scheduled for November.***

Once this has been done the Assembly can begin to evaluate why some functions were carried out and were successful, whilst others did not succeed so well. It is important that the assessment be carried out in a spirit of true Bahá'í consultation: that is, it should be full and frank, but also impartial and friendly. Assembly members must not engage in negative criticism of friends associated with unsuccessful activities. For example, an evaluation of the above activity might be as follows:-

The first project in which we were involved was successful in that those community members who participated enjoyed themselves and made good friends with members of the environmental group, who were likewise very pleased to have the assistance and impressed that we had offered. The Assembly is concerned, however, that not many community members came, despite advance notice. We need to encourage greater participation in the next project in November. The Assembly recognises that some friends have transport problems and will undertake to arrange lifts for these people in future.

To aid the consultation it may be useful for the Secretary to prepare in advance a draft review so that the Assembly has something on which to base its consultation. This draft review should, however, confine itself to listing the proposed activities, the degree to which each was achieved, and the steps taken with regard to each. It should not include an evaluation of the reasons why a project succeeded, or did not succeed, which the Assembly may wish to consider during its meeting.

16.3.4 *Why is reviewing essential?*

To review and assess one's actions is an important part of spiritual growth:-

> *Bring thyself to account each day ere thou art summoned to a reckoning; for death, unheralded, shall come upon thee and thou shalt be called to give account for thy deeds.*
>
> (Bahá'u'lláh, "The Hidden Words" no.31)

Just as individuals need to review their actions in order to learn how to improve them, so too, do Assemblies. A mid-year review, for example, might result in the Assembly recognising that it needs to 'fine tune' its activities, as in the example cited above. The major value of a review, however, is that it enables the Assembly to measure the community's progress with its goals and to give a constructive account of its own activities to the community and to the National Spiritual Assembly.

CHAPTER SIXTEEN

16.4 FEEDBACK

16.4.1 *What response may the Local Spiritual Assembly expect from the National Spiritual Assembly?*

The written reaction of the National Spiritual Assembly to the Annual Report submitted by a Local Spiritual Assembly is the main feedback and guidance it will receive from this Institution. The Local Spiritual Assembly should, therefore, give careful and detailed attention to this response. In addition, Local Spiritual Assemblies must send copies of their Minutes to the National Spiritual Assembly. The National Spiritual Assembly will follow progress with the Local Spiritual Assemblies' plans through this means also and may sometimes send comments in response to the Minutes.

16.4.2 *What should the Local Spiritual Assembly do if it disagrees with the comments it receives from the National Spiritual Assembly?*

It is bound to happen that not all Local Spiritual Assemblies will agree with all the comments they receive from the National Spiritual Assembly. When this occurs, the Local Spiritual Assembly must bear in mind the principles of obedience to the National Spiritual Assembly, as explained by Shoghi Effendi:-

> *...the Guardian wishes me to again affirm his view that the authority of the National Spiritual Assembly is undivided and unchallengeable in all matters pertaining to the administration of the Faith...and that, therefore, the obedience of individual Bahá'í, delegates, groups, and Assemblies to that authority is imperative, and should be whole-hearted and unqualified. He is convinced that the unreserved acceptance and complete application of this vital provision of the Administration is essential to the maintenance of the highest degree of unity among the believers, and is indispensable to the effective working of the administrative machinery of the Faith in every country.*

(letter written on behalf of Shoghi Effendi, to a National Spiritual Assembly, dated June 11, 1934)

This means that the Local Spiritual Assembly has a duty to carefully consider the advice of the National Spiritual Assembly, even if it is not in full agreement with this advice. The Local Spiritual Assembly is, however, also free to write to the National Spiritual Assembly and explain why it does not agree with its comments. The National Spiritual Assembly, in its turn, then has a duty to carefully consider the Local Spiritual Assembly's point of view.

16.4.3 *What about feedback from the local community?*

The Local Spiritual Assembly is obliged to consult with the local community and give due consideration to any recommendations brought forward at the Feast, including recommendations concerning progress with the plan. The Assembly is also obliged to remind the friends periodically of the plan during the year. It may be that the Assembly will choose to modify its plan as a result of the community's recommendations. As previously noted in the 'Introduction', the Local Spiritual Assembly must consult with the community at the time of drawing up the plan and it must present the final plan to the community at the Annual General Meeting. There are opportunities here also, therefore, for the community to have input into the plan.

16.5 NOTES FOR REGISTERED GROUPS

Registered groups may find this method of planning useful for organising their activities and, therefore, are encouraged to consider implementing those aspects relevant to them. This

CHAPTER SIXTEEN

will be good practise for the time when they achieve Assembly status.

16.6 **SAMPLE PLAN**

16.6.1 *This sample plan assumes a community of 20 adults, 8 youth and 10 children. It also assumes a united, active and stable community. All communities are different of course, and therefore, will have different priorities. All communities should, however, attach primary importance to developing an active teaching campaign.*

(Please note that the headings under which the activities are listed below relate to this plan only. Your Assembly may choose quite different headings, according to the activities you choose.)

ITEM	RESPONSIBILITY	DATE
1. Teaching Activities		
Set a goal of substantially increasing the size of the community this year. This is to be achieved by:-		
a) holding regular fortnightly community firesides to support individual teaching efforts	local teaching committee	
b) holding a Nine Day Teaching Campaign with a stand in the local shopping centre and nightly firesides	local teaching committee	June
c) buying 200 copies of the Peace Message for distribution during the Campaign and making them freely available to the community for giving to contacts	local teaching committee	
d) place an ad, in the local paper once a month	public information officer	
e) to assist the goal of the South helping the North, encourage the youth to form travel teaching teams to go North in their school holidays; provide the youth with financial assistance to enable them to do this	local youth committee	
f) find a family from this community, or another community, to homefront pioneer to the community's extension goal area	local teaching committee	
2. Involvement in Society/ Social and Economic Development Projects		
a) foster closer association with a local environmental group by assisting their activities e.g. tree planting projects	appiont an Assembly member to liaise with the group	
b) work with neighbouring Bahá'í communities to organise a one day seminar on 'Unity in Diversity" which will include non-Bahá'í speakers and multicultural entertainment in the evening	Assembly	
c) organise public meetings to mark U.N. World Environment Day (June 5) and United Nations Day		

(October 24); have Bahá'í and non-Bahá'í speakers; hold the meetings in the community's extension goal area	Assembly and local teaching committee

3. Promote Greater Use of Bahá'í Literature

a) prepare a list of books available in the local Bahá'í library and disseminate the list to community members	community librarian
b) buy a copy of the revised Lights of Guidance and more Persian titles	community librarian
c) check whether Bahá'í books in the local civic library are being used and change them if not	community librarian
d) investigate the possibility of placing Bahá'í books in local school libraries	Assembly

4. Maturation of the Local Community/ Spiritual Enrichment of Individual Believers

a) improve the quality of the Feast by encouraging more universal participation e.g. involving the children and youth more; translating, verbally, the most important messages received into Persian	Assembly
b) invite the assistants to advise and be involved in the teaching activities and to address the community at the Feast at least once during the year	Assembly
c) establish a community newsletter to come out each Feast	appoint a community member

d) hold community deepenings on:
  i. importance of giving to the Fund
  ii. Bahá'í relations with society
  iii. family life
	local deepening committee

e) have community prayers each Saturday morning	Assembly
f) appoint a social and welfare committee to hold two community social functions during the year; keep in touch with individual believers; organise welcomes for new believers	community members
g) establish a local women's group	Assembly
h) continue holding weekly local children's classes	local children's committee
i) improve Assembly functioning by holding an Assembly deepening on consultation and invite the assistant for protection to conduct it	Assembly

CHAPTER SEVENTEEN

Chapter 17

17. Local Committees

17.1 FUNCTIONS OF COMMITTEES

17.1.1 *What is the purpose of setting up local committees?*

The purpose of setting up local committees is to assist the Local Spiritual Assembly to carry out its various functions:-

> *In whatsoever locality the Cause has sufficiently expanded, and in order to insure efficiency and avoid confusion, each of these manifold functions will have to be referred to a special Committee...*
>
> (Shoghi Effendi, "Bahá'í Administration", p.39)

> *The local committees are the hands of the Spiritual Assembly that has appointed them...*
>
> (letter written on behalf of Shoghi Effendi to an individual believer, dated February 16, 1939)

Addressing a National Spiritual Assembly, Shoghi Effendi stated that the purpose of having committees is to relieve the Assembly of the details of the work. He warned that an Assembly that keeps too much of the work to itself cannot function efficiently. On the other hand, he also warned against delegating too much power to the committees as this would jeopardise the status of the Assembly, which is the body in which supreme authority must always remain. The Bahá'í standard is a balance between the two:-

> *The absorption of the petty details of Bahá'í administration by the personnel of the National Spiritual Assembly is manifestly injurious to efficiency and an expert discharge of Bahá'í duties, whilst the granting of undue discretion to bodies that should be regarded in no other light than that of expert advisers and executive assistants would jeopardise the very vital and pervading powers that are the sacred prerogatives of bodies that in time will evolve into Bahá'í National Houses of Justice.*
>
> (Shoghi Effendi, "Bahá'í Administration", p.142)

This instruction, although it was given to a National Spiritual Assembly, is equally true of the relationship that should exist between the Local Spiritual Assembly and its committees. Shoghi Effendi also said that a Local Spiritual Assembly should find ways to make use of the talents of its community members, otherwise they may divert their energies elsewhere:-

> *The first quality for leadership both among individuals and Assemblies is the capacity to use the energy and competence that exists in the rank and file of its followers. Otherwise the more competent members of the group will go at a tangent and try to find elsewhere a field of work and where they could use their energy.*
>
> (letter written on behalf of Shoghi Effendi to a National Spiritual Assembly, dated August 30, 1930)

The establishment of local committees or working groups is a useful way of doing this.

CHAPTER SEVENTEEN

17.1.2 **Does the Local Spiritual Assembly have to implement all the procedures outlined in this Chapter?**

No. The procedures outlined in this Chapter should only be implemented to the extent that the Assembly feels is necessary and possible, taking into account the size and maturity of the Assembly and its local community. A new Assembly may not have the need to establish committees along the formal lines set out here. It may prefer to set up occasional working groups or to appoint individual believers to carry out specific tasks, rather than committees.

17.1.3 **What kinds of committees could an Assembly have?**

The number and type of committees a Local Spiritual Assembly may require will depend on the size of the local community and the kinds of activities it intends to pursue; however, in a letter to a National Spiritual Assembly, dated July 30, 1972, the Universal House of Justice singled out the following functions for which Local Assemblies commonly appoint committees:-
- teaching
- observance of Feasts and Anniversaries
- solution of personal problems

During the Seven Year Plan the Universal House of Justice stated:-

> *National Assemblies should consider calling upon every Local Assembly to...appoint a local teaching committee wherever it is desirable to do so and has not already been done.*

> (letter written on behalf of the Universal House of Justice to all National Spiritual Assemblies, Naw-Rúz 1979)

In view of this advice from the Universal House of Justice, the National Spiritual Assembly encourages all Local Assemblies to consider appointing a local teaching committee. Other specific committees the Local Spiritual Assembly may wish to consider are:-
- deepening committee
- youth committee
- child education committee
- women's committee

17.1.4 **When should local committees be appointed?**

Shoghi Effendi has said that local committees should be appointed annually; however, the Universal House of Justice points out that this does not mean that it is necessary for terms of appointment to end at Ridván. Indeed, in order to preserve continuity, it may be advisable to begin the committee year in June or July:-

> *As regards the appointment of committees on a yearly basis, we refer to the Guardian's instructions on page 141 of "Bahá'í Administration" that "...the renewal, the membership, and functions...should be reconsidered separately each year by the incoming National Assembly...". Individuals appointed to committees should identify themselves with functions and objectives which normally extend beyond the term of their appointment. Just as members of the National Assembly relate themselves to goals of the Nine Year Plan, members of Local Assemblies and committees should do likewise, so that a single dynamic spirit may animate the important work for which each Assembly or committee is responsible.*

> *It is not necessary, however, that the term of committee appointments*

CHAPTER SEVENTEEN

expire at Ridván. It may be advisable, in order to provide continuity, to begin the committee year in June or July. Furthermore, the fact that, generally speaking, there are few radical changes in committee personnel should also make for continuity of thought and action.

(letter from the Universal House of Justice to a National Spiritual Assembly, dated January 23, 1967)

The National Spiritual Assembly has followed this advice and makes its own committee appointments in June and July each year. The Local Spiritual Assemblies are free to make up their own minds about this, but are advised to give due consideration to the advice of the Universal House of Justice, as outlined above.

17.1.5 **What is the difference between a committee and a working group?**

A committee is appointed by an Assembly for a term of 12 months and functions similarly to an Assembly insofar as it must have office bearers, must conduct regular meetings, keep minutes, and so on. A working group may be set up by an Assembly to carry out a specific task, on completion of which it then disbands. It does not have to have office bearers or conduct its meetings with the formality of a committee. It must, however, in common with a committee, report its activities to the Assembly on a regular basis. Bahá'í principles of consultation apply equally to working groups and committees. Not every task needs to be carried out by a committee or a working group. The Local Assembly is also free to ask individual believers to undertake specific projects.

17.1.6 **What is the relationship between a local committee and other regional or national committees with similar functions? (eg. Local Teaching Committee - Regional Teaching Committee - National Bahá'í Teaching Committee)**

Local committees are encouraged to keep in touch with their regional and national counterparts to exchange information and ideas and, if necessary, seek assistance with coordination of their activities. The National Bahá'í Youth Committee, for example, asks Local Youth Committees to communicate regularly with the Regional and National Youth Committees. It also requests that a copy of the Local Committee's Annual Report be sent to the National Bahá'í Youth Committee.

All such communications are governed by the general principle that local committees are directly and solely responsible to the Assembly that appoints them. The Local Spiritual Assembly is, therefore, responsible for overseeing the communications of its local committees.

17.1.7 **What is the relationship between a Local Spiritual Assembly and a national committee?**

In a letter written on his behalf, Shoghi Effendi has said that Local Assemblies should cooperate with national committees:-

He feels that the Local Assemblies should be encouraged to realise that National Committees are constituted to serve their needs, not to dictate arbitrarily to them and to unify the work of the Cause...Assemblies...should certainly cooperate with National Committees and not refuse their assistance.

(letter written on behalf of Shoghi Effendi to a National Spiritual Assembly, dated November 5, 1948)

CHAPTER SEVENTEEN

17.2 MEMBERSHIP OF COMMITTEES

17.2.1 *Is a believer obliged to serve on a committee if appointed?*

Yes:-

> ...*The Guardian wishes you to make clear to all the believers that membership in a Bahá'í Assembly or Committee is a sacred obligation which should be gladly and confidently accepted by every loyal and conscientious member of the community, no matter how humble and inexperienced.*
>
> (letter written on behalf of Shoghi Effendi, "Dawn of a New Day", p.79)

17.2.2 **Do committee members have to be appointed each year?**

Yes:-

> ...*Although National Assemblies and Local Assemblies may provide for continuity of Committee personnel by re-appointment of members each year, Assemblies should not appoint members of Committees for a term of more than one year.*
>
> (letter from the Universal House of Justice to a National Spiritual Assembly, dated December 20, 1966)

17.2.3 *How many members should a Local Spiritual Assembly appoint to a committee?*

In a letter written on its behalf to a National Spiritual Assembly, dated September 2, 1981 the Universal House of Justice said:-

> ...*it is preferable to have an odd number of members appointed to a committee. This would lessen the chance of a tie vote result.*

17.2.4 *Can Local or National Assembly members be appointed to local committees?*

Yes. Shoghi Effendi has said that the only condition of appointment is that those chosen must be the people best suited to do the work:-

> *Those who are best fitted for the specific work assigned to the committees should be elected, irrespective of their membership on either national or local Assemblies. The greater the pressure on those who shoulder both committee and Assembly responsibilities, the greater the reward and the richer the blessings vouchsafed to those who willingly and gratefully sustain this double burden.*
>
> (Shoghi Effendi, "Principles of Bahá'í Administration", p.50)

At the same time, however, the Assembly should bear in mind the desirability of appointing believers not serving on the National or Local Assembly, in order that they may have the opportunity to develop administrative skills. The following advice was conveyed to a National Spiritual Assembly, but is also relevant to Local Spiritual Assemblies:-

> *In the list of national committees for 1983-84, it was noted that eight members of the National Assembly had been appointed to serve. Indeed, your Treasurer will be on three committees, and your Secretary on two. While it is understandable that those elected to a National Spiritual Assembly generally have great capacity to assume manifold duties, the House of Justice points out that the opportunity for non-members of Assemblies to develop administrative skills is lost when*

CHAPTER SEVENTEEN

members of a National Assembly serve on a large number of national committees.

(letter written on behalf of the Universal House of Justice to a National Spiritual Assembly, dated December 28, 1983)

17.2.5 **Can youth who have not yet reached the age of 21, serve on committees?**

Yes. The Local Assembly is free to appoint youth to any of its committees if it believes they have the talents necessary for such service:-

The question of young Bahá'ís being permitted to serve on Committees other than the Youth Committee has been raised in a number of letters recently, and in considering the matter he felt that Bahá'í young people under 21 should not be denied the privilege of Committee work. Though they cannot be voting members of Bahá'í Communities (or exercise the electoral vote at all until they reach that age), and though they cannot, likewise, be elected to Assemblies, there is no reason why they should not serve the Cause on various Committees as all Committees, National or Local, are subordinate to Assemblies and their members not elected but appointed, and appointed by Assemblies. We have many devoted and talented young believers who can be of great assistance to the Cause even though not yet legally of age.

(letter written on behalf of Shoghi Effendi to a National Spiritual Assembly, dated February 28, 1945)

17.2.6 **Can a Local Assembly appoint a person outside its area of jurisdiction to serve on a local committee or working group?**

As a general principle this is not permissible:-

We are asked to say that it is not administratively correct for a Local Assembly to appoint believers who do not reside within its jurisdiction to membership in its local committees. However, committees of Spiritual Assemblies are perfectly entitled to seek the advice either through consultation or correspondence of anybody they wish, Bahá'ís or non-Bahá'ís, and this would of course include any believer outside the jurisdiction of the Spiritual Assembly to which they are responsible.

(letter written on behalf of the Universal House of Justice to a National Spiritual Assembly, dated January 7, 1987)

It is, however, permissible for an individual to serve on another Assembly's local committee in either of the following circumstances:-
1. if the person wishes to do so and his or her own Local Spiritual Assembly does not object. It is also permissible for an isolated believer or member of a group to serve on a local committee in another community if the person wishes to do so.
2. if the National Spiritual Assembly initiates a project and gives overall responsibility for it to a Local Spiritual Assembly; however, the project extends beyond the boundary of that Local Spiritual Assembly. In this instance, with the permission of the National Spiritual Assembly, that Local Assembly may invite representatives of the neighbouring communities to assist.

17.2.7 **What attitude should a Local Spiritual Assembly take when disunity amongst committee members is disrupting the work?**

In the first instance the Local Spiritual Assembly should be careful to appoint to its committees,

CHAPTER SEVENTEEN

believers whom it has reason to consider will work well together. Should the Assembly nevertheless find that disharmony is disrupting the work of the committee, it has a duty to try and reconcile the friends:-

> *We are asked by the Universal House of Justice to acknowledge your letter in which you ask for guidelines on the following questions:*
>
> *a) What attitude should a National Spiritual Assembly take when believers accept appointment to a committee but do not attend its meetings because of what you term incompatible personalities or lack of unity with other members of the committee, and yet they do not resign from the committee?*
>
> *As you are already aware, in your choice of members for committees, you must use careful judgement and discretion, with the aim of appointing a membership, which, from the outset, has good prospects of operating with full force. If, despite your efforts to do this, there is disharmony among the committee members, the following extract from a letter of 13 May 1945 written on behalf of the beloved Guardian may be helpful to you.*
>
> *Regarding the matter of...and the inharmony that seems to exist among certain of the friends. When Bahá'ís permit the dark forces of the world to enter into their own relationships within the Faith they gravely jeopardise its progress; it is the paramount duty of the believers, the Local Assemblies, and particularly the National Spiritual Assembly to foster harmony, understanding and love amongst the friends. All should be ready and willing to set aside every personal sense of grievance - justified or unjustified - for the good of the Cause, because the people will never embrace it until they see in its Community life mirrored what is so conspicuously lacking in the world: love and unity.*
>
> *(letter written on behalf of the Universal House of Justice to a National Spiritual Assembly, dated August 19, 1985)*

17.3 DELEGATION OF AUTHORITY TO COMMITTEES

17.3.1 *How much authority can a Local Spiritual Assembly delegate to a committee?*

The degree of authority given to a committee will vary according to the functions it has to perform. This is a matter that remains within the power of the Local Assembly to decide. Generally speaking, a committee should be given the degree of authority necessary to carry out the functions it has to perform and these functions should be defined as clearly as possible. The Local Spiritual Assembly may like to draw up Terms of Reference along the lines suggested below; otherwise, it must at least provide the committee with a clear statement of its designated functions and the boundaries of its authority. However the Assembly decides, Shoghi Effendi has made it quite clear that ultimate responsibility for the actions of a committee remains vested in the Local Assembly. This responsibility cannot be delegated to any other body:-

> *The local Spiritual Assembly cannot delegate to any one of the local committees the authority to exercise any control or supervision over any other committee or body which it has itself appointed. All local committees are directly and solely responsible to the local Assembly*

CHAPTER SEVENTEEN

which alone can exercise the power of supervision over them.

(Shoghi Effendi, "Principles of Bahá'í Administration", p.51)

17.3.2 ***In what manner should authority be delegated to the committee?***

When the National Spiritual Assembly appoints a national committee it draws up Terms of Reference for that committee. These Terms of Reference include:-
- a statement of the overall purpose of the committee
- a list of the functions it is to perform
- an outline of its methods of operation

Local Spiritual Assemblies may like to draw up similar Terms of Reference for their committees, following the example set out below. Terms of Reference should begin by stating who appointed the committee; to whom the committee is responsible; and by whom it is being funded. This should be followed by a statement of the committee's overall purpose. An example of a statement of overall purpose for a committee might be:-

To promote the development of women within the local community and enable them to fulfil the high aspirations held for them in the Bahá'í Writings. A committee having such a purpose might then be given the following list of functions:-

1. To encourage women to be active in teaching and consolidation work.
2. To encourage mothers to understand the importance of their role in the education of children.
3. To organise deepenings for the community related to the role of women.
4. To organise a function to celebrate United Nations International Women's Day (March 8) each year.
5. To promote an awareness of issues relating to peace within the local Bahá'í community.

The methods of operation should cover such things as:-

1. procedures for reporting to the Local Spiritual Assembly

It is provided in Art. XI(4) of the By-Laws of a Local Spiritual Assembly that committee reports shall be presented at the Annual General Meeting of the community. This is usually done by incorporating the committees' reports into the Assembly's Annual Report. It is necessary, therefore, that the Assembly provide its committees with a submission date for their annual reports sufficiently in advance of the Annual General Meeting to enable the Assembly to incorporate its committees' reports into its own Report. Similarly, if the committee is provided with funds, its annual financial statements need to be incorporated into the Assembly's Annual Financial Statement to the community and, therefore, need to be submitted at the same time as the annual reports.

2. preparation of an annual plan

The National Spiritual Assembly requires its committees to follow a planning and review cycle based on the drawing up of an annual plan which must be submitted for approval to the National Spiritual Assembly. Local Spiritual Assemblies may consider implementing this cycle, or parts of it, with their local committees also. [For further information, see Chapter 16 on Planning in this Handbook.] The Local Spiritual Assembly also needs to decide how it will allocate funds to its local committees. It may, for example, provide them with a budget, or it may require them to request funds from the Local Spiritual Assembly as necessary.

3. lines of communication

As a general principle, the Local Spiritual Assembly is responsible for all communications made by its committees. The Assembly, therefore, will need to determine appropriate procedures for overseeing its committees' communications;

CHAPTER SEVENTEEN

for example, it may require all correspondence to be submitted to the Local Spiritual Assembly for approval and forwarding on Assembly letterhead; or it may simply request that it be copied with all correspondence sent by the committee. There may also be circumstances in which a Local Spiritual Assembly wishes to authorise a committee to communicate with other Bahá'í or non-Bahá'í institutions directly. It is within the Local Assembly's discretion to do this, provided the Assembly itself has authority to communicate with that institution.

4. **to meet regularly** and send a copy of its minutes to the Local Spiritual Assembly

A sample Terms of Reference for a local committee is contained in section 6 of this Chapter.

17.3.3 *How should the Local Spiritual Assembly supervise its committees?*

The Local Spiritual Assembly should remain in close contact with its local committees. It should attempt to meet with them regularly, to encourage them and provide constructive feedback on their activities. The Secretary of the Assembly should regularly check the minutes of local committees to ensure that they are continuing to act on their Terms of Reference.

17.4 **THE COMMITTEE IN OPERATION**

17.4.1 *Are office bearers appointed by the Assembly or elected by the committee?*

In a letter written on his behalf, Shoghi Effendi stated his preference that committee officers be elected by the committee:-

> *He feels that committees must assume more responsibility and exercise freedom of choice and judgment in electing their officers, and function as a corporate body with a corporate spirit. More especially so as now that the Cause is growing in numbers, and its responsibilities are being multiplied, national committees are acquiring added importance, and must seek, ever-increasingly, to follow the pattern of Bahá'u'lláh and assume responsibility for the election of their officers. These committees must develop, become mature, and forge ahead courageously, relying more on united effort and less on personal leadership, as is now the case with local and national Assemblies.*
>
> (Shoghi Effendi through his Secretary, "Principles of Bahá'í Administration", p.51)

More recently, in a letter written on its behalf to a National Spiritual Assembly, dated December 10, 1975, the Universal House of Justice repeated this preference but added that in exceptional circumstances an Assembly may be justified in appointing a particular person to be Secretary of a committee:-

> *...generally it is desirable for committees to elect their own officers as indicated by the Guardian's instructions...This is not inconsistent with the statement from the letter of the Universal House of Justice dated February 12, 1971 suggesting that at least one member of a committee should have secretarial skills and be capable of carrying the heavy burden of correspondence. Nevertheless, there may be exceptional circumstances requiring your National Assembly to specify which of the committee members shall be Secretary, as was no doubt the case with your ... Committee.*

17.4.2 *How is the first meeting of the committee convened?*

When the Local Spiritual Assembly appoints the members of a committee, it must also appoint one person as the Convenor. This person is responsible for calling the first meeting of the committee. The first meeting should be held as soon as possible after the committee is appointed to elect office bearers, discuss its designated functions and decide on regular meeting times. The Convenor will chair the meeting until a Chairman is elected.

17.4.3 *How are the office bearers elected?*

The procedure for electing the officers of a committee is the same as for electing the officers of the Local Spiritual Assembly.

17.4.4 *What are the duties of the officers?*

Generally, the duties of committee officers are the same as those of Local Spiritual Assembly officers.

The following specific points should also be noted:-
1. **Chairman** - must ensure that the committee's consultation remains within the boundaries of its designated functions.
2. **Secretary** - a copy of the minutes approved by the committee and signed by the Chairman should be sent to the Local Spiritual Assembly.
3. **Treasurer** - must liaise with the Local Spiritual Assembly's Treasurer regarding payment of bills and other financial matters.

17.4.5 *Who is responsible for calling meetings?*

Normally a committee will decide on a schedule of meetings when it is first convened. The only requirements are that all the members be notified well in advance so that they have the opportunity to attend and there must be a quorum present for the committee to be able to make valid decisions. In any committee there is a quorum when more than 50% of the members are present. For example, in a committee of 7 members, a quorum is 4 members or more.

17.4.6 *How are urgent matters to be dealt with?*

If an urgent matter arises, a quorum of the committee must be consulted before a decision can be made. This could be arranged either through a special meeting or by telephone.

17.4.7 *How should a committee organise its work?*

If the Local Spiritual Assembly requires the committee to draw up an annual plan, the committee's actions will be determined by the tasks specified in that plan. Otherwise, its activities will be determined by reference to its designated functions. Should a committee ever wish to engage in an activity not clearly permitted by its designated functions, it must seek the permission of the Local Spiritual Assembly before proceeding.

17.5 **NOTES FOR REGISTERED GROUPS**

Registered Groups will obviously not have the resources to establish local committees, unless they are quite large, in which case they may consider setting up a teaching committee. The information in this Chapter should, therefore, primarily be considered as deepening material, until such time as the Group achieves Assembly status.

17.6 **SAMPLE TERMS OF REFERENCE**

17.6.1 *Following is an example of the way in which Terms of Reference for a local committee*

CHAPTER SEVENTEEN

may be set out.

Local Bahá'í Women's Committee

APPOINTED BY: The Local Spiritual Assembly
RESPONSIBLE TO: The Local Spiritual Assembly
FUNDING FROM: The Local Spiritual Assembly

OVERALL PURPOSE:

To promote the development of women within the local community and enable them to fulfil the high aspirations held for them in the Bahá'í Writings.

FUNCTIONS:

1. To encourage women to be active in teaching and consolidation work.
2. To encourage mothers to understand the importance of their role in the education of children.
3. To organise deepenings for the community related to the role of women.
4. To organise a function to celebrate United Nations International Women's Day (March 8) each year.
5. To promote an awareness of issues and activities relating to peace within the local Bahá'í and non-Bahá'í community.

METHODS OF OPERATION:

1. To draw up a list of proposed activities for the year in February and submit this to the Local Spiritual Assembly for approval.
2. To meet regularly and send a copy of minutes to the Local Spiritual Assembly.
3. To submit an annual report to the Local Spiritual Assembly by March 31 each year for inclusion in the Assembly's report to the community at the Annual General Meeting.
4. To keep the National Bahá'í Women's Committee informed of its activities.
5. To send all correspondence to the Local Spiritual Assembly for approval and forwarding. The committee may apply for permission to correspond directly with certain individuals on a case by case basis.
6. To request funds from the Local Spiritual Assembly as the need arises.

EXAMPLE ONLY

CHAPTER EIGHTEEN

Chapter 18

18. Insurance

18.1 THE POLICY

18.1.1 ***What type of insurance policy does the National Spiritual Assembly have?***

The National Spiritual Assembly has taken out a Public/Products Liability insurance policy. This policy covers claims made by third parties for personal injuries or damage to property in those circumstances in which the National Spiritual Assembly is legally liable to pay compensation (excluding punitive or exemplary damages). Legal liability only arises when the National Spiritual Assembly, Local Spiritual Assembly, Registered Group or local or national committee has acted negligently. In brief, this policy only covers us against our own negligence. The sum insured for is $10,000,000.00.

18.1.2 ***Who is covered by this policy?***

The National Spiritual Assembly, all Local Spiritual Assemblies and their committees, Registered Groups and national committees are covered by this policy.
In what situations are Local Spiritual Assemblies covered by this policy?
As a general principle this policy is applicable to any function organised by a Local Spiritual Assembly in which other individuals or other people's property are involved; for example, hire of a public hall.

18.1.3 ***What situations are not covered by this policy?***

The policy states that the insurance Company shall not be liable for claims in respect of:-

Personal Injury or Property Damage caused by or arising out of the ownership, possession, maintenance or use by the Insured of any vehicle,
1. which is registered or,
2. in respect of which insurance is required by virtue of any legislation relating to motor vehicles or,
3. which is otherwise insured in respect of the same liability.

From time to time, Local Assemblies either hire or borrow vehicles such as trucks or trailers for use in events such as a festival. It is important to note that, under the terms of the above exception, the National Spiritual Assembly's policy does not cover the Assembly for any liability that may arise as a result of an accident to or by that vehicle. Only the owners of vehicles may insure them. Before taking delivery of a borrowed or hired vehicle for use in a Bahá'í activity, therefore, the Local Spiritual Assembly should check that it has been fully insured by its owner. Otherwise, in the event of an accident, the community could be up for unnecessary and significant costs. There are other exceptions to the National Spiritual Assembly's policy also. For your ease of reference some of these have been lifted from the policy and are set out below:-

The Company shall not be liable for claims in respect of:

Personal Injury or Property Damage arising directly or indirectly out of or caused by or in connection with:
1. the ownership, possession or use of any aircraft aerial device or air cushion vehicle by the Insured or by another on its behalf.
2. the ownership possession or use by or on behalf of the Insured of any watercraft

whilst afloat except where the watercraft is less than 8 (eight) metres in length.

Personal Injury or Property Damage caused by or arising out of contaminating or polluting substances discharged dispersed or released, into or upon the land atmosphere or water where such discharge dispersal or release is not caused by a sudden unexpected and unintended happening. Additionally the Company shall not be liable for expenses incurred by the Insured for the prevention of such contamination or pollution.

Personal Injury or Property Damage
1. for which insurance against such liability (whether the insurance is limited in amount or not) is or would have been provided under a policy in a form prescribed or approved under or issued in pursuance of any Workers or Workmen's Compensation Legislation applicable to the Insured or any extension of such policy granted on request as a matter of usual practice by insurers authorised to issue such policies.
2. to or of any person in the service of the Insured and where such claims arise from a liability imposed by any Industrial Award or Agreement or Termination.
Personal Injury to any employee of the Insured arising out of his employment in the Insured's business. But this exclusion does not apply with respect to liability to other persons for damages arising out of Personal Injury to any employee where the Insured has assumed such liability by way of written contract.

Property Damage to property belonging to or in the physical or legal control of the Insured but the Company shall be liable for claims arising in connection with
1. Premises (including contents thereof) not owned or leased by the Insured but temporarily occupied by them for the purpose of doing work
2. Personal effects of Directors Employees and Visitors of the Insured
3. Vehicles not belonging to or used by or on behalf of the Insured or in the physical or legal control of the Insured whilst within a car park owned or operated by the Insured unless part of the Insured's business is the operation of a car park for reward or the provision of a motor vehicle repair or maintenance service
4. Premises (including landlord's fixtures and furnishings) leased or rented to the Insured in respect of Property Damage caused by:-
a) fire or explosion
b) (water discharge or leaking from any pipe or water system
c) impact by any vehicle

Provided that in respect of each occurrence in (a) and (b) the Insured shall be responsible for the first $100 of such Property Damage in addition to any other excess specified in the Schedule.

18.1.4 *What should a Local Spiritual Assembly do if a claim arises?*

If a claim arises, the Local Spiritual Assembly should notify the National Office immediately and provide full details, so that the National Spiritual Assembly may advise the insurance company. It is most important that the Local Spiritual Assembly not admit liability to anyone, regardless of whether the claim is valid or not. In the event of property damage occurring the Local Spiritual Assembly should not make any repairs without the consent of the insurance company.

18.1.5 *Where can Local Spiritual Assemblies obtain more information about the insurance policy?*

If a Local Spiritual Assembly needs more details about the insurance policy it should contact the Treasury Assistant at the National Office.

CHAPTER EIGHTEEN

18.2   **NOTES FOR REGISTERED GROUPS**

As noted in Section 1 of this Chapter, the National Spiritual Assembly's insurance policy also covers Registered Groups.

18.3   **COPY OF NATIONAL ASSEMBLY'S PUBLIC/PRODUCTS LIABILITY POLICY**

18.3.1 *Attached is a copy of the National Spiritual Assembly's Public/Products Liability insurance policy. Please note that in any instance in which an Assembly is required to make copies of this policy to outside bodies, only the necessary sections of the policy should be copied. Please also check the date on the covering page to ensure that you possess the current policy, before supplying details to outside bodies.*

NZI Insurance

CONFIRMATION OF CURRENCY

INSURANCE COMPANY	:	NZI Insurance Australia Ltd
CLASS OF INSURANCE	:	Public & Products Liability
POLICY NUMBER	:	42 HMB3527 LIA
DUE DATE	:	1st July 1996
INSURED	:	National Spiritual Assembly of the Baha'is of Australia Incorporated
SITUATION	:	Anywhere in Australia
INTERESTED INSURED	:	Legal Liability to Third Parties
SUM INSURED/LIMIT	:	$10,000,000
APPROVED BY	:	
DATE	:	6th July 1995

NZI Insurance Australia Limited
A.C.N. 001 948 278
A member company of General Accident Group

CHAPTER NINETEEN

Chapter 19

19. Properties

19.1 LOCAL SPIRITUAL ASSEMBLY PROPERTIES

19.1.1 *What forms of property may a Local Spiritual Assembly own?*

An Assembly may own the following property:
- burial ground in a cemetery
- endowment land
- local Bahá'í Centre

19.1.2 *What is the purpose of acquiring a local Bahá'í Centre?*

The purpose of acquiring a local Bahá'í Centre is to provide a focal point for the 'spiritual, social and administrative activities' of the community.

(letter from the Universal House of Justice to the National Spiritual Assembly of Australia, dated January 1981).

Specific functions for which local Bahá'í Centres are used around the world include:
- administrative centre for the Local Spiritual Assembly

> dawn prayers
> Nineteen Day Feasts
> Holy Days and Anniversaries
> deepening classes
> youth gatherings
> women's activities
> teaching the Faith
> general social functions
> tutorial schools and other development projects

(from "The Seven Year Plan" 1979-86 Statistical Report (published by the Universal House of Justice), p.86).

19.1.3 *What is the relationship between a local Bahá'í Centre, local Hazíratu'l-Quds and Mashriqu'l-Adhkár*

The local Bahá'í Centre may be regarded as an embryonic Hazíratu'l-Quds. The Bahá'í Writings anticipate the establishment of Hazíratu'l-Quds at both the national and local levels, to serve as administrative headquarters for the Faith:-

Simultaneous with the establishment and incorporation of local and national Bahá'í Assemblies, with the formation of their respective committees, the formulation of national and local Bahá'í constitutions and the founding of Bahá'í endowments, undertakings of great institutional significance were initiated by these newly founded Assemblies, among which the institution of the Hazíratu'l-Quds - the seat of the Bahá'í National Assembly and pivot of all Bahá'í administrative activity in the future - must rank as one of the most important...

Based, with permission, on "Bahá'í Properties" in "Developing Distinctive Bahá'í Communities":

CHAPTER NINETEEN

Guidelines for Spiritual Assemblies 1989 by the National Spiritual Assembly of the Bahá'ís of the United States.

> *Complementary in its functions to those of the Mashriqu'l-Adhkár - an edifice exclusively reserved for Bahá'í worship - this institution, whether local or national, will, as its component parts, such as the Secretariat, the Treasury, the Archives, the Library, the Publishing Office, the Assembly Hall, the Council Chamber, the Pilgrims' Hostel, are brought together and made jointly to operate in one spot, be increasingly regarded as the focus of all Bahá'í administrative activity, and symbolise, in a befitting manner, the ideal of service animating the Bahá'í community in its relation alike to the Faith and to mankind in general.*
>
> (Shoghi Effendi, "God Passes By", p.339-40)

The Writings also anticipate the establishment of a Mashriqu'l-Adhkár in each local community, surrounded by various dependencies to serve the needs of humanity. The local Bahá'í Centre can further be seen as a first step towards the creation of these institutions:-

> *A symbol of this process [social and economic development] may be seen in the House of Worship and its dependencies. The first part to be built is the central edifice which is the spiritual heart of the community. Then, gradually, as the outward expression of this spiritual heart, the various dependencies, those 'institutions of social service as shall afford relief to the suffering, sustenance to the poor, shelter to the wayfarer, solace to the bereaved, and education to the ignorant' are erected and function. This process begins in an embryonic way long before a Bahá'í community reaches the stage of building its own Mashriqu'l-Adhkár, for even the first local centre that a Bahá'í community erects can begin to serve not only as the spiritual and administrative centre and gathering place of the community, but also as the site of a tutorial school and the heart of other aspects of community life.*
>
> (letter written on behalf of the Universal House of Justice to a National Spiritual Assembly, dated May 8, 1984)

Shoghi Effendi has said that in the future the administrators of the Faith, working in the Hazíratu'l-Quds, will derive the necessary inspiration for their work from visits to the Mashriqu'l-Adhkár.

> *;From the Mashriqu'l-Adhkár, ordained as a house of worship by Bahá'u'lláh in the Kitáb-i-Aqdas, the representatives of Bahá'í communities, both local and national, together with the members of their respective committees, will, as they gather daily within its walls at the hour of dawn, derive the necessary inspiration that will enable them to discharge, in the course of their day-to-day exertions in the Hazíratu'l-Quds - the scene of their administrative activities - their duties and responsibilities as befits the chosen stewards of His Faith.*
>
> (Shoghi Effendi, "God Passes By", p.340)

The Bahá'í Centre presently serves as a general gathering place for the community because size and lack of resources prevent the establishment of the above institutions as yet:-

CHAPTER NINETEEN

As in most cases the Bahá'ís have no other meeting-place in the city which has a Hazíratu'l-Quds, and the Hazíratu'l-Quds is a building that has a number of rooms, he sees no objection in allowing the youth to have their meetings there with their non-Bahá'í friends ... Bahá'í weddings and funerals can likewise be conducted in the Hazíratu'l-Quds. The Hazíratu'l-Quds, although Feasts and Holy Days are celebrated in it, must not be confounded with a Temple; it is an administrative headquarters. No doubt in the future it will be used for purely administrative purposes, but for the time being it must fill the role of being a true Centre and rallying-point for the Bahá'í Community.

(letter written on behalf of Shoghi Effendi to a National Spiritual Assembly, dated February 15, 1947)

When a Local Spiritual Assembly acquires a Bahá'í Centre, it should regard this meeting place as an embryonic Hazíratu'l-Quds and should do everything possible to foster in the community a proper attitude of respect for the Centre...

When a community grows in size and in the resources at its disposal, the Assembly may well acquire a community centre for recreational and other uses, in addition to the Bahá'í Centre. However, if it is able to acquire only one centre, that meeting place should be designated as the Bahá'í Centre since it is the focus of Bahá'í community activity and the seat of the Spiritual Assembly, in addition to its being identified with the Bahá'í Faith in the eyes of the public.

(letter written on behalf of the Universal House of Justice to a National Spiritual Assembly, dated July 26, 1989)

19.1.4 **Are Local Spiritual Assemblies encouraged to acquire local Bahá'í Centres?**

The Universal House of Justice has discouraged the acquisition of Bahá'í Centres when they are not among the goals of a community in the current Plan:-

Because of the need to commit our resources to the overall objectives of a particular global plan, the use of those resources for acquisition of properties not called for in the Plan is discouraged, but in exceptional circumstances it can be permitted.

(letter written on behalf of the Universal House of Justice to a National Spiritual Assembly, dated August 21, 1980)

As the Bahá'í House of Worship and Yerrinbool Bahá'í School are national institutions, established according to the directives of the World Centre, the National Spiritual Assembly, at the present time (June, 1994), places a higher priority on maintaining and developing these institutions, and on the establishment of State Information Centres - as part of the Entry by Troops effort - than on the acquisition of local Bahá'í Centres. In accordance with the directives of the Universal House of Justice the National Assembly would likewise prefer to see Local Assemblies concentrating on increasing the size of their communities. They may, nevertheless, acquire Bahá'í Centres if they choose, provided they have the resources at the local level to do so. [See further Section 2 of this Chapter.]

19.1.5 *May Local Spiritual Assemblies build Mashriqu'l-Adhkárs at the present time?*

No. The Universal House of Justice has advised, however, that they may build a 'prayer hall', which may be incorporated into a Hazíratu'l-Quds:-

> Re yr email ... concerning Temple site ... it would be entirely fitting to build a hall for worship and prayer, but it would not be appropriate to apply the term Mashriqu'l-Adhkár to the building to be erected at this time. It is suggested that the structure might be designated as a "Prayer Hall".

(message from the Universal House of Justice to a National Spiritual Assembly, dated February 4, 1988)

19.2 FACTORS TO CONSIDER BEFORE ACQUIRING A LOCAL BAHÁ'Í CENTRE

19.2.1 *How may a Local Spiritual Assembly acquire a Bahá'í Centre?*

A Bahá'í Centre is typically bought or may be donated to the community by a Bahá'í friend. An incorporated Local Spiritual Assembly may lease a Centre; however, unincorporated Assemblies may not do so in the name of the Assembly.

19.2.2 *What general factors should a Local Spiritual Assembly take into account when deciding whether to buy, lease, or accept a donation of a Bahá'í Centre?*

The Local Spiritual Assembly should consider the following general factors:

1. Does the community need a Bahá'í Centre?
   That is, can the community's activities be adequately catered for in private homes or by renting facilities as the need arises? If so, the Assembly does not need to acquire a Centre. A related factor is whether or not the majority of community members want to have a Centre.
2. Is the community sufficiently mature to accept responsibility for a Bahá'í Centre?
   The decision to acquire a Bahá'í Centre should be based on the community's readiness for one, regardless of whether someone has offered to donate a building or whether sufficient funds to purchase a building are available. Often it will be wisest for Spiritual Assemblies to rent facilities as needed for specific events. At a later stage of development, the Assembly will have acquired the experience to rent on a long-term basis or acquire a facility of its own. A Local Spiritual Assembly must clearly understand all aspects of owning property and be able to handle the extra financial, physical and administrative requirements. A Bahá'í Centre should not be viewed as 'a way to save money' or as an investment. The day-to-day operating costs of a facility can soon absorb any anticipated savings. An Assembly may decide to begin saving funds for that time in the future when the community is ready for a Hazíratu'l-Quds. The Local Spiritual Assembly may like to consider investing this money in the National Spiritual Assembly's Property Development Investment Fund, thereby assisting the national funds of the Faith also.
3. Does the community have the necessary resources to acquire, maintain and run a local Bahá'í Centre?

To decide if the community has the necessary resources the Assembly must first decide exactly what the Centre is to be used for. There are many possible uses It is not likely that the building will fulfil them all, therefore, the Assembly must decide where its priorities lie, based on the needs of the community. The Universal House of Justice has advised that it is important that Bahá'í properties be fully used for the purposes for which they are acquired:-

CHAPTER NINETEEN

> *It is also important to make full use of the properties of the Faith for the purposes for which they were acquired. Well maintained and regularly used properties will not only be a means of fostering Bahá'í community life, but will add to the prestige and dignity of the Faith in the eyes of the non-Bahá'í public.*
>
> (letter written on behalf of the Universal House of Justice to all National Spiritual Assemblies, Naw-Rúz 1979)

The Universal House of Justice has also warned that the original cost and responsibility of running and maintaining a Bahá'í Centre may, far from enhancing the community's development, become too great a burden and create an adverse effect:-

> *The House of Justice does not feel that ... the building or buying of a Local Centre will necessarily infuse the friends with a dynamic spirit for community development and inspire them to actively teach. On the contrary, the original cost and responsibilities of operation and maintenance may impose a heavy burden on them and create an adverse effect.*
>
> (letter written on behalf of the Universal House of Justice to an individual believer, dated July 9, 1978)

For example, it may drain the community's financial resources; pose significant demands on the friends for upkeep of the property, both in time and money; cause divisions within the community over financial and maintenance problems; require supervision that the community does not have the manpower to provide; convey a poor image of the Faith if upkeep of the structure and its grounds is not exemplary. If the Assembly intends to use the Centre for, Feasts or firesides, it needs to consider whether the desired atmosphere can be maintained in a Centre, as opposed to a private home. Would it become too formal; would it stifle spontaneity?

The following questions in this Section explore five major technical issues that the Assembly must consider before making a decision to acquire a Centre. These are:
1. financial requirements
2. physical considerations
3. property operation
4. property maintenance
5. legal considerations

Only the rudimentary issues are considered. The particular facts and requirements will be different for every situation, locality, property, and building. When looking at building codes and zoning requirements, for example, the laws will not only be different from state to state, but often from town to town, and the zoning restrictions may vary within the same block. It is therefore advisable for local Assemblies to obtain local professional advice on each of the above areas. It is suggested that the Local Spiritual Assembly draw up a one or two page 'Statement of Purpose' focussing on the above issues. This will help the Assembly to clarify its thinking and make a final decision as to whether or not to acquire a Centre.

19.2.3   **What financial considerations must the Local Spiritual Assembly take into account?**

The Universal House of Justice has said:-

> *As far as possible, local Hazíratu'l-Quds and other local properties should be kept up by the local friends themselves.*

CHAPTER NINETEEN

(letter written on behalf of the Universal House of Justice to all National Spiritual Assemblies, Naw-Rúz 1979)

The Assembly must first consider the financial status of its community. For example:
- all Local Spiritual Assemblies and individuals have a responsibility to contribute to the National, International and Continental Funds of the Faith. If the Assembly decides to acquire a local Centre it must ensure that contributions to the Centre are made additional to contributions to these Funds, not as a substitute for them.

The health of the Local Fund must be assessed. For example, are contributions to the Local Fund regular and consistent, or do occasional large contributions make up for thin months? If the Fund is supported in large part by contributions from a few individual believers, what would happen if one or two of these persons moved out of the community? Does the Fund allow for a safety margin in case of unexpected expenses?

The Universal House of Justice has warned that the financial outlay required must not interfere with the discharge of other responsibilities in the current Plan:-

> *We have been asked to say that there is no objection to the Local Assembly looking for a property to purchase for their Hazíratu'l-Quds, but ... They should ... decide whether they can manage the financial outlay required without interfering with the discharge of their other responsibilities toward the success of the Five Year Plan [1974-79]*

(letter written on behalf of the Universal House of Justice to a National Spiritual Assembly, dated February 6, 1975)

The Assembly must secondly consider the financial costs involved in acquiring a Centre. The Universal House of Justice has pointed out that this involves both the initial cost of acquisition and continuing maintenance costs:-

> *We have been asked to say that there is no objection to the Local Assembly looking for a property to purchase for their Hazíratu'l-Quds, but they should be reminded that in addition to the initial cost of acquisition they must be prepared to assume the continuing costs of upkeep, maintenance, and services.*

(letter written on behalf of the Universal House of Justice to a National Spiritual Assembly, dated February 6, 1975)

> *In addition to the purchase price, a breakdown of these costs includes:*
> - *expert advice as to the condition of any building the Assembly considers*
> - *cost of rehabilitation*
> - *alterations*
> - *improvements*
> - *furnishings*

(letter from the Universal House of Justice to a National Spiritual Assembly, dated January 28, 1974)

Other costs may include:
- monthly rental or mortgage (note: only an incorporated Assembly may borrow money to purchase a Bahá'í Centre; unincorporated Assemblies may not)
- insurance
- electricity, water and telephone.
- upkeep and repair of furnishings and grounds
- routine maintenance costs

CHAPTER NINETEEN

The Assembly should also budget to maintain a reserve Fund for major repairs and replacements of building components.

19.2.4 *How can the Local Spiritual Assembly acquire, in advance, an indication of the financial support it could expect from its community for a local Centre?*

The Universal House of Justice has suggested that a Local Spiritual Assembly could call for pledges from the friends:-

> *Pledges can be useful as a means of encouraging contributions and of bringing the financial needs of the Cause to the attention of the friends. This method can be particularly helpful in a situation where a Spiritual Assembly has a major task to perform, such as building of a Ḥaẓíratu'l-Quds or the establishment of a tutorial school, and needs to have some idea in advance of whether the funds for the project will be available.*
>
> (Memorandum of Comments and Suggestions attached to a letter from the Universal House of Justice to all National Spiritual Assemblies, dated August 7, 1985)

19.2.5 *Is financial assistance available from the National Spiritual Assembly?*

No. The state of the National Fund does not permit the National Spiritual Assembly to provide financial assistance to Local Spiritual Assemblies for local Bahá'í Centres.

19.2.6 *What physical considerations need to be taken into account?*

The following physical considerations need to be taken into account:

1. appearance
- when looking for property, the Assembly must remember that a Bahá'í facility has to meet standards of dignity and quality. Bahá'í properties convey a public image of the Faith, which can enhance the prestige of the Cause and contribute to relations with the community at large.

2. location
- this will generally be determined by the purpose of the Centre. For example:
- if the primary purpose for purchasing a Centre is to proclaim the Faith, the property must be visible. A Centre may be a teaching and proclamation project supported by Bahá'ís from throughout the state. In such a case, the building may not be necessarily the primary meeting place for local Bahá'ís;
- if the primary purpose for the Bahá'í Centre is as a meeting place, it may be important that it be centrally located. It may be unnecessary for it to be highly visible;
- if an Assembly wants to reach a particular population, locating the Bahá'í Centre near that population may prove helpful;
- the Local Spiritual Assembly should consider whether it is important for the Centre to be located close to public transport.

3. size and physical arrangements
- these too will be determined by the purpose of the Centre. If the Assembly needs adequate space for the Nineteen Day Feasts, for example, the primary meeting room should be large enough to hold the community members and their guests, although rental of a large hall may sometimes be necessary for special events. Again, if the Bahá'í Centre is to be used for community meetings and child education classes, it may be helpful to have at least two large rooms so that the arrangements for children's classes do not have to be dismantled frequently. These issues should be clarified in

the Statement Purpose referred to above.

4. civil law requirements- these may include:
- access for the handicapped
- parking
- compliance with building codes
- life-safety features such as smoke detectors, emergency lighting, emergency exits

19.2.7 ***How is the Centre to be managed?***

The Assembly should appoint a Centre manager who will be responsible to the Local Spiritual Assembly but given the duty to provide for the Centre's overall operation, including beautification, regular cleaning and other necessary care. The manager would also schedule all activities to be held in the Centre. The terms of reference for the Centre manager should be in writing so that all responsibilities are clear. If other managers are employed, they must understand exactly what is expected of them, or their jobs can easily evolve into virtually every task undertaken at the Centre. Without a clear understanding of the manager's duties, expectations can easily arise that are not shared by all parties involved.

19.2.8 ***How is the Centre to be maintained?***

The Assembly should set aside a regular sum for the maintenance of the Centre and appoint a special committee to be in charge of maintenance. This committee can recommend to the Assembly a maintenance budget each year:-

> *The Treasurer should advise the Assembly to set aside sufficient sums on a regular basis to provide for the repair and maintenance of properties owned by the Faith, so that these can be kept in good condition and so that the normal work of the Cause is not interrupted by sudden requirements of large sums for repairs. Usually the task of maintaining the properties is assigned to a special committee or committees, which should be consulted by the Assembly and can suggest a suitable amount to be set aside annually.*
>
> (letter written on behalf of the Universal House of Justice to a National Spiritual Assembly, dated July 13, 1981)

This committee should be given the responsibility of ensuring that the Centre is kept in good condition, and of making recommendations to the Assembly for necessary improvements. Ideally the Centre manager should be a member of the committee. The Assembly must also decide whether the committee will be given its own budget or whether it should request funds from the Assembly as needed.
[See further Chapter 17 of this Handbook for guidelines on setting up local committees]

Incidental costs for general upkeep and repair may include the following:
- tools, locks, keys, light bulbs, fuses, etc.
- rubbish removal, upkeep of yard and landscaping
- window, carpet, bathroom and general cleaning
- heating and air conditioning service
- refurbishment of drapes, carpets and furnishings
- office equipment and mailing supplies
- cups, plates, towels and refreshments for public meetings
- pest control
- roof plumbing, electrical, window and heating repairs
- parking lot and sidewalk patching, sealcoating and stripping
- gas, water, electricity and telephone

CHAPTER NINETEEN

- permits, inspections, property taxes and assessments
- alterations required by local government codes

The use of volunteer Bahá'ís with professional skills may reduce these costs somewhat, however, licensed repair personnel and permits are required by law for some work such as electrical, plumbing, heating, and structural modifications.

What legal considerations need to be taken into account?

The following legal considerations need to be taken into account:

1. **ownership (or rental)**
   In Australia Local Spiritual Assemblies may own their own property if they are incorporated. The National Spiritual Assembly will hold a property on behalf of an unincorporated Assembly on the condition that it has been totally paid for. When this Assembly becomes incorporated ownership of the property will revert back to it. All stamp duty and legal costs related to the transfer of ownership back to the Local Spiritual Assembly must be borne by that Assembly. As noted above, incorporated Local Spiritual Assemblies may also rent properties; however, the National Spiritual Assembly's policy is that unincorporated Assemblies may not do so. Such rental agreements may be entered into by individual Bahá'ís on behalf of the unincorporated Assembly. For all properties either owned or leased, a written purchase, transfer, or rental agreement is essential. Once the Local Spiritual Assembly has decided on the property it wishes to lease, or have transferred to its ownership, it must consult a lawyer to ensure that the transaction is properly completed.
2. **council rates**
   It may be possible to obtain exemption from paying rates. The Local Council should be approached regarding this matter. Whether exemption is granted will depend on the purpose to which the Assembly intends to put the building.
3. **liability and insurance**
   A Local Spiritual Assembly that owns or rents property should have the following insurance:
- public liability - all Local Spiritual Assemblies are covered by the National Spiritual Assembly's insurance policy for public liability
- property insurance including fire, theft and burglary - a Local Spiritual Assembly that owns its own property must insure both the property and its contents for fire, theft and burglary. A Local Spiritual Assembly that is leasing property may need to insure contents owned by the Assembly for fire, theft and burglary.
- voluntary workers' accident policy (if applicable) -Local Spiritual Assemblies should seek advice from a reputable broker or insurance company.
4. **zoning and building/alteration controls**
- the Assembly must ensure that it is able to use the building for the purpose intended, before committing the Assembly to lease or purchase of the property. It is, therefore, essential to know the zoning of the property the Assembly has in mind and whether re-zoning is necessary in order to use it for that purpose. For example, in New South Wales, a permit would not be necessary to use a building as a residence in a residential zone; however, the local council's consent would be necessary for such purposes as use of a building in a residential area for a drop-in centre, hostel, or community facility.
- if the Assembly wishes to alter, construct, or demolish a building, it will require a permit from the local council to do so.

- before making a commitment to lease or purchase any property, it is advisable for the Assembly to consult with the Town Planning Department of the local council so as to possible problems and to learn the proper procedures to follow regarding both planning permits and building and alteration permits. (above three points taken from Redfern Legal Centre, "The Law Handbook" (3rd edition), p.655-6).
- zoning laws and building codes may require a minimum number of parking places or limit the number of people who can be in the building or in particular rooms at any one time.

5. protection of Bahá'í properties

- the Local Spiritual Assembly must ensure that the property is protected. The Universal House of Justice has noted that, in some parts of the world, where properties have been infrequently visited by the friends, squatters have settled, involving the Bahá'í community in extra expenses, both in time and money, to regain occupancy:-

> *We have noticed from various reports and Minutes received at the World Centre that in a number of cases where National or Local Spiritual Assemblies own plots of land located in areas infrequently visited by the friends, squatters have settled. In most cases the Assemblies concerned have succeeded in removing such occupants, but in some cases, in view of the nature of the law of the land, Bahá'í properties are in jeopardy of being lost, or else compensation is being paid from Bahá'í funds to remove the squatters.*

(letter from the Universal House of Justice to all National Spiritual Assemblies, dated November 15, 1971)

19.3 OTHER MATTERS- MISCELLANEOUS

19.3.1 *May a Local Spiritual Assembly rent out Bahá'í property to non-Bahá'ís?*

It is permissible to rent out Bahá'í property to non-Bahá'ís provided their activities and conduct are compatible with Bahá'í attitudes and standards:-

> *We have reviewed your letter of July 6, 1970 inquiring if it would be permissible to rent or lend Bahá'í school property for periods between Bahá'í summer and winter schools sessions to non-Bahá'í humanitarian or educational organisations. Decision in these matters is left to the discretion of your National Assembly and the exercise of wisdom in considering all the factors involved. Obviously, you should be certain that such organisations are not objectionable from the Bahá'í viewpoint and that their presence on Bahá'í school property would not adversely reflect on Bahá'í standards of conduct.*

(letter from the Universal House of Justice to a National Spiritual Assembly, dated August 11, 1970)

It is also permissible to use the income generated for general Bahá'í purposes.

19.3.2 *May a Local Spiritual Assembly rent its property to an organisation that may wish to bring alcohol on to the premises?*

The general principle involved is that the Assembly should not knowingly allow alcohol to be served on Bahá'í-owned premises. Should alcohol be served without the Assembly's knowledge it would incur no responsibility for this; however, should the Assembly become aware of alcohol being served it would then have the responsibility to do everything possible to put an end to this practise. These principles are contained in the following statement of

CHAPTER NINETEEN

the Universal House of Justice:-

> *Concerning his comments about renting Bahá'í properties to non-Bahá'í organisations which may wish to bring alcoholic beverages onto the premises, we have been asked to say that when the National Spiritual Assembly of Iran asked the beloved Guardian about the sale of alcoholic drinks at Bahá'í owned premises and restaurants, his Secretary, in a letter dated 6 November 1935, wrote on his behalf, '... he asked me to point out that this practice is highly improper and reprehensible and would be tantamount to encouraging acts that are forbidden in the Faith. It is indeed the conscientious duty of every true Bahá'í to abandon such practices. However, should a Bahá'í owner rent his property without himself taking any part whatever in the business, or giving aid to the tenant, then he would incur no responsibility. Nevertheless the landlord should resort to every possible means to rid his premises of the defilement of this degrading business: how far more injurious if he himself were engaged in such repugnant affairs.'*
>
> (letter written on behalf of the Universal House of Justice to a National Spiritual Assembly, dated April 24, 1983)

Problems can be avoided by the Assembly making it a condition of renting the property that no alcohol be brought onto the premises, and ensuring that the organisation to whom it is being rented knows this before it enters into a rental agreement.

19.3.3 *May a Local Spiritual Assembly rent its property to a political organisation?*

Shoghi Effendi has provided the guidance that a political organisation may use a Bahá'í Centre occasionally for a meeting entirely free of political involvement; however, such an organisation should not be allowed to use the Centre on a regular and permanent basis:-

> *The Guardian's Secretary also wrote the following on his behalf to the Local Spiritual Assembly of Bombay, on 23 July 1932, regarding ... the use of the Hazíratu'l-Quds:*
>
> *Regarding the Brahma Somaj community, he said that there is no objection for them to hold occasionally at the Bahá'í Hazíratu'l-Quds a meeting which would be entirely free from any tinge of political involvement. It would not be appropriate, however, for this group to use the Bahá'í Headquarters on a regular and permanent basis. This matter should be explained to them with kindness and due deference.*
>
> (letter written on behalf of the Universal House of Justice to a National Spiritual Assembly, dated April 24, 1983)

19.3.4 *Is dancing permitted in a local Bahá'í Centre?*

Only traditional dances associated with the expression of a culture are permissible in Bahá'í Centres and then only if the theme of the dance is in harmony with the high ethical standards of the Faith:-

> *We are asked to say that it is not appropriate for dancing to occur in a local or national Bahá'í Centre. When a Local Spiritual Assembly acquires a Bahá'í Centre, it should regard this meeting place as an embryonic Hazíratu'l-Quds and should do everything possible to foster in the community a proper attitude of respect for the Centre.*

CHAPTER NINETEEN

Traditional dances associated with the expression of a culture are permissible in Bahá'í Centres. However, it should be borne in mind that such traditional dances generally have an underlying theme or a story being represented. Care must be exercised to ensure that the themes of such dances are in harmony with the high ethical standards of the Cause and are not portrayals that would arouse base instincts and unworthy passions.

(letter written on behalf of the Universal House of Justice to a National Spiritual Assembly, dated July 26, 1989)

19.3.5 **Is it permissible to hold Bahá'í functions on the premises of other religious organisations?**

This is permissible provided it will not tend to identify the Faith with that religious organisation in the eyes of the public:-

Generally there is no objection to holding other Bahá'í functions in places or facilities owned and operated by non-Bahá'í religious bodies, provided such use does not tend to identify the Faith, in the eyes of the public, with other religions. The House of Justice leaves the application of this principle to your discretion.

(letter written on behalf of the Universal House of Justice to a National Spiritual Assembly, dated June 3, 1982)

The National Spiritual Assembly leaves the application of this principle to the discretion of the Local Spiritual Assembly.

19.3.6 **Does the Local Spiritual Assembly have to report the acquisition of, or changes to, property holdings, to the National Spiritual Assembly?**

Yes. Local Spiritual Assemblies should report any major changes to their property holdings to the National Spiritual Assembly as soon as possible. This includes the purchase, donation, long term (more than one year) lease, sale or transfer, new construction or demolition of property. In the case of sale or transfer, new construction or demolition of property, Local Spiritual Assemblies are strongly advised to contact the National Spiritual Assembly before proceeding, especially if it is owned in the name of the National Spiritual Assembly. The Local Spiritual Assembly should also prepare a Property Report, noting any changes to the property during the year, and attach this, as a separate piece of paper, to the copy of its Annual Report sent to the National Office. The National Spiritual Assembly needs this information because it must report annually on any changes in property holdings at the local and national level to the Universal House of Justice.

19.3.7 **May a Local Spiritual Assembly accept a gift of free land from a non-Bahá'í source for Bahá'í use?**

The circumstances under which a Local Spiritual Assembly may accept a gift of free land for Bahá'í use are covered by the following statements of the Universal House of Justice and Shoghi Effendi:-

1. *The principle of not accepting gifts from non-Bahá'ís for strictly Bahá'í purposes applies to receiving free grants of land from non-Bahá'ís, whether individuals, institutions or governments.*
2. *There is no objection, however, to accepting free plots of land from the government or civic authorities if such plots are used for Bahá'í cemeteries or for such institutions as are charitable or humanitarian in nature, such as schools.*
3. *In countries where the ONLY method to acquire property is to be granted by the*

CHAPTER NINETEEN

authorities free USE of land, there is no objection to receiving such allocation of land (which excludes ownership) for the building of institutions of a strictly Bahá'í nature, such as a Ḥaẓíratu'l-Quds, a Summer School, or a Teaching Institute.

4. *If the government offers gifts of land to all religious communities in recognition of their status as a religious entity in the country, Bahá'ís may accept such properties under the provisions of points 1 and 2 above. They should make it clear to the government that they can embark upon the establishment of institutions of a humanitarian or charitable nature, only when conditions favourable to the establishment of such institutions are present.*

(letter written on behalf of the Universal House of Justice to a National Spiritual Assembly, dated September 19, 1985)

As you have stated in your letter it is not possible for the Bahá'ís to accept gifts from non-Bahá'ís for Bahá'í work. The Guardian feels that if the piece of property which was offered by a friend of the Faith in the ... District, were purchased at a ridiculously low price, it would be tantamount to a gift and therefore would not be consistent with Bahá'í principles. The Guardian feels that what might be done is to have the property valued at a fair price and then purchase it on that basis. In other words, you would be sure that you are not paying more than the property is worth, particularly if it is valued by someone who would establish a fair valuation.

(letter written on behalf of Shoghi Effendi to a National Spiritual Assembly, dated August 23, 1957)

19.3.8 *How may a Local Spiritual Assembly use the proceeds from the sale of property purchased with earmarked funds?*

The Universal House of Justice has provided the following guidance:-

As to the proceeds from the sale of Bahá'í property ... If the property was donated or purchased with funds earmarked for that specific purpose, the proceeds of the sale of the property retain the earmarking unless the donor has specifically provided otherwise. If the donor or donors are living, they may, of course, release the earmarking. If the donor or donors are not living, or refuse to release the earmarking, the proceeds should be used for the same purpose. If that purpose has already been fulfilled (ie. an alternate property has already been acquired), the surplus should be used to the extent possible in a manner having regard for the original intention of the donor or donors, eg. to maintain or improve the property.

(letter written on behalf of the Universal House of Justice to a National Spiritual Assembly, dated August 21, 1980)

19.3.9 *May a Local Spiritual Assembly purchase a church for use as a Bahá'í Centre?*

A Local Spiritual Assembly may purchase a building used as a church for a Bahá'í Centre, provided it does not have the distinctive characteristics of a church and that there are no conditions attached to the sale concerning the use of the property. A building that has the architectural characteristics normally incorporated into a church or has other institutions such as a cemetery surrounding it, may not be used. Church properties, as distinct from church buildings, may be purchased:-

The Universal House of Justice has received your letter...requesting guidance on purchasing old church buildings for use as Bahá'í Hazíratu'l-Quds, and has asked us to convey the following to you. A number of factors must be examined in each specific case. For instance, if the building is constructed not *as an ordinary secular structure, but with the architectural characteristics normally incorporated in a church, or if there are institutions, such as a cemetery, surrounding the church building, it would not be appropriate to purchase such buildings for use as Bahá'í Hazíratu'l-Quds. On the other hand, there are denominations which use a building for church services without the building itself having the distinctive characteristics of a church, and such a building could be purchased and converted into a Bahá'í Hazíratu'l-Quds if financially and practically suitable. Church properties, as distinct from church buildings, can be purchased at any time that these become available. These transactions are possible only when the church authorities attach no conditions to the sale concerning the use of the property. If such property can be purchased by anyone and used for any purpose, there is no reason why a Bahá'í institution cannot buy it for use as an administrative centre.*

(letter written on behalf of the Universal House of Justice to a National Spiritual Assembly, dated May 16, 1982)

19.4 NOTES FOR REGISTERED GROUPS

Registered Groups may not own or lease property. In the event of a Registered Group having the opportunity to obtain property for the Faith, eg. through donation, the matter should be referred to the National Spiritual Assembly.

19.5 BIBLIOGRAPHY

The following works were used to draft this Chapter:

1. "Developing Distinctive Bahá'í Communities", Guidelines for Spiritual Assemblies, Chapter 14 (published by the National Spiritual Assembly of the United States, Bahá'í Publishing Trust, 1989)
2. "The Law Handbook", 3rd edition (Redfern Legal Centre Publishing, New South Wales, 1988).

CHAPTER TWENTY

Chapter 20

20. Publishing and Distribution of Bahá'í Literature

20.1 PUBLISHING LITERATURE

20.1.1 *May a Local Spiritual Assembly publish Bahá'í literature?*

Yes. Although Local Spiritual Assemblies are encouraged to arrange for publication through Bahá'í Publications and Distribution Services Australia (BPDSA), they are not obliged to do so. They may make their own arrangements for publication. The decision whether to publish a work must be based on whether there is a need for the work within the community; for example, will it help further the teaching effort? It is not the function of a Local Spiritual Assembly to go into business in order to raise funds

In its 'Memorandum on Establishing and Operating a Bahá'í Publishing Trust', May 1974, the Universal House of Justice lays down the principle that Bahá'í literature must be made available at as low a price as possible. At the same time the Trust must be able to build up a sound business. To this end the Trust must price its works as cheaply as possible whilst also enabling itself to recover its costs and to make a small surplus so as to build up capital. The same principle applies to Local Spiritual Assemblies if they decide to publish literature; that is, they should aim to supply it as cheaply as possible, calculating only to recover costs and make a modest surplus if they intend to continue publishing. The Local Spiritual Assembly must also comply with the following requirements:

BEFORE PUBLICATION
a) make sure the work is reviewed
b) make sure all copyright laws - Bahá'í and civil - are obeyed
c) obtain an ISBN (International Standard Book Number) from the National Library of Australia, Canberra, ACT 2600 and print this on the 'publisher's details' page.

AFTER PUBLICATION
a) send nine copies of the publication to the National Office. Four copies are for the National Spiritual Assembly and will be paid for at cost. Five copies are required for lodgement at the World Centre and these are to be donated freely.
b) send one free copy to the National Library of Australia (Canberra, ACT, 2600), marked 'for legal deposit'.
c) send one free copy to the State Library of the State in which the work is published.
d) in New South Wales, send one free copy to the Fisher Library of the University of Sydney, addressed to the 'Copyright Office'. In other States, legislation may require free deposit with a designated University Library.
e) optionally, two free copies may be sent to Association for Bahá'í Studies, Canada, for deposit in their library.
If the work has been prepared for the local community but could have more than local value, Local Spiritual Assemblies are encouraged to send a copy to BPDSA for consideration for national and overseas distribution. The sharing of resources in this way helps to prevent duplication of effort. Similarly, before making a decision to publish its own work, the Local Spiritual Assembly should check that the item is not already available from some other source, such as BPDSA.
[For further information on publishing Bahá'í literature see "Lights of Guidance"{revised edition}, nos. 346-71.]

CHAPTER TWENTY

20.2 REVIEWING LITERATURE

20.2.1 *Which institution is responsible for reviewing works about the Faith before publication?*

A work about the Faith published at the local level must be reviewed, before publication, by the Local Spiritual Assembly within whose area of jurisdiction it will be distributed. Any work intended for distribution in more than one Local Spiritual Assembly area must be reviewed, before publication, by the National Spiritual Assembly. This applies whether the publisher is a Bahá'í or a non-Bahá'í:-

> *At this early stage of the Cause all works by Bahá'ís which deal with the Faith, whether in the form of books, pamphlets, translations, poems, songs, radio and television scripts, films, recordings, etc. must be approved before submission for publication, whether to a Bahá'í or non-Bahá'í publisher. In the case of material for purely local consumption the competent authority is the Local Spiritual Assembly, otherwise the National Spiritual Assembly (through its Reviewing Committee) is the approving authority.*
>
> (Universal House of Justice, 'Memorandum on Bahá'í Publishing' - Ridván 1971, p.1)

Works for review by the National Spiritual Assembly should be sent to the National Office.

20.2.2 *What is the purpose of review?*

> *...The purpose of review is to protect the Faith against misrepresentation by its own followers at this early stage of its existence when comparatively few people have any knowledge of it.*
>
> (letter written on behalf of the Universal House of Justice to an individual believer, dated October 8, 1980)

20.2.3 *What standards apply to reviewing works?*

In its 'Memorandum on Bahá'í Publishing' - Ridván 1971 p.2, the Universal House of Justice said the following standards must be upheld:
a) conformity with the Teachings
b) accuracy
c) dignity in presentation

In a letter to a National Spiritual Assembly dated March 11, 1965 the Universal House of Justice noted that this function of review may include

> 'verification of any quotations from Bahá'í writings'; also that it 'should not be confused with evaluation of the literary merit of a work or of its value as a publication which are normally the prerogative of the publisher...'

Local Assemblies conducting a review should therefore confine themselves to the above three points and not turn down a proposed publication on other grounds. Of course, even if a work passes review the Local Spiritual Assembly may not be able to proceed if there are other practical difficulties, eg. a lack of funds to finance the publication.

20.3 COPYRIGHT

20.3.1 *Are Spiritual Assemblies and individuals free to quote in their publications from any of the Writings of the three Central Figures of the Faith without obtaining*

clearance from the copyright holder?

Yes:-

> ...Spiritual Assemblies and individual believers are free to quote in their publications from any of the Writings of the three Central Figures of the Faith or from the writings of the beloved Guardian, whether in the original language or in translation, without obtaining clearance from the copyright holder, <u>unless</u> the copyright holder in the case of a translation is an individual or is a non-Bahá'í institution...
>
> The ruling is made to ensure that the Sacred Scriptures of our Faith and the writings of the beloved Guardian may be freely used by the believers; it does not change the existing requirements for individual believers to submit their works on the Faith for review before publication, neither does it relieve Spiritual Assemblies of their responsibility to protect the dignity of the Faith and uphold the proper standard of reverence in the use of its Sacred Scriptures. Thus, if any Assembly sees that one of the friends is making use of any of the Holy Texts in an unbefitting manner, it should remonstrate with him and, if necessary, require him to stop doing so.
>
> (letter written on behalf of the Universal House of Justice to a National Spiritual Assembly, dated September 4, 1981)

Individuals and institutions may quote in their own publications from the published works of the Universal House of Justice and its agencies. If a work of the Universal House of Justice or its agencies has not been published neither individuals nor institutions may use extracts from it in their own publications without first checking with the National Spiritual Assembly.

20.3.2 ***What about other publications, musical and artistic works, audio-visual material (eg. video tapes), computer software programmes, and so on?***

All such items are usually covered by copyright. Permission to copy or use extracts from these works must, therefore, be sought from the copyright holder. This applies when the copyright holder is a Bahá'í individual or institution, as well as when the copyright holder is not a Bahá'í. In all cases of doubt, Local Spiritual Assemblies and individuals are advised to carefully check the legal requirements. Penalties for failure to comply with the law can be severe.

20.4 **DISTRIBUTING LITERATURE**

20.4.1 ***May a Local Spiritual Assembly sell works it has published outside its own area of jurisdiction?***

As previously noted, any work intended for distribution outside a single Local Spiritual Assembly area must be reviewed by the National Spiritual Assembly. If the work passes review it may be distributed nationwide and even overseas. Local Spiritual Assemblies are encouraged to negotiate a marketing agreement with Bahá'í Publications and Distribution Services Australia (BPDSA), but they are not obliged to do so. They may distribute their works independently. The same principle applies as is set out in 'May Local Spiritual Assemblies publish Bahá'í literature?'; that is, the work should be made available as a service to the community. It should be priced as cheaply as possible, only allowing the Assembly to cover its costs and make a modest margin.

20.4.2 *May a Local Spiritual Assembly set up a sales outlet?*

According to Article III of the "By-Laws of a Local Spiritual Assembly", the Local Spiritual Assembly has a responsibility to 'make available the published literature of the Faith' within its area of jurisdiction. One way in which it may do this is to establish a sales outlet. A Local Spiritual Assembly may set up a sales outlet if there is sufficient demand in the community for the outlet to be financially self-sufficient. Items may only be sold outside the Assembly's are of jurisdiction if the Assembly obtains the written consent of those Assemblies within whose area of jurisdiction it wishes to sell. A local sales outlet may order its materials from any source. Sales outlets which elect to import material directly from overseas are required to comply with the law relating to any sales tax or customs duties which may be applicable. Failure in the past on the part of Bahá'í travellers and on the part of Bahá'í Assemblies to properly declare goods to Customs has resulted in a loss of good name. The effect for a time was that all importations of Bahá'í books into Australia was slowed down by the imposition of thorough inspections. The limitations have now been lifted, but if any individual or Assembly again misbehaves or is careless of the law the same restrictions will be imposed, perhaps more severely than before. Further information on setting up a sales outlet and on applicable taxes and duties is available from BPDSA.

20.5 ENCOURAGING THE USE OF BAHÁ'Í LITERATURE

20.5.1 *How may a Local Spiritual Assembly encourage the use of Bahá'í literature within its community?*

The Local Spiritual Assembly should establish a reference and lending library for the community and should encourage the friends to make use of it. New works should be brought to the attention of the friends at Bahá'í meetings. Bahá'í Publications and Distribution Services Australia (BPDSA) recommends the appointment of a 'Literature Distribution Representative' to receive and present material from BPDSA to the friends. Further information on how to set up a community library is available from BPDSA. Another way of encouraging the use of Bahá'í literature is to set up a sales outlet.

20.6 NOTES FOR REGISTERED GROUPS

Members of registered groups may publish and distribute literature on the same terms as individuals within the Faith. They may not review works. Any work produced for distribution in the Registered Group's area must be passed to the National Spiritual Assembly for review. Registered Groups may not set up sales outlets. They may, of course, establish community libraries.

CHAPTER TWENTY ONE

Chapter 21

21. Bahá'í Societies at Tertiary Institutions

21.1 BAHÁ'Í SOCIETIES AT TERTIARY INSTITUTIONS

21.1.1 What is the purpose of Bahá'í Societies at tertiary institutions?

The purpose of the formation of a Bahá'í Society on a campus is to promote the study of the Bahá'í Faith.

21.1.2 What is the responsibility of the Local Spiritual Assembly for Bahá'í Societies at tertiary institutions?

A Local Spiritual Assembly that has a tertiary institution within its area of jurisdiction has the following responsibilities:
- if there is no current Bahá'í Society at the institution, to meet with the Bahá'í students and go about forming one;
- to become involved in the Bahá'í Society, to meet with the students
- and encourage activities for the up-coming year. The Local Spiritual Assembly should meet with students, and support their activities;
- the Local Spiritual Assembly has to take the initiative to make sure Societies are formed and continue to be active.

21.1.3 What is the procedure for the formation and operation of a Bahá'í Society?

The procedure for the formation of a Bahá'í Society and the operation of the Society are:
1. Every campus with a Student Union has a mechanism for forming a Society
2. There are guidelines for Societies which can be obtained
3. Societies can be financial affiliates
4. An Executive of a Bahá'í Society is elected with a Chairperson, Vice Chairperson, Secretary and Treasurer
5. An office bearer of the Bahá'í Society should attend every second meeting (at least) of the Student Union (this is important as non-attendance may cause de-registering of a Bahá'í Society)
6. The Local Spiritual Assembly should obtain the Student Union Handbook and Guidelines for Societies and study these carefully. There are benefits given to Societies, such as:
   - Money can be received from the Union for reimbursement of secretarial expenses, refreshments, posters, annual dinners
   - Money may be reimbursed if you go as a delegate from your Society to a National Conference. These moneys should be used exclusively for the Bahá'í Society. They may not be contributed to other Bahá'í Funds.
7. The Local Spiritual Assembly could consider formulating plans with the Society based on the semester system.

21.1.4 Are there detailed terms of reference available for Bahá'í Societies at tertiary institutions?

Yes. The National Spiritual Assembly has prepared a 'Constitution for Bahá'í Societies in Tertiary Institutions' which sets out in detail the purpose, membership and methods of operation of a Bahá'í Society. The Society should operate according to this Constitution. Copies are available from the Bahá'í National Office.

21.1.5 **What is the role of the Association for Bahá'í Studies Australia Committee in relation to Bahá'í Societies at tertiary institutions?**

The Association for Bahá'í Studies Australia has the role of stimulating, and encouraging the formation and development of Bahá'í Societies on campuses.

21.2 **NOTES FOR REGISTERED GROUPS**

Registered Groups, not being administrative institutions, cannot take on formal responsibility for any Bahá'í Societies at tertiary institutions in their area, however, they are encouraged to assist such Societies in their activities.

A D D E N D U M

A STUDY GUIDE TO CHAPTER 2 OF THIS HANDBOOK

INTRODUCTION

What is Bahá'í consultation?

Bahá'í consultation is a tool for individuals and institutions to use when making and implementing decisions on issues of concern to them. Its purpose, 'Abdu'l-Bahá has said, is "the investigation of truth."

("The Promulgation of Universal Peace", p.72)

The power of Bahá'í consultation lies in its implementation of the most fundamental principle of the Faith - "unity in diversity" - at the decision- making level. On the one hand, by turning their thoughts to the divine kingdom and entering into consultation in a spirit of love and harmony, the institutions or individuals concerned ensure that unity is maintained at their meeting. On the other hand, by implementing the right and obligation of every believer to express his views freely and frankly, they ensure that a diversity of viewpoints are brought to bear on the issue under consideration. The necessity of considering a variety of viewpoints enables the assembled believers to arrive at the best possible solution. The necessity of maintaining unity ensures both that the consultation will proceed to a solution and that, the decision having been made, it can be effectively implemented. When both these elements are present we have Bahá'í consultation. It should be remembered that one of the Australian community's continuing goals is to: "Foster the practice of consultation in the conduct of human affairs and the resolution of conflicts at all levels of society." Clearly, the place to begin is within the Bahá'í community itself. The material in this chapter is intended to assist the Local Spiritual Assembly in its practice of Bahá'í consultation.

Other useful works on the subject are the Universal House of Justice compilation, "Bahá'í Consultation, The Lamp of Guidance" and John E. Kolstoe, "Consultation, A Universal Lamp of Guidance". Both are available from the national and regional book distribution outlets.

CONSULTATION WITHIN THE LOCAL SPIRITUAL ASSEMBLY

What are the major principles to be kept in mind during consultation?

The members thereof must take counsel together in such wise that no occasion for ill-feeling or discord may arise. This can be attained when every member expresseth with absolute freedom his own opinion and setteth forth his argument. Should anyone oppose, he must on no account feel hurt for not until matters are fully discussed can the right way be revealed. The shining spark of truth cometh forth only after the clash of differing opinions.

('Abdu'l-Bahá, in "Bahá'í Administration", p.21)

The following principles can be derived from this statement:-
(1) Every member has not only the right, but also the obligation to put forward his point of view. Concerning the right of each member to his own point of view, Shoghi Effendi has said: *"...at the very root of the Cause lies the principle of the undoubted right of the individual to self-expression, his freedom to declare his conscience and set forth his views."* ("Principles of Bahá'í Administration", p.44) Concerning the obligation of each member to express his opinion, Shoghi Effendi has said: *"...it is not only the right but the sacred obligation of every*

ADDENDUM

member to express freely and openly his views, without being afraid of displeasing or alienating any of his fellow-members."
(letter written on behalf of Shoghi Effendi to an individual believer, dated October 28, 1935)

It follows from this that no Assembly member has the right to remain silent if he has an opinion that has not yet been expressed. Nor can he ask another to speak on his behalf:-
...the Guardian would advise you to give up the method of asking other members to voice your opinion and suggestions. This indirect way of expressing your views to the Assembly not only creates an atmosphere of secrecy which is most alien to the spirit of the Cause, but would also lead to many misunderstandings and complications. The Assembly members must have the courage of their convictions...
(from a letter written on behalf of Shoghi Effendi to an individual believer, dated October 28, 1935)

(2) Once an opinion is expressed it becomes the property of the Assembly and must be considered on its own merits, without regard to the personality of the member whose opinion it is. 'Abdu'l-Bahá has said: *"it is in no wise permissible for one to belittle the thought of another..."*("Bahá'í Administration", p.22) Similarly, it is not correct for the one who has put forward an idea to feel that he has a duty to defend it, in the face of opposition from other Assembly members. 'Abdu'l-Bahá makes this clear when he says: *"...They must in every matter search out the truth and not insist upon their own opinion, for stubborness and persistence in one's views will lead ultimately to discord and wrangling and the truth will remain hidden."*

("Bahá'í Administration", p.22)

(3) Remember, it is the opinions and not the people that are to clash. Assembly members must focus their attention on the constructive ideas that are generated by the collision of opinions. They must not focus on the collision itself and certainly not on the members whose views are in conflict.(Kolstoe, p.30) If an Assembly meeting degenerates into personal conflict the discord will prevent an effective decision being made, much less put into practice.

What is the procedure for consultation?

(1) Define the matter to be decided.
Make a clear statement of the issue and ensure that all the members agree with it.

(2) Ascertain all the facts of the matter and agree on them.
This involves collecting basic information about the what, when, where, how and why of an issue. If the Assembly is consulting for the purpose of making plans, it should have a clear understanding of the goal it is aiming at, as well as of the means by which it can achieve it.
There are three major steps to be taken -
(a) separate the relevant from the irrelevant facts and be sure to distinguish between impressions and facts
(b) discover the background
- determine whether or not the stated problem is the real one or if there is an underlying issue which needs to be addressed (Kolstoe, p.27)
(c) examine different perspectives
- the same 'facts' will look different to different people, therefore, it is important to be aware of how each person concerned with the issue If the Assembly finds that it does not have all the information necessary it may have to postpone discussion on the matter to another meeting.

(3) Identify the spiritual and administrative principles that relate to the issue. Available

ADDENDUM

sources are:
(a) the Writings of Bahá'u'lláh, 'Abdu'l-Bahá, Shoghi Effendi and the Universal House of Justice
(b) this Local Spiritual Assembly Handbook and other works mentioned in its chapters
(c) Continental Counsellors, Auxiliary Board Members and their assistants
(d) the National Spiritual Assembly Sources (a) and (b) should be researched first before consulting sources (c) and (d).

(4) Consult together, applying the principles of consultation outlined above. The purpose of consultation is to arrive at a decision. During consultation two extremes need to be avoided. One is cutting the discussion short before every member has had the opportunity to fully express a view. The other is to carry the consultation on beyond a useful point. If a resolution has been arrived at, continuing discussion may cause the decision to become diluted.(Kolstoe, p.28) The time factor also needs to be taken into account. If the Assembly has many items on its agenda it cannot afford to spend too long on one issue. Nevertheless, cutting off discussion too early may prevent the formation of a unanimous decision. The Assembly must take all these factors into account and strive for a balanced approach. One method of generating a range of possible solutions is 'brainstorming'. The procedure here is for the members of the Assembly to simply put forward any ideas that come into their heads. No idea is challenged, no matter how unlikely it may seem. When the period of brainstorming is over, the Assembly can sift through the ideas put forward and see if they offer any fresh perspectives on, or solutions to, the issue at hand. If the Assembly chooses to have a brainstorming session, it is advisable to set a time limit at the start. The Secretary must also be sure to write down all the ideas presented. Consultation may also be made more effective in an Assembly meeting if the procedure is followed of having members raise their hand when they want to speak and then waiting to be recognised by the Chairman. This will help to ensure that everyone is given the opportunity to speak and the consultation remains orderly. It is, however, up to the Assembly to decide whether it wishes to use this method or not.

(5) Make a clear statement of the provisional conclusion.
When it seems that the discussion has arrived at a point of conclusion the Chairman, or some other person designated by the Assembly, should summarise the discussion and make a clear statement of the tentative decision. The purpose is to ensure that everyone understands and agrees on the proposition that is to be voted on. If the Assembly feels it is necessary, the temporary decision may be expressed as a motion. This is simply a more formal way of putting the proposed decision. To put a motion before the Assembly a formal proposition must be 'moved' by one member and 'seconded' by another. The wording of the motion, if carried when voted upon, becomes the form of the decision made and recorded in the minutes. If a member wishes to alter the motion, he must move an amendment. This in turn must be seconded. An amendment should change the original motion by omitting or substituting words. It must not negate the original motion. If the Assembly votes against the amendment the original motion stands. There is no limit to the number of amendments that can be moved. They should be voted on in the order they are moved. A successful amendment alters the original motion and a later successful amendment alters the motion as previously amended. If the mover and seconder of the original motion are in agreement with the amendment they may withdraw their original motion and allow a new motion to be moved, thus simplifying the voting procedure. It is up to the Assembly to decide whether or not to use this more formal method of establishing the proposed decision. It may help to clarify the issue under discussion and ensure that the wording of the decision is agreeable to everyone. On the other hand, if consultation is flowing smoothly, the use of such formal procedures may be an unnecessary hindrance.

ADDENDUM

(6) Make a decision by consensus or majority vote.
If the tentative decision is read out and it is clear that everyone agrees to it, a vote will not be necessary. The Universal House of Justice has clearly stated that: *"The ideal of Bahá'í consultation is to arrive at a unanimous decision."*
(letter to a National Spiritual Assembly, dated March 6, 1970)

It is clear, therefore, that unanimity is to be preferred wherever possible; however, it is not obligatory. 'Abdu'l-Bahá has said: *"...if, the Lord forbid, differences of opinion should arise, a majority of voices must prevail."*
("Bahá'í Administration", p.22)

Therefore, if the members are not agreed the decision must be put to the vote. At this point, a member of the Assembly has the right to ask for more information if he does not yet feel able to make up his mind. The Universal House of Justice has said that it is then *"for the Assembly to decide whether or not further consultation is needed before voting."*
(letter to a National Spiritual Assembly, dated March 6, 1970)

If the Assembly does choose to re-open consultation it may find that, with fresh ideas and information, it is now able to reach a consensus. If the Assembly chooses not to re-open consultation, a vote must be taken and the majority opinion prevails. The instructions of Shoghi Effendi must be kept in mind at this point:-
And, when they are called upon to arrive at a certain decision, they should, after dispassionate, anxious and cordial consultation, turn to God in prayer, and with earnestness and conviction and courage record their vote and abide by the voice of the majority...
("Bahá'í Administration", p.64)

(7) Record the decision in the minutes.
Check that the members agree on the recorded decision by having the Secretary read it back to the Assembly.

(8) Decide how the decision will be carried out.
Consultation is not complete until the task is performed. The Assembly must be sure that the member or members who are to carry out the decision have a clear understanding of what they must do. If the task includes conveying information to another person it must be decided how this will be done:- letter, phone, or personal contact?

Can an Assembly member absent himself from the consultation when the issue under discussion involves him personally?

The relevant guidance is contained in the following statements by the Universal House of Justice:-
In your letter of 4 April you inquire further about the principles governing the presence of a member of the National Assembly when a matter concerning him or her personally is being discussed. The first principle to bear in mind is that every member of an Assembly has an absolute and incontrovertible right to be present at every meeting of that body and to be fully informed of every matter coming before it. The second principle is that of detachment in consultation. The members of an Assembly must learn to express their views frankly, calmly, without passion or rancour. They must also learn to listen to the opinions of their fellow members without taking offence or belittling the views of another. Bahá'í consultation is not an easy process. It requires love, kindliness, moral courage and humility. Thus no member should ever allow himself to be prevented from expressing frankly his view because it may

ADDENDUM

offend a fellow member; and, realising this, no member should take offence at another member's statements.
The third principle is that if a believer feels that he has been done an injustice by the Assembly, he should appeal the decision in the normal way.
(letter from the Universal House of Justice to a National Spiritual Assembly, dated August 26, 1965)

We note on page 2 that ... left the room while the National Assembly discussed ways and means of helping her. Naturally, if one wishes to absent himself while his own situation is being discussed by the National Assembly, there is no objection. The National Assembly cannot require a member to remove himself from the consultation, and he is fully entitled to remain.
(letter from the Universal House of Justice to a National Spiritual Assembly, dated February 23, 1965)

It should also be understood that a member may wish to absent himself from a meeting at which subjects in which he is personally involved are to be discussed. In such cases he may do so unless the Assembly requires him to be present.
(letter from the Universal House of Justice to the International Teaching Centre, dated January 22, 1975)

It is clear from the above statements that an Assembly member has the right to remain present at all meetings of the Assembly, regardless of whether the issue under discussion involves him personally. He must remember the principle of not allowing himself to be upset by the opinions of others. The other Assembly members, for their part, must keep in mind the importance of discussing the problem, not the person. They have a responsibility to be honest but loving, so as not to alienate the individual concerned. If, however, the Assembly member prefers to absent himself, he has the right to do so, unless the Assembly specifically asks him to remain present.

Should any Assembly member feel that he has been unjustly treated by an Assembly he has the right to appeal against its decision in the usual way. [For further information on the right of appeal see the relevant section later in this chapter.] [For further information about consultation between an Assembly and an individual see the section in this chapter, "Consultation Between the Local Spiritual Assembly and an Individual".]

When problems arise in consultation how can we solve them?

Bahá'í consultation is about effective communication between a diverse group of individuals in order to achieve certain tasks. In any such situation there is the possibility of conflicts of personality. The Universal House of Justice has pointed out that: *"Bahá'í consultation is not an easy process. It requires love, kindliness, moral courage and humility."*
(letter from the Universal House of Justice, to a National Spiritual Assembly, dated August 26, 1965)

When conflicts do arise there are two responses that have been specifically forbidden by Shoghi Effendi:-
(1) A believer cannot resign from, or stop attending the meetings of, an Assembly -
The remedy to Assembly inharmony cannot be in the resignation or abstinence of any of its members. It must learn, in spite of disturbing elements, to continue to function as a whole, otherwise the whole system would become discredited through the introduction of exceptions to the rule. The believers, loving the Cause above all else and putting its interests first, must be ready to bear the hardships entailed, of whatever nature they may be. Only through such persistence and self-sacrifice can we ever hope to preserve on the one hand our divine

ADDENDUM

institutions intact, and on the other force ourselves to become nobler, better instruments to serve this glorious Faith.

(letter written on behalf of Shoghi Effendi to an individual believer, dated November 20, 1941)

(2) The Assembly members must not take sides -
The Bahá'ís must learn to forget personalities and to overcome the desire - so natural in people - to take sides and fight about it.
(letter written on behalf of Shoghi Effendi to a National Spiritual Assembly, dated June 30, 1949)

Remember there are no 'sides' in Bahá'í consultation, only different points of view. It is clear, therefore, that whatever problems arise, the Assembly members must be prepared to put the good of the Cause before their own interests and must strive to maintain the unity of the Assembly at all costs. Without unity the Assembly cannot hope to function effectively. Problems must be solved within this context. There are two issues to address. One is promotion of the right attitude on the part of Assembly members. The other is the practical steps the Assembly can take to work through problems.
(1) The right attitude.
'Abdu'l-Bahá said that two conditions must be present for consultation to be effective. The first is unity, which is to be attained through the promotion of love and harmony amongst Assembly members. The second is the focussing of one's attention on the Abhá Kingdom through prayer. Together they create the necessary atmosphere of cooperation and common purpose:-
The first condition is absolute love and harmony amongst the members of the Assembly. They must be wholly free from estrangement and must manifest in themselves the Unity of God, for they are the waves of one sea, the drops of one river, the stars of one heaven, the rays of one sun, the trees of one orchard, the flowers of one garden. Should harmony of thought and absolute unity be non-existent, that gathering shall be dispersed and that Assembly be brought to naught. The second condition:-They must when coming together turn their faces to the Kingdom on High and ask aid from the Realm of Glory.

("Bahá'í Administration", p.22)

The promotion of love and harmony requires more than a mere tolerance for one another's points of view. It means that Assembly members must strive to acquire a real understanding of and respect for, one another. They must learn to see and encourage the good in each other and overlook faults. They need to be aware of and to understand differences of background, especially cultural differences.

One means by which love and harmony may be fostered is by setting aside a period of time before the meeting to share personal and community concerns. This could take the form of a shared meal or other social gathering. If a member is experiencing particular difficulties with consultation, the other members will then be better able to understand why and offer support to that individual. When prayers are being said, special prayers for assistance for members with particular problems can also be offered. In general, love and harmony will be better achieved if the members of the Assembly make a real effort to mix with and get to know one another outside of Assembly meetings. Once in the meeting, it is important that every member focus his attention on the purpose for which he is present. That is, service to the Cause of God, and more specifically, to his Bahá'í community:-
...The members of these Assemblies, on their part, must disregard utterly their own likes and dislikes, their personal interests and inclinations, and concentrate their minds upon those measures that will conduce to the welfare and happiness of the Bahá'í Community and promote the common weal.

ADDENDUM

("Principles of Bahá'í Administration", p.41)

Turning to the Abhá Kingdom before consultation begins helps focus the mind on the purpose of the meeting, as well as requesting the necessary divine assistance. During the meeting, a useful way of guarding against dissension is to keep a picture of 'Abdu'l-Bahá in a clearly visible place. This will remind each member to conduct himself as though he was in the presence of 'Abdu'l-Bahá. Indeed, communication between 'Abdu'l-Bahá and every Assembly properly constituted is promised:-

'Abdu'l-Bahá is constantly engaged in ideal communication with any Spiritual Assembly which is instituted through the divine bounty, and the members of which are in the utmost devotion turning to the divine kingdom and are firm in the Covenant. To them He is heartily attached and with them He is linked by everlasting ties. Thus correspondence with them is sincere, constant and uninterrupted.

("Bahá'í World Faith", pp. 410-11)

The promotion of a positive, friendly attitude within the Assembly makes problems easier to deal with when they arise.
(2) Practical action.

In his book, "Consultation, A Universal Lamp of Guidance" (pp. 180-82), John Kolstoe outlines 7 different methods that can be used to cope with conflict:-

(1) Postpone discussion. 'Abdu'l-Bahá has made it clear that if disunity reaches a point where enmity and threats are about to occur, the discussion must immediately be halted until another time:-

The honoured members of the Spiritual Assembly should exert their efforts so that no differences may occur, and if such differences do occur, they should not reach the point of causing conflict, hatred and antagonism, which lead to threats. When you notice that a stage has been reached when enmity and threats are about to occur, you should immediately postpone discussion of the subject, until wranglings, disputations, and loud talk vanish, and a propitious time is at hand.

(Universal House of Justice compilation, "Bahá'í Consultation", p.7, extract from previously untranslated Tablet)

If feelings are running particularly high, it may even be necessary to end the meeting altogether and wait for another time when emotions have cooled. If the problem concerns one particular member and continues over time, it may be necessary to consult with an Auxiliary Board Member or the National Spiritual Assembly.

(2) Consult about it. If a particular difficulty is recurring there is no point in continually ignoring it and hoping it will go away. The following points should be remembered in addition to the general rules of consultation -
(a) If the Assembly knows it is being lied to, it should confront the individual concerned with the fact. If there is no proof, only a general feeling that all is not being said, there are two options. One is to raise the issue at the meeting. The other is to be patient, wait for the offender to trip himself up, then deal with the issue.(Kolstoe, pp 164-5)
(b) If an individual, on or off the Assembly, is taking a confrontationist attitude towards an Assembly member, or towards the Assembly as a whole, the Assembly or the particular individual concerned, must not react and take the confrontation as a challenge. Rather, it should try and address the basic issue without being drawn into an argument. (Kolstoe, p.163) Be prepared to postpone other important business and spend as much time as is required to restore understanding and goodwill amongst the Assembly members.

ADDENDUM

(3) Pray for unity. Even if only two or three believers are aware of a problem, a prayer campaign may solve it.

(4) Resolve differences. If there is conflict between just two members they could meet together to resolve it. Or they may invite a third person to act as a mediator.

(5) Intervene in disputes. If the dispute is between only some Assembly members, the other should not sit back and leave it to those members to work out. Rather, they should intervene and resolve the dispute so that the Assembly can get back to business.

(6) Exercise patience and long-suffering. Realise that some problems can only be solved with time and that some are not solvable but must simply be endured. In the case of a contentious individual who refuses to cooperate there may be no other alternative except to wait and pray for a change of attitude in him. In the meantime, work that has to be done should not be neglected. (Kolstoe, p.168)

(7) Problems between people are shortened by acts of kindness. Find the courage to make a sincere friendly gesture even if you have mixed feelings towards that particular individual. Assemblies should also evaluate their consultations regularly. They should consider how their consultation has improved; what weak areas remain, and which particular area to work on next.

How can consultation be made to work more effectively?

Following is a list of DOs and DON'Ts for Assembly members to keep in mind during a meeting:-

DO
- listen carefully to what other people are saying
- criticise ideas not people
- listen to ideas on their merits, not according to who suggests them
- address the meeting rather than the person who has just spoken
- keep your contribution brief and to the point: think before you speak
- prepare before the meeting for discussion on major issues so that the discussion is informed and therefore valid
- try to respond to the speaker's INTENTION even though his words may be inadequate or tactless
- see your own point of view as a contribution, not as an unalterable fact
- express what you are feeling as well as what you are thinking
- be sensitive to the emotional climate and help resolve tensions
- be supportive and trusting of others
- be honest and open in your dealings with others
- try to keep negative feelings under control
- be prepared to admit you are wrong
- attend meetings regularly and be punctual
- support the decisions of the Assembly even if you don't agree with them
- keep in mind the ultimate purpose of the meeting: service to the Faith
- remember that 'Abdu'l-Bahá is present
- be willing to experiment
- pay attention to future actions rather than past errors

DON'T
- speak with the intention to hurt
- belittle another's thoughts or achievements

ADDENDUM

- burden others with unwarranted or biting criticism
- allow yourself to be upset by other people's opinions
- be discouraged by differences of opinion
- engage in fruitless and hair-splitting discussions
- insist on speaking if another has expressed essentially the same view
- insist on your own opinion
- monopolise the conversation by jumping in repeatedly with your opinion
- be immoderate in expressing your views
- be afraid to express your opinion
- say the first thing that comes into your head
- set out to persuade
- back-bite
- be repetitive
- interrupt another person while they are speaking
- wave your hand wildly while another person is speaking
- scold another member for something he has done wrong
- be so concerned about procedure that the spirit of Bahá'í consultation is lost
- quote Bahá'u'lláh, 'Abdu'l-Bahá, Shoghi Effendi, or the Universal House of Justice out of context to strengthen your point of view
- insist on speaking after the Assembly has voted to adjourn
- criticise a decision of the Assembly in or out of the meeting
- become complacent about the standard of consultation, the achievements of the Assembly, or your own spiritual well-being

CONSULTATION BETWEEN THE LOCAL SPIRITUAL ASSEMBLY AND AN INDIVIDUAL

On what matters should an individual consult with the Assembly?

An individual is obliged to obey and, if necessary, consult with his Assembly on any matter pertaining to the Cause. He may also take personal matters to the Assembly if he chooses; however, he is not obliged to. A believer who does take a personal problem to an Assembly is not bound to follow its advice, but he should bear in mind the general principle of obedience to Assembly decisions. He is bound to consider the advice he receives very carefully. Alternatively, an individual may choose to consult with friends, family, or professional counsellors, eg. a lawyer, or doctor. Or he may solve the problem by himself. The following statement by the Universal House of Justice to a National Spiritual Assembly, dated March 19, 1973, clarifies this issue:-

When a believer has a problem concerning which he must make a decision, he has several courses open to him. If it is a matter that affects the interests of the Faith he should consult with the appropriate Assembly or committee, but individuals have many problems which are purely personal and there is no obligation upon them to take such problems to the institutions of the Faith... A Bahá'í who has a problem may wish to make his own decision upon it after prayer and after weighing all the aspects of it in his own mind; he may prefer to seek the counsel of individual friends or of professional counsellors such as his doctor or lawyer so that he can consider such advice when making his decision; or in a case where several people are involved, such as a family situation, he may want to gather together those who are affected so that they may arrive at a collective decision. There is also no objection whatever to a Bahá'í asking a group of people to consult together on a problem facing him.

(letter to a National Spiritual Assembly, dated March 19, 1973)

ADDENDUM

The principle that confession is forbidden should also be noted in this context. If an individual takes a problem to the Assembly, he does so in order to find a solution to the problem. Talking about our sins and shortcomings merely for the sake of talking serves no good purpose and is forbidden in the Faith. The Universal House of Justice made this clear in the same letter cited above:-

It should be borne in mind that all consultation is aimed at arriving at a solution to a problem and is quite different from the sort of group baring of the soul that is popular in some circles these days and which borders on the kind of confession that is forbidden in the Faith. On the subject of confession the Guardian's Secretary wrote on his behalf to an individual believer: *"We are forbidden to confess to any person, as do the Catholics to their priests, our sins and shortcomings, or to do so in public, as some religious sects do. However, if we spontaneously desire to acknowledge we have been wrong in something, or that we have some fault of character, and ask another person's forgiveness or pardon, we are quite free to do so. The Guardian wants to point out, however, that we are not obliged to do so. It rests entirely with the individual."*

Can an individual bring a problem to the Local Spiritual Assembly if other parties to the problem do not wish to involve the Assembly?

Yes. Shoghi Effendi has said:-
Regarding consultation: Any person can refer a matter to the Assembly for consultation whether the other person wishes to or not.

("Principles of Bahá'í Administration", p.58)

Can a Local Spiritual Assembly intervene in a conflict against the will of the parties involved?

Yes. An Assembly can intervene in a matter that affects the Cause where this is necessary to protect the Faith as a whole, or individual communities or believers:-
In matters which affect the Cause the Assembly should, if it deems it necessary, intervene even if both sides do not want it to, because the whole purpose of the Assemblies is to protect the Faith, the Communities, and the individual Bahá'ís as well.

("Principles of Bahá'í Administration", p.58)

Can the Assembly delegate a committee or individual to counsel a believer?

Yes. In a letter to a National Spiritual Assembly, dated March 27, 1966, the Universal House of Justice said:-
Although Local Spiritual Assemblies are primarily responsible for counselling believers regarding personal problems, there may be times, when in the judgement of the National or Local Assembly, it would be preferable to assign counselling or advisory duties to individuals or committees. This is within the discretion of the Assembly. In larger communities especially, the Assembly may find it useful to delegate responsibility to a committee or individual. Otherwise it may find too much of its time being taken up with counselling.

What is the procedure for consultation between the Local Spiritual Assembly and an individual?

When counselling an individual, the Assembly's aim must be to help that individual find a realistic solution to his problem. The advice it gives may be that the individual seek professional advice elsewhere. Or the Assembly may work out a course of action itself for

ADDENDUM

the individual to follow. In either case the Assembly is bound to give the individual moral support and encouragement to carry the solution through.

The following steps should be taken by the Assembly when conducting a meeting with an individual:-

(1) Welcome the individual and invite him to say a prayer

(2) If necessary, explain the general principles of consultation to the individual -
(a) Remind the individual about the importance of maintaining confidentiality
(b) Mention that statements made by individual Assembly members during the consultation are not to be taken as decisions of the Assembly

(3) Conduct the interview in a courteous, orderly manner -
(a) Avoid interrupting those who are speaking
(b) Avoid giving personal opinions or advice but ask questions to clarify matters if necessary
(c) Listen attentively
(d) If appropriate, ask the individual to summarise what he is requesting from the Assembly

(4) Excuse the individual from the meeting -
(a) Express appreciation to the individual for meeting with the Assembly
(b) Provide assurances to the individual about the confidentiality of what was said

(5) Consult on the problem, following the procedure outlined previously and arrive at and record a decision

(6) Decide how the decision of the Assembly will be communicated to the individual-
(a) A future meeting with the individual if appropriate
(b) Communication in writing
(c) Appoint a delegate or delegates to meet with the individual
When communicating the decision, be sure to point out the spiritual principles involved and encourage the individual to pray and meditate on these principles.

Also assure him of the prayers of the Assembly.
(7) Have some follow up actions prepared if necessary -
(a) If a person is having difficulty following the Assembly's recommendation, he may be assisted by being given specific tasks
(b) He may also be asked to report his progress periodically to the Assembly The above procedure may also be followed when an Assembly itself initiates the consultation. This will occur if an Assembly wishes to counsel an individual on his behaviour and to assist him in obeying the laws of the Faith.

CONSULTATION BETWEEN INDIVIDUALS

How should individuals settle disputes?

Shoghi Effendi has specifically discouraged believers from settling disputes by going to the civil courts, even over issues not affecting the Faith:-
The Guardian wishes to emphasise the importance of avoiding [reference to civil courts] of cases of dispute between believers, even in non-Bahá'í issues. It is the Assembly's function to endeavour to settle amicably such disputes, both in order to safeguard the fair name and prestige of the Cause, and to acquire the necessary experience for the extension of its functions in the future.

ADDENDUM

("Directives from the Guardian", no.36)

Kolstoe (p.91) suggests 4 other courses of action that are open to the individuals concerned:-
(1) They may talk out their problems themselves and come to an amicable agreement.

(2) The matter can be referred to the Local Assembly. There is no obligation to do this, however, and the Assembly may choose not to become involved.

(3) They may turn to an Auxiliary Board Member or Assistant for help. Their function is not to arbitrate the dispute, but they can help those concerned to review the situation and work out solutions. They may also be able to advise when a matter should be referred to the other branch of the Administrative Order.

(4) They may select other trusted Bahá'ís who are not involved, and consult with them. The advice received would not be binding, but again, it may be helpful in finding a solution. Obviously, if all else fails a dispute may have to go to court; however, this must remain a last resort.

REFERENCES

The following works were used to compile this chapter:-

PRIMARY

Universal House of Justice, "**The Constitution of the Universal House of Justice**". Bahá'í World Centre, Haifa, 1972

"**Bahá'í Consultation, The Lamp of Guidance**" (compilation). Bahá'í Publications Australia, 1978. National Spiritual Assembly of the Bahá'ís of the United Kingdom

"**Principles of Bahá'í Administration**" (compilation). Third Edition. Bahá'í Publishing Trust, London, 1973

H. Hornby, "**Lights of Guidance**", A Bahá'í Reference File. Bahá'í Publishing Trust, New Delhi, 1983.

SECONDARY

Bahá'í Comprehensive Deepening Program, "**The Development of Local Spiritual Assemblies.**" Second Revised Edition. Bahá'í Publishing Trust, Wilmette, Illinois, 1976.

G. Coy, "**Counsels of Perfection**", A Bahá'í Guide to Mature Living. George Ronald, Oxford, 1978.

J. Hatcher, "**Love and Unity Among Assembly Members**", "Bahá'í Canada, April 1988.

J. E. Kolstoe, "**Consultation, A Universal Lamp of Guidance**". George Ronald, Oxford, 1985.

B. Na<u>kh</u>javání, "**Response**". George Ronald, Oxford, 1981.

H. Reed, D. Cameroon, D. Spanks, "**Stepping Stones, Crossing the river of Local Group Despair**". Revised Edition. Community Management Training Scheme, Hurstville, 1985.

ADDENDUM

WORKSHOP 1

BAHÁ'Í MARRIAGE WITHOUT CONSENT

Facts:

Two members of the Bahá'í community - Joe and Jackie - were married in a civil ceremony. During the six months or so previous to the ceremony the couple had attempted to get consent to marry. A year earlier, the young man (white) had introduced his fiance (black) to his family and his parents had written their approval for the marriage. The couple decided to postpone their marriage for a few months and did not realise that his parents would be antagonistic toward the Bahá'í Faith. Therefore, Joe did not keep his parents' letter of consent. When the couple attempted to get consent again from all parents, Joe's parents adamantly refused, on the grounds of religious prejudice, rather than on the fact that this would be an interracial marriage. Not being able to secure the necessary consents, the couple were married in a civil service although both were aware of the Bahá'í laws on marriage.

Problem:

Principles:

Principles applied to the facts:

Decisions:

A D D E N D U M

WORKSHOP 2

APPEARANCE OF DRINKING

Facts:

The Local Spiritual Assembly has received a report that Edward, a member of its community, has been seen drinking alcohol in an area restaurant. The Assembly invites Edward to consult with it about the report. He informs the Assembly that he often has business luncheons at the restaurant where non-Bahá'ís present order alcoholic drinks, but he only orders soft drinks. He feels that the person making the report mistakenly felt that his soft drink contained alcohol since everyone else at the table was drinking alcoholic beverages. The Local Assembly is satisfied with Edward's explanation and, because it has never had reason to question his obedience to Bahá'í laws in the past, decides to let the matter drop. Later in the week Edward requests another meeting with the Assembly at which he states that the report about his possible drinking has deeply disturbed him. He is concerned that his integrity as a Bahá'í has been called into question and states that his feelings have been hurt. He states that if he is not trusted by his fellow believers, it will be difficult for him to participate in community events.

Problem:

Principles:

Principles applied to the facts:

Decisions:

WORKSHOP 3

PREDOMINANTLY PERSIAN COMMUNITY

Facts:

Community A has about fifty members. For economic reasons it is difficult for people to move out of the community. Sixty percent of these members are Persian, most of them having arrived in Australia from Iran within the last five years, and some as recently as twelve months ago. At Feasts and other official Bahá'í functions they often speak Persian, although efforts have been made to emphasise English. The believers actively participate in Feasts, Assembly meetings and other community activities, but the participation rate of non-Persian Bahá'ís has dropped to only twenty percent of their number (that is, only four out of the twenty non-Persians regularly attend). There have been two declarations of local people in the last two years, but the new declarants are inactive. The community has tried various teaching programmes but found that, although these projects enthused the community for a while, they lost momentum and teaching stopped again.

Problem:

Principles:

Principles applied to the facts:

Decisions:

ADDENDUM

WORKSHOP 4

DOMINANT PERSONALITIES

Facts:

For many years Community B has had only nine or ten adult members and only just manages to reform its Local Spiritual Assembly at Ridván. There is friction in the community between two long standing believers who have strong personalities and are dominant at community meetings, and other community members who feel they are being continually criticised by these two believers, but also feel too intimidated to do anything about the situation. These two members are also on the Local Spiritual Assembly. The community is active. It holds the Feasts and other meetings regularly, with good attendance, and has had no problems with believers breaking Bahá'í laws or in any way bringing the Faith into disrepute; however, there is always tension at community gatherings and in Assembly meetings. Individual teaching initiatives have been successful in bringing people into the Faith; however, a constant movement of Bahá'ís out of the community means that overall numbers never increase. Everybody knows the problem is the underlying disharmony within the community, but nobody wants to be the one to bring the problem out into the open. There is also some feeling that it would be wrong to disrupt the surface unity of the community as unity is a fundamental principle of the Faith.

Problem:

Principles :

Principles applied to the facts:

Decisions:

INDEX

Numbers refer to Chapter. Section. Sub-Section

A

Aboriginal
    Assemblies 1.1.7
    teaching 5.7.2
Administrative principles 3.1
Administrative procedures (see Procedures of a Local Spiritual Assembly)
Age of maturity 8.3.8
Alcohol 9.5
    non-alcoholic wines 9.5.2
    ownership of business that sell 9.5.5
    serving to non-Bahá'ís 9.5.3, 9.5.4
Annual Report 3.8
Archives 3.9
Area of jurisdiction 1.1.6
Auctions 4.6.7 (see also Bahá'í Funds: fund-raising)
Auxiliary Board Members and Assistants 7
    assisting inter-community activities 13.1.9
    functions of
        Assistants 7.3
        Auxiliary Board Members 7.2
    relations with individuals 7.5
    relations with Local Spiritual Assembly 7.4
    rulers and the learned 7.1

B

Bahá'í Anniversaries 6.8
Bahá'í Burial 12
    Fund 12.6.1
    laws 12.3
        and the Local Spiritual Assembly 12.5
        binding upon believers in the West 12.3.2
        binding on the Persian friends 12.3.3
    ring 12.3.7
    service 12.4
Bahá'í Cemeteries 12.6
Bahá'í Centre, Local 19
Bahá'í Communities
    working together (see Inter-Community Activities)
Bahá'í engagement 10.4
Bahá'í Funds 4
    an obligation 4.1.2
    Annual Financial Report 4.4.9, 4.4.10
    budget 4.4.7, 4.4.8
    contributions 4.3
        to overseas Bahá'í projects 4.2.7
    deepening on 4.4.13
    Deputisation Fund 5.5.9
    different funds 4.2
        Bahá'í Investment Fund 4.2.5
        National Fund 4.2.2, 4.2.3
        Area Delegates' Funds 4.2.4
        Huqúqu'lláh 4.8
    endowments 4.7
    fund-raising 4.6, 6.6.8
    importance 4.1.1
    responsibilities of Local Spiritual Assembly 4.4
    spiritual principles underlying contributions 4.1.6
    tax deductible donations 4.2.6
    voluntary nature 4.1.3
    who may contribute 4.1.4, 4.1.5
Bahá'í Holy Days 6.6, 6.7, 6.8
    children stay at home 6.7.5, 8.3.17
    exchange of gifts 6.6.3
    fund-raising 6.6.8
    holding of marriages on 10.6.4
    how to observe 6.6.2
    importance of observing 6.6.1
    in local community 6.6.6
    obligatory to observe on the prescribed day 6.6.4
    marriages 6.6.9
    responsibility of Local Spiritual Assembly 6.6.7
    suspension of work 6.7
Bahá'í Investment Fund 4.2.5
Bahá'í Law 9
    administering a violation of Bahá'í Law 9.3
    alcohol, drugs and tobacco 9.5
    application 9.1
    behaviour that damages the reputation of the Faith or causes disunity 9.6
    behaviour that disrupts community life 9.6.4
    confidentiality 9.1.8
    consequences of not intervening in a situation 9.1.6
    debts 9.6.5
    dishonest or fraudulent behaviour 9.6.3
    disobedience to civil law 9.7
        deprivation of voting rights 9.7.2
    divorce 9.8
    domestic violence 9.9
    duty of the Assembly towards the community 9.1.3
    ethical standards 9.6.2
    gambling 9.6.6
    general principles 9.1
    homosexuality 9.10.9, 9.10.10
    immoral relationships 9.10
    inactive believers 8.4.4
    loss of voting rights 9.2
    marriage 9.11 (see also Marriage)
    membership in unacceptable organisations 9.12
    morality 9.10
    political activities 9.12
    rehabilitation and restoration of voting rights 9.4

INDEX

shared accommodation 9.10.5, 9.10.6, 9.10.7
    violation of 9.3
Bahá'í Sales Outlet 20.4..2
Bahá'í Societies at Tertiary Institutions 21
    purpose of 21.1.1
    procedure for formation and operation 21.1.3
    role of Association for Bahá'í Studies in 21.1.5
    responsibility of the Local Spiritual Assembly 21.1.2
    terms of reference 21.1.4
By-election 1.6.2

C

Challenge facing the Bahá'í Community 14.2.1
Charity fund raising 15.1.5
Chinese
    teaching 5.7.3, 5.7.4
Civil Law
    disobedience to 9.7
Civil Court
    role of Local Spiritual Assembly in enforcing decisions of 11.7.5
    swearing an oath or affirmation 9.7.4
Committees, Local 17
    appointing a person outside its area of jurisdiction 17.2.6
    believers are not obliged to serve if appointed 17.2.1
    convenor 17.4.2
    delegation of authority to 17.3
    difference between a committee and a working group 17.1.5
    disunity amongst committee members 17.2.7
    functions of 17.1
    membership of 17.2
        children 8.3.16
        Local or National Spiritual Assembly members as members of 17.2.4
        period of appointment 17.1.4, 17.2.2
        size of 17.2.3
    office bearers 17.4.1
        duties 17.4.4
        election of 17.4.3
    organising the work 17.4.7
    operation 17.4
    procedures for urgent matters 17.4.6
    purpose in setting up 17.1.1
    relationship with other regional or national committees 17.1.6
    sample terms of reference 17.6
    supervision by Local Spiritual Assembly 17.3.3
    youth on 17.2.5
Communications 3.10
    form 3.10.2
    from the Assembly 3.10.3
    letterhead design 3.10.5

local newsletters 3.10.6
on behalf of the Local Spiritual Assembly 3.10.1
protocol for addressing institutions 3.10.4
with Hands of the Cause, a Continental Board of Counsellors or individual Counsellor 3.10.10
with an overseas National Spiritual Assembly 3.10.9
with Universal House of Justice 3.10.7
Confidentiality 3.3, 7.5.3, 9.1.8
Consultation 2
    right of appeal 2.5
        against a decision of the National Spiritual Assembly 2.5.2
    with an individual 2.3
        right of appeal 2.5.1
    with a committee 2.4
    with the community 2.2, 16.1
    within the Local Spiritual Assembly 2.1
Copyright 20.3
Covenant, The 14.4
    importance of studying 14.4.2
    meaning 14.4.1
Covenant-breakers 14.4.4, 14.4.5, 14.4.6, 14.4.7
Covenant-Breaking 14.4.3, 14.4.8, 14.4.9
Credentials 8.6
Cremation 12.3.8, 12.3.9, 12.5.3, 12.5.4, 12.5.6

D

Death at sea 12.7
Declaration (see Membership in the Bahá'í Community)
Deepening 5.4.2
De Facto relationships 10.11
Delegation of authority 17.3
Deputisation Fund 5.5.9
Distributing literature 20.4
Disunity 14.2.3, 14.2.4, 14.2.5, 14.2.7
    behaviour that causes 9.6
Divorce 9.9, 11
    annulment 11.8
    approved marriage counselling and pre-marital education organisations 11.10
    arrangements after the 11.7
    civil divorce law 11.4
        relationship between Bahá'í and civil divorce laws 11.5
    involvement of Local Spiritual Assembly 11.7.3
    preventing 11.1
    reconciliation 11.2
    responsibilities of the Local Spiritual Assembly 11.6
    year of patience 11.3
Dowry 10.5
Drugs 9.5

INDEX

E
Election of Local Spiritual Assembly 1.3-1.6
    procedures 1.3
        voting 1.4
Election of Officers 1.5
    mid-term 1.6.3
Encouraging Unity 14.2
Enemies of the Faith (see Opposition)
Enrolment
    children and youth 8.3
Entry by Troops (see Teaching)
Ethical standards 9.6.2
Euthanasia and life-support systems 12.7.4

F
Filing 3.7
Formation of Local Spiritual Assembly 1
    general principles 1.1
Functions
    of Assembly officers 1.5.7
    of the Propagation Board 7.2.1
    of the Protection Board 7.2.2
    of the Secretary 3.4
    of the Treasurer 4.5
Fund-raising (see Bahá'í Funds)

H
Hazíratu'l-Quds 19.1.3
Homosexuality 9.10.9, 9.10.10
Huqúqu'lláh (see Bahá'í Funds)

I
Incorporation 3.11
    lapsed 3.11.5
    responsibilities 3.11.4
    value 3.11.1
    wind up of 3.11.3
Immorality within the community 9.10.2, 9.10.8
    flagrant 9.10.3
Inactive believers 8.4
Individual
    action to be taken if he or she becomes aware of Covenant-breaking activities 14.4.8
    action to be taken if he or she becomes aware of opposition to the Faith 14.3.4
    answering mail from Covenant-breakers 14.4.7
    appealing against a decision of the Local Spiritual Assembly 2.5.1
    communicate directly with Hands of the Cause, a Continental Board of Counsellors or individual Counsellors 3.10.11
    communicate directly with the Universal House of Justice 3.10.8
    confidentiality 9.9.14
    consultation with the Local Spiritual Assembly 2.3
    right of appeal 2.5.1
    deprivation of voting rights 9.2.2
    domestic violence 9.9
    duty to make a will 12.1.2
    ecclesiastical activities of other groups 9.12.1
    expulsion from the Faith 9.2.3
    government jobs 15.4.1
    ignorance of the law 9.2.8
    joining the armed forces 15.4.3
    loss of voting rights 9.2
    partial loss of voting rights 9.2.4
    participation in coordinated campaigns 15.4.5
    participation in protests or demonstrations 15.4.6
    political activities 9.12.1
    problems with other members of the community 14.2.8
    public comment on current issues 15.4.7
    raise funds for non-Bahá'í causes 15.1.16
    reading the writings of Covenant-breakers 14.4.6
    rectifying an injustice 15.4.9
    relations with Auxiliary Boards 7.5
    responding to claims made by Covenant Breakers in the press 14.4.5
    strikes 15.4.4
    swearing an oath or affirmation in a Court of Law 9.7.4, 9.7.5
    voting in civil elections 15.4.2
    writing to the government 15.4.8
Insurance 18
    copy of National Spiritual Assembly's Public/Products Liability Policy 18.3
    policy 18.1
Inter-community Activities 13
    definition 13.1
    joint activity 13.2

L
Libraries
    books written by enemies of the Faith 14.3.7 (see also Opposition)
Literature 20
    copyright 20.3
    distributing 20.4
    encouraging the use of literature 20.5
    publishing 20.1
    reviewing 20.2

M
Malaysians
    teaching 5.7.6
Marriage, Bahá'í 10.1
    age of maturity 10.1.2
    annulment 11.8
    Bahá'í engagement 10.4

INDEX

between relatives 10.1.3
consent of both parties 10.2
consent of parents 10.3
counselling and pre-marital education organisations 11.10
de facto relationships 10.11
domestic violence 9.9
dowry 10.5
celebrants 10.8
ceremony
    importance of 10.7
    nature of 10.6
notifying the marriage celebrant 10.9
on Bahá'í Holy Days 6.6.9
reponsibilities of the Local Spiritual Assembly 10.10
requirements for 10.1.4
Mashriqu'l-Adhkár 19.1.5
Meetings of Local Spiritual Assembly 3.2
    attendance at 3.2.11
    calling a meeting 3.2.1
    conducting 3.2.2
    banning smoking 9.5.10
    confidentiality 3.3
    dissatisfaction with one of its officers 3.2.10
    elected office absent 3.2.9
    election of a temporary member 3.2.12
    emergencies 3.2.8
    frequency 3.2.4
    materials which should be brought to 3.2.3
    quorum 3.2.5, 3.2.6
    routine action between meetings 3.2.7
Membership List 3.6
    inactive believers 8.4
    transfers (see Credentials)
Membership in the Bahá'í Community 8
    credentials 8.6
    declaration and enrolment 8.1, 8.2
    de facto relationships 10.11
    enrolment of children and youth 8.3
    inactive believers 8.4
    resignation of believers 8.5
Membership in unacceptable organisations 9.12
Membership of Local Spiritual Assembly 1.2
    vacancies 1.6
Memorial gatherings 12.4.9
Mentally Ill
    teaching 5.7.8
Minutes 3.5
Mixed flatting 9.10.5, 9.10.6, 9.10.7
Morality 9.10
Muslims
    teaching 5.7.5

N

National Committees

liaising with 13.1.8
National Spiritual Assembly
    appealing against a decision of 2.5.2
    encourage inter-community activities 13.1.2
    notifying results of election 1.5.5
New Bahá'ís
    nurture 5.4.3, 5.4.4
    stop drinking alcohol or taking drugs immediately 9.5.11
    stop selling alcohol immediately 9.5.12
Nineteen Day Feast 6
    attendance 6.4
    fund-raising during 4.6.2
    joint Feast 6.2.5
    origins of 6.1.1
    preparation of and for 6.2
    programme 6.3
    purpose of 6.1.2
    time and place 6.5
Non-Bahá'í Movements 15.1
    co-operate with 15.1.1, 15.1.2, 15.1.3
    fostering association with 15.1.14
    individuals 15.1.12
    order of priorities 15.1.4
    political activities 15.1.6, 15.1.7
    raising funds for charity 15.1.15, 15.1.16
    sanctions 15.1.8
Non-Bahá'í Organisations 15.2
    affiliation 15.2.3, 15.2.4
        if uncertain 15.2.10
        individuals 15.2.11
        may affiliate with 15.2.9
    appoint a representative 15.2.15
    association 15.2.1, 15.2.2
        issues to be considered 15.2.8
    be office bearers in 15.2.13
    membership of
        secret society 15.2.7
        society that practices discrimination 15.2.6
        trade unions 15.2.12
    religious 15.2.5, 15.2.5
    rules of conduct governing participation 15.2.17
Notification of marriage form 10.10.5

O

Opposition 14.3
Organisations Bahá'ís may be affiliated members of in Australia 15.8

P

Participation
    cultural/religious festivals 6.9
Pilgrimage 8.6.17, 8.6.18
Pioneering 5.5
Planning 16

INDEX

feedback 16.4
introduction 16.1
process 16.2
reviewing 16.3
sample plan 16.6
Political activities 9.12
Politics 15.1.6, 15.1.7, 15.1.8, 15.1.9
Procedures of a Local Spiritual Assembly 3.1
   aboriginal teaching 5.7.2
   administering the Year of Patience 11.6
   administering a violation of Bahá'í Law 9.3
   administrative 3
   appealing against a decision of the National Spiritual Assembly 2.5.2
   assisting a couple to make a division of assets, custody of children, etc 11.7.3, 11.7.4
   becoming a Bahá'í 5.1.5, 5.7.8
   Chinese teaching 5.7.3, 5.7.4
   credentials 8.6
   contacting the media 5.2.7
   declaration and enrolment - general 8.1
   declaration and enrolment - special cases 8.2
   dissemination of Bahá'í literature 5.2.8
   election procedures 1.3
   enrolment of children and youth
   establishing its own procedures 3.1.3, 3.1.4
   inactive believers 8.4
   loss of voting rights 9.2
   making contact with local dignitaries 5.2.11
   Muslim teaching 5.7.5, 5.7.6
   overseas travel 8.6.16
   pilgrimage 8.6.17, 8.6.18
   publicity campaigns 5.2.5
   public meetings 5.2.10
   resignation 8.5
   restoration of voting rights 9.4
   social and humanitarian activities 5.2.12
   transferring (see Credentials)
   transferring in Iranian Bahá'ís 8.6.13
   transferring in Southeast Asian Bahá'ís 8.6.14
   transferring Bahá'ís out of the community 8.6.15
   violation of ethical standards 9.6.2
   voting procedures
Proclamation 5.2
Properties 19
   consumption of alcohol on Bahá'í-owned premises 9.5.6
   dancing in a local Bahá'í centre 19.3.4
   factors to consider before acquiring a local Bahá'í centre 19.2
   gift of free land from a non-Bahá'í source for Bahá'í use 19.3.7
   holding Bahá'í functions on the premises of other religious organisations 19.3.5
   Local Spiritual Assembly 19.1
   purchasing a church for use as a Bahá'í Centre 19.3.9
   renting out 19.3.1, 19.3.2, 19.3.3
   reporting the acquisition of, or changes to, property holdings to the National Spiritual Assembly 19.3.6
   use of proceeds from the sale of property purchased with earmarked funds 19.3.8
Protection 14
   Covenant, the 14.4
   encouraging unity 14.2
   opposition 14.3
   responsibilities of the Local Spiritual Assembly 14.1
Publishing literature 20.1

R

Relations with Auxiliary Board 7.4
Relations with Society 15
   association and affiliation with non-Bahá'í organisations 15.2
   general principles 15.1
   public comment on a current issue 15.3.1
   signing an appeal or protest directed to its own and/or other governments 15.3.3
   submissions to government 15.3.2
   support for a march or demonstration 15.3.4
Relationship with national committees 17.1.7
Resignation of believers 8.5
Responsibilities of the Local Spiritual Assembly
   administering the Year of Patience 11.6
   as protector of the Cause of God 14.1
   burial service 12.5.2
   Bahá'í Holy Days 6.6.7
   homefront pioneering 5.5.4
   maintaining graves 12.6.2
   marriage 10.10
   nurture new believers 5.4.3, 5.4.4
   pioneering and travel teaching 5.5.1, 5.5.2, 5.5.8
   register of births 8.3.2
   register of deaths 12.5.8
   reputation of the Faith 9.6
   teaching 5.6
Restoration of voting rights 9.4
Reviewing literature 20.2
Right of Appeal 2.5

S

Sample letters
   commencement of Year of Patience
   end of Year of Patience
   finalisation of Bahá'í divorce
   to funeral director 12.9
Sample committee terms of reference 17.6
Sample plan 16.6

INDEX

Secretary of the Assembly
  functions 3.4
Smoking tobacco 9.5.9
  ban during Bahá'í meetings 9.5.10
Social and economic activities (see Procedures of a Local Spiritual Assembly)
Statistics 5.2.13, 8.3.15
Suicide 12.7.5
Summer Schools 5.4.5

T

Teaching 5
  aboriginal 5.7.2
  challenge facing the Australian Bahá'í community 5.1
  consolidation 5.4
  entry by troops 5.1.3
  expansion 5.3
  institutes 5.4.6
  minorities 5.7
  pioneering 5.5
  proclamation 5.2
  responsibilities of the Local Spiritual Assembly 5.6
  travel teaching 5.5
Tobacco 9.5

U

United Nations Day and events 15.7
Unity 14.2

V

Vacancies on the Local Spiritual Assembly 1.6
Voting procedures 1.4
Voting Rights 9.2, 9.4
  birth of a child out of wedlock 9.10.4
  children of Bahá'ís who have lost voting rights 8.3.6
  deprivation of 9.2.2, 9.7.2
  dishonest or fraudulent behaviour 9.6.3
  failing to repay his or her debts 9.6.5
  gambling 9.6.6
  loss of 9.2
  mixed flatting 9.10.5, 9.10.6, 9.10.7
  restoration of 9.4

W

Wills 12.1
  and Local Spiritual Assembly 12.2
  donation of body to medical science 12.7.2
  donation of organs 12.7.3
  solicitors outline 12.8

Y

Youth
  enrolment 8.3.13

Iranian declarations 8.3.14
re-affirmation 8.3.8, 8.3.9, 8.3.10
statistical report 8.3.15